'2

D1439034

Prints and Engraved Illustrations
By and After Henry Fuseli

A Catalogue Raisonné

Prints and Engraved Illustrations
By and After Henry Fuseli

A Catalogue Raisonné

D. H. Weinglass

S COLAR
PRESS

Published by
SCOLAR PRESS
Gower House
Croft Road
Aldershot
Hants GU11 3HR
England

Ashgate Publishing Company
Old Post Road
Brookfield
Vermont 05036
USA

British Library Cataloguing in Publication Data

Weinglass, David H.
 Prints and Engraved Illustrations By and After
 Henry Fuseli: A Catalogue Raisonné
 I. Title
 769

ISBN 0-85967-882-2

The paper in this publication meets the requirements
of the U.S. National Standard for long-life paper.

Printed in Great Britain at the University Press, Cambridge

CONTENTS

ACKNOWLEDGEMENTS

This catalogue has been in preparation since the mid-1980s and has entailed extensive travel to visit collections in the United States, Britain and Switzerland. I wish to express my sincere thanks to the Pro Helvetia Swiss Arts Council for their generosity in making me a grant which allowed me to pursue my investigations during the period August through November 1985 in Switzerland. Grateful acknowledgements are likewise due to the University of Missouri and the Weldon Spring Endowment for their support to me as a Weldon Spring Humanities Fellow, which enabled me to continue research in the Folger Shakespeare Library and the Huntington Library, and to make visits to Chicago, Princeton and Philadelphia. I also owe a debt of gratitude to the Research Council of the University of Missouri-Kansas City for funding on several occasions since 1982 that allowed research at various locations in the United States and Britain. Thanks are also due to the National Endowment for the Humanities for a Travel to Collections Grant (1986) to visit the Huntington Library.

For their generous assistance in underwriting the cost of the photographs for the 356 illustrations in the present work, thereby significantly enhancing its usefulness as a reference tool, I extend grateful thanks to the Paul Mellon Centre for Studies in British Art, London, and its Director, Professor Michael Kitson, for a grant-in-kind for photography done on my behalf in the British Museum; and to the University of Missouri-Kansas City Office of Research and the Acting Dean of Graduate Faculties and Research, Ronald A. MacQuarrie, for funding to help defray other photography costs. For funding to cover the cost of a laser printer I thank Marvin R. Querry, Vice-Provost for Academic Affairs, University of Missouri-Kansas City.

My indebtedness to Gert Schiff, whose incomparable scholarship will always remain the rock upon which Fuseli studies rest, is writ large on every page of this book. I have also received valuable support from other scholars. I wish to thank in particular Robert N. Essick who gave of his time and experience during my early struggles with my growing mass of materials to instruct me about the essential qualities of a critical catalogue, and thus helped me develop an appropriate format. He also provided generous access to the Fuseliana in his personal print collection. However, I alone must bear responsibility for the form the catalogue finally assumed. Special thanks are also due to Max Browne, who has not only shared his collections with me, but out of friendship on my behalf has also 'sometimes been obliged to run half over London in order to fix a date correctly'. Particularly heartfelt acknowledgements are due to Detlef Dörrbecker and Marilyn Carbonell for their pointed and indispensable advice in bibliographic and art historical matters whenever I felt myself floundering. I likewise gratefully acknowledge the assistance of David Alexander, from whom I have frequently solicited information and advice, although he is of course not to blame for any unextirpated errors.

My thanks also go to Leonard Koenig who designed the title page; to Michael Mardikes for his expertise in computer set-up and Greek fonts; to Carol Rust who took all of my word processing problems in her stride; to Lois Spatz for help with Greek and Latin quotations; to Ann Thorne for advice on graphic layout; to the Interlibrary Loan Department of the UMKC Library; and to my enthusiastic Fuseli-scouts Janet Beets, Brenda Dingley, and Kevin McCarrison.

I have received uniformly courteous and helpful treatment in the many print rooms and libraries where I have been privileged to pursue my research. To all of these I extend grateful thanks, but I hope I will be forgiven for singling out for their particular kindness Hilary Williams and the other staff members of the Department of Prints and Drawings of the British Museum; the members of the Departments of Prints and Drawings and Rare Books of the Yale Center for British Art, and Anne-Marie Logan, the Center's Head Reference Librarian and Photo Archivist; and the Librarian of the Shakespeare Library, Birmingham, Niki Rathbone.

INTRODUCTION

The current interest in the work of Henry Fuseli (1741-1825) is rivalled only by the phenomenal popularity of William Blake (1757-1827), who many still think of, incorrectly, as having been a sort of guru to the older man, who is reported to have said that Blake was 'd----d good to steal from'. The steady spate of articles, books, and exhibitions dealing with Fuseli reflects the continuing upward evaluation of his reputation on several fronts.

Long recognised as a superb and intensely dramatic draughtsman, few now carp at what used to be considered his distracting Michelangelesque pretensions. Similarly, in the wake of Gert Schiff's brilliant elucidation of Fuseli's supposedly impenetrable iconography,[1] there is a juster appreciation of the remarkable erudition and familiarity with the Greek and Latin classics, the Bible, Shakespeare, and the western epic tradition from Homer and Virgil, through the *Nibelungenlied*, Dante, Spenser and Milton that underpin Fuseli's art. As a result he can now be seen as a seminal figure in the rise of Romanticism. His originality—part of his vastly different conception of creativity from that of any previous age—goes hand in hand with his prodigious knowledge of art and theory, and his eclecticism, exemplified in his ability to transpose appropriate attitudes or figures from the works of other artists into his own, with incomparable effect.[2] At the same time his characteristic interest in 'the vague and insubstantial phantoms which haunt like dim dreams the oppressed imagination'[3] is of a piece with his fascination with bizarre and violent 'Sado-Mannerist'[4] scenes with their disturbing psychological overtones. But it is an oversimplification that does not hold up to the informed scrutiny of individual works to 'see' his pictures overall as 'more interesting from a literary and psychological perspective than as paintings per se'.[5]

Johann Heinrich Füssli, better known in England as Henry Fuseli,[6] was the offshoot of a Swiss family whose lineage, extending back into the Middle Ages, was studded with artists and

---

[1] The standard work on Fuseli is Gert Schiff's *Johann Heinrich Füssli, 1741-1825*, 2 vols., Zurich and Munich, 1973. A new updated edition in English, translated and edited by D.H. Weinglass, is forthcoming, from Yale University Press. The Schiff numbers cited below and throughout this catalogue are from the German edition; they will not necessarily correspond to those in the new English edition.

[2] For Fuseli's own discussion of this process, which he referred to as 'the judicious adoption of figures in art', see Lecture III: 'Invention', Knowles 1831, II, 181-182. Sir Joshua Reynolds called such eclecticism 'Pasticcio', and in his *Discourse* VI praises the artist, 'who borrows an idea ... and so accommodates it to his own work, that it makes a part of it, with no seam or join appearing'. Such imitation, he asserts, 'is a perpetual exercise of the mind, a continual invention'. Edward Hodnett's view that Fuseli's numerous and pervasive borrowings are 'disheartening' to the viewer and 'cast doubt on [*Fuseli's*] ethics as well as his originality' (*Image and Text*, 1982, 74) is fortunately only a minority one.

[3] 'The Late Mr. Fuseli', *New Monthly Magazine*, May 1831, 435.

[4] This is Jeffery Daniels' coinage; see his 'Sado-Mannerism', *Art & Artists*, 9 (February 1975), 22-29.

[5] Hallman B. Bryant in his brief, and by no means error-free, entry on Fuseli in Garland Publishing's *Encyclopedia of Romanticism: Culture in Britain, 1780s-1830s* (sic), ed. Laura Dabundo, 1992, 212.

[6] On his first arrival in England his name tended to be anglicised as 'Tussle' or 'Fussle' or 'Fusseli'. He adopted the italianate form, 'Fuseli', during the near-decade he spent in Rome, but when he returned to London his correspondents frequently rendered this as 'Fusely', 'Fusili', 'Fuzeli' or 'Fuzelli': such spellings seem to correspond to two variant pronunciations—viz., with an unstressed (Fusĕli) or a stressed (Fuséli) penultimate syllable. But at least one contemporary, Sir Henry Holland, who attended him on his deathbed was misled by his name and 'passionately eccentric' temperament into thinking he was 'a compatriot of Ugo Foscolo', i.e. an Italian (*Recollections of Past Life*, New York, 1872, 255).

artisans. The future painter of the hobgoblin world of the *Nightmare* was born in Zurich on 6th February 1741, the second of three sons and two daughters of Johann Caspar Füssli (1706-1780), a much-travelled portrait painter and writer on art. All five children were artistically talented; to underline the family's uncommon dedication to the art of painting, the father proudly dubbed his household 'Domus Fueselinorum artis pingendi cultrix'.[7] However, for reasons it is difficult to comprehend given Henry's obvious gifts, Johann Caspar was adamantly set against his son's becoming a painter; he intended him to become a clergyman. Fortunately, this did not deter young Fuseli. His earliest surviving drawings, made surreptitiously and in defiance of his father's wishes, are dated 1751. The career to which he so audaciously committed himself at ten years of age would usher in a lifetime's 'unremitting exertion of fancy'. His formal stint as an ordained Zwinglian minister left some traces on his mind but was both brief and uneventful, notable mainly for the Sternean choice of the Biblical text he took for his first sermon: 'What will this babbler say?' In contrast, for the next seven decades, 'Art, like love, excluded all competition and absorbed the man'.[8]

Fuseli's art always remained deeply rooted in literature. As is clear from his surviving juvenilia, the most formative examples of art with which he became familiar at this stage were engraved book illustrations, above all from the Bible, and Roman and Helvetic history and legend. He even did drawings that deliberately imitated the techniques of the woodcut.[9] His father's substantial collection was particularly rich in drawings and prints by Swiss artists, many of whom were notable for their strong mannerist tendencies.[10] We should, therefore, not underestimate their influence upon him in terms both of subject matter and style. This early predisposition to seek out subjects from such sources explains why from the very beginning 'Nature only put him out'. As William Blake noted, 'If you have not Nature before you for Every Touch, you cannot Paint Portrait; & if you have Nature before you at all, you cannot Paint History':[11] thus, many of Fuseli's apparently most realistic sketches, such as the precocious teenager's remarkable gallery of Swiss artists at work in their studios (1754-1756; Schiff nos. 130-141), prove not to be from the life at all. Throughout this cycle of imaginary portraits, the ubiquitous book located within handy reach of the painter is seen as part of normal studio paraphernalia and thus becomes a tangible symbol of the imaginative interdependence of the sister arts (*ut pictura poesis*).

As a history painter, Fuseli consistently sought to render in befittingly heroic style the painterly subjects and high moral themes that he found embodied in literature, history and legend. His

---

[7] All six family members are commemorated under this title in a series of engravings, dated 1771, perhaps after portraits executed by the eldest son, Johann Rudolf (1737-1806) (Zentralbibliothek, Zurich, KK 3628). For accounts of his father and two brothers, see Fuseli's edition of Pilkington's *Dictionary of Painters* (1805, 1810)—from which he seems to have deliberately omitted his sisters, Elisabeth (1744-1780) and Anna (1749-1772), both flower painters.

[8] Aphorism 3; Knowles 1831, III, 63.

[9] e.g. Schiff nos. 98, 103, and 286.

[10] Such artists include Jost Amman, Conrad Meyer, Rudolf Meyer, Christoph Murer, and Gotthard Ringgli. In Appendix 8 to her article, 'Johann Caspar Füssli und sein Briefwechsel mit Jean-Georges Wille' in the *Jahrbuch des Schweizerischen Instituts für Kunstwissenschaft 1974-1977* (Zurich, 1978, 162-171), Yvonne Boerlin-Brodbeck lists the artists whose works formed part of Johann Caspar Füssli's art collection; as part of her documentation, she cites from Schiff all Fuseli's drawings after or inspired by any given artist in the collection.

[11] William Blake to Thomas Butts, 22 November 1802; Keynes 1980, 43.

remarkable erudition and literary versatility stood him in good stead in this pursuit. However, he never dwindled into a mere book-illustrator or bent his ear to what he called mediocrity's 'common expletive';[12] he always denied any implication that the painter's invention was confined to the 'poet's or the historian's alms'.[13] It is salutary in this respect to compare him with Thomas Stothard (1755-1834), whose uncommon but more facile productivity made him the most prolific *illustrator* of his age. Estimates of the number of Stothard's designs range from between five and ten thousand;[14] although predominantly for book illustrations (including vignettes in school books, cookery books, and sporting books), they were also executed for everything from bank notes, concert tickets, silverwork, sculpture and ceramics. While Stothard's works, with their characteristic charm and delicacy, have an undeniably strong appeal, these qualities unfortunately do not always assort with his pretensions as a history painter as may be seen, for example, in his illustrations for Du Roveray's editions of the *Iliad* (1805) and Glover's *Leonidas* (1798). Indeed, the vast differences between the two artists' outlook and achievement in this respect are strikingly exemplified in Fuseli's dissatisfaction with the final product of his efforts to capture the sublimity of Homer within the confines of Kitcat size paintings. 'He never can be great who honours what is little', Fuseli declares in his Aphorism 238.[15] But these illustrations, which Fuseli deprecates as representing 'Heroes and Heroines ... convulsed or slain by puny pangs &c in puny battles',[16] are certainly far from the 'pigmy' art he so disdained.

He favoured large paintings and grandiose projects, but none more remarkable than the vast exhibition cycle, upon which he embarked single-handedly in the early 1790s, and with which his name will always be associated. For this undertaking—certainly 'glory sufficient for an ambitious man', in Sir Joshua Reynolds' phrase—he executed more than fifty paintings, many of them as large as 12 x 10 feet, to illustrate John Milton's life and works, exhibiting forty-seven of them in his ill-fated Milton Gallery (1799, 1800). He had earlier contributed nine paintings to Alderman Boydell's Shakespeare Gallery, constantly trying to wheedle from the Proprietor extra inches of canvas beyond already generous allotments ranging up to 8 x 12 feet for *Lear*. Yet it was in the modest compass of the reproductive print, capable of being multiplied at will, that his fame and that of his fellow painters was wafted abroad—whereby the engraved image might appear at times to have evoked a more intense frisson than the original.[17] The point stressed by the organisers of a recent exhibition of prints after J.M.W. Turner, that engraving was his 'primary means of communication with the public at large' is equally applicable to Fuseli. What is more, for Fuseli, like Turner, 'the

---

[12] Aphorism 48 (Corollary); Knowles 1831, III, 78.

[13] Aphorism 21, Knowles 1831, III, 68.

[14] A.C. Coxhead, *Thomas Stothard, R.A. An Illustrated Monograph*, 1906, 29-30. For another study with a professedly rather different focus, see Shelley M. Bennett, *Thomas Stothard: The Mechanisms of Art Patronage in England circa 1800*, 1988.

[15] Knowles 1831, III, 148.

[16] To William Roscoe, 15 November 1803; *Letters*, 290. All ten of the works in question were intended for F.I. Du Roveray's 6-vol. *Iliad of Homer, Translated by A. Pope. A New Edition. Adorned with Plates* (1805) (**Nos. 227-236**).

[17] Matthias Vogel informs me that he has found no published newspaper comments in 1782 on the painting of the *Nightmare* as compared to later references to the engraving. In terms of such 'shuddering images', it is worth noting that Henry Kirke White's panegyric to Fuseli as the 'Genius of Horror and romantic awe' was inspired by 'seeing Engravings from his Designs' (*Ode, Addressed to H. Fuseli, Esq. R.A.*, reprt. Knowles, 1831, I, 431-434).

xiv

large body of reproductive engravings after [*his*] work constitutes the most neglected area of his output'.[18]

It says much for Fuseli's grip on the imagination of his age that more than 300 subjects—about one-eighth of his total production—were engraved after him. Apart from anything else, it means they had also demonstrated their worth as marketable commodities. But Fuseli was never so unworldly as to ignore the reality that certain subjects, particularly those on specifically Swiss themes, such as his exemplary patriotic celebration of the legendary founders of the Helvetic Confederation, the *Oath on the Rütli* ('my best work and the quintessence of my powers'), were just not 'saleable' in England either in the form of paintings or engravings.[19] No reproduction of the *Oath on the Rütli* (**No. 282**) was available to even a Swiss audience until it was engraved in outline for the *Sämmtliche Werke*, published in Zurich, 1807-1809. Another Swiss subject, *William Tell's Leap from the Boat*, was elevated into a powerful political icon of great universality only when it was imported into the new revolutionary milieu of France in 1789-1790, where it was disseminated in the form of the engraving (**No. 82**) by the Paris-based engraver-publisher Carl Gottlieb Guttenberg. Fuseli's image transformed William Tell into an emblem of the common citizen as revolutionary freedom fighter: in 1790 a copy of Guttenberg's engraving was formally installed in the 'Temple of Virtue' established in the Guillaume Tell arrondissement at Paris. In contrast, the rule of thumb that Boydell impressed upon Northcote as the prerequisite for success as an art entrepreneur—'We want a picture [*illustrating the great national poet*] according to the common, popular story!'[20]—would sufficiently explain the fact that in the last resort the raw materials of his greatest history paintings are preponderantly English.

For the artist, the illustration[21] of works of literature and drama is an act of both creative imagination and translation; for purposes of our discussion, we exclude purely literal representations of stage settings, actual productions, and costume portraits. A successful illustration of a text undoubtedly gains in effect as an imaginative catalyst when physically located within the book in proximity to the passage or scene of which it is meant to provide a visualisation. Of the two usual alternatives, the illustration as a full-page engraving separately inserted into the book, or the normally much smaller vignette, which constituted an integral part of the page of text, Fuseli would have preferred the former, since vignettes clearly tended to be viewed rather as ornament than as

---

[18] Nicholas Serota ('Foreword'), Anna Lyles & Diane Perkins, *Colour Into Line: Turner and the Art of Engraving* (Tate Gallery), 1989, 5, 7.

[19] To J.C. Lavater, 18 October 1781; Muschg 1942, 199. The converse of this is that on the Continent there was little call for engravings of English, and in particular, Miltonic subjects. Both Lessing (*Laocoon,* trans. E.A. McCormick, 1962, 74)—'Milton cannot fill picture galleries'—and Winckelmann (*History of Ancient Art,* trans. G.H. Lodge, 1968, I, 61)—'the astonishing, partly fearful pictures, in which Milton's greatness consists ... are absolutely unfit to be painted'—discount him as a suitable subject for poetical painting (cited by Ravenhall 1980, 543).

[20] *Conversations of James Northcote R.A. with James Ward on Art and Artists*, ed. Ernest Fletcher, 1901, 116.

[21] The use of 'illustrate' in the exclusively pictorial sense dates only from about 1813-1816 (*Oxford English Dictionary*). Hence, *The Christian's Complete Family Bible* (**Nos. 25B, 26A**)(1804), in common with works like *The Christian's Universal Family Bible* (**No. 30B**)(1810, 1812), is described on the title page as being 'illustrated with Notes and Annotations ... in which the most difficult passages are rendered clear and familiar'.

an effective visual narrative accompaniment.[22] (The mixture of plates and vignettes in Lavater's *Essays on Physiognomy*, for example, in both the French and English editions was clearly the choice of the author and publisher(s), determined by the format of the work.) It is true that the editor of one multi-volume edition of Shakespeare[23] rejected 'separate engravings, as making ... merely an appendage to the work [*rather than*] an integral part of it', in favour of vignettes. But, given the enormous expense of full-page illustrations as also his expressed desire to avoid the expense of any notes or commentary, he may have been making a virtue of a necessity in seeking less costly but 'elegant ornaments of the pencil' to accompany the work.

A frontispiece, although usually placed opposite the title page, may refer to a specific scene later in the book, or it may attempt to serve as some sort of broad general pictorial statement about the thrust or subject matter of the whole work, as for example in *Two Hovering Geniuses Summoning a Seated Young Man to Virtue* (**No. 14**) or *The Priestess Unveiling the Statue of the Goddess of Nature* (**No. 173**). This may also be particularly appropriate in a work such as John Bonnycastle's *Introduction to Astronomy* (**No. 75**) where other plates are explicitly technical in nature. At a period when such embellishments had come to be taken for granted even in cheaper editions of books, a frontispiece could, thus, be seen as minimally satisfying the obligatory requirement for some form of illustration.

Although the visual expectations of different periods and epochs may vary widely, the most striking works of illustration will survive the vicissitudes of mere taste and continue to please and enlighten later ages. However, it is to be noted that Fuseli's illustrations in the form of drawings almost always make far greater demands on the spectator than his engraved illustrations, which tend to depict more traditional subjects of history painting. In fact, *Garrick as Duke of Gloucester Waiting for Lady Anne at the Funeral Procession of her Father-in-law, King Henry VI*, c. 1766 (Schiff no. 340),[24] is one of only three such quasi-documentary theatrical renderings in Fuseli's oeuvre. It is thus possible for us to generalise that Henry Fuseli is more likely to give us archetypes than stereotypes (clichés) even in a drawing such as this, based on memories of an actual performance. Comparison with its unpublished 'universalised' counterpart in the Art Institute of Chicago (not in Schiff 1973) shows the remarkable level of timeless abstraction regularly attained by Fuseli in his imaginative re-creations. Another rendering of this sort, '*Garrick and Mrs. Pritchard as Macbeth and Lady Macbeth after the Murder of Duncan*', c. 1766 (Schiff no. 341),[25] was later engraved after a reconceptualised version in oils, stripped of its realistic trappings of costume ('*I've Done the Deed*'; **No. 183**). Such treatment accords with our recognition of the critical paradox that 'grotesquely unrealistic' scenes like Gloucester's wooing of Lady Anne over the corpse of her father-in-law, murdered by the selfsame Richard, are in fact a staple of Shakespeare's dramatic genius rather than a mere anomaly. But we should also remember (*a.*) that Shakespeare was not Fuseli's only source of theatrical subjects—witness his illustrations for *Bell's British Theatre* (**Nos. 126-130**); and (*b.*) that his most dramatic subjects certainly did not always

[22] See for example the vignette headpieces to the plays in Capell's Dublin edition of the *Plays of Shakespeare*, published by Thomas Ewing, 1771.

[23] *The Plays of Shakespeare. Printed from the Text of Samuel Johnson, George Steevens, and Isaac Reed.* 12 vols. London: Longman, Hurst, Rees and Orme; Edinburgh: A. Constable, 1807, I, iii.

[24] Reproduced Tomory 1972, pl. 12, and in the catalogues of the exhibitions held in Zurich 1969 (121), Hamburg 1974-1975 (10), London 1975 (43) and Paris 1975 (92).

[25] Reproduced Tomory 1972, pl. 160, Schiff-Viotto 1977, pl. D11, and in the catalogues of the exhibitions held in Zurich 1969 (122), Hamburg 1974-1975 (11), London 1975 (32), Paris 1975 (81).

come from the theatre. As Kenneth Clark reminds us, one of Fuseli's hallmarks is 'a sense of visual drama which is not trivially descriptive'.[26]

There are engraved illustrations, namely Fuseli's etchings (e.g. **Nos. 76, 81, 111, 112**), as also his lithograph *Heavenly Ganymede* (**No. 172**), which approximate drawings both in their spontaneity and in their less transparent subject matter. This is manifested in particularly striking form in the deliberately rather enigmatically inscribed outline engraving 'Der Kronenräuber', i.e. 'The Usurper' (**No. 280**), after Fuseli's Roman drawing (Schiff no. 445). In this design, exemplifying his aphorism that 'Genius either discovers new materials of nature, or combines the known with novelty',[27] Fuseli transposes the details of a scene of homosexual seduction, depicted on a 4th century attic vase, to the murder of Hamlet's father by his brother Claudio, in order to explicate the complex light-darkness metaphor that underlies Hamlet's reference to his father as 'Hyperion to a satyr'.

Freed from concerns with the actors' entrances and exits on a real-life stage, the artist can narrow the frame of the action to as small and intense a compass as he desires, capturing a single figure or a whole group, reducing architectural detail to a minimum, if not totally eliminating it (Fuseli has typically more drapery than architectural elements), and telescoping details from past and future scenes. Among the interesting theoretical questions raised by this kind of allusiveness is the extent to which illustrations, insofar that they are complete in themselves, must be self-explanatory, or indeed whether a fully self-explanatory illustration is ever a wholly feasible proposition. Given the perennially vexing practical and theoretical problem of mimesis, i.e. imitation of nature, one must assume for this genre of representative art a certain knowledge by the spectator of the iconographic conventions involved and a shared fund of literary knowledge. Such considerations explain, in fact, why history painting in England was by the 1840s being overwhelmingly displaced in the public's favour by smaller-sized anecdotal narrative paintings by followers of the Dutch tradition.[28]

But there is a related question, which raises other important issues. Robert R. Wark warns us against 'becom[*ing*] over-sophisticated in attributing intentions to artists' or 'interpreting illustrations to a work of literature as an indication of changing attitudes towards it'. The factors controlling most artists' illustrations, Wark suggests, are 'much more pedestrian': even if we assume that 'the choice of scene is not made by the publisher but the artist, he seems more likely to go to the illustrations by his predecessors for inspiration than to the text itself'.[29] Ralph Cohen, on the other hand, distinguishes between 'the illustration as interpretation' and 'the illustration as independent work of art' and concludes that even 'a "bad" engraving may still be a valuable commentary upon artistic tradition'.[30] Indeed, if we assume the inherent interdependence of text and pictorial design, posited by Joseph A. Wittreich, Jr., it is certainly plausible, given Fuseli's abiding interest in Milton, to see the illustrations of his works by an artist of Fuseli's calibre, as a form of non-verbal criticism.[31]

Mary Ravenhall has effectively shown in this regard the extent to which Fuseli takes issue in

---

[26] Kenneth Clark, *The Romantic Rebellion: Romantic versus Classic Art*, 1972, 62.

[27] Aphorism 5; Knowles 1831, III, 63.

[28] A good sample of such paintings may be seen in John Hadfield's *Every Picture Tells a Story: Images of Victorian Life*, 1985.

[29] Robert R. Wark, *Drawings from the Turner Shakespeare*, 1973, 15.

[30] Cohen 1964, 259.

[31] See Joseph A. Wittreich, Jr. on 'Illustrators' in *A Milton Encyclopedia*, 1978, IV, 55-58.

his strongly sensual illustrations of Adam and Eve with such authoritative eighteenth-century critics of Milton as Addison, Voltaire and Richardson, who praise the poem 'for its delicate portrayal of innocent love';[32] Fuseli also departs from Milton's text, e.g. in *The Triumphant Messiah* (**No. 169**), 'to make the fall of Satan the central theme of his illustration';[33] in *The Expulsion* (**No. 170**) Fuseli diverges from both Milton and other artists in seeing the consolation of Adam and Eve as lying 'not so much [*in*] God's promise of salvation as [*in*] the ability man retains to find happiness during his brief life on this earth'.[34]

All but a handful of Fuseli's designs were transferred to copper by professional engravers. The designs from which the engraver worked ran the gamut from highly finished oil paintings and drawings to rapid sketches and even rather rudimentary jottings, requiring considerable working up by the engraver in consultation with the artist. Ideally most engravers would have preferred a wash drawing approximately the same size as the intended plate. Whatever the shock effect of so many of Fuseli's stormy inventions, including, for example, the disquieting sexual overtones of the *Nightmare* (**Nos. 67, 68**) or of *An Incubus Leaving Two Sleeping Women* (**No. 135**), the resulting engravings, like his paintings, are clearly intended for public display, in contrast to that class of his drawings, 'the firstlings of his hand', characterised by Lord Clark as being 'of a ferocious obscenity more frightening than provocative'[35], that tended to be consigned to the covert domain of his 'unofficial' art.

The majority were executed in line engraving (a process aptly described by Blake as 'Eternal work'),[36] which despite its laborious nature enjoyed greater prestige than other reproductive media, in part because it was generally associated with history painting. One of the most serious criticisms of Boydell's Shakespeare Gallery prints, often repeated, was their 'inferior quality' due to the use of the roulette and similarly spiked tools to implement the hybrid process, known as stipple, which combined etching, drypoint and engraving, rather than relying more single-mindedly on the burin as in line engraving. Benjamin West disapproved strongly of 'Such a mixture of *dotting* and engraving.—& such a general defficiency in *respect of drawing*, which He observed the Engravers

---

[32] Ravenhall 1980, 556, is also eager to note that 'Fuseli's interest in *Paradise Lost* was not confined to the sublimity of Satan but [*embraced also*] the beauty and pathos of the story of Adam and Eve ... recognised by Fuseli as the heroes of Milton's poem' (554).

[33] Ravenhall 1980, 558. She maintains that 'Fuseli's subject is not really to be found anywhere in the text of Book VI': not only does Fuseli oppose Satan directly to Messiah in contradiction to Milton's account of the fall of the rebel angels, but he also 'rejects the distinction Milton drew between Father and Son' by depicting the Son with shaggy hair and beard without armour (557).

[34] Ravenhall 1980, 584. Among other differences from other artists in their representation of Milton's conclusion, Fuseli focuses not on what lies ahead but upon Adam's determination to meet his fate manfully (580) and continue as Eve's comfort and support.

[35] Kenneth Clark, *The Romantic Rebellion: Romantic versus Classic Art* (1973), 65. For a fuller discussion of Fuseli's erotic art, particularly his hair fetishism, see Gert Schiff, 'Fuseli, Lucifer and the Medusa', in *Henry Fuseli 1741-1825*, 1975, 9-20, and my '"The Elysium of Fancy": Aspects of Henry Fuseli's Erotic Art', in *Erotica and the Enlightenment*, ed. Peter Wagner (Frankfurt: Peter Lang), 1991, 294-353.

[36] Blake told Dr. Trusler (26 August 1799; Keynes 1980, 9f.) that he found it '[infinitely more laborious] To Engrave after another Painter ... than to Engrave one's own Inventions'; he alternately 'curse[*d*] & bless[*ed*] Engraving ... because it takes so much time & is so untractable, tho' capable of such beauty & perfection' (to William Hayley, 12 March 1804; Keynes 1980, 83).

seemed to know little of'.[37] Another immediate and 'sufficiently known' advantage of line engraving pointed out by Woodmason in his prospectus for 'The New Shakespeare Gallery' (1794) was that such 'a Stroke-engraved Plate ... when well executed, is capable of producing at least *Two Thousand* good Prints'[38]

However, an interesting group of Fuseli's illustrations was engraved in mezzotint, which was traditionally, although since the 1760s no longer exclusively, the preserve of the portrait; the medium was not inappropriate for the representation of the gloomy dungeon-like settings and rather stagey theatrical postures of the figures in the seven subjects engraved after Fuseli in the 1780s (six of them by John Raphael Smith).

The popularity of the etching medium ('so peculiarly a painter's art') resides in the fact that it allows the draughtsman to draw directly onto the grounded plate from which he will multiply his design without inhibiting the spontaneity of his line and, consequently, without need for the intermediacy of the professional engraver. Only sixteen of Fuseli's etched designs (plus two lithographs) from the artist's own hand are now known; there were undoubtedly more. In 1785 he refers to proposals for unidentified 'Etchings that may not be ready perhaps for another twelve months', which appear to be connected with two paintings, also unidentified, that he had just sent off to his correspondent.[39] The following year we find William Roscoe urging Fuseli to publish what may or may not have been a suite of four etchings, conceivably associated with Roscoe's poem denouncing the slave trade, *The Wrongs of Africa* (Parts I-II, 1787-1788).[40] A decade later, as he struggled to complete his Milton Gallery, although he had not 'been able to procure Subscriptions in Sufficient number to make thoughts of publication at present adviseable', Fuseli was already planning himself to execute the engravings to accompany the exhibition. He had therefore begun to 'exercise [*himself*] in preparatory Essays ... in *Acqua Tinta*, [*Aqua*]*fortis* [*and*] *tallow* [*i.e. soft-ground etching*]' so that he might 'lose the '*far leccato*' [*i.e. injudicious exactness*] of the Engraver [*and*] gain the hand of the master'.[41]

There are indications that an indeterminate number of early illustrations after his designs other than etchings may have been lost or not yet identified. For example, his drawing *Rococo Lady with Sheet of Music* [1758-1760] (not in Schiff 1973), appears to have been indented for transfer, i.e. used as a template to trace the contour lines of the image directly on to a grounded copper plate as

---

[37] *Farington Diary*, 26 May 1804; VI (1979), 2331. Thirty years later W.J. Linton attacked one of Samuel Freeman's engravings as 'scarcely worthy of a Slave' because 'Stippling and the line manner are mingled in its mode of execution ... without principle, apparently by some person whose mind and hand, formed in conventional trammels, by and for a mercenary age, has probably no suspicion that the art which he nominally exercises, is, in its inherent capabilities, aught better than the merest of mechanic trade' (cited by F.B. Smith, *Radical Artisan: William James Linton 1812-97*, 1973, 6).

[38] See Catalogue, p. 170.

[39] To Sir Brooke Boothby, c. 15 January and 22 January 1785; *Letters*, 24-26.

[40] To Roscoe, 24 August 1786; *Letters*, 32. Mrs. Roscoe's resentment at '[*Fuseli's*] and Johnsons conduct about the *Wrongs*' expressed in a letter to her husband dated 3 April 1791 (*Letters*, 63) might refer to an abortive agreement with Joseph Johnson to publish the work (?possibly with illustrations by Fuseli). The poem appeared under the imprint of Faulder.

[41] To William Roscoe, 14 September 1796; *Letters*, 162. I have adapted the phrase 'injudicious exactness' from that used by Sir Joshua Reynolds, referring to the way his engraver, Edward Fisher 'wasted his time in making the precise shape of every leaf with as much care as he would bestow on features of a portrait' (James Northcote, *Memoirs of Sir Joshua Reynolds*, 1813 [no page no. given], cited by Carol Wax in *The Mezzotint, History and Technique*, 1990, 56f.).

a preliminary to engraving it, albeit no such print has been found. Fuseli's biographer, John Knowles, informs us that Fuseli received 'ample employment' from the London booksellers and was generously treated by them when he first arrived in London. Millar, for example, gave Fuseli 'the whole proceeds' from his translation of Winckelmann's *Reflections on the Painting and Sculpture of the Greeks* (**Nos. 9-10**), 'after deducting only the expenses of paper and printing'.[42] Joseph Johnson lodged Fuseli in his house (both before and after his return from Italy) in return for drawings and an 'occasional piece of writing', such as his translation of Dragonetti's *Treatise on Virtues and Rewards* (**Nos. 14-16**),[43] and possibly his *Remarks on Rousseau* (**No. 11**), neither of which brought Johnson any real financial return. Although it cannot be documented whether Fuseli ever actually executed the commission, there is nothing implausible in Fuseli's report to Salomon Dälliker that he had committed himself to do 'fifty small Quarto-drawings' for an unnamed friend for £100.[44] His employments at this time certainly allowed him considerable leisure, which he devoted to improving his drawing skills. Among other lost designs from this period are those he grudgingly executed for Klopstock's *Messiah*: 'I sent off the drawings to Klopstock's bookseller but did not reply to him.'[45] On the other hand, it is difficult to fault Dr. Johann Georg Zimmermann for his decision not to have Fuseli's scatological *Apothecary and Doctor Visiting a Patient Suffering from Dysentery* (1766; Schiff no. 344) engraved as frontispiece to his tract on the depredations of the disease the previous year in Brugg.[46] A notation appended by Lavater to Fuseli's drawing from the late 1770s, *Young Woman Asleep in a Window Seat, with a Book beside her that has Fallen from her Hand* (not seen) (Weimar; Schiff no. 557), suggests it might have been engraved, though the engraving remains untraced.[47]

The later re-engravings of Fuseli's productions are at least equally numerous, although certain popular works and themes (e.g. from Shakespeare) are represented in disproportionate numbers; the more recondite subjects were rarely if ever reissued. Artists received a one-time payment for their originals: Fuseli would have merely shrugged to see the five reissues of his designs for Smollett's *Peregrine Pickle* that appeared in six new editions between 1769 and 1784 (**Nos. 17-20 - 17E-20E**) and the great variation in their quality; he could expect no further remuneration, nor did he have any say in the extensive changes his images often suffered later. There are sometimes such great differences between engravings as first issued and certain late-generation re-engravings that one almost has to rely upon the presence of the artist's name in the margin to confirm they are really after him. This would appear to be more or less the case, for example, in the reissued plates of Fuseli's *Death of Goliath* and *Isaiah's Vision* (1815) (**Nos. 27C, 30C**)(not reproduced) that had first appeared in Willoughby's *Practical Family Bible* of 1772 (**Nos. 27, 30**).

However, not all reissued plates needed to be re-engraved. As G.E. Bentley documents, Francis Isaac Du Roveray financed his new editions by selling the rights in his already published

[42] Knowles 1831, I, 32.

[43] To J.C. Lavater, 23 June 1769; Muschg 147.

[44] To Salomon Dälliker, 12-15 November 1765; Muschg 1942, 104.

[45] To Salomon Dälliker, 12-15 November 1765; Muschg 1942, 111.

[46] To J.C. Lavater, 25 June 1766; Muschg 1942, 134-136. Dr. Zimmermann's tract, *Von der Ruhr unter dem Volke im Jahr 1765*, appeared in 1767 with a small and conventional title vignette by another artist.

[47] Lavater's note reads: 'Engrave this bagatelle in a smaller format and more sharply defined' ('radirt diese Nonchalance einmal kleiner und netter').

editions together with the copperplates to other publishers.[48] The plates accompanying the 1808 trade-share edition of *Paradise Lost* (**Nos. 165B-170B**), acquired in the above fashion from Du Roveray, were merely given a new imprint, i.e. Du Roveray's name was burnished out on the original copperplates which were then re-lettered to indicate the new publisher's name and publication date ('Vernor, Hood & Sharpe, Poultry, 1808'). This operation would have been very economical at a cost of about 7s.5d. per plate, or just under £4.10s. for all twelve plates.[49] Joseph Johnson went one better, saving time and avoiding all engraving and other expenses, by purchasing for his edition of the *Iliad* and the *Odyssey* in Cowper's translation (1810) proof impressions of plates, originally intended for the large paper copies of Du Roveray's own Homer edition (**Nos. 227-236, 237-243**) that had been destroyed in a warehouse fire. Series of engravings, issued either bound or in portfolio form but without accompanying text, such as the forty plates illustrative of Homer's *Iliad* and *Odyssey* (see headnote to **Nos. 227-236**) become a fairly typical phenomenon during this period, although this particular collection is now very rare. However, as examples of this tendency, we may rank the five different 'Series of Engravings ... by Heath, Hall, Rhodes, Fitler', published by John Murray, Alfred Woodmason and H. McLean to illustrate the works of Shakespeare and Milton (**Nos. 132-134, 182-183**), and the two editions of outline 'Illustrations to Shakespeare from the Plates in Boydell's edition', published by A.J. Valpy (**Nos. 117E-125E**).

Thackeray's vivid recollection at almost forty years' remove from his childhood of Boydell's 'black and ghastly gallery' (**Nos. 117-124**), with its 'murky Opies, glum Northcotes, [*and*] straddling Fuselis ... Lear, Oberon, Hamlet, with starting muscles, rolling eyeballs, and long pointing quivering fingers',[50] bears witness not only to Fuseli's imaginative force but also to the curious phenomenon whereby the Boydell illustrations became canonical examples of 'the older nobler style of acting', and were reused in various modified forms throughout the century to embellish successive generations of Shakespeare editions.[51] Such secondary versions were usually copied from other engravings rather than by reference to an original, and thus the duplicate image is often given in reverse—whereas a surprisingly large proportion of primary engravings after Fuseli were reproduced in the same sense as his originals. Although re-engravings of the 'large Boydell' plates were frequently reduced in size, Chidley's thirty-sixmo Shakespeare (**Nos. 17G-18G, 122G-124G**) was an unusually small format to accommodate these illustrations, especially in view of the fact that they were line engravings rather than the more common outline engravings, popularised in the 1830s by such engravers as Normand fils, Starling and Réveil in their embellishments for Valpy's, Baudry's and Virtue's editions of Shakespeare (by this date engraving on steel was the norm).

---

[48] Du Roveray II, 74-81.

[49] I base this calculation on the unit price for 'Engraving writing on 37 Plates' given *infra* in the 'Publication Expenses for Chalmers' Shakespeare' (p. 358).

[50] [William Makepeace Thackeray], '*Pictures of Life and Character*. By John Leech, London, 1854', *Quarterly Review*, 96 (December 1854), 75.

[51] Geoffrey Ashton, 'The Boydell Shakespeare Gallery: Before and After', in *The Painted Word*, 1991, 40. The popularity of engraved illustrations of Shakespeare in the eighteenth and early nineteenth century may be measured by the 212 editions included in Ashton's forthcoming 'Catalogue of illustrated editions of Shakespeare, 1709-1850', (*The Painted Word*, 43, note 1). For her part, Esther Gordon Dotson, in her 'English Shakespeare Illustration and Eugène Delacroix', suggests a baseline figure of over 650 separate designs of scenes from Shakespeare's plays published between 1780 and 1810 in editions of the plays or in collections of Shakespeare prints (*Marsyas*, Suppl. II, 1965, 47 note). She deliberately excludes from this number separately published prints like those in the Boydell Gallery and other miscellaneous collections.

Other productions, such as *Robin Goodfellow-Puck* (**No. 125**) and Haughton's stipple, *Solitude (Twilight)* (**No. 178**) reappear as wood-engravings. The woodblock became the most widely used kind of printed illustration in the early Victorian period, owing to the comparative cheapness that resulted from single printing of pages containing both type and picture.[52] When *Robin Goodfellow* and the other 'small Boydell' plates were translated into woodcut headpieces for Sherwood's editions of Shakespeare's plays (**No. 125B**), the accompanying reduction in size eliminated a great deal of detail. This did not detract from their attraction for the Hartford, Connecticut publisher, Silas Andrus and his successors, for whom they became standard embellishments in a remarkable series of twenty different popular American editions (**No. 125C**) between 1828 and 1854.

Throughout much of the eighteenth century, book-illustration and printselling served as a market for artists' and engravers' skills and as a means of stimulating public interest in both the arts and literature. But Northcote was correct in asserting that before Boydell and his Shakespeare Gallery no entrepreneur had ever 'been at the expense and risk of setting a mighty machine to work'[53] to create a demand for history paintings as opposed to portraits. With the proliferation of such galleries and the commissions they generated a radical shift occurred in the traditional patronage system, transforming print publishers into new patrons of the arts. The wars with France by interdicting the export of prints to the Continent crippled the trade and fatally undermined Boydell's Shakespeare Gallery, the first and most famous of such schemes. Even so, Boydell had demonstrated that the publication of engravings could be very profitable, while also shaping the taste for literary illustration, particularly of Shakespeare, and promoting the careers of certain artists. But though Fuseli eventually became with Moses Haughton his own publisher (see the items listed under his name in the 'Index of Publishers'), he was never able to make the sale of prints after his own work a meaningful source of income,[54] perhaps because, unlike Lawrence, he was disinclined to cater to the popular print market by 'an[y] attempt of uniting the Goddess with the Belle'.[55] Fuseli's one real possibility 'to lay, hatch and Crack' such a profitable egg for himself[56] was thwarted, when plans for a sumptuously illustrated edition of Milton to be edited by William Cowper and published by Joseph Johnson as an adjunct to the exhibition of Fuseli's Milton paintings

---

[52] Eric de Maré, *Victorian Woodblock Illustrators*, 1981, 7.

[53] *Conversations of James Northcote R.A. with James Ward*, ed. Ernest Fletcher, 1901, 121f.

[54] Compare in this respect, the profitable 'joint-stock adventure' with painter and engraver as 'sole proprietors' initiated in 1812 by Wilkie and Raimbach to publish engravings after Wilkie's paintings. Under this arrangement Wilkie received one-third (later reduced to one quarter) and Raimbach two-thirds (later increased to three quarters) of the proceeds (Abraham Raimbach, *Memoirs and Recollections*, 1843, 112).

[55] By the 1820s Lawrence's work had become so popular that Hurst and Robinson were paying him £3,000 a year for the right of engraving his pictures (Douglas Goldring, *Regency Portrait Painter: The Life of Sir Thomas Lawrence, P.R.A.*, 1951, 295). Fuseli's phrase is cited by Kenneth Garlick, who concludes, however, that while Lawrence adapted his style to the mood of the day, he never lowered his professional standards or pandered to the taste of the readers of *The Keepsake*, *The Bijou* and *The Amulet* (*Sir Thomas Lawrence*, 1955, 14). For a closely-documented discussion of the extent to which the demand for prints influenced the art of another fashionable painter, i.e. Angelica Kauffman, whose work became 'the major inspiration for a new kind of decorative print', see David Alexander, 'Kauffman and the Print Market in Eighteenth-century England' in *Angelica Kauffman A Continental Artist in Georgian England*, ed. Wendy Wassying Roworth, 1992, 140-178.

[56] To William Roscoe, 17 August 1790; *Letters*, 61. Fuseli cites here as one example of this, Benjamin West's 'prints from English History and the Late advertisement of Allegorical prints to be published from his designs by Bartolozzi'.

had to be abandoned due to a recurrence of Cowper's insanity.[57]

There were fewer opportunities for exhibition in the wake of Boydell's collapse and the general decay of the other historical galleries but not necessarily a dearth of commissions for painters such as Fuseli, for whom literature still remained the major source of their inspiration. The patronage function of the galleries passed instead in great measure to the publishers of such popular series of small-format illustrated editions as C. Cooke's 'Pocket Library of the Original & Complete Works of Select British Poets ... Novels [*and*] Sacred Classics' (for which Fuseli did not execute any commissions); and John Sharpe's 'British Theatre' (**No. 184**), 'British Classics' (**Nos. 185-186**), 'The Works of the British Poets' (**Nos. 180-181**), and 'The Works of the Greek and Roman Poets' (**No. 294**); and above all, from the point of view of Fuseli, the connoisseur Francis Isaac Du Roveray (1772-1849), active as a publisher from 1798 to 1806, for whose neatly printed octavo editions of the classic eighteenth-century English poets (which included Alexander Pope's translation of Homer) Fuseli supplied thirty designs, all but four in the form of oil paintings, representing over a quarter of Du Roveray's 114 published illustrations. Fuseli's services were also in demand by better known members of the publishing establishment ('The Trade'), and we might note that in this same period Fuseli was selected to execute a total of sixty-nine designs as sole illustrator of A. Chalmers' *Shakespeare* (**Nos. 189-225**) for the 'Proprietors' headed by F.C. & J. Rivington; Cowper's *Poems* (**Nos. 267-274**) and other authors (**Nos. 142-145, 146-149, 173-176**) for Joseph Johnson; and Wieland's *Oberon*, translated by W. Sotheby (**Nos. 244-255**) for Cadell & Davies. The first decade of the new century was thus one of Fuseli's most productive periods, albeit still characterised by the lack of 'a Public,—the only Legitimate and effectual patron of the Arts'.[58]

Fuseli was fortunate to live in an age of great engravers. Joseph Strutt's boast in 1785 that 'The Art of Engraving was never more encouraged than at the present day, especially in England, where every man of taste is in some degree a collector of prints',[59] coincided with a spate of artistic and publishing projects intended to enshrine Shakespeare, Spenser and Milton in illustration. At last both the typography of their works and the illustrations which embellished them truly reflected their literary stature. In this process engravers also had a starring role, often producing works more striking and atmospheric than the paintings on which they were based. According to Pye it was the 'spirit of rivalry' and the concentration on book-embellishments of this sort, called forth by the lack of 'more important employment' after the mid-1790s, which inculcated in British line-engravers the skills, exemplified 'in the plates of Raimbach and Warren', which enabled them to 'render proofs of their works highly finished pictures in black and white'.[60] Yet, by the 1850s the reproductive engraver, as a species, was in the throes of extinction, wiped out by the rapid advances in photo-mechanisation. 'Men of taste', the Redgraves proclaimed in elegiac tones in 1866, 'do not now care to collect engravings; the art has deteriorated, and the greatest of our living engravers are neglected'.[61]

---

[57] The project was described in the *Proposals*, dated 'London, Sept. 1, 1791', for 'Engraving and Publishing by Subscription | Thirty Capital Plates, | From Subjects in | Milton; | To be Painted Principally, if not Entirely, by | Henry Fuseli, R.A.' (Copy at Yale in the Beinecke Library).

[58] To William Roscoe, 25-29 April 1802; *Letters*, 248. This is also the tenor of Fuseli's Twelfth Lecture: 'On the Present State of the Art, and the Causes which Check its Progress', Knowles 1831, III, 41-59.

[59] Joseph Strutt, *A Biographical Dictionary; Containing an Historical Account of all the Engravers, from the earliest period of the Art of Engraving to the Present Time*, 2 vols., 1785, I, v.

[60] John Pye, *Patronage of British Art, An Historical Sketch*, 1845, 372.

[61] Samuel & Richard Redgrave, *A Century of British Painters*, 1866, I, 464.

Fuseli and his fellow-Academicians had always taken the importance of engraving to their own endeavours for granted, considering it as no more than a refined handicraft. Joseph Farington reports a discussion on this subject in his *Diary*, where a remark had been made to the effect that '*Musical men* [were] generally ... ignorant silly fellows, but that Painters ... were men of more talent & power than any other body of men'. To this Sir George Beaumont added that '*executive musicians* He would compare to Engravers, who only execute with skill the ideas of others'.[62] Fuseli unqualifiedly shared this view, notwithstanding the importance of the engraved print in his own education and in consolidating his artistic reputation in the public mind. 'Translation and engraving', he tells us in his Aphorism 138, 'however useful to man or dear to art is the unequivocal homage of inferiority offered by taste and talent to the majesty of genius'.[63] This is not far removed from the view expressed by Jean-Baptiste Du Bos, contrasting the workaday or 'mechanic' productions of 'de vils ouvriers & des manoeuvres, dont il faut payer les journées' and those of true genius.[64] It is a telling comment on the engraver's status that when Farington was approached about helping a deaf and dumb youth who 'loved to be employed in drawing', Farington agreed that 'He might be taught the Art of Engraving. Painting was mentioned but given up as being less certain'.[65]

Fuseli's prejudice was of long standing. He was not prepared to waste 'great thoughts and noble lines', he once told Lavater, on a dull engraver who was only capable of seeing the most blatantly obvious.[66] He ungraciously informed Du Roveray that if engravers 'deserve[d] to be employed at all', they had no excuse for delay, 'Considering the Comparative facility of their task which has nothing of the precariousness of the Painter's, who is often obliged to wait for happy moments',[67] reinforcing what he had earlier told Du Roveray, 'In a work of Taste Time must or ought to wait on Fancy'.[68] His reaction to John Landseer's petition to the Prince Regent in 1812 to allow engravers into the Academy on the same footing as other academicians is, thus, hardly surprising: he considered it 'a subversion of the physical and moral principles of the Institution'.[69] It was not until 1853 that the rules of the Royal Academy were changed concerning membership of engravers; the first full-fledged Academician Engraver was elected in 1855.[70]

John Singleton Copley's opinion that 'the difficulties of a Painter began when his picture was finished, if an engraving from it should be his object',[71] was obviously shared by Fuseli. In an anonymous review of Macklin's Gallery of British Poets, Fuseli praises his own painting, *Prince*

---

[62] *Farington Diary*, 13 April 1806; VII (1982), 2718.

[63] Knowles 1831, III, 113.

[64] '... low workmen and labourers, paid by the day'. J.B. Du Bos, *Réflexions critiques sur la poësie et sur la peinture*, 1746, II, 6-7, cited by John Barrell, *The Political Theory of Painting from Reynolds to Hazlitt*, 1986, 41.

[65] *Farington Diary*, 20 May 1814; XIII (1984), 4519.

[66] To J.C. Lavater (declining to execute very small designs for his *Physiognomy*), 2 November 1770; Muschg 1942, 161.

[67] To F.I. Du Roveray, 2 August 1799; Freies Deutsches Hochstift, Goethe-Museum, Frankfurt a/M (HS 22214).

[68] To F.I. Du Roveray, 2 April 1798; *Letters*, 183.

[69] Minute Books of the General Assembly, Royal Academy of Arts, III, 91.

[70] Sidney C. Hutchison, *The History of the Royal Academy 1768-1968*, 1968, 115.

[71] *Farington Diary*, 21 November 1794; I (1978), 262.

Arthur's Vision ('Arthur's soul seems to have transfused itself into the painter's eye, when he conceived this vision'!), but indicts Bartolozzi's handling of *Queen Katharine's Dream* (**No. 77**), begging the public not to do the painter an injustice by judging his picture by the engraving: '*Katharine* and *Patience* have lost their character and individual expression, *Griffith* his limbs, the *Vision* its splendor'.[72] Fuseli's letter of 27 September 1802 to Du Roveray respecting Bromley's failure to achieve 'adequate transcripts' of his paintings *Satan Calling up his Legions* (**No. 165**) and *Satan Starting from the Touch of Ithuriel's Spear* (**No. 168**) is a typical analysis of his engraver's performance: the former is 'too much of one depth ... the Shadows want more work; ... the feet, the hands, the knees of Satan want more precision ... the figure of Beelzebub Labours under the Same defects ... the Sky is insipid', etc.; in the latter 'the atmosphere in which Satan moves is rendered dim by the Want of Strength ... the face wants grandeur and truth in the Outline, and the foot a toe. ... The Shadows of the drapery ought to be much more Vigorous', etc.[73] Fuseli is equally critical about Isaac Taylor's work on *Briseis Led Away by the Heralds* (**No. 227**), the first of Fuseli's Homer illustrations, where Achilles has a double chin and 'Seems more fit to hold a Living than a Spear', while his 'Lower part ... is too puny for the upper'.[74]

Yet much as he fulminated against them ('All the best Engraver can do is mar your work and empty your pocket'), Fuseli was generally well served by his engravers, whose ranks included many of the foremost practitioners of the art. His bold and imaginative designs tended to work to his advantage in this respect, and he was undoubtedly on occasions the beneficiary of the generally recognised power of the good engraver to heighten the artistic force of his original. 'Considered as a whole of Light and Shade', Raphael Smith's mezzotint of *Lady Macbeth Walking in Her Sleep* [**No. 71**], had exceeded Fuseli's expectation and did him 'more than Engraver's justice'.[75] Despite his difficulties in 'obtaining a light Style from Copying pictures So much loaded with Colour',[76] Isaac Taylor showed commendable initiative in his attempts to accurately render Fuseli's Homer pictures. It is unusual to have such detailed commentaries by an engraver on his overall strategy and techniques as we find in Taylor's letters to Du Roveray. In his plate of *Odysseus Addressing the Shade of Ajax in Tartarus* (**No. 239**), Taylor 'adopted a novel method of representing the Spectre ... which gives to the Engraving all that aerial insubstantiality which the painter Secures by his blue and green tints'. He had had 'a stroke' laid with the ruling machine 'over the Sky and the ghost [*thereby*] uniting him to the Air itself and ... made out his Shape and effect by delicate Strokes on him the way of the drawing'.[77]

Charles Warren was no less ingenious in trying to decipher Fuseli's design (now lost) for *Lady Macbeth Walking in her Sleep* (**No. 203**) for Chalmers' Shakespeare (1805). Warren was extremely

---

[72] [H. Fuseli], Review of 'A Catalogue of the Second Exhibition of Pictures, painted for Mr. Macklin ... by the Artists of Great Britain, illustrative of the British Poets', *The Analytical Review*, IV (July 1789), 369.

[73] *Letters*, 252-253.

[74] To F.I. Du Roveray, 22 November 1803; Collection D.H. Weinglass. Fuseli also recommended to Taylor 'a Careful examination of the Lines of the Picture; if the Eye fail, there is Little to be hoped from the Ear in anything of this Kind'.

[75] To Unknown Addressee, c. September 1783; *Letters*, 21. See also Antal 1956, who considers that 'thanks partly to the engravers' the engravings after Fuseli for Chalmers' edition of Shakespeare 'have an appearance of greater reality than is usual in Fuseli' (125).

[76] Isaac Taylor to F.I. Du Roveray, 9 October 1806; *Letters*, 353.

[77] Isaac Taylor to F.I. Du Roveray, 24 June 1806; *Letters*, 345.

puzzled by 'two extraordinary projectiles placed a little above [*Lady Macbeth's*] head ... totally unlike anything he had ever seen on a female head [*but*] concluded they must be symbols designed by the imaginative Fuseli to express in some way or other, her savage character or night-walking propensities. ... At length clapping his hand to his forehead, "By Jove", said he ... "how could I be so stupid as not to think of it before? Wings! ... bat's wings—flying by night—blood suckers too—just as she is". ... Thus congratulating himself, he set to work, engraved the plate, and took the proof impression to Fuseli, who considered it attentively. "What's *that?*" said he pointing to the Lady's forehead. "Wings, sir; you meant them for wings, did you not?" "Not I", replied Fuseli; "I meant nothing but her night-cap. ... Never mind, let them stand". The plate was accordingly so published, with wings standing out from Lady Macbeth's temples'.[78] As it happens, in his depictions of the *Nibelungenlied*—and in the remarkable series of transmogrified portraits of his wife—Fuseli does frequently draw women's hair in the form of Gorgon wings or the winged head-dress of a Medusa, as a symbol of the dominating wife or virago (i.e. sadistic or virilised woman). From this point of view, Mary Balmanno's story at first struck me as being purely apocryphal; but after re-examining the handful of surviving drawings from the original thirty-seven from which the engravers prepared the plates to this edition of Shakespeare, I am now inclined rather to see the anecdote as reflecting the unfinished quality of the sketches from which the engravers were expected to work.

A special relationship is often invoked between Fuseli and Blake, based on the premise that Fuseli would never have provided the engraver with such cursory designs to work up into full-fledged compositions as those for **Nos. 80, 115, and 162**, unless he had an exceptionally trusting relationship with Blake. It is true that Fuseli was particularly close to Blake at least during the 1790s and that they shared a great many mythographic concerns. Yet overall it does not appear to have been uncommon for Fuseli to submit quite rudimentary sketches to engravers other than Blake to work up in similar if not always such extensive fashion. This may be the case with several of Fuseli's (missing) designs for Willoughby's *Practical Family Bible*, assuming, for example, that the Swedish National Museum's *David and Goliath* is in fact the preliminary sketch for the plate (**No. 27**) and not a Roman reworking of the same theme. Chalmers' Shakespeare designs also seem to have been substantially modified; it is indicative of the haste and informality with which they were prepared, that Schiff nos. 1405 and 1411 each have a second design on the verso. Such practices do not appear to have been particularly unusual, witness the leeway Turner allowed his engravers in the initial stages of preparing their plates: although 'of little value *as drawings*', the slightest of Turner's sketches sufficed for his engravers, who understood him 'perfectly' and thus knew how to '*make* [them] *out*'; they could count on Turner to 'touch & retouch' their plates to achieve certain desired effects.[79] Fuseli also closely supervised his engraver, making 'it a rule in any capital Engraving made from Paintings or Drawings by him, to have Impressions taken from the plates in various Stages of it', as is borne out by at least one collector's '5 proofs in different Stages [*of the Witches' meeting Macbeth on the Heath*,] one [*with*] Corrections by Fuseli himself for the Engraver' (**No. 120**).[80] William Bromley was clearly not the only engraver who feared the artist's predictable reaction to an unsatisfactory performance, when he expressed his feeling to Du Roveray that it would be 'plainly ... dangerous to [*his*] interest to shew *Celadon and Amelia* [**No.**

---

[78] Mary Balmanno, 'Henry Fuseli, Esq., R.A.', in *Pen and Pencil* (New York: D. Appleton, 1858), 199.

[79] Cited by Luke Herrmann, *Turner Prints: The Engraved Work of J.M.W. Turner*, 1990, 183.

[80] Note by the unidentified grangeriser ('G:') of an extra-illustrated copy of a 'small Boydell Shakespeare' now in the Folger Library (PR2752.1802 Copy 2, Vol. 4, before p. 61).

163] in an imperfect state to Mr. Fuseli'.[81] Perhaps not all engravers would have agreed with Isaac Taylor about the particular stage in the process when the painter should be consulted about 'touching a proof'. He considered that 'the Engraver Should first make out his effect and do all but the last harmonizings and Scratchings before he troubles the painter for his opinion[—]While the Engraver Sees before him much to do why Should he ask directions[?]'[82]

Such cases tend to mitigate the stern finality of Thomas Griffiths Wainewright's declaration, in his persona as C. Van Vinkbooms, that 'The first essential of a print is implicit fidelity to the original'.[83] The master engraver, like the artist who illustrated a work of literature, was no servile copyist, but rather translated a painting to the plate, using his own very different set of graphic conventions to convert colour, tone and painterly mass into line. John Timbs, citing William Sharp's 'transcendent work from West's *Lear*', did not hesitate to assert that 'the power of a first-rate engraver, even of other men's designs, does not lie within the scope of mere talent; but that it is *genius*, and of a higher order than that displayed by many a painter, who looks upon engravers as artists much below him'.[84] Landseer viewed 'Engraving [*as*] no more an art of *copying* Painting, than the English language is *an art of copying* Greek or Latin. Engraving is a distinct language of Art'.[85] Robert Hartley Cromek saw its essential quality exemplified in the work of Louis Schiavonetti as 'a harmony analogous to that of composition in painting, of numbers [*i.e. verse*] in poetry, and of sounds in music'.[86] The most desirable qualities of a print are characterised in a typical critique by Robert Hunt as the 'vigour', 'energy and exactness' of the copy, the 'spirit and richness of its forms', the judicious 'gradations of light and shade', and its overall 'refinement, mellowness' and 'harmony'.[87] The constituents of these latter qualities ('delicacy, clearness and richness of Style') are specifically located by Isaac Taylor in 'the middle tints' of the plate. 'The light tints Scarcely catch the eye enough to give it either pleasure or disgust[;] the dark tints cut away the Copper So much that there is Scarcely white enough between the Strokes to Show them out with any beauty'.[88] The engraver's practice of requesting from the publisher 'a proof of one of his best engravings' in order to avoid 'varying too much the work and colour of the one they are now about',[89] thereby conforming the whole range of different prints intended to embellish a particular work is in keeping with the above aesthetic intent.

Engravers capable of such virtuosity invariably commanded fees commensurate with their reputation, and considerably higher than those paid to the artists whose paintings they made accessible to the public. Thus, William Woollett (1735-1785) received between £6,000 and £7,000

---

[81] W. Bromley to F.I. Du Roveray, 18 November 1801; *Letters*, 243-244.

[82] To F.I. Du Roveray, 18 March 1803; *Letters*, 265.

[83] *Essays and Criticisms by Thomas Griffiths Wainewright*, collected by W. Carew Hazlitt, 1880, 192, 194.

[84] John Timbs, 'Henry Fuseli, R.A.', *Anecdote Lives of William Hogarth, Sir Joshua Reynolds, Thomas Gainsborough, Henry Fuseli, Sir Thomas Lawrence, and J.M.W. Turner*, 1860 (reprt. 1887), 221.

[85] John Landseer, *Lectures on the Art of Engraving, Delivered at the Royal Institution of Great Britain*, 1807, 177.

[86] Obituary of Louis Schiavonetti, *The Examiner*, 1810, 413.

[87] *The Examiner*, 1812, 234.

[88] Isaac Taylor to F.I. Du Roveray, 17 September 1806; *Letters*, 352.

[89] Louis Schiavonetti to F.I. Du Roveray, 14 October 1803; Philadelphia Free Library, 'Autograph Letters of Engravers', vol. S-T.

for his engraving of Benjamin West's *Death of Wolfe*;[90] Louis Schiavonetti was paid 840 guineas for engraving Stothard's painting of *The Procession of Chaucer's Canterbury Pilgrims*, while for his four years' work on Copley's *Death of Lord Chatham* William Sharp received 1,200 guineas.[91] (One of the amenities of the good life which an élite engraver like James Fittler enjoyed, and that Sharp also shared, at least 'in the meridian of his career', was 'a servant in livery').[92] From this point of view, it is instructive to compare Fuseli's remuneration for his large Boydell paintings with the payments his various engravers received. The highest price paid Fuseli was £294 for *Titania and Bottom* in *A Midsummer Night's Dream*; Simon's reward was £367. In every case but one (viz., *Falstaff and Doll Tearsheet*, for which Leney received £105 and Fuseli £63), the engraver's fee exceeded the highest paid the painter: for engraving *Lear* Earlom received £420, as opposed to the £262 that Fuseli earned; *Macbeth* garnered £383 for Caldwell and Trotter in contrast to Fuseli's £210. This latter was the same amount Fuseli received for *Hamlet* and the *Tempest*: Thew and Simon were each remunerated £315. For *King Henry V Condemning the Conspirators*, Thew again received £315, whereas Fuseli's labours were adjudged at a mere £63.[93]

Fuseli's commissions round the turn of the century tended to be for smaller paintings, paid at a much lower rate than those he executed for Boydell. The twelve illustrations to *Oberon* (**Nos. 244-255**) that Fuseli executed for Cadell & Davies (each approx. 24 x 18 inches) carried a price tag of ten guineas per painting; the eighteen guineas per plate for *Oberon* seems to be an average payment for an engraver during this period, although Anker Smith and William Sharp probably averaged at least two guineas more for each of their plates; the engravers selected to execute the Cowper plates all received twenty-five guineas. Fuseli's fee was probably closer to the '15 guineas a piece' that he received in 1797 for the four small pictures from *Hamlet* and *Macbeth* (£63), that he executed for 'Heath's Shakespeare' (1807), and which were commissioned by the engraver-publisher himself.[94] Only two of these were actually engraved (**Nos. 182-183**) before being auctioned off by the engraver in 1808.[95] An 1806 letter from Landseer to Du Roveray indicates that Du Roveray had given 'some Years ago ... 60 Guineas for 4 of Fuseli's pictures'.[96] Unfortunately, it is not clear whether these 'pictures' were paintings or large highly finished watercolours, although the context seems to suggest the latter.

In the mid-1760s Fuseli's going price for his designs had been two guineas.[97] Forty years later, Fuseli accepted three guineas per drawing from Rivington, on behalf of the booksellers, for thirty-seven designs for Chalmers' edition of Shakespeare (1805). Disadvantageous as this might appear in comparison with Du Roveray's prices, from whom Fuseli received £31 for *The Cave of Spleen* (**No. 153**) and £21 for *The Descent of Odin* (**No. 157**), we should note that three guineas was the same rate at which Stothard was employed by 'the Trade' at this period. The drawings for Du

---

[90] John Pye, *Patronage of British Art, An Historical Sketch*, 1845, 244.

[91] G.E. Bentley, Jr., 'The Great Illustrated-Book Publishers of the 1790s and William Blake', in *Editing Illustrated Books*, ed. William Blissett, 1980, 62 and 92 (notes 9, 10).

[92] Abraham Raimbach, *Memoirs and Recollections*, 1843, 36, note 55.

[93] These prices are tabulated in Friedman 1974, 222-223.

[94] To William Roscoe, 5 December 1797; *Letters*, 175.

[95] Fredericksen 1990, II, Pt. 1, 378.

[96] John Landseer to F.I. Du Roveray, 2 February 1806; *Letters*, 339-340.

[97] To J.C. Lavater, 20 August 1766 (from Tours); Muschg 1942, 137; where he boasts to his correspondent that he receives 'at least' this amount 'for the worst' of his efforts.

Roveray were finished enough to be exhibited at the Royal Academy, whereas the designs for Rivington were much sketchier productions.

We certainly should not imagine, looking at some of the fees cited above, that all engravers lived on easy street. For most engravers there was little 'chance of escape from the thraldom of devoting the labours of a whole life to the end of their being shut up in a book'.[98] Many were forced to augment their income by dealing in prints on the side. Nor were publishers uniformly generous or well disposed towards those who depended on them for employment. Du Roveray, who was generally fair rather than generous towards his engravers, not only solicited them to purchase the commissioned pictures they had just engraved but regularly attempted to get them to accept as much as half their payment in the form of books rather than cash.[99] His correspondence with them was often 'distinctly acerbic' even before they organised their boycott against him in early 1803. G.E. Bentley adduces that it was Du Roveray's 'continued inability to make [*his engravers*] perform like reliable mechanicks [*sic*] and deliver their work at the promised times, [*that*] fostered his disillusionment with publishing as a profession'.[100] Raimbach never forgot his indignation at John Stockdale's offer of two guineas instead of Raimbach's then-standard fee of six guineas; he eventually received four guineas. Likewise, he always remembered the 'air of conscious superiority [*with which*] the rather pompous gentleman-publisher [*C. Cooke*] ... dispensed his patronage among the hungry artists [*i.e. engravers, sometimes*] under the implied condition of "No cure no pay"—that is, if Cooke did not approve, [*the engraver*] was to expect nothing'.[101]

Among the collection of manuscript 'Letters of Engravers' in the Philadelphia Free Library is one written by W. Harrison Craig from 'Felons Side, Newgate', 'this melancholy abode of wretchedness & misery'. A not inconsiderable proportion of such engravers' letters (of which more are preserved in the 'Du Roveray collection' at the Huntington Library) is taken up with requests for advances and or loans to tide them over. Joseph Farington's *Diary* abounds with references to engravers who have become destitute as a result of the excessive demands they made upon their health in the course of their labours. For example, Farington notes in 1813 that three engravers had died within the previous three years of consumption and over-application; another practitioner had told him that as a result of an extended stint of 14-hour workdays, 'his head was in such a state as to cause Him to think the House in which he was wd. fall over him'.[102] (For the grueling work-regimen of engravers, see also Basil Hunnisett's *Steel-engraved Book Illustration in England*, Scolar, 1980). The lucky engravers among the smaller fry were those who had something else to fall back on. When commissions during the wars with France became 'like angels' visits ... few and far between', Abraham Raimbach turned to painting in miniature to eke out his 'extremely scanty income'.[103] Isaac Taylor, probably not untypically, could count upon his daughter Jane to

---

[98] Abraham Raimbach, *Memoirs and Recollections*, 1843, 112.

[99] Re purchase, see John Landseer and R.H. Cromek (*Letters* 339-340, 363), and William Bromley (3 February 1806; Philadelphia Free Library, 'Letters of Engravers', vol. B-C, 88); both Thomas Holloway (*Letters* 194) and Isaac Taylor (15 March 1803; 'Letters of Engravers', vol. S-T, 8), were prepared to take copies of books.

[100] Du Roveray III, 100-103.

[101] Abraham Raimbach, *Memoirs and Recollections*, 1843, 23-24; 25.

[102] *Farington Diary*, 25 February 1813; XII (1983), 4304-4305.

[103] Abraham Raimbach, *Memoirs and Recollections*, 1843, 28.

share his drudgery, by completing at least the backgrounds of plates he was working on.[104] When for similar reasons Taylor too fell on slack times as an engraver, he became a nonconformist minister, first at Colchester and then at Ongar in Essex. Fate was even kinder to Henry Hole of Liverpool who immediately retired as a wood engraver when he came into an inheritance.

Once the decision was arrived at to publish a book in a given format, embellished with a certain number of engraved prints,[105] the publisher would proceed as rapidly as possible to commission artists and engravers and assign them their respective subjects so that he could set about advertising the work and issuing 'Proposals' to attract subscribers, whose earnest money would help cover some of the initial costs of production. As to the painter's choice of subject, he probably generally had less leeway in this than we tend to assume (see *supra* p. xvi). Du Roveray's consistent use of at least two different artists whose designs complemented each other to illustrate his various editions, certainly seems to suggest close control in this respect, although Fuseli clearly retained considerable independence in choosing his own subjects from Homer.[106]

Irrespective of whether the engraver himself picked up the painter's design, or other arrangements were made to convey paintings from London to distant engravers like Isaac Taylor, who lived in Colchester,[107] it was usual for the publisher to supply the engraver with the copper plate(s) he would need for his task.[108] The proofs submitted to the artist for his judgment (the process of taking impressions from a plate in progress was commonly referred to by contemporary engravers as 'proving') were normally taken off by copperplate printers,[109] rather than the engraver himself. Characteristic of this diversification within the structure of the trade was the full-blown development by now of new areas of specialisation for engravers, such as laying in ground,

---

[104] See Isaac Taylor to F.I. Du Roveray, 13 January 1806; Philadelphia Free Library, 'Letters of Engravers', vol. S-T, 24. Taylor in his *Memoirs of the Late Jane Taylor* (available to me only in the first American ed., Lowell, Mass., 1829) relates how the 'active and laborious' Jane's 'cares of family were suffered, but in a small degree, to infringe upon the customary hours devoted to engraving' (38), although Jane herself complained that despite getting up at six a.m. and 'getting every thing in order before breakfast [*and*] with all [*her*] endeavours' she could not 'begin engraving before eleven; to which I sit down again half an hour after dinner' (40).

[105] The booksellers, Cadell and Davies, had always relied heavily on Roscoe's literary judgment (see Robert D. Thornton's detailed account in *James Currie, The Entire Stranger and Robert Burns*, 1963, of his important advisory role in the publication of Robert Burns's *Works*, 1800), but Fuseli's letter of 21 June 1804 (*Letters*, 300), alerting Roscoe that Cadell and Davies will be requesting his opinion about the 'choice of Subjects [*and*] Number' of illustrations in *Oberon* shows how much weight they placed on his advice in artistic matters. It is interesting also to learn here that the artist had a say in deciding whether 'the prints' should be engraved after 'designs or pictures', one of the criteria being 'if the Sale of the work warrant the expence'.

[106] Du Roveray III, 142-144.

[107] To F.I. Du Roveray, 5 July 1803 (acknowledging safe arrival of the 'Case Containing two of Fuseli's pictures'); *Letters*, 272.

[108] See the letters of similar import among the 'Letters of Engravers' in the Philadelphia Free Library from William Bromley (7 December 1805; vol. B-C, 87) and R.H. Cromek (8 August 1803; vol. E-G, 131) to F.I. Du Roveray, requesting that 'the Picture by Mr Fuseli together with a plate for engraving the same' be sent by the bearer.

[109] Thus, according to Du Roveray, John Dixon, Tottenham Street (fl. 1799-1836), was 'universally allowed to be the best [copperplate] printer'; but Du Roveray 'could not bear Gravel's proofs [James Gravel, Red Lion Court, fl. 1790-1806], on account of their flatness and want of Spirit' (*Letters*, 348).

engraving borders, aquatinting margins, lettering, and even hotpressing the prints/proofs. Examples of etched proofs are illustrated in **Figures 12 and 13** accompanying **Nos. 235 and 239**. It is interesting to note that 'India paper' was not at first a preferred medium for proof impressions.[110] One reason for this was that 'it frequently came loose and started from the paper'. Robert Balmanno, who was an occasional etcher (see **No. 287**) solved this problem, c. 1810, by 'Boydelling' items 'in that started state' by taking them to Boydell's printing office, where he had the printer 'brush the back of the proof with thin paste, lay it on [*a polished*] plate [*of copper*], the paper over and then run it through the press. It answered to perfection'.[111]

As earlier noted, a design in the form of a drawing could be transferred to the grounded plate by indenting the outlines with a stylus. However, in the case of a painting the procedure obviously called for an intermediate stage: the painting was 'squared' i.e. covered with a grid of chalked lines, thereby enabling the engraver to produce an appropriately reduced drawing. William Sharp's squared working drawing for the never-completed engraving of Fuseli's *Macbeth and the Armed Head* is reproduced in Susan Lambert's *The Image Multiplied*, pl. 36. It had long been customary for engravers to engrave large distant paintings by reference to copies prepared by another artist for this purpose. But when Sharp began work on Fuseli's huge painting *Satan, Sin and Death* (13 x 10 feet), Fuseli characteristically insisted on giving him 'the picture itself, not a Copy'. However, because of the painting's size he enlisted the bridge-building skills of Thomas Paine, author of the *Rights of Man*, 'who is a Mechanic as well as a Demogorgon ... to Contrive a roller' on which to install it in Sharp's house.[112]

This obvious interdependence of painter and engraver resulted in what Carol Wax aptly refers to as 'complex symbiotic relationships' between these two related factions. It also encouraged the best engravers and painters to seek each other out.[113] The association between Fuseli and Blake with its glamorous overtones of two creative artists sharing mythographic, artistic and literary concerns has always overshadowed the less well known working collaboration, lasting seventeen years, between Fuseli and Moses Haughton, particularly since the latter relationship may have been based on little beyond Haughton's youthful malleability and his skill as a reproductive engraver. But it is this which links Haughton and Fuseli to such other durable and productive pairings of engraver and painter as Allan Ramsay and David Martin (1737-1798), Sir Joshua Reynolds and Giuseppe Filippo Liberato Marchi (1737?-1808), David Wilkie and Abraham Raimbach (1776-1843), and Sir Thomas Lawrence and Samuel Cousins (1801-1887).

I have outlined in the Catalogue (pp. 187, 222-223) the important stages in the relationship between Fuseli and Haughton, from the early rather dismissive reference to the young neophyte who had 'travestied' his figures[114] ('it is done with more freedom than taste ... it wants much more finishing ... to be intitled to the pompous Fecit under it'),[115] to the warm accolade four years later ('he has, with other qualifications, those which are the most Valuable in an Engraver, fidelity,

---

[110] Abraham Raimbach to F.I. Du Roveray, 31 January 1803; Philadelphia Free Library, 'Letters of Engravers', vol. N-R, 17.

[111] Robert Balmanno to John Sartain, 26 March 1860; Balmanno papers, Manuscript Division, NYPL.

[112] To William Roscoe, 29 May 1792; *Letters*, 81.

[113] Carol Wax, *The Mezzotint History and Technique*, New York, 1990, 56.

[114] To William Roscoe, 4 January 1799; *Letters*, 192.

[115] To William Roscoe, 17 August 1798; *Letters*, 187.

diligence and taste'),[116] and finally his anointing as Fuseli's engraver-in-residence, when he moved into Fuseli's house in Berner's Street in 1803, later accompanying him to Somerset House when Fuseli became Keeper. I wish to explore here briefly some of the implications not discussed in the Catalogue of Fuseli's thus 'buying up' the services of a promising engraver. The action itself appears to have been unusual only in its successful outcome: a 'tempting offer' by Lawrence to Samuel Cousins in 1826 was rebuffed.[117]

However, for Haughton, in the financial sense at least, the price he paid for subordinating his craft to the needs of Fuseli's genius was substantial, although Fuseli was insistent that this was 'intirely *his own offer and more in his interest than mine*' (Fuseli's italics).[118] But as Haughton wrote to Roscoe in a letter, dated 27 June 1806, requesting payment of his outstanding 'little account': 'so much of my time for the last three Years having been spent on a work that as yet [']as made so little return for my labour ... I am nearly Pennyless— ... I am very unwell owing to incessant labour, and never having been out of the smoke of London for the last three Years, and am led to believe that an excursion for a few days would restore my strength and render me capable of pursuing with vigour my speculation in the Prints'.[119] To this we might add that Haughton seems to have assumed with his role of engraver-in-residence also the more indeterminate one of Fuseli's assistant, although we must be careful not to overstate this. Thus, we find Haughton squaring canvases for Fuseli;[120] sending off paintings for him;[121] and collecting money due him from the booksellers.[122]

Fuseli had very exact ideas of what he wanted from his engraver; hence the arrangement which lasted until 1819 served Fuseli's purposes eminently well. There was considerable truth in Edward Roscoe's jesting comment that Haughton received Fuseli's commands with 'all submission'.[123] What Fuseli wanted from his single engraver was the kind of stylistic and tonal uniformity that he was hardly likely to find in the deliberate diversity of individual styles that the bookseller often sought in dividing up the engraving assignments for a given set of book-illustrations among several individuals. An older, more experienced engraver would have been less compliant about receiving the kind of detailed guidance that Fuseli surely insisted on giving his engraver. For Bryan Troughton, one of Du Roveray's select clientele of affluent amateurs, the 'chief object' in taking Fuseli's new Milton subjects was his conviction that they were to be 'executed under the immediate superintendance of Fuseli [*and thus*] would have at least the merit of being faithful copies of that great master's painting and manner'—to which he adds, somewhat surprisingly perhaps, 'tho' I cannot much admire the execution of them in general—I am told that Mr. [*Thomas*] Holloway speaks of them in very high terms'.[124] Troughton would have been pleased at Fuseli's statement that 'Moses Houghton [*sic*] is now finishing in my Study, the traced out Lines for a large print

---

[116] To William Roscoe, 20 August 1802; *Letters*, 250.

[117] Alfred Whitman, *Samuel Cousins*, London, 1904, 15, where the cited phrases are used in reference to Lawrence's overtures to the latest recruit on the engraving scene.

[118] To William Roscoe, 15 March 1803; *Letters*, 264.

[119] *Letters*, 345-346.

[120] To William Roscoe, 11 February 1803; *Letters*, 263.

[121] To George Bullock, 21 August 1804; *Letters*, 307.

[122] To Cadell & Davies, 13 June 1805; *Letters*, 318.

[123] Edward Roscoe to Mrs. Jane Roscoe, 10 March 1804; *Letters*, 294.

[124] To F.I. Du Roveray, 19 March 1805; Huntington Library, Du Roveray Collection.

from the *Lazarhouse*,[125] just as he would have applauded the emphasis that Fuseli placed on Haughton's beginning 'the Milton Series ... under my Inspection'.[126]

Haughton's engraving style, although criticised in a harsh review on the publication of *Lycidas* and *The Dream of Eve* as 'extremely singular',[127] was exactly the instrument Fuseli desired. It is clear from his expressed intention, three years before his first Milton Gallery exhibition, 'to execute the work myself in *Acqua Tinta, fortis* or *tallow*',[128] that he did not consider line engraving an appropriate medium for this purpose. He was correct in assuming that a more painterly effect, with greater richness and a fuller tone could be achieved in prints 'of the acqua tinta kind with dotting'.[129] Another of the advantages of stipple over line engraving was the greater ease with which changes could be made on the plate, thereby allowing the engraver more effectively to heighten the effects sought by the painter and to make minor changes more easily.

Haughton's eight smaller plates after Fuseli for Darwin's *Temple of Nature* (**Nos. 173-176**) and Joel Barlow's *The Columbiad* (**Nos. 256-259**) are clearly not in the same category as the fourteen prints engraved 'from Milton, Shakespeare and Dante after Paintings by Fuseli' (out of the intended total of fifty announced in the lost prospectus issued early in 1804).[130] Ranging in size from 29.0 x 24.0 cm to a maximum of 54.0 x 66 cm, all of these prints, particularly the six in horizontal format, exemplify the increased expressiveness and other aesthetic advantages cohering to separate plates and underlined by their significant difference in size from smaller book illustrations in octavo and quarto. Detlef Dörrbecker's point is well taken that they were conceived as what he calls 'furniture prints', and were intended to be viewed as substitutes for paintings.[131] A remark by Du Roveray's client, Bryan Troughton, who was a subscriber to Haughton's plates, may have some bearing on the question of Fuseli's stylistic criteria for these plates. Troughton comments that 'the delay in the publication of the 2nd No [?*The Dream of Eve*] is owing I hear to an alteration in the style of the engraving which was necessary in my opinion and will be for the advantage of the undertaking'.[132] This alteration seems to have entailed increasing the size of subsequent prints and involving the rising aquatint engraver, F.C. Lewis, more closely in the preparation of several later plates. One can only hope that this and other questions relating to the too-long overlooked collaboration of Moses Haughton and Henry Fuseli will receive the further study they deserve.

I have tried in this Introduction to touch on some of the intricate interrelationships between artist, engraver, printer and publisher as exemplified in the engraved illustrations after a major artist. I hope that the documentation assembled in the Catalogue will serve to further advance our understanding of the special role of the print and the illustrated book in the eighteenth and nineteenth centuries.

D.H. Weinglass
Kansas City, April 1993.

---

[125] To William Roscoe, 20 August 1802; *Letters*, 250.

[126] To William Roscoe, 15 November 1803; *Letters*, 291.

[127] *Monthly Magazine*, April 1804, 268.

[128] To William Roscoe, 14 September 1796; *Letters*, 162.

[129] To William Roscoe, 20 August 1802; *Letters*, 250.

[130] To William Roscoe, 27 March 1804; *Letters*, 296.

[131] D.W. Dörrbecker, *Konvention und Innovation: Eigenes und Entliehenes in der Bildform bei William Blake und in der britischen Kunst seiner Zeit*, Berlin: Wasmuth, 1992, 307, 327.

[132] To F.I. Du Roveray, 28 November 1804; Huntington Library, Du Roveray Collection.

ORGANISATION OF THE CATALOGUE
AND EDITORIAL PRINCIPLES

The present catalogue represents a massive expansion of my earlier *Henry Fuseli and the Engraver's Art* (1982). As compared to the 82 entries a decade ago, this comprehensive work contains 306 primary entries, of which 80% (*circa* 240) are book illustrations and 20% (*circa* 66) are separate plates. The secondary versions, i.e. later re-engraved or reissued plates, are about equal in number to the plates in their primary form. The period covered extends from 1764 (the date of the first known engravings after Fuseli) to 1850, by which time reproductive engraving had begun to fall into decline. However, certain items after this date are also represented (among them, pastiches of the *Nightmare*, versions of the Boydell Shakespeare plates up until 1863, and Rudolf Rey's lithograph of *Fuseli and Bodmer in Conversation*, 1878), although all photomechanical reproductions have been excluded. Since my aim is to show as comprehensively as possible the range of Fuseli's illustrations, in whatever media, all engraved reproductions between my stated time limits are considered worthy of inclusion in the catalogue, notwithstanding the inevitable variation in quality.

Entries are organised chronologically; secondary versions are given alternate numbers with appended letters (e.g. **142A, 142B**) and are interpolated within the main numerical sequence. Since the dates of the reissued plates within such interpolated series may range over an extended period—secondary versions of the Boydell plates, for example, are documented from as early as 1799 (**117A-123A**) to 1863 (**117K-124K**) and beyond—users of the catalogue might find it helpful in such cases to refer to the running heads or the finding aids noted below.

Book illustrations are grouped under the heading of the printed work in which they occur: titles, imprints and dates of all pertinent editions are given in these headers in full (in capitalised form), together with line divisions, but without regard to different typefaces, etc. In order to provide as much pertinent information as possible about the engravings, their preparation and distribution, I have actively sought printed prospectuses and proposals to incorporate into the entries. However, many of these have proved elusive, in part because such ephemeral materials were often discarded rather than being bound into the book. Whenever available, such information forms part of my brief preliminary accounts of the publishing history of specific book illustrations and separately issued plates, including details of payments made to artist and engraver, etc.

Each entry contains a full physical description of the print named, keyed whenever possible to the copy in the British Museum, Department of Prints and Drawings ('BM'), or in the British Library ('BL'). 'Other locations' of copies in major collections are also listed. Every print is identified by its accession no. or the call no. of the book containing it. Prints from 'BM' may normally be assumed to be 'Plates only', i.e. book illustrations separated from the book in which they are supposed to appear. The publisher's 'Imprint' and all other parts of the 'Inscription' are reproduced verbatim, including all raised letters and words in capitals. However, both here, in the headers to entries, and in transcriptions of prospectuses certain words have been given in **bold** type to indicate the use of particularly large lettering in the original. Single slashes (|) indicate divisions between lines; double slashes (||) indicate a line divided in two halves. The main entry normally corresponds to the 'final' published form of the print, in the collection indicated in parentheses in the dimensions line, although this may not be the source of the photographic illustration. Unless otherwise indicated in the first line of the entry identifying the engraver and his medium (e.g. 'Unsigned outline engraving by J.H. Lips'; 'Mezzotint engraved by William Ward'; 'Wood engraving by unknown engraver'; 'Soft ground etching by Henry Fuseli', etc.), the medium designated by the term 'engraved' is to be understood as line-engraving.

All measurements are given height before width in centimetres (cm) as well as in inches (in divisions of sixteenths of an inch), although the measurements in centimetres should be considered as the authoritative ones. Some variation in the measurements of individual prints is inevitable and should not be considered in and of itself as significant. 'Nothing is more uncertain than Copperplate printing', Du Roveray tells us, 'as it depends upon so many causes which cannot be controuled [*sic*], such as the humour of the men, the state of the weather and ... the Due wetting of the paper' (*Letters*, 348).

Since an engraved design may occur with or without a frame around it, I provide in each case the 'Dimensions' of the image alone (indicated by the symbol ■), and, wherever appropriate, the external dimensions of the outermost frame surrounding the image (represented by the symbol of the image within its frame, thus: ▣). In certain cases the dimensions are given 'to the platemark.'

Earlier states are described and ranked (in ascending order from the earliest proof to the one closest to the published form) under the heading 'Variants', which I have preferred to the usual 'states' because I do not, in fact, enumerate the fine distinctions that the latter term connotes. My variants represent gross differentiations such as 'etched state before letters', where the distinction is made on the basis of the addition of letters rather than more subtle and less easily determined changes in the etching itself.[†]

The binding height of Large Paper copies of books containing engraved illustrations is indicated as 'H=26.0 cm'.

'Schiff nos.' refer to entry numbers in Gert Schiff's *Johann Heinrich Füssli, 1741-1825* (1973) (**1-1826** or '**Lost Works 1-90**'). Whenever applicable this number appears together with the dimensions recorded in Schiff 1973, as the first of the bibliographic citations listed under the heading 'Lit.'; thus, *Japhet Beholds the Daughters of Sipha*, 1764 (**No. 1.**) is identified as 'Schiff 291; 13.0 x 9.4 cm'. Additional citations for the given engraving follow in chronological order. Unfortunately, the new Schiff numbers from the forthcoming enlarged English edition of Gert Schiff's work were not yet available for incorporation into the present catalogue; nor will they necessarily be the same as in the German edition of 1973. If a given engraving was exhibited, place and date of the exhibition, together with the number in the exhibition catalogue, are recorded under the heading 'Exh.'.

In order to make it easier to find a given engraving in this catalogue, all engravings are indexed by Titles (pp. 401-404), by Engravers (pp. 377-387), and by Publishers (pp. 395-400). There is also a listing of Locations of engravings by entry nos. (pp. 410-412). Further finding aids are given in the form of an alphabetical list, by author, of 'Books Containing Engraved Illustrations after Fuseli' (pp. 389-393), and a 'Conspectus of Subjects' (pp. 405-407). For short titles used in the 'Introduction', please see 'Abbreviated References and Bibliography' (pp. 361-375).

From its inception my project was intended to serve not merely as an exhaustive descriptive catalogue, but also within feasible limits as a census of Fuseli illustrated-book and print holdings in selected collections in Britain, the United States and Switzerland. There is, however, one egregious and unintended omission in this respect. To my great regret, I was not able to visit the Harvard University libraries, which should, therefore, not be automatically discounted as owners of given materials, even if they are not specifically cited as such.

[†] Compare in this respect Essick's five proof impressions of *Tornado* (**No. 116**), which 'lack the same work in the design, including the diagonal crossing strokes in the sea and air lower left' (*Blake's Commercial Illustrations*, 1991, no. XXI, p. 48).

LIST OF COLLECTIONS CITED

American Antiquarian	The American Antiquarian Society, Worcester, Massachusetts
Arizona	University of Arizona, Tucson, Arizona
Art Institute Chicago	The Art Institute of Chicago, Chicago, Illinois
Basel	Kupferstichkabinett, Öffentliche Kunstsammlung, Basel, Switzerland
UB Basel	Universitätsbibliothek, Basel, Switzerland
Bern	Schweizerische Landesbibliothek, Bern (National Library of Switzerland)
SB Bern	Stadtbibliothek, Bern, Switzerland
Birmingham	Birmingham Shakespeare Library
BL	British Library, London
BM	Department of Prints and Drawings, British Museum, London
Bodleian	Bodleian Library, Oxford University
Browne	Collection of Max Browne, Esq., London
Cambridge	Cambridge University Library
Chicago	University of Chicago, Chicago, Illinois
Coburg	Kunstsammlungen der Veste Coburg, Coburg, Germany
DHW	Collection of D.H. Weinglass and M. Carbonell, Kansas City, Missouri
Dörrbecker	Collection of Detlef W. Dörrbecker, Trier, Germany
Dr. Williams's	Dr. Williams's Library, London
Duke	Duke University, Durham, North Carolina
Essick	Collection of Robert N. Essick, Altadena, California
ETH	Eidgenössische Technische Hochschule, Zurich
Fitzwilliam	The Fitwilliam Museum, Cambridge
Folger	The Folger Shakespeare Library, Washington, D.C.
Fribourg	Bibliothèque Publique et Universitaire, Fribourg, Switzerland
Geneva	Bibliothèque Publique et Universitaire, Geneva, Switzerland
Georgia	University of Georgia, Athens, Georgia
Goucher	Goucher College, Towson, Maryland
Harvard	Harvard University Libraries, Cambridge, Massachusetts
Hornby, Liverpool	Hornby Library, Liverpool City Libraries
Hunterian	Hunterian Art Gallery, University of Glasgow, Scotland
Huntington	The Henry E. Huntington Library, San Marino, California
Illinois	University of Illinois at Champaign-Urbana, Urbana, Illinois
Iowa	University of Iowa, Iowa City, Iowa
Kentucky	University of Kentucky, Lexington, Kentucky
KHZ	Kunsthaus Zürich, Zurich, Switzerland
Lausanne	Bibliothèque Publique et Universitaire, Lausanne, Switzerland
LC	The Library of Congress, Washington, D.C.
Lewis Walpole	Lewis Walpole Library, Farmington, Connecticut
Library Co.	The Library Company of Philadelphia, Philadelphia, Pennsylvania
Lucerne	Zentralbibliothek, Lucerne, Switzerland
McGill	McGill University, Montreal, Québec, Canada
Michigan	University of Michigan, Ann Arbor, Michigan
MMA	The Metropolitan Museum of Art, New York, N.Y.
Monash	Monash University, Clayton, Victoria, Australia
Newberry	The Newberry Library, Chicago, Illinois
NYPL	New York Public Library, New York, N.Y.
Old Dominion	Old Dominion University, Norfolk, Virginia
Pennsylvania	University of Pennsylvania, Philadelphia, Pennsylvania

Pierpont Morgan	The Pierpont Morgan Library, New York, N.Y.
Princeton	Princeton University, Princeton, New Jersey
Rice	Rice University, Houston, Texas
Royal Academy	Royal Academy of Arts, London
Ryskamp	Collection of Charles Ryskamp, New York, N.Y.
St. Louis	St. Louis Public Library, St. Louis, Missouri
Southern California	University of Southern California, Los Angeles, California
Tampa	University of Tampa, Tampa, Florida
University College	University College, London
V & A	Victoria and Albert Museum, London
Vanderbilt	Vanderbilt University, Nashville, Tennessee
Virginia	University of Virginia, Charlottesville, Virginia
Warren	Collection of Leland E. Warren, Manhattan, Kansas
Widener College	Widener College, Wilmington, Delaware
Winterstein	Collection of Dr. Alfred Winterstein, Munich
Winterthur	Stadtbibliothek, Winterthur, Switzerland
Wisconsin	University of Wisconsin-Milwaukee, Milwaukee, Wisconsin
Witt	Witt Library, Courtauld Institute, London
Yale	Yale University Libraries, New Haven, Connecticut
YCBA	Yale Center for British Art, New Haven, Connecticut
ZBZ	Zentralbibliothek, Zurich, Switzerland

Publisher's note

The illustrations of the prints itemised in this Catalogue regularly include any engraved inscriptions. However, in a few instances, the inscription proved too faint to reproduce, so it was omitted and the image only reproduced.

Catalogue
of the Engravings

Nos. 1 - 8.
Johann Jakob Bodmer.
DIE | NOACHIDE | IN | ZWÖLF GESÄNGEN | = |
BERLIN | BEY CHRISTIAN FRIEDRICH VOSS.
1765 (8/12 illus. + t.-vign.).

While Herder a decade after the fact (14
November 1774) considered 'Fuseli's engraving
in the *Noachide*' as the performance of 'a young
Michelangelo' (Mason, p. 69), the artist himself
was less than satisfied with the engraver's
performance—and told Lavater (25 June 1766;
Muschg 1942, 136) that he had thrown the prints
into the fire as soon as he saw them. He also
complained bitterly to Bodmer about his 'botched'
drawings (9 September 1766; Muschg 1942, 139).
But Tomory (*Life and Art of Henry Fuseli*, 1972)
is incorrect when he says that the eight
illustrations 'were so mangled by the engraver
that they were never used' (p. 12): they are
described below.

It is, however, true that four of the twelve
illustrations Fuseli had prepared for this purpose
were replaced with designs by Bernhard Rode
when Fuseli's failed to arrive (HF to Sulzer, 17
April 1765; Federmann 1927, 113). This is the
only 18th-century German epic which appeared
with engraved illustrations after Fuseli. He did
accede grudgingly to Klopstock's request for some
drawings—now lost—for his *Messias*, but sent
them off to Klopstock's publisher without
answering the poet's letter (to Dälliker, 12-15
November 1765; Muschg 1942, 111). Fuseli
considered the *Messias* and Gessner's *Death of
Abel* fit only for the 'poor in spirit' ('die Armen
im Geiste') (to Bodmer, 10 June 1767; Federmann
1927, 117).

For a discussion of the artistic quality of
Fuseli's originals in comparison with the
engravings after them, see Schiff 1973, 62-63.

1.

1. *Japhet Beholds the Three Beautiful Daughters
of Sipha in Paradise*, 1764
(Book I, 121-137)
(facing title page)

Etched by Christian Gottfried Mathes (1738-
1805?)
Inscription: Fussli. del | | C.G. Mathes fec. 1764. |
Iᵉʳ. Gesang.
Dimensions (excluding inscription): 13.0 x 9.4 cm
| 5²/16" x 3¹¹/16" (BL 11521.b.19)
Other locations: UB Basel A.k. IV.2; Bern
(between pp. 2-3); SB Bern (after t.p.);
Vanderbilt PT1820.B8N63 1765; Lucerne H
19,084 (facing p. 2); Princeton 3434.7.368 (after
t.p.); Winterthur BRH 5978; ZBZ ZM 2822 (after
t.p.)

1

Lit.: Schiff 291 (13.0 x 9.4 cm); Hammelmann 1975, 33.

During Noah's absence from his dwelling in the secluded valley, exploring with the Seraph the cities of the unrighteous in the lowlands, Japhet, one of his three sons, discovers an unfamiliar path leading up into the mountains. As the early sun fills the right half of the picture with its resplendent rays, he emerges into a paradisiacal garden abloom with rare flowers and fruits, although there is little effort to show this cornucopia naturalistically. The illustration focuses upon the moment when Japhet catches sight of the three beautiful daughters of Sipha before their bower. One of the maidens has already turned to flee; the second, carrying a basket of flowers upon her hip is about to do so. The third, who is compared to a rose unfolding at daybreak, holds her ground to hear him speak despite her alarm, at the same time vainly attempting to cover her bare bosom with her tunic. The Edenic setting is suggested by the fruitful palm and luxuriant bush in the centre, and what might be a small pineapple or similar plant at Japhet's feet.

Apart from such awkwardly rendered details as the placement of Japhet's right leg, the engraver seems to have imbued the scene with a quality of coyness and archness more characteristic of the French rococo than ever was true of Fuseli's style.

2. *Asa, Poisoned by Selima, Murders his Father, Zippor, in the Temple at Yarmut*, 1764
(Book II, 605-657)
(facing p. 38)

Etched by Christian Gottfried Mathes (1738-1805?)
Inscription: Füssli. inv & del||C G Mathes. fec 1764.|IIer. Gesang.
Dimensions (excluding inscription): 13.0 x 9.5 cm | 5²/16" x 3¾" (BL 11521.b.19)
Other locations: UB Basel A.k.IV2; Bern L.10.052; SB Bern H.VIII.44; Lucerne H19,084; Princeton 3434.7.368; Vanderbilt PT1820.B8N63 1765; Winterthur BRH 5978; ZBZ ZM 2822
Lit.: Schiff 292 (13.0 x 9.5 cm); Hammelmann 1975, 33.

II.ter *Gesang*.

2.

Upon his return from his travels with Raphael through the nations of the earth, Noah gives an account of the wickedness of mankind he has witnessed in Cush, Assur, and finally Havila, which has been devastated by the fanatical followers of the self-proclaimed prophet, Selima. Only the city of Yarmut, spurred on by Zippor, has managed to withstand Selima's murderous hordes. Selima promises Zippor that if the city will surrender, he will crown Zippor king and restore to him his long-lost son, Asa, who had been carried off as a child by robbers. These offers Zippor rejects out of hand, although Selima is finally allowed into the city under a flag of truce. The illustration depicts the inevitable outcome of Selima's treachery. Zippor lies expiring beneath the altar in the temple of the Sun stabbed to death by his own son, the zealous and unwitting tool of the prophet. With the arrival on the scene of Sua, the robber, Asa discovers he has murdered his own father; stricken with the enormity of his deed, he is prevented from killing himself by the dying patriarch—only to succumb to the poison administered to him by Selima. The dagger plucked from his son's hand is about to fall from Zippor's own. Grouped in the centre of the picture in a pyramid shaped configuration the black robed prophet stands over the prostrate bodies of Zippor and Asa. Behind him looms the statue of Apollo. Sua, wearing a turban-like headdress, is seen entering the temple on the right, his hand raised to his mouth in horror. He is surrounded by roughly sketched figures wearing wreaths of laurel upon their heads that identify them as temple acolytes.

sacrifice and have been entertained by his beautiful daughters. Love and admiration have already blossomed between the couples. With much rejoicing they set out for Noah's dwelling in the valley. One of the brothers, represented only by his head and shoulders, hovers uncertainly in the centre of the composition. As in the previous illustration, the action is largely static.

3.

4.

3. *Sipha Embraces the Sons of Noah*, 1764
(Book III, 596-621)
(facing p. 66)

Etched by Christian Gottfried Matthes (1738-1805?)
Inscription: Fussli. del||C.G. Matthes. fec 1764| III^{ter}. Gesang.
Dimensions excluding inscription): 12.8 x 9.5 cm | 5^2/16" x 3¾ " (BL 11521.b.19)
Other locations: UB Basel A.k.IV.2; Bern L.10.052; SB Bern H.VIII.44; Lucerne H19,084; Princeton 3434.7.368; Vanderbilt PT1820.B8N63 1765; Winterthur BRH 5978; ZBZ ZM 2822
Lit.: Schiff 293 (12.7 x 9.5 cm); Hammelmann 1975, 33.

Sipha greets with joy his old friend Noah's sons who arrived while he was absent at his morning

4. *Sipha Marries his Three Daughters to the Sons of Noah*, 1764
(Book IV, 645-655)
(facing p. 96)

Etched by Christian Gottfried Matthes (1738-1805?)
Inscription: Füssli del||C G. Matthes fec 1764| IV^{ter}. Gesang.
Dimensions (excluding inscription): 12.7 x 9.5 cm | 5^2/16" x 3¾ " (BL 11521.b.19)
Other locations: UB Basel A.k.IV.2; Bern L.10.052; SB Bern H.VIII.44; Lucerne H19,084; Princeton 3434.7.368; Vanderbilt PT1820.B8N63 1765 (13.0 x 9.5 cm); Winterthur BRH 5978; ZBZ ZM 2822
Lit.: Schiff 294 (12.7 x 9.5 cm); Hammelmann 1975, 33.

While the happy party approach their destination, borne 'on the wings of the most tender love', God is informing Noah of the coming flood. Noah and Sipha withhold the fearful news from their children. However, they consent to the immediate marriage of the brothers and the three maidens. This is the ceremony we see being performed in the illustration, as Noah (at the right of the altar) unites Shem with Debora, Ham with Tamar, and Japhet with Kerenhapuch, while Sipha (half hidden behind the bridegroom at the left) pronounces the conjugal blessing.

5.

5. *Noah Exhorts Fallen Dagon to Repent*, 1764 (Book V, 639-647)
(facing p. 122)

Etched by Christian Gottfried Mathes (1738-1805?)
Inscription: Füssli del||C G, Matthes fec 1764.|
V.^ter. Gesang.
Dimensions (excluding inscription): 12.9 x 9.4 cm
| 5²/16" x 3¾" (UB Basel A.k.IV.2)
Other locations: Bern L.10.052; SB Bern
H.VIII.44; Lucerne H19,084; Princeton
3434.7.368; Vanderbilt PT1820.B8N63 1765;
Winterthur BRH 5978; ZBZ ZM2822

Lacking plate: BL 1152.b.19
Lit.: Schiff 295 (12.9 x 9.4 cm); Hammelmann 1975, 33.

Schiff identifies this illustration as Dagon speaking to the Fallen Giant of Assur, but in fact the scene represents Noah, after the destruction of the infernal airship intended to ferry the invaders up to the Garden of Paradise, standing beside the broken body of Dagon exhorting him to acknowledge God over Satan:

> Dagon war unweit Noah gefallen, ihm waren
>   die Glieder
> Sehr zerstossen, ihm rann das schwarze Blut aus
>   den Wunden....
> Als er da ringt mit dem Tode, vermahnt ihn
>   Noah, der Hölle
> Abzusagen und mindestens im Sterben den
>   Schöpfer zu Ehren.
> Sagst du den Satanen ab, so gieb mit der Hand
>   mir ein Zeichen,
> Rief er ihm zu. Der Gottlose starb und gab ihm
>   kein Zeichen.

(Dagon fell not far from Noah: most of his limbs were broken, the dark blood trickled from his wounds....As he wrestles with death, Noah exhorts him to renounce Hell and at least in dying to honour the Creator. 'If you renounce Satan, hold up your hand as a signal,' he cried to him. The godless one died and made no sign.)

The Poussinesque design (the extended right arm), no less than the subject of deathbed repentance, is strongly reminiscent of later depictions by Fuseli of the Death of Beaufort (No. **177** and Schiff 1260).

There is some divergence in detail from the text. Thus, the pyramid in the background is here freestanding, although it is, in fact, supposed to be built into the north side of the mountain in order to allow the giant descendants of Cain and Seth to invade Paradise. Also lacking are the marble steps extending up the huge structure and the platform at its peak, level with the lower terrace of the sacred mountain. There is some telescoping of events here too, since at this point in the narrative the pyramid had already been destroyed by a divinely inspired earthquake.

6.

6. *Shem Finds Sipha Dead Beside the Sacrificial Altar*, 1764
(Book VIII, 1-42)
(facing p. 208)

Etched by Christian Gottfried Mathes (1738-1805?)
Inscription: Füssli del | | C G Mathes fec 1764 | VIII<u>ter</u>. Gesang.
Dimensions (excluding inscription): 12.8 x 9.7 cm | 5^{1}/16" x 3^{13}/16" (BL 11521.b.19)
Other locations: UB Basel A.k.IV.2; Bern L.10.052; SB Bern H.VIII.44; Lucerne H19,084; Princeton 3434.7.368; Vanderbilt PT1820.B8N63 1765); Winterthur BRH 5978; ZBZ ZM2822
Lit.: Schiff 296 (12.8 x 9.6 cm); Hammelmann 1975, 33.

At the end of Book VII Sipha had been visited by angel who announced to him his imminent death. On the morning of the fourth day, as Sipha meditates at the altar in the grove, the angel of death fulfils his warning by piercing the old man through the heart, albeit with one of his least painful darts ('sanfteste Pfeile') dipped in soothing balm. Shem discovers Sipha not long afterwards still seated beside the altar with his head supported on his arm. In the evening after a

day of lamentation and mourning, they give the body a befitting burial.

Like so many other scenes in the work, the subject is not particularly dramatic, nor does Fuseli's treatment infuse it with any real intensity. Compare, from this point of view, Fuseli's rendering of Huon's and Amanda-Rezia's discovery of Alphonso's body in Canto IX of *Oberon* (No. **252**).

7.

7. *The Poet Begs the Muse to Relate to him How the Ark Escapes the Flood*, 1764
(Book IX, 2-4, 442-446)
(facing p. 240)

Etched by Christian Gottfried Matthes (1738-1805?)
Inscription: Füssli. del | | CG Matthes fec 1764 | IX<u>ter</u>. Gesang.
Dimensions (excluding inscription): 12.9 x 9.4 cm | 5^{1}/16" x 3^{11}/16" (BL 11521.b.19)
Other locations: UB Basel A.k. IV.2; Bern L.10.052; SB Bern H.VIII.44; Lucerne H19,084; Princeton 3434.7.368; Winterthur BRH 5978; Vanderbilt PT1820.B8N63 1765; ZBZ ZM2822
Lit.: Schiff 297 (12.9 x 9.4 cm); Hammelmann 1975, 33.

Fuseli's illustration seems to do double duty,

representing both the Bard addressing his muse at the beginning of Book IX as he observes the Ark upon the waters —

> …Entfalte die tödlichen Scenen,
> Muse, wie allein vor der Arche vorüber
>   gegangen,
> Als sie auch Eden zerstört' und der Gärten
>   Gottes nich schonte;
> Sage, wie sie die Riesen in ihren Sünden
>   erhaschte!

(Relate, o Muse, the fatal scenes: how the Ark alone remained unscathed by the storm; not even the Paradise of God was spared, and Eden too was destroyed; tell of the destruction that overwhelmed the giants sunk in their sinful ways.) —

as also the 'later' Bard [*Milton*], 'whose song ranged over all the scenes of man ... soaring on wings of fire towards Heaven, and explored [*the wonders of*] Divine Providence' (... [*der*] ... alle Scenen des Menschen gesungen | Und indem er ... sang mit Flügeln cherubischen Feuers | Oft gen Himmel hinauf stieg, und Gottes Wege durchforschte—IX, 442-446).

8.

8. *Lamech Speaks to the Spirit of Tydor on the Purgatorial Moon*, 1764
(Book X, 442-515)
(facing p. 268)

Etched by Christian Gottfried Matthes (1738-1805?)
Inscription: Füssli. del | | CG, Mathes. fec. 1764. | X^ter Gesang
Dimensions (excluding inscription): 12.9 x 9.5 cm | 5 1/16" x 3¾" (BL 1152.b.19)
Other locations: UB Basel A.k.IV.2; Bern L.10.052; SB Bern H.VIII.44; Lucerne H19,084; Princeton 3434.7.368; Winterthur BRH 5978; Vanderbilt PT1820.B8N63 1765; ZBZ ZM2822
Lit.: Schiff 298 (12.9 x 9.4 cm); Hammelmann 1975, 33.

On one of his visits to the Ark, Raphael gives Noah an account of his departed father, Lamech, who as a reward for his lifelong perseverance in the ways of righteousness and love of God, has been elevated to 'the assembly of fathers in the highest Heavens' ('die Versammlung der Väter im Empyreum'). Having descended to the sun and viewed the earth and the Ark floating upon the waters, Lamech is returning to heaven when he sees a small moon crowded with myriads of spirits. The illustration depicts a hovering Lamech, reminiscent of one of Raphael's saints, parting the shadows shrouding the Angel of Death's dismal world and awakening one of the spirits by breathing upon him with his 'animating breath' ('Olympischer Atem'). The naked figure of Tydor is shown sitting upright among the heaped and scattered spirits of the sinners who had drowned in the Flood asleep upon the flowers of asphodel (as unlikely as it might strike the reader to find them blooming in the icy wastes described by Bodmer). The expression upon Tydor's face as he shields his eyes against Lamech's radiance and the desolation of his surroundings reflects his horror at this premature awakening and his torment as the agonies of conscience, temporarily mitigated by his deathlike sleep, renew their onslaught.

In the following lines, before he sinks back into his slumber Tydor recounts his past history, leaving the horrified Lamech to wonder if this wretch was indeed a man or merely the concealed instrument of Satan's malice, disguised in human form. (The English version is taken with modifications and amplifications from Collyer's translation.)

Ich war der unmenschliche Tydor,
Unter den Sclaven der erst', und der Herr der
　Sclaven des Sultans;
Von mir ward sein zerschmetternder Arm
　geleitet, ich würgte
Jeden, der seine Befehle nicht gleich den
　göttlichen ehrte,
Immer besorgt, dass er das Reich nicht
　verlöhr', und verlöhre
Weil er zu sehr sich scheute das sclavische Blut
　zu vergiessen.
Magog sollte der einzige sein, dem zu wollen
　erlaubt wär',
Alle die andern nur folgen, und wer nicht
　folgte, nicht leben.
Sein Wort musste mit keiner geringern
　Gewissheit geschehen,
Als notwendig das Ziel ein wohlgerichteter Pfeil
　trifft.
Vor ihm musste die Ehrfurcht des Kinds, die
　Gesetze der Ehre,
Zärtliche Liebe der Mutter und Liebe des
　Bräutigams schweigen,
Seine verzehrende Wut empfing die Flamme
　von meiner.
Deinem Gebot, so sprach ich zu ihm, den
　Gehorsam verweigern,
Ist fluchwürdig Verbrechen und fordert
　fluchwürdige Strafen;
Aber dein Sclav, der Chusit, hat einen Nacken
　von Kiesel,
Ihm ist der Tod ein Spiel, und nur die Todesart
　furchtbar.
Soll ihn der Tod erschüttern, so muss er in
　neuen Gestalten
Vor ihn treten. : : : Mein war die Gabe, die
　seltsamsten Tode
Auszusinnen; noch glückt' es mir nicht die
　Grossmut zu töten.

(I was the inhuman Tydor, lord of the prince's slaves; his destroying arm was committed to my guidance, and I pointed it against all who did not reverence his commands as those of the deity, lest he should lose his kingdom through excess of scruples to spill the blood of his slaves. I was, next to Magog, the delegate of omnipotence. Subjection—or death—was the portion of all others. I caused his most cruel commands to be executed with as much certainty as the well-aimed dart hits the mark. Before him filial duty, the laws of honour, maternal affection and bridal love, were to keep silence. It was I who kindled his consuming fury. 'He who hesitates to fulfill thy command,' I told him, 'commits a heinous crime for which he must pay with his life. But the Chusites, thy slaves, have a neck of flint. They despise death, and find only the manner of dying fearful. To render it terrible, it must assume new forms.' I had the gift of inventing new modes of dying; even so I could not destroy their elevated mind.)

******

Nos. 9 - 10.
Johann Joachim Winckelmann.
REFLECTIONS | ON THE | PAINTING AND SCULPTURE | OF | THE GREEKS: | WITH | INSTRUCTIONS FOR THE CONNOISSEUR, | AND | AN ESSAY ON GRACE IN WORKS OF ART. | TRANSLATED FROM | THE GERMAN ORIGINAL OF THE ABBÉ WINKELMANN, | LIBRARIAN OF THE VATICAN, F.R.S. &C. &C. | BY HENRY FUSSELI, A.M. | [Vignette] | LONDON: | PRINTED FOR THE TRANS[-] LATOR, AND SOLD BY A. MILLAR, | IN THE STRAND. 1765 (2/2 illus.).

...THE SECOND EDITION, CORRECTED. | [Vignette] | LONDON: | PRINTED FOR A. MILLAR AND T. CADELL IN THE STRAND. | MDCCLXVII [1767].

As the research of Eudo C. Mason has shown ('Heinrich Füssli und Winckelmann', 1971), notices of the official publication of the work appeared in the London newspapers of 25 April 1765. To judge by other advertisements in the *London Chronicle* and *St. James's Chronicle* an undetermined number of copies were subscribed and paid for in advance:

Such Noblemen and Gentlemen that have subscribed to the Translator are desired to send for their Books as above, with his Receipt.

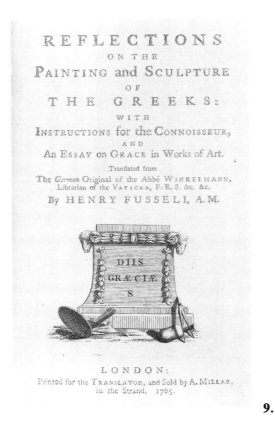

9.

REFLECTIONS
ON THE
PAINTING and SCULPTURE
OF
THE GREEKS:
WITH
INSTRUCTIONS for the CONNOISSEUR,
AND
An ESSAY on GRACE in Works of Art.

Translated from
The *German* Original of the Abbé WINCKELMANN,
Librarian of the VATICAN, F. R. S. &c. &c.

By HENRY FUSSELI, A.M.

DIIS
GRÆCIÆ
S

LONDON:
Printed for the TRANSLATOR, and Sold by A. MILLAR,
in the Strand, 1765.

The book does not seem to have sold well—perhaps because of the eccentric English style of the translation—and almost a year later, between 11 and 13 March 1766, a somewhat misleading notice appeared in *The Public Advertiser*, the *St. James's Chronicle*, and the *London Chronicle* reporting that the *Reflections* had been 'This day...published'. Even more misleading was the announcement in the *Gazetteer* and other London papers of 4 - 7 May 1767 of the publication of 'the Second Edition, corrected, price 4s in boards, or 5s. bound *Reflections on the Painting and Sculpture of the Greeks* etc.', which Mason does not accept as a genuine second edition. He is convinced rather that this purported new edition consists merely of unsold copies with a new title page. Mason feels it to be particularly significant from this point of view that the work would be republished on the same day and by the same publisher as his *Remarks on Rousseau*.

Fuseli's father, J. C. Füssli, was a friend and patron of Winckelmann, and Fuseli early imbibed his Neoclassical ideas. But this admiration later faded and in his maturity Fuseli rejected his former oracle. Winckelmann became in Fuseli's eyes 'the parasite of the fragments that fell from the conversation or tablets of Mengs...[and he] reasoned himself into frigid reveries and Platonic dreams on beauty' (Introduction, *Lectures on Painting*, 1820, p. xvi; Knowles, II, 13f.)

9. *Diis Graeciae Sacrum*, 1765

Unsigned title-vignette after Fuseli's design engraved by [Charles Grignion (1721-1810)] Inscription: Diis | Graeciae | S[*acrum*]. Dimensions (to platemark): 6.5 x 8.0 cm | 2⁹/16" x 3²/16" (BL 564.a.13) Other locations: BL 1560/267 (1767); Cambridge 7400.d.62; DHW; DHW (H=22.0 cm); Folger N5630.W3; Goucher College 709.38 W76Bf (1767); Huntington 318764; Library Company Is 3282.0 (H=26.0 cm); YCBA N5630.W513; ZBZ XXV 957
Lit.: Schiff 299 (5.3 x 7.0 cm); Hammelmann 1975, 33; Schiff-Viotto 1977, repr. p. 84, centre row, left; Hall 1985, 29-34, repr. 34.
Exh.: Kansas City 1982 (2).

Lying at the foot of an altar 'Dedicated to the Gods of Greece' are, on the left, a palette, brush, malstick, and sheet of paper; on the right a sculptor's mallet and compasses.

10. *Graiis Ingenium*, 1765
(p. [1])

Unsigned ornamental headpiece in the form of a motto in an engraved cartouche by Charles Grignion (1721-1810) after Fuseli's lost design. Inscription: GRAIIS INGENIUM | &c. Dimensions (to platemark): 5.2 x 10.9 cm | 2¹/16" x 4¼" (BL 564.a.13) Other locations: BL 1560 (1767); Cambridge 7400.d.62; DHW; DHW (H=22.0 cm); Folger N5630.W3; Goucher College 709.38 W76Bf (1767); Huntington 318764; Library Company Is 3282.0 (H=26.0 cm); YCBA N5630.W513; ZBZ XXV 957
Lit.: Schiff 300 (4.5 x 9.5 cm); Hammelmann 1975, 33.

The Latin motto translates as 'the invention of the Greeks'.

******

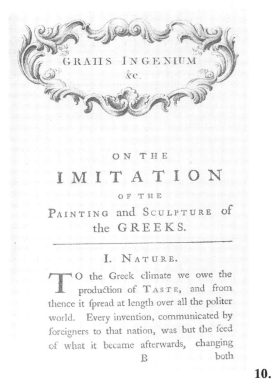

10.

11.

No. 11.
[Henry Fuseli].
REMARKS | ON THE | WRITINGS AND
CONDUCT | OF J.J. ROUSSEAU. | *Dead flies*
cause the ointment of the apothecary to send |
forth a stinking savour: so doth a little folly, him |
that is in reputation for wisdom and honour. |
SOLOMON. | —*on n'a jamais ouï dire qu'un*
peintre, qui expose | *en public un tableau, soit*
obligé de visiter les yeux | *des spectateurs, et de*
fournir des lunettes à tous ceux | *qui en ont besoin.*
LETTR. à MR. GRIM. | = | LONDON: | PRINTED
FOR T. CADELL, (SUCCESSOR TO MR.
MILLAR) IN THE STRAND; J. JOHNSON
AND B. DAVENPORT; | AND J. PAYNE, IN
PATER-NOSTER-ROW. | MDCCLXVII [1767]
(1/1 illus.).

11. *Justice and Liberty Hanged, while Voltaire*
Rides Monster Humanity and Jean-Jacques
Rousseau Takes his Measure, 1767
(facing title page)

Engraved frontispiece by Charles Grignion (1721-
1810).

Inscription (bottom right): C. Grignion Sculp.
Dimensions: ■ 13.2 x 8.5 cm | 5¼" x 3^{11}/16";
■ 3.5 x 8.9 cm | 5^{5}/16" x 3½" (BL
11826.aaa.14)
Other locations: Bern A10.704; Bern A14.719
Res. (cropped) (13.5 x 8.0 cm); DHW; Essick;
Geneva Hf.4970; Huntington 355724; Library
Company O Eng Fues 568; Newberry
Y762.R793; NYPL NKC Rousseau; Pforzheimer;
Princeton Ex 3288.682.c.2 (Robert Balmanno's
copy); Yale Hfd.25.25
Plate only: BM 1863-5-9-72
Lacking plate: Cambridge S735.e.76.10; Folger
PQ2053.A3F8; ZBZ AX 6177; Princeton Ex
3288.682 c.1.
Lit.: Schiff 301 (13.3 x 8.9 cm); Mason 1951,
134-136; Antal 1956, 19; Mason 1962, 54-55, 57;
Hammelmann 1975, 33; Schiff-Viotto 1977, repr.
84, middle row, centre; *Letters*, 8-9; Hall 1985,
47-49, repr. 48.
Exh.: Kansas City 1982 (1); Hamburg 1989 (44).

Fuseli's admiration of Rousseau and 'devotion
to his divine morality' began at the age of 18. But
the quarrel between Rousseau and David Hume,
which in 1767 provoked the *Remarks*, also

perceptibly cooled Fuseli's feelings for his former idol, whom he considered to have 'betrayed himself to exchange [*in return*] for the *baseless fabric of a vision* the solid merit of generosity and gratitude' (*Remarks*, ed. Mason, 102).

The *Remarks* had 'a short life and a bright ending' (Cunningham, II, 266), and is now an extremely rare book. Most of the edition is presumed to have been burned in a fire at the house of Joseph Johnson (1738-1809), the radical publisher, in 1770.

In his satirical *Lettre au Docteur Pansophe* (1766) against Rousseau, Voltaire had exhorted the citizens of London to return to nature and eat grass in Hyde Park. Fuseli's illustration is a striking visual translation of Voltaire's witty reductio ad absurdum of Rousseau's ideas. As Mason shows (*Remarks*, 54, 57), Fuseli was able to draw for inspiration on James Boswell's caricature of Rousseau as 'The Savage Man,' published 30 January 1767, where Voltaire riding a hobby-horse, whips the shaggy Apostle of Nature with a handkerchief, crying out: 'I'll whip him into Humanity' (repr. C.B. Tinker, *Young Boswell*, 1922, p. 60). (See fig. 1). Carol Hall notes the strong resemblance between Fuseli's crawling savage and a crawling figure in the frontispiece to Vol. III of William Kendrick's translation of Rousseau's *Émile* (1767).

In an anonymous review of his own book, published in the *Critical Review* (May 1767), Fuseli provides a detailed interpretation of his often misunderstood frontispiece, while at the same time characteristically puffing the author (himself) as 'a gentleman, a scholar, a philosopher, a genius and a man of wit.'

[*In this*] ingenious, well-designed satirical frontispiece,...Voltaire is introduced, in a fine flowing peruke, with a pair of jackboots and spurs, and a whip in his hand, bestriding a monster which he has bridled, saddled and brought to the ground. Over his head, pendant by their necks upon a gibbet, are Justice and Liberty, upon the beam of which is seen all that remains of the temple of Liberty. On the right side of the piece, in front, upon a little eminence, stands an arch, shrugging figure, representing Rousseau, in a furred gown and cap, pointing with his right hand to the beast and his burthen, and with the plummet of Truth in his left, sounding as we may suppose, the sincerity and real estimation of the rider.

We own that we are much affected at the awkward situation of our darling principles, Justice and Liberty; and are entirely ignorant of what they have done to deserve to be gibbeted.

If the little gentleman in fur, by virtue of his plummet and line, has found out, as he seems to insinuate, that Voltaire has been their executioner, we are of opinion that he ought to be hanged up in their stead (Mason 1951, 136).

Robert Balmanno may be overstating the case when he comments in a handwritten note in his personal copy of the work: 'This early performance of my dear Friend and Testator, Henry Fuseli, in latter years, gave him sincere pain and he did all he could to suppress it.'

******

Fig. 1. *The Savage Man.* After J. Boswell.

A N
E S S A Y
ON THE
FIRST PRINCIPLES
OF
GOVERNMENT;
AND ON THE NATURE OF
Political, Civil, and Religious
L I B E R T Y.

By JOSEPH PRIESTLEY, LL.D. F.R.S.

LONDON:
Printed for J. DODSLEY, in Pall-Mall; T. CADELL (fuc-ceffor to Mr. Millar) in the Strand; and J. JOHNSON, Nº. 8, Pafter-nofter Row.

MDCCLXVIII.

12.

No. 12.
Joseph Priestley.
AN ESSAY | ON THE | FIRST PRINCIPLES | OF | GOVERNMENT; | AND ON THE NATURE OF | POLITICAL, CIVIL, AND RELIGIOUS | LIBERTY. | BY JOSEPH PRIESTLEY, LL.D. F.R.S. | [Vignette]. | LONDON: | PRINTED FOR J. DODSLEY, IN PALL-MALL; T. CADELL (SUC- | CESSOR TO MR. MILLAR) IN THE STRAND; AND J. JOHNSON, | NO. 8, PATERNOSTER ROW. | MDCCLXVIII [1768] (1/1 illus.).

12. *Sphinx and Cherub with Cap of Liberty*, 1768

Engraved title-vignette by Charles Grignion (1721-1810) after Fuseli's untraced drawing.
Inscription: Fuseli inv. | | Grignion Sc.
Dimensions: 4.7 x 7.5 cm | 1¹⁴/16" x 3" (BL 232.i.31)
Other locations: BL T1611.(1.); BL T1116.(11.); Bodleian Gdwn.Pamph. 2700(12); Cambridge Acton.c.48.187; Dr. Williams's Library 5609.K.14; Dr. Williams's PP.1.40.12; Huntington 83092; Newberry Case JO.713; NYPL *C p.v.87 (3)

Lit.: Schiff 302 (?7.5 x 5.0 cm); Hammelmann 1957, 354; Hammelmann 1975, 34

The plate was reused on the last page of Fuseli's anonymous translation of Giacinto Dragonetti's *Treatise on Virtues and Rewards* (1769) (see Nos. **14 - 16** below) but was not reissued in Priestley's 2nd corrected and enlarged edition of 1771.

******

13. *The Apparition Appears to Dion Wielding a Broom*, 1768
(Plutarch, *Dion*, 55)

Etched by Henry Fuseli (hand coloured)
Inscription (lower left within plate): HF | **Spectrum Dioneum.** | Vide Plut. in Dione.
Dimensions: ■ 46.0 x 59.0 cm | 18²/16" x 23¼" (BM 1931-4-13-237)
Lit.: Schiff 330 (45.7 x 69.0 cm); Knowles, I, 42

This 'large scale' etching was among the portfolio that inspired Sir Joshua Reynolds to say that 'were he at [*Fuseli's*] age and endowed with the ability of producing such works, if any one were to offer him … a thousand pounds a-year, on condition of being anything but a painter, he would, without the least hesitation, reject the offer.'

Dion of Syracuse was a friend of Plato. He overthrew the tyrant Dionysius. Beset by conspiracies, he saw a fearful apparition:

He was sitting late in the day in the vestibule of his house, alone and lost in thought, when suddenly a noise was heard at the other end of the colonnade, and turning his gaze in that direction he saw (for it was not yet dark) a woman of lofty stature, in garb and countenance exactly like a tragic Fury, sweeping the house with a sort of broom. He was terribly shocked, and, becoming apprehensive, summoned his friends, told them what he had seen, and begged them to remain and spend the night with him, being altogether beside himself, and fearing that if he were left alone the portent would appear to him again. This, indeed, did not occur a second time. But a few days afterwards his son, who was hardly a boy any more, in a fit of angry displeasure caused by some trivial and childish grievance, threw himself headlong from the roof and was killed. (Trans. Bernadotte Perrin).

13.

No. 13A.
[*Heinrich Füssli, Johann Jakob Horner & Felix Nüscheler*].
[Overall title]: HEINRICH FUESSLI'S SÄMMTLICHE WERKE | NEBST EINEM VERSUCHE SEINER BIOGRAPHIE. | — | ZÜRICH, 1807. | IN DER KUNSTHANDLUNG VON FUESSLI UND COMPAGNIE.

[Wrappers]: HEINRICH FUESSLI'S | SÆMMTLICHE WERKE. | — | ERSTES HEFT. [ZWEYTES HEFT.] | ZÜRICH, 1807. [1809.] | IN DER KUNSTHANDLUNG VON FUESSLI UND COMPAGNIE. (16/16 illus.).

For the other illustrations in this work see also Nos. **70A-71A, 72C, 73E, 74A, 275-283**.

13A. *The Apparition Appears to Dion Wielding a Broom*, 1806
(Plutarch, *Dion*, 55)
(Part I, No. 2, facing p. 1)

Re-engraved as unsigned outline engraving by Johann Heinrich Lips (1758-1817)

Inscription (bottom centre): **Das Gespenst des Dion.**
Dimensions: ■ 21.8 x 28.6 cm | 8⁹/16" x 11¼"
(ZBZ KK 307)
Other locations: Bern A16.441; DHW; KHZ D33; Lucerne H36gr.fol.; YCBA folio B.N.29(not seen)
Plate only: MMA 55.526.13
Lit.: Schiff 330; Lonchamp 1920, no. 225; Federmann 1927, 73.

Variants:
I. Proof before letters: ETH 545/136
Other locations: ETH 1524a; KHZ C4/IIIA, 1214

Nos. 14 - 16.
Giacinto Dragonetti.
A | TREATISE | ON | VIRTUES AND REWARDS. | [Vignette] | LONDON: | PRINTED FOR JOHNSON AND PAYNE, IN PATER-NOSTER- | ROW, AND J. ALMON, IN PICCADILLY. | M.DCC.LXIX [1769] (4/4 illus.).

For the reused illustration in this work from Priestley's *Essay* (1768), see No. **12**.

LONDON:

Printed for JOHNSON and PAYNE, in Pater-nofter-
Row, and J. ALMON, in Piccadilly.

M.DCC.LXIX.

14.

14. *Two Hovering Geniuses Summoning a Seated Young Man to Virtue*, 1769

Title-vignette engraved by Charles Grignion (1721-1810) after Fuseli's preliminary sketch in a private collection.
Inscription (left): ΣΥΜΠΟΡΕΥΘΕΙΣ ΘΕΩ [Θεῷ]|(bottom left): F||C. Grignion sc.
Dimensions: 6.0 x 5.8 cm | 2⁶/16" x 3" (BL 8407.D10) (H=19.1 cm)
Other locations: DHW (H=22.0 cm) (hole punched through—'A'—the first word of title)
Lit.: Schiff 1728a (6.0 x 5.8 cm); Hammelmann 1957, 354f.; Hammelmann 1975, 34

The Greek inscription is from Plato, *Phaedrus*, 249C: 'our soul once *journeyed with God*'.

The two Geniuses hovering above the seated young man summon him to Virtue. Like Rousseau in No. **11**, the youth holds in his left hand 'the plummet of Truth'. The vignette is framed on the right by tendrils of ivy (the symbol of immortality) in which are perched two doves, the emblems of love. The triangle within the circle inscribed on the socle represents the Holy Trinity.

This edition of Dragonetti appears to be very rare. I am aware of only the two copies listed.

15.

15. *ΘΕΟΙΣ*, 1769
(p. [5])

Vignette engraved by Charles Grignion (1721-1810) at head of Fuseli's Dedication to Lord Viscount Chewton after Fuseli's lost design.
Inscription: ΘΕΟΙΣ|F|C Grignion Sc.
Dimensions (to platemark): 6.7 x 8.1 cm | 2²/16" x 3³/16" (BL 8407.D10) (H=19.1 cm)
Other locations: DHW (H=22.0 cm)
Lit.: Schiff 1728b (?7.3 x 5.5 cm) (not illustrated); Hammelmann 1975, p. 34.

This allegorical headpiece depicts Virtue seated at the left beside a cornucopia—in allusion to the 'Rewards' of the work's title—facing Modesty accompanied by a cherub.

16. *Discite Justitiam Moniti*, 1768
(p. 182)

Vignette engraved by Charles Grignion (1721-1810) after Fuseli's lost design.
Inscription: Discite|Justitiam|Moniti|F||C Grignion Sc
Dimensions (to platemark): 5.5 x 8.1 cm | 2²/16 x 3³/16" (BL 8407.D10) (H=19.1 cm)
Other locations: DHW (H=22.0 cm)
Lit.: Schiff 1728c (7.5 x 5.0 cm); Hammelmann 1957, 354f.; Hammelmann 1975, 34

This tailpiece shows three young men kneeling before an altar before which they are laying a

crown and sceptre. The sense of the quotation
(from Vergil, *Aeneid*, VI, 620) is 'Learn justice
from being admonished'.

16.

Nos. 17 - 20.
[Tobias Smollett.]
THE│ADVENTURES│OF│PEREGRINE
PICKLE.│IN WHICH ARE INCLUDED,│
MEMOIRS│OF A│LADY OF QUALITY.│—│IN
FOUR VOLUMES.│—│VOL. I [-VOL. IV].│—│
Respicere exemplar vitae morumque jubebo│
Doctum imitatorem, & veras hinc ducere voces.│
HOR.│—│THE FOURTH EDITION.│=│
LONDON:│PRINTED FOR R. BALDWIN, Nº.
47. AND ROBINSON│AND ROBERTS, Nº. 25.
IN PATER-NOSTER-ROW; AND│T. BECKET
AND T. CADELL, IN THE STRAND.│
MDCLXIX [1769] (4/4 illus.).

For the re-engravings of 1769, 1773-1778, 1776,
1779, 1784 see Nos. **17A - 20A, 17B - 20B, 17C
- 20C, 17D - 20D,** and **17E - 20E** below.

Fuseli's four illustrations to *Peregrine Pickle*
are not limited, as assumed by Hammelmann and
Schiff, to the 4th edition of 1769. There are in
fact *two* 4th editions in that year, distinguished on
the title page by the placement of the word
'HOR.' either directly following the quotation on
the same line, or offset a line below. The same
designs reappear with the signature of J. Lodge as
the engraver in 1773 (5th ed.) and 1778 (6th ed.),
as also in unsigned form and unspecified editions
in 1776, 1779, and 1784. Their rarity value may
hence lie more in the fact that *Peregrine Pickle*
was the only work of English fiction for which

Fuseli provided illustrations. Ganz (1949, 30)
suggests (inaccurately) that these illustrations
appeared in 1765.

They are characterised by their 'neat
Hogarthian realism' and their 'concentrated
composition made interesting through a
combination of layers and lively diagonals'
(Antal).

17.

17. *Gamaliel Pickle Observes Commodore*
Trunnion and Lieutenant Hatchway Duel at the
Inn, [1769]
(Chapter 2)
(Vol. I, facing title page)

Engraved frontispiece by Charles Grignion (1721-
1810).
Inscription (top left): Vol. 1.│(bottom right): C.
Grignion Sculp.
Dimensions: ■ 12.2 x 7.7 cm │ 4¹³/16" x 3" (BL
1206.b.1) (H=16.9 cm)
Other locations: Bodleian Vet. A5.e.5782/1;
DHW; Essick
Plate only: BM 1863-5-9-69
Lit.: Schiff 303 (12.2 x 7.7 cm); Hammelmann
1957, 355; Hammelmann 1975, 34.

The choleric Commodore Trunnion and his household are particularly characteristic of Smollett's love of the eccentric and the grotesque.

...he has been a great warrior in his time, and lost an eye and a heel in the service—Then he does not live like any other Christian land-man; but keeps garrison in his house, as if he were in the midst of his enemies, and makes his servants turn out in the night, watch and watch (as he calls it) all the year round. His habitation is defended by a ditch, over which he has laid a draw-bridge, and planted his courtyard with patereroes continually loaded with shot, under the direction of one Mr. Hatchway, who had one of his legs shot away, while he acted as lieutenant on board of the commodore's ship; and now being on half-pay, lives with him as his companion. The lieutenant is a very brave man, a great joker, and, as the saying is, hath got the length of his commander's foot—Though he has another favourite in the house called Tom Pipes, that was his boatswain's mate, and now keeps the servants in order. Tom is a man of few words, but an excellent hand at a song concerning the boatswain's whistle, hussle-cap and chuck-farthing—there is not such another pipe in the county.

This plate represents Trunnion, who is sitting in the parlour of the inn with his cohorts, taking umbrage at one of the lieutenant's jokes:

Ay, ay, Jack, everybody knows your tongue is no slander; but howsomever, I'll work you to an oil for this, you dog.' So saying, he lifted up one of his crutches, intending to lay it gently a-cross Mr. Hatchway's pate; but Jack, with great agility, tilted up his wooden-leg, with which he warded off the blow, to the no small admiration of Mr. Pickle, and utter astonishment of the landlord, who, by the bye, had expressed the same amazement, at the same feat, at the same hour, every night for three months before.
...Tom, who indeed had no words to spare, sat smoking his pipe with great indifference....

18. *Peregrine in the Palais Royal*, 1769
(Ch. 42)
(Vol. II, facing title page)

18.

Engraved frontispiece by Charles Grignion (1721-1810)
Inscription (top left): Vol. 2.|(bottom right): C. Grignion Sculp
Dimensions: ■ 12.1 x 7.9 cm | 4¾" x 3²/16" (BL 1206.b.1) (H=16.9 cm)
Other locations: Bodleian Vet. A5.e.5782/2; DHW; Essick
Lit.: Schiff 304 (12.0 x 7.8 cm); Antal 1956, 19, 26 (erroneously assumes the edition containing Fuseli's illustrations was never published); Hammelmann 1957, 355; Hammelmann 1975, 34

Standing before a painting in the Palais Royal at Paris, Mr. Pallet, the English painter, and his travelling companion, the physician, discuss—very much at cross purposes—the picture's merits with the Swiss attendant, while Peregrine observes with amusement from the side:

...the Swiss, who sets up for a connoisseur, looking at a certain piece, pronounced the word *magnifique*! with a note of admiration; upon which Mr. Pallet, who was not at all a critic in the French language, replied with great vivacity, '*Manufac*, you mean, and a very indifferent piece of manufacture it is; pray, gentlemen, take notice, there is no keeping in those heads upon the background, nor no relief in the principle figure: then you'll observe the shadings are harsh to the last degree;—and come a little closer this way—don't you perceive that the fore-shortening of that arm is monstrous—agad, sir! there is an absolute fracture in the limb—doctor, you understand anatomy, don't you think that muscle evidently misplaced? Hark ye, Mr. what d'ye call um (turning to the attendant) what is the name of the dauber who painted that miserable performance!' The Swiss imagining that he was all this time expressing his satisfaction, sanctioned his supposed commendation, by exclaiming *sans prix*. 'Right, cried Pallet, I could not recollect his name, though his manner is quite familiar to me. We have a few pieces in England done by that same Sangpree; but there they are in no estimation; we have more taste among us, than to relish the productions of such a miserable gout...

With its quotations from Latin and Greek (not given here) and its satirical comment on the nature and appreciation of art, the passage contains elements of obvious appeal to Fuseli.

According to Ronald Paulson, Smollett's model for Mr. Pallet was none other than William Hogarth (*Hogarth: His Life, Art and Times*, 1971, II, 130-131). However, in Fuseli's illustration Pallet does not appear to be a portrait of Hogarth.

19. *Cadwallader Disguised as a Magician Receives the Lady and her Maid*, 1769
(Ch. 82)
(Vol. III, facing title page)

Engraved frontispiece by Charles Grignion (1721-1810)
Inscription (top left): Vol. 3. | (bottom right): C. Grignion Sculp.
Dimensions: ■ 11.4 x 7.7 | 4½" x 3¹/16" (BL 1206.b.1) (H = 16.9 cm)
Other locations: DHW; Essick
Plate only: BM 1863-5-9-74
Lacking plate: Bodleian Vet.A5.e.5782/3
Lit.: Schiff 305 (11.5 x 7.8 cm); Hammelmann 1957, 355; Hammelmann 1975, 34

To ridicule the fashionable world, Peregrine

19.

sets up Cadwallader Crabtree, as a fortune teller, and surrounds him with such apparatus 'as globes, telescopes, ... a skeleton, a dried monkey [*and*] ... an alligator'. Here we see him 'habited in a black gown and fur-cap, ... his countenance ... improved by a thick beard white as snow', with a black cat upon each shoulder, being consulted by two women who have changed roles to confuse him. The 'lady' in the foreground is actually the servant, while her mistress is dressed as the maid:

Their conductor advancing to the table, presented his offering, and pointing to the *suivante*, told him, that lady desired to know what would be her destiny in point of marriage. The philosopher, without lifting up his eyes ... turned his ear to one of the sable familiars that purred upon his shoulder, and taking up the pen, wrote upon a detached slip of paper these words, which Peregrine, at the desire of the ladies, repeated aloud, 'Her destiny will, in a great measure, depend upon what happened to her about nine o'clock in the morning, on the third day of last December'.

This sentence was no sooner pronounced, than the counterfeit lady uttered a fearful scream, and ran out into the antichamber, exclaiming, 'Christ have mercy upon us! Sure he is the devil incarnate!'

20.

20. *Peregrine Places the Beggar-woman's Daughter in Pipes's Charge*, 1769
(Ch. 87)
(Vol. IV, facing title page)

Engraved frontispiece by Charles Grignion (1721-1810)
Inscription (top left): Vol. 4. | (bottom right): C. Grignion Sculp.
Dimensions: ■ 12.1 x 7.9 cm | 4¾ " x 3²/16" (BL 1206.b.1) (H=16.9 cm)
Other locations: Bodleian Vet.A5.e.5782/4; DHW; Essick
Lit.: Schiff 306 (12.0 x 7.8 cm); Hammelmann 1957, 355, repr. facing p. 54

Since he had been 'disdained' by Emilia, Peregrine 'vowed within himself [*to*] seek consolation in the possession of the first willing

wench he should meet upon the road'. The 'proper object for the performance of his vow' turns out to be the daughter of a beggar-woman:

> The girl was about the age of sixteen, and notwithstanding the wretched equipage in which she appeared, exhibited to his view a set of agreeable features, enlivened with the complexion of health and cheerfulness. ... He therefore entered into a conference with the mother, and for a small sum of money purchased her property in the wench, who did not require much courtship and intreaty, before she consented to accompany him to any place that he should appoint for her habitation.

The illustration shows Peregrine, 'after having laid strong injunctions upon [*his servant*] to abstain from all attempts upon her chastity', sending off the girl in charge of Pipes to the Garrison, where his friend is instructed 'to receive this hedge-inamorata, and direct her to be cleaned and cloathed in a decent manner'.

******

Nos. 17A - 20A.
[Tobias Smollett.]
THE | ADVENTURES | OF | PEREGRINE PICKLE. | IN WHICH ARE INCLUDED, | MEMOIRS | OF A | LADY OF QUALITY. | — | IN FOUR VOLUMES. | — | VOL. I. [-VOL. IV.] | — | *Respicere exemplar vitae morumque jubebo* | *Doctum imitatorem, & veras hinc ducere voces.* HOR. | — | THE FOURTH EDITION. | = | LONDON: | PRINTED FOR R. BALDWIN, Nº. 47. AND ROBINSON | AND ROBERTS, Nº. 25. IN PATER-NOSTER-ROW; AND | T. BECKET AND T. CADELL, IN THE STRAND. | MDCCLXIX [1769] (4/4 illus.).

17A. *Gamaliel Pickle Observes Commodore Trunnion and Lieutenant Hatchway Duel at the Inn*, 1769
(Ch. 2)
(Vol. I, facing title page)

Unsigned frontispiece engraved by anonymous engraver (image not reversed from No. **17**)
Inscription (top left): Vol. 1.
Dimensions: ■ 12.1 x 7.4 cm | 4¾ " x 2¹⁵/16"
(BL 12614.bbb.10)

Other locations: Bodleian Vet.A5.f.476; DHW; Folger PR3694.A4 1769; LC PR3694.P4 1769

18A. *Peregrine in the Palais Royal*, 1769
(Ch. 42)
(Vol. II, facing title page)

Unsigned frontispiece engraved by anonymous engraver (image not reversed from No. **18**)
Inscription (top left): Vol. 2
Dimensions: ■ 12.1 x 7.8 cm | 4^{13}/16" x 3^{1}/16"
(BL 12614.bbb.10)
Other locations: Bodleian Vet.A5.f.477; DHW; Folger PR3694.A4 1769; LC PR3694.P4 1769
Exh.: Kansas City 1982 (72)

19A. *Cadwallader Disguised as a Magician Receives the Lady and her Maid*, 1769
(Ch. 82)
(Vol. III, facing title page)

Unsigned frontispiece engraved by anonymous engraver (image reversed from No. **19A**)
Inscription (top left): Vol 3
Dimensions: ■ 11.4 x 7.6 cm | 4½" x 3" (BL 12614.bbb.10)
Other locations: Bodleian Vet.A5.f.478; DHW; Folger PR3694.A4 1769; LC PR3694.P4 1769

20A. *Peregrine Places the Beggar-woman's Daughter in Pipes's Charge*, 1769
(Ch. 87)
(Vol. IV, facing title page)

Unsigned frontispiece engraved by anonymous engraver (image reversed from No. **20**)
Inscription (top left): Vol 4
Dimensions: ■ 11.7 x 7.8 cm | 4^{10}/16" x 3^{1}/16"
(BL 12614.bbb.10)
Other locations: Bodleian Vet.A5.f.479; DHW; Folger PR3694.A4 1769; LC PR3694.P4 1769
Plate only: BM 1863-5-9-73

******

Nos. 17B - 20B.
[Tobias Smollett.]
THE | ADVENTURES | OF | PEREGRINE PICKLE. | IN WHICH ARE INCLUDED, | MEMOIRS | OF A | LADY OF QUALITY. | — | IN

FOUR VOLUMES. | — | VOL. I. [-VOL. IV]. | — | *Respicere exemplar vitae morumque jubebo* | *Doctum imitatorem, & veras hinc ducere voces.* | *HOR.* | — | THE FIFTH EDITION. | = | LONDON PRINTED FOR R. BALDWIN, NO. 47. AND ROBINSON AND ROBERTS, NO. 25. IN PATER-NOSTER-ROW; AND T. BECKET AND T. CADELL, IN THE STRAND. 1773 (4/4 illus.).

...THE SIXTH EDITION. | = | LONDON: | PRINTED FOR W. STRAHAN, J. RIVINGTON AND SONS, | R. BALDWIN, G. ROBINSON, T. LOWNDES, T. BECKET, | T. CADELL, AND W. GOLDSMITH. | MDCCLXXVIII [1778].

17B. *Gamaliel Pickle Observes Commodore Trunnion and Lieutenant Hatchway Duel at the Inn*, 1773
(Chapter 2)
(Vol. I, facing title page)

Frontispiece re-engraved by John Lodge
Imprint: Publish'd according to Act of Parliament Octr. 5th. 1773.
Inscription (top left): Vol. 1. | (bottom right): J. Lodge sculp.
Dimensions: ■ 12.0 x 7.8 cm | 4¾" x 3^{1}/16" (BL 12612.b.20) (H=17.0 cm)
Other locations: BL 1508/1284 (1778) (H=17.1 cm); Bodleian 256.f.2418; Cambridge 7720.d.493; Cambridge S727.d.77.9 (1778); Chicago PR3694.A2 1773; DHW (1773); Illinois x823.Sm7a.1778; Newberry Case Y1565.S66 1778; Yale IM.sm79.751.cl (1778)

18B. *Peregrine in the Palais Royal*, 1773
(Ch. 42)
(Vol. II, facing title page)

Frontispiece re-engraved by John Lodge
Imprint: Publish'd according to Act of Parliament Octr. 5th. 1773.
Inscription (top left): Vol. 2. | (bottom right): J. Lodge sculp.
Dimensions: ■ 12.1 x 7.9 cm | 4¾" x 3^{2}/16" (BL 12612.b.20) (H=17.0 cm)
Other locations: BL 1508/1284 (1778) (H=17.1 cm); Bodleian 256.f.2419; Cambridge 7720.d.494; Cambridge S72.d.77.10 (1778); Chicago PR3694.A2 1773; DHW (1773); Illinois

x823.Sm7a.1778; Newberry Case Y1565.S66 1778; Yale IM.sm79.751.cl (1778)

19B. *Cadwallader Disguised as a Magician Receives the Lady and her Maid*, 1773
(Ch. 82)
(Vol. III, facing title page)

Frontispiece re-engraved by John Lodge
Imprint: Publish'd according to Act of Parliament Octr. 5th. 1773.
Inscription (top left): Vol. 3. | (bottom right): J. Lodge sculp.
Dimensions: ■ 11.3 x 8.0 cm | 4^7/16" x 3^2/16" (BL 12612.b.20) (H=17.0 cm)
Other locations: BL 1508/1284 (1778) (H=17.1 cm); Bodleian 256.f.2420; Cambridge 7720.d.495; Cambridge S727.d.77.11 (1778); Chicago PR3694.A2 1773; DHW (1773); Illinois x823.Sm7a.1778; Newberry Case Y1565.S66 1778; Yale IM.sm79.751.c.1

20B. *Peregrine Places the Beggar-woman's Daughter in Pipes's Charge*, 1773
(Ch. 87)
(Vol. IV, facing title page)

Frontispiece re-engraved by John Lodge
Imprint: Publish'd according to Act of Parliament Octr. 5th. 1773.
Inscription (top left): Vol. 4. | (bottom right): J. Lodge sculp.
Dimensions: ■ 11.9 x 7.9 cm | 4^{11}/16" x 3^2/16" (BL 12612.b.20) (H=17.0 cm)
Other locations: BL 1508/1284 (1778) (H=17.1 cm); Bodleian 256.f.2421; Cambridge 7720.e.496; Cambridge S727.d.77.12 (1778); Chicago PR3694.A2 1773; DHW (1773); Illinois x 823.Sm7a.1778 (facing p. 49); Newberry Case Y1565.S66 1778; Yale IM.sm79.751.cl (1778)

******

Nos. 17C. - 20C.
[Tobias Smollett.]
THE | ADVENTURES | OF | PEREGRINE PICKLE. | IN WHICH ARE INCLUDED, | MEMOIRS | OF | A | LADY OF QUALITY. | IN FOUR VOLUMES. | VOLUME I. [-VOLUME II.] | — | *Respicere exemplar vitae morumque jubebo | Doctum imitatorem, & veras hinc ducere*

voces. HOR. | — | = | LONDON: | PRINTED FOR R. BALDWIN, N^O. 25. IN PATER-NOSTER-ROW; AND | T. BECKET AND | T. BECKET AND T. CADELL, IN THE STRAND. | MDCCLXXVI [1776].

17C. *Gamaliel Pickle Observes Commodore Trunnion and Lieutenant Hatchway Duel at the Inn*, 1776
(Ch. 2)
(Vol. I, facing title page)

Unsigned frontispiece re-engraved by unknown engraver
Inscription (top left): Vol. 1
Dimensions: ■ 11.9 x 7.2 cm | 4^{11}/16" x 2^{13}/16" (BL 1607/1505) (H=15.6 cm)
Other locations: Huntington 400866

18C. *Peregrine in the Palais Royal*, 1776
(Ch. 42)
(Vol. II, facing title page)

Unsigned frontispiece re-engraved by unknown engraver
Inscription (top left): Vol. 2
Dimensions: ■ 12.0 x 7.6 cm | 4¾" x 3' (BL 1607/1505) (H=15.6 cm)
Other locations: Huntington 400866

19C. *Cadwallader Disguised as a Magician Receives the Lady and her Maid*, 1776
(Ch. 82)
(Vol. III, facing title page)

Unsigned frontispiece re-engraved by unknown engraver
Inscription (top left): Vol. 3
Dimensions: ■ 11.1 x 7.5 cm | 4^6/16" x 2^{15}/16" (BL 1607/1505) (H=15.6 cm)
Other locations: Huntington 400866

20C. *Peregrine Places the Beggar-woman's Daughter in Pipes's Charge*, 1776
(Ch. 87)
(Vol. IV, facing title page)

Unsigned frontispiece re-engraved by unknown engraver

Inscription (top left): Vol. 4
Dimensions: ■ 11.4 x 7.5 cm | 4½" x 3" (BL
1607/1505) (H=15.6 cm)
Other locations: Huntington 400866

******

Nos. 17D. - 20D.
[Tobias Smollett.]
THE | ADVENTURES | OF | PEREGRINE
PICKLE. | IN WHICH ARE INCLUDED, |
MEMOIRS | OF A | LADY OF QUALITY. | IN
FOUR VOLUMES. | VOLUME I. [VOLUME II.]
| — | *Respicere exemplar vitae morumque jubebo* |
Dictum imitatorem, & veras hinc ducere voces.
HOR. | — | — | LONDON: | PRINTED FOR R.
BALDWIN, NO. 47. AND ROBINSON AND
RO- | BERTS, NO. 25. IN PATER-NOSTER-
ROW; AND T. BECKET AND | T. CADELL, IN
THE STRAND. | M,DCC,LXXIX [1779].

...MEMOIRS | OF A | LADY OF QUALITY. | IN
FOUR VOLUMES. | VOLUME III. | — | *Respicere*
exemplar vitae morumque jubebo | *Doctum*
imitatorem, & veras hinc ducere voces. HOR. | — |
— | LONDON: | PRINTED FOR R. BALDWIN,
Nº. 47. AND ROBINSON | AND ROBERTS,
Nº. 25. IN PATER-NOSTER-ROW: AND | T.
BECKET AND T. CADELL, IN THE STRAND.
| MDCCLXXIX [1779].

17D. *Gamaliel Pickle Observes Commodore*
Trunnion and Lieutenant Hatchway Duel at
   the Inn, 1779
(Ch. 2)
(Vol. I, facing title page)

Unsigned frontispiece re-engraved by anonymous
engraver
Inscription (top left): Vol. 1
Dimensions: ■ 11.7 x 7.3 cm | 4¹⁰/16" x 2¹⁴/16"
(BL 1608/1541) (H=19.1 cm)
Other locations: Iowa xPR3694.P4.1779; L.E.
Warren

18D. *Peregrine in the Palais Royal*, 1779
(Ch. 42)
(Vol. II, facing title page)

Unsigned frontispiece re-engraved by anonymous
engraver
Inscription (top left): Vol. 2

Dimensions: ■ 11.8 x 7.8 cm | 4¹⁰/16" x 3¹/16"
(BL 1608/1541) (H=19.1 cm)
Other locations: Iowa xPR3694.P4.1779; L.E.
Warren

19D. *Cadwallader Disguised as a Magician*
Receives the Lady and her Maid, 1776
(Ch. 82)
(Vol. III, facing title page)

Unsigned frontispiece re-engraved by anonymous
engraver
Inscription (top left): Vol. 3
Dimensions: ■ 11.0 x 7.6 cm | 4⁵/16" x 3"
(BL 1608/1541) (H=19.1 cm)
Other locations: Iowa xPR3694.P4.1779; L.E.
Warren

20D. *Peregrine Places the Beggar-woman's*
Daughter in Pipes's Charge, 1779
(Ch. 87)
(Vol. IV, facing title page)

Unsigned frontispiece re-engraved by anonymous
engraver
Inscription (top left): Vol. 4
Dimensions: ■11.3 x 7.7 cm | 4⁷/16" x 3¹/16"
(BL 1608/1541) (H=19.1 cm)
Other locations: Iowa xPR3694.P4.1779

******

Nos. 17E. - 20E.
[Tobias Smollett.]
THE | ADVENTURES | OF | PEREGRINE
PICKLE. | IN WHICH ARE INCLUDED, |
MEMOIRS | OF A | LADY OF QUALITY. | IN
FOUR VOLUMES. | VOLUME I. [VOLUME
IV.] | *Respicere exemplar vitae morumque jubebo* |
Doctum imitatorem, & veras hinc ducere voces.
Hor. | — | — | LONDON: | PRINTED FOR R.
BALDWIN, NO. 47. AND ROBINSON AND
ROBERTS, | NO. 25. IN PATER-NOSTER-ROW;
AND T. BECKET AND T. CADELL, | IN THE
STRAND. M,DCC,LXXXIV [1784].

17E. *Gamaliel Pickle Observes Commodore*
Trunnion and Lieutenant Hatchway Duel at
   the Inn, 1784
(Ch. 2)
(Vol. I, facing title page)

Unsigned frontispiece re-engraved by anonymous engraver
Inscription (top right): Vol. 1
Dimensions: ■ 11.7 x 7.6 cm | 4^{10}/16" x 3";
▣ 11.9 x 7.7 cm | 4^{11}/16" x 3^{1}/16" (Illinois x823.sm7a.1784)

18E. *Peregrine in the Palais Royal,* 1784
(Ch. 42)
(Vol. II, facing title page)

Unsigned frontispiece re-engraved by anonymous engraver
Inscription (top right): Vol. 2.
Dimensions: ■ 11.7 x 7.5 | 4^{10}/16" x 2^{15}/16";
▣ 11.9 x 7.7 cm | 4^{11}/16" x 3" (Illinois x823.sm7a.1784)

19E. *Cadwallader Disguised as a Magician Receives the Lady and her Maid,* 1784
(Ch. 82)
(Vol. III, facing title page)

Unsigned frontispiece re-engraved by anonymous engraver
Inscription (top right): Vol. 3.
Dimensions: ■ 11.5 x 7.6 cm | 4^{9}/16";
▣ 11.7 x 7.7 cm | 4^{10}/16" x 3^{1}/16" (Illinois x823.sm7a.1784)

20E. *Peregrine Places the Beggar-woman's Daughter in Pipes's Charge,* 1784
(Ch. 87)
(Vol. IV, facing title page)

Unsigned frontispiece re-engraved by anonymous engraver
Inscription (top right): Vol. 4.
Dimensions: ■ 11.8 x 7.7 cm | 4^{10}/16" x 3";
▣ 12.0 x 7.8 cm | 4^{11}/16" (Illinois x823.sm7a.1784)
Other locations: L.E. Warren (Vol. 4 only)

******

[No. 21.]
[Unidentified edition]
[Tobias Smollett.]
[THE ADVENTURES OF PEREGRINE PICKLE. (N.d.)]

21.

21. Proof Illustration, perhaps to *Peregrine Pickle,* [1769]

Unsigned proof, engraved probably by Charles Grignion (1721-1810)
Dimensions: ■ 12.9 x 8.6 cm | 5^{2}/16" x 4^{5}/16"
(BM 1863-5-9-71)
Lit.: Schiff 307

******

No. 22.
[Unidentified edition].
Thomas Southern.
[OROONOKO. (N.d.)]

22. Proof Illustration to *Oroonoko,* [1764-1769]
(Thomas Southern, *Oroonoko,* II, iii)

Unsigned proof engraving by anonymous engraver
Inscription (top centre): [*illegible*] (trimmed)
Dimensions: ■ 16.7 x 11.3 cm | 6^{9}/16" x 4^{7}/16"
(BM 1863-5-9-57)
Lit.: Schiff 309 (16.7 x 11.4 cm)

23.

22.

24.

The Indians have attacked the colony and have stolen the slaves, among them the beautiful slave, 'Clemene', with whom the Governor has fallen in love. But while the Governor considers it useless to attempt to rescue Clemene and the other captives, Oroonoko, the noble savage, does not hesitate, for he has recognised Clemene as his beloved Imoinda. Seizing a sword he places himself at the head of the Planters and successfully attacks the Indians, crying: 'I'll lead you on, be bold, and follow me'.

******

23. *Perseus and the Graeae*, [1770-1774]
(Ovid, *Metamorphoses*, IV, 770ff.)

Monotype finished with pen and tempera by Henry Fuseli.
Dimensions: 33.3 x 40.2 cm | 13²/16" x 15¹³/16"
(Dr. Alfred Winterstein, Munich)
Lit.: Schiff 405-405a
Exh.: Munich 1958 (49) (as 'Allegorical Scene'); Hamburg 1974-1975 (17a); London 1975 (ex cat.); Paris 1975 (52).

The Graeae, the two daughters of Phorcys, are the only ones who know the secret location of the leather bag, the mirror and the winged shoes that Perseus needs in order to cut off the head of the Medusa. Guided by Athena Perseus seizes the single eye that the two sisters share; faced by the threat of perpetual blindness they reveal the information he needs. While the goddess hovers above, the hero prepares to snatch the eye as it is passed from one sister to the other. This monotype, the only one in Fuseli's artistic corpus, is a close version of his drawing (Schiff 405A; 1771) in the Kunsthalle, Hamburg.

******

No. 24.
[Unidentified edition.]
Guillaume-Thomas Raynal.
[A | PHILOSOPHICAL AND POLITICAL | HISTORY | OF THE | SETTLEMENTS AND TRADE | OF THE | EUROPEANS | IN THE | EAST AND WEST INDIES. | — | REVISED, AUGMENTED, AND PUBLISHED, | IN TEN VOLUMES, | BY THE ABBÉ RAYNAL. | — |

NEWLY TRANSLATED FROM THE FRENCH, | BY J.O JUSTAMOND, F.R.S. | WITH A | NEW SET OF MAPS, ELEGANT ENGRAVINGS ADAPTED | TO THE WORK, AND A COPIOUS INDEX. | = | VOLUME THE FIRST. [-SIXTH.] | DUBLIN: | PRINTED FOR JOHN EXSHAW, GRAFTON STREET | AND LUKE WHITE, DAME STREET. | MDCCLXXXIV.]

24. *Proof Illustration, probably to A History of the East and West Indies*, [post 1770]

Unsigned engraving by unknown engraver
Dimensions (from photocopy): ■ 14.2 x 9.0 cm | 5⁹/16" x 3½" (the late Frederic V. Grunfeld) (plate only—location unknown)
Inscription (from photocopy): The Dress and manner of living of the | SPANIARDS in SOUTH-AMERICA.
Lit.: Frederic V. Grunfeld, *The Art and Times of the Guitar*, 1969, repr. 171.

Variants:
Lacking inscription (proof?)
Dimensions: ■ 14.3 x 10.5 cm | 5⁹/16" x 4²/16" (BM 1863-5-9-66) (plate only)
Lit.: Schiff 310 ('1764-1769')(14.6 x 10.5 cm)

The illustration appears to correspond to the description in Raynal (below), the English text of which is taken from the 1784 Dublin edition (III, 153-154). However, since the first edition of Raynal did not appear until 1770, Schiff's dating of '1764-1769' would be too early.

The charms of the Peruvian women are superior to the terror which the spiritual arms of Rome inspire. The majority of them, especially the women of Lima, have eyes sparkling with vivacity, a fair skin, a complexion that is delicate, animated, full of sprightliness and life, and a slender and well formed shape; a foot better turned and smaller than that of the Spanish women themselves; thick and black hair, flowing as if by chance, and without ornament, over their neck and shoulders, which are extremely white.
These various natural graces are heightened by every improvement that art can add to them. The clothing of the women is most sumptuous,

and they use an unbounded profusion of pearls and diamonds, in every kind of dress in which it is possible to introduce them.

... Such are the pleasures which the women, who are all dressed rather with elegance than modesty, taste and diffuse at Lima. But it is particularly in those delicious saloons where they receive company, that they appear seducing. There, carelessly reclined on a couch, which is a foot and a half high, and five or six feet wide, and upon carpets and superb cushions, they pass their days in tranquillity and in delicious repose. The men, who are admitted to their conversation, seat themselves at some distance, unless their adorers, from greater intimacy, be permitted to come up to the couch, which, as it were, the sanctuary of worship of the idol. Yet these goddesses choose rather to be affable than haughty; and, banishing ceremony, they play on the harp and guitar, and sing and dance when they are desired.

The woman's pose resembles that of the stock allegories of America, which often incorporated the armadillo (foreground). Fuseli may have been familiar with this animal from Conrad Gesner's *Historia Animalium*, Zurich, 1544, where it was first illustrated. For Grunfeld 'the lady's shocking deshabille represents another link in the tradition that associates the guitar with loose living.'

******

Nos. 25 - 35.
A | PRACTICAL FAMILY BIBLE; | ON A PLAN ENTIRELY NEW. | CONTAINING THE SACRED TEXT OF THE | OLD AND NEW TESTAMENT; | ALSO THE | APOCRYPHA; | ACCOMPANIED WITH NOTES, | EXPLAINING OBSCURE PASSAGES, VINDICATING THOSE THAT HAVE BEEN CONTROVERTED, AND DEDUCING | FROM EVERY PART OF SCRIPTURE | USEFUL, PLAIN, AND PIOUS ADMONITIONS; | TENDING TO ENLIGHTEN THE UNDERSTANDING, AND PURIFY THE HEART, | BY PROMOTING | THE KNOWLEDGE AND PRACTICE OF TRUE RELIGION, | ON WHICH DEPENDS | THE HAPPINESS OF IMMORTAL SOULS. | THE NOTES ARE CHIEFLY COLLECTED FROM THE PRINTED SERMONS OF SUCH ENGLISH DIVINES, WHOSE EMPLOY- | MENT THROUGH LIFE HAS BEEN TO UNFOLD THE WORD OF GOD, AND WHO

HAVE DISTINGUISHED THEMSELVES FOR THEIR | ABILITIES AND SUCCESS THEREIN; OR FROM THE CONTRIBUTIONS OF A NUMBER OF LEARNED AND PIOUS CLERGYMEN, | WHOSE ASSISTANCE THE EDITOR HAS SOLICITED TO FURTHER SO LABORIOUS A DESIGN. | THE WHOLE DIGESTED, AND SUPPLIED WITH OCCASIONAL ELUCIDATIONS FROM THE BEST COMMENTATORS, BY | THE HON. AND REV. FRANCIS WILLOUGHBY, D.D. RECTOR OF UPCOT, IN YORKSHIRE. | EMBELLISHED WITH A SET OF BEAUTIFUL ENGRAVINGS OF THE MOST INTERESTING HISTORICAL PASSAGES IN THE SACRED | SCRIPTURES, ENGRAVED FROM THE BEST COPIES OF CAPITAL PAINTINGS BY ABLE ARTISTS. | LONDON: PRINTED FOR J. WILKIE, NO. 71, ST. PAUL'S CHURCH YARD. MDCCLXXII [1772-1773] (11/38 illus. + 1 frontis. + 3 maps).

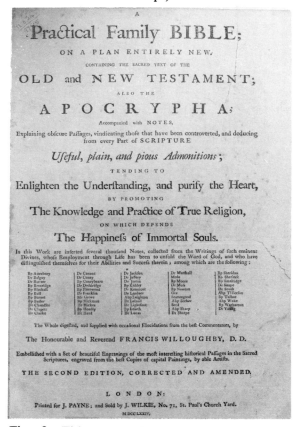

Fig. 2. Title page of Francis Willoughby's *A Practical Family Bible*, second edition, 1774

...IN THIS WORK ARE INSERTED SEVERAL
THOUSAND NOTES, COLLECTED FROM
THE WRITINGS OF SUCH EMINENT |
DIVINES WHOSE EMPLOYMENT THROUGH
LIFE HAS BEEN TO UNFOLD THE WORD
OF GOD, AND WHO HAVE | DISTINGUISHED
THEMSELVES FOR THEIR ABILITIES AND
SUCCESS THEREIN; AMONG WHICH ARE
THE FOLLOWING: |

[*col. 1*]:	[*col. 2*]	[*col. 3*]
Bp Atterbury	Dr Conant	Dr Jackson
Dr Balguy	Dr Coney	Dr Jeffery
Dr Barrow	Dr Coneybeare	Dr Jortin
Bp Beveridge	Dr Doddridge	Bp Kidder
Bp Blackall	Bp Fleetwood	Dr Kennicot
Bp Bull	Dr Franklin	Dr Lardner
Bp Burnet	Mr Grove	Abp Leighton
Bp Butler	Bp Hickman	Dr Lightfoot
Dr Chandler	Dr Hickes	Bp Lowth
Dr Clagett	Bp Hoadly	Dr Lucas
Dr Clarke	Dr Hurd	

[*col. 4*]	[*col.5*]
Dr Marshall	Bp Sheridan
Mede	Bp Sherlock
Bp Moore	Bp Smalridge
Dr Moss	Dr Snape
Bp Newton	Dr South
Orr	Abp Tillotson
Scattergood	Bp Talbot
Abp Secker	Abp Wake
Seed	Bp Warburton
Abp Sharp	Dr Young
Dr Sharpe|	

THE WHOLE DIGESTED, AND SUPPLIED
WITH OCCASIONAL ELUCIDATIONS FROM
THE BEST COMMENTATORS, BY | THE
HONOURABLE AND REVEREND FRANCIS
WILLOUGHBY, D.D. | EMBELLISHED WITH
A SET OF BEAUTIFUL ENGRAVINGS OF
THE MOST INTERESTING HISTORICAL
PASSAGES IN THE SACRED | SCRIPTURES,
ENGRAVED FROM THE BEST COPIES OF
CAPITAL PAINTINGS, BY ABLE ARTISTS. |
THE SECOND EDITION, CORRECTED AND
AMENDED. | LONDON: | PRINTED FOR J.
PAYNE; AND SOLD BY J. WILKIE, NO. 71,
ST. PAUL'S CHURCH YARD. | MDCCLXX
[1774], 1773

25.

25. *The Expulsion from Paradise*, 1772
(*Genesis*, 3:1-24)
(facing sig. [C2])

Engraved by Charles Grignion (1721-1810)
Inscription (in cartouche above): The Expulsion
from | PARADISE. | Gen: ch.3. | (below): Fuseli
delin. | | C Grignion sculp | (in cartouche below):
To the Reverend the Clergy of Derbyshire, | and to
the CONGREGATIONS committed to their
charge; | This Plate is most respectfully Inscribed,
by their fellow Labourer | and obedient Servant, | F.
Willoughby.
Dimensions: ■ 16.3 x 9.9 cm | 6^7/16" x 3^{14}/16"
(BL L.15.f.2) (H=41.0 cm)
Other locations: Chicago BS 185. f 1772 (facing
sig. [C]; Chicago BS 185 f. 1773b (1774); Dr.
Williams' Library 1113.M6 (1774)
Lit.: Schiff 311 (16.4 x 9.9 cm); Hammelmann
1975, 34, pl. 43.

25A.

26.

27.

25A. *The Expulsion from Paradise*

Unsigned proof before letters (reversed) perhaps
engraved by Charles Grignion (1721-1810)
Dimensions: ■ 23.8 x 18.5 cm | 9⁷/16" x 7¼"
(BM 1863-5-9-10)
Lit.: Schiff 311A (23.8 x 18.4 cm)

26. *Cain and Abel*, 1772
(*Genesis*, 4:15)
(facing sig. [C3])

Engraved by John Collyer (1708-1786)
Inscription (in cartouche above): CAIN & ABEL|
Where is Abel thy brother|Gen: chap. 4. v. 15.|
(bottom): Fussels delin.||J Collier sculp.|To the
right rev^d: father in God Fred^k. Lord Bishop of|
Exeter to the rev^d: the Clergy of the County of
Devon,|and to the CONGREGATIONS
committed to their charge;|This Plate is most
respectfully Inscribed by his Lordship's|dutiful
Son, and their fellow Labourer|and humble
Servant,|F. Willoughby.

Dimensions: ■ 16.3 x 9.9 cm | 6⁷/16" x 3¹⁴/16"
(BL L.15.f.2) (H=41.0 cm)
Other locations: Chicago BS 185. f 1772; Chicago
BS 185 f. 1773b (1774); Dr. Williams' Library
1113.M.6 (1774) (facing sig. I3)
Lit.: Schiff 312 (16.3 x 9.9 cm); Hammelmann
1975, 34.

27. *David and Goliath*, 1772
(*Samuel*, 17:44)
(facing sig. [4A3]

Engraved by John June (c. 1725-1780) after
Fuseli's sketch (reversed) in the Swedish National
Museum.
Inscription (top centre): David & Goliah. | (bottom
centre): 1 Samˡ. ch. XVII. ver. 44. | | J. June
sculp. | And the Philistines said to David, come to
me, & I will give thy flesh unto the Fowls of the
Air—
Dimensions: ■ 24.6 x 18.3 cm | 9¹¹/16" x 7²/16"
(BL L.15.f.2) (H=41.0 cm)
Other locations: Chicago BS 185. f 1772 (facing
sig. [4A2]; Chicago BS 185 f. 1773b (1774)
Ref.: Schiff 313 (24.6 x 18.3)

28. *The Withering of King Jeroboam's Hand*, 1772
(1 *Kings*, 13: 4-9)
(facing sig 4P)

Unsigned engraving
Inscription (top): Engraved for the HISTORY and
ILLUSTRATION of the HOLY BIBLE, by the
Revᵈ. Dʳ. WILLOUGHBY. | (bottom): And it
came to pass, when King Jeroboam heard the
saying of the man of God, which had cried against
the altar in | Bethel, that he put forth his hand from
the altar, saying, Lay hold on him. And his hand
which he put forth against | him dried up so that he
could not pull it in again to him. I. Kings Chap.
XIII. Ver. 4.
Dimensions: ■ 25.7 x 20.1 cm | 10²/16" x 7¹⁵/16"
(BL L.15.f.2) (H=41.0 cm)
Other locations: Chicago BS 185. f 1772; Chicago
BS 185 f. 1773b (1774); Dr. Williams' Library
1113.M.6 (1774)
Refs: Schiff 314 (25.9 x 20.3 cm)

Jeroboam, the 'mighty man of valour' who had
'made Israel to sin' and worship false gods, is
seen sacrificing at the altar to the golden calves.

28.

29. *Ahab's Seventy Sons Slain by the Rulers of Samaria*, 1772
(2 *Kings*, 10:7)
(facing sig. 4X)

Engraved by Henry Fuseli
Inscription (top): Ahab's Seventy Sons slain by
the Rulers of Samaria II King's ch. X. ver. 7.; |
(bottom): Fusseli inv. et delin. | | Fusseli sculp. | To
the revᵈ the CLERGY of NORTHUMBERLAND,
and to the Congregations com- | mitted to their
charge, this Plate is most respectfully Inscribed
BY F. Willoughby.
Dimensions: 18.0 x 22.0 | 7" x 8¹³/16" (Dr.
Williams' Library 1113.M.6) (1774).
Other locations: Chicago BS 185 f. 1773b (1774)
Plate only: Basel 1948.64

Variants:
I. Lacking the Dedication: BL L.15.f.2
(H=41.0 cm)
Dimensions: 17.8 x 22.3 cm
Other locations: Chicago BS 185. f 1772
Plate only: Basel 1948.64
Lit.: Schiff 315 (17.8 x 22.3 cm)

Elijah had called for the complete extirpation of the house of wicked King Ahab—a judgement finally carried out at the command of Jehu.

Ifaiah's Vision. Chap.VI.ver.6.

30.

30. *Isaiah's Vision*, 1772
(*Isaiah*, 6:6)
(facing sig. [7ɪ2])

Engraved by Henry Fuseli
Inscription (bottom right): Fuseli inv. & delin. | | **Isaiah's Vision**. Chap. VI. ver. 6.
Dimensions: 24.5 x 17.6 cm (BL L.15.f.2) (H=41.0 cm)
Other locations: Chicago BS 185. f 1772
Lit.: Schiff 316 (24.5 x 17.6 cm)

Variants:
I. Reissued (1774) with added dedication and repositioned title: Dr. Williams' Library 113.M.6
Inscription (top): Isaiah's Vision. Isa. ch. VI. ver. 6. | (bottom): To the Rev^d. the Clergy of RUTLANDSHIRE, and to the Congregations committed to their charge; | This PLATE is most respectfully Inscribed by their humble Servant, | F. Willoughby.
Other locations: BM 1870-10-08-2794; Chicago BS 185 f. 1773b (1774) (facing sig. [7H])

Isaiah, beholds the Lord and his retinue in a vision and bewails his 'unclean lips'. Whereupon a seraph takes a live coal from the altar (here in the form of a burning brazier) and places it upon Isaiah's mouth, declaring his iniquity taken away and his sin purged.

Unlike the seraph with its six wings, Fuseli's angel has only one pair to fly and another (small) pair upon his head; he has none upon his feet.

31. *The Breaking of the Potter's Vessel*, 1772
(*Jeremiah*, 19:1-10)
(facing sig. [7T2])

Engraved by Antoine Benoist (1721-1770) with aquatint by Henry Fuseli
Inscription (top): ENGRAVED for D^r. WILLOUGHBY'S ILLUSTRATION of the HOLY BIBLE. | (Bottom): H. Fusseli Inv: & inc: aq: fort: | | Benoist Sculp. | Thus saith the Lord, Go, & get a Potter's earthen bottle, & take of the Antients of y^e. People, & of y^e. Antients of y^e. Priests, & go forth into y^e. Valley of the Son of Hinnom & say, Hear the | word of y^e. Lord, O Kings of Judah, & Inhabitants of Jerusalem; &c.—Then shalt thou break the bottle in the sight of the men that go with thee, Jeremiah Chap. XIX. Verses 1. 2. 3. &c.
Dimensions: 19.5 x 25.0 cm | 7^{11}/16" x 9^{14}/16" (BL L.15.f.2) (H=41.0 cm)
Other locations: Chicago BS 185. f 1772
Plate only: BM 1867-12-14-418; Huntington 49000, 4850 (top line cropped)
Lit.: Schiff 317 (19.6 x 25.0 cm)

This plate is not present in the 2nd edition of 1774, where it has been replaced by an illustration engraved by Walker after Wale.

By breaking the bottle, the Prophet demonstrates God's intention to 'break this people and this city, as *one* breaketh a potter's vessel, that cannot be made whole again', for they had 'hardened their necks' and rejected God's word (*Jeremiah*, 19: 11, 15).

29.

31.

32. *Jonah's Indignation*, 1772
(*Jonah*, 4:8)
(between sigs. [8z4] and 9A)

Engraved in aquatint by Henry Fuseli

Inscription (top): Jonah's Indignation. | (bottom left): Fuseli inv. del. et in aq.fort excudit. | And it came to pass when the Sun did arise, that God prepared a vehement east Wind; and the Sun beat

upon | the head of Jonah, that he fainted, & wished
in himself to die, & said, it is better for me to die
than to live. Jonah. ch. IV. ver 8.
Dimensions: ■ 23.4 x 18.1 cm | 9¼" x 7²/16"
(BL L.15.f.2.) (H=41.0 cm)
Other locations: Chicago BS 185. f 1772 (between
sigs. 8Z2 and 9A); Chicago BS 185 f. 1773b
(1774); Dr. Williams' Library 1113.M.6 (facing
sig. [8Z3]) (23.6 x 18.4 cm)
Plate only: BM 1856-12-13-144 (cropped top and
bottom); BM 1870-10-8-2795
Lit.: Schiff 318 (23.4 x 18.1 cm)

Not present in the Chicago copy of the 1774
edition (BS 185 f. 1773b), where it has been
replaced by an illustration engraved by Page after
Wale.

Fuseli is one of only a very small number of
biblical illustrators ever to treat this subject,
which depicts Jonah nursing his anger at God's
decision not to destroy Nineveh.

32.

33.

33. *Salome Receives the Head of John the
Baptist*, 1772
(*Matthew*, 14: 10, 11)
(facing sig. [H2])

Engraved by Charles Grignion (1721-1810)
Inscription (top): John Baptist Head brought in a
Charger Matt. XIV. 10. 11. | (bottom): Fusseli
inv: & del | | C. Grignion sculp: | To the Revᵈ. the
Clergy of Westmoreland, and to the
Congregations committed to their charge, | This
Plate is most respectfully Inscribed by their
humble Servant, | F. Willoughby.—
Dimensions: ■ 25.1 x 18.6 cm | 9¹⁴/16" x 7⁶/16"
(BL L.15.f.2) (H=41.0 cm)
Other locations: Chicago BS 185. f 1772 (between
sigs. H-[H2]); Chicago BS 185 f. 1773b (1774);
Dr. Williams' Library 1113.M.6 (1773) (25.3 x
18.9 cm)
Lit.: Schiff 319 (24.8 x 18.4 cm); Boase 1963,
162, pl. 22d; Hammelmann 1975, 34, pl. 44.

Variants:
I. Proof before letters: BM 1863-3-12
Dimensions: 25.2 x 19.1 cm

For Fuseli's explanation of Salome's vine-wreathed thyrsus, one of the attributes of a maenad, see No. **98**.

34.

34. *The Childhood of Jesus*, 1772
(*Luke*, 2: 51-52)
(facing sig. [Y4])

Engraved by Antoine Benoist (1721-1770)
Inscription (top): **Engraved for Dʳ. Willoughby's Practical Family Bible.** | (bottom): Fusseli invᵗ. | | Benoist scᵖ. | And he went down with them, & came to Nazareth, & was subject unto to them: but his mother kept all | these sayings in her heart.—And Jesus increased in Wisdom & Stature, & in favour with God and Man. | Luke CHAP. II. verses 51, 52.
Dimensions: 23.8 x 17.6 cm | 9⁶/16" x 6¹⁵/16" (BL L.15.f.2) (H=41.0 cm)
Other locations: Chicago BS 185. f 1772; Chicago BS 185 f. 1773b (1773); Dr. Williams' Library 1113.M.6 (1773)

Lit.: Schiff 320 (23.9 x 17.6 cm); Boase 1963, 162, pl. 22a.

35.

35. *The Temptation of Jesus*, 1772
(*Luke*, 4:3)
(facing sig. Z)

Engraved by Johann Sebastian Müller (1715-*post* 1785)
Inscription (top): Engraved for Dʳ. WILLOUGHBY'S practical family BIBLE. | (bottom): H. Fusseli Inv: | Müller Sculp. | If thou be the Son of GOD, command this Stone that it be made bread. Luke Chap. IV. ver. 3.
Dimensions: 23.5 x 17.9 cm | 9¼" x 7¹/16" (BL L.15.f.2) (H=41.0 cm)
Other locations: Chicago BS 185 f.1773b
Lacking plate: Dr. Williams' Library 1113.M.6
Lit.: Schiff 321 (23.6 x 18.0 cm)

Variants:
I. Proof before letters: BM 1870-10-8-2796
II. Reissued with changed inscriptions (new title at head; below: dedication in lieu of verse): Chicago BS 185 f. 1772

Inscription (top): Christ Tempted. Luke ch. IV. ver. 3.; (bottom): H. Fusseli Inv:│ │ Müller Sculp.│To the Rev^d" the Clergy of SHROPSHIRE, and to the Congregations committed to their charge;│This PLATE is most respectfully Inscribed by their humble Servant│ F. Willoughby.

******

Nos. 25B, 26A
THE│CHRISTIAN'S│COMPLETE│FAMILY BIBLE;│OR,│UNIVERSAL LIBRARY OF DIVINE KNOWLEDGE,│CONTAINING THE SACRED TEXTS OF THE│OLD AND NEW TESTAMENTS,│WITH THE│APOCRYPHA, AT LARGE.│ILLUSTRATED WITH│NOTES AND ANNOTATIONS,│HISTORICAL, CHRONOLOGICAL, BIOGRAPHICAL, GEOGRAPHICAL, THEOLOGICAL, MORAL SYSTEMA-│TICAL, PRACTICAL, ADMONITORY, DIVINE, AND EXPLANATORY;│IN WHICH THE MOST DIFFICULT PASSAGES ARE RENDERED CLEAR AND FAMILIAR, THE SEEMING CONTRADICTIONS RECONCILED, THE MIS-TRANSLATIONS RECTIFIED, AND IMPORTANT TRUTHS CONFIRMED; SO AS TO CONFUTE THE INFIDEL, DISPEL THE MISTS OF DARKNESS, ENLIGHTEN THE IGNORANT, ENCOURAGE THE DIFFIDENT, RECLAIM THE VICIOUS, RECONCILE THE DOUBTFUL, LEAD THE│WAVERING INTO THE PATHS OF TRUTH, AND IMPLANT IN THE MIND OF EVERY CHRISTIAN THAT DIVINE KNOWLEDGE WHICH IS ESSENTIALLY NECESSARY TO SALVATION.│FORMING A COMPLETE TREASURY OF│DIVINE REVELATION.│ BEING A FULL EXPLANATION OF THE VARIOUS BOOKS IN THE│OLD AND NEW TESTAMENTS.│AND AS A FARTHER ILLUSTRATION WILL BE GIVEN,│A GENERAL INDEX, OR CONCORDANCE, CLEARLY POINTING OUT EVERY MATERIAL TRANSACTION RECORDED IN THE SACRED WRITINGS;│A CHRONOLOGICAL INDEX OF TRANSACTIONS FROM ADAM TO THE TIME OF OUR BLESSED SAVIOUR;│A GEOGRAPHICAL INDEX OF PLACES MENTIONED IN THE HOLY SCRIPTURES; A BRIEF ACCOUNT OF THE APOSTLES AND THEIR SUCCESSORS, WHO PROPAGATED THE CHRISTIAN RELIGION, BY PRESIDING OVER THE APOSTOLIC│CHURCHES OF ANTIOCH, JERUSALEM, &C.│THE WHOLE FORMING A│COMPLETE BODY OF CHRISTIAN DIVINITY;│EXPLAINED AND ILLUSTRATED IN SUCH A MANNER, AS TO GUIDE THE READER THROUGH THE PATHS OF HAPPINESS IN THIS WORLD, AND LEAD HIM TO│THE MANSIONS OF ETERNAL BLISS IN THAT WHICH IS TO COME.│=│ILLUSTRATED AND EXPLAINED BY SEVERAL EMINENT DIVINES.│=│EMBELLISHED AND ENRICHED WITH FORTY ENGRAVINGS, ILLUSTRATIVE OF THE VARIOUS TRANSACTIONS RECORDED IN THE SACRED WRITINGS FROM│GENESIS TO THE END OF THE REVELATION.│=│LIVERPOOL,│PRINTED BY J. NUTTALL, NO. 21, DUKE STREET.│=│1804 (2/40 illus.).

25B. The Expulsion from Paradise, 1803
(*Genesis*, 3:1-24)
(facing sig. [B2])

Re-lettered reissue of engraving by Charles Grignion (1721-1810)
Inscription (in cartouche above): The Expulsion from│PARADISE.│Gen: ch.3.│(below): Fuseli delin.│ │C Grignion sculp│(in cartouche below): Engrav'd for│NUTTALLS' FAMILY BIBLE,│1803.
Dimensions: ■ 16.4 x 9.9 cm │ 6⁷/16" x 3¹⁵/16" (BL L.14.g.8)

26A. Cain and Abel, 1803
(*Genesis*, 4:15)
(facing sig. [C])

Re-lettered reissue of engraving by John Collyer (1708-1786)
Inscription (in cartouche above): CAIN & ABEL│where is Abel thy brother│Gen: chap 4. v. 15.│(below): 'Fussels delin.'│ │'J Collier sculp'.'│Engrav'd│for NUTTALL'S│FAMILY BIBLE,│1803.
Dimensions: ■ 16.4 x 9.8 cm │ 6⁷/16" x 3¹⁴/16" (BL L.14.g.8)

No. 30B.

THE|CHRISTIAN'S UNIVERSAL|FAMILY BIBLE;|OR|LIBRARY OF DIVINE KNOWLEDGE;|CONTAINING|THE SACRED TEXTS OF THE|OLD AND NEW TESTAMENTS,|WITH THE APOCRYPHA AT LARGE.|EXPLAINED AND ILLUSTRATED| WITH CHOICE NOTES AND VALUABLE ANNOTATIONS,|THEOLOGICAL, HISTORICAL, CHRONOLOGICAL, CRITICAL, PRACTICAL, MORAL, AND EXPLANATORY;|FOR THE PECULIAR AND IMPORTANT PURPOSES OF|REMOVING THE DOUBTS AND ENCOURAGING THE HOPES OF THE WEAK AND DIFFIDENT, INSTRUCTING THE IGNORANT, EXPLAINING OBSCURE AND DIFFICULT PASSAGES, RECTIFYING MIS[-]TRANSLATIONS,|AND VINDICATING THE GENUINE PURITY OF THE SACRED SCRIPTURES; INCLUDING WHATSOEVER CAN BE OF IMPORTANCE TO EDIFY AND ENLIVEN THE PIOUS AND WELL-MEANING CHRISTIAN, OR|DEPRESS THE PRESUMPTION OF THE WICKED AND CARELESS OFFENDER; BY RAISING THE MOST STRIKING INFERENCES FROM THE MORE INTERESTING PASSAGES OF THE SACRED VOLUMES,|EXCITING THE SERIOUS AND RATIONAL ATTENTION OF PERSONS OF ALL DESCRIPTIONS, ROUSING THE WRETCHED AND PROFANE SINNER TO A SENSE OF HIS DEPLORABLE CONDITION, AND PIERCING|THE HEART OF THE STUBBORN AND OBDURATE ATHEIST AND INFIDEL; THAT ALL MAY BE BROUGHT TO THE KNOWLEDGE OF THE TRUTH, THROUGH THE MERITS AND MERCIES OF OUR GRACIOUS|REDEEMER, AND THEREBY SECURE THE BLESSINGS AND COMFORTS OF THIS LIFE, AND A WELL-GROUNDED HOPE OF THAT WHICH IS TO COME.|WITH AN INTRODUCTION PREFIXED TO EACH BOOK,|FROM GENESIS TO THE REVELATION,|CONTAINING A SUMMARY OF ITS DOCTRINES AND HISTORY; AND A CONCLUSION ANNEXED, COMPREHENDING THE MOST IMPORTANT |PRACTICAL OBSERVATIONS, WITH SUITABLE REFLECTIONS ON EACH.|TO WHICH WILL BE ADDED|AN INDEX CHRONOLOGICAL AND GEOGRAPHICAL;|

THE PROPER NAMES USED IN THE SCRIPTURES CLEARLY EXPLAINED; USEFUL TABLES OF SCRIPTURE WEIGHTS, MEASURES, AND COINS, WITH THE| METHOD OF REDUCING THEM TO THOSE USED IN ENGLAND; BY THE BISHOP OF PETERBOROUGH. INCLUDING ALSO ALL THE|MARGINAL READINGS WHICH IN THE LEAST AFFECT THE SENSE OF THE TEXT, &C. &C.|THE WHOLE FORMING A COMPLETE|COMMENTARY ON THE HOLY BIBLE,|ADAPTED AND RENDERED EASY, PLEASANT, AND PROFITABLE, BOTH IN FAITH AND PRACTICE, TO EVERY CAPACITY; AND CALCULATED TO PROMOTE THE TEMPORAL|COMFORT AND ETERNAL HAPPINESS OF CHRISTIAN FAMILIES;|CHIEFLY EXTRACTED FROM THE VALUABLE WRITINGS OF THE MOST EMINENT|DIVINES, ANCIENT AND MODERN, WITH OBSERVATIONS AND PRACTICAL REFLECTIONS, BY|THE REV. JOHN MALHAM,|VICAR OF HELTON IN DORSET, AUTHOR OF TWO VOLUMES OF SERMONS, DICTIONARY OF THE COMMON PRAYER, &C. &C.|—|EMBELLISHED WITH ELEGANT ENGRAVINGS,|ILLUSTRATIVE OF SOME OF THE MOST IMPORTANT SUBJECTS IN THE HOLY BIBLE.|=|*Search the Scriptures; for in them ye think ye have eternal life, and they are they which testify of me.-John v. 39.*|*These were more noble than those in Thessalonica, in that they received the word with all readiness of mind, and searched the*|*Scriptures daily whether those things were so.—Acts XVII.II.* |=| LONDON:PRINTED FOR THOMAS KELLY, NO. 52, PATERNOSTER-ROW,|BY W. CLOWES, NORTHUMBERLAND-COURT, STRAND.|—| 1810 (1/41 illus.).

[*With added title page*]: THE|HOLY BIBLE| WITH NOTES AND ANNOTATIONS|BY THE REV[D] JOHN MALHAM.|[Vignette]|*Pollard Sculp.*|*Writg. by G. King.*| LONDON: PRINTED BY THOMAS KELLY, 52, PATERNOSTER ROW. NOV[R]. 28—1812.

30B. *Isaiah's Vision,* 1811
(*Isaiah,* 6:6)
(facing sig. 8I[4]

Re-engraved perhaps by Robert Pollard

Imprint: London, Published by Thomas Kelly, Paternoster row, March 23— 1811.
Dimensions: 15.8 x 12.5 cm (BL L.21.aa.16)
Lit.: Eugene C. Worman, 'George Virtue and the British "Numbers" Game', *AB Bookman's Weekly*, 15 June 1987, 2648.

According to Worman, the 80,000 full copies that Kelly sold of this Bible, which appeared in 173 parts at 8d. each, brought in £460,000.

******

Nos. 27C, 30C.
HOLY BIBLE, | WITH NOTES AND ANNOTATIONS | BY THE REV^D. MATTHEW HENRY: | ABRIDGED FOR THE USE OF FAMILIES, | BY THE REV^D. THOMAS SMITH. | [Vignette] | LONDON. | PRINTED BY THOMAS KELLY | | 53, PATERNOSTER ROW. | 1815 (2/35 illus.).

The advertisement is dated 'Spa-Fields, Dec. 3, 1814'.

27C. *The Death of Goliath*, 1813
(*Samuel*, 17:44)
(facing sig. 4E)

Re-engraved in smaller format by — Grainger, composition much changed
Imprint: London. Pub by Thomas Kelly, Paternoster row, May 22— 1813
Inscription: Fuseli del. | | Grainger Sc. | THE DEATH OF GOLIAH. | 1. Samuel, Chap. XVII, ver. 57.
Dimensions: ■ 17.0 x 13.8 cm | 6^{11}/16" x 5^7/16";
■ 20.8 x 17.5 cm | 8^3/16" x 6^{14}/16" (BL LR.280.d.8)

30C. *Isaiah's Vision*, 1812
(*Isaiah*, 6:6)
(facing sig. 7[O4])

Re-engraved (reversed) in reduced format by — Grainger
Imprint: London, Published by Thomas Kelly, Paternoster row. March 23— 1812.
Inscription: Fuseli del. | | Grainger sculp. | ISAIAH'S VISION. | Isaiah. Chap. VI. ver. 6.
Dimensions: ■ 15.8 x 12.2 cm | 6^3/16" x 4^{14}/16";
■ 19.4 x 16.1 cm | 7^{10}/16" x 6^5/16" (BL LR.280.d.8)

******

Nos. 36 - 37.
Johann Caspar Lavater.
PHYSIOGNOMISCHE FRAGMENTE, | ZUR BEFÖRDERUNG | DER MENSCHEN[-] KENNTNISS UND MENSCHENLIEBE, | VON | JOHANN CASPAR LAVATER. | — | *Gott schuf den Menschen sich zum Bilde!* | -ERSTER VERSUCH. [-VIERTER VERSUCH.] | MIT VIELEN KUPFERN. | [Vignette] | — | LEIPZIG UND WINTERTHUR, 1775. [-1778] | BEY WEIDMANNS ERBEN UND REICH, UND HEINRICH STEINER UND COMPAGNIE (2/827 illus.).

An important role was played in the publication and—in some sections—the composition of the *Physiognomische Fragmente* by J.W. von Goethe, who acted as Lavater's intermediary in the negotiations with the publisher; Goethe also helped see the volumes through the press. The text was printed by the firm of Dürre in Leipzig, while Lavater was responsible for providing the plates. Seven hundred and fifty copies were published. Lavater's compensation amounted to almost 25,000 fl. (Schulte-Strathaus 1913, no. 77a citing Karl Buchner, *Aus den Papieren der Weidmannschen Buchhandlung*, Berlin, 1873). But from this sum Lavater also had to pay his engravers. The extent of such expenses, both for this and the French edition, may be gauged from the account books of one of Lavater's principal engravers, Johann Rudolf Schellenberg, preserved in the Kunstmuseum Winterthur (copy in the Stadtbibliothek, Ms. 8° 549). A later numbered list of Schellenberg's engravings, 1766-1805, with prices, is in the National Library, Bern ('Verzeichniss der von I: R: Schellenberg ... gestochenen Kupferplatten', Ms. 7361).

36. *Head of a Dying Man*, 1775
(Vol. IV, facing p. 415, Plate No. XLVI)

Unsigned stipple engraving by Johann Rudolf Schellenberg (1740-1806) after Fuseli's lost painting
Inscription (top right): **Nach Fuessli.**
Dimensions: ■ 21.6 x 17.5 cm | 8½" x 6^{14}/16";
■ 22.0 x 17.9 cm | 8^{11}/16" x 7" (Newberry fB56.48)

Other locations: UB Basel Kp.V.71 (not seen);
Bern A 15.089; BL 29.g.10 (H=34 cm); Bodleian
4Δ156; ETH A111/8 (Vol. IV of plates); ETH
3545 (between pp. 414-415); Fribourg A 2062;
Lucerne D50 fol.; Winterthur a362; ZBZ
Lav.Dr.22f.; ZBZ Lav. H 103
Lit.: Schiff 1735 (?21.0 x 17.8); Hammelmann
1975, 34 (Refers to 'a few illustrations' by
Fuseli); Schiff-Viotto 1977, no. 15[1]

Variants:

I. Proof before frame: ZBZ Lav. Ms.
96.e/A.67

Inscription (top right): **Nach Fuessli**.

Schellenberg charged 4 fl for etching this (April
1775) (Ms. 7361, no. 326: 'Ein Sterbender').

According to Lavater the 'seven times more
expressive original' was drawn 'with seven
brushstrokes on a raw canvas'.

36.

37. *Head of a Dying Man*, 1778
(Vol. IV, p. 415)

Engraved in smaller format by Johann Rudolf
Schellenberg (1740-1806) after Fuseli's lost
drawing
Inscription (bottom left): J.R. Schellenberg. fec.
Dimensions (to platemark): 8.7 x 8.4 cm |
3½" x 3⁵⁄₁₆" (Newberry fB56.48)

Other locations: Bern A 15.089; BL 29.g.10
(H=34 cm); Bodleian 4Δ156; ETH A111/4 (text
vol.); ETH 3545; Fribourg A 2062; Lucerne
D50.fol.; ZBZ Lav.Dr.22f; ZBZ Lav.H.103
Lit.: Schiff 1735 (8.2 x 8.1 cm) (engraved 'F.
Schellenberg')

Entered in the engraver's ledger (no. 535,
January [1779]) as 'Eine Vignette. Ein Sterbender
Kopf'. Schellenberg's fee was 2.20 fl.

******

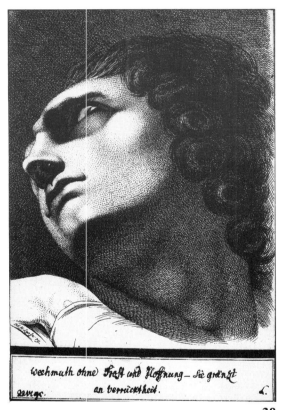

38.

38. *Head of Ugolino*, 1779
(Dante, *Inferno*, XXXIII)

Engraved by Johann Heinrich Lips (1758-1817)
after Fuseli's painting in the Staatliche Kunst-
sammlungen, Weimar ([1770-1778]; Schiff 361)
Inscription (bottom left): Joh: H: Lips fec: 79
Dimensions: 13.8 x 10.2 cm | 5⁷⁄₁₆" x 4" (KHZ
C4/I, 589)
Other locations: ZBZ F.A.Lav.Ms.84 e/c
Lit.: Schiff 361; Schiff-Viotto 1977, no. 8

Lavater's inscription mounted beneath his copy
of the print (ZBZ) reads in English: 'Melancholy
without consolation and hope verges on madness'.

Nos. 39 - 63.
Johann Caspar Lavater.
ESSAI | SUR LA | PHYSIOGNOMONIE, |
DESTINÉ | À FAIRE CONNOITRE L'HOMME
& À LE FAIRE AIMER. | PAR JEAN GASPARD
LAVATER, CITOYEN DE ZURICH ET
MINISTRE DU ST. EVANGILE. | PREMIÈRE
PARTIE. [-TROISIEME PARTIE] | *Dieu créa
l'Homme à son Image.* | IMPRIMÉ À LA HAYE |
1781 [-L'AN 1786] (25/827 illus.).

For the re-engravings of 1806, 1820 and 1835 see
Nos. **39A - 63A** and **39B - 63B** below.
For Lavater's commentaries accompanying the
individual plates, see the entries for the English
edition, 1789-1798 (Nos. **84-110**).

The French edition was more than a mere
translation: Lavater extensively reworked the
Physiognomische Fragmente before it was
translated and most of the engraved illustrations
were also new. The bulk of the engravings were
done by Johann Heinrich Lips and Johann Rudolf
Schellenberg. The work was printed at the Hague
at Lavater's expense but was distributed by
Heinrich Steiner & Co. of Winterthur (see
Schulte-Strathaus 1913, no. 77d). The fourth
volume was announced for the end of 1788 but
did not in fact appear until 1803. No copy has
been located of the prospectus published 1
October 1781 (see 'L'Avis au Public', dated 1
August 1787).

39. *Head of a Trans-Tiberine*, 1779
(Vol. II, facing p. 34, Plate IV)

Engraved by Johann Heinrich Lips (1758-1817)
after Fuseli's drawing in the Santa Barbara
Museum of Art ([1777-1779]; Schiff 1741)
Inscription (top right): IV. P. 34. | (lower left,
along line of neck): H. Fuesli del: | (lower right):
H: Lips sculp: 79. | **un Trasteverin.**
Dimensions (to platemark): 26.5 x 19.8 cm |
10⁷/16" x 7¾" (ZBZ NNN 116)
Other locations: Basel 1942.11; Bern L.Theol.22
Res; BL 29.g.6; Geneva Md 411; KHZ Dg251b;
Lausanne AVC 55; Lucerne D51.fol.; MMA
68.526.18; Newberry Wing fZP746.K45; NYPL
MEB+; Winterthur BRH 5219 (not seen); ZBZ
KK 2405a; ZBZ Lav.H.16; ZBZ LL56
Plate only: KHZ C4/I, 582 (cropped inside
platemark)

Lit.: Schiff 765 (26.0 x 19.7 cm); Hammelmann
1975, 34.
Exh.: Coburg 1989 (57)

Variants:
I. Proof before all letters (lacking vol. and page
nos.): ETH 545
Inscription: H. Fuesli del: | (lower right): H:
Lips sculp: 79. | (bottom): **un Transteverin.**

IV.P.34.

un Trasteverin.

39.

40. *Head of Brutus*, 1779
(Vol. II, facing p. 252, Plate LVIII)

Engraved by Robert Brichet (unfinished study in
the Kunsthaus, Zurich [1778-1780]; Schiff 498)
Inscription (top right): LVIII. P. 252. | (top left in
plate): **Brutus.** | (lower right in plate): R. Brichet
sculp.
Dimensions: ■ 22.4 x 18.3 cm | 8¹³/16" x 7³/16";
■ 22.6 x 18.6 cm | 8¹⁴/16" x 7⁵/16" (ZBZ NNN
116)
Other locations: Basel 1942.11; Bern L.Theol.22;
BL 29.g.6; Geneva Md 411; KHZ Dg251b;

Lucerne D51.fol.; MMA 65.526.18; Newberry Wing fZP746.K45; NYPL MEB+;ZBZ Lav.H.16
Lit.: Schiff 766 (22.5 x 18.5 cm)

Variants:

I. Punctuation of plate no. altered: ZBZ KK 2405a
Inscription (top right): LVIII: P. 252.|(top left in plate): **Brutus.**|(lower right in plate): R. Brichet sculp.
Other locations: ETH 3545A; Lausanne AVC 55; ZBZ LL57

40.

41. *Mary, Sister of Martha*, 1779
(*Luke*, 10: 38-42)
(Vol. II, facing p. 253, Plate LIX)

Engraved by Johann Heinrich Lips (1758-1817) after Fuseli's drawing in the Kunsthaus, Zurich ([1778-1779]; Schiff 501)
Inscription (top right): LIX. P. 253.|H: Fuessli pinx.||H: Lips sculp: 1779.|**Marie Soeur de Mathe**
Dimensions: ■ 24.2 x 19.0 cm | 9½" x 7^7/16"; ▣ 24.3 x 19.2 cm | 9^6/16" x 7^9/16" (ZBZ NNN 116)
Other locations: Basel 1942.11; Bern L.Theol.22; BL 29.g.6; Geneva Md 411; Luzern D51.fol.;

MMA 68.2526.18; Newberry Wing fZP746.K45; NYPL MEB+
Lit.: Schiff 767 (24.2 x 19.3 cm)

Variants:

I. Before page and plate no.: Basel 1942.11
Inscription: H: Fuessli pinx.||H: Lips sculp: 1779.|**Marie Soeur de Mathe.**
Exh.: Coburg 1989 (56)
II. Punctuation of plate no. altered ('LIX: P. 253'): ZBZ KK 2405a
Other locations: ETH 3545A; Lausanne AVC 55; ZBZ Lav.H.16; ZBZ LL57
III. Spelling of name corrected ('Marthe'): KHZ Dg.251b

Marie Soeur de Marthe .

41.

42. *St. John the Baptist*, 1779
(Vol. II, facing p. 254, Plate LX)

Engraved by Johann Heinrich Lips (1758-1817) after Fuseli's lost drawing, for which a preliminary sketch survives in the Nationale Forschungs und Gedenksstätten der klassischen deutschen Literatur (Goethe's collection) ([1778-1779]; Schiff 502)

Inscription (top right): LX. P. 254. | (along line of neck): Joh: H: Lips sculp: 79. | Joh: H: Fuessli del. | (bottom right, inside frame): **S. Jean.**
Dimensions: ■ 26.2 x 18.6 cm | $10^5/16$" x $7^5/16$"; ■ 26.5 x 18.9 cm | $10^7/16$" x $7^7/16$" (ZBZ NNN 116)
Other locations: Basel 1923.12; Bern L.Theol.22; BL 29.g.6; Geneva Md 411; KHZ Dg251b; Lucerne D51.fol.; MMA 68.526.18; NYPL MEB+; Newberry Wing fZP746.K45; ZBZ Lav.H.16
Lit.: Schiff 768 (26.2 x 19.0 cm); Jaton 1988, repr. 140
Exh.: Coburg 1989 (55)

42.

Variants:
I. Proof before frame and all letters (lacking plate and page nos. and title): ETH 545
Inscription: Joh. H: Lips sculp: 79. | Joh: H: Fuessli del.
Dimensions (to platemark): 28.4 x 21.0 cm
Other locations: KHZ C4/I, 590
II. Punctuation of Plate no. altered: ZBZ KK 2405a

Inscription (top right): LX: P. 254. | (along line of neck): Joh: H: Lips sculp: 79. | Joh: H: Fuessli del. | (bottom right, inside frame): **S. Jean.**
Other locations: ETH 3545A; Lausanne AVC 55; ZBZ LL57

43.

43. *Satan*, 1779
(Vol. II, facing p. 255, Plate LXI)

Engraved by Johann Heinrich Lips (1758-1817)
Inscription (top right): LXI. P. 255 | Satan | | d'après F. | (lower left): H: Lips sculp: 79. | H: Fuessli del.
Dimensions (to platemark): 28.9 x 21.5 cm | $11^6/16$" x $8^7/16$" (ZBZ NNN 116)
Other locations: Basel 1923.12; Bern L.Theol.22; BL 29.g.6; Geneva Md 411; KHZ Dg251b; Lausanne AVC 55; Lucerne D51.fol.; MMA 68.526.18; Newberry Wing fZP746.K45; NYPL MEB+; ZBZ Lav.H.16
Lit.: Schiff 769 (28.0 x 21.3 cm); Federmann 1927, 164; Tomory 1972, pl. 168; Jaton 1988, repr. 140
Exh.: Coburg 1989 (58)

Variants:
I. Proof before all letters (signatures only):
ETH 545
Inscription: H: Lips sculp: 79|H: Fuessli del.
Other locations (plate only): KHZ C4/I, 588
II. Punctuation of Plate no. altered ('LX: P.
254.'): ZBZ KK2405a
Other locations: ETH 3545A; ZBZ LL57

Writing to Lavater, 17 September 1779, Fuseli
expressed annoyance that Lavater had let Lips 'so
diabolically cheapen his devil' (Federmann 1927,
164).

45.

44.

44. *Murdered Abel*, 1779
(Vol. II, top of p. 256)

Unsigned engraving
Dimensions: ■ 4.2 x 18.8 cm | 1¹⁰/₁₆" x 7⁷/₁₆"
(ZBZ NNN 116)
Other locations: Bern L.Theol.22; BL 29.g.6;
ETH 3545A; Geneva; KHZ Dg251b; Lausanne
AVC 55; Lucerne D51.fol.; MMA 68.526.18;
Newberry Wing fZP746.K45; NYPL MEB+;
ZBZ KK 2045a; ZBZ Lav.H.16; ZBZ Lav.H.16;
ZBZ LL57
Lit.: Schiff 770 (4.2 x 18.6 cm)

45. *Cain*
(Vol. II, bottom of page 256)

Unsigned engraving
Dimensions (to platemark): 8.8 x 6.0 cm |
3⁶/₁₆" x 2⁶/₁₆" (ZBZ NNN 116)
Other locations: Bern L.Theol.22; BL 29.g.6;
ETH 3545A; Geneva Md 411; KHZ Dg251b;
Lausanne AVC 55; Lucerne D51.fol.; MMA
68.526.18; Newberry Wing fZP746.K45; NYPL
MEB+; ZBZ KK 2045a; ZBZ Lav.H.16; ZBZ
LL57
Lit.: Schiff 771 (8.8 x 6.0 cm)

46.

46. *Balaam Blessing the People of Israel Whom
He Intended to Curse*
(*Numbers*, 23: 7-11)
(Vol. II, p. 257, f)

Engraved by Robert Brichet
Inscription (bottom left in plate): R. Brichet Sculp

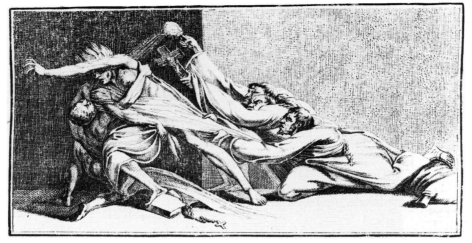

47.

48.

Dimensions: 12.8 x 9.8 cm | 5¹/16" x 3¹⁴/16"
(ZBZ NNN 116)
Other locations: Basel 1923.12; Bern L.Theol.22;
BL 29.g.6; ETH 3545A; Geneva Md 411; KHZ
Dg251b; Lausanne AVC 55; Lucerne D51.fol.;
MMA 68.526.18; Newberry Wing fZP746.K45;
NYPL MEB+ (H=33.0 cm); ZBZ KK 2045a;
ZBZ Lav.H.16; ZBZ LL57
Lit.: Schiff 772 (12.7 x 9.7 cm)

47. *The Escapee*
(Vol. II, p. 258, g)

Unsigned engraving after Fuseli's drawing in the
British Museum ([1772]; Schiff 515)
Dimensions: ■ 5.9 x 11.4 cm | 2⁵/16" x 4⁷/16";
▣ 6.1 x 11.5 cm | 2⁶/16" x 4½" (ZBZ NNN
116)
Other locations: Basel 1923.12; Bern L.Theol.22;
BL 29.g.6; ETH 3545A; Geneva Md 411; KHZ
Dg251b; Lausanne AVC 55; Lucerne D51.fol.;
MMA 68.526.18; Newberry Wing fZP746.K45;
NYPL MEB+; ZBZ KK 2045a; ZBZ Lav.H.16;
ZBZ LL57
Lit.: Schiff 773 (6.1 x 11.5 cm)

48. *The Witch of Endor Summoning up for Saul the Spirit of Samuel*
(I *Samuel*, 28: 7-25)
(Vol. II, top of p. 259, h)

Unsigned engraving
Dimensions: ■ 8.3 x 15.4 cm | 3¼" x 6¹/16"
(ZBZ NNN 116)
Other locations: Basel 1923.12; Bern L.Theol.22;
BL 29.g.6; ETH 3545A; Geneva Md 411; KHZ
Dg251b; Lausanne AVC 55; Lucerne D51.fol.;
MMA 68.526.18; Newberry Wing fZP746.K45;
NYPL MEB+; ZBZ KK 2045a; ZBZ Lav.H.16;
ZBZ LL57
Lit.: Schiff 774 (8.2 x 15.4 cm)

49. *Young Man Sitting Underneath a Tree with Landscape in Background*
(Vol. II, bottom of p. 259)

Oval vignette engraved by Johann Rudolf
Schellenberg (1740-1806) after a similar motif by
Fuseli, with independent addition of the landscape
Inscription: Schellenberg f.
Dimensions (to platemark): 5.5 x 7.5 cm |
2³/16" x 2¹⁴/16" (ZBZ NNN 116)
Other locations: Basel 1923.12; Bern L.Theol.22;
BL 29.g.6; ETH 3545A; Geneva Md 411; KHZ
Dg251b; Lausanne AVC 55; Lucerne D51.fol.;
MMA 68.526.18; Newberry Wing fZP746.K45;
NYPL; ZBZ KK 2045a; ZBZ Lav.H.16; ZBZ
LL57
Lit.: Schiff 775 (5.0 x 6.5)

49A. *Young Man Beneath a Tree*

Unused engraving perhaps by Johann Rudolf

Schellenberg (1740-1806) (image reversed)
Dimensions: (ZBZ F.A.Lav.MS.)

49.

50. *Three Heads of Damned Souls from Dante*
(Vol. II, top of p. 260, i)

Unsigned engraving after the two Fuseli paintings
in the Art Institute Chicago (no Schiff number)
Inscription: 1.||2.||3.|
Dimensions (to platemark): 8.2 x 18.5 cm |
3¼" x 7¼" (ZBZ NNN 116)
Other locations: Bern L.Theol.22; BL 29.g.6;
ETH 3545A; Geneva Md 411; KHZ Dg251b;
Lausanne AVC 55; Lucerne D51.fol.; MMA
68.526.18; Newberry Wing fZP746.K45; NYPL;
ZBZ KK 2045a; ZBZ Lav.H.16; ZBZ LL57
Lit.: Schiff 776 (8.2 x 18.5 cm); Schiff-Viotto
1977, repr. p. 84, bottom row, centre; W.
Hartmann, *Die Wiederentdeckung Dantes in der
deutschen Kunst*, 1969, 56-57.

50.

51.

53.

52.

54.

51. *Fourth Head of a Damned Soul from Dante*
(Dante, *Purgatorio*, XIII, 58-62)
(Vol. II, bottom of p. 260)

Unsigned engraving
Dimensions (to platemark): 7.8 x 8.0 cm |
3^1/16" x 3$^{1}\!/\!4$" (ZBZ NNN 116)

Other locations: Basel 1923. 12; Bern L.Theol.22;
BL 29.g.6; ETH 3545A; Geneva Md 411; KHZ
Dg251b; Lausanne AVC 55; Lucerne D51.fol.;
MMA 68.526.18; Newberry Wing fZP746.K45;
NYPL MEB+; ZBZ KK 2045a; ZBZ Lav.H.16;
ZBZ LL57

Lit.: Schiff 776 (8.2 x 18.5 cm); Schiff-Viotto 1977, repr. p. 84, bottom row, centre.

52. *Salome Receiving the Head of John the Baptist*
(Vol. II, facing p. 261)

Unsigned outline engraving
Inscription (top right): LXII. P. 261. | Salome. | d'après Füsslin.
Dimensions: ■ 22.5 x 18.4 cm | 8¹⁴/16" x 7¼";
■ 23.0 x 18.7 cm | 9¹/16" x 3⁷/16"
(ZBZ NNN 116)
Other locations: Bern L.Theol.22; BL 29.g.6; Geneva Md 411; KHZ Dg251b; Lucerne D51.fol.; MMA 68.526.18; Newberry Wing fZP746.K45; NYPL MBE+; ZBZ Lav.H.16
Lit.: Schiff 777 (23.0 x 18.7 cm)

Variants:
I. Punctuation of plate no. altered: ZBZ KK2045a
Inscription (top right): LXII: P. 261. | (bottom within frame): Salome. | d'après Füsslin.
Other locations: ETH 3545A;ETH 3545A; Geneva Md 411; KHZ Dg251b; Lausanne AVC 55; ZBZ LL57

53. *Rechab with the Head of Ishbosheth*
(II *Samuel*, 4:)
(Vol. II, p. 261, Plate No. 62)

Unsigned engraving
Inscription: PLANCHE LXII.
Dimensions (to platemark): 7.9 x 11.8 cm | 3²/16" x 4²/16" (ZBZ NNN 116)
Other locations: Bern L.Theol. 22; BL 29.g.6; ETH 3545A; Geneva Md 411; KHZ Dg251b; Lausanne AVC 55; Lucerne D51.fol.; MMA 68.526.18; Newberry Wing fZP746.K45; NYPL MBE+; ZBZ KK 2045a; ZBZ Lav.H.16; ZBZ
Lit.: Schiff 778 (7.9 x 11.3 cm) (as 'Executioner Displaying the Head of John the Baptist')

54. *Patriarch or Prophet*
(Vol. II, p. 262, l)

Unsigned engraving by Johann Rudolf Schellenberg (1740-1806) after Fuseli's drawing

sold Christie's, London, 9 July 1991 (60)
Dimensions (to platemark): 15.2 x 11.2 cm | 5¹⁵/16" x 4⁷/16" (ZBZ NNN 116)
Other locations: Bern L.Theol.22; BL 29.g.6; ETH 3545A; Geneva Md 411; KHZ Dg251b; Lausanne AVC 55; Lucerne D51.fol.; MMA 68.526.18; Newberry Wing fZP746.K45; NYPL MBE+; ZBZ KK 2045a; ZBZ Lav.H.16; ZBZ LL57
Lit.: Schiff 779 (15.2 x 11.3)

55.

55. *Head of Christ*
(Vol. II, p. 263)

Unsigned engraving
Dimensions: 11.4 x 9.0 cm | 4½" x 3½" (ZBZ NNN 116)
Other locations: Bern L.Theol.22; BL 29.g.6; ETH 3545A; Geneva Md 411; KHZ Dg251b; Lausanne AVC 55; Lucerne D51.fol.; MMA 68.526.18; Newberry Wing fZP746.K45; NYPL MBE+; ZBZ KK 2045a; ZBZ Lav.H.16; ZBZ LL57
Lit.: Schiff 780 (11.4 x 9.0 cm)

56.

57.

56. *Count Ezzelin Musing over the Body of Meduna, Slain by him for Infidelity*, 1779 (Vol. II, p. 264, n)

Engraved by Johann Heinrich Lips (1758-1817) after the painting in the Soane Museum, London (1779; Schiff 360)
Inscription (bottom): H: Fuessli del. | | H. Lips fec 79
Dimensions: ■ 10.7 x 14.8 cm | 4³/16" x 5¹³/16" (ZBZ NNN 116)

Other locations: Bern L.Theol.22; BL 29.g.6; ETH 3545A; Geneva Md 411; KHZ Dg251b; Lucerne D51.fol.; MMA 68.526.18; Newberry Wing fZP746.K45; NYPL MBE+; ZBZ KK 2405a; ZBZ Lav.H.16; ZBZ LL57
Plate only: KHZ C4/I, 584
Lit.: Schiff 781 (?11.8 x 14.8 cm)

57. *Christ at the Sepulchre*, 1779 (Loosely based on the engraving by Ennea Vico) (Vol. II, p. 265, o)

Engraved by Johann Heinrich Lips (1758-1817) after Fuseli's study in the British Museum ([1770-1778]; Schiff 689)
Inscription: J: H: Fuessli del.||Joh. H. Lips sculp. 1779.
Dimensions: 13.7 x 23.5 cm | 5⁶/16" x 9¼" (ZBZ NNN 116)
Other locations: Bern L.Theol.22; BL 29.g.6; ETH 3545A; Geneva Md 411; KHZ Dg251b; Lucerne D51.fol.; MMA 68.526.18; Newberry Wing fZP746.K45; NYPL MBE+; ZBZ KK 2405a; ZBZ Lav.H.16; ZBZ LL57
Lit.: Schiff 782 (13.6 x 23.4 cm)

Variants:
I. Proof, with additional lettering: KHZ C4/I, 601
Inscription: Joh: H. Fuessli del||Joh. H Lips sculp 1779

58.

58. *Martha Hess*, 1780
(Vol. II, p. 284)

Unsigned engraving by Johann Heinrich Lips (1758-1817) after Fuseli's drawing in the Kunsthaus, Zurich ([1778-1779]; Schiff 575)
Dimensions (to platemark): 16.3 x 11.0 cm | 6⁷/16" x 4⁵/16" (ZBZ NNN 116)
Other locations: Bern L.Theol.22; BL 29.g.6; ETH 3545A; Geneva Md 411; KHZ Dg251b; Lausanne AVC; Lucerne D51.fol.; MMA 68.526.18; Newberry Wing fZP746.K45; NYPL MBE+; ZBZ KK 2405a; ZBZ Lav.H.16; ZBZ LL57
Plate only: KHZ C4/1, 612 (17.2 x 10.6 cm)
Lit.: Schiff 783 (16.2 x 10.5); Jaton 1988, repr. 72, right

Engraver's name and date have been determined from Lips' own copy among his collected engravings in the Kunsthaus, Zurich

59.

59. *Youth Sitting Under a Tree*
(Vol. II, p. 346)

Unsigned engraving
Dimensions (to platemark): 9.5 x 13.3 cm | 3¹³/16" x 5¼" (ZBZ NNN 116)
Other locations: Bern L.Theol.22; BL 29.g.6; ETH 3545A; Geneva Md 411; KHZ Dg251b; Lucerne D51.fol.; MMA 68.526.18; Newberry Wing fZP746.K45; ZBZ KK 2045a; ZBZ Lav.H.16; ZBZ LL57
Lit.: Schiff 784 (9.6 x 13.3 cm)

60.

61.

60. *Sibyl with Open Book in her Lap*
(Vol. III, p. 82)

Unsigned engraving
Dimensions (to platemark): 5.0 x 7.6 cm |
2" x 2¹³/16" (ZBZ NNN 117)
Other locations: Bern L.Theol.22; BL 29.g.7;
ETH 3545A; Geneva Md 411; KHZ Dg251c;
Lucerne D51.fol.; MMA 68.526.18; N Wing
fZP746.K45; NYPL MEB+; ZBZ KK 2405a;
ZBZ Lav.H.17; ZBZ LL58
Lit.: Schiff 785 (5.2 x 7.7 cm)

61. *Naked Muscular Man Sitting with Left Leg Crossed*
(Vol. III, p. 120)

Unsigned engraving
Dimensions (to platemark): 9.6 x 6.4 cm |
3¾" x 2½" (ZBZ NNN 117)
Other locations: Bern L.Theol. 22; BL 29.g.7;
ETH 3545A; Geneva Md 411; KHZ Dg251c;
Lausanne AVC 55; Lucerne D51.fol.; MMA
68.526.18; Newberry Wing fZP746.K45; NYPL
MEB+; ZBZ KK 2405a; ZBZ Lav.H.17; ZBZ
LL58
Lit.: Schiff 786 (9.6 x 6.4 cm)

62. *Woman's Hand and Arm with Bracelet round the Wrist*
(Vol. III, p. 347)

Unsigned engraving after Fuseli's sketch in the
Kunsthaus, Zurich ([1778-1779]); Schiff 505)
Dimensions (to platemark): 10.0 x 23.1 cm |
3¹⁵/16" x 9²/16" (ZBZ NNN 117)
Other locations: Bern L.Theol.22; BL 29.g.7;
ETH 3545A; Geneva Md 411; KHZ Dg251c;
Lausanne AVC 55; Lucerne D51.fol.; MMA
68.526.18; Newberry Wing fZP746.K45; ZBZ
KK 2405a; ZBZ Lav.H.17; ZBZ LL58
Lit.: Schiff 787 (10.0 x 23.1 cm); Jaton 1988,
repr. 119

63. *Man's and Woman's Crossed Hands*
(Vol. III, p. 348)

Unsigned engraving by Johann Heinrich Lips
(1758-1817) after Fuseli's sketch at Winterthur
([1778-1779]; Schiff 507)
Dimensions (to platemark): 17.0 x 22.1 cm |
6¹¹/16" x 8¹¹/16" (ZBZ NNN 117)
Other locations: Bern L.Theol.22; BL 29.g.7;
ETH 3545A; Geneva Md 411; KHZ Dg251c;
Lausanne AVC 55; Lucerne D51.fol.; MMA
68.526.18; Newberry Wing fZP746.K45; NYPL;
ZBZ KK 2405a; ZBZ Lav.H.17; ZBZ LL58
Plate only: KHZ C4/I, 574
Lit.: Schiff 788 (17.0 x 21.8 cm); Jaton 1988,
repr. 118

Engraver's name and date have been determined
from Lips' own copy among his collected
engravings in the Kunsthaus, Zurich.

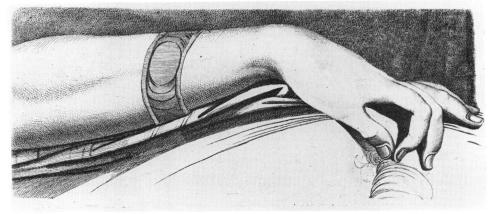

62.

63.

Nos. 39A. - 63A.
Johann Caspar Lavater.
L'ART|DE CONNAITRE LES HOMMES|PAR
LA PHYSIONOMIE,|PAR GASPARD
LAVATER.|NOUVELLE EDITION,
CORRIGÉE ET DISPOSÉE DANS UN ORDRE
PLUS METHODIQUE, PRÉCÉDÉE D'UNE|
NOTICE HISTORIQUE SUR L'AUTEUR;
AUGMENTÉE D'UNE EXPOSITION DE
RECHERCHES OU DES|OPINIONS DE LA
CHAMBRE, DE PORTA, DE CAMPER, DE
GALL, SUR LA PHYSIONOMIE; D' UNE|
HISTOIRE ANATOMIQUE ET PHYSIO[-]
LOGIQUE DE LA FACE AVEC DES FIGURES
COLORIÉES; ET D'UN|TRÈS-GRAND
NOMBRE D'ARTICLES NOUVEAUX SUR LES

CARACTÈRES DES PASSIONS, DES
TEMPÉRA-|MENS ET DES MALADIES; PAR
M. MOREAU, DOCTEUR EN MEDECINE.|
AVEC 500 GRAVURES EXECUTÉES SOUS
L'INSPECTION DE M. VINCENT, PEINTRE,|
MEMBRE DE L'INSTITUT.|[Vignette]|TOME
I. [-TOME VIII, IX.]| PARIS|1806 [-1807,
1809]|CHEZ|L. PRUDHOMME, RUE DES
MARAIS| LEVRAULT, SCHOELL ET C^E. RUE
DE SEINE.   (21/599 illus.).
...NOUVELLE ÉDITION, CORRIGÉE ET
DISPOSÉE DANS UN ORDRE PLUS
MÉTHODIQUE; PRÉCÉDÉE D'UNE|NOTICE
HISTORIQUE SUR L'AUTEUR; AUGMENTÉE
D'UNE EXPOSITION DES RECHERCHES OU
DES OPINIONS|DE LA CHAMBRE, DE

PORTA, DE CAMPER, DE GALL, SUR LA PHYSIONOMIE; D'UNE HISTOIRE ANA-| TOMIQUE ET PHYSIOLOGIQUE DE LA FACE, ETC.; PAR M. MOREAU (DE LA SARTHE), PROFESSEUR À|LA FACULTÉ DE MEDECINE DE PARIS;|ORNÉE DE PLUS DE 600 GRAVURES, DONT 82 COLORIÉES ET EXECUTÉES SOUS L'INSPECTION|DE M. VINCENT, PEINTRE, MEMBRE DE L'INSTITUT.|[Vignette]| PARIS,| DEPELAFOL, LIBRAIRE, RUE DES GRANDS-AUGUSTINS, NO 21.|—|1820.

...L'ART|DE CONNAITRE LES HOMMES| PAR|LA PHYSIONOMIE|PAR GASPARD LAVATER.|NOUVELLE ÉDITION|CORRIGÉE ET DISPOSÉE DANS UN ORDRE PLUS MÉTHODIQUE,|AUGMENTÉE|D'UNE EXPOSITION DES RECHERCHES OU DES OPINIONS DE LA CHAMBRE,|DE PORTA, DE CAMPER, DE GALL, SUR LA PHYSIONOMIE;|D'UNE HISTOIRE ANATOMIQUE ET PHYSIOLOGIQUE DE LA FACE;|PRÉCÉDÉE D'UNE NOTICE HISTORIQUE SUR L'AUTEUR,|PAR MOREAU (DE LA SARTHE),|PROFESSEUR À LA FACULTÉ DE MEDECINE DE PARIS.| ORNÉE DE 600 GRAVURES EN TAILLE-DOUCE, DONT 82 TIRÉES EN COULEUR,| ET EXECUTÉES SOUS L'INSPECTION DE VINCENT, PEINTRE.|—| TOME PREMIER. [TOME DIXIÈME.]| PARIS.|DEPELAFOL, LIBRAIRE-EDITEUR,|RUE GIT-LE-COEUR, 4.|—|MDCCXXXV [1835].

Vol. IX (1809) contained the general index.

39A. *Un Trasteverain*, 1806
(Vol. VI, facing p. 29)

Unsigned etching re-engraved by an unknown engraver, perhaps Louis-François Couché fils (1782-1849)
Inscription (at top): Tom. 6.||Pl. 266
Dimensions (to platemark): 21.7 x 15.3 cm | 8½" x 6" (ZBZ Res 141)
Other locations: BL 721.1.6; LC BF843.L32 (facing p. 190);
(1820) (facing p. 31): Bern A17.452; Geneva Md 637; Lausanne 468; NYPL YEZA; ZBZ KK3216; ZBZ LL 355e
Lacking plate: ETH 911,511 (1820)

Variants:
I. Reissued (1835) (between pp. 30-31) with page no. added: ZBZ Res 426
Inscription (top): Tom. 6.||Pl. 266.||Page 31.
Other locations: Bern L.Theol.3.308

40A. *Brutus à la Vue d'un Spectre*, 1806
(Vol. V, facing p. 184)

Unsigned etching with stipple re-engraved by an unknown engraver., perhaps Louis-François Couché fils (1782-1849)
Inscription (top): Tom. 5.||Pl. 208.
Dimensions: 14.8 x 11.4 cm | 5^{13}/16" x 4½" (ZBZ Res 174)
Other locations: BL 721.1.6 (facing p. 190); LC BF843.L32; (15.0 x 11.4 cm); ZBZ Res 140; **(1820)**: Bern A17.452; ETH 911511; Geneva Md 637 (15.1 x 11.5 cm); Lausanne 468 (15.0 x 11.4 cm); NYPL YEZA; ZBZ KK3215

Variants:
I. Reissued (1835) (facing p. 184) with page no. added: ZBZ Res 425
Dimensions: 15.0 x 11.3 cm
Inscription (top): Tom. 5.||Pl. 208.||Page 184.
Other locations: Bern L.Theol.3.308

41A. *Marie, Soeur de Marthe*, 1807
(Vol. VII, facing p. 202)

Unsigned etching in outline re-engraved by an unknown engraver, perhaps Louis-François Couché fils (1782-1849)
Inscription (top): Tom. 7.||Pl. 435.
Dimensions (to platemark): 22.5 x 15.6 cm | 9" x 6^3/16" (ZBZ Res 176)
Other locations: BL 721.1.7.; LC BF843.L32; ZBZ Res 142; **(1820)** (facing p. 220): Bern A17.452; Geneva Md 637; Lausanne N468; NYPL YEZA; ZBZ KK3217; ZBZ LL 355f; **(1835)** (facing p. 220): Bern L.Theol.3.308 (facing p. 205); ZBZ Res 427 (facing p. 205)
Lacking plate: ETH 911511 (1820)

42A. *St. Jean*, 1807
(Vol. VII, facing p. 202)

Unsigned etching in outline re-engraved by an unknown engraver, perhaps Louis-François Couché fils (1782-1849)

Inscription (top): Tom. 7.| |Pl. 436.
Dimensions (to platemark): 23.0 x 15.8 cm | 9" x 6³/16" (ZBZ Res 176)
Other locations: BL 721.l.7; ZBZ Res 142; LC BF843.L32 (facing p. 203); (**1820**) (facing p. 206): Bern A17.452; Geneva Md 637; Lausanne N468; NYPL YEZA; ZBZ KK 3217; ZBZ LL 355f; (**1835**) (facing p. 206): Bern L.Theol.3.308; ZBZ Res 427
Lacking plate: ETH 9111511 (1820)

43A. *Satan*, 1807
(Vol. VII, facing p. 217)

Unsigned etching re-engraved by an unknown engraver, perhaps Louis-François Couché fils (1782-1849)
Inscription (top): Tom. 7.| |Pl. 446.
Dimensions (to platemark): 23.0 x 16.0 cm | 9" x 6³/16" (ZBZ Res 176)
Other locations: BL 721.l.7.; LC BF843.L32; ZBZ Res 142
(**1820**) (facing p. 220): Bern A17.452; Geneva Md 637; Lausanne N468; NYPL YEZA; ZBZ KK3217; ZBZ LL 355f
(**1835**) (facing p. 220): Bern L.Theol.3.308; ZBZ Res 427
Lacking plate: ETH 911511 (1820)

44A-45A. *La Mort d'Abel* and *Cain*, 1806
(Vol. VII, facing p. 220)

Unsigned etching (two designs on one plate) re-engraved by unknown engraver (perhaps Louis-François Couché fils (1782-1849)
Inscription (top): Tom. 7.| |Pl. 447.
Dimensions (to platemark): 21.5 x 15.0 cm | 8½" x 5¹⁵/16" (ZBZ Res 176)
Other locations: BL 721.l.7; LC BF843.L32
(**1820**) (facing p. 223): Bern A17.452; Geneva Md 637; Lausanne N468; NYPL YEZA; ZBZ KK3217; ZBZ LL 355f
(**1835**) (facing p. 223): Bern L.Theol.3.308; ZBZ Res 427
Lacking plate: ETH 911511 (1820)

46A. *Le Magicien Balaam*, 1807
(Vol. VII, facing p. 221)

Unsigned etching re-engraved by an unknown

engraver (perhaps Louis-François Couché fils (1782-1849)
Inscription (top): Tom. 7.| |Pl. 448.
Dimensions: 13.2 x 10.1 cm | 5³/16" x 4" (ZBZ Res 176)
Other locations: BL 721.l.7; LC BF843.L32; ZBZ Res 142
(**1820**) (facing p. 224): Bern A17.452; Geneva Md 637; Lausanne N468; NYPL YEZA; ZBZ KK3217; ZBZ LL 355f
(**1835**) (facing p. 224): Bern L.Theol.3.308; ZBZ Res 427
Lacking plate: ETH 911511 (1820)

47A. *Une Tête très-expressive* (**The Escapee**), 1807
(Vol. VII, facing p. 222)

Unsigned etching in outline re-engraved by an unknown engraver (perhaps Louis-François Couché fils (1782-1849)
Inscription (top): Tom. 7.| |Pl. 449.
Dimensions: 7.5 x 11.3 cm | 2¹⁵/16" x 3¹⁵/16" (ZBZ Res 176)
Other locations: BL 721.l.7; LC BF843.L32; ZBZ Res 142
(**1820**) (facing p. 225): Bern A17.452; Geneva Md 637; Lausanne N468; NYPL YEZA; ZBZ KK3217; ZBZ LL 355f
(**1835**) (facing p. 225): Bern L.Theol.3.308; ZBZ Res 427
Lacking plate: ETH 911511 (1820)

48A. - 49A. *La Pythonisse d'Endor Evoquant l'Ombre de Samuel* and *Jeune Homme*, 1807
(Vol. VII, facing p. 223)

Unsigned etching re-engraved by an unknown engraver, perhaps Louis-François Couché fils (1782-1849)
Inscription (top): Tom. 7.| |Pl. 450.
Dimensions: ■ 6.8 x 12.5 cm | 2¹¹/16" x 4¹⁵/16"; ■ 4.6 x 6.5 cm | 1¹³/16" x 2⁹/16" (ZBZ Res 176)
Other locations: BL 721.l.7; LC BF843.L32; ZBZ Res 142
(**1820**) (facing p. 226): Bern A17.452; Geneva Md 637; Lausanne N468; NYPL YEZA; ZBZ KK3217; ZBZ LL 355f
(**1835**) (facing p. 220): Bern L.Theol.3.308; ZBZ Res 427

50A. - 51A. *Quatre Visages d'après le Dante*,
1807
(Vol. VII, facing p. 224)

Unsigned etching (four designs on one plate) re-engraved by an unknown engraver, perhaps
Louis-François Couché fils (1782-1849)
Inscription (top): Tom. 7. | | Pl. 451.
Dimensions (to platemark): 23.0 x 15.8 cm | 9" x
6³/16" (ZBZ Res 176)
Other locations: BL 721.1.7; LC BF843.L32;
ZBZ Res 142
(1820) (facing p. 227): Bern A17.452; Geneva
Md 637; Lausanne N468; NYPL YEZA; ZBZ
KK3217; ZBZ LL 355f
(1835) (facing p. 227): Bern L.Theol.3.308; ZBZ
Res 427
Lacking plate: ETH 911511 (1820)

52A. *Salomé*, 1807
(Vol. VII, facing p. 205)

Unsigned etching in outline re-engraved by an
unknown engraver, perhaps Louis-François
Couché fils (1782-1849)
Inscription (top): Tom. 7 | | Pl. 437.
Dimensions: 14.7 x 11.5 cm | 5¾" x 4⁹/16"
(ZBZ Res 176)
Other locations: BL 721.1.7; LC BF843.L32;
ZBZ Res 142
(1820) (facing p. 208): Bern A17.452; Geneva
Md 637; Lausanne N468; NYPL YEZA; ZBZ
KK3217; ZBZ LL 355f
(1835) (facing p. 208): Bern L.Theol.3.308; ZBZ
Res 427
Lacking plate: ETH 911511 (1820)

53A. *Un Satellite*, 1807
(Vol. VII, p. 205)

Unsigned etching re-engraved by an unknown
engraver, perhaps Louis-François Couché fils
(1782-1849)
Inscription (top right): Pl. 438. | (bottom):
T.7. | | 52
Dimensions (to platemark): 8.0 x 7.5 cm | 3²/16"
x 3" (ZBZ Res 176)
Other locations: BL 721.1.7; LC BF 843.L32;
ZBZ Res 142
Lacking plate: ETH 911511 (1820)

Variants:
I. Reissued (1835) on separate page (between
pp. 208-209) with Vol. no. in Roman numerals
(ZBZ Res 427)
Inscription (top): Tome VII. | | Page 208. | | Pl.
438
Dimensions (to platemark): 10.0 x 10.0 cm |
3¹⁵/16" x 3¹⁵/16"
Other locations: Bern L.Theol.3.308
II. Re-issued (1820) with reduced inscription
(bottom of p. 208) (ZBZ LL 355f)
Inscription (top right): Pl. 438
Other locations: Geneva Md 637; Lausanne
N468; NYPL YEZA; ZBZ KK 3217

54A. *Tête de Patriarche*, 1807
(Vol. VII, facing p. 206)

Unsigned etching re-engraved by an unknown
engraver, perhaps Louis-François Couché fils
(1782-1849)
Inscription (top): Tom. 7. | | Pl. 439.
Dimensions (to platemark): 21.5 x 15.0 cm | 8½"
x 5¹⁴/16" (ZBZ Res 176)
Other locations: BL 721.1.7; LC BF843.L32
(1820) (facing p. 209): Bern A17.452; Geneva
Md 637; Lausanne N468; NYPL YEZA; ZBZ
KK3217; ZBZ LL 355f
(1835) (facing p. 209): Bern L.Theol.3.308; ZBZ
Res 427

[55A. Not reproduced in these editions.]

56A. *Un Chevalier à la Vue de sa Maîtresse qu'il
vient d'assassiner*, 1806
(Vol. VI, facing p. 14)

Unsigned etching in outline re-engraved by an
unknown engraver, perhaps Louis-François
Couché fils (1782-1849)
Inscription (top): Tom. 6. | | Pl. 256.
Dimensions: ■ 10.7 x 14.7 cm | 4¼" x 5¾"
(ZBZ Res 141)
Other locations: BL 721.1.7.; LC BF843.L32;
ZBZ Res 142
(1820) (facing p. 220): Bern A17.452; Geneva
Md 637; Lausanne N468; NYPL YEZA; ZBZ
KK3217; ZBZ LL 355f
(1835) (facing p. 220): Bern L.Theol.3.308; ZBZ
Res 427

Lacking plate: ETH 911511 (1820)

Variants:
I. Reissued (1835) (facing p. 14) with page no. added (ZBZ Res 426)
Inscription (top right): Page 14. | Tom. 6. | | Pl. 256
Other locations: Bern L.Theol.3.308 (facing p. 15)

57A. *Un Groupe Représentant Jésus-Christ Mourant, et à qui on Donne des Secours*, 1807
(Vol. V, facing p. 201)

Unsigned etching in outline re-engraved by an unknown engraver, perhaps Louis-François Couché fils (1782-1849)
Inscription (top): Tom. 5 | | Pl. 216.
Dimensions: 11.4 x 19.2 cm | 4½" x 7⁹/16"
(ZBZ Res 174)
Other locations: BL 721.1.6; LC BF843.L32; ZBZ Res 140
(1820) (facing p. 194): Bern A17.452; ETH 911511; Geneva Md 637 (11.5 x 19.4 cm); Lausanne N468; NYPL YEZA; ZBZ KK3215; ZBZ LL 355d

Variants:
I. Reissued (1835) (facing p. 194) with page no. added (ZBZ Res 425)
Inscription (top): Tom. 5. | | Page 194. | | Pl. 216.
Other locations: Bern L.Theol.3.308

Dissatisfied with this rendering of Raphael, the French editor criticises it in the following terms:

Note: Ce groupe, que nous avons fait graver conformément à la planche qui se trouve dans l'ouvrage de LAVATER, n'est, il faut l'avouer, qu'une misérable traduction d'un chef-d'oeuvre; et cependant, dans cette copie infidèle, dans ce dessin inexact, on connaît encore Raphaël, on sent encore le charme de son style; et, ce qui caractérise peut-être plus particulièrement ce grand peintre, c'est de ne pouvoir jamais être entièrement défiguré dans les plus mauvaises gravures.

58A. *Martha Hess*, 1806
(Vol. II, facing p. 20 top)

Unsigned etching in outline re-engraved by an

unknown engraver, perhaps Louis-François Couché fils (1782-1849) (2 designs on one plate)
Inscription (top centre): Pl. 38. | 1.
Dimensions: ■ 8.0 x 5.7 cm | 3¹/16" x 2⁵/16"
(ZBZ Res 171)
Other locations: BL 721.1.4; LC BF843.L32; ZBZ Res 137 (24.8 x 17.0 cm)
(1820): Bern A17.452; Geneva Md 637; Lausanne N468; NYPL YEZA; ZBZ KK 3212; ZBZ LL 355a
Lacking plate: ETH 911511 (1820)

Variants:
I. Reissued (1835) with Vol. and page nos. added (ZBZ Res 422)
Inscription (top): Tome II. | | Page 20. | Pl. 38. | 1.
Other locations: Bern L.Theol.3.308

59A. *Un Penseur*, 1807
(Vol. VII, bottom of p. 137)

Unsigned etching re-engraved by an unknown engraver, perhaps Louis-François Couché fils (1782-1849)
Inscription (top right): 395. | (bottom left): T.7. | (bottom right): 35
Dimensions (design only): 9.0 x 10.5 cm | 3½" x 4³/16" (ZBZ Res 176)
Other locations: BL 721.1.7; LC BF843.L32; ZBZ Res 142

Variants:
I. Reissued (1835) (facing p. 141) with page no. added, Vol. no. given in Roman numerals (ZBZ Res 427)
Inscription (top): Tome VII. | | Page 141. | | 395.
Other locations: Bern L.Theol.3.308
II. Reissued (1820) (p. 141) with reduced inscription (ZBZ LL 355f)
Inscription (top right): 395.
Other locations: Bern A17.452; Geneva Md637; Lausanne N468; NYPL YEZA; ZBZ KK 3217
Lacking plate: ETH 911511

60A. *Sybille*, 1809
(Vol. X, title page)

Unsigned title vignette re-engraved by an unknown engraver, perhaps Louis-François Couché fils (1782-1849)

Printed in brown
Dimensions (to platemark): 6.8 x 8.5 cm | 2⁹/16"
x 3⁷/16" (ZBZ LL 355h)
Other locations: LC BF8943.L32
Lacking plate: BL 721.1.10
(**1820**): Bern A17.452; ETH 911511; Geneva Md
637; Lausanne N468; NYPL YEZA; ZBZ
KK3219

Variants:
I. Reissued (1835) (facing title page) as
frontispiece with inscription (ZBZ Res 429)
Sepia impression
Inscription (top): Tome IX. | | Frontispice
Other locations: Bern L.Theol.3.308

61A. *Homme Assis*, 1807
(Vol. VIII, p. 142)

Unsigned etching re-engraved by an unknown
engraver, perhaps Louis-François Couché fils
(1782-1849)
Inscription (top right): 510
Dimensions (to platemark): 11.1 x 10.8 cm |
4⁶/16" x 4¼" (ZBZ Res 177)
Other locations: BL 721.1.7; LC BF843.L32;
(**1820**) (facing p. 141): Bern A17.452; ETH
911511; Geneva Md 637; Lausanne N468; NYPL
YEZA; ZBZ KK3218; ZBZ LL 355g

Variants:
I. Reissued (1835) (facing p. 141) with
expanded inscription (ZBZ Res 428)
Inscription (top): Tome VIII. | | Page 141. | 510
Other locations: Bern L.Theol.3.308

62A. *Une Main très-expressive*, 1806
(Vol. III, facing p. 8)

Unsigned etching in outline re-engraved by an
unknown engraver, perhaps Louis-François
Couché fils (1782-1849)
Inscription (top): Pl. 107.
Dimensions (to platemark): 14.5 x 21.1 cm | 5¾"
x 8⁵/16" (ZBZ Res 138)
Other locations: BL 721.1.5; LC BF843.L32
(**1820**): Bern A17.452; Geneva Md 637; Lausanne
N468; NYPL YEZA; ZBZ KK3213; ZBZ LL
355b

Lacking plate: ETH 911511 (1820)

Variants:
I. Reissued (1835) with expanded inscription
(ZBZ Res 423)
Inscription (top): Tome III. | | Pl. 107. | | Page 8.
Other locations: Bern L.Theol.3.308

63A. *Deux Mains d'une grande Valeur
physiognomonique*, 1806
(Vol. III, facing p. 9)

Unsigned etching re-engraved by an unknown
engraver, perhaps Louis-François Couché fils
(1782-1849)
Inscription (top): Pl. 108.
Dimensions (to platemark): 14.7 x 21.3 cm | 5½"
x 8⁷/16" (ZBZ Res 138)
Other locations: BL 721.1.5; LC BF843.L32
(?sepia)
(**1820**): Bern A17.452; Geneva Md 637; Lausanne
N468; NYPL YEZA; ZBZ KK3213; ZBZ LL
355b
Lacking plate: ETH 911511 (1820)

Variants:
I. Reissued (1835) (facing p. 9) with expanded
inscription (ZBZ Res 423)
Inscription (top): Tome III. | | Page 9. | Pl. 108
Other locations: Bern L.Theol.3.308

******

64. *Hands*, 1778

Unsigned engraving by Johann Heinrich Lips
(1758-1817) after an untraced drawing
Unused designs
Inscription (in pencil): Hände nach Füssli
Dimensions (sheet): 23.5 x 18.8 cm | 9¼" x
7⁶/16" (KHZ C4/I, 573)

These two illustrations of a man's right hand in
different positions, engraved on one plate, were
perhaps modelled on the same hand, distinguished
by the markedly spatulate form of the fingers,
illustrated in Nos. **63** and **110** (Schiff 788, and
972). These designs seem not to have been used
by Lavater in his *Physiognomy*.

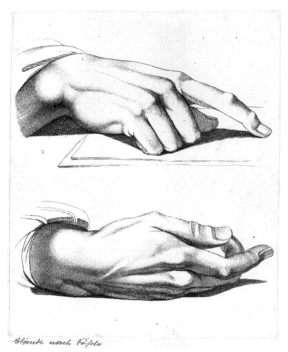

64.

66.

65. *Ezzelin Musing over the Body of his Wife Meduna, Slain by him for her Infidelity During his Absence on the Crusades*, 1781

Mezzotint engraved by John Raphael Smith (1752-1812) after the painting exhibited (1780/77) at the Royal Academy, and now in the Soane Museum, London (1779; Schiff 360)
Imprint: London publishd 31st March 1781 by J R Smith N°. 10 Batemans Buildings Soho Square.
Inscription: Painted by H Fusley||Engraved by J R Smith|Ezzelin Count of Ravenna, surnamed Bracciaferro or Iron arm, musing over the body of Meduna, slain by him for infidelity during his absence in the Holy Land.
Dimensions: 44.0 x 55.4 cm | 17^6/16" x 21¾" (BM 1870-5-14-1612).
Lit.: *Neue Bibliothek der schönen Wissenschaften*, XXVI (1781), 353-354; Frankau 1902, no. 133; *Letters*, 20, 74

Variants:
I. Signature abbreviated in inscription (Frankau 133/I) (not seen)
Inscription: Painted by Fus.||Engraved by J R Smith|[&c.]
II. Reissued (1781) with corrected inscription ('Braccioferro') and changed imprint: BM 1877-6-9-1771
Imprint: London, Publish'd May 1781 by Ja^s., Birchall, No. 473 Strand.
Inscription: Painted by H. Fusely||Engraved by J. R. Smith|**Ezzelin, Count of Ravenna**, Surnamed, **Braccioferro** or Iron Arm; musing over the Body of **Meduna**, slain by him for infidelity during his absence in the Holy Land.
Other locations: MMA 59.570.363
Lit.: Frankau 1902, no. 133/II

J.R. Smith probably received the painting to copy when it was returned at the end of the Royal Academy Exhibition. By early September the mezzotint was 'in great forwardness and promis[ed] to be a very good one' (to Sir Robert Smyth, 3 September 1780).
This subject like the saga of Percival and Belisane was one that Fuseli had himself 'Combined' (to William Roscoe, 22 October 1791). Many years later, when asked by Lord Byron to identify the source of this unknown story, Fuseli also told him he had invented it (*Diary*, 20 March 1814).

65.

No. 66.
[Joseph Ritson.]
A | SELECT | COLLECTION | OF | ENGLISH
SONGS. | IN THREE VOLUMES. | VOLUME
THE FIRST. [-VOLUME THE THIRD.] |
[Vignette] | —*APIS MATINAE* | *MORE MODOQUE*
| *GRATA CARPENTIS THYMA PER LABOREM* |
PLURIMUM. | *HOR.* | LONDON: | PRINTED
FOR J. JOHNSON IN ST. PAULS
CHURCHYARD. | MDCCLXXXIII [1783] (1/1
pl. + 16 vignette headpieces and tailpieces).

**66. *Young Man with Flute and Young Woman
with Musical Scroll*, 1783**
(Frontispiece)
(Vol. I, facing title page)

Engraved frontispiece by James Heath (1757-
1834)
Inscription (top right): Frontispiece.
Dimensions: ■ 12.9 x 8.6 cm | 5^1/16" x 3^6/16";
■ 13.4 x 9.1 cm | 5¼" x 3^9/16" (BL 13025)
Other locations: BL 239.137; Essick

Plate only: BM 1863-5-9-68 (damaged)
Lit.: Schiff 308 (12.7 x 8.0 cm) (source not
identified; dated as '1764-1769'); Bertrand H.
Bronson, *Joseph Ritson: Scholar-at-Arms*, 1938,
II, 753-755 (full bibliographic description of
work)

The illustration seems to be emblematic of the
role of music and song as lyric impulse in the
ideal natural world (cf. *Remarks*, Ch. VII).

Instead of Fuseli's frontispiece some copies of
the first edition (e.g. BL 992.a.13) contain a plate
engraved by Grignion after Stothard; Bronson
considers these 'quite rare'. The 2nd ed. (1813) is
not illustrated. According to Bronson, the *St.
James's Chronicle* announced the *Songs* as
published on 11/14 and 14/16 September 1784.
The price was 12s. or 15s. bound. 'A few Copies
[*were*] printed on finer paper'. The size was
inaccurately described as 'Crown Octavo'.

Although Bronson identified the plate as after
Fuseli (II, 354), the unaccompanied plate in the
British Museum was only recently re-associated
with Ritson's *Select Collection* by Robert Essick.

THE NIGHTMARE

67.

67. *The Nightmare*, 1783

Engraved in stipple by Thomas Burke (1749-1815) after the painting exhibited at the Royal Academy (1782/64) and now in the Detroit Institute of Arts ([1781]; Schiff 757).
Imprint: London Publish'd Jany. 30th 1783 by J.R. Smith N°. 83 Oxford Street.
Inscription: Painted by H. Fusley. | | Engraved by T. Burke. | THE NIGHT MARE. |

[*left*]
—on his Night-Mare, thro the evening fog,
Flits the squab fiend o'er fen, and lake, and
  bog,

[*right*]
Seeks some love-wilder'd maid, by sleep
  opprest,
Alights and grinning, sits upon her breast.

Dimensions: ■ 19.2 x 23.1 cm | 7^9/16" x 9^2/16";
■ 19.5 x 23.4 cm | 7^11/16" x 9¼" (BM 1873-12-13-620).
Other locations: BM 1870-5-14-1610

Lit.: Schiff 757; Powell 1973, 15, 98, repr. [14]; *Neue Bibliothek der schönen Wissenschaften*, XXX (1785), 158; *Letters*, 22-23.
Exh.: New Haven 1980 (135).

This was the authorised version for which Fuseli was paid twenty guineas. According to Knowles, 'Smith acknowledged to have gained upwards of five hundred pounds for the sale of the prints, although vended at a small price' (I, 64). The cost according to *NBSW* was 5 shillings.

Erasmus Darwin's poem, *The Botanic Garden* (Part II), from which the lines in the inscription are taken, was not published until 1789, although Fuseli was already acting as intermediary between Darwin and Joseph Johnson about its publication as early as 1784, when Darwin reports Fuseli had been 'so kind as to promise some ornament for the work.' However, all the engraved versions of the *Nightmare* originally appeared as separate (octavo) plates, although from 1799 Holloway's version (No. **68**) was specifically used as a book illustration. None of the quarto editions call for a plate of the *Nightmare*.

67A. *The Nightmare*, 1782

Stipple engraving by — Laurede, printed in
brown ink (not reproduced in the catalogue)
Imprint: Sold by le Noir Printseller to his Majesty
under the Arches of the Royal Palace No. 43.
Inscription: Painted by H. Fusley. | | Engraved by
Laurede. | THE NIGHT MARE. |

[*left*]
—on his Night Mare, thro the evening fog,
Flits the squab fiend o'er fen, and lake, and
  bog,

[*right*]
Seeks some love-wilder'd maid, by sleep
  opprest,
Alights, and grinning, sits upon her breast.

Dimensions: ■ 19.2 x 22.1 cm | $7^9/16"$ x $8^{11}/16"$;
▣ 19.5 x 23.4 cm | $7^{11}/16"$ x $9¼"$ (MMA
59.608.46).
Lit.: Powell 1973, 98 (as presumably pirated).

67B. *Le Cochemar*, 1784

Colour aquatint etched by de Ville Neuve
Imprint: A Paris chez De Ville Neuve.
Inscription: H. Fusley inv. & pinx. Londini. | | M.
De Ville Neuve sculp. Parisis 1784. | **Le
Cochemar** |

[*left*]
D'un songe affreux, aimable Devonshire,
Fusley nous peint ici les effets douleureux:

[*right*]
Notre âme en est émue, et notre coeur soupire,
En désirant le sort du monstre trop heureux.

Dimensions: ■ 13.0 x 15.5 cm | $5^2/16"$ x $6^2/16"$;
▣ 13.5 x 16.0 cm | $5^5/16"$ x $6^5/16"$ (KHZ
1940/111)
Lit.: Powell 1973, 98; *Neue Bibliothek der
schönen Wissenschaften*, XXX, Pt. 1 (1785), 363.

The verses read in English: 'Fuseli paints here,
dear Lady Devonshire, the painful effects of a
fearful dream: our soul is moved by it and our
heart sighs, desiring the lot of the happy monster'.

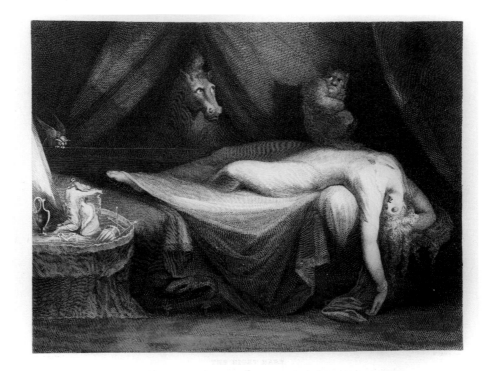

67D.

67C. *The Nightmare*, 1802

Reissue of the engraving (1783) by Thomas Burke (1749-1815), with new imprint
Imprint: London, Pub^d. July 1st. 1802, by S.W. Fores, 50 Piccadilly.
Inscription: Painted by H. Fusley.||Engraved by T. Burke|THE NIGHT MARE.|[*verses*]
Dimensions: ■ 19.2 x 23.3 cm | 7^9/16" x 9^3/16";
◼ 19.5 x 23.5 cm | 7^{11}/16" x 9¼" (BM 1875-7-10-3381)
Other locations: DHW; KHZ

Variants

I. Hand-coloured impression (cropped): BM 1868-11-14-497.
Imprint: Pub^d. July 1st. 1802, by S.W. Fores, 50 Piccadilly.
Other locations: BM 1875.7.10.3381; Essick; KHZ 1940/109 (cropped within frame); KHZ 1940/110 (cropped)

67D. *The Nightmare*, 1827

Engraved (India paper) by W. Raddon (fl. 1816-1862) after a lost version of the painting.
Imprint: London, Pub. April 20. 1827, by W. Raddon, 38, Sidmouth Street, Gray's Inn Road, & M. Colnaghi, Cockspur Street.
Inscription: H. Fuseli RA. Pinx^t.||W. Raddon Sculp^t.|THE NIGHT MARE.|

[*left*]
—-on his Night-Mare, thro the evening fog,
Flits the squab fiend o'er fen, and lake, and bog,

[*right*]
Seeks some love wilder'd maid, by sleep opprest,
Alights, and grinning, sits upon her breast.

Engraved from the Original Picture in the||
Collection of the R^t. Honb^e. the Countess of Guilford,|to whom by Permission, this Print is||respectfully inscribed, by her Obliged Servt. W. Raddon.
Dimensions: ■ 18.4 x 23.0 cm | 7¼" x 9^1/16" (BM 1848-11-11-3) (formerly Earl of Harrowby)
Other locations: Essick; KHZ 1931/44
Lit.: Schiff 757A (?8.6 x 14.4 cm); Tomory 1972, 202, pl. 222; Powell 1973, 99, pl. 55

Variants:

I. Proof before all letters (signatures and imprint only): BM 1864-6-25-2
Handwritten dedication (in ink): E. Goodall Esqr. with W. Raddon's Compt^s.
Imprint: London, Published April 20, 1827, by W. Raddon, 38, Sidmouth Street, Gray's Inn Road.
Inscription: H. Fuseli RA Pinx^t.||W. Raddon Sculp^t.
Other locations: V & A E.1194-1886

In a letter of 3 September 1827 to Fuseli's cousin Heinrich Füssli in Zurich, accompanying a fine proof print on India paper of the *Nightmare*, John Knowles described this version as 'one of the last of the productions of Fuseli,' differing from the former 'inasmuch as he has introduced an episode of the fairies on the dressing table' (Zentralbibliothek, Zurich, Ms. Lind. 73). A horned owl has also been added. The reviewer in the *London Literary Gazette and Journal of Belles Lettres* of 12 May 1827 describes it as 'very cleverly executed in a bold and expressive manner … the subject faithfully preserved, and the wild and supernatural parts a happy mixture of the grotesque and terrible' (p. 300).

No. 67E.
SARTAIN'S|UNION MAGAZINE|OF|LITERATURE & ART.|1849

67E. *The Nightmare*, 1849
(July 1849)
(Vol. V, between pp. 38-39)

Re-engraved in mezzotint in reduced format by Samuel Sartain (1830-1906) after Raddon's plate
Inscription (top): SARTAIN'S MAGAZINE.|
(bottom): ENGRAVED BY SAMUEL SARTAIN.
—THE ORIGINAL BY H. FUSELI.|THE NIGHTMARE.|Printed by Jas. Irwin & Co. Phil^a.
Dimensions: 12.6 x 16.5 cm | 4^{15}/16" x 6½" (NYPL *DA)
Other locations: BL P.P. 6382; Huntington 198850 (frontis.); LC AP2.S147 (bound in as 1/5 plates between Vol. IV and Vol. V); Newberry A5.83; NYPL (Berg) (frontis.); Pierpont Morgan E-3.90.E (2 vols. in 1)(bound in as 1/5 five plates between Vol. IV and Vol. V)
Lacking plate: BL P.P.6382.a; DHW

The print was intended to illustrate the
following poem by G.G. Foster:

THE NIGHTMARE
(See Engraving.) [*In the original*]

What a mad mystery is the world of sleep!
With phantom horrors and unreal joys
So mixed and crowded, that the lapsing soul
Thrills with prophetic transports, or shrinks
back,
Already shuddering with the pangs of hell!
Who guides the sleeping spirit?—who controls
Its world-wide wanderings through the realms
of dreams?
Or, irresponsible in those dim hours,
Is't left to mock itself and life, uncurbed
By reason or by possibility?
Perchance God has spread out the world of
sleep,
With all its ghostly and misjointed horrors,
That we might know what *this* world would
become,
Were it from His strong guiding love
withdrawn.
And were it so, what wretch would dare to live,
Risking to meet the monsters of the night—
Demons and gibbering nightmares, and foul
hags
Blasting the senses with their horrent kisses—
Blue corpses stalking playfully about,
Twining in festive dances with the shapes
Stark Madness sees within her crooked mirror—
And by and by the chance of being like them!

Last year a young and gentle lady lived
In a sweet bower, whose truant vines and leaves
In their midsummer pride above my wall
Peeped saucily—breathing the while such odours
As love and beauty shed on all around them.
Oh, she was lovely! Laughter was the air
She breathed and, and music but the echoing
Of her clear voice through its harmonious
caverns.
But she was pensive too, and oft at night,
When the pale profile of the moon looked out
From its entablature of azure sad and cold,
The lady's being would subside to sorrow,
Even as the day subsided into night;
And I have heard, floating across the garden
That lay a fragrant sea between us, sounds
So exquisitely plaintive, I have deemed

That sorrowing angels had come down from
heaven
To mourn over a blind, unhappy world.
One night, when moon was none and darkness
howled
Ravenously, as 'twould devour the world,
And timid hearts felt terror even in life,
This lady, shuddering with vague thoughts and
fears,—
Yet striving still to laugh at what she felt,—
Bravely at last her silent chamber sought,
Disrobed her lovely self, and wooed repose.
The dim lamp, wavering in the gloomy dark,
As if in sympathy with the wind without,
Soon leaped its last into the air and died,
Ere sleep had wrapt the lady in its pall.
But even fear grows weary—and at length
Her veined lids closed o'er their wondrous orbs,
And the soft form grew marble in repose—
All but the bosom, where the gentle tide
Of life still swelled and sank within its bounds.

Anon the fears that wakefulness had banished,
Arming themselves in frightful, haggard
forms—
Grinning faces, eyes that leered maliciously,
Nostrils dilate and breathing pale blue fire,
Shapes foul and monstrous that 'twould scarcely
seem
A lady's soul could even dream about—
Came back, and in the luminous darkness of her
trance,
Chattered and mewed and mocked at her—and
one,
More horrible than can be written of,
Half-satyr and half-demon, leaped upon
Her muse-like form, and crouching on her
breast,
Made the night gleam with his malignant eyes,
Sparkling with fiendish pleasure. With a groan,
That said farewell to life, one mighty struggle
The poor girl made. Her beauteous head fell
back,
And her fair ringlets, parted in her agony,
Knotted themselves in spiral, snake-like folds.
Her glorious arms fell stark and stiff; and now
The undulations of her breast stood still.—
In one dread instant she had passed from life
And all its direful phantasms, and reclaimed
Her star-throne in the shadowless spirit world.

******

No. 67F.
NEW SERIES. | VOLUME VII. | THE | ART-JOURNAL. | 1861. | JAMES S. VIRTUE, LONDON; AND 26, JOHN STREET, NEW YORK. (3/37 full page illus.).

For the other illustrations in this work see Nos. **117J - 118J.**

67F. *The Nightmare*, 1861
(James Dafforne, '*British Artists: Their Style and Character....No. LVII.—Henry Fuseli, R.A.*')
(Vol. VII n.s., p. 325)

Engraved on steel perhaps by James Dafforne (d. 1880)
Inscription: THE NIGHTMARE.
Dimensions: 10.3 x 13.9 cm | 14⁷/₁₆" x 5½" (BL P.P.1931.PC).
Other locations: DHW

No. 67G.
M.W. Bürger [i.e. Théophile-Étienne-Joseph Thoré.]
HISTOIRE DES PEINTRES DE TOUTES LES ÉCOLES | ÉCOLE ANGLAISE | PAR | M.W. BÜRGER. | [Medallion]. | PARIS: | Vᵛᴱ JULES RENOUARD, LIBRAIRE-EDITEUR | DIRECTEUR-GERANT: G ÉTIENNE-PERON | RUE DE TOURNON, N° 6, FAUBOURG SAINT-GERMAIN | — | MDCCCLXIII [1863]. (4/5 illus. + portr. = Fuseli essay [pp. 1-12] only.)

For the other illustrations in this work see Nos. **117K - 118K, 124K.**

67G. *The Nightmare*, 1863
(2. série. *Les peintres anglais*)
(p. 5)

Engraved on steel by Jean Baptiste Amédée Guillaume (1822-1893) after a drawing by Ulysse Parent (d. 1879)
Inscription: UL. PARENT D. | | FUSELI. P | | J. GUILLAUME SC. | LE CAUCHEMAR.
Dimensions: ■ 11.5 x 14.0 cm | 4½" x 5⁹/₁₆" (BL 2262.G1).
Other locations: Basel A204

68.

No. 68.
[**Erasmus Darwin.**]
THE | BOTANIC GARDEN, | A POEM. | IN TWO PARTS. | = | PART I. | CONTAINING | THE ECONOMY OF VEGETATION. | = | PART II. | THE LOVES OF THE PLANTS. | = | WITH | PHILOSOPHICAL NOTES. | = | THE FOURTH EDITION. | = | LONDON: | PRINTED FOR J. JOHNSON, ST. PAUL'S CHURCH-YARD. | — | 1799 (3/11 illus.)

THE | POETICAL WORKS | OF | ERASMUS DARWIN, | M.D. F.R.S. | CONTAINING THE BOTANIC GARDEN, IN TWO PARTS; | AND THE TEMPLE OF NATURE. | WITH PHILOSOPHICAL NOTES AND PLATES. | IN THREE VOLUMES. | VOL. I. | CONTAINING THE ECONOMY OF VEGETATION. | LONDON: | PRINTED FOR J. JOHNSON, ST. PAUL'S CHURCH-YARD, | BY T. BENSLEY, BOLT COURT, FLEET STREET. | 1806 (3/11 illus.).

For the other two illustrations in these works see Nos. **114A - 115A**.

This illustration was originally published as a separate plate in octavo format and, therefore, does not appear in the quarto editions of the *Botanic Garden*, except in rare instances as an obvious extra-illustration. It is formally included only in the London edition of 1799 and the *Poetical Works* of 1806 (both in octavo).

68. *The Nightmare*, 1791
(*Loves of the Plants*, III, 51-
(Vol. II, facing p. 126)

Engraved by Thomas Holloway (1748-1827) after the later version of the painting in the Goethe-Museum, Frankfurt am Main ([1790-1791]; Schiff 928).
Imprint: London, Published June 1= 1791. by J. Johnson, S^t. Pauls Church Yard.
Inscription: H Fuseli RA Pinxit. | | T. Holloway Sculp^t. | **Nightmare**.
Dimensions: ■ 12.2 x 9.8 cm | 4^{13}/16" x 3^{14}/16";
▣ 12.7 x 10.2 cm | 5" x 4^1/16" (BL 1465.g.23)
Other locations: BL 19262; BL 19263; Bodleian Vet.A5.d.32; Dr. Williams's Library 1110.H.9 (1806); DHW; DHW; Essick; Fribourg ANT 9847 (1806); Illinois 821 D25b; Iowa 581.5.D22.b; Library Company O Eng Darw Bot 1799 (H=22.4 cm); Newberry Y185.D25 (1806); Yale Im D259e
Plate only: DHW; Dr. Williams's Library 1009.S.20 (loosely inserted Vol. II, facing p. 97) (1795); V & A E1195-1886 (no imprint—possibly cropped)
Lacking plate: Lausanne 1M.2727
Lit.: Schiff 975; Powell 1973, *passim*; Boime 1987, 289-292, pl. 4.8; Andersen 1989, 280, repr. 205.
Exh.: Kansas City 1982 (4).

Variants:
I. Proof before letters and frame: BM 1853-12-10-564

No. 68A.
[Erasmus Darwin].
THE | BOTANIC GARDEN. | IN TWO PARTS. | — | PART I. | CONTAINING | THE ECONOMY OF VEGETATION. | — | PART II. | THE LOVES OF THE PLANTS. | — | WITH |

PHILOSOPHICAL NOTES. | = | THE SECOND AMERICAN EDITION. | = | NEW=YORK: | PRINTED AND SOLD BY T. & J. SWORDS, PRINTERS TO THE FACULTY OF PHYSIC | OF COLUMBIA COLLEGE, NO. 160 PEARL-STREET. | — | 1807 (3/23 illus.).

For the other two illustrations in this work see Nos. **114C - 115C**.

68A. *The Nightmare*, 1807
(Vol. II, facing p. 71)

Re-engraved by John Boyd (fl. 1807-1827) from the *Poetical Works*
Inscription: H. Fuseli R.A. Pinx^t. | | J. Boyd Sc. | **Nightmare**.
Dimensions: ■ 12.4 x 10.0 cm | 4^{14}/16" x 3^{15}/16";
▣ 12.7 x 10.3 cm | 5" x 4^1/16" (Library Company)
Other locations: NYPL *KL Darwin; Yale (Medical History) 18-Cent

******

PARODIES AND PASTICHES OF **THE NIGHTMARE**

69A.

69A. *The Night Mare or Hag Ridden Minister*, 1783

Engraved by John Boyne (1750?-1810)
Imprint: London Publishd as the Act Direct [*sic*] March 4 1783 by R Rusted N°. 3 Bridge St.^{t} Ludgate Hill.
Inscription: THE NIGHT MARE or Hag Ridd,n [*sic*] MINISTER.

Dimensions: ■ 17.5 x 25.4 cm | 6¹⁴/₁₆" x 10"
(BM 1865-6-10-1141)
Lit.: George 6184

For the term 'hag' in the sense of nightmare,
see *O.E.D.* and David J. Hufford, *The Terror that
Comes in the Night*, Philadelphia, 1982.

The body of a sleeping man is supported on the
points of eight pyramids, inscribed respectively:
'It shall be Recomen'd [*sic*] Congress to Cut the
Loyalists'; '16 Artic¹.'; '14 Artˡᵉ'; '10ᵗʰ Artˡᵉ'; '6
Artˡᵉ.'; '11 Artˡᵉ'; '7 Art'; '4 Artˡᵉ'. An incubus
in the form of a dog with a human head crouches
on his chest, saying 'If He opens his mouth I Will
be down his Throat'. A man in a bottom wig
crouches at the sleeper's head. He is saying: 'take
Comfort me Lord, for you I Will be allways
Dunning'. A disembodied head hovering over the
feet remarks: 'the North fog Rot Him'.

69B. *The Night Mare, or Prime Minister Hag-Ridden*, 1783

Re-issued (colour impression), with new
publisher's imprint
Imprint: Pubᵈ 29ᵗʰ March 1783 by W Humphrey
Nᵒ 227 Strand
Dimensions: (BM—no number, stamped 'Smith
Coll' on verso)
Lit.: George 6184A.

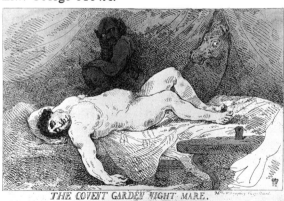

THE COVENT GARDEN NIGHT MARE,

69C.

69C. *The Covent Garden Night Mare*, 1784

Etched by Thomas Rowlandson (1756-1827) after
the original drawing in the Broadley Collection,
Westminster Public Library
Imprint (bottom right): Pubᵈ by W Humphry Nᵒ
227, Strand

Inscription: THE COVENT GARDEN NIGHT
MARE,
Dimensions: ■ 22.2 x 33.1 cm | 8¾" x 13" (BM
1859-9-1-195)
Other locations: Fitzwilliam P.761.1948
Lit.: Grego, I, 129; George 6543; Tomory 1972,
pl. 223; Powell 1973, 101, pl. 3.

According to Powell, Rowlandson's print
(published c. 20 April 1784) appears to be the
first English political caricature based on the
travesty of a painting. Fox is represented stretched
in an uneasy slumber, oppressed by a large
incubus upon his chest, while the head and
shoulders of a supernatural mare are shown
making their appearance through the bed-curtains.
On a table by Fox's side are shown the dice and
dicebox, emblematic of Fox's notorious passion
for gambling.

69D. *The Nightmare of the Aristocracy (Le Cauchemar de l'Aristocratie)*, [1792]

Stipple engraving, in colour, engraved by Benoît-
Louis Provost (Prévost) after Jacques-Louis Copia
(1764-1799)
Inscription: Copia Sc. | | Sauvage pinxit
Dimensions (oval): 9.0 x 10.7 cm | 3½" x 4³/₁₆"
(Bibliothèque Nationale, coll. Hennin no. 12.479)
Lit.: M. Vovelle, *La Révolution française. Images
et récits*, 1986, IV, 268.
Exh.: Paris 1989 (779)

In this reflection upon the French Revolution,
Fuseli's image serves once again as a vehicle for
political comment, although Piat-Joseph Sauvage's
source appears to have been a wall painting from
Herculaneum or Pompeii, to which he had
frequent recourse for his paintings. Within an
oval pictorial area a woman naked to the waist,
perhaps a courtesan (David Bindman, Paris 1989),
who is also a representative of the aristocracy, lies
in uneasy slumber 'poised or posed' between the
new and the old emblems of power: suspended
above her are the levelling plumb and Liberty cap;
on the floor beside her bed are scattered a family
escutcheon, a tiara, a sceptre and two crowns. A
slender ewer stands at the foot of the bed with its
handle in the form of a semi-erect monkey.

This composition appears to have been very
popular: after engraving Copia's design, Provost
then re-engraved it; both versions were published
by Sébastien Desmarest (**69E.**).

LE CAUCHEMAR DE L'ARISTOCRATIE

A Paris chez Desmarest, Rue J.J. Rousseau, M^{on} de Bullion.

69E.

69E. *Le Cauchemar de l'Aristocratie*, [1792]

Re-engraving (colour impression) by Benoît-Louis
Provost (or Prévost) after Jacques-Louis Copia
(1764-1799)
Imprint: A Paris chez Desmarest, Rue J.J.
Rousseau M^{on}. de Bullion.
Inscription: LE CAUCHEMAR DE
L'ARISTOCRATIE
Dimensions (oval): 9.0 x 10.9 cm | 3½" x 4¼";
(to platemark): 12.3 x 12.6 cm | 4¹⁴/16" x 5"
(NYPL MES1)
Other locations: Bibliotèque Nationale; Hamburg
Lit.: Aubert & Roux 1921, II, no. 3620; repr.
cover *Bulletin of Research in the Humanities*,
Spring 1982

    Both versions are very close in time to
Desmarest's pendant to his *Cauchemar*, *Le
Jéhovah des Français*, which is has been dated to
post January 1793.
    Desmarest was particularly known for his
revolutionary calendars and his small format
allegorical productions.

**69F. *The Conquest of Equality or The
Countering of the Plots (La Conquête de
l'Égalité ou Les Trames déjouées)*, 1792**

Aquatint by an anonymous engraver

Inscription (top): LA CONQUÈTE DE
L'ÉGALITÉ|Ou les trames déjouées Allégorie de
la Journée du 10. Août 1792. Dédié aux
Répúbliquains Français——|(bottom):

    Ha! Ha! il faut donc sélérats que nous nous
     lêvions encore une fois; Nôtre tollerance
    vous à fait ourdir de Nouvelles trames; Hé bien!
     qu'a cette fois il vous souviennent
    que nous voulons être libres, Et que le souvenir
    seul de Cette Journé, vous donne pour
    toujours le Cochemard, et malgré touts vos
    projets nous Jurons que Ça ira Ça ira ....,

Dimensions: 19.2 x 27.1 cm | 7⁹/16" x 10¹¹/16"
(Bibliothèque Nationale, Inv. no. Qb¹ 101.362)
Lit.: Aubert & Roux 1921, III, no. 4905; M.
Vovelle, *La Révolution française. Images et récits*,
1986, III, 148.
Exh.: Paris 1989 (780).

69G.

69G. *A Nightmare*, 1794

Aquatint (coloured impression) etched by Richard
Newton (1777-1798)
Imprint (bottom right): London Pub by W Holland
October 26 1794 N° 50 Oxford Street
Inscription: DRAWN and ETCH^d. by R^d.
NEWTON.
Dimensions: ■ 25.0 x 31.4 cm | 9¹³/16" x
12⁶/16"; ▣ 25.3 x 32.0 cm | 10" x 12½" (BM
??)
Other locations: V & A E.943-1970
Lit.: Tomory 1972, pl. 224; Powell 1973, 101,
pl. 4; George 8555; Andersen 1989, repr. 204

A couple lie in a truckle bed. On the woman, who is asleep, sits a grotesque demon, smoking a pipe and holding up a lantern; he glares fiercely at her. The man stares terror-struck. A horse (or mare) puts its head through the open casement window on the left of the picture.

THE NIGHT MARE

69H.

69H. *The Night Mare*, 1795

Engraved by unknown engraver perhaps after Temple West
Imprint: Pub Augst. 13 1795 by S W Fores N° 50 Piccadilly the Corner of Sackville St Folioes of Caracatures lent out for the Evening
Inscription (bottom right): 13. Aug. 1795. | (handwritten): West | THE NIGHT MARE
Dimensions: ■ 22.6 x 34.2 cm | 8^{15}/16" x 13½" (BM 1868-8-8-6461)
Other locations: Huntington Pr. Box 212.12/38
Lit.: George 8671; Powell 1973, 101, pl. 38.

A political travesty of the *Nightmare*, satirising the burdens of war and dearth in 1795. John Bull lies on his back in bed, his mouth gaping; a goblin, representing Pitt, sits on his chest, holding above his upturned head a load inscribed *13 Pence*. Pitt has a huge head with starting eyeballs; his hair stands up and the bag of his queue, inscribed *Taxes* flies out behind him. A fantastic French republican, with bulging eyeballs and fang-like teeth, glares at John Bull through a casement window on the left; from his neck hangs the model of a guillotine. Behind his head is a waning moon. Beside him are the words: *Republic War and Famine for Ever*. Beneath the bed is a chamber-pot inscribed *John Bull*; beside it is a chair on which stands a candle.

69I.

69I. *The Night Mare or the Source of the Nile*, 1798

Engraved by an anonymous engraver
Inscription: NB the greatest rarity in Europe constantly on sale. | The Night Mare.
Dimensions: Unknown (seen only in reproduction)
Lit.: Powell 1973, 83, 101, pl. 42.

Emma Hamilton is shown in the attitude of woman oppressed by the Nightmare lying upon a huge round bed. Nelson is shown seated upon Emma's breast in the act of lifting her diaphanous nightdress. The inscription on the chamber-pot ('Source of [*the*] Nile') and the partial title of the book on the chair beside the bed ('Bruce's | Travels &c') seem to refer to James Bruce's *Travels to Discover the Source of the Nile* (London, 1790). The allusion is probably to Nelson's victory at the Battle of the Nile at Aboukir (1 August 1798), which cut off the French army from France.

No. 69J.
THE | ANTI-JACOBIN | REVIEW AND MAGAZINE; | OR, | MONTHLY POLITICAL AND LITERARY CENSOR. | FROM | APRIL TO AUGUST (INCLUSIVE,) | —1799— | WITH AN APPENDIX, | CONTAINING | AN AMPLE REVIEW OF FOREIGN LITERATURE. | = | *In vitium LIBERTAS excedit, et vim dignam LEGI Regi. HORAT.* | = | VOL. III. | (EMBELLISHED WITH PLATES.) | LONDON: | PRINTED, FOR THE PROPRIETORS, AT THE ANTI-JACOBIN PRESS, BY T. CROWDER, | OF GUN-STREET, SPITALFIELDS. | AND PUBLISHED AT THE

ANTI-JACOBIN OFFICE, PETERBOROUGH COURT, FLEET|STREET, BY J. WHITTLE, AND BY C.CHAPPLE, BOOKSELLER, PALL MALL;|T. PIERSON, BIRMINGHAM; BELL AND BRADFUTE, EDINBURGH; BRASH|AND REID, GLASGOW; J. MILLIKEN, DUBLIN; AND BY W. COBBETT,|PHILADELPHIA.|—| 1799.

69J.

69J. *The Night Mare*, 1799
(*The Anti-Jacobin Review*, III, 99)

Etched by J[?ohn] Chapman (fl. 1790-1820) after R. S. (coloured impression)
Imprint (bottom left): Publish'd May 1. 1799, by T. Whittle, Peterboro' Court Fleet Street—for the Anti Jacobin Review.
Inscription (bottom right in plate): R S 1799|
(bottom right): J. Chapman, Aq. for sc|THE NIGHT MARE.
Dimensions: ■ 19.6 x 25.0 cm | 7¾ " x 9¹⁴/₁₆";
■ 20.1 x 25.4 | 7¹⁵/₁₆" x 10" (BL P.P. 3596)
Other locations: BL 261.i.3; Huntington 147113; LC AP4.A66 (facing p. [1]); V & A E.946-1970
Lit.: George 9371; Powell 1973, p. 102 (5.)

The following explanatory verses are given facing the print:

THE NIGHT MARE.

'Hic vir, hic est, titii quam promitti saepius
    audis.'   Virgil.

From toil and trouble, wrangling and debate,
The arch seceder, *patriot* like,* retires,
And dooms his country to th' impending fate,
Nor cares he aught to quench th' anarchic fires.

Lo! demons hov'ring o'er his *patriot* head—
Torment his soul—convulsions shake his
    frame—
In pangs reclining in somnific dread;
Struggling for sense, to fly his tort'ring dream.

Father of anarchy ! your child behold!
In *night-mare form* ascend—he firmly plants
THAT Freedom's flag the sons of Gallia hold,
On the black breast that for SUCH freedom
    pants.

War's phantom, too, horrific shape assumes,
The Ægyptian hero's form, hell's fit viceroy,
With Murder's sword, and Death's awe-moving
    plumes,
Salutes the patriot in rude frantic joy!

'Patron of earthly liberty!
'I'm Anarchy's chaotic son,
'Come to greet thee—do not sigh !
'Yet thy course thou hast not run:
'Still the world shall by thy spell
'Be made to taste the pangs of hell,
'And Jacobins shall rally round,
'And raise *this Freedom's banner* on a
    deathly mound.'

As thus the spectre, Ephialtian said,
The vision ceas'd, and vanish'd into shade.
May, 1799.   UCALOGON. [*Mr. Stevens*]

*[*Original footnote*]: 'According to the language of Jacobins, all *seceders* from duty, and *oppositionists* to the constitution of their country, are termed *true patriots* and *constitutional-men*!'

******

69K. *Singular Dream of a Lady at York*, 1802

Coloured impression of an engraving by John Ke[?], perhaps from a chap-book.
Imprint (on open pages of book held by incubus): John|Ke [*one or two letters obscured*]|May|15ᵗʰ|1802
Inscription: [*T*]he singular DREAM of a LADY at YORK
Dimensions: 13.5 x 8.9 cm | 5⁵/₁₆" x 3½" (BM 1868-8-8-13306)
Lit.: George 9946; Powell 1973, 102.

This adaptation of the *Nightmare* (perhaps from a chapbook) depicts a sleeping young woman. A nearly naked monster, gripping a long spear and holding up an open book, squats on her chest. A horse is looking through a window at the left.

he fingular DREAM of a LADY at YORK

69K.

DUTCH NIGHT-MARE
OR THE FRATERNAL HUG RETURNED WITH A DUTCH SQUEEZE

69L.

69L. *The Dutch Night Mare or the Fraternal Hug Returned with a Dutch Squeeze*, 1813

Engraved by Thomas Rowlandson (1756-1827) (coloured impression)
Imprint: Pubᵈ Novʳ 29. 1813 by R Ackermann N° 101 Strand—

Inscription: DUTCH NIGHT-MARE | OR THE FRATERNAL HUG RETURNED WITH A DUTCH SQUEEZE
Dimensions: 30.9 x 23.0 cm | 12³/16" x 9¹/16" (BM 1868-8-8-8089)
Lit.: George 12105; George 1959, 145, pl. 56; Powell 1973, 102

Variants:
I. Dutch copy lacking imprint, 1813 (not seen)
Lit.: Van Stolk 1908, no. 6224; George 1959, 150

Napoleon lies in bed, his right arm hanging down over the edge, his feet projecting from under the coverlet. He stares up, terrified, at the fat Dutchman in a high-crowned hat, with a large (orange) cockade, seated on his chest, squeezing his neck between his legs and puffing tobacco smoke at his face, and saying *Orange Boven*. The Dutchman has his left hand in the pocket of his ample breeches. The curtains and counterpane are patterned with eagles; the curtains hang from a circular canopy topped by a large crown and a trophy of sword, sceptre and eagle. They are drawn aside to frame the two figures. On the fringed pelmet eagles alternate with crowns and a papal tiara, emblem of the humiliation of the Papacy. On the right stand two enormous fasces with projecting lictor's axes, the blades turned towards Napoleon. On a stool in front of the bed are the Emperor's bicorne and sword.

69M.

No. 69M.
[William Combe.]
THE LIFE OF | NAPOLEON. | A | HUDIBRASTIC POEM | IN | FIFTEEN CANTOS | BY | DOCTOR SYNTAX, | EMBELLISHED WITH | THIRTY ENGRAVINGS, | BY | G. CRUIKSHANK. |

LONDON. PRINTED FOR T. TEGG, 111
CHEAPSIDE, WM ALLASON, 31 NEW BOND
STREET & J. DICK, EDINBURGH 1815 (1/30
illus.).

69M. *Napoleon Dreaming in his Cell at the Military College*, 1814
(Plate 1, facing p. 6)

Unsigned aquatint in colour engraved by George
Cruikshank (1792-1878)
Imprint: London, Published by Thomas Tegg, Nº.
111, Cheapside, Nov. 10th. 1814
Inscription: NAPOLEON DREAMING IN HIS
CELL AT THE MILITARY COLLEGE.
Dimensions: ■ 11.5 x 19.5 cm | 4½" x 7¹⁰/16"
(BL C.116.f.4.)
Other locations (plate only): BM 12455; DHW
Lit.: Bourguignon 1936, I, 20; George 12455;
Reid 1871, no. 4651; Douglas 1903, 256; Cohn
1924, 153; Powell 1973, 102, pl. 40.

Variants:
I. Uncoloured impression: BM ??call no.

Napoleon, who had entered the Military School
at Paris in 1784, is shown here as a young cadet
in his bed (his head on the left of the picture)
dreaming of fame and glory while a phantom
jackass with pricked ears ridden by a demon
straddles his chest. Beside the bed are a wash-
stand and a three-legged stool with a book of
devotion, kept open by a cross.

******

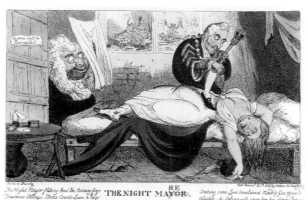

69N.

69N. *The Night Mayor*, 1816

An unsigned caricature designed and etched by
George Cruikshank (1792-1878), based on
Fuseli's painting.
Imprint (right half of first line): Pubᵈ. 25th.
Novemʳ. 1816 by S W Fores 50 Piccadilly.
Inscription: Painted by Fuzely. | THE NIGHT
MAYOR | RE. |

[*left*]
The Night Mayor flitting thro' the Evening fogs
Traverses Alleys, Strees [sic] Courts Lane &
bogs

[*right*]
Seeking some Love-bewilder'd Maid by Gin
oppress'd
Alights— & Ogling sits upon her her [sic]
downy breast.

(at right, by hand): 25 Nov. 1816.
Dimensions: 20.0 x 33.2 cm | 7¹⁴/16" x 13¹/16"
(BM 1868-8-8-8351)
Other locations: BM 1862-6-12-1280
Lit.: George 12817; Reid 599; Douglas 1073;
Cohn 1789; Powell 1973, 102, pl. 5 (as by
'Anonymous'); Allentuck 1976, 46f., pl. 4

Variants:
I. Later impression with the redundant 'her' in
the 4th line of the verse removed: (BM 1862-
12-17-543)

This adaptation of Fuseli's *Night Mare* satirises
Matthew Wood, Lord Mayor of London, and his
campaign against the prostitutes in the City.
Wood, wearing his mayoral gown, is represented
as the incubus squatting on the bosom of a large
and apparently drunken prostitute. Fuseli's horse
is replaced by John Silvester, the City Recorder,
notorious for his harsh and reactionary views on
crime and punishment, who is shown peeping
around a scanty curtain, exclaiming, 'Thy deeds
shall be <u>Recorderded</u>.' The two large prints
hanging on the wall depict other scenes of
nightmares: (1) A demon holding up a birch-rod
and scourge bestrides the sleeping forms of a man
in bed between two women in a wretched room.
(2) A demon squats on a man lying in irons in a
prison cell, holding up a lantern and some
instrument of torture.

69O. *Louis the Fat Troubled with the Night Mare and Dreams of Terror*, 1823

Coloured engraving by [Isaac] Robert Cruikshank (1789-1856) (not reproduced in the catalogue)
Imprint: Pub^d May 1823 by J Fairburn Broadway Ludgate Hill (not reproduced in the catalogue)
Inscription: *LOUIS* THE *FAT* TROUBLED WITH THE *NIGHT MARE* AND *DREAMS* OF *TERROR*. !!! — | A Hint to the Bourbons, 1823. | R. Cruikshank fecit.
Dimensions: 8^6/16" x 12^14/16" (BM ???)
Lit.: Powell 1973, 117, pl. 41 (as by George Cruikshank).

69P.

69P. *John Bull's Night Mare*, 1828

Engraved by Robert Seymour (1798-1836) (as 'Shortshanks') after his own design
Imprint: London, Pub^d. by Thos. M^c.Lean, 26, Haymarket.
Inscription: Seymour Del Shortshanks Sculpt | JOHN BULL'S NIGHT MARE. |

[*left*]   When this unfortunate Gent. (having nothing | to keep him awake) retires after a hearty meal |

[*right*] to sleep he always dreams of one or more of | those terrific Specters sometimes of all together.

Dimensions: 25.0 x 34.5 cm | 8^10/16" x 12^10/16" (BM 1868-8-8-8844)

Other locations: Huntington 180644/76 (coloured)
Lit.: George 15497; Powell 1973, 103, pl. 39.

69Q.

69Q. *Fatal Effects of Gluttony: A Lord Mayor's Day Night Mare*, 1830

Lithograph by M G
Imprint: Published by Thos. McLean 26, Haymarket Nov: 4th 1830.
Inscription (top): FATAL EFFECTS OF GLUTTONY | (right): Printed by C. Motte 23 Leicester Sq^re.. | A LORD MAYOR'S DAY NIGHTMARE. | Dedicated to all the City Gourmands.—to be had at all the Taverns in the United Kingdom
Dimensions: 23.5 x 33.5 cm | 9¼" x 13^3/16"; (with border): 10½" x 14" (BM 1868-8-8-9243)
Other locations: V & A E.953.1970
Lit.: George 16429

A glutton lies in bed, asleep, assailed by the fish, flesh, and fowl of a City dinner. A huge turtle is on top of him, a lobster pinches his nose, a pheasant swoops to peck an eye. A big frog points a spear on which three small frogs are spitted. On his bedside table besides candle, box of 'Dixon's Pills,' basin, &c., is a bill of fare, listing: 'Turtle & fresh Cod | Roast beef & a la mode | Veal and Mutton | Pork and Venison | Pheasants & Pigeons | Lobster & Sturgeon | Turkey & Capon | Goose and Salmon | Turbot & Ducks | Shrimps in Pots | Frogs a la Crapodine | Anguille & a la diabletine.'

Nos. 69R - 69T.
[Unlocated edition.]
LES MACEDOINES, 1830.

69R. *Diabolic Scene*, 1830

Lithograph by Paul-Guillaume-Sulpice Gavarni (1804-1866) (not reproduced in catalogue)
Inscription: [Scène diabolique]
Dimensions: Unknown (seen only in reproduction)
Lit.: Tomory 1972, 202, pl. 226

69S. *Diabolic Reverie*, 1830

Lithograph vignette by Charles Ramelet (1805-1851) (not reproduced in catalogue)
Inscription: [Rêverie diabolique]
Dimensions: Unknown (seen only in reproduction)
Lit.: Tomory 1972, 202, pl. 227

69T. *Female Seated on a Demon*, 1830

Lithograph by — Callot (not reproduced in catalogue)
Dimensions: Unknown (seen only in reproduction)
Lit.: Tomory 1972, 202, pl. 228

69U. *Le Rêve*, 1830

Lithographed by V. Ratier after Toni Johannot (1803-1852) (not reproduced in the catalogue)
Inscription (left): Toni Johannot.|(right): Lith. de V. Ratier.

A cloud of monsters hover above a young woman lying in the same attitude as the woman in the *Nightmare*.

No. 69V.
Michel Raymond [i.e. Raymond Brucker]
LES INTIMES,|PAR MICHEL RAYMOND,|AUTEUR DU MAÇON.|I. [-II.]|SECONDE ÉDITION.|[Vignette]| PARIS,|EUGÈNE RENDUEL,|RUE DES GRANDS-AUGUSTINS, N° 22.|1831.

69V. *Le Cauchemar*, 1831
(Vol. II, title vignette)

Title vignette engraved on wood by 'Andrew' (fl. 1828-1852) after a drawing by Toni Johannot (1803-1852) (not reproduced in catalogue)
Inscription: JOHANNOT|ANDREW.
Dimensions: 9.0 x 8.6 cm | 3½" x 3⁶/16"

(Wisconsin PQ 2347.M8I58).
Lit.: Powell 1973, 91-93, pl. 52.

******

Nos. 69W - 69X.
FIGARO IN LONDON.|—|VOL. I. [-VOL. VIII.]|FOR THE YEAR 1832. [-1839.]|LONDON; PRINTED BY W. MOLINEUX, ROLLS BUILDINGS, FETTER LANE.|PUBLISHED BY WILLIAM STRANGE, 21, PATERNOSTER ROW;|AND MAY BE HAD OF ALL BOOKSELLERS.

69W.

69W. *Britannia's Nightmare*, 1832
(Vol. I, 118; No. 30. 30 June 1832)

Woodcut engraved by —- Lee after Robert Seymour (1798-1836)
Inscription (bottom right): Lee
Dimensions: ■ 6.2 x 7.6 cm | 2⁷/16" x 3" (BL P.P. 5264)
Other locations: Arizona AP101.F46; NYPL *DX+
Lit.: George 17162 (2)

At the centre of the picture lies Britannia in the throes of a nightmare. The representation of Britannia with the incubus crouched upon her chest has been taken over almost verbatim from Holloway's engraving, although she has been given a spear and a shield, emblazoned with the Union Jack, and ancillary figures have been added. To the left, at Britannia's head stands a man in a cocked hat (the Duke of Wellington). Three geese fly overhead, screaming 'War,|

Famine, | Taxes, Troubles | shall cease.' At the
foot of the bed Hercules is poised with his club
raised over his head, under the inscription 'Peace
and Truth | shall reign.' In the right foreground is
a drummer boy, wearing a busby. These various
elements constitute an extension of and visual
commentary on the series of transparently utopian
prophecies by 'Figaro,' which I cite in abridged
form:

> ...at the commencement of 1833, a reformed
> parliament will be *sitting*, while a great deal of
> public business will be standing. A proposition
> will be made in the course of the year for
> extending the elective franchise to all persons
> unstained by moral crime, or rendered unable
> by idiotcy to use their mental capacities....
> About June, several sinecurists will be reduced
> to beggary....
>   Mr. Cobbett suddenly becomes respectful in
> his language towards the Government....
>   In December the Duke of Wellington beats the
> Whig ministry by proposing the Ballot,
> Universal Suffrage, and Annual Parliaments....
> Sir Robert Peel does the same in the Commons
> ....
>   At the close of the year the members of the
> Carlton club take the benefit of the Insolvent
> act, and here a number of horrors ensue which
> we dare not describe, but they will have a
> felicitous issue, as the caricature beneath doth
> testify.

The astrological signs at the top of the picture
denote that Jupiter and Mars are in opposition to
Saturn—since both of these are consistently
unfavourable aspects, they further underline the
blatantly unrealistic expectations about the
political and social gains that passage of the
Reform Bill is supposed to bring.

69X. *Ireland's Political Nightmare*, 1834
(Vol. III, top of col. 1, p. 98)
(Issue No. 30, 21 June 1834)

Wood engraving after Robert Seymour (1798-
1836)
Dimensions: 8.3 x 8.3 cm | 3¼" x 3¼" (BL P.P.
5264)
Other locations: NYPL *DX+; Pennsylvania
AP101

This caricature was inspired by the

69X.

consciousness 'that it is in contemplation to renew
the persecution of Ireland, and that the Coercion
Bill is to continue in force under the mild and
merciful direction of the Whig government.' As
the text below notes:

> ...the above caricature...is designed to show the
> condition to which poor Ireland has been
> reduced by the system that has invariably been
> pursued towards her. She has, as it were, been
> continually subject to the oppression of a
> political nightmare, and such is the incubus, that
> even at this moment the Whig ministers are
> preparing to continue in force against her. We
> trust the opposition they will experience may be
> decisive, and we certainly shall be ready to
> assist the laudable efforts of those who meet
> them with defiance.

Beneath a blood-spattered Union Jack decorated
with a pair of clasped hands (symbolising the
intent of the Act of Union), Ireland is pictured as
young woman in tortured sleep, her head and
shoulders hanging over the edge of her bed so that
her hair and both her hands touch the ground.
The squat and cloven-footed incubus crouched
upon her chest wears a liberty hat decorated with
a cockade and is wrapped in a judicial looking
cloak from under which a long tail emerges,
ending in a hissing serpent's head. He holds a
paper inscribed 'Rent' in his left hand; the dagger
in his right has begun to pierce the maiden's

chest, while blood dribbles from the wound between her exposed breasts. To the right on the other side of the bed the head of a horse appears between the curtains snorting a cloud of steam. To enhance her woeful plight, in the foreground next to the bed stands an Irish harp with all its strings broken; the upper two sides of its characteristic triangular form are represented by the body of a naked woman supported on her stiff wings.

******

THE BIRMINGHAM NIGHT MARE.

69Y.

No. 69Y.
M^C. LEAN'S MONTHLY SHEET OF CARICATURES, N°. 31.|OR THE|LOOKING GLASS|OR|CARICATURE ANNUAL|—|1832. |-VOL. 3.-| LONDON (THOMAS MCLEAN| 26, HAYMARKET).

69Y. *The Birmingham Night Mare*, 1832 (*McLean's Monthly Sheet of Caricatures*, No. 31, p. 4)

Lithographed by Robert Seymour (1798-1836) [1 July 1832]
Inscription: THE BIRMINGHAM NIGHT MARE.
Dimensions: 7.8 x 12.2 cm | 3^1/16" x 4^{13}/16" (V & A E.5264-1904)
Lit.: George 17177; Powell 1973, 103, pl. 6

With head and arms thrown back Britannia lies on a low bed, her shield, spear, and helmet beside her. Seated on her chest and staring at her face is Thomas Attwood, the political Radical of the

Birmingham Political Union, cloaked in black. A horse puts its head in at the window, glaring and snorting savagely at the dreamer.

******

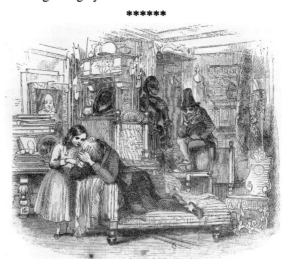

69Z.

No. 69Z.
Charles Dickens.
MASTER HUMPHREY'S CLOCK.|BY CHARLES DICKENS.|—|WITH ILLUSTRATIONS|BY| GEORGE CATTERMOLE AND HABLOT BROWNE.|VOL. I [-VOL. II.]| LONDON:| CHAPMAN AND HALL, 186, STRAND.| MDCCCXL [-XLI]. [1840-1841]

THE OLD CURIOSITY SHOP.|A TALE.|BY CHARLES DICKENS.|-|WITH ILLUSTRATIONS |BY|GEORGE CATTERMOLE AND HABLOT K. BROWNE.|-| COMPLETE IN ONE VOLUME.| -| LONDON:|CHAPMAN AND HALL, STRAND. |MDCCCXLI. [1841] (1/54 illus.)

69Z. *Quilp Observing Nell and her Grandfather* (Charles Dickens, *The Old Curiosity Shop*, Ch. IX)

Wood engraving by Ebenezer Landells (1808-1860) after George Cattermole
Inscription (bottom centre): E. LANDELLS.
Dimensions: 10.8 x 11.7 cm | 4¼" x 4^{10}/16" (Glenn Book Shop, Kansas City, Missouri)

There are a number of indications throughout *The Old Curiosity Shop* that Dickens was familiar with Fuseli's *Nightmare*, probably in its engraved form. Indeed, the way in which Daniel Quilp, the grotesque dwarf, is repeatedly tagged as a 'nightmare' would seem to represent one of Dickens's most typical techniques of characterisation (see for example pages 81f., 159, 228, and 239, in the Penguin English Library edition of the novel). Not only does Quilp become a 'perpetual nightmare' to Nell, 'who was constantly haunted by a vision of his ugly face and stunted figure' (p. 288), but he is even seen 'looking at his insensible wife like a dismounted nightmare' (p. 462). As the strong compositional echoes here of the 1791 engraving suggest, the illustrator seems to have picked up on the author's verbal hints—albeit in his image he might almost appear to have conflated an Irish leprechaun figure with that of the incubus.

******

69AA.

No. 69AA.
Charles Nodier.
CONTES|DE|CHARLES NODIER|Trilby.—Le Songe d'or.—Baptiste Montauban.|—La Fée aux Miettes. La Combe de l'Homme Mort.—Inès de las Sierras.|—Smarra.—La Neuvaine de la Chandeleur.|—La Légende de la Soeur Béatrix.| —EAUX FORTES PAR TONY JOHANNOT.| [Vignette]| PARIS PUBLIÉ PAR J. HETZEL, RUE RICHELIEU, 76, ET RUE MENARS 10. 1846 (1/8 illus.)

...|PARIS|[*left*] VICTOR LECOU|10, RUE DU BOULOI|[*right*] J. HETZEL ET CIE|76, RUE RICHELIEU|[1852]

...|PARIS|MAGNIN, BLANCHARD ET CIE| ANCIENNE MAISON L. JANET.|RUE HONORE-CHEVALIER, 3|—|1859

69AA. *Smarra*, 1845
(Charles Nodier, *Smarra*)
(facing p. [241])

Frontispiece (India paper) etched by Toni Johannot (1803-1852) after his own design.
Inscription: Tony Johannot 1845
Dimensions: ■ 10.4 x 8.0 cm | 4^1/16" x 3^2/16"
(NYPL NKV)
Other locations: LC PQ2376.N6C7 1846; MMA 66.698; ZBZ AL 284 (1852); ZBZ AL 241 (1859) (facing p. [247])
Lit.: Powell 1973, 93f., 112, pl. 53

I have not been able to locate the 1845 edition of *Smarra ou les démons de la nuit* cited by Powell to which this plate purportedly served as a frontispiece. Powell considers this illustration to be an elaboration of Johannot's earlier title-vignette *Cauchemar* (**69V.**)

******

No. 69BB.
LE CHARIVARI.|16 JANVIER 1851.| PUBLIANT CHAQUE JOUR UN NOUVEAU DESSIN ET LITHOGRAPHIE|OU GRAVURES, ET VIGNETTES SUR BOIS|1851

69BB. *Nightmare of a Good Old Parisian Bourgeois Who Lives in Place St. Georges*, 1851
(*Charivari*, 16 January 1851)

Lithograph by Honoré Daumier (1808-1879) (not reproduced in the catalogue)
Inscription (top right): 52.; (bottom left in plate): h.D.|Chez Aubert & Cie Pl. de la Bourse 29. Paris.||Imp. de Me Ve Aubert, 5. r. de l'Abbaye Paris|Un Cauchemar d'un bon petit bourgeois de la Place S^t. Georges.
Dimensions: ■ 20.0 x 25.1 cm | 8^4/16" x 9^{14}/16"
KHZ Delteil 2082
Lit.: Hazard & Delteil, 1904, no. 2793; Delteil 1925-1930, no. 2082
Exh.: Bern 1991 (489)

Variants:
I. Proof before letters (Delteil) (not seen)

An elderly Frenchman (perhaps representing Thiers) wearing a nightcap is lying asleep in bed, his head resting on a pillow on top of a bolster. Upon the sleeper's chest sits the nightmare in the form of a youthful figure of indeterminate sex wearing a republican cap. The incubus/succubus has a malicious grin and is making a derisive gesture ('cocking a snook') in the dreamer's face. Circling the head of the nightmare with a halo whose radiance illuminates the darkness is the inscription '1851 AN 4 DE LA REPUBLIQUE'. In this context, the Phrygian cap is emblematic of the revolutionary political temper of the infant republic brought forth in 1848, now entering its fourth year of existence, while the conventional nightcap equates the troubled sleeper with bourgeois conservativism.

******

No. 69CC.
PUNCH | [Title illustration signed 'JT'] | — | VOL 50 | LONDON: | PUBLISHED AT THE OFFICE, 85, FLEET STREET, | AND SOLD BY ALL BOOKSELLERS. | 1866.

69CC.

69CC. *London's Nightmare*, 1866
(*Punch, or the London Charivari*, 10 March 1866)
(Vol. 50, p. [101])

Full-page wood-engraving after Sir John Tenniel (1820-1914) (verso blank)

Inscription (top): PUNCH, OR THE LONDON CHARIVARI.—MARCH 10, 1866.; (at lower right within plate): JT [*ligature*]; (bottom centre): LONDON'S NIGHTMARE.
Dimensions (including running head at top):
■ 24.6 x 18.1 cm | 9¹¹/16" x 7²/16";
■ 24.3 x 17.3 cm | 9⁹/16" x 7" (BL P.P. 5270)
Other locations: BL P.P. 5270. ah.
Lit.: Eric de Mare, *The Victorian Woodblock Illustrators*, 1981, repr. 79.

London's Nightmare is one of the approximately 2,300 full-page political cartoons which Sir John Tenniel (1820-1914) provided during his more than thirty-year tenure at *Punch* whose staff he joined in 1851. The cartoon shows Bumble, the heartless and corrupt beadle in Charles Dickens' *Oliver Twist*, seated like an incubus upon the breast of London, here shown as a nightmare-ridden woman with clenched fists under the crushing weight of 'Bumbledom'. The meaning is explained in 'Punch's Essence of Parliament' on page 98:

> 'London's Nightmare', Bumbledom, that is to say, the conflicting jurisdictions of folks who ought to have no jurisdiction at all, and who job, blunder, squabble, and utterly misgovern the metropolis of the world, was well lectured upon by LORD ROBERT MONTAGU.
>
> [*The following day*] Another onslaught upon Bumbledom was made, and the 'system', if such a chaos may be called by a name implying order, was further illustrated, and much contempt expressed for its components. A Select Committee has been appointed to consider the subject.

*****

69DD.
PUCK | ILLUSTRIRTES | HUMORISTISCHES WOCHEN-BLATT | KEPPLER & SCHWARZMANN, HERAUS-GEBER. | | TRADE MARK REGISTERED 1878. | | PUCK BUILDING, ECKE HOUSTON & MULBERRY ST. [NEW YORK].

69DD. *Restless Nights*, 1887
(*Puck*, 16 March 1887)
(Vol. XXI, no. 523, pp. [44-45])

Centrefold in colour lithography after Joseph Keppler (1838-1894) (not reproduced in catalogue).

Imprint: J. Ottman, Lith. PUCK BUILDING, N.Y.
Inscription (top centre): PUCK. | (Bottom centre) RESTLESS NIGHTS. | (Signed, bottom right corner of plate): J. Keppler.
Dimensions (sheet): 34.5 x 51.0 cm | 13¹⁰/₁₆" x 20²/₁₆" (LC AP 101.P75).
Other locations (plate only): DHW

This late reminiscence of the *Nightmare*, attacking publisher Joseph Pulitzer, is explicated with heavy irony in the 'Cartoons and Comments' section (p. 38) as follows:

It is pretty hard for a practical politician and a strict party-man to toil away, day after day, editing a great paper and moulding public opinion at two or three cents per daily mould, and to see public opinion doing its own moulding, all the time, in just the way it should not. It is disheartening — it is hard on a truly great editor. And yet to such misery are some of our most prominent moulders subjected. They toil unceasingly to show to President Cleveland the error of his ways — giving the public an incidental glimpse — and the more they show it to him, the less he sees it — and the less the public sees it. He goes on and does his work as he promised to do it, and the public seems to be thoroughly well pleased with him. But it is hard on the moulders.

In the German-language version a long verse narrative (p. 424) relates the events taking place in the picture.

For an account of Joseph Keppler, see Richard S. West, *Satire on Stone: The Political Cartoons of Joseph Keppler*, Urbana & Chicago, 1988.

******

70.

70. *Belisane and Percival under the Enchantment of Urma*, 1782

Mezzotint engraved by John Raphael Smith (1752-1812) after the lost original exhibited at the Royal Academy (1783/28).
Imprint: London Publish'd August 25. 1782 by J.R. Smith N°. 31 King Street Covent Garden.

Inscription: Painted by H, Fusley||Engrav'd by J,R, Smith|BELISANE & PARCIVAL under the ENCHANTMENT of URMA|from the provenzal tale of Kyot

Dimensions: ■ 43.5 x 55.1 cm | 17²/16" x 21¾" (BM 1873-8-9-236)

Other locations: KHZ B43a; KHZ B43; ETH 1925, 44/433

Lit.: Schiff 717 (40.7 x 56.0 cm); Schiff-Viotto 1977, no. 35; Frankau 1902, no. 32

Variants

I. Address changed in imprint: BM 1870-5-14-1613

Imprint: London Publishd August 25. 1782 by J. R. Smith N°. 83 Oxford Street.

Other locations: YCBA B1977.14.114.97; Essick; MMA 59.570.362

II. Coloured impression (KHZ 1940/140)

Like *Ezzelin and Meduna*, this subject was invented by Fuseli himself. Fuseli's other painting illustrating this fictional saga, *Percival Delivering Belisane from the Enchantment of Urma* (1783; Schiff 718), was not engraved. For his two invented episodes, Fuseli appears to have combined motifs from *Parzival* and Book III of the *Faerie Queene*. 'Like Klinschor and Spenser's Busirane, Urma is a magician who separates women and knights from those they love and holds them in bondage by means of a spell. ... As in *Parzival* and the *Faerie Queene* the spell is a symbol for the enslavement of the soul by bodily desires' (see *Henry Fuseli 1741-1825*, London, 1975, no. 124).

For No. **70A** see the combined entry for *Fuessli's Sämmtliche Werke* following No. **74A**.

******

71.

71. *Lady Macbeth Walking in her Sleep*, 1784
(W. Shakespeare, *Macbeth*, V, i)

Mezzotint engraved by John Raphael Smith (1752-1812) after Fuseli's painting exhibited at the Royal Academy (1784/66) and now in the Louvre ([1781-1784]; Schiff 738).
Imprint: London Publish'd Jany. 6 1784 by I.R. Smith. N° 35 King Street Covent Garden.
Inscription: Painted by H. Fusley||Engrved by J,R, Smith,|**Lady Macbeth** Act, 5th|one, two; why then 'tis time to do't.
Dimensions: 62.5 x 45.2 cm | 24½" x 17¾" (KHZ 1940/136)

Other locations: BM 1870-5-14-1616 (not seen)
Lit.: Schiff 738-A (62.1 x 45.0 cm); Schiff-Viotto 1977, no. 61; Frankau 225

Variants:
I. Address changed in imprint (Frankau 225) (not seen).
Imprint: London Publish'd Jany. 6 1784 by J.R. Smith No 83 Oxford Street.

******

For No. **71A** see the combined entry for *Fuessli's Sämmtliche Werke* following No. **74A**.

******

72.

72. *Lear Awakens to Find Cordelia Beside his Bed*, 1784
(Shakespeare, *King Lear*, IV, vi)

Mezzotint engraved by John Raphael Smith (1752-1812) after Fuseli's lost painting (1784; Schiff 741)

Imprint: London Publish'd May 21 1784 by I: R: Smith N°. 83 Oxford Street.
Inscription: Painted by H. Fuseli||Engrav'd by J: R: Smith, Mezzotinto Engraver, to|his Royal Highness the Prince of Wales.|LEAR & CORDELIA|

[*left*]
Cor.   Sir do you know me.

[*right*]
Lear.   You are a spirit I know, where did
          you die.
          King Lear Act 4th. |

(right): From the Original in the possession of
W^m. Locke Esqr.
Dimensions (cropped on two sides inside
platemark): ■ 43.7 x 55.0 cm | 17⁷/₁₆" x 21¾"
(BM 1867-12-14-203)
Other locations: KHZ B43
Lit.: Schiff 741 (45.4 x 56.0 cm); Schiff-Viotto
1977, no. 64

Variants:

I. Address changed in imprint: ETH
433/1925,44
Imprint: London Publish'd May 21. 1784 by
I:R: Smith N°. 31 King street Covent Garden
II. Source of the quotation in the inscription
changed:... Vide Shakespears King Lear Act
4th. (Frankau 212—not seen).
Lit.: Frankau 1902, no. 212

Having cast out Cordelia, his only truly loving
daughter, Lear soon discovers the true nature of
Regan's and Goneril's professions of love.
Stripped of all his kingly attributes and illusions,
Lear goes mad and wanders the heath, buffeted by
the storm. Kent brings him to Dover where
Cordelia's tender care helps him regain his
reason. Here we see the joyful reunion as the old
man awakens and recognises Cordelia.

72A *Lear Awakens to Find Cordelia Beside his*
Bed, [n.d.]

Re-engraving on steel in reduced format by
unknown engraver (unsigned)
Proof before all letters
Inscription (bottom, open letters): KING LEAR. |
Act 4. Scene 7.
Dimensions: ■ 10.7 x 8.2 cm | 4³/₁₆" x 3¼"
(Birmingham 190562,465)
Other locations: Huntington 140092, Vol. IX, 1/4
between pp. 450-451

Variants:

I. Proof before letters: BM 1863-5-9-50

72B.

No. 72B.
WILLIAM SHAKSPEARES | SCHAUSPIELE. |
— | NEUE GANZ UMGEARBEITETE
AUSGABE. | — | VON | JOHANN JOACHIM
ESCHENBURG. | [Vignette] | ERSTER BAND.
[-ZWÖLFTER BAND.] | — | ZÜRICH, | BEI
ORELL, GESSNER, FÜSSLI UND
COMPAGNIE. | 1798-1805 (1/12 illus. + portr.
frontis.).

Also issued (1798-1806) with added t.p. and
commentaries to each play, substantially changing
the pagination of each volume.

ZWÖLF SCENEN | AUS | SHAKSPEARE'S
SCHAUSPIELEN | NEBST | DESSELBEN
PORTRAIT. | GESTOCHEN | VON | HEINRICH
LIPS. | — | ZÜRICH, | BEY ORELL, FÜSSLI
UND COMPAGNIE. | 1808 (1/12 illus.).

72B. *Lear Awakens to Find Cordelia Beside his*
Bed, 1804
(*King Lear*, IV, vi)
(Vol. XI, title page)

Reduced version of John Raphael Smith's
mezzotint in the form of title vignette engraved in
aquatint by Johann Heinrich Lips (1758-1817)

Imprint: Zürich, | bei Orell, Füssli und
Compagnie. | 1805.
Inscription (bottom left): H. Lips fec. | König
Lear: Act V. Sc III.
Dimensions: ■ 4.7 x 7.0 cm | 1¹³/16" x 2¾" (BL
11763.bb.19)
Other locations: Coburg V.115,85 (1798-1806);
KHZ C6/IIIA, 1134; LC PR2780.E7 (1798-1806);
ZBZ AX 2076 (1808) (facing p. 17); ZBZ BB
615; ZBZ IV.R110bk

Plate only: Birmingham 190562,750
Lacking plate: Folger PR2796.G3 1798-1805a;
Yale Ig.5n.775b
Exh.: Coburg 1989 (197)

******

For No. **72C** see the combined entry for *Fuessli's
Sämmtliche Werke* following No. **74A**.

******

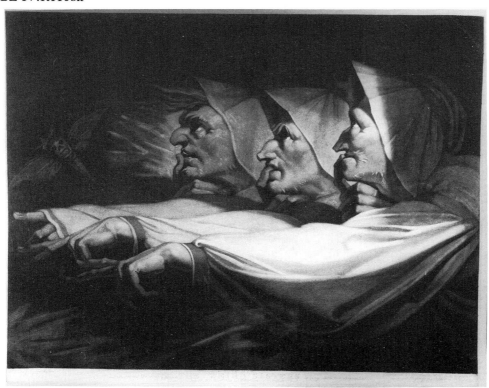

73.

73. *The Weird Sisters*, 1785
(W. Shakespeare, *Macbeth*, I, iii)

Mezzotint engraved by John Raphael Smith (1752-
1812) after the original painting exhibited
(1783/10) at the Royal Academy and now in the
Kunsthaus Zurich ([1783]; Schiff 733).
Imprint: London Publishd March 10ᵗʰ. 1785. by
J.R. Smith N° 83. Oxford Street.
Inscription: Shakespear Macbeth Act 1ˢᵗ. | Painted
by H. Fuseli | | Engraved by J.R. Smith
Mezzotinto Engraver to | his Royal Highness the
Prince of Wales | THE WEIRD SISTERS |

[left]
—each at once her choppy finger

[right]
laying upon her skinny Lips.

Dimensions: ■ 43.5 x 55.0 cm | 17²/16" x
21¹³/16" (BM 1870-5-14-1615)
Other locations: KHZ 1940/138 (44.0 x 55.0 cm);
MMA 59.570.361
Lit.: Schiff 733; Schiff-Viotto 1977, no. 55;
Calloway 1981, 62, repr. 63.

Variants:
I. Address in imprint changed: V & A Dyce
2928
Imprint: London Published March 10ᵗʰ. 1785.
by J.R. Smith N° 31 King Street Covent Garden
Other locations: Essick

73A. *The Weird Sisters*, 1786
(Shakespeare, *Macbeth*, I, iii)

Re-engraved in stipple by Peltro W. Tomkins
(1760-1840)
Imprint: London Published Augt. 30th. 1786 by T.
Macklin.
Inscription: H. Fuseli pinx^t. | | P.W. Tomkins
sculp^t. Pupil of F. Bartolozzi. | THE WITCHES. |

[*left*]
_____What are these
So wither'd, and so wild in their attire,
That look not like th'inhabitants o' th' earth,
And yet are on't? Live you or are you ought

[*right*]
That man may question? You seem to
   understand me
By each at once her choppy finger laying
Upon her skinny lips.
                    Shakespear__Macbeth.

Dimensions: ■ 19.9 x 25.2 cm | 7^13/16" x 9^15/16";
◼ 20.3 x 25.5 cm | 8" x 10^2/16" (YCBA
B1976.1.206).
Other locations: Essick (imprint cropped);
Huntington 181067, XX, 47 (23.4 x 26.0 cm)
Lit.: Schiff 733.
Exh.: New Haven 1981 (49).

Variants:
I. Proof before all letters (lacking title and
verse): BM 1849-5-12-256
Imprint: Publishd as the Act Directs Augt 1
1786 by T. Macklin
Other locations: Huntington 181067, XX, 46
II. Re-issued (1809) with new imprint: KHZ
1940/108
Imprint: Pub^d July 21. 1809, by T. Palser,
Surry Side, Westminster Bridge
Other locations: DHW

No. 73B.
THE | PLAYS AND POEMS | OF | SHAKSPEARE
| ACCORDING TO THE | IMPROVED TEXT OF
EDMUND MALONE, | INCLUDING THE
LATEST REVISIONS, | WITH, | A LIFE
GLOSSARIAL NOTES, AN INDEX, | AND |
ONE HUNDRED AND SEVENTY

ILLUSTRATIONS | FROM DESIGNS BY
ENGLISH ARTISTS. | EDITED BY | A.J.
VALPY, A.M. | FELLOW OF PEMBROKE
COLLEGE, OXFORD. | IN FIFTEEN
VOLUMES. | VOL. I. [-VOL. XV.] | LONDON: |
HENRY G. BOHN, YORK STREET, COVENT
GARDEN. | 1842.

For the other illustrations in this work, see Nos.
117D - 125D.

73B.

73B. *The Three Witches*, 1842
(front covers of Vols. V, VI)

Design embossed in gilt in panel on front cover
after No. **73.** by unknown engraver
Inscription (left): [*illegible*] ... Y
Dimensions (centre panel): ■ 7.7 x 9.8 cm |
3^1/16" x 3^14/16" (Illinois)

The same design is blind-stamped on the rear
covers of Vols. VII and X.

**73C. *Weird Sisters; Ministers of Darkness;
Minions of the Moon*, 1791**

Aquatint by James Gillray (1757-1815), parodying
Fuseli's *Weird Sisters*.
Imprint (lower right corner inside design):
Published Decr 23^d. 1791 | by H. Humphrey N°.
18. Old Bond Street.

Inscription (top): To H: Fuzelli Esq'. this attempt in the Caricatura-Sublime, is respectfully dedicated. | (bottom): WIERD-SISTERS; MINISTER'S of DARKNESS; MINIONS of the MOON. | -'They should be Women!-and yet their beards forbid us to interpret, - that they are so' - Dimensions (to plate mark): 25.5 x 35.5 cm | 10" x 14" (BM 1868-8-8-6144)
Other locations: Birmingham 190563,341; Fitzwilliam P.248-1948
Lit.: George 7937; D. Hill, *Fashionable Contrasts*, 138; Tomory 1972, pl. 249; Feaver 1981, repr. in colour top of p. 54

Exh.: New Haven 1981 (55).

Two years after the Regency crisis of 1789, Gillray expresses the persistent concern for the state of George III's sanity. The Home Secretary, Lord Dundas (1742-1811), the Prime Minister, William Pitt the Younger (1759-1806), and the Lord Chancellor, Lord Thurlow (1732-1806), are caricatured as Fuseli's three witches (here reversed). Thrumming their 'skinny lips' with their 'choppy finger,' the three members of the cabinet anxiously scan the profiles of Queen Charlotte and George III, representing the bright and dark sides of a double-faced moon.

73D.

No. 73D.
THE WORKS | OF | JAMES GILLRAY, | FROM THE | ORIGINAL PLATES, | WITH | THE ADDITION OF MANY SUBJECTS NOT BEFORE COLLECTED. | [Vignette] | LONDON: | PRINTED FOR HENRY G. BOHN, YORK STREET, COVENT GARDEN, | BY CHARLES WHITING. [1851] (1/582 illus.)

A facsimile reprint was published by Benjamin Blom (New York & London, 1968) under the title *The Works of James Gillray*. The volume includes a Supplement with the 45 'Suppressed Plates'.

73D. *Weird Sisters; Ministers of Darkness; Minions of the Moon*, 1851
(Plate No. 68)

Reissue (1851) of Gillray's aquatint with Plate no. ('68') added (Huntington 225625)
Other locations: Browne
Exh.: Kansas City 1982 (31).

******

For No. **73E** see the combined entry for *Füssli's Sämmtliche Werke* following No. **74A**.

******

No. 73F.
W.J. Linton.
THIRTY PICTURES | BY | DECEASED BRITISH ARTISTS | ENGRAVED EXPRESSLY FOR | THE ART-UNION OF LONDON | BY | W.J.LINTON. | LONDON (1860)

73F. *The Three Witches*, 1860
(No. XVI)

Engraved by William James Linton (1812-1898) from a drawing after Fuseli by William Bell Scott (1811-1890)
Dimensions: 15.0 x 20.0 cm | 15^{14}/16" x 7^{14}/16" (V & A E.223-1905)
Inscription (bottom left, within plate): W.J. LINTON | FUSELI. | | No. XVI.
Other locations: Ashmolean sm. fol. 928.9 Ein
Plate only: DHW

Variants:
I. Proof (India paper): NYPL MEM L.761.T

No. 73G.
THE|PORTFOLIO|AN ARTISTIC
PERIODICAL.|EDITED BY|P.G.
HAMERTON.|WITH NUMEROUS
ILLUSTRATIONS.| LONDON:|SEELEY,
JACKSON, AND HALLIDAY, FLEET
STREET.|1873 (1/45 illus.).

73G. *The Three Witches*, 1873
(Sidney Colvin, 'From Rigaud to Reynolds:
Characteristics of French and English Paintings in
the 18th Century. XIV. Henry Fuseli (1741-
1825)', pp. 50-48 [56])
(facing p. 52)

Drawn on stone by E.H. Mitchell after Fuseli.
Dimensions: ■ 17 x 21.7 cm | $6^{11}/16''$ x $8^9/16''$
(BL P.P. 1931.pcd)
Other locations: NYPL

******

74. *The Death of Oedipus*, 1785
(Sophocles, *Oedipus at Colonus*, 1606-1628)

Mezzotint engraved by William Ward (1766-1826)
after the painting exhibited at the Royal Academy
(1784/147) and now in the Walker Art Gallery,
Liverpool (1784; Schiff 712)
Imprint: London Publish'd Augt. 26th 1785 by J R
Smith N° 83 Oxford Street.
Inscription: Painted by H. Fuseli.||Engraved by
W. Ward.|THE DEATH OF OEDIPUS|

[*left*]
Κτυπησε μεν Ζεὺς χθόνιος αἱ δὲ παρθὲνοι
῾Ρίγησαν ως ἤκουσαν, ἐς δὲ γόυνατα
Πατρὸς πεσουσαι, κλωον.—ΣΟΦ. Ο. ΕΠΙ
ΚΟΛ.

[*right*]
In Thunders call'd the god beneath the blast
with horror struck his Daughters, on his knees
they fell and wept.

Dimensions: ■ 44.0 x 55.3 cm | $17^5/16''$ x 21¾ "
(KHZ 1940/128)
Other locations: MMA 59.570.360
Lit.: Julia Frankau, *William Ward A.R.A.*, 1904,
no. 86 (p. 179); Schiff 712; Macandrew 1959-
1960, 24f.; Schiff-Viotto 1977, no. 23.

Variants:
I. Change in address (not in Frankau): DHW
Imprint: London Publish'd Augt. 26th 1785 by
JR Smith N° 31 King's S^t. Covent Garden.
II. Other locations: V & A Dyce 3027

Fuseli's illustration depicts blind Oedipus in the
grove of the Eumenides at Colonus receiving the
summons of death. The scene is described by
Allan Cunningham thus:

> The desolate old man is seated on the ground,
> and his whole frame seems inspired with a
> presentiment of the coming vengeance of
> heaven. His daughters [*Antigone and Ismene*]
> are clasping him wildly, and the sky seems
> mustering the thunder and fire in which the
> tragic bard made him disappear. 'Pray, Sir,
> what is that old man afraid of?' said some one
> to Fuseli when the picture was exhibited.
> 'Afraid, Sir', exclaimed the painter, 'why
> afraid of going to hell!' (*Lives of the British
> Painters*, 2nd ed., 1830, II, 290).

Gert Schiff lists two mezzotints of this subject,
one supposedly by John Raphael Smith and the
other by Ward (1973, nos. 712, 712A; Schiff-
Viotto 1977, no. 23); however, I have been
unable to locate any version by J.R. Smith. Since
this engraving is also not documented in Julia
Frankau's catalogue (1902), I assume that Schiff's
reference is an oversight.

******

For No. **74A.** see the combined entry for *Fuessli's
Sämmtliche Werke* following No. **74.**

******

Nos. 70A - 71A, 72C, 73E, 74A.
**[Heinrich Füssli, Johann Jakob Horner & Felix
Nüscheler].**
[Overall title]: HEINRICH FUESSLI'S
SÄMMTLICHE WERKE,|NEBST EINEM
VERSUCH SEINER BIOGRAPHIE.|—|
ZÜRICH, 1807.|IN DER KUNSTHANDLUNG
VON FUESSLI UND COMPAGNIE.

[Wrappers]: HEINRICH FUESSLI'S|
SÆMMTLICHE WERKE|—|ERSTES HEFT.
[ZWEYTES HEFT.]| ZÜRICH, 1807. [-1809.]|
IN DER KUNSTHANDLUNG VON FUESSLI
UND COMPAGNIE (16/16 illus.).

For the other illustrations in this work see also
Nos. **13A, 275-283.**

THE DEATH OF OEDIPUS

74.

70A. *Belisane and Percival Under the Enchantment of Urma*, 1807
(Part II, No. 16, facing p. 16)

Unsigned outline engraving by Johann Heinrich Lips (1758-1817)
Inscription: **Belisane und Perceval**
Dimensions: ■ 22.2 x 28.4 cm | 8¾" x 11³/16" (ZBZ KK 307)
Other locations: DHW; ETH 1524a; KHZ D33
Plate only: MMA 55.526.6
Lit.: Schiff 717; Lonchamp 1920, no. 225; Schiff-Viotto 1977, no. 35

Variants:
I. Proof before letters: KHZ C4/IIIA, 1220

71A. *Lady Macbeth Walking in her Sleep*, [1807-1809]
(Shakespeare, *Macbeth*, V, i)
(Part I, No. 4, between pp. 2-3)

Outline engraving by Christoph G. Oberkogler (1774-1850)
Inscription: **Lady Macbeth.** | (bottom left, in pencil): Chr. G. Oberkogler

Dimensions: ■ 28.0 x 20.4 cm | 11" x 8" (KHZ D33)
Other locations: DHW; ETH 1524a; ETH 545/133; Bern A16,441 (facing p. 3); Lucerne H36 gr.fol.; YCBA folio B.N.29 (not seen)
Lit.: Lonchamp 1920, no. 225; Schiff-Viotto 1977, no. 61

72C. *Lear Awakens to Find Cordelia Beside his Bed*, 1809
(Shakespeare, *King Lear*, IV, vi)
(Part I, No. 10, facing p. 10)

Outline engraving by Johann Heinrich Lips (1758-1817)
Inscription (bottom right): H. Lips. sc. | **Lear und Cordelia**
Dimensions: ■ 22.0 x 27.6 cm | 8¹⁰/16" x 10¹⁴/16" (KHZ D33)
Other locations: DHW; ETH 545/130 (in pencil: 'H Füssli inv:'); ETH 1524a; Bern A16.441; Lucerne H.36 gr.fol.; YCBA folio B.N.29; ZBZ KK307
Lit.: Schiff 741; Lonchamp 1920, no. 225

Variants:
I. Proof before letters: KHZ C6/IIIA, 1267

73E. *The Three Witches*, [1807-1809]
(Shakespeare, *Macbeth*, I, iii)
(Part I, No. 11, before p. 11)

Outline engraving by Johann Heinrich Lips (1758-1817)
Inscription (bottom right): H Lips. sc.│**Die drey Hexen**
Dimensions: ■ 21.8 x 28.0 cm │ 8¹⁰/16" x 11"
(ZBZ KK307)
Other locations: Bern A16.441 (facing p. 11);
DHW; ETH 1524a; ETH 545/129 (in pencil: 'H Füssli inv:'); Lucerne H 36 gr.fol. YCBA folio B.N.29 (not seen); ZBZ KK 307 (facing p. 11)
Lit.: Schiff 733 (as by 'F.Hegi'); Lonchamp 1920, no. 225; Todd 1947, repr. 77; Schiff-Viotti 1977, no. 55

74A. *The Death of Oedipus*, [1807-1809]
(Sophocles, *Oedipus at Colonus*, 1605-1607)
(Part I, No. 9, facing p. 9)

Outline engraving by Franz Hegi (1774-1850)
Inscription (bottom right): F Hegi sc.│**Der Tod des Oedipus**
Dimensions: ■ 22.8 x 30.3 cm │ 8¹⁵/16" x 11¹⁵/16" (ZBZ KK 307)
Other locations: Bern A16,441; DHW; ETH 1524a; KHZ D33 (between pp. 8-9); Lucerne H.36 gr.fol; YCBA folio B.N.29 (not seen)
Plate only: MMA 55.526.11 (defaced)
Lit.: Appenzeller 602; Schiff 712; Schiff-Viotto 1977, no. 23

******

No. 75.
John Bonnycastle.
AN│INTRODUCTION│TO│ASTRONONOMY.│
IN A│SERIES OF LETTERS,│FROM A│
PRECEPTOR TO HIS PUPIL.│IN WHICH THE
MOST USEFUL AND INTERESTING PARTS
OF THE│ SCIENCE ARE CLEARLY AND
FAMILIARLY EXPLAINED.│ILLUSTRATED
WITH COPPER-PLATES.│─│BY JOHN
BONNYCASTLE,│OF THE ROYAL MILITARY
ACADEMY, WOOLWICH.│—*Docuit quae
maximus Atlas,│Hic canit errantem Lunam,
Solisque labores.│*VIRGIL.│— │ LONDON,│
PRINTED FOR J. JOHNSON, NO. 72, ST.
PAUL'S│CHURCH-YARD.│MDCCLXXXVI
[1786] (1/21 illus.).

...THE SECOND EDITION, CORRECTED
AND IMPROVED.│—*Docuit quae maximus*

*Atlas,│Hic canit errantem Lunam, Solisque
labores.│* VIRGIL.│*Into the heav'ns I have
presum'd,│An earthly guest, and drawn empyreal
air.│MILTON.│* LONDON,│PRINTED FOR J.
JOHNSON, NO. 72, ST. PAUL'S│CHURCH-
YARD.│MDCCLXXXVII [1787].

...IN WHICH THE MOST USEFUL AND
INTERESTING│PARTS OF THE SCIENCE
ARE CLEARLY AND│FAMILIARLY
EXPLAINED.│—│THE FOURTH EDITION,
CORRECTED AND IMPROVED.│BY JOHN
BONNYCASTLE│PROFESSOR OF
MATHEMATICS IN THE ROYAL ACADEMY,
│WOOLWICH.│-│[*Verses*]│—│ LONDON:│
PRINTED FOR J. JOHNSON, NO. 72, ST.
PAUL'S│CHURCHYARD.│=│1803.

...THE FIFTH EDITION, CORRECTED AND
IMPROVED.│[*Verses*]│—│LONDON:│PRINTED
FOR J. JOHNSON, NO. 72, ST. PAUL'S│
CHURCHYARD.│=│1807 (1/19 illus.).

...THE SIXTH EDITION, CORRECTED AND
IMPROVED.│—│[*Verses*]│—│ LONDON:│
PRINTED FOR J. JOHNSON AND CO.,│ST.
PAUL'S CHURCH-YARD.│1811 (1/17 illus.).

...THE SEVENTH EDITION,│CORRECTED,
AND GREATLY IMPROVED.│—│[*Verses*]│=│
LONDON:│PRINTED FOR J. NUNN; LAW
AND WHITTAKER; CADELL│AND DAVIES;
LONGMAN, HURST, REES, ORME AND CO.;
│J. RICHARDSON; J. MAWMAN; BALDWIN,
CRADOCK, AND│JOY; GALE AND FENNER;
AND J. ROBINSON.│—│1816.

...THE EIGHTH EDITION.│CORRECTED,
AND GREATLY IMPROVED.│—│[*Verses*]│—│
LONDON:│PRINTED FOR J. NUNN; CADELL
AND DAVIES; LONGMAN, HURST,│REES,
ORME AND BROWN; JOHN RICHARDSON; J.
MAWMAN;│BALDWIN, CRADOCK AND
JOY; T. HAMILTON; G. AND W.B.│
WHITTAKER; JOHN ROBINSON, AND
SIMPKIN AND MARSHALL.│1822.

**75. *Aratus the Poet and Urania the Muse of
Astronomy*, 1786**
(facing the title page)

Engraved frontispiece by John Keyse Sherwin
(1751-1790)

Imprint (across full width of page): London
Published as the Act directs 17 May 1786 by J.
Johnson in S^t. Pauls Church Yard
Inscription (top left): Frontispiece. | (bottom right):
I.K. Sherwin sculp^t.
Dimensions: ■ 15.3 x 8.6 cm | 6^1/16" x 3^7/16";
▣ 15.5 x 8.8 cm | 6^2/16" x 3½" (NYPL 3-OMP)
Other locations: BL 8562.dd.5 (1796) (hand
coloured); BL 8561.e.22 (1803); Bodleian
(Radcliff) (not seen) (1803); DHW (1803)
Plate only: BM 1863-5-9-38; Huntington 140092
(Vol. V, after title page) (globe marked with
continents); R.A. Anderdon, X, 118 (imprint
cropped, top line of inscription shaved)
Lit.: Schiff 790 (15.6 x 8.8); Hammelmann 1975,
34 (as 'unsigned frontispiece').
Exh.: Kansas City 1982 (8).

Variants:
I. Globe not marked: BL 531.i.9
Inscription (top centre): FRONTISPIECE. |
(bottom right): I.K. Sherwin sculp^t.
Other locations: Cambridge L.51.9; Bodleian
Douce BB 698; Library Company Io Bonn

Aratus of Soli in Cilicia (315?-239? B.C.) was
the poet of the *Phaenomena* (or 'Heavenly
Display') and of *Diosemia* (or Prognostics), a
treatise on the signs of the weather. These works
enjoyed great popularity in antiquity, particularly
among the Romans, who produced three
translations of the *Phaenomena*.

Fuseli's illustration is in the spirit of the verses
cited by Bonnycastle (p. 3) from Dryden's
translation of Vergil's *Georgics* (II, 673-684):

Ye sacred Muses! with whose beauty fir'd,
My soul is ravish'd, and my brain inspir'd;
Whose priest I am, whose holy fillets wear;
Would you your poet's first petition hear;
Give me the ways of wand'ring stars to know,
The depths of heav'n above, and earth below:
Teach me the various labours of the moon,
And whence proceed th' eclipses of the sun;
Why flowing tides prevail upon the main,
And in what dark recess they shrink again;
What shakes the solid earth; what cause delays
The summer nights, and shortens winter days.

75A. 1787 (without inscription)
Imprint: Pub. 27 May. 1786. by J. Johnson. S^t.
Pauls Church Yard London.
Dimensions: 15.2 x 8.5 cm (BL 8562.d.16)
Other locations: Geneva KB 85; NYPL OMP

75.

75B. 1807, 1811
Imprint: Pub. 27. May 1786, by J. Johnson S^t.
Pauls Church Yard London.
Inscription (bottom right): Fuseli Delin^t. | | Sherwin
Sculp^t.
Dimensions: ■ 15.2 x 8.6 cm (BL 8561.e.23)
Other locations: BL 8562.dd.7 (1811); Bodleian
Rigaud.e.57 (title on spine: 'Bonnycastle
Trigonometry'); Huntington 25077 (Keats's copy);
LC QB45.B7 1807; Princeton 8407.197
Lit.: Hammelmann 1975, 34 (inscription given as
'Fuseli delineavit')

75C. 1816, 1822
Imprint: Published June 18. 1816, by J Robinson,
Paternoster Row, London.
Inscription: Fuseli Delin^t. | | Sherwin Sculp^t.
Dimensions: ■ 15.1 x 8.5 cm (BL 8561.d.29)
Other locations: BL 8562.d.8 (1822); Duke
520.B718I; Essick; Geneva Kb 86; Lausanne AZ
2222; ZBZ AS 390

******

76.

No. 76.
Theophilus Swift.
The | Temple of Folly, | in Four Cantos. | By
Theophilus Swift, Esq. | Εξαπατασθαι αυτον ὑφ᾽
αυτου, παντων χαλεπωτατον. | *PLAT. CRAT.* |
[Flower vignette] | LONDON: | PRINTED FOR J.
JOHNSON, Nº 72, ST. PAUL'S CHURCH
YARD. | M.DCC.LXXXVII [1787] (1/1 illus.)

[Half-title]: — | THE | TEMPLE OF FOLLY. | — |
[PRICE FIVE SHILLINGS.]

The quotation on the title page is from Plato's
Cratylus (D428). It translates as 'The worst of
all deceptions is self-deception.'

76. *The Mighty Mother Sails Through the Air*,
1787
(*The Temple of Folly,* Canto IV)
(facing title page)

Etched frontispiece by Henry Fuseli after his own
pen and ink drawing in the British Museum
([1787]; Schiff 843)
Imprint (bottom left): Published June 1ˢᵗ. 1787 by
J. Johnson Nº. 72 Sᵗ. Pauls Church Yard London.
Inscription (at lower right on globe):
Πανδαματωϱ

Dimensions: 23.3 x 18.8 cm | 9³/16" x 7⁶/16" (BL
1346.i.46) (H=27.6 cm).
Plate only: YCBA B1977.14.11499 (inscr. in
pencil, in unknown hand): Etched by Fuseli.

Variants:
I. Lacking imprint: Newberry Case.Y185.S9751
(H=24.2 cm)
Other locations: Bodleian Pamph.1709.11 (not
seen); Monash (not seen); NYPL NCI p.v.191
(3) (hand coloured)
Plate only: BM 1863-5-9-6 (Sheet=31.0 cm)
Lit.: Schiff 844 (as 'Fortune Hovering Over the
Globe') (23.3 x 18.8 cm)

The eccentric Irish controversialist, Theophilus
Swift (1746-1815), was the son of Deane Swift,
the cousin and biographer of Jonathan Swift.
Fuseli had probably met the latter-day satirist at
the house of the publisher Joseph Johnson. The
relationship of the two men is otherwise
undocumented and was probably slight. However,
Fuseli would no doubt have found considerable
appeal in the substantial allusions to Greek
literature and mythology in Swift's learned satire
in the form of a dream vision. There is no way of
knowing to what extent, if any, Fuseli might in
fact have contributed to its philological waggery.

Traditionally considered to represent *Fortune
Hovering Over the Globe*, Fuseli's unsigned
etching was only recently identified by Robert N.
Essick as an illustration to *The Temple of Folly*,
when he found it reproduced as the frontispiece to
bookseller Stuart Bennett's catalogue X, *English
Verse 1751-1800*. Fuseli's design is strongly
reminiscent of Dürer's two depictions of *Fortuna*
as *das Grosse* and *das Kleine Glück* (Walter L.
Strauss, *The Complete Engravings, Etchings and
Drypoints of Albrecht Dürer*, 1981, nos. 37 and
7), but with conflated attributes.

Fuseli's figure, with her fools cap surmounted
by a crescent moon, represents Folly. Two
separate elements from Dürer, Fortune's cane and
the spray of the thistle-like plant eryngium that
she is holding in her hand, have been combined to
form Folly's wand, while the blossoms or berries
of the eryngo have become the round objects—
whether seeds or worlds—being shaken into
Folly's goblet. The globe on which Folly stands is
a balloon rather than the globular stone or the
'sphere of uncertainty' in Dürer's engravings.

The 1780s' fascination with 'aerostatics' in the aftermath of the first successful balloon ascents in France and England was reflected in the numerous cartoons of the period. Swift was thus not the first to attempt to mine the subject for literary satire. F. Nevill Jackson quotes from a contemporary satire which makes a very similar point about human pridefulness to that being made in Swift's poem: Lunardi's ascents represent a danger to the East India Company since these might teach 'the Company's servants, who are already above their masters, to ascend still higher' ('Balloon Caricatures', *Connoisseur*, May-August 1915, 84).

Moria/Folly is conceived by Swift in the spirit of Pope's Goddess of Dulness (*Dunciad*) or Dryden's 'Mother-Strumpets' (*Mac Flecknoe*, 64-73). This enables him to relate Folly as the 'Mighty Mother' explicitly to the mythological 'Magna Mater', i.e. to 'Cybele, who was the supposed mother of all the gods' (I, 281 & note). Fuseli is clearly aware that Dürer's image 'places her among the matriarchs' (Strauss, 76). Hence also the Greek word, Πανδαματωρ, that Fuseli appends below Folly's right foot to designate the Great Mother, although the word is used in Homer to refer rather to 'all-conquering' sleep. (Cf. Book IV of the *Dunciad*, 639-640:

> Thus at her felt approach, and secret might,
> *Art* after *Art* goes out, and all is night.)

There is also a certain discrepancy between Swift's text and Fuseli's illustration, insofar that it is actually Moria's daughter, 'the court belle, possessed of every *accomplishment* that can adorn a well-bred woman' ('Argument to the Second Canto', p. 28), whose 'ambitious spirit mounts the moon,|Thron'd with Lunardi in his proud Balloon' (II, 195f.).

******

Nos. 77 - 78.
Thomas Macklin.
BRITISH POETS, [ONE HUNDRED PICTURES |PRINTS ILLUSTRATIVE OF THE MOST CELEBRATED BRITISH POETS...WITH LETTER-PRESS EXPLANATORY OF THE SUBJECT, EXTRACTED FROM THE WRITINGS OF THE RESPECTIVE POETS. PARTS I-VI]. 1788-1799 (2/24 illus.).

PROSPECTUS
(National Library of Wales)

PROPOSALS
FOR
MACKLIN'S BRITISH POETS.

This Work is, by Permission, dedicated to|HIS ROYAL HIGHNESS THE PRINCE OF WALES;|And illustrative of the most celebrated BRITISH POETS;|PARTICULARLY,|Chaucer, Skelton, Sydney, Spencer, Shakespeare, Drayton, Johnson, Fletcher, Massinger, Phineas Fletcher, Milton, Donne, Crashaw, Randolph, Cowley, Waller, Denham, Butler, Otway, Dryden, Southern, Smith, Phillips, Congreve, Rowe, Addison, Pope, Swift, Gay, Prior, Parnell, Young, Collins, Hammond, Savage, Thomson, Mallet, Ramsay, Akenside, Armstrong, Cunningham, Churchill, Goldsmith, Gray, Jago, Johnson, Chatterton, Mason, Warton, Hayley, Jerningham, Cowper, Pinkerton, Sargent, T. Swift, Burns, Gregory, Williams, Carter, Barbauld, Seward, More, Smith, &c.

CONDITIONS.
I. One hundred Pictures of the most interesting Subjects from the Poets of *Great Britain*, to be painted by the following Masters:

[*col. 1*]
Sir Joshua Reynolds,
  President of the Royal Academy.
Mr. Artaud.
Mr. Barry, Professor of Painting
  to the Royal Academy, and R.A.
Mr. Bigg.
Mr. Cosway, Painter to His Royal
Highness the Prince of Wales,
  and R.A.
Mrs. Cosway
Mr. Fuseli.
Mr. Gainsborough, R.A.
Mr. Hamilton, R.A.
Mr. Harding.
Mr. Hoare

[*col. 2*]
Mrs. Angelica Kauffman, R.A.
Mr. Loutherbourg, R.A
Mr. Martin.

Mr. Nixon.
Mr. Opie, R.A.
Mr. Pocock, of *Bristol*.
Mr. Peters, R.A. whose Subjects, already engaged for, are from *Milton*, and *Young*.
Mr. Rigaud, R.A.
Mr. Stothard.
Mr. West, Historical Painter to His Majesty, and R.A.
And others as may be found equal to this Undertaking.

II. This work will be engraved from the beforementioned Pictures, by Mr. *Bartolozzi*, his School, and other eminent Artists.
III. The Work will be published in Numbers, each Number containing FOUR PRINTS; with Letter-Press, explanatory of the Subject, extracted from the Writings of the respective Poets: the Size of each Print to be 18 inches by 14: the Price, to Subscribers, Three Guineas; to Nonsubscribers, Four Guineas. Proofs, Six Guineas; and in Colours, Eight Guineas the Number.

Half the Money to be paid at the Time of subscribing, and the Remainder on Delivery of each Number.

The Numbers shall be delivered in the Order they are subscribed for.

Two Numbers will be published each Year, till the Design is completed.

The scheme was never completed: the series was suspended in 1799 after six numbers (24 prints) had appeared (see Boase 1963, 148-155). Macklin died in 1800 and his pictures were sold by Peter Coxe, Burrell, & Foster, 27-30 May 1801. For details of the pictures auctioned, see Fredericksen 1988-, I, 9f., 1011.

QUEEN KATHARINE'S DREAM
No 1 of the British Poets

77.

77. *Queen Katharine's Dream*, 1788
(Shakespeare, *King Henry VIII*, IV, ii)
(No. 1)

Stipple engraving in brown by Francesco
Bartolozzi (1725-1815)
Imprint: London, Publish'd April 4th. 1788 by
Thos. Macklin No. 39 Fleet Street.
Inscription: Fuseli Pinxt.||F. Bartolozzi R,A, &
Engraver to his Majesty Sculpt.|QUEEN
KATHARINE'S DREAM|Vide Shakespear's
Henry 8th.|No. 1 of the British Poets.
Dimensions: 35.5 x 45.4 cm | 14" x 17¹⁵/₁₆" (BL
3.tab.43)
Other locations (plate only): BM 1859.7.9.732;
BM 1859-7-9-731; BM 1863-5-9-51; Browne;
Essick; ETH 428 (cut down inside platemark;

imprint lacking); Basel 1938.83; KHZ B41;
YCBA B1976.1.107 P55
Lit.: Schiff 729 (45.7 x 35.5 cm); de Vesme
1928, no. 1427; Boase 1963, 153, pl. 20c;
Hammelman 1975, 34, pl. 45; Schiff-Viotto 1977,
no. 50, pl. 50¹
Exh.: Kansas City 1982 (20)

Variants:
I. Unfinished proof (etched state) (de Vesme
1427/I) (not seen)
Imprint (scratched letters): 'July 20 1787.'
II. Proof before all letters (inscription erased)
(de Vesme 1427/2) (not seen).
III. Proof (title in open letters) (de Vesme
1427/3) (not seen).
IV. Coloured impression: YCBA B1978.43.232
(35.3 x 45.0 cm)

PRINCE ARTHURS VISION.
Nº 1 of the British Poets.

78.

This engraving shows Queen Katharine, the divorced queen of King Henry VIII, the night before her execution, when the 'Spirits of peace' appear to her in a dream to console her and dance and pay reverence to her. Fuseli depicts them clad in white and wearing garlands but omits their 'golden vizards'. The sleeping Queen is represented 'as it were by inspiration [*making*] signs of rejoicing' and holding up her hands to heaven. This was the only Shakespearean subject published in Macklin's series of British Poets.

78. *Prince Arthur's Vision*, 1788
(Edmund Spenser, *The Faerie Queene*, I, ix, 13)
(No. 1)

Aquatint engraving in brown by Peltro W. Tomkins (1760-1840)
Imprint: London Publish'd April 4. 1788 by Thos. Macklin Nᵒ. 39 Fleet Street.
Inscription: H. Fuseli pinxt.||P. W. Tomkins Sculpt. late Pupil of F. Bartolozzi|PRINCE ARTHURS VISION.|Vide Spencers Fairy Queen|Nᵒ. 1 of the British Poets.
Dimensions: 45.2 x 35.4 cm | 17¾" x 13¹⁴/16" (BL 3.tab.43)
Other locations (plate only): Basel 1936.39 (cut down within platemark); BM 1859-7-9-731 (not seen); Browne; DHW; ETH 422; KHZ B43; MMA 42.119.356; V & A E.1189-1886 (imprint cut off); V & A E.1188-1886 (not seen)
Lit.: Vesme & Calabi, 1928, no. 1430; Boase 1963, 153, pl. 20d; Schiff 721A; Tomory 1972, pl. 157; Hammelmann 1975, 35; Bradley 1980, 39, pl. 10a-10b; *Letters*, 33, 231-232.

Variants:
I. Proof before all engraved letters (lacking title), dated 1787: Essick
Imprint (scratched letters): London Publish'd as the Act directs Aust. 16 1787 by T Macklin Fleet Street.
Inscription (scratched letters): Painted by H Fuseli||Engravd by P W Tomkins late pupil of F Bartolozzi
II. Proof (title in open letters) (de Vesme 1430/2) (not seen)
III. Colour-printed impression (cropped) (lacking imprint and all but 1st line of inscription): Essick

Prince Arthur has come to Faerie Land to find

the Faerie Queen with whom he had fallen in love after being visited by her in a dream as in this illustration of the following lines:

> For-wearied with my sports, I did alight
> From loftie steed, and downe to sleepe me layd;
> The verdant gras my couch did goodly dight,
> And pillow was my helmete fair displayd:
> Whiles every sence the humour sweet embayd,
> And slombring soft my hart did steal away,
> Me seemed, by my side a royall Mayd
> Her daintie limbes full softly down did lay:
> So faire a creature yet saw never sunny day.

But for Fuseli the next two stanzas, describing the love-wildered knight's sorrow and despair upon finding her gone, provide 'soul, action, passion' (undated letter, c. 1800). In contrast to Fuseli's interpretation of Gloriana's character in his earlier drawing of 1769 (Schiff 337), Laurel Bradley sees Fuseli in this design deflating in typically ironic fashion a lofty subject: the 'powerful upright figure [*of Gloriana*] in a clinging garment and fashionable hat gestur[*ing*] imperiously' towards the passive knight becomes 'a materialisation of Arthur's erotic dreams rather than a spirit inspiring virtuous action' (1980, 47).

******

79. *Theseus Receiving the Thread from Ariadne*, 1788
(Virgil, *Aeneid*, VI, 27)

Mezzotint engraved by John Raphael Smith (1752-1812) after the original painting exhibited at the Royal Academy (1788/235) and now in the Kunsthaus, Zurich (1788; Schiff 714).
Imprint: London Publish'd July 14ᵗʰ 1788: by J.R. Smith Nᵒ 31: King Street Covent Garden.
Inscription: Painted by H. Fuseli.||Engraved by J.R. Smith. Mezzotinto Engraver to His Royal|Highness the Prince of Wales & His Serene Highness the Duke of Orleans|ARIADNE and THESEUS.|

[*left*]
When to your hands the fatal clew I gave,
Which thro' the winding Laby'rinth led you safe
Then how you lov'd! Dryden

[*right*]
Hic Labor ille domus, et inextrcabilis error.
—Ipsa dolos tecti ambagesque resolvit
Caeca regens filo vestiga. virg. AEn. VI.

Dimensions: 61.7 x 45.3 cm | 24⁶/16" x 17¹³/16" (BM 1887-7-22-209)
Other locations: KHZ B43
Lit.: Schiff 714A (61.6 x 45.2 cm) (not reproduced); Frankau 1902, no. 13.

Variants:
I. Coloured impression (imprint cropped): KHZ 1940/137
Inscription: 'inextricabilis'
II. 'loved,' 'inextrcabilis,' 'vestiga': Basel 16256

As related by Ovid (*Metamorphoses*, VIII, 172-173) and Virgil, each year Athens was required to send as a tribute to Crete seven youths and maidens to be sacrificed to the minotaur. This monster, half animal and half man, the fruit of Pasiphae's unnatural passion for a favourite bull, dwelt in the impenetrable labyrinth built by Daedalus. Fuseli's illustration shows Theseus, the peripatetic hero, receiving from a besmitten Ariadne the clue, i.e. the ball of thread which will allow him to retrace his path after he has slain the monster.

Following the authority of Virgil, Fuseli has depicted the minotaur as a centaur-like figure with a human torso and head equipped with short curved horns on a bull's body rather than as a beast with a bull's head on a human body. Tradition sanctions both forms of representation: early Greek vases depicted the creature rather arbitrarily in both fashions, while the Middle Ages almost always portrayed him as a centaur (A.G. Ward, et al., *The Quest for Theseus*, 1970, 32, 165, 189).

In a later rendering of the subject, circa 1815-1820 (Schiff 1488; not engraved), Fuseli places more emphasis on the actual contest with the minotaur rather than dwelling, as here, almost exclusively on the romantic aspects of the hero's relationship with Ariadne.

79.

80.

No. 80.
John Caspar Lavater.
APHORISMS ON MAN: | TRANSLATED |
FROM THE ORIGINAL MANUSCRIPT | OF |
THE REV. JOHN CASPAR LAVATER, |
CITIZEN OF ZURIC. | — | *è coelo descendit* γνωθι
σεαυτον. | *Juv. Sat. IX.* [sic] | — |
LONDON: | PRINTED FOR J. JOHNSON, ST.
PAUL'S CHURCH-YARD. | — |
MDCCLXXXVIII [1788] (1/1 illus.)

...SECOND EDITION. | = | LONDON, |
PRINTED BY T. BENSLEY, | FOR J.
JOHNSON, ST. PAUL'S CHURCH-YARD. | — |
M,DCC,LXXXIX [1789].

...THIRD EDITION. | = | LONDON, | PRINTED
FOR J. JOHNSON, ST. PAUL'S CHURCH- |
YARD. | — | M,DCC,XCIV [1794].

80. *Seated Man, Perhaps Representing the
Author of the Aphorisms, Consulting a Tablet in*

Greek Held up to Him by the Muse, 1788
(facing title page)

Frontispiece engraved by William Blake (1757-
1827) after Fuseli's sketch in the Essick
collection, Altadena, California (1788; Schiff
831a-b)
Inscription (bottom right): Blake. sc
Dimensions: ■ 12.1 x 7.5 cm | 4¾ " x 2¹⁵/₁₆"
(BL 98.a.20).
Other locations: Bern L Theol.3.304 (1794); BL
8413.aa.26 (1794) (H=16.2 cm); BL 08407.e.53
(1789); Bodleian 270.g.282; Bodleian 2784.f.8
(1789); Bodleian Vet.A5f.3583 (bound with
'Fuseli's Aphorisms on Art'); Cambridge
7180.d.174; Dörrbecker (1789); Essick; Essick
(1789); Fitzwilliam P.566.1985; Huntington 57431
(Blake's own annotated copy); Iowa xPT
2392.L2A3.1794; NYPL YFH (1789); Yale
Hkc7.280r (1794); ZBZ AX 6474 (1789)
Plate only: BM 1863-11-14-487 (1789); Essick;
LC Rosenwald 1838.13 (iii)
Lacking plate: Library Company Ia Lava;
Princeton Ex 3467.85.312.6.1788
Lit.: Schiff 789, 831a-b; Russell 1912, no. 68;
Hammelmann 1957, 355f., repr. facing 350;
Bentley & Nurmi 1964, no. 389; Todd 1971-
1972, 173-181; Hammelmann 1975, 34; Schroyer
1977, 23-26, repr. 24; Schiff-Viotto 1977, repr.
84; Easson & Essick 1979, no. XXXII; Essick
1980, 19-20, 51-52; Schroyer 1980; Hall 1985,
127-137, repr. [126]; Essick 1988, 10-11; Essick
1991, no. XVIII
Exh.: Kansas City 1982.

Variants:

I. Plate reworked (1794): LC Rosenwald 1831
Other locations: Essick; LC PT2392.L2A3 1794
Toner; Princeton Ex 3467.85.312.6 (1794)
Plate only: LC Rosenwald 1838.13 (i)

Essick (1991, 40f.) interprets this design as
representing Lavater composing his aphorisms,
'and perhaps also Fuseli in the act of translating
and editing his friend's words. The hovering
presence is the muse, revealing the insights into
human nature communicated by the aphorisms in
the volume'. The Greek motto was inscribed on
the temple at Delphi; it is quoted by Juvenal in his
eleventh Satire. This line, given on the title page
of Lavater's work, translates as 'From heaven
descends the maxim, *Know thyself* (Juvenal, *The*

Sixteen Satires, trans. Peter Green, Penguin, 1967, 228).

Essick provides a detailed description of the reworkings that characterise the second and third states of the plate, which 'appear with about equal frequency in copies of the 1794 edition'.

As was also the case with his design for the *Fertilization of Egypt* (No. **115**), Fuseli provided Blake with only a sketchy outline for the frontispiece to the *Aphorisms*. Ruthven Todd is undoubtedly correct when he says that 'for a short period, roughly from late 1787 to early 1792, [*Fuseli and Blake*] were in closer contact and enjoyed more absolute sympathy with each other than at any other time during their friendship' (1971-1972, 179), but it should be noted that Fuseli also gave other engravers to whom he was much less close similar rough visual hints to work up. See, for example, the sketch in the Swedish National Museum from which John June engraved *David and Goliath* (No. **27**) for Willoughby's *Practical Family Bible*, 1772.

Carol Louise Hall has shown how far Fuseli went beyond the usual role of translator in his treatment of Lavater's aphorisms: he also made important editorial decisions, selecting and modifying Lavater's *Regeln*, and creating others out of whole cloth, to give them appropriate English dress and transform loose sayings into pithy aphorisms (131-137).

******

No. 80A.
John Caspar Lavater.
APHORISMS ON MAN. | TRANSLATED | FROM THE ORIGINAL MANUSCRIPT | OF | THE REV. JOHN CASPAR LAVATER, | CITIZEN OF ZURIC. | — | è coelo descendit γνωθι σεαυτον. | *JUV. Sat. IX.* [sic] | — | THIRD EDITION. | = | DUBLIN, | PRINTED BY W. SLEATER, DAME-STREET, | AND P. BYRNE, GRAFTON-STREET. | — | M,DCC,XC [1790] (1/1 illus.).

80A. *Seated Man Consulting a Tablet in Greek Held up to Him by the Muse*, 1790 (Facing title page)

Re-engraved (1790) by Patrick Maguire (fl. 1790-1820) from frontispiece of the first edition.

Inscription: P. Maguire Sculpt.
Dimensions: 11.8 x 7.4 cm | 4¹⁰/16" x 2¹⁴/16" (Cambridge Hib.7.790.27)
Other locations: DHW; Library Company Dg.1024.D; Library Company; Western Ontario
Lacking plate: BL 8407.cc.20
Lit.: Bentley and Nurmi 389A, who state there is no plate in this Dublin edition (Since rectified in Part III of 'A Supplement to *Blake Books*,' *Blake*, XI, 1977-1978), 149);Schroyer 1977, 26, repr. 25

******

No. 80B.
John Caspar Lavater.
APHORISMS ON MAN. | TRANSLATED | FROM THE ORIGINAL MANUSCRIPT | OF THE | REV. JOHN CASPAR LAVATER, | CITIZEN OF ZURIC. | — | —è coelo descendit γνωθι σεαυτον. | *JUV. Sat. IX.* [sic] | = | THIRD EDITION. | = | T&JS | = | LONDON: PRINTED. | NEW YORK: RE-PRINTED BY T. AND J. SWORDS, | FOR BERRY AND ROGERS, HANOVER-SQUARE. | — | M,DCC,XC [1790] (1/1 illus.).

80B. *Seated Man Consulting a Tablet in Greek Held up to Him by the Muse*, 1790 (Facing title page)

Frontispiece re-engraved by Cornelius Tiebout (1777-1830?)
Inscription (top): Frontispiece. | (bottom right): Tiebout Sculpᵗ.
Dimensions: ■ 12.0 x 7.1 cm | 4¹¹/16" x 2¹³/16" (Library Company Am 1790 Lav.)
Other locations (plate only): LC P & P PAGA4-AA-1921 R:1
Lacking plate: NYPL *KD 1790
Lit.: Schroyer 1980, xv.

******

No. 80C.
John Caspar Lavater.
APHORISMS ON MAN. | TRANSLATED | FROM THE ORIGINAL MANUSCRIPT | OF THE | REV. JOHN CASPAR LAVATER, | CITIZEN OF ZURIC. | — | è coelo descendit γνωθι σεαυτον. | *JUV. SAT. IX.* [sic] | — | = | FOURTH EDITION. | PRINTED AT BOSTON, | BY I. THOMAS AND E.T. ANDREWS. | AT FAUST'S STATUE, NO. 45, NEWBURY STREET. | SOLD

BY THEM AT THEIR BOOKSTORE, BY D. WEST, IN MARLBOROUGH|STREET, BY E. LARKIN, JUN. IN CORNHILL, AND BY|I. THOMAS, IN WORCESTER.|=|MDCCXC. [1790] (1/1 illus.)

80C. *Seated Man Consulting a Tablet in Greek Held up to Him by the Muse*, 1790 (Facing title page)

Re-engraved by an anonymous American engraver (perhaps Isaiah Thomas, 1749-1831).
Imprint: Published by Thomas & Andrews, at Boston.
Inscription (top centre): FRONTISPIECE.
Dimensions: ■ 11.8 x 7.5 cm | $4^{10}/16$" x $2^{15}/16$" (Yale Hkc 7.280y)
Other locations: NYPL 8-*KD 1790
Lit.: Schroyer 1980, xv.

81.

81. *Sleeping Woman with a Cupid*, [1780-1790]

Etching designed and executed in drypoint by Henry Fuseli after his own pencil and chalk drawing in the Oeffentliche Kunstsammlung, Basel ([1780-1790]; Schiff 842)
Imprint: Publish'd by R Pollard Spafields London.
Inscription (bottom left, in plate): Fuseli.
Dimensions (sheet): ■ 22.8 x 35.1 cm | $8^{15}/16$" x $13^{13}/16$" (MMA 56.644.16)
Other locations: BM 1882-4-11-1320
Exh.: New York 1981 (3) (as 'Zita')

Variants:
I. Proof (without eye): BM 1852-2-14-90
II. Before letters: Basel 1918.44
III. Lacking imprint: BM 1863-1-10-94
Inscription (handwritten): Designed and etch'd

by the late H; (in the plate): Fuseli.
Other locations: BM 1870-10-8-2844; V & A E.1192-1886 (22.2 x 32.3 cm)
IV. Printed in brown: Essick (from the collection of Sir Thomas Lawrence with his collection mark)
Lit.: Schiff 842A (22.5 x 35.0 cm); Essick, 1980, repr. 59.

The etching depicts a half-reclining woman asleep on a chaise longue beside a pillar inscribed 'ΣΙΓΑ' ('Hush!' or 'Silence!'). The book she appears to have been reading has fallen from her hand. The mating butterflies in the foreground serve as a dream-symbol, while simultaneously reinforcing the erotic nature of the woman's dreams suggested by the hovering cupid with his bow.

Although no narrative source has been found for this illustration, the attitude of the sleeping woman with her exposed breasts is almost identical with that of the central figure of Belinda in Fuseli's painting *Belinda's Dream* (1780-1790; Schiff 1751), where mating butterflies also occupy a prominent position. The etching and the reversed drawing of the same subject may thus be associated in some preliminary or retrospective fashion with that painting, particularly in view of

the presence of the sylph hovering over Belinda.

Fuseli was left-handed, but if this plate appears to be that of a right-hander, i.e. with the hatched lines going from the upper right of the plate towards the bottom left, rather than from the upper left to the bottom right, it is because the etched image is reversed when the plate is printed. This explains why in his original drawing Fuseli printed the Greek letters inscribed on the pillar backwards.

82.

82. *William Tell's Leap from the Boat*, [1788-1790]

Engraved by Carl Gottlieb (or Gottfried) Guttenberg (1743-1790) after Fuseli's lost painting [1780-1787].
Imprint: A Paris Rue S^t. Hyacinthe, N°. 5.
Inscription: Peint par Fuessli, à Londre. | | Gravé à Paris par Charles Guttenberg. |

[*left*]   WILLHELM TELL,
GESLER despotischer Landvogt in der Schweiz,

liess auf oeffentlichen Platze seinen Hut auf eine Lanze setzen, und befahl den Inwohnern, bei Strafe, den selben im vorübergehen demüthig zu grüssen; TELL aber, ein berühm-|ter Bogenschütz war grossmüthig genug den Befehl zu verspotten. GESLER gerieth deswegen in Zorn: er wollte den Verwegenen züchtigen. Kanst du, sprach er zu ihm, deinem. Sohne dort den Apfel vom Kopfe schiessen? | so vergebe ich dir dein Verbrechen. TELL traf glücklich den Apfel! und was soll der andere Pfeil, den du bei dir hast? hätte ich zu meinem Leide, meinen Sohn, war die Antwort, getödtet, so hätte dich dieser getroffen, | Auf dieses liess der Landvogt den beherzten Mann in Ketten schliessen, und verdammte ihn im Schlosse Kusenach ewig gefangen zu leben. Das Schloss liegt im Lucerner See. GESLER lies den Gefangenen zu Schiffe bringen, und | begleitete ihn selber, damit er sicher dahin käme. Aber die Winde wehten heftig; ein Sturm entstand, die Wellen droheten dem Schiffe den Untergang: selbst die Schiffer bebten und baten den Landvogt den Geschlossenen als einen geübten See- | mann loszulassen, damit er das Ruder regire. Beides geschah—schon war man dem Lande nahe. Schnell und Kühn, eingeflammet vom Geiste der Freiheit raffte TELL Pfeil und Bogen zu sich, und sprang an Strand: das Schiff wankte | vom Stosse des Trittes zurück; Doch GESLER kam bald, und grimmig ans Gestade, er tratt aus, entschlossen dem entflohenen nachzueilen, Aber TELL erschoss aus dem Gebusche den Tirannen.

[*right*]   GUILLAUME TELL,
Trois des plus courageux habitans des Cantons de Schwitz, d'Ury et d'Unterwald, nommés, Melchtal, Stauffacher et Walter-Fürst avoient resolu d'affranchir leur pays des traitemens barbares qu'exercoient les Gouv.^{eurs} que leur avoit donnés | Albert d'Autriche. Ils avoient attiré dans leur parti neuf autres amis surs, et déjà le jour du soulevement étoit fixé, lorsque GESLER Gouv.^{eur} d'Ury s'avisa d'un genre de Tyrannie aussi horrible que ridicule. Il fit mettre son chapeau sur une | perche dans la place du Marché d'Altorff, et il ordonna qu'on saluat ce chapeau, sous peine de la vie. GUILLAUME TELL un des douze conjurés, ayant refusé de saluer GESLER le condamna à mourir, lui offrant cependant sa grace à condition | que d'un seul coup de flèche, il abattroit une pomme placée sur la tête de son fils. Le Père tira et fut assez heureux pour abattre la pomme. Pourquoi donc avois tu deux flèches, lui demanda le Gouv.^{eur} Si j'avois blessé mon fils, répondit TELL, la seconde t'étoit | destinée. Le Tyran furieux le fait enchainer, et veut qu'il soit transporté sur le champ au Chateau de Kusnach, situé au milieu du Lac de Lucerne; lui même se charge de l'y conduire, et il descend dans la même barque. Une violante tempete s'élève.

Les Mate- | Lots s'écrient qu'ils sont perdus si TELL ne prend le gouvernail. On le dechaine, et bientôt on approche du rivage. Alors TELL saisit un moment favorable, et transporté par le Génie de la Liberté, il s'élance de la Barque, que, du même mouv.^{ment}, il a repous^{sé}, | dans les flots. Muni de ses Armes toujours sûres, qu'il a sçu enlever avec lui, il se cache dans des brossailles pour y attendre le moment de la vengeance. A peine GESLER a-t[-]il mis pied a terre, qu'il est atteint de la flèche mortelle.

Cette action intrepide affermit | les Conjurés dans leur résolution. |

Dimensions: 43.8 x 59.5 cm | 17¼" x 23½" (KHZ 1940/141)
Other locations: Basel: no inv. no. (Rep. UU); BM 1870-8-13-990; BM 1870-10-8-2792; ETH 500B
Lit.: Schiff 719 (43.8 x 59.5 cm); Weinglass 1988, 145f., repr. 144; Weinglass 1992, 67
Exh.: Bern 1991 (64)

The legend of William Tell the mythic champion of Swiss liberty is well known. Gessler, the despotic Austrian governor, sets his hat on a pole for the Swiss to salute. When Tell refuses, Gessler places an apple on the head of Tell's son and forces the father to shoot at it. Tell's aim is true and he splits the apple. But when the marksman reveals that he would have killed Gessler if his son had been hit, the governor orders Tell to be taken in chains to the castle of Kussnach in the middle of Lake Lucerne. En route, a terrible storm threatens to sink the boat and Tell's chains are removed so that he can take the rudder. But Tell leaps to safety and escapes when the boat nears the shore. The narrative accompanying the illustration compresses the action: as Gessler comes ashore Tell shoots him with his crossbow; this deed serves as the catalyst for the rising against the Austrian oppressors organised by the three confederates from the Forest Cantons of Uri, Schwyz, and Unterwalden.

Even before the French Revolution, William Tell had become a European symbol of the republican ideal; he would soon also be regarded as the champion of the Revolution and the rights of man. In Paris there was even a Guillaume Tell arrondissement: in 1790 *Le Courier de Provence* describes the formal installation of Guttenberg's engraving in the district's 'Temple of Virtue'.

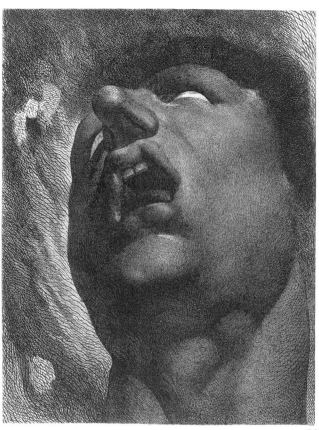

83.

83. *Head of a Damned Soul, Perhaps Ruggieri degli Ubaldini, Archbishop of Pisa*, [1789-1790] (Dante, *Inferno*, XXXIII, 14ff.)

Engraved (dot and lozenge) by William Blake (1757-1827) perhaps after ?Fuseli's painting on panel (offered at Sotheby's, London, 4 October 1978, lot 304)
Proof
Inscription (in pencil, below image bottom left): Fuseli Pinxit||W. Blake [Sculpsit?]
Dimensions: ■ 34.7 x 26.1 cm | 13^{11}/16" x 10^{6}/16" (BM 1856-7-12-209)
Other locations: BM 1874-7-71-149; Fitzwilliam P. 423.1985; Hunterian; Huntington Msc. Blake (trimmed inside plate mark); Ryskamp
Lit.: Schiff 946 (35.0 x 26.5 cm); Bentley 1977, no. 450E.; Bindman 1978, no. 79; Easson & Essick 1979, 87-91; Essick 1983, no. XXXII; Weinglass 1991, 67
Exh.: Cambridge 1965 (12); Princeton 1969 (28) (Ryskamp copy); New York 1974 (?); New Haven 1982-1983 (28); London 1986 (29)

This design is very similar to the first of the 'Three Heads of Damned Souls from Dante's Inferno' in the French and English editions (1781-1786, 1789-1798) of Lavater's *Essays on Physiognomy* (respectively Nos. **50.** and **96.**), but it is clearly distinct from these smaller engraved versions. The differences between the engraved and painted versions of the *Head of the Damned Soul* (photograph Mellon Centre Archive, London) and the study for the Lavater engraving (Art Institute of Chicago), with the more sharply defined features and shape of the head in the former, suggest Fuseli's desire to improve and individualise the earlier somewhat grotesque portrait, thereby giving the subject a more specifically Dantean and less physiognomical focus and intent.

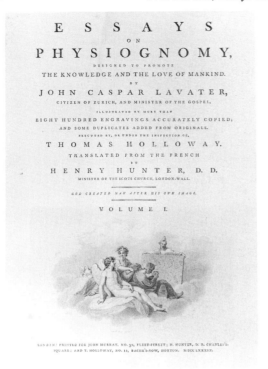

Fig. 3. J.C. Lavater, *Essays on Physiognomy*, 1789. Title page, Vol. I.

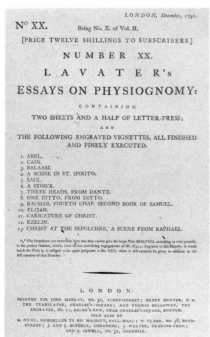

Fig. 4. Part No. XX of J.C. Lavater, *Essays on Physiognomy*, dated December 1791.

Nos. 84 - 110.
Johann Caspar Lavater.
ESSAYS|ON|PHYSIOGNOMY,|DESIGNED TO PROMOTE|THE KNOWLEDGE AND THE LOVE OF MANKIND.|BY|JOHN CASPAR LAVATER,|CITIZEN OF ZURICH, AND MINISTER OF THE GOSPEL.|ILLUSTRATED BY MORE THAN|EIGHT HUNDRED ENGRAVINGS ACCURATELY COPIED;|AND SOME DUPLICATES ADDED FROM ORIGINALS.|EXECUTED BY, OR UNDER THE INSPECTION OF,|THOMAS HOLLOWAY.|TRANSLATED FROM THE FRENCH|BY|HENRY HUNTER, D.D.|MINISTER OF THE SCOTS CHURCH, LONDON-WALL.|—|*God created man after his own Image.*|—|VOLUME I.|[Vignette]| LONDON:|PRINTED FOR JOHN MURRAY NO. 32, FLEET-STREET; H. HUNTER, D.D., CHARLES'S-|SQUARE; AND T. HOLLOWAY, NO. 11, BACHE'S-ROW, HOXTON. MDCCLXXXIX [1789] (27/800+ illus.).

...VOLUME II.|[Vignette]| LONDON: PRINTED FOR JOHN MURRAY, NO. 32, FLEET-STREET; H. HUNTER, D.D. BETHNAL-|GREEN ROAD; AND T. HOLLOWAY, NO. 11, BACHE'S-ROW, HOXTON. MDCCXCII [1792].

...VOLUME III.|[Vignette]|LONDON: PRINTED FOR MURRAY AND HIGHLEY, NO. 32, FLEET-STREET; H. HUNTER, D.D.| BETHNAL-GREEN ROAD; AND T. HOLLOWAY, NO. 11, BACHE'S-ROW, HOXTON. MDCXCVIII [1798].

...ILLUSTRATED BY|ENGRAVINGS, ACCURATELY COPIED;|AND SOME DUPLICATES ADDED FROM ORIGINALS.| EXECUTED BY, OR UNDER THE INSPECTION OF,|THOMAS HOLLOWAY.| TRANSLATED FROM THE FRENCH|BY| HENRY HUNTER, D.D.|MINISTER OF THE SCOTS CHURCH, LONDON-WALL.|=|*God Created Man After His Own Image.*|=| VOLUME I. [VOLUME III.]|[Vignette]| LONDON: |PRINTED BY T. BENSLEY, BOLT COURT, FLEET STREET,|FOR JOHN STOCKDALE, PICCADILLY.|1810.

PROPOSALS
(BM 1860.10.13.157)

London, June, 1787.

PROPOSALS
FOR
PUBLISHING BY SUBSCRIPTION,
A Translation of that ingenious and instructive work, | ESSAYS ON PHYSIOGNOMY, | BY | JOHN GASPARD LAVATER, | Citizen of Zurich and Minister of the Gospel. | The Translation, from the superb edition in French, revised and corrected by the Author, and collated with the original German, will be accompanied with Notes critical, historical, and explanatory, and will be enriched with exact Copies of all the original Engravings, executed in the most capital Style, and Duplicates of some of the most interesting Subjects, from original Paintings or Drawings, to which the English Artist can have Access, and which Mr. Lavater frequently laments he had not the Means of consulting.

The Translator and the Artist have already made considerable Progress in the Work, and it will be ready for Publication according to the Conditions undermentioned.

The Letter-Press will be executed in the most superb Manner, and the Plates (exclusive of Vignettes) printed on the best French Paper: and every Effort of British Art and Industry will be employed to render the Book, in its new Dress, superior to every former foreign Edition.

CONDITIONS.

I. The Work will be printed on Imperial Paper, equally adapted to receive the Letter-Press and Vignettes, and with a Type cast on Purpose.

II. Each Number will contain at least Three Sheets of Letter-Press, accompanied with from Eight to Twelve capital Engravings, including Vignettes, designed to illustrate the different Subjects.

III. The Work will be comprized, as nearly as can be computed in Forty Numbers [*actually, forty-one*] which will make four magnificent Volumes in Quarto.

IV. Subscribers to pay one Guinea Deposit, for which they are to have a Receipt from the Proprietors; in order to be ensured Proof Impressions of the Plates as Security for completing their Purchase, and to enable the Proprietors to do Justice to the Undertaking.

V. The Price to Subscribers for first Impressions, 12s. each Number.

VI. The Price to Non-Subscribers for second Impressions, 15s. a Number.

VII. Subscribers will be faithfully supplied with their Copies according to the Order of their Subscription.

VIII. The Names of Subscribers to this Work will be printed.

IX. No. I. on these Conditions will be published on Tuesday the 1st of January, 1788.

To the PUBLIC.

The professed Aim of this curious, entertaining, and instructive Work, is to promote the Knowledge and the Love of Mankind.

The Plan is perfectly original, and the Subject universally interesting and important. In the Execution there are incessantly discovered Marks of an enlarged Mind, a pentrating Genius, an ardent and pious Spirit, a warm and benevolent Heart. The Style of the Author is elegant, correct, and perspicuous; his Figures, of which he makes abundant Use, are, in general, just, bold, and striking; his Sentiments frequently noble and sublime.

To various Descriptions of Readers, the Editor flatters himself, the Translation and the Embellishments of these singular Essays will be highly acceptable. Artists in all the Branches of Design will be furnished with innumerable Hints respecting the Principles and the Improvement of their Art. The Philosopher will find himself conducted into a new, extensive, and useful Field of Speculation. Mr. Lavater's FRAGMENTS, as he modestly terms them, afford a rich Repast to the Lovers of polite Learning, who will be supplied with ample Matter to exercise, to gratify, perhaps to correct their Taste. To the Friend of Virtue it must yield heart-felt Satisfaction to meet with another generous, manly, spirited Attempt to promote the Cause of Humanity, Goodness and Truth: while the Man of Piety will rejoice in the animated and affecting Views which are continually presented of the great CREATOR'S Power, Wisdom, and Beneficence.

The daring, fervid Spirit of Lavater, it is acknowledged, frequently hazards a Flight, which the Calm and Timid will be apt to tax with Rashness and Extravagance. But the very

Wildness and Eccentricity of Genius please infinitely more than all the frigid, laborious Correctness of Phlegm and Apathy.

Neither the Author nor the Editor pretend to offer this to the Public as a perfect and finished Work. They are abundantly sensible that the Science of Physiognomy is yet in its Infancy; but they are confident it is a Subject of successful, though of difficult Investigation. The learned, acute, and enterprizing Swiss has made a respectable Beginning, and a Meritorious Progress. Why may it not be reserved for British Ingenuity, Spirit, and Perseverance to complete his Design; to supply the Materials which still wanting, to clear away what may be found superfluous, and to rear the Fabrick to its highest possible Pitch of Beauty, Solidity, Grandeur, and Usefulness?

*₊*Subscriptions are taken in by *John Murray*, Bookseller, No. 32, Fleet-Street, by HENRY HUNTER, D.D. the Translator, Charles-Square; and by THOMAS HOLLOWAY, the Engraver, No. 11, Bache's Row, near Charles'-Square, Hoxton.

Also by G. NICOL, Bookseller to His Majesty; J. SEWELL, No. 32, Cornhill; J. WALTER, Corner of Spring-Gardens, Charing-|Cross; J. STOCKDALE, and J.DEBRETT, Piccadilly; R. FAULDER, Bond-Street; J. and J. FLETCHER, Oxford; J. and J.|MERRILL, Cambridge; and by W. CREECH, at Edinburgh.

In 1799, the Proprietors published a prospectus (now untraced), which was reviewed in *Monthly Magazine*, VII (December 1799), 903, where it is described in some detail: it contained 'a list of the plates, comprising portraits, with physiognomical analyses of the most illustrious characters in Europe, of the last and present century. Among them the British characters make a distinguished figure; and ... are given in their full spirit'. It is also noted that 'some very fine copies of the work' remain available: 'These, when properly arranged, make five similarized royal quarto volumes; the second and third of the French original being divided into two each, with a separate title-page to the second part'. The price of the five volumes is quoted as £27 in boards, or £30 'elegantly half bound with Morocco backs and corners'.

84.

84. *Head of a Trans-Tiberine Roman*, 1789
(Vol. II, facing p. 36, Plate 55)
(Issued in Part No. XI, December 1789)

Engraved by Thomas Holloway (1748-1827) after the drawing in the Santa Museum of Art ([1777-1779]; Schiff 1741)
Inscription: Fuzeli Delinᵗ,||Holloway Sc.|A TRANS-TIBERINE (TRASTEVERINO)|A Race of Men who inhabit the South side of the Tiber, they consider themselves as the Legitimate Descendants of|the Ancient Romans, and all the rest of the Inhabitants as bastards of Transalpine Barbarians.—|55
Dimensions (to platemark): 26.9 x 22.5 cm | 10¹⁰/16" x 8¹⁴/16" (NYPL Arents) (in parts)
Other locations: YCBA (in parts); BL 30.g.2; Bodleian Arch. Antiqq: A.I.23; DHW; Dr. Williams's Library 1124.L2 (II.I); Essick; Essick (1810); Huntington 224203; Huntington 43910 (1810) (facing p. [37]) (1810); Lucerne 853 fol (1810); Newberry B56.4845; NYPL YEZA+; NYPL YEZA+ (1810); Princeton 6453.568.12q (not seen); ZBZ BX 421
Plate only: BM 1863-5-9-84
Lit.: Schiff 947 (26.7 x 22.1 cm); Hughes/Moir 1976, 272-273.

Lavater's commentary (II, 36) emphasises the 'masculine austerity' of the Trans-Tiberine in contrast with the 'softness' of the infant in the vignette on the facing page:

Nature has marked very distinctly the line of separation which bounds the faculties of the being whose image is before us. If she had not given to to the look the most piercing vivacity, to the mouth an expression of wisdom, and a candor which approaches to goodness—the obstinate and harsh character of that brazen forehead, those eyebrows, thick and strongly marked, that nose, which announces so much force and activity, would excite in us an emotion of terror. Nature intended that face to be firm and inflexible. She had need of such a boundary, of such a key-stone of the arch, where she has placed it. Dare any one ask her the reason?

Hughes suggests that Fuseli has 'flattered the Trans-Tiberine pretensions to ancient lineage, by basing this image on some Roman bust of the third or fourth centuries A.D.'

85. *Brutus at the Moment the Ghost of Caesar Appears to him*, 1791
(Vol. II, facing p. 282, Plate 90)
(Issued in Part No. XXI, December 1791)

Engraved by Thomas Trotter (1756-1803)
Inscription: Fuseli del.||Trotter sculp.|
BRUTUS.|(bottom right): [*Plate No.*] 90.
Dimensions: ■ 16.6 x 13.6 cm | 6½" x 5⁶/16"
(NYPL Arents) (in parts)
Other locations: YCBA (in parts); BL 30.g.2;
Bodleian Arch Antiqq: A.I.23; DHW; Dr.
Williams' Library 1124.L.3; Essick; Essick
(1810); Huntington 224203; Huntington 439103
(1810); Lucerne 853 fol. (1810); NYPL YEZA+;
NYPL YEZA+ (1810); Princeton 6453.568.12q;
ZBZ BX 422
Plate only: Folger PR2752.1807c c.4 (Vol. IV,
between pp. 26-27) (lacking inscription);
Huntington, XXIV, 157
Lit.: Schiff 948 (16.4 x 13.5 cm)

Lavater's commentary reads as follows:

Here is...a Brutus, at the instant when the Ghost appears to him. The copy has been cruelly disfigured, especially in what regards the mouth and root of the nose; but whatever

may be its faults, a vigorous mind alone could have seized a character of such force. The terror painted on this face announces a soul filled with agitation and uneasiness, yet still possessing itself sufficiently to think and to reflect. Uncertainty, boldness, contempt and fear are legible in the eye, and the mouth. The contours of the eyes, the eye-brows, and the nose want correctness and dignity, but a character of greatness, which does honour to the feeling and the efforts of the Designer, is strikingly apparent in the whole taken together. In the chin, particularly, there is an expression of obstinacy, courage and haughtiness.

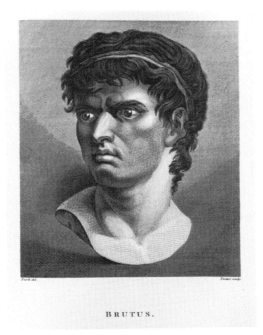

BRUTUS.

85.

86. *Mary Sister of Martha*, 1792
(*Luke*, 10: 38-42)
(Vol. II, between pp. 282-283; Plate 103)
(Issued in Part No. XXIV, July 1792)

Engraved by Thomas Holloway (1748-1827)
Imprint: Published as the Act directs, 2 July, 1792, by J. Murray, T. Holloway and the other Proprietor.
Inscription: H. Fuseli delᵗ.||T. Holloway sculpᵗ.|
MARY Sister of MARTHA.|This Print is engraved after an entirely new drawing by Mʳ. Fuseli, he being unwilling that the preceding Outline should pass as his Idea of Mary.|But Mʳ.

Lavater's remarks rendered it necessary to the English Editor to give a fac-simile of the French engraving. | (bottom right): [*Plate No.*] 103
Dimensions: ■ 19.0 x 15.6 cm | 7½" x 6²/16" (NYPL Arents) (in parts)
Other locations: YCBA (in parts); BL 30.g.2; Bodleian Arch. Antiqq: A.I.23; DHW; Dr. Williams's Library 1124.L.3; Essick; Essick (1810); Huntington 224203; Huntington 439103 (1810) (facing p. 283); Lucerne H583.fol (1810) (facing p. 283); NYPL YEZA+ (facing p. 283); NYPL YEZA+ (1810); Princeton 6453.5.68.12q (facing p. 283); ZBZ BX 422
Plate only: BM 1863-5-9-15
Lit.: Schiff 949 (18.6 x 15.4 cm)

86.

Lavater's commentary (II, 283) is not applicable to this illustration, and has therefore been appended to No. **87.** According to a note to the commentary, the engraving after Fuseli's new drawing 'endeavour[s] to regain what was lost or disfigured by the Engraver of the head in the French edition. It is left to the Reader to determine, whether the criticisms of the Author, on spurious deformities, were worth retaining at the expence of propriety and beauty'.

MARY SISTER OF MARTHA.

87.

87. *Mary Sister of Martha*, 1792
(*Luke*, 10: 38-42)
(Vol. II, facing p. 283; Plate 99)
(Issued in Part No. XXIV, July 1792)

Unsigned outline engraving, facsimile of Johann Heinrich Lips's engraving in the French edition
Inscription: MARY SISTER OF MARTHA. |
(bottom right): [*Plate No.*] 99
Dimensions: ■ 23.8 x 19.3 cm | 9⁶/16" x 7¹⁰/16"; ■ 24.2 x 19.9 cm | 9½" x 7¹³/16" (NYPL Arents) (in parts)
Other locations: YCBA (in parts); BL 30.g.2; Bodleian Arch. Antiqq: A.I.23; DHW; Dr. Williams's Library 1124.L.3; Essick; Essick (1810); Huntington 224203; Huntington 439103 (1810) (between pp. 282-283); Lucerne H853.fol (1810) (between pp. 282-283); Newberry B56.4845; NYPL YEZA+ (between pp. 282-283); NYPL YEZA+ (1810); Princeton 6453.568.159 (between pp. 282-283); ZBZ BX 422
Plate only: DHW
Lit.: Schiff 950 (24.2 x 19.7 cm)

Lavater's commentary on this illustration is highly critical:

A mixture of gentleness and harshness, of enthusiasm and sensuality. The forehead and the nose are too coarse, and [*out of*] accord with the mild and docile character of a disciple of Jesus. The eye, on the contrary, expresses perfectly well a religious attention, great mental vigour. ...The mouth is much too coarse [*but*] this fault must be imputed to the copyer [*and it*] preserves an air of devotion, languor and tenderness. ...

The attitude of the hand is very fortunate [*but*] too weak and too delicate for the hand of a man, it has neither the grace nor pliancy of the beautiful hand of a woman.

All these traits in general are too strong for a female figure. The ear [*has*] both delicacy and precision; but it is too far from the nose, besides somewhat too large, and badly placed.

Dimensions: ■ 16.4 x 11.6 cm | [6⁷/16" x 4⁹/16"]; ■ 16.7 x 11.9 cm | 6¹⁰/16" x 4¹¹/16" (NYPL Arents) (in parts)
Other locations: YCBA (in parts); BL 30.g.2; Bodleian Arch. Antiqq: A.I.23; DHW; Dr. Williams's Library 1124.L.3; Essick; Essick (1810); Lucerne H853.fol (1810); Newberry B56.4845; NYPL YEZA+; NYPL YEZA+ (1810); ZBZ BX422
Plate only: BM 1870-10-8-2791; Witt (plate no. cropped)
Lit.: Schiff 951 (16.6 x 11.8 cm)

In a footnote Fuseli considers Lavater's designation of his 'unpremeditated Lines' as the head of 'Saint-John-Baptist in the ecstasy of contemplation' to be 'fanciful'—'the foreign Engraver [*had*] done [*all*] in his power to make it worse'.

Lavater for his part suggests that Fuseli should have 'listened to the voice of truth, rather than followed the wanderings of a wild imagination!'

S. JOHN.

88.

88. *St. John the Baptist*, 1791
(Vol. II, facing p. 284; Plate 81)
(Issued in Part No. XVIII, March 1791)

Engraved by Thomas Holloway (1748-1827)
Inscription: Fuseli Delin'. | T Holloway Direxit. | Sᵀ. JOHN. | (bottom right): [*Plate No.*] 81.

S A T A N.

The Engraver has consulted the Designer, and followed the Original,
the mouth of which expresses contempt instead of fear.

89.

89. *Head of Satan*, 1790
(Vol. II, facing p. 285; Plate 79)
(Issued in Part No. XVII, December 1790)

Engraved by Thomas Holloway (1748-1827)
Inscription (along line of shoulder): Fuseli
Delin| |Holloway Sc.|SATAN.|The Engraver has
consulted the Designer and followed the
Original,|the mouth of which expresses contempt
instead of fear.|(bottom right): [*Plate No.*] 79
Dimensions (to the platemark): 23.5 x 19.4 cm |
9¼" x 7¹⁰/16" (NYPL Arents) (in parts)
Other locations: YCBA (in parts); BL 30.g.2;
Bodleian Arch. Antiqq: A.I.23; DHW; Dr.
Williams's Library 1124.L.3; Huntington 224203
(1810) Lucerne H853.fol (1810); Newberry
B56.4845; NYPL YEZA+; NYPL YEZA+
(1810); ZBZ BX 422
Plate only: BM 1863-5-9-18 (sheet trimmed)
Lit.: Schiff 952 (14.7 x 11.5 cm)
Exh.: Kansas City 1989 (3)

This design is indicative of Fuseli's persistent
interest in the character of Satan, while it also
looks forward to his later portrayals in the Milton
Gallery and Du Roveray's edition of *Paradise
Lost* (1802). Lavater criticises its 'borrowed and
affected manner: that original sin of all Painters
who have genius, or who imagine that they have
it.' But he also notes:

> ...this image represents a Being powerful,
> extraordinary, more than human, the sworn
> enemy of every thing that belongs to gentle
> simplicity and dignity of sentiment.
>   Harshness and obstinacy are engraven on that
> front of brass.
>   The same character is visible also in the eye-
> brow, if that name may be given to the
> capricious trait which the Painter has substituted
> in its place....
>   Under these disfigured traits you cannot
> however but distinguish the fallen Angel: you
> perceive still, some traces of his ancient
> greatness—and in this consists...the principal
> merit of the piece.

90.

90. *The Death of Abel*, 1791
(Vol. II, top of p. 286, plate E)
(Issued in Part No. XX, December 1791)

Engraved by Charles Grignion (1721-1810)
Inscription (bottom centre): Grignion sculp.
Dimensions: ■ 4.2 x 18.6 cm | 1¹¹/16" x 7⁵/16"
(NYPL Arents) (in parts)
Other locations: YCBA (in parts); BL 30.g.2;
Bodleian Arch. Antiqq: A.I.23; DHW; Dr.
Williams's Library 1124.L.3; Lucerne H853.fol
(1810); Newberry B56.4845; NYPL YEZA+;
NYPL YEZA+ (1810); ZBZ BX 422
Plate only: BM 1863-5-9-81
Lit.: Schiff 953 (4.2 x 18.6 cm)

Lavater remarks of this and its counterpart,
Cain, below:

> The death of Abel, the first victim sacrificed
> to envy, furnishes a bold subject for the pencil
> of our Artist; and suffering innocence is here
> presented in manly and energetic traits, under
> the form of a Hero. The same vigorous touch
> is discernible in all the Works of this Painter.
> A manner feeble or pitiful were altogether
> unsuitable to his original genius. You remark,
> in his designs, rather a sort of tension, which in
> truth is not common, but which he some-times
> pushes to extravagance, even at the expence of
> correctness.

91.

92.

91. *Cain*, 1791
(Vol. II, bottom of p. 286)
(Issued in Part No. XX, December 1791)

Engraved by Charles Grignion (1721-1810)

Inscription (bottom left of design): Fuseli Delin |
(bottom centre): Grignion sculp.
Dimensions (to platemark): 9.2 x 6.6 cm |
3¹⁰/16" x 2¹⁰/16" (NYPL Arents) (in parts)
Other locations: YCBA (in parts); BL 30.g.2;
Bodleian Arch. Antiqq: A.I.23; DHW; Dr.
Williams's Library 1124.L.3; Lucerne H853.fol
(1810); Newberry B56.4845; NYPL YEZA+;
NYPL YEZA+ (1810); ZBZ BX 422 (8.9 x 6.5
cm)
Plate only: BM 1854-12-10-560
Lit.: Schiff 954 (8.9 x 6.6 cm)

92. *Balaam Blessing the Children of Israel*, 1791
(*Numbers*, 23: 7-11)
(Vol. II, p. 287, plate F)
(Issued in Part No. XX, December 1791)

Engraved by Thomas Holloway (1748-1827)
Inscription: H Fuseli Delin. | | T Holloway Sculp.
Dimensions (to platemark): 16.0 x 13.5 cm |
6⁵/16" x 5⁵/16" (NYPL Arents) (in parts)
Other locations: YCBA (in parts); BL30.g.2;
Bodleian Arch. Antiqq: A.I.23; DHW; Dr.
Williams's Library 1124.L.3; Lucerne H853.fol
(1810); Newberry B56.4845; NYPL YEZA+;
NYPL YEZA+ (1810); ZBZ BX 422
Plate only: BM 1863-5-9-14
Lit.: Schiff 955 (?12.7 x 10.0 cm)

The plate illustrates the following Bible passage:
[And the Lord put a word in Balaam's mouth]
And he took up his parable and said, Balak the
king of Moab hath brought me from Aram, out
of the mountains of the east, *saying* Come,
curse me Jacob, and come, defy Israel.

How shall I curse, *whom* God hath not cursed?
or how shall I defy, *whom* the Lord hath not
defied?

For from the top of the rocks I see him, and
from the hills I behold him: lo, the people shall
dwell alone, and shall not be reckoned among
the nations.

Who can count the dust of Jacob, and the
number of the fourth *part* of Israel? Let me die
the death of the righteous, and let my last end
be like his!

And Balak said unto Balaam, What hast thou
done unto me? I took thee to curse mine
enemies, and behold, thou hast blessed *them*
altogether.

Lavater describes the scene as follows:

This figure must strike, even without our knowing what it is intended to represent; and it is surely not the production of an ordinary genius. A single design such as this announces more than a methodical Artist, more than an Artist merely intelligent. And if I further add that this figure represents the Magician of Balaam on the summit of the Mountain, blessing the Children of Israel, whom he intended to curse—could any one refuse to the Author a genius kindled with the fire of a Michel-Angelo?

93. *The Escapee: A Real Scene in the Hospital of San Spirito at Rome*, 1791
(Vol. II, p. 288, plate G)
(Issued in Part No. XX, December 1791)

Engraved by Thomas Holloway (1748-1827) after Fuseli's drawing in the British Museum ([1772]; Schiff 515)
Imprint: Published as the Act directs, by T. Holloway, 20. Oct. 1791.
Inscription: Fuseli delin'. | | Holloway sc. | Drawn from memory after a real Scene in the Hospital of S. Spirito at Rome. Mr. Lavater has given only the terrific part of the Scene. The Designer |

having indulged the English Artist with the original Drawing complete, he thought it would be acceptable to the Public to give the whole in this Ed- | (ition.
Dimensions: ■ 10.3 x 16.1 cm | 4¹/16" x 6⁶/16" (NYPL Arents) (in parts)
Other locations: YCBA (in parts); BL.g.2; Bodleian Arch. Antiqq: A.I.23; DHW; Dr. Williams's Library 1124.L.3; Lucerne H853.fol (1810); Newberry B56.4845; NYPL YEZA+; NYPL YEZA+ (1810); ZBZ BX 433
Plate only: BM 1907-11-6-5
Lit.: Schiff 956 (9.9 x 15.9 cm) (year of date mistakenly given as '1792');
Exh.: Kansas City 1982 (14).

Lavater says of this:

Fury and force, an energy uniformly supported, and ever active—this is what distinguishes most of the figures and compositions of this masculine genius. Spectres, Demons, and madmen; fantoms, exterminating angels; murders and acts of violence—such are his favourite objects; and yet, I repeat it, no one loves with more tenderness. The sentiment of love is painted in his look—but the form and bony system of his face characterize in him a taste for terrible scenes, and the energy which they require.

93.

94.

94. *The Witch of Endor Summoning up the Spirit of Samuel*, 1791
(I *Samuel*, 28: 7-25)
(Vol. II, top of p. 289, plate H)
(Issued in Part No. XX, December 1791)

Engraved by Thomas Holloway (1748-1827) after Fuseli's drawing in the Kunsthaus, Zurich ([1777]; Schiff 373)
Imprint: Published as the Act directs by T Holloway Octr 20 1791.
Inscription: Fuseli Delin^t. || Holloway Sculp^t.
Dimensions: ■ 8.3 x 14.4 cm | 3¼" x 5^{11}/16" (NYPL Arents) (in parts)
Other locations: YCBA (in parts); BL 30.g.2; Bodleian Arch. Antiqq: A.I.23; DHW; Dr. Williams's Library 1124.L.3; Lucerne H853.fol (1810); Newberry B56.4845; NYPL YEZA+; NYPL YEZA+ (1810); ZBZ BX 422 (8.2 x 14.1 cm)
Plate only: BM 1863-5-9-34
Lit.: Schiff 957 (8.2 x 14.1 cm).
Exh.: Kansas City 1982 (15).

In disfavour with the Lord and fearful about the outcome of the pending battle at Gilboa, Saul seeks out the Witch of Endor, who summons up for him the spirit of Samuel. Fuseli's illustration of the biblical story depicts Saul fainting in the arms of a soldier upon hearing Samuel's dire prophecies—that his kingdom will be reft from him to be given to David, and that his army will be delivered into the hands of the Philistines.

Lavater describes the Witch of Endor thus:

Her face presents a mixture of greatness and littleness, of originality and caricature. Her attitude expresses energy and astonishment.

The figure which represents the Spirit of Samuel is in every respect admirable.

That of Saul equally merits the highest praise, and is perfectly suitable to the Hero whom we see fainting in the arms of a Soldier inured to dreadful scenes.

95.

95. *Youth Sitting Beneath a Tree in a Pastoral Landscape*, 1792
(Vol. II, bottom of p. 289)
(Issued in Part No. XX, December 1791)

Oval vignette engraved by Isaac Taylor, Jr. (1759-1829)
Inscription: Isaac Taylor Junr Sculp.
Dimensions: 5.2 x 6.5 cm | 2^1/16" x 2^9/16" (NYPL Arents) (in parts)

Other locations: YCBA (in parts); BL 30.g.2;
Bodleian Arch. Antiqq: A.I.23; DHW; Dr.
Williams's Library 1124.L.3; Lucerne H853.fol
(1810); Newberry B56.4845; NYPL YEZA+;
NYPL YEZA+ (1810); ZBZ BX 422
Plate only: BM 1863-5-9-76
Lit.: Schiff 958 (5.2 x 6.5 cm).
Exh.: Kansas City 1982 (16).

This vignette was intended to serve as a contrast
to *The Witch of Endor* above it on the same page,
by presenting 'the image of calmness and
wisdom.' It is designated in the listing on the
cover of Part No. XX as 'A Stoick'.

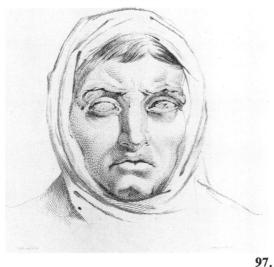

97.

96. *Three Heads from Dante's Inferno*, 1791
(Vol. II, top of p. 290)
(Issued in Part No. XX, December 1791

Engraved by Thomas Holloway (1748-1827)
Inscription (top): I.|1||2||3|; (bottom): H Fuseli
Delin¹,||T Holloway sculp.

Dimensions (to platemark): 9.2 x 25.0 cm | 3⁹/16"
x 9¹⁴/16" (NYPL Arents) (in parts)
Other locations: YCBA (in parts); BL 30.g.2;
Bodleian Arch. Antiqq: A.I.23; DHW; Dr.
Williams's Library 1124.L.3; Lucerne H853.fol
(1810); Newberry B56.4845; NYPL YEZA+;
NYPL YEZA+ (1810); ZBZ BX 422
Plate only: BM 1863-5-9-86
Lit.: Schiff 959 (9.2 x 25.0 cm); Turner 1985, pl.
1 (as 'Head Illustrating Sloth from Dante's
Inferno')

97. *Fourth Head from Dante*, 1791
(Vol. II, bottom of p. 290)
(Issued in Part No. XX, December 1791)

Engraved by Thomas Holloway (1748-1827)
Inscription: H. Fuseli Del.||T. Holloway sculp.
Dimensions (to platemark): 10.4 x 10.4 cm |
4²/16" x 4²/16" (NYPL Arents) (in parts)
Other locations: YCBA (in parts); BL 30.g.2;
Bodleian Arch. Antiqq: A.I.23; DHW; Dr.
Williams's Library 1124.L.3; Lucerne H853.fol
(1810); Newberry B56.4845; NYPL YEZA+;
NYPL YEZA+ (1810); ZBZ BX 422
Lit.: Schiff 959A (10.4 x 10.0 cm)

Although these four heads 'express the most
horrible sufferings ... even in this state they
announce characters naturally energetic, though
destitute of true greatness'. Lavater characterises
them as 'no ordinary sinners [*but*] men rugged
and relentless, who never knew what pity was:
and therefore judgement without mercy, has been
pronounced against them'.
Wolfgang Hartmann in his dissertation, 'Die
Wiederentdeckung Dantes in der deutschen Kunst'
(Bonn, 1969, pp. 56-57), suggests that head no. 1
represents Camicion dei Pazzi, 'who had lost

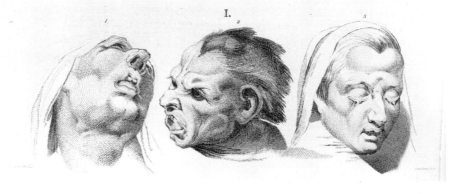

96.

both his ears on account of the cold' (*Inferno*, XXXII, 52f.). However, I suggest this is more probably Ruggieri degli Ubaldini, Archbishop of Pisa (*Inferno*, XXXIII, 14ff.). Head no. 2 portrays perhaps Bocca degli Abati, the traitor to Florence (*Inferno*, XXXII, 106f.). While nos. 3 and 4 may represent two of the unnamed sinners among the envious whose eyes had been sewn up with wire (*Purgatorio*, XIII, 58-62).

98.

98. *Salome Receiving the Head of John the Baptist (I)*, 1792
(*Matthew*, 14: 10-11)
(Vol. II, facing p. 291; [*Plate No.*] 89
(Bound in Part No. XX, but first listed as issued in Part No. XXIV, July 1792)

Unsigned outline engraving [by Thomas Holloway (1748-1827)] (reversed) after the original plate engraved by Charles Grignion (1721-1810) for *Willoughby's Practical Family Bible* (1772)
Inscription: SALOME.|(bottom right): [*Plate No.*] 89.
Dimensions: ■ 21.7 x 18.3 cm | 8⁹/16" x 7³/16";
■ 21.9 x 18.6 cm | 8¹⁰/16" x 7⁵/16" (NYPL Arents) (in parts)
Other locations: YCBA (in parts); BL 30.g.2; Bodleian Arch. Antiqq: A.I.23; DHW; Dr. Williams's Library 1124.L.3; Lucerne H853.fol (1810) (between pp. 290-291); Newberry

B56.4845; NYPL YEZA+; NYPL YEZA+ (1810); ZBZ BX 422 (between pp. 290-291)
Plate only: DHW
Lit.: Schiff 960 (21.9 x 18.6);
Exh.: Kansas City 1982 (10).

Lavater finds this representation ('one of our Artist's earliest productions') unsatisfactory on several accounts:

> The face of the daughter of Herodias is neither sufficiently young or feminine. ... The too narrow forehead ... can produce a good effect neither for the physiognomy, nor as a picture; besides, it forms a singular contrast with the length and delicacy of the hand. ... The head of Saint-John is at least forty years too old. I discern in it ... a noble energy, but not by far the sublimity 'of the greatest of those who are born of woman.'

99.

99. *Salome Receiving the Head of John the Baptist (II)*, 1798
(*Matthew*, 14: 10-11)
(Vol. II, between pp. 290-291; Plate No. 174)
(Issued in Part No. XLI, March 1799, but first announced in Part No. XXIV, July 1792)

Engraved by Thomas Holloway (1748-1827)
Imprint: Published as the Act directs by T.
Holloway & the other Proprietors April 25. 1798.
Inscription: Henʸ. Fuseli Esqʳ. R.A. delinᵗ. | | T.
Holloway sculpᵗ. | THE DAUGHTER OF
HERODIAS | [*Plate No.*] 174
Dimensions: ■ 30.4 x 21.5 cm | 11¹⁵/16" x 8⁷/16"
(NYPL Arents) (in parts)
Other locations: YCBA (in parts); BL 30.g.2;
Bodleian Arch. Antiqq: A.I.23 (lacks
imprint—cropped?); DHW; Dr. Williams's
Library 1124.L.3 (plate no. cropped); Lucerne
H853.fol (1810) (facing p. 291); MMA;
Newberry B56.4845 (imprint cropped); NYPL
YEZA+; NYPL YEZA+ (1810) (plate no.
cropped); ZBZ BX 422
Plate only: BM 1863.5.11.9; KHZ B43 (imprint
and plate no. cropped)
Lit.: Schiff 961 (30.5 x 21.1 cm); Schiff-Viotto
1977, no. 19; Weinglass 1991, 307f., pl. 25.
Exh.: Kansas City 1982 (11).

A note in Part No. XXIV announced that since
'Mr. Lavater's remarks necessarily required ... a
fac-simile of the French print', Fuseli would
furnish a new drawing: he 'disowned' the earlier
'mutilated and altogether deformed' version.

In a long note appended to his 'Advertisement'
in Vol. I (Sig. [b4]), he justifies 'representing the
Nymph and her Companion in the attire and with
the attributes of Bacchantes,' by suggesting that
Salome, who had been taught to dance by her
Greek mother, would thus have performed for
Herod the 'orgic ballet' of Autonoe and her
sisters, Ino and Agave, who tore off the head of
Pentheus. The onlookers would have been
reminded forcibly of 'the similarity of the insult
offered by John to Herod's love and the
profaneness of Pentheus,' as related by Euripides
in the *Bacchae*.

100. *Rechab Displaying the Head of Ishbosheth*, 1791

(Vol. II, p. 291)
(II *Samuel*, 4: 1-12)
(Issued in Part No. XX, December 1791)

Engraved by James Gillray (1757-1815)
Inscription: H. Fuseli delᵗ. | | J. Gillray sculpᵗ.
Dimensions (to platemark): 10.5 x 12.2 cm |
4³/16" x 4¹³/16" (NYPL Arents) (in parts)

Other locations: YCBA (in parts); BL 30.g.2;
Bodleian Arch. Antiqq: A.I.23; DHW; Dr.
Williams's Library 1124.L.3; Lucerne H853.fol
(1810); Newberry B56.4845; NYPL YEZA+;
NYPL YEZA+ (1810); ZBZ BX 422
Lit.: Schiff 962 (10.3 x 12.2 cm) (as 'Executioner
Displaying the Head of John the Baptist')

Variants:
I. Proof before printing on verso: BM 1863-5-9-75
Inscription: H. Fuzelli delᵗ. | | J. Gillray sculpt.

The subject and source are identified on the
cover of Part No. XX. The caption in Moore's
edition (1793) is similar.

The biblical story reads thus:

And [*Saul's captains, Baanah and Rechab*]
came about the the heat of the day to the house
of Ishbosheth, who lay on a bed at noon.
   And they came thither ... and they smote him,
... and slew him, and beheaded him....
   And they brought the head of Ishbosheth unto
David to Hebron, and said to the king, Behold
the head of Ishbosheth the son of Saul thine
enemy....
   And David answered, ... when wicked men
have slain a righteous person in his own house
... shall I not therefore now require his blood of
your hand, and take you away from the earth?
   And David commanded his young men, and
they slew them....

H.Fuseli delᵗ.   J.Gillray sculpt.

100.

101.

102.

101. *Patriarch or Prophet*, 1791
(Vol. II, p. 292, plate L.)
(Issued in Part No. XX, December 1791)

Engraved by William Bromley (1769-1842)
Imprint: Published as the Act directs 20 Oct^r.
1791 by T. Holloway.
Inscription: Fuseli del^t. | | Bromley sculp^t.
Dimensions (to platemark): 17.9 x 13.4 cm |
7' x 5^5/16" (NYPL Arents) (in parts)
Other locations: YCBA (in parts); BL 30.g.2;
Bodleian Arch. Antiqq: A.I.23; DHW; Dr.
Williams' Library 1124.L.3; Lucerne H853 fol
(1810); Newberry B56.4845; NYPL YEZA+;
NYPL YEZA+ (1810); ZBZ BX 422
Plate only: BM 1863-5-9-17
Lit.: Schiff 963 (17.0 x 12.7 cm)

This figure is designated on the cover of Part
No. XX as 'Elijah.' Lavater describes it as being,

... full of fire, of dignity and energy, but
defective in respect of truth and correctness. I
imagine it represents a Patriarch or a Prophet
bestowing his benediction. Nothing can be
more solemn than this face. If that mouth had
anathemas to pronounce, it would strike terror
into the most obdurate hearts. Who could resist
the adjuration of such a person?

102. *Head of Christ*, 1791
(Vol. II, p. 293, plate M.)
(Issued in Part No. XX, December 1791)

Engraved by John Corner (1768?-1825?)
Inscription (bottom centre): J. Corner sc.
Dimensions: ■ 10.8 x 8.6 | 4¼" x 3^6/16" (NYPL
Arents) (in parts)
Other locations: YCBA (in parts); BL 30.g.2;
Bodleian Arch. Antiqq: A.I.23; DHW; Dr.
Williams' Library 1124.L.3; Lucerne H843.fol
(1810); Newberry B56.4845; NYPL YEZA+;
NYPL YEZA+ (1810); ZBZ BX 422
Plate only: DHW; V & A E.1198-1886
Lit.: Schiff 964 (10.4 x 8.4 cm)

This head is listed on the cover of part No. XX
as 'Caricature of Christ'. Lavater criticises its
'savageness' and 'vehemence', but as stated in
the footnote, it is not Fuseli's 'Idea of Christ' but
is copied from Andrea Verrocchio. Lavater states:

The oblong square of this face adds nothing ...
to the expression of its grief ... the less harsh
the forms, the better they express the afflictions
of the soul, the more susceptible they are of
dignity and energy. ... This [*face*] presents only
the grimace of a forced character, only an
assemblage of traits absolutely heterogeneous.

Fuseli Pinx.^t   Holloway Sculp.^t

Ezzelin Count of Ravenna, surnamed Braccaferro or Iron arm, musing over the body of Meduna, slain by him for infidelity during his absence in the Holy Land.

Published as the Act directs by J. Holloway 20 Oct. 1791.

103.

Published as the Act directs by J. Holloway 20 Octobr. 1791.

J. Holloway sculp.^t

104.

103. *Count Ezzelin Bracciaferro Musing over the Body of Meduna Slain by Him for Infidelity While he was Away on a Crusade*, 1791
(Vol. II, p. 294, plate N)
(Issued in Part No. XX, December 1791)

Engraved by Thomas Holloway after Fuseli's lost painting sent (1781) to Caspar Escher vom Wollenhof in Zurich
Imprint: Published as the Act directs, by T. Holloway, 20. Oct. 1791.
Inscription: Fuseli Pinx^t: | | Holloway Sculp^t. | Ezzelin Count of Ravenna, surnamed Bracciaferro or Iron arm, musing over the body of Meduna, slain by him for infidelity during his absence in the Holy Land.—
Dimensions: ■ 13.4 x 16.9 cm | 5¼" x 6^{11}/16" (NYPL Arents) (in parts)
Other locations: YCBA (in parts); BL 30.g.2; Bodleian Arch. Antiqq: A.I.23; DHW; Dr. Williams's Library 1124.L.3; Lucerne H853.fol (1810); Newberry B56.4845; NYPL YEZA+; NYPL YEZA+ (1810); ZBZ BX 422
Plate only: DHW; V & A E.1198-1886
Lit.: Schiff 965 (12.9 x 16.6 cm); Hammelmann 1975, 35; Schiff-Viotto 1977, no. 32
Exh.: Zurich 1941 (144r)

Variants:
I. Proof before printing on verso: BM 1853-12-10-565

Lavater describes Ezzelin's state of mind as follows:

Fettered by remorse of conscience, accused by the presence of his victim, he deplores his madness, but repents it not; he detests it, and yet still applauds himself for it. A character of such force was capable of committing a premeditated crime in cold blood. Before giving himself up to it, he beheld it not in all its blackness: and even after the fatal blow, he does not yet feel it in all its enormity.

104. *Christ at the Sepulchre: A Scene from Raphael*, 1791
(After the engraving by Ennea Vico after Raphael)
(Vol. II, p. 295)
(Issued in Part No. XX, December 1791)

Engraved by Thomas Holloway (1748-1827)

Imprint: Published as the Act directs by T Holloway 20 October 1791.
Inscription: H. Fuseli del^t | | T. Holloway sculp^t
Dimensions: ■ 13.8 x 23.1 cm | 5^7/16" x 9" (NYPL Arents) (in parts)
Other locations: YCBA (in parts); BL 30.g.2; Bodleian Arch. Antiqq: A.I.23; DHW; Dr. Williams's Library 1124.L.3; Lucerne 853.fol (1810); NYPL YEZA+; NYPL YEZA+ (1810); ZBZ BX 422 (13.3 x 22.5 cm)
Plate only: BM 1849-5-12-257; V & A E.1207-1886 (13.7 x 23.0 cm)
Lit.: Schiff 966 (13.3 x 22.5 cm)

Of this 'beautiful composition, drawn from memory', Lavater declares:

This copy* pronounces at once the elogium of our Artist's genius and sensibility; and after the many proofs we have produced of his ardent imagination, one was wanting to establish his gentle and loving character. Is it not self evident that this piece is singularly delicate? Every thing in it breathes tranquility, softness, tenderness. You love to hang over it; You feel an inclination to assist the persons employed in rendering to Jesus Christ services so affecting.

*[*Footnote signed H.H.*] Whoever chooses to compare this copy with the original will find that *all* of it does not belong to Raphael.

105. *Martha Hess*, 1791
(Vol. II, p. 316, pl. Addition L)
(Issued in Part XX, December 1791, though not listed)

Engraved by Thomas Holloway (1748-1827) after the drawing in the collection of Edward Croft-Murray ([1785-1792]; Schiff 848)
Inscription: Fuseli del^t. | | Holloway Sc. | If the Author's Criticism should to the English Reader appear unfounded on comparing the Text with | the Plate, he is informed, that the Designer of the Original Head claims the right of restoring his own | Lines, and leaves the Engraver to the French Edition, in full possession of the Censure.
Dimensions: ■ 11.9 x 8.3 cm | 4^{10}/16" x 3¼" (NYPL Arents) (in parts)
Other locations: YCBA (in parts); BL 30.g.2; Bodleian Arch. Antiqq: A.I.23; DHW; Dr. Williams's Library 1124.L.3; Lucerne H853.fol

(1810) (11.7 x 8.1 cm); Newberry B56.4845; NYPL YEZA+; NYPL YEZA+ (1810); ZBZ BX 422 (11.6 x 8.1 cm)
Plate only: BM 1863-5-9-16 (12.1 x 8.1 cm)
Lit.: Schiff 967 (11.6 x 8.1 cm)

105.

Once again Fuseli asks the reader to judge Lavater's critical comments by comparing Holloway's engraving with the earlier version in the French edition (No. **58**).

Nature had imprinted on this physiognomy the image of gentleness and benignity ... but the irregular design of the eye, the immoderate lengthening of the nose, and the harshness of several other features, produce a heterogenous effect, which does not belong to the character of this face. The painter intended to give it an antique form, to introduce an expression of greatness, but ... that expression has degenerated into hardness; and in this, perhaps, he has only lent it his own character, little formed apparently for sensibility.

106. *Young Man Sitting Underneath a Tree*, 1792
(Vol. II, p. 388)
(Issued in Part No. XXIV, July 1792)

Engraved vignette by Thomas Holloway (1748-1827)
Imprint: Published as the Act directs by J Murray T Holloway & the other Proprietors.
Inscription: Fuseli Delin'. | | Holloway Sc
Dimensions (to platemark): 10.3 x 12.7 cm | 4¹/16" x 5" (NYPL Arents) (in parts)
Other locations: YCBA (in parts); BL 30.g.2; Bodleian Arch. Antiqq: A.I.23; DHW; Dr. Williams' Library 1124.L.3; Lucerne 853.fol (1810); NYPL YEZA+; NYPL YEZA+ (1810); ZBZ BX 422
Plate only: BM 1863-5-9-83
Lit.: Schiff 968 (10.2 x 12.6 cm)

The figure is described on the cover of Part No. 24 as a 'Beautiful male figure (lax meditation)'

106.

107.

107. *Sibyl with Open Book in her Lap*, 1793
(Vol. III, p. 90)
(Listed on the cover of Part No. XXVI, but first issued in Part No. XXVII, April 1793)

Engraved vignette by Charles Grignion (1721-1810)
Inscription: Fuseli Delin. | Grignion sculp
Dimensions (to platemark): 8.6 x 11.0 cm | 3⁶/16" x 4⁵/16" (NYPL Arents) (in parts)
Other locations: YCBA (in parts); BL 30.g.3; Bodleian Arch. Antiqq: A.I.23; DHW; Dr. Williams' Library; Lucerne H853 fol (1810); Newberry B56.4845; NYPL YEZA +; NYPL YEZA+ (1810); ZBZ BX 423
Lit.: Schiff 969 (8.6 x 11.0 cm); Tomory 1972, pl. 110

Variants:
I. Proof before printed verso: BM 1863-5-9-77

108.

108. *Seated Muscular Male Nude*, 1793
(Vol. III, p. 133)
(Listed on the cover of Part No. XXVIII, but contained in No. XXIX, September 1793)

Engraved by Thomas Holloway (1748-1827)
Inscription: Fuseli Del'. | |Holloway Sc.
Dimensions (to platemark): 9.0 x 6.6 cm | 3⁹/16" x 2¹⁰/16" (NYPL Arents) (in parts)
Other locations: YCBA (in parts); BL 30.g.3; Bodleian Arch. Antiqq:; DHW; Dr. Williams' Library 1124.L.4; Lucerne H853.fol (1810); Newberry B56.4845; NYPL YEZA +; NYPL YEZA+ (1810); ZBZ BX 423
Plate only: BM 1863-5-9-32
Lit.: Schiff 970 (8.9 x 6.5 cm)

Variants:
I. Proof before printing on reverse: V & A E.1209-1886

According to Lavater:
Solid and calm strength manifests itself by a well-proportioned stature, rather too short than too tall; by a thick nape, broad shoulders, a face rather bony than fleshy, even in a state of perfect health. [III, 132]

109. *Woman's Hand and Arm with a Bracelet Around the Wrist*, 1797
(Vol. III, p. 424, pl. Addition B)
(Listed on cover of Part No. XXXIX, but first issued in Part No. XL, May 1797)

Engraved by Thomas Holloway (1748-1827) after Fuseli's sketch in the Kunsthaus, Zurich ([1778-1779]; Schiff 505)

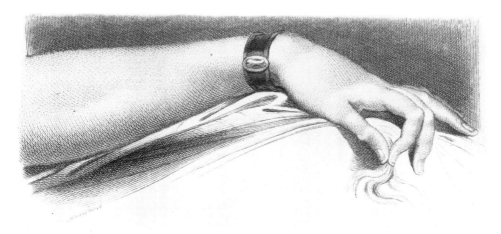

109.

Inscription (bottom left): T Holloway Direxit.
Dimensions (to plate mark): 10.8 x 22.5 cm |
4¼" x 8¹⁴/16" (NYPL Arents) (in parts)
Other locations: YCBA (in parts); BL 30.g.3;
Bodleian Arch. Antiqq: A.I.23; DHW; Dr.
Williams' Library 1124.L.5; Lucerne H853.fol
(1810); Newberry B56.4845; NYPL YEZA+;
NYPL YEZA+ (1810); ZBZ BX 424
Lit.: Schiff 971 (10.5 x 22.5 cm).
Exh.: Kansas City 1982 (17).

Lavater finds this hand, which exemplifies for
him 'the trick and finesse of coquetry',

...immoderately lengthened, too much on the
stretch, and of a delicacy affectedly refined ...
whose archetype is no where to be found in
nature. ... [*This*] drawing proves ... that
[*Fuseli's*] genius does not exclude agreeable and
soft expression. Whatever impression this hand
may make on minds purely sensual, to me it
appears *cold*.

110. *Crossed Man's and Woman's Hands*, 1797
(Vol. III, p. 425, pl. Addition C)
(Listed on the cover of Part No. XXXIX, but first
issued in Part No. XL, May 1797)

Engraved by Thomas Holloway (1748-1827) after
the sketch in the Nationale Forschungs- und
Gedenkstätten der klassischen deutschen Literatur,
Weimar ([1778-1779]; Schiff 508)
Inscription (bottom left): T. Holloway Direxit
Dimensions (to plate mark): 12.0 x 18.3 |
4¾" x 7²/16" (NYPL Arents) (in parts)
Other locations: YCBA (in parts); BL 30.g.3;
Bodleian Arch. Antiqq: A.I.23; DHW; Dr.
Williams' Library 1124.L.5; Lucerne H853.fol
(1810); Newberry B56.4845; NYPL YEZA+;
NYPL YEZA+ (1810); ZBZ BX 424
Lit.: Schiff 972 (?10.5 x 22.5 cm).
Exh.: Kansas City 1982 (18).

Lavater describes this design as an attempt

...to contrast the delicacy of the female hand
with the energy of that of the male: probably
[*Fuseli's*] own hand served him as a model for
this last. The uppermost indicates calmness and
repose; the other ... seems made for execution.
The former needs to be guided; the latter directs
itself. ... [*However,*] this is not a brilliant
production, either as to correctness of design, or
elegance of fore-shortening.

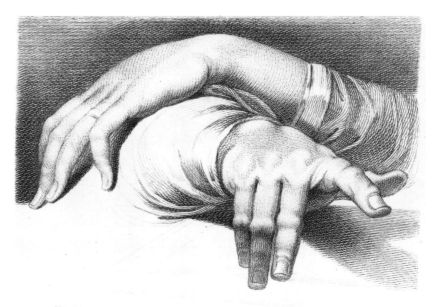

110.

Nos. 84A - 85A, 87A - 98A, 100A - 105A,
109A -110A, 109B - 110B.
John Caspar Lavater.
LAVATER'S | ESSAYS ON PHYSIOGNOMY. |

WITH | ORNAMENTAL CARICATURES, |
AND | FINISHED PORTRAITS. | TRANSLATED
FROM THE LAST PARIS EDITION, | BY THE
REV. C. MOORE, LL.D. F.R.S. | [Vignette] |

[VOLUME I.] | LONDON: | PRINTED BY AND FOR W. LOCKE, RED-LION STREET, | HOLBORN. [n.d.].

[*Intended to accompany*]: THE | CONJUROR'S MAGAZINE, | OR, | MAGICAL AND PHYSIOGNOMICAL MIRROR. | INCLUDING | A SUPERB EDITION | OF | LAVATER'S | ESSAYS ON PHYSIOGNOMY. | VOL. I. | — | LONDON: | PRINTED FOR W. LOCKE, NO. 12, RED-LION STREET, HOLBORN. | 1792.

ESSAYS ON PHYSIOGNOMY. | CALCULATED TO EXTEND | THE KNOWLEDGE AND THE LOVE OF MANKIND. | WRITTEN BY | THE REVEREND JOHN CASPAR LAVATER, | CITIZEN OF ZURICH. | TRANSLATED FROM THE LAST PARIS EDITION, | BY THE REV. C. MOORE, LL D. F.R.S. | ILLUSTRATED BY | SEVERAL HUNDRED ENGRAVINGS, | ACCURATELY COPIED FROM | THE ORIGINALS. | [Vignette] | VOLUME II. | — | LONDON: | PRINTED FOR W. LOCKE, NO. 12, RED LION-STREET, HOLBORN. | 1793.

[*Engraved title page*]: ESSAYS | ON | PHYSIOGNOMY; | CALCULATED TO EXTEND | THE KNOWLEDGE AND THE LOVE OF MANKIND. | WRITTEN BY | THE REV. JOHN CASPAR LAVATER, | CITIZEN OF ZURICH. | TRANSLATED FROM THE LAST PARIS EDITION, | BY THE REV. C. MOORE, LL.D. F.R.S. | ILLUSTRATED BY | SEVERAL HUNDRED ENGRAVINGS, | ACCURATELY | COPIED FROM THE ORIGINALS. | [Vignette] | VOLUME I. [-VOLUME III.] | = | LONDON: | PRINTED FOR W. LOCKE, N°. 12, RED LION STREET, HOLBORN. | — | 1793, 1794.

...ILLUSTRATED BY | SEVERAL HUNDRED ENGRAVINGS, | ACCURATELY | COPIED FROM THE ORIGINALS. | [Vignette] | VOLUME I. [VOLUME IV.] | = | LONDON: | SOLD BY H. D. SYMONDS, N°. 20, PATERNOSTER ROW. | 1797.

[*Reissued as*]: THE | WHOLE WORKS OF LAVATER | ON | PHYSIOGNOMY; | WRITTEN BY | THE REV. JOHN CASPAR LAVATER, | CITIZEN OF ZURICH. | TRANSLATED FROM THE LAST PARIS EDITION | BY GEORGE GRENVILLE ESQR. | ILLUSTRATED BY | SEVERAL HUNDRED ENGRAVINGS. |

[Vignette] | VOLUME. I [-VOLUME. IV]. | = | LONDON. | PRINTED FOR W. BUTTERS, & SOLD BY W. SIMMONDS, PATERNOSTER ROW. [n.d.]

84A. *A Trans-Tiberine Roman*, [1792]
(Gathered at the end of Vol [II], as plate [11])

Engraved by John Barlow (1760-1810?)
Inscription (along bottom left-hand edge of cloak): Fuseli delin. | | Barlow sculp. | A TRANS-TIBERINE (TRASTEVERINO) | A Race of Men who inhabit the South side of the Tiber, they consider themselves as the legitimate Descendants | of the Ancient Romans, and all the rest of the Inhabitants as bastards of Transalpine Barbarians. | (lower right): From Lavater.
Dimensions: ■ 11.0 x 9.1 cm | $4^6/16$" x $3^9/16$" (Bodleian Per 930.e.663)
Other locations: Illinois Baldwin 4579 (1793) (Vol. II, between pp. 274-275) (10.5 x 9.1 cm)

Variants:
I. Reissued (1797) in truncated form but with Volume, page and plate nos. ('82') added (BL 1509.1034) (Vol. II, facing p. 32) (9.9 x 9.0 cm)
Inscription (top): Page 32. | | A TRANS TIBERINE | | Vol. II. | (bottom): [*Plate no.*] 82
Other locations: Bern L9.895 (1797); Bern A16.776 (Grenville); BL 7410.tt.8 (Grenville); Library Company Id 7835.0 (1797); Widener College BF843.L3 1797; ZBZ AX 658 (1797); ZBZ AX 658; ZBZ Lav.H.610a (Grenville)
Lacking plate: Library Company Ia Lav. (1797); Newberry B56.485 (Grenville)

Announced on the title page of *The Conjuror's Magazine* as appearing in the January 1792 issue (copies: Bodleian Per.930.e.663 and British Library P.P. 5441.ba).

85A, 87A. *Heads of Brutus and Mary Magdalen*, [1793]
(Vol. II, facing p. 259) (1794)

Two separate portraits within a single frame, engraved by John Barlow (1760-1810?)
Inscription (top): Page 259. | | A | | B | | Vol. II.
Dimensions: ■ 7.7 x 6.6 cm | $3^2/16$" x $2^{10}/16$"; ■ 8.5 x 14.3 cm | $3^7/16$" x $5^{10}/16$" (ZBZ AG 913)

Other locations (lacking plate): Illinois Baldwin 4579

Variants
I. Reissued (1797) with plate no. ('172') added (Vol. III, facing p. 259): BL 1509.1034
Other locations: Bern L9.895 (1797); Bern A16.776 (Grenville); BL 7410.tt.8 (Grenville) (facing p. 257); Library Company Ia Lav. (1797); Library Company Id 7835.0 (1797); Newberry B56.485 (Grenville); NYPL YEZA 1797; Widener College BF843.L3 1797; ZBZ AX 659 (1797); ZBZ Lav.H.610b (Grenville)

88A. *St. John the Baptist in the Ecstasy of Contemplation*, [1792]
(Gathered at the end of Vol. [II], as plate [31])

Engraved by John Barlow (1760-1810?)
Inscription (bottom): Fuseli delin. | | Barlow sculp. | S^t. JOHN. | From Lavater.
Dimensions (to platemark): 17.6 x 11.2 cm | 6^{15}/16" x 4^9/16" (Bodleian Per 930.e.663)
Other locations: Illinois Baldwin 4579 (1793) (Vol. II, facing p. 261); ZBZ AG 913 (1793, 1794)

Variants:
I. Reissued (1797) with Volume, page and plate nos. ('173') added (Vol. III, facing p. 261): BL 1509.1034
Inscription (top): Page 261. | | Vol II. | (bottom): Fuseli delin. | | Barlow sculp. | S^t. JOHN. | From Lavater. | [*Plate No.*] 173.
Other locations: Bern L9.895 (Vol. II, facing p. 260); Bern A16.776 (Grenville); BL 7410.tt.8; Library Company Ia Lav. (1797); Library Company Id 7835.0 (1797); Newberry B56.485 (Grenville); NYPL YEZA 1797; Widener College BF843.L3 1793 (facing p. 262); ZBZ AX 659; ZBZ Lav.H.610b (Grenville)

This 'Highly finished Head of ST. JOHN, drawn by Fuseli' was one of the 'Capital Engravings, all faithfully copied from LAVATER' announced on the cover of the October 1791 issue of *The Conjuror's Magazine*.

89A. *Head of Satan*, [1792]
(Gathered at end of Vol. [II] as plate no. [5])

Engraved by John Barlow (1760-1810?)

Inscription (along bottom of neck): Drawn by Fuseli. | | Engraved by Barlow. | SATAN. | From Lavater.
Dimensions (to platemark): 17.8 x 11.3 cm | 6^{15}/16" x 4^9/16" (Bodleian Per 930.e.663)
Other locations: Illinois Baldwin 4579 (1793) (Vol. II, facing p. 274); ZBZ AG 913 (1793, 1794)

Variants:
I. Reissued (1797) with Volume, page and plate nos. ('174') added: BL 1509.1034 (Vol. III, between pp. 262-263)
Inscription (top): Page 262. | | Vol. II. | (along bottom of neck): Drawn by Fuseli. | | Engraved by Barlow. | SATAN. | From Lavater. | [*Plate No.*] 174.
Other locations: Bern L9.895 (Vol. II, facing p. 262); Bern A16.776 (Grenville) (facing p. 262); BL 7410.tt.8 (Grenville); Library Company Ia Lav. (1797); Library Company Id 7835.0 (1797); Newberry B56.485 (Grenville); NYPL YEZA 1797; Widener College BF843.L3 1793; ZBZ AX 659; ZBZ Lav.H.610b (Grenville)

This was one of the 'Three Capital Copper-Plates...accurately copied from LAVATER' announced on the cover of the September 1791 issue of *The Conjuror's Magazine*.

90A. *The Death of Abel*, [1792]
(Gathered at the back of Vol. I as plate no. [14])

Engraved by John Barlow (1760-1810?)
Inscription (bottom): Fuseli delin. | | Barlow sculp. | ABEL | the first victim sacrificed to envy. | from Lavater.
Dimensions: ■ 7.6 x 15.7 cm | 2^{15}/16" x 6^3/16"; ■ 7.8 x 15.9 cm | 3^1/16" x 6^5/16" (Bodleian Per 930.e.663)
Other locations: Illinois Baldwin 4579 (1793) (Vol. II, between pp. 274-275); ZBZ AG 913 (Vol. II, between pp. 262-263)

Variants:
I. Reissued (1797) with Volume, page and plate nos. ('176') added (Vol. III, between pp. 262-263): BL 1509.1034
Inscription (top): Page 263. | | Vol. II | (bottom): Fuseli delin. | | Barlow sculp. | ABEL | the first victim sacrificed to envy. | from Lavater. | [*Plate No.*] 176

Other locations: BL 7410.tt.8 (Grenville); Bern L9.895 (1797); Bern A16.776 (Grenville) (facing p. 263); Library Company Ia Lav. (1797); Library Company Id 7835.0 (1797); Newberry B56.485 (Grenville); NYPL YEZA 1797 (Vol. III, between pp. 262-263); Widener College BF843.L3 1793 (facing p. 263); ZBZ AX 659 (1797); ZBZ Lav.H.610b (Grenville)

'ABEL lying murdered on the Ground' was one of the 'elegant Copper Plates...accurately copied from LAVATER, and drawn by FUSELI,' announced on the cover of the February 1792 issue of *The Conjuror's Magazine*.

91A. *Cain*, 1792
(Gathered at the end of Vol. II as plate no. [18])

Engraved by John Barlow (1760-1810?)
Inscription: Fuseli delin| |Barlow sculp|CAIN.| From Lavater
Dimensions (to platemark): 17.3 x 11.0 cm | 6^{13}/16" x 4^5/16" (Bodleian Per 930.e.663)
Other locations: Illinois Baldwin 4579 (1793) (Vol. II, between pp. 262-263); ZBZ AG 913 (Vol. II, between pp. 262-263)

Variants:
I. Reissued (1797) with Volume, page and plate nos. ('175') added: BL 1509.1034
Inscription: Page 263.| |Vol. II.|(bottom): Fuseli delin| |Barlow sculp|CAIN.|From Lavater.|[Plate No.] 175
Other locations: Bern L9.895 (1797); Bern A16.776 (Grenville); BL 7410.tt.8 (Grenville); Library Company Ia Lav. (1797) (facing p. 263); Library Company Id 7835.0 (1797); Newberry B56.485 (Grenville); NYPL YEZA 1797 (Vol. III, between pp. 262-263); ZBZ AX 659 (1797); ZBZ Lav.H.610b (Grenville)

'CAIN ruminating on the Murder of ABEL.- Engraved by Barlow' was one of the 'elegant Copper Plates, all accurately copied from LAVATER, and drawn by FUSELI' announced on the cover of the March 1792 issue of *The Conjuror's Magazine*.

92A. *Balaam Blessing the Children of Israel*, [1792]
(Gathered at the end of Vol. [I] as plate no.[12])

Engraved by John Barlow (1760-1810?)
Inscription (bottom): Fuseli delin.| |Barlow sculp.|THE MAGICIAN BALAAM|Blessing the Children of Israel whom he intended to Curse|From Lavater
Dimensions (to platemark): 16.8 x 11.1 cm | 6^1/16 x 4½" (Bodleian Per 930.e.663)
Other locations: Illinois Baldwin 4579 (1793) (Vol. II, between pp. 274-275); ZBZ AG 913 (1793, 1794) (Vol. II, facing p. 262)

Variants:
I. Reissued (1797) with Volume, page and plate nos. ('177') added (facing p. 263): BL 1509.1034
Inscription (top): Page 263.| |Vol II.|(bottom): Fuseli delin.| |Barlow sculp.|THE MAGICIAN BALAAM|Blessing the Children of Israel whom he intended to curse|From Lavater| [Plate No.] 177.
Other locations: Bern L9.895; Bern A16.776 (Grenville) (facing p. 264); BL 7410.tt.8 (Grenville); Library Company Ia Lav. (1797); Library Company Id 7835.0 (1797) (facing p. 263); Newberry B56.485; NYPL YEZA 1797 (Vol. III, between pp. 262-263); Widener College BF843.L3 1793 (facing p. 262); ZBZ AX 659; ZBZ Lav.H.610b (Grenville)

This was one of the 'Three Capital Copper Plates, purposely engraved for this Work,' announced as embellishment no. 3 on the cover of the January 1792 issue of *The Conjuror's Magazine*.

93A. *The Escapee: A Real Scene in the Hospital of S. Spirito at Rome*, [1793]
(Vol. II, facing p. 264)

Unsigned engraving [by John Barlow (1760-1810?)]
Inscription (top): Page 264.| |Vol. II.|(bottom centre): G
Dimensions: ■ 8.3 x 14.5 cm | 3^5/16" x 5^{11}/16" (Illinois Baldwin 4579)
Other locations: ZBZ AG 913 (1794)

Variants:
I. Reissued (1797) with plate no. ('178') added (Vol. III, facing p. 264): BL 1509. 1034
Other locations: Bern L9.895 (1797) (8.4 x 14.5 cm); Bern A16.776 (Grenville) (Vol. III,

between pp. 264-265); BL 7410.tt.8 (Grenville);
Library Company Ia Lav. (1797); Library
Company Id 7835.0 (1797); Newberry B56.485
(Grenville); NYPL YEZA 1797; ZBZ AX 659
(1797); ZBZ Lav.H.610b (Grenville) (between
pp. 264-265

94A. *The Witch of Endor*, [1793]
(Vol. II, between pp. 264-265)

Unsigned engraving [by John Barlow (1760-
1810?)]
Inscription (top): Page 264. | | Vol.II. | (bottom): H
Dimensions: ■ 8.2 x 14.2 cm | 3¼" x 5¹⁰/16"
(Illinois Baldwin 4579)
Other locations: ZBZ AG 913 (1794)

Variants:
I. Reissued (1797) with plate nos. ('177 | | 179')
added (Vol. III, between pp. 264-265): BL
1509.1034
Other locations: Bern L9.895; Bern A16.776
(Grenville); BL 7410.tt.8 (Grenville); Library
Company Ia Lav. (1797); Library Company Id
7835.0 (1797); NYPL YEZA 1797; ZBZ AX
659 (1797); ZBZ Lav.H.610b (Grenville)

95A., 96A.-97A. *Calmness* and *Four Horrible
Faces from Hell*
(Vol. II, facing p. 265)

Unsigned engraving by John Barlow (1760-1810?)
Inscription (top): Page 265. | | Vol. II. | Calmness. |
(bottom): I
Dimensions: ■ 14.7 x 8.3 cm | 5¹²/16" x 3⁴/16";
▣ 14.8 x 8.5 cm | 5¹³/16" x 3⁶/16" (Illinois
Baldwin 4579)
Other locations: ZBZ AG 913 (1794) (between
pp. 264-265)

Variants:
I. Reissued (1797) with plate no. ('181') added
(Vol. III, facing p. 265): BL 1509.1034
Other locations: Bern L9.895 (1797) (Vol. II,
facing p. 266); Bern A16.776 (Grenville)
(between pp. 264-265); BL 7410.tt.8 (Grenville)
(between pp. 264-265); Library Company Ia
Lav. (1797); Library Company Id 7835.0
(1797) (between pp. 264-265); Newberry

B56.485 (Grenville) (between pp. 264-265);
NYPL YEZA 1797; ZBZ AX 659 (1797)
(between pp. 264-265); ZBZ Lav.H.610b
(Grenville) (between pp. 264-265)

98A. *Salome with the Head of John the Baptist
in a Charger*
(Vol. II, between pp. 264-265)

Unsigned outline engraving [by John Barlow
(1760-1810?)]
Inscription (top): Page 265. | | Vol. II. | (bottom): K
Dimensions: ■ 14.1 x 8.9 cm | 5⁹/16" x 3½"
(Illinois Baldwin 4579)
Other locations: ZBZ AG 913 (1794) (Vol. II,
facing p. 265)

Variants:
I. Reissued (1797) with plate no. ('182') added
(Vol. III, between pp. 264-265): BL 1509.1034
Other locations: Bern L9.895 (1797) (Vol. II,
between pp. 266-267); Bern A16.776
(Grenville) (facing p. 265); Library Company Ia
Lav. (1797); Library Company Id 7835.0
(1797) (facing p. 265); Newberry B56.485;
NYPL YEZA 1797; ZBZ AX 659 (1797)
(facing p. 265); ZBZ Lav.H.610b (Grenville)
(facing p. 265)

100A. *Rechab with the Head of Ishbosheth*, 1792
(Vol. II, between pp. 274-275)

Engraved by John Barlow (1760-1810?)
Inscription: Fuseli delin. | | Barlow sculp. |
RECHAB with the Head of ISHBOSHETH. | 4ᵗʰ.
Chap. 11ᵗʰ. Book of Samuel. | From Lavater.
Dimensions: ■ 13.9 x 9.7 cm | 5⁷/16" x 3¹³/16"
(Illinois Baldwin 4579)
Other locations: Newberry B56.485 (Grenville);
Widener College BF843.L3.1793 (1797) (Vol. IV,
facing title page); ZBZ AG 914 (1794) (Vol. III,
facing title page)
Lacking plate: Bern L9.895 (1797); Bern A16.776
(Grenville); BL 1509.1034; BL 7410.tt.8;
Bodleian Per 930.e.663 (1792); Library Company
Ia Lav. (1797); Library Company Id 7835.0
(1797); NYPL YEZA 1797; ZBZ AX 660 (1797);
ZBZ Lav.H.610a-c

This was one of the 'elegant Copper Plates, all
accurately copied from LAVATER, and drawn by

FUSELI,' announced on the cover of the February 1792 issue of *The Conjuror's Magazine*.

101A. *Elijah Bestowing his Benediction*
(Vol. II, facing p. 266)

Unsigned engraving by John Barlow (1760-1810?)
Inscription (top): Page 266. | | Vol II. | (bottom): L
Dimensions: ■ 14.3 x 8.9 cm | 5^{10}/16" x 3½"
(Illinois Baldwin 4579)
Other locations: ZBZ AG 913 (1794)

Variants:
I. Reissued (1797) with plate no. ('180') added (Vol. III, facing p. 266): BL 1509.1034
Other locations: Bern L9.895 (1797) (Vol. II, between pp. 266-267); Bern A16.776 (Grenville); BL 7410.tt.8 (Grenville); Library Company Ia Lav. (1797) (between pp. 265-266); Library Company Id 7835.0 (1797); Newberry B56.485 (Grenville); NYPL YEZA 1797; ZBZ AX 659 (1797)

102A. *Head of Christ*, 1793
(Vol. II, facing p. 267)

Re-engraved by John Barlow (1760-1810?)
Inscription (bottom right): Barlow sculp. | CHRIST. | From Lavater.
Dimensions(Oval): ■9.9 x 7.8 cm | 3^{14}/16" x 3^1/16"; ■ 10.3 x 8.3 cm | 4^1/16" x 4¼"; (rectangle): ■12.3 x 8.5 cm | 4^{13}/16" x 3^5/16; ■13.0 x 9.1 cm | 5^2/16" x 3^9/16" (Illinois Baldwin 4579)
Other locations: ZBZ AG 913 (1793, 1794) (between pp. 266-267)

Variants:
I. Reissued (1797) with Volume, plate and page nos. ('183') added (Vol. III, between pp. 266-267): BL 1509.1034
Inscription (top): Page 267. | | Vol II. | (bottom right): Barlow sculp. | CHRIST. | From Lavater. | [*Plate No.*] 183
Other locations: Bern L9.895 (1797) (Vol. II, between pp. 266-267); Bern A16.776 (Grenville) (Vol. III, between pp. 266-267); BL 7410.tt.8 (Grenville) (Vol. III, between pp. 266-267); Library Company Ia Lav. (1797); Library Company Id 7835.0 (1797) (between

pp. 266-277); Newberry B56.485 (Grenville) (Vol. III, between pp. 266-267); NYPL YEZA 1797 (Vol. III, facing p. 267); Widener College BF843.L3.1793 (1797); ZBZ AX 659 (1797) (Vol. III, between pp. 266-267); ZBZ Lav.H.610b (Grenville) (Vol. III, between pp. 266-267)

103A. *Count Ezzelin Musing over the Body of Meduna, Slain by him for Infidelity*
(Vol. II, between pp. 266-267)

Unsigned engraving by John Barlow (1760-1810?)
Inscription (top): Page 267. | | Vol. II.
Dimensions: ■ 8.8 x 11.6 cm | 3^7/16" x 4^9/16"
(Illinois Baldwin 4579)
Other locations: ZBZ AG 913 (1794) (facing p. 267)

Variants:
I. Reissued (1797) with plate no. ('184') added (Vol. III, between pp. 266-267): BL 1509.1034
Other locations: Bern L9.895 (1797) (Vol. II, facing p. 267); Bern A16.776 (Grenville) (Vol. III, facing p. 267); BL 7410.tt.8 (Grenville) (Vol. III, facing p. 267); Library Company Ia Lav. (1797) (between pp. 265-266); Library Company Id 7835.0 (1797) (facing p. 267); Newberry B56.485 (Grenville) (facing p. 272); NYPL YEZA 1797; ZBZ AX 659 (1797) (facing p. 267); ZBZ Lav.H.610b (Grenville) (facing p. 267)

104A. *Christ at the Sepulchre*, [1794]
(Vol. II, facing p. 268)

Unsigned re-engraving by John Barlow (1760-1810?)
Inscription: Page 268. | | Vol. II.
Dimensions: ■ 8.7 x 14.2 cm | 3^7/16" x 5^9/16"
(ZBZ AG 913)

Variants:
I. Reissued (1797) with plate no. ('185') added (Vol. III, facing p. 268): BL 1059.1034
Other locations: Bern L9.895 (1797) (Vol. II, facing p. 268); Bern A16.776 (Grenville); BL 7410.tt.8 (Grenville); Library Company Ia Lav. (1797); Library Company Id 7835.0 (1797); Newberry B56.485 (Grenville); NYPL YEZA

1797; ZBZ AX 659 (1797); ZBZ Lav.H.610a (Grenville)

105A. *Head of of a Woman Expressive of Gentleness and Benignity*, [1792]
(Gathered at the end of Vol. [I] as plate no. [24])

Engraved by John Barlow (1760-1810?)
Inscription: Fuseli Del.|⎮Barlow Sculp.|
GENTLENESS and BENIGNITY.|From Lavater.
Dimensions: ■ 11.9 x 8.2 cm | $4^{10}/16$ x $3^3/16$;
▣ 12.9 x 9.2 cm | $5^2/16$" x $3^{10}/16$" (Bodleian Per 930.e.663)
Other locations: Illinois Baldwin 4579 (1793) (Vol. II, between pp. 274-275); ZBZ AG 913 (1793, 1794) (Vol. II, facing p. 284)

Variants:
I. Reissued (1797) with Volume, page and plate nos. ('189') added (Vol. II, facing p. 284): BL 1059.1034
Inscription: Page 284.|⎮Vol. II.|Fuseli Del.|⎮ Barlow Sculp.|GENTLENESS and BENIGNITY.|From Lavater.|[*Plate No.*] 189
Other locations: Bern L9.985 (Vol. II, facing p. 284); Bern A16.776 (Grenville) (between pp. 284-285); BL 7410.tt.8 (Grenville) (between pp. 284-285); Library Company Ia Lav. (1797) (between pp. 284-285); Library Company Id 7835.0 (1797); Newberry B56.485 (Grenville); NYPL YEZA 1797 (Vol III, facing p. 284); Widener College BF 843.L3.1793; ZBZ AX 659 (1797) ZBZ Lav.H.610b (Grenville)

This 'Portrait of GENTLENESS and BENIGNITY' was the first of three 'elegant Engravings, all accurately copied by BARLOW, from LAVATER' announced on the cover of the June 1792 issue of *The Conjuror's Magazine*.

109A. *Hand of a Woman*, 1794
(Vol. III, facing p. 328)

Unsigned engraving [by John Barlow (1760-1810?)]
Inscription (top): Vol. III.
Dimensions: ■ 8.6 x 16.2 cm | $3^6/16$" x $6^6/16$";
▣ 8.8 x 16.3 cm | $3^7/16$" x $6^7/16$" (ZBZ AG 914) (1794)
Variants:
I. Reissued (1797) with page and plate nos.

('315') added (Vol. III, facing p. 328): BL 1059.1034
Inscription (top): Page 328.|⎮Vol. III.|
(bottom): [*Plate No.*] 315
Other locations: Bern L9.895 (1797); Bern A16.776 (Grenville) (facing p. 328); BL 7410.tt.8 (Grenville) (facing p. 328); Library Company Ia Lav. (1797) (facing page 328); Library Company Id 7835.0 (1797); Newberry B56.485 (Grenville); NYPL YEZA 1797 (Vol. IV, between pp. 328-329); Widener College BF843.L3 1797; ZBZ AX 660 (facing p. 328); ZBZ Lav.H.610c (Grenville) (facing p. 328)

110A. *Two Hands*
(Vol. III, between pp. 328-329)

Unsigned engraving by John Barlow (1760-1810?)
Inscription (top): Vol. III.
Dimensions: ■ 9.8 x 14.4 cm | $3^{14}/16$" x $5^{11}/16$" (ZBZ AG 914) (1794)

Variants:
I. Reissued (1797) with page and plate nos. ('316') added (Vol. III, between pp. 328-329): BL 1509.1034
Inscription (top): Page 328.|⎮Vol. III.|[*Plate No.*] 316
Other locations: Bern L9.895 (1797) (Vol. III, facing p. 328); Library Company Ia Lav. (1797) (between pp. 328-329) (page and vol. nos. cropped); Library Company Id 7835.0 (1797); NYPL YEZA 1797 (Vol. IV, facing p. 328); Widener College, BF843.L3 1797 (between pp. 328-329); ZBZ AX 660 (1797) (between pp. 328-329) (top left hand edge cropped)

109B, 110B. *Man and Woman's Crossed Hands; Woman's Hand and Arm with a Bracelet Around the Wrist*, [post 1797]
(Vol. IV, between pp. 328-329; Plate 316)
(Grenville's edition only)

Unsigned engraving by John Barlow (1760-1810?)
Inscription (top): Page 328.|⎮Vol. III.|[*Plate No.*] 316.
Dimensions: ■ 9.6 x 14.4 cm | $3^{14}/16$" x 5¾" (BL 7410.tt.8)
Other locations: Bern A16.776; Newberry B56.485

******

111. *Alcibiades accompanied by Phrynia and Timandra Visits Timon in his Cave*, 1790
(Shakespeare, *Timon of Athens*, IV, iii)

Etched by William Blake (1757-1827) after
Fuseli's pen and wash drawing in the Auckland
City Art Gallery (1783; Schiff 1755)
Imprint: Publishd by W Blake Poland St. July 28:
1790.
Dimensions: ■20.2 x 29.6 cm | 7¹⁵/16" x 11¹⁰/16"
(BM 1863-11-14-87)
Lit.: Essick 1980, 61-63, pl. 55; Essick 1983, no.
XXXIII, pls. 74-75
Exh.: Florence 1979 (5)

Reduced to beggary by excessive generosity and
embittered by the ingratitude of his friends in his

time of need, Timon becomes a misanthrope and
goes to live in a cave near the seashore, focusing
all of his hatred on Athens and its citizens. As he
digs for roots, he uncovers a cache of gold, which
he will give to Alcibiades to support his siege of
Athens. (Alcibiades had been unjustly exiled from
Athens.) Fuseli's design shows Alcibiades arriving
at the cave with his 'brace of harlots', Phrynia
and Timandra, while Timon sits brooding at the
entrance to the cave. A shovel leans against the
wall and coins from the treasure trove are
scattered on the ground.

Fuseli's later illustration of the play for
Chalmers' edition of *Shakespeare* (1805) reprises
this scene but in a vertical format omitting
Alcibiades and his mistresses (No. **215**).

111.

112. *Allegory of a Dream of Love*, [c. 1790]

Etched by William Blake (1757-1828)
Inscription (within the composition): FALSA AD
COELUM MITTUNT INSOMNIA MANES
Dimensions: 22.0 x 35.0 cm | 8¹⁰/16" x 13¾"
(BM 1882-8-12-221)
Lit.: Schiff 1348 (22.0 x 35.9 cm) (dated as 'c.

1800-1805'); Keynes 1957, no. XXXV; Bindman
1978, no. 80; Essick 1980, 61-63, fig. 56; Essick
1983, no. XXXIV
Exh.: London 1957 (22/8) (as 'Falsa ad Coelum
Mittunt Insomnia Manes')

According to Gert Schiff, Fuseli's allegory is
based upon the description in Virgil (*Aeneid*, VI,
893-896) of the two gates in the bowers of sleep:

True dreams pass through the gate of 'transparent horn'; from the gate of 'polished ivory' come forth, as expressed in Virgil's words inscribed on the floor, those 'false visions that the nether powers speed therefrom to the heaven above' (trans. H.R. Fairclough). The sleeping woman's dream, with its strongly erotic tenor, falls into the category of delusive visions—hence the moth (on the woman's thigh), which is always associated in Fuseli's work with the demonic and the erotic. But the offspring of such visions (including the cupids) are driven out by the rising sun, represented here by the Egyptian god Harpocrates (in the form of a herm), who epitomises truth.

Schiff sees the elephant-headed man at the lower right as Fuseli's own visualisation of Homer's play upon the Greek words for 'ivory' and 'deceive' (*Odyssey*, XIX, 562-567). Essick (1983, 175-176) suggests a possible association with Ganesa, the Hindu god of knowledge and prudence. (The *Index to the First Eighteen Volumes of the Asiatic Researches*, Calcutta, 1835, notes a reference to 'Ganésa and Janus, the identity of' in the first volume of that journal, 1799, and there are further entries for other early issues; might there not be other sources of this kind earlier in the 1790s through which Fuseli could have learned about Ganesa?).

My dating for *Falsa ad Coelum* is that suggested by Essick, 'based on the great similarity between its graphic style and that of *Timon and Alcibiades*'. While very confident that the same hand etched *Timon and Alcibiades* and *Falsa ad Coelum*, Essick feels 'one cannot completely rule out the possibility that Fuseli, or Fuseli and Blake working together, executed both plates' (1983, 175). See also above, No. **81**. *Sleeping Woman with a Cupid*.

******

112.

113. *Beatrice Eavesdropping on Hero and Ursula*, 1791
(Shakespeare, *Much Ado About Nothing*, III, i)

Mezzotint engraved by John Jones (1745?-1797) after the original painting exhibited (1789/40) at the Royal Academy and now in the Gemälde-galerie, Dresden ([1789-1791]; Schiff 748).
Imprint: Pub^d. as the Act directs Jany. 6th. 1791 by J. Jones N°. 75, Great Portland Street

Inscription: Painted by H Fuseli R,A, | | Engraved by John Jones. | Principal Engraver to his Royal Highness Duke of York. | **Beatrice listening to Hero, & Ursula,** | Vide Shakespeare's Much Ado about nothing | Act E^d [*sic*] Sc.
Dimensions: ■ 49.7 x 45.5 cm | 20" x 17¾" (BM ??call no.)
Other locations: Folger Art File S528m.6 no. 26; YCBA B1977.14.11496

Lit.: Schiff 748; John Chaloner Smith, *British Mezzotinto Portraits*, 1883-1884, II, 776.

Variants:
I. Proof before title: YCBA B1976.1.162
Other locations: V & A Dyce 2891
II. Last line of inscr. changed: KHZ 1940/139
Inscription:...Vide Shakespeare's Much Ado about Nothing Act E^d [sic] Sc 1st.
Other locations: V & A Dyce 2892

Hero and Ursula are plotting to get Benedick and Beatrice to fall in love with each other, so they pretend not to see Beatrice eavesdropping on them, and talk as if poor Benedick is pining for love of the heartless Beatrice. Chaloner Smith thinks Beatrice may be a portrait of Mrs. Dorothy Jordan (1762-1816), and Hero a likeness of Miss Harriet Murray (1783-1844).

113.

Nos. 114 - 116.
[Erasmus Darwin.].
THE | BOTANIC GARDEN. | PART I. | CONTAINING | THE ECONOMY OF VEGETATION. | A POEM. | WITH | PHILOSOPHICAL NOTES. | = | *It Ver, et Venus; et Veneris Praenuncius ante.* | *Pennatus graditur Zephyrus vestigia propter;* | *Flora quibus mater, praespergens ante viai* | *Cuncta. coloribus egregiis et odoribus opplet. LUCRET.* | = | LONDON, |

PRINTED FOR J. JOHNSON, ST. PAUL'S CHURCH-YARD. | ····· | MDCCXCI [1791]. (2/10 illus.).

...THE SECOND EDITION. | = | LONDON, | PRINTED FOR J. JOHNSON, ST. PAUL'S CHURCH-YARD. | ····· | MDCCXCI. [1791] (2/10 illus.).

THE | BOTANIC GARDEN. | A POEM, | IN TWO PARTS. | = | PART I. | CONTAINING | THE ECONOMY OF VEGETATION. | = | PART II. | THE LOVES OF THE PLANTS. | = | WITH | PHILOSOPHICAL NOTES. | = | THIRD EDITION | = . | LONDON: | PRINTED FOR J. JOHNSON, ST. PAUL'S CHURCH-YARD. | — | MDCCXV [1795]. | ENTERED AT STATIONERS' HALL. (3/11 illus.).

These are all editions in Quarto format.
There is a facsimile ed. by Scolar Press (1973).

114.

114. *Flora Attired by the Elements*, 1791
(*The Economy of Vegetation*, I, 69-80)
(Vol. I, facing title)

Frontispiece engraved by Anker Smith (1759-1819)

Imprint (bottom left): Published June 1ˢᵗ 1791, by J. Johnson, in Sᵗ. Pauls Church Yard London.
Inscription (top right): Frontispiece, Vol. 1.| FLORA attired by the ELEMENTS.|(bottom right): Design'd by H. Fuseli, Engraved by Anker Smith
Dimensions: ■ 24.5 x 17.4 cm | 9¹⁰/16" x 7¹/16"; ■ 24.8 x 17.8 cm | 9¾" x 7" (BL 448.f.16)
Other locations: BL 642.1.14 (2d ed.); BL 642.1.15 (3rd ed.); BL 1502/21, BL 78.g.1; Bodleian Vet.A5.d.44; Cambridge CCA.24.61 (Charles Darwin's copy); Cambridge Syn.4.79.6 (top cropped); Cambridge Syn.4.79.13; Dörrbecker; Dr. Williams' Library 1009.S.20 (3rd ed.); Essick (3rd ed.); Folger PR3396.B6 1791; Folger PR3396.B6 1791a (2d ed.); Fribourg ANT 589; Huntington 387423 (2d ed.); Illinois xq821 D25b 1791a (Geoffrey Keynes' copy); LC Rosenwald PR3396.A7 1795 c.2; Yale Im D259+789b (bottom line cropped)
Plate only: BM 1863-5-9-63; Royal Academy Anderdon VII, 109
Lit.: Schiff 973 (14.0 x 9.3 cm); Tomory 1972, pl. 173; Hammelmann 1975, 35.
Exh.: Kansas City 1982 (6) (as illustrating latin motto on title page)

Variants:
I. Proof before letters and before oval frame: BM 1902-4-15-1
Dimensions: 21.3 x 15.3 cm (Sheet=25.5 x 18.0 cm
II. Proof before all letters: DHW
Inscription: FLORA attired by the ELEMENTS.|Engraved by Anchor Smith
III. MMA 63.611.2 (cropped at top)

A pencilled notation on the copy in the Metropolitan Museum of Art (Variant III) indicates, 'There is also a folio version of the same design,' but this statement is erroneous.

The design illustrates the 'hieroglyphic figures of the Elements, or of the Genii presiding over their operations' (line 73 note), gathered around the seated figure of 'Fair Spring'. Darwin refers to the four elements, Earth, Air, Fire and Water, by the names given them in Rosicrucian doctrine:

Pleas'd GNOMES, ascending from their earthy beds,
Play round her graceful footsteps, as she treads;
Gay SYLPHS attendant beat the fragrant air

On winnowing wings, and waft her golden hair;
Blue *Nymphs* emerging leave their sparkling streams,
And *Fiery Forms* alight from orient beams;
Musk'd in the rose's lap fresh dews they shed,
Or breathe celestial lustres round her head.

The sylph attending to Flora's hair wears a hat ornamented with a butterfly wing and antennae. The fiery element is represented as a hovering figure with wings on her head, which is capped with flames. The nymph is the sad-eyed figure at the right with bare arms, her left hand on an urn. Strongly foreshortened, the gnome's head and arms are seen emerging from the Earth in the foreground, as he extends two jewelled rings towards Flora, emblematic of the treasures of the underworld. Her attendant holds a basket of flowers; more flowers wreathe the oval frame.

Lavater's remarks on the 'immoderately lengthened' *Female Hand* (No. **109**), 'too much on the stretch ... whose archetype is nowhere found in nature', are also eminently applicable to the exaggeratedly elongated female figure of Flora.

Fertilization of Egypt.

London. Published Decʳ 1ˢᵗ 1791 by J. Johnson Sᵗ Pauls Church Yard.

115.

115. *Fertilization of Egypt*, 1791
(Part I, III, 129-138)
(Vol. I, facing p. 127)

Engraved by William Blake (1757-1827) after
Fuseli's pencil sketch (1791; Schiff 1038)
Imprint: London, Publish'd Decr. 1st. 1791. by J.
Johnson, S^t. Pauls Church Yard.
Inscription: H Fuseli. RA: inv||W Blake. sc.|
Fertilization of Egypt.
Dimensions: ■ 19.7 x 15.2 cm | 7¾" x 6" (BL
448.f.16)
Other locations: BL 642.1.15 (3rd ed.); BL
1502/21; BL 78.g.1; Bodleian Vet.A5.d.44;
Dörrbecker; Dr. Williams's Library 1009.S.20
(3rd ed.); Essick; Essick (2d ed.); Essick (3rd
ed.); Folger PR3396.B6 1791 (facing p. 127);
Folger PR3396.B6 1791a; Fribourg ANT 589
(lacking imprint); Huntington 387423 (2d ed.);
LC PR3396.A7 1795 c.2 (3rd ed.); Yale Im
D259+789b (imprint cropped)
Plate only: BM 1870-10-8-2793; Essick;
Fitzwilliam P.547.1985; Huntington 49000, 1831
(imprint cropped); LC Rosenwald 1838.15; LC
Rosenwald 1838.15; Royal Academy Anderdon
XIII, 271
Plate lacking: BL 1642.1.14 (2d ed.)
Lit.: Schiff 974 (13.0 x 7.8 cm octavo edition
only, 1799, 1806), 1038; A.S. Roe, 'The
Thunder of Egypt', in *William Blake: Essays for
S. Foster Damon*, ed. Alvin H. Rosenfeld, 1969,
159-164, 169f., 178; Tomory 1972, pl. 141;
Easson & Essick 1979, no. XXXVI.1(1.); Essick
1985, 210 (11A); *Letters*, 187; Essick 1991, no.
XXI.1, pls. 67-69
Exh.: Princeton 1969-1970 (33b); Normal 1971
(8); Kansas City 1982 (7); New Haven 1982-1983
(27); Hamburg 1989 (436)

The lines illustrated are:

Sailing in air, when dark *Monsoon* inshrouds
His tropic mountains in a night of clouds;
Or drawn by whirlwinds from the Line returns,
And showers o'er Afric all his thousand urns;
High o'er his head the beams of *Sirius* glow,
And, Dog of Nile, *Anubis*, barks below.
Nymphs! you from cliff to cliff attendant guide,
In headlong cataracts the impetuous tide;
Or lead o'er wastes of Abyssinian sands
The bright expanse to *Egypt*'s shower-less
  lands.

Here, as in the illustrations for Lavater's
Aphorisms on Man (No. **80**) and the fantasy
portrait of Michelangelo, Fuseli reveals his great
confidence in Blake as his engraver, although
there were undoubtedly oral instructions as the
work proceeded, for the composition is blocked
out in quite cursory fashion, leaving much detail
to his discretion, such as the representation of of
the rain-bringer (Jupiter Pluvius), borrowed from
Bernardus de Montfaucon. Fuseli explicitly
recommended Blake's performance to Moses
Haughton as the model for an aspiring young
engraver to emulate (to William Roscoe, 17
August 1798). The star to which the dog-headed
god Anubis raises his hands in prayer is 'Sirius,
or the dog-star', that rises 'at the time of the
commencement of the flood'.

Tornado.

116.

116. *Zeus Battling Typhon*, 1795
(III, 771-780)
(Vol. I, facing p. 168) (3rd ed. only)

Engraved by William Blake (1757-1827)

Imprint: London, Published Augt. 1st. 1795, by J. Johnson, S^t. Paul's Church Yard.
Inscription: H. Fuseli RA: inv: | | W Blake: sc: |
Tornado.
Dimensions: ■ 21.0 x 16.9 cm | 8^9/16" x 6^{11}/16" (BL 642.1.15)
Other locations: Dr. Williams' Library 1009.S.20; Essick; Illinois 821.D25b 1795; LC PR3396.A7 1795 c.2
Plate only: Fitzwilliam P.546.1985; LC Rosenwald 1838.15 (Moss Coll.); LC Rosenwald 1838.15
Lit.: Schiff 976; Easson & Essick 1979, no. XXXVI.6; Essick 1991, no. XXI.6, pl. 74.

Variants

I. Proof before all letters (signatures only): BM 1863-5-9-19
Inscription: H. Fuseli RA: inv: | | W Blake: sc:
Other locations: BM 1978.u.1742; Essick

Essick describes five proof impressions of the plate: their number and 'the presence of an imprint on one of them suggest that they were printed for use in the book or sale to collectors'.

The design illustrates Darwin's personification of 'Tornado ' in the following lines:

You seize TORNADO by his locks of mist,
Burst his dense clouds, his wheeling spires
    untwist;
Wide o'er the West when borne on headlong
    gales,
Dark as meridian night, the Monster sails,
Howls high in air, and shakes his curled brow,
Lashing with serpent-train the waves below,
Whirls his black arm, the forked lightning
    flings,
And showers a deluge from his demon wings.

Essick's pithy commentary on this illustration is exemplary: Fuseli's design represents two combatants as compared to the single figure described by Darwin. Schiff's title, *Zeus in Combat with Typhon*, thus, suggests that Fuseli's interpretation of Darwin's text is based on Hesiod's account of the destruction by Zeus of the giant with a hundred serpent heads (*Theogony*, 820-860).

*****

Nos. 114A - 115A.
Erasmus Darwin.

THE | BOTANIC GARDEN, | A POEM. | IN TWO PARTS. | = | PART I. | CONTAINING | THE ECONOMY OF VEGETATION. | = | PART II. | THE LOVES OF THE PLANTS. | = | WITH | PHILOSOPHICAL NOTES. | = | THE FOURTH EDITION. | = | LONDON: | PRINTED FOR J. JOHNSON, ST. PAUL'S CHURCH-YARD. | — | 1799 (3/11 illus.).

THE | POETICAL WORKS | OF | ERASMUS DARWIN, | M.D. F.R.S. | CONTAINING THE BOTANIC GARDEN, IN TWO PARTS; | AND THE TEMPLE OF NATURE. | WITH PHILOSOPHICAL NOTES AND PLATES. | IN THREE VOLUMES. | VOL. I. | CONTAINING THE ECONOMY OF VEGETATION. | LONDON: | PRINTED FOR J. JOHNSON, ST. PAUL'S CHURCH-YARD, | BY T. BENSLEY, BOLT COURT, FLEET STREET. | 1806 (3/11 illus.).

It is not known why these *octavo* plates are dated 1791 since all editions prior to 1799 are *in quarto*. For the other illustration in these eds. see No. **68**.

114A. *Flora Attired by the Elements*, 1799
(Vol. I, facing title page)

Frontispiece vignette (oval) re-engraved in reduced format by Anker Smith (1759-1819)
Imprint: London, Published June 1st. 1791, by J. Johnson, S^t. Paul's Church Yard.
Inscription (bottom left): Fuseli inv^t. | (bottom right): A. Smith sc. | **Flora attired by the Elements.**
Dimensions: ■ 14.0 x 9.3 cm | 5^9/16" x 3^{11}/16" (BL 1465.g.23)
Other locations: BL 19262; Bodleian Vet.A5. d.31; Dörrbecker; Dr. Williams's Library 1110.H.9 (1806) (imprint cropped?); Essick (imprint cropped); Fribourg ANT 9847 (facing p. [1]); Illinois 821 D25b; Iowa 581.5.D22.b; Lausanne 1M.2727; Library Company O Eng Darw Bot 1799 (H=22.4 cm); Newberry Y185.D25 (1806); Yale [??call no.]
Plate only: Fitzwilliam P.715.1985
Lit.: Schiff 973; Boime 1987, 293, pl. 4.9 (identified as '1791 edition').
Exh.: Kansas City 1982 (6).

Variants:
I. Proof before letters: BM 1849-5-12-300
II. Reissued (1806) with Volume and page numbers added: BL 11641.dd.11
Inscription (top right): Frontispiece Vol. I.
Other locations: Essick; Huntington 421361
Plate only: BM 1863-5-9-64

115A. *The Fertilization of Egypt*, 1799
(Vol. I, facing p. 145)

Unsigned re-engraving in reduced format by William Blake (1757-1827) (reversed from 1791)
Imprint: London, Published Decr. 1st. 1791, by J. Johnson, S^t. Pauls Church Yard.
Inscription: **Fertilization of Egypt.**
Dimensions: ■ 13.1 x 7.9 cm | 5^2/16" x 3^2/16"
(BL 1465.g.23)
Other locations: BL 19262; Bodleian Vet.A5.d.31; Dörrbecker; Dr. Williams's Library 1110.H.9 (1806); Essick (facing p. [129]); Essick (1806); Fribourg ANT 9847; Huntington 421361 (1806); Illinois 821.D25b; Iowa 581.5 D22b; Lausanne 1M.2727; Library Company O Eng Darw Bot 1799 (H=22.4 cm); Newberry Y 185.D25 (1806); Yale [?call no]
Plate only: Fitzwilliam P.552.1985; Rosenwald 1838.15 (i) (imprint cropped); Rosenwald 1838.15 (ii)
Lit.: Schiff 974 (13.0 x 7.8 cm); Easson & Essick 1979, no. XXXVII.1(2); Essick 1991, no. XXI.7.

Nos. 114B - 115B.
Erasmus Darwin.
O | JARDIM BOTANICO | DE DARWIN. | PARTE I. | OU | A ECONOMIA DA VEGETAÇAO, | POEMA | COM NOTAS FILOSOFICAS, | TRADUZIDO DO INGLEZ | POR | VICENTE PEDRO NOLASCO DA CUNHA. | — | LISBOA. M.DCC.III.[-M.DCCC.IV.] | — | NA REGIA OFICINA TYPOGRAFICA. | POR ORDEM SUPERIOR. [1803-1804] (2/3 illus.).

114B. *Flora Attired by the Elements*, 1804
(Vol. I, facing title page)

Oval frontispiece vignette re-engraved in reduced format by an anonymous Portuguese engraver
Inscription: **Flora adornada pelos Elementos**
Dimensions: 11.8 x 7.8 cm. | 4^{10}/16" x 3^1/16"
(BL 11641.a.17)

Other locations: Yale Im.D259 Ej803 (facing p. 1)

115B. *The Fertilization of Egypt*, 1804
(Canto IV)
(Vol. I, facing p. 263)

Re-engraved in reduced format by an anonymous Portuguese engraver
Inscription: **Afertilizaçaõ do Egypto**
Dimensions: ■ 11.1 x 6.6 cm | 4^6/16" x 2^{10}/16"
(BL 11641.a.17)
Other locations: Yale Im.D259 Ej803 (facing p. 119)

******

No. 114C - 115C.
Erasmus Darwin.
THE | BOTANIC GARDEN. | IN TWO PARTS. | — | PART I. | CONTAINING | THE ECONOMY OF VEGETATION. | — | PART II. | THE LOVES OF THE PLANTS. | — | WITH | PHILOSOPHICAL NOTES. | = | THE SECOND AMERICAN EDITION. | = | NEW = YORK: | PRINTED AND SOLD BY T. & J. SWORDS, PRINTERS TO THE FACULTY OF PHYSIC | OF COLUMBIA COLLEGE, NO. 160 PEARL-STREET. | — | 1807 (3/23 illus.).

For the other illustration to this work see No. **68A**.

The first American edition (1798), also published by T. & J. Swords, omits these three plates as being 'merely ornamental' ('Advertisement').

114C. *Flora Attired by the Elements*, 1807
(Frontispiece)
(Vol. I, facing the title page)

Oval vignette frontispiece re-engraved by Gideon Fairman (1774-1827)
Inscription: Fuseli Del^t. | G. Fairman Sc^t. | (below): FLORA attired by the ELEMENTS.
Dimensions (oval): 14.8 x 9.8 cm | 5^{13}/16" x 3^{14}/16" (NYPL *KL Darwin)
Other locations: Library Company

115C. *The Fertilization of Egypt*, 1807
(Vol. I, facing p. 81)

Re-engraved by Peter Maverick (1780-1831)
Inscription: H. Fuseli R.A. del. | | P. Maverick
sculp. | (bottom): **Fertilization of Egypt.**
Dimensions: ■ 11.9 x 9.0 cm | 4^{11}/16" x 3^9/16";
■ 12.2 x 9.3 cm | 4^{13}/16" x 3^{11}/16" (Library
Company)
Other locations: NYPL *KL Darwin (lacks plate)

＊＊＊＊＊＊

No. 115D.
Erasmus Darwin.
THE | BOTANIC GARDEN, | A POEM, IN TWO
PARTS; | CONTAINING | THE ECONOMY OF
VEGETATION | AND THE | LOVES OF THE
PLANTS. | WITH | PHILOSOPHICAL NOTES. |
— | BY ERASMUS DARWIN, M.D. | — |
LONDON: | PUBLISHED BY JONES &
COMPANY, | 3, ACTON PLACE, KINGSLAND
ROAD. | 1824, 1825. (1/9 illus. + portr. frontis.).

[Printed paper covers]: *Jones's University Edition*
of the MODERN POETS. | Dr. DARWIN's
POETICAL WORKS, comprising the Bo- | tanic
Garden—Loves of the Plants, and Temple of
Nature; | with numerous Engravings, complete for
7s. | = | THE | BOTANIC GARDEN, | A POEM,
IN TWO PARTS; | CONTAINING | THE
ECONOMY OF VEGETATION, | AND THE |
LOVES OF THE PLANTS, | WITH |
PHILOSOPHICAL NOTES; | ALSO | THE
TEMPLE OF NATURE, | A POEM. | — | BY
ERASMUS DARWIN, M.D. | — | LONDON: |
PUBLISHED BY JONES & COMPANY | 3,
ACTON PLACE, KINGSLAND ROAD. | — |
1824.

115D. *The Fertilization of Egypt*, 1824
(Bound in at end—see binder's instructions)

Re-engraved by anonymous engraver (unsigned)
Imprint: London, Published by Jones & Co. July
1, 1824.
Inscription: **Fertilization of Egypt.**
Dimensions: ■ 12.9 x 7.7 cm | 5^1/16" x 3^1/16";
■ 13.3 x 8.1 cm | 5¼" x 3¼" (NYPL NCL)
Other locations: Bodleian 280.e.3909; Huntington
121577-78; Missouri—Columbia (facing title
page); NYPL NCL (1825) (misbound: facing p.
16 of *Temple of Nature*); Princeton Ex
3706.5.32.1824 (facing title page); Princeton Ex
3598.211

Plate only: Rosenwald 1838.15

＊＊＊＊＊＊

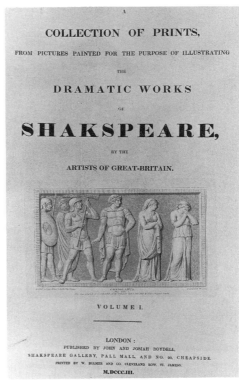

Fig. 5. J. & J. Boydell, *Collection of Prints*, 1803.
Title page, Vol. I.

Nos. 117 - 124.
[John & Josiah Boydell.]
A | COLLECTION OF PRINTS, | FROM
PICTURES PAINTED FOR THE PURPOSE OF
ILLUSTRATING | THE | DRAMATIC WORKS |
OF | SHAKSPEARE, | BY THE | ARTISTS OF
GREAT-BRITAIN. | [Vignette] | VOLUME I.
[-VOLUME II.] | = | LONDON: | PUBLISHED
BY JOHN AND JOSIAH BOYDELL, |
SHAKSPEARE GALLERY, PALL MALL, AND
NO. 90, CHEAPSIDE. | PRINTED BY W.
BULMER AND CO. CLEVELAND ROW, ST.
JAMES'S. | M.DCCC.III [1803]. (8/96 illus. + 2
portrait fpcs. + 2 title vignettes).

THE | AMERICAN EDITION | OF | BOYDELL'S |
ILLUSTRATIONS OF THE DRAMATIC
WORKS | OF | SHAKSPEARE, | BY THE MOST |
EMINENT ARTISTS OF GREAT BRITAIN. |
[Vignette] | VOL. I. [-VOL. II.] | = | NEW
YORK: | RESTORED AND PUBLISHED WITH

ORIGINAL DESCRIPTIONS OF THE PLATES|
BY SHEARJASHUB SPOONER, A.B. M.D.,|
AUTHOR OF A BIOGRAPHICAL AND
CRITICAL DICTIONARY OF PAINTERS,
ENGRAVERS, SCULPTORS AND
ARCHITECTS.|1852.

...PHILADELPHIA:|RICE, RUTTER & CO.
[n.d.]

For the re-engravings of 1799-1802, 1810-1812,
1825, 1828-1841, 1831-1832-1839, 1832-1834-
1887, 1837, 1843, 1845, 1847-1848, n.d. (c.
1840), 1861, 1863, 1871, see Nos. **117A, 120A -
121A, 123A, 120B - 122B, 127B, 125C, 117C -
119C, 123C, 117D - 125D, 117E, 117F - 118F,
122F - 124F, 117G, 119G, 125H, 117I -118I,
and 117J - 118J, 124J.**

A number of facsimile editions have been
published, among them:

The Shakespeare Gallery: A [photographic]
*Reproduction in Commemoration of the
Tercentenary Anniversary of the Poet's Birth.*
London: L. Booth, 1864.
*The Boydell Gallery. ...Reproduced from the
Originals in Permanent Woodburytype by Vincent
Brooks, Day & Son.* London: Bickers, 1874.
*The Gallery of Illustrations for Shakespeare's
Dramatic Works ... Published by John Boydell,
reduced and re-engraved by the heliotype process
with selections from the text,* ed. by J. Parker
Norris. Philadelphia: Gebbie & Barrie, 1874.
The Boydell Shakespeare Prints. New York: B.
Blom, 1968 (reprt. Arno Press, 1979).

PROSPECTUS
(DHW)
[bound in *A Catalogue of the Pictures in
the Shakspeare Gallery,* 1789]

May 1, 1789.
SHAKSPEARE GALLERY PALLMALL.

MR. ALDERMAN BOYDELL, JOSIAH
BOYDELL,|AND GEORGE NICHOL,|
PROPOSE TO PUBLISH BY SUBSCRIPTION
|A MOST MAGNIFICENT AND ACCURATE
EDITION|OF THE PLAYS OF SHAKSPEARE,|
IN NINE VOLUMES|Of the largest QUARTO
SIZE, on the finest ROYAL ATLAS PAPER,|
fabricated for that Purpose by Mr.
WHATMAN.|And Printed with TYPES cast in

the Proprietors' House, upon a Principle|
calculated to unite Beauty with Utility.|The
TEXT to be regulated, and the LITERARY
PART of the Undertaking| conducted,|By
GEORGE STEEVENS, Esq.|
To Accompany this Work|MESSIEURS
BOYDELL|Intend to Publish|A SERIES OF
LARGE AND CAPITAL PRINTS,|After
PICTURES Painted by the following
ARTISTS,|from the most striking Scenes of
SHAKSPEARE:|

Sir JOSHUA REYNOLDS,
Portrait-Painter to his MAJESTY, and President
of the Royal Academy,|

ANGELICA KAUFFMAN, R.A.	Mr. NORTHCOTE, R.A.
Mr. BARRY, R.A. Professor of	Mr. OPIE, R.A.
Painting to the Royal Academy.	Rev. W. PETERS, R.A.
Mr. JOSIAH BOYDELL.	Mr. RIGAUD, R.A.
Mr. COPLEY, R.A.	Mr. ROMNEY.
Mr. DOWNMAN.	Mr. SMIRK.
Mr. DURNO.	Mr. WEST, R.A. History-
Mr. FUSELI	Painter to his Majesty.
Mr. HAMILTON, R.A.	Mr. RAPHAEL WEST.
Mr. KIRK.	Mr. WRIGHT, &c. &c.
Mr. MILLER.	

TO BE ENGRAVED BY

Miss CAROLINE WATSON.	Mr. HEATH.
Mr. BARTOLOZZI, R.A.	Mr. LEGATT.
Historical Engraver	
to his Majesty.	Mr. MICHEL.
Mr. COLLIER, A.	Mr. OGBORNE.
Mr. EARLOM.	Mr. RYDER.
Mess. FACIUS.	Mr. SHARPE.
Mr. FITTLER, Marine Engraver	Mr. SIMON.
to his Majesty.	Mr. A. SMITH.
Mr. HALL.	Mr. THEW.
Mr. HAWARD, A.	Mr. TROTTER, &c. &c.

The PICTURES will be of various Sizes,
many as large as Life.

As fast as they are finished, and at Liberty
from the Engraver, they will be hung up in the
GALLERY, which has been built on Purpose to
receive them—into which the Proprietors mean
to give the Subscribers *Perpetual Free
Admission.*

[Page] (2)
CONDITIONS
I. SEVENTY-TWO Scenes will be painted
(perhaps more) being two appropriated to each
of the Plays of SHAKSPEARE. —As, however,

some of them exhibit more interesting Subjects than others, the Plates will be given without regard to any certain Number for each Drama.

II. The Whole to be published in Numbers, each containing at least, four CAPITAL PRINTS. The Size of the largest to be about 19 Inches by 24 long.

III. Beside the four large Prints each Number will consist of four smaller Prints, engraved from the same Pictures, of a proper Size to bind up with the Letter-press.

IV. The Letter-press of each Number will contain two Plays, printed in a Manner, it is hoped, superior to any Thing hitherto executed in this Country, of which a Specimen may now be seen.

V. The Price to Subscribers will be Three Guineas at the Time of subscribing, and Two Guineas on the Delivery of the Number.

VI. On Account of the unexampled Magnificence and Decorations of this Edition of our immortal Author (the Expence of which will considerably exceed *One Hundred Thousand Pounds*) it is expected, that on receiving each Number, the Subscribers will deposit Three Guineas, as the first Payment of the next Number.

VII. To accommodate those who, being contented with their present Editions of SHAKSPEARE, would only wish to be possessed of the large Prints—A separate Subscription is opened, on the following Terms:—For each Number consisting of four or more large PRINTS, Two Guineas are to be paid at the Time of subscribing, and One Guinea on Delivery of the Prints.

VIII. And to accommodate those, who only wish to have this magnificent Edition of the Text of SHAKSPEARE, with the smaller Plates of a proper Size to bind up with it—It is proposed, that the Subscription to each Number shall be One Guinea at the Time of subscribing, one One Guinea on the Delivery of it.

IX. That one Number, at least, shall be published annually.—The Proprietors hope, nay are confident, they shall be enabled to produce two Numbers within the Course of every Year, as soon as the first Number is published; but do not choose to promise absolutely what they may not with Certainty perform.

It may be some Satisfaction to the Subscribers to know, that Forty of the Pictures are nearly finished—Thirty-four of which are now exhibiting—And that Eighteen of the Plates are in the Hands of the Engravers, some of them nearly finished, and most of them in great forwardness.

A prospectus for the American edition of the plates was issued by S. Spooner of New York on 1 November 1848. The prospectus went through at least six editions (the 6th is dated 1852), each being considerably augmented by the texts of the numerous newspaper reviews that had appeared to that date. In the following transcription, the reviews have been omitted.

PROSPECTUS
FOR PUBLISHING
AN
AMERICAN EDITION
OF
BOYDELL'S
ILLUSTRATIONS OF SHAKSPEARE.
NEW YORK: | S. SPOONER, 106 LIBERTY-STREET | J.J. Reed, Printer, 16 Spruce-st. | — | 1849.

The subscriber having, by a train of fortunate circumstances become possessed of all the original one hundred copper-plates of Boydell's folio Illustrations of Shakspeare, and believing [*p. 2*] that he would render the public a service by restoring them to their original beauty, applied himself with diligence to effect this object. As a work of art, in design, in execution, in unlimited outlay of time and money, in the employment of the best talent in Great Britain, and in the patronage and cordial support of the king, [*p. 3*] nobility and gentry of England, Boydell's Illustrations of Shakspeare stands pre-eminent and wholly unrivalled.

After having finished a number of the plates, the most worn and difficult to be restored, and taken proofs from them, all the most distinguished artists, engravers, and connoisseurs, in [*p. 4*] the city of New York, were invited to examine and scrutinize the work, and to compare critically these proofs with the best copies in America, some of which were engraver's proofs before the letter. The result of this trial has been most satisfactory; and the subscriber has, upon their decision, and by the advice of his friends and the [*p. 5*] lovers of the Fine Arts, determined to push the work to its entire completion as rapidly as the necessity for accuracy and care will admit.

To those who may not be acquainted with this great work, the subscriber begs leave to say that it contains 100 plates, all of which are perfect studies, having from ten to twenty full-length fig- [*p. 6*] ures in the foreground, most of which are genuine portraits, in every variety of grouping and composition, and every human passion faithfully delineated, forming a series of the most original pictures ever executed. It is also believed that nothing can be done that will have so great a tendency to cultivate a taste for the fine arts, in our country [*p. 7*] as a general circulation of these splendid prints, illustrating as they do the genius of the great poet, and emanating from the most distinguished British artists, as Sir Joshua Reynolds, Sir Benjamin West, Sir William Beechy, Fuseli, Romney, Northcote, Westall, Smirke, Opie, as painters; and Sharpe, Bartolozzi, Earlom, Thew, Si- [*p.8*] mon, Middiman, Watson, Fyttler, Wilson, and many others, as engravers. We have few public galleries of paintings, and must therefore mostly form our taste for this branch of the fine arts, from engravings; and these plates are fit to grace the drawing room or portfolio of any gentleman. Nothing, it is conceded, has a greater [*p. 9*] tendency to refine the mind, than the cultivation of the fine arts, and it certainly adds greatly to our pleasure. If the subscriber can be instrumental in assisting to cultivate the growing taste for the fine arts, he will not consider his undertaking fruitless, even though he should fail in reaping the pecuniary recompense, which he [*p. 10*] trusts a liberal public will feeling willing to bestow upon a project of this nature, involving as it does a very heavy outlay of capital in the commencement, and much risk of loss in its prosecution. The subscriber pledges himself to spare no efforts or expense in perfecting the work, and making it in every way worthy of its magnitude, [*p. 11*] and of the subjects illustrated. He proposes to publish the work in monthly parts of two or more plates each, at the unprecedented low price of one dollar per plate, to subscribers. Boydell's subscription price was two guineas ($10) per plate, for the first 300

proofs, and one guinea per plate, for the prints; besides, may noblemen and others made handsome donations, in addition to their subscriptions, to encourage the work; and yet he failed for the enormous sum of two hundred and fifty thousand pounds sterling. During the lifetime of the Boydells it was never sold for less than one hundred guineas per set. Some of the proofs in former years have brought at pub- [*p.13*] lic sales, fifteen guineas each in London, and twenty-five dollars in New York.

The work will be printed on thick linen paper, 24 by 30 inches, weighing 140 lbs. to the ream. Each print will be accompanied with stereotype letter-press description of the same, with quotations from the text which it illustrates, [*p. 14*] printed on the best hot-pressed linen paper, of the same size as the print, with tissue paper between, which will add greatly to the beauty and interest of the work. In Boydell's editions, there is no description of the plates, nor tissue paper; and only a list of the plates at the end of the volumes. The work, when completed, will form [*p. 15*] two volumes of surpassing beauty, far superior to any of the old copies now in the country.

TERMS.

To subscribers, $1,00 per plate, including the two vignettes which embellish the titel-page of each volume. [*p. 16*]

Terms cash on the delivery of every number. All letters and orders must be post-paid. These terms are not above one fifteenth part of the present English publishing price for prints of the same size and class, as will be seen by the extracts given below.

The plates are numbered in small figures, from [*p. 17*] 1 up to 100, in the lower left hand corner, for the direction of the binder, and for the convenience of those sending orders. This is important, for hardly a copy of the original work can be found in which some of the plates are not misplaced; and, as there are many worn impressions in the [*p. 18*] market, this will be a certain mark, by which to distinguish the restored prints.

A list of all the patrons of the work, with a preface, will be given in the concluding part to be bound up with it.

S. SPOONER.

117.

117. *Prospero, Miranda, Caliban and Ariel*,
1797
(*The Tempest*, I, ii, 325
(Vol. I, Plate IV)

Stipple engraving by Jean-Pierre Simon (1750?-
1810?) after Fuseli's painting No. 1 in the
'Shakspeare Gallery' of which the only surviving
fragment is the head of Prospero now in the City
of York Art Gallery (1789; Schiff 743).
Imprint: Publish'd Septr. 29, 1797, by J. & J.
BOYDELL, at the Shakspeare Gallery, Pall Mall;
& at N°. 90, Cheapside.
Inscription: Painted by H. Fuseli, R.A. | |
Engraved by I.P. Simon. | SHAKSPEARE. |
Tempest. | ACT I. SCENE II. | The inchanted
Island: before the Cell of Prospero.—Prospero,
Miranda, Caliban, & Ariel. |

[*left*]
Pro. For this, be sure, tonight thou shalt have
   cramps,
Side-stitches that shall pen thy breath up;
   urchins
Shall, for that vast of night that they may work,

[*right*]
All exercise on thee: thou shalt be pinch'd
As thick as honey-combs, each pinch more
   stinging
Than bees that made them.

Dimensions: ■ 43.6 x 58.5 cm | 17²/16" x 22¹⁵/16"
(Bodleian Sutherland 172)
Other locations: Essick; Essick; Folger Art Flat
b1 c.1; Folger Art Flat b1-2 c.2; Folger Art Flat
b1-2 c.3; Huntington 21148; LC NE 1713.B6 fol.
('gray' caps); LC NE1713.B7 fol.; Newberry
Case +YS 65.11; YCBA L 198.212(fB)
Plate only: Basel 1938.74; BM Dd 6 No 9; DHW;
V & A Dyce 2921; YCBA B1977.14.11602
Lit.: Schiff 742 (43.2 x 58.0 cm); Schiff-Viotto
1977, no. 67; Boydell, *Catalogue of Plates*
(1803), xix, 4; Friedman 1976, 223; *Letters*, 47
Exh.: London, Boydell, 1790, 1794 (XXXVI),
1802 (II); Chicago 1978 (7); Kansas City 1982
(32); London, Heim, 1991 (76).

Variants:
I. Unfinished proof (etched state) before letters:
Folger Art Flat b1 c.4

Other locations: Folger Art Flat b1 c.1
II. Proof before all letters (lacking verse): KHZ
1940/133
Imprint: Publishd Sept 29 1797 by J & J
BOYDELL at the Shakspeare Gallery Pall Mall
& at N° 90 Cheapside
Inscription: Painted by H Fuseli RA||Engraved
by IP Simon|SHAKSPEARE. (open letters)|
Tempest|ACT I SCENE II|The inchanted
Island: before the Cell of Prospero [*open space*]
Prospero Miranda Caliban & Ariel
Other locations: KHZ B43
III. Coloured impression: DHW
IV. Reworked and reissued (1852) with plate
number ('6') added bottom left: Folger Art Flat
b10 c.1
Other locations: Birmingham 386911; Folger
Art Flat b1 c.4; Folger Art Flat b10 c.1; Folger
Art Flat b10 c.2; Folger Art Flat b10 c.3 (42.7
x 58.5 cm); Folger Art Flat b3 (Rice); LC
NE1713.B72 fol.; NYPL *NDC+ + + 1852

During 12 years of exile, Prospero accompanied
by his daughter Miranda has ruled by magic over
an enchanted island inhabited by ethereal spirits
and the strange, mis-shapen, brutish Caliban,
'half a fish and half a monster.' In Fuseli's
rendering, Prospero like one of Michelangelo's
prophets castigates Caliban, whose irredeemable
bestial nature, on which 'Nurture can never
stick,' is plainly revealed in every glowering
feature of his canine head, his pointed ears, and
long claw-like nails and hooked nipples. In a later
painting of the same subject, c. 1806-1810
(Indiana University), Caliban resembles rather
Milton's defiant Satan than misbegotten witch's
seed.

Allan Cunningham in his *Gallery of Pictures By
the First Masters of the English and Foreign
Schools* (see Nos. **117G-119G**) commends Fuseli
for the 'grand and commanding expression,' of
Prospero, the 'power of anatomical display' in
Caliban, and the exquisite and beautifully
conceived and drawn figure of Ariel. However,
Fuseli's 'peculiar' representation of Miranda is
criticised: 'In seeking to invest her person with an
expression of disgust and disdain at Caliban, he
has given her a masculine and mock-heroic
character.' Cunningham concludes that the
composition is 'a work of no common genius in
art; one which the mere common-place painter

could never reach, though he would undoubtedly
avoid its errors.'

Fuseli was paid £210 (200 guineas), while the
engraver received £315 (300 guineas).

118. *Titania and Bottom with the Ass's Head*,
1796
(*A Midsummer Night's Dream*, IV, i)
(Vol. I, Plate XX)

Stipple with aquatint by Jean-Pierre Simon (1750?-
1810?) after Fuseli's painting No. 2 in the
Shakspeare Gallery in the Tate Gallery, London
([1780-1790]; Schiff 753).
Imprint: Published Sept. 29. 1796 by J. & J.
BOYDELL at the Shakspeare Gallery Pall Mall &
at N°. 90 Cheapside London.
Inscription: Painted by H Fuseli R.A.||Engraved
by I.P. Simon.|SHAKSPEARE.|**Midsummer-
Nights Dream.**|ACT IV. SCENE I.|A Wood. -
Titania, Queen of the Fairies, Bottom, Fairies
attending &c. &c.|

[*left*]
Bot. Scratch my head, Pease-blossom.—Where's
monsieur Cobweb?
Cob. Ready.
Bot. Monsieur Cobweb, good monsieur, get
your weapons in your hand, and
kill me a red-hip'd bumble bee on the top of a
thistle; and, good monsieur,
bring me the honey-bag. Do not fret yourself
too much in the action, mon-
sieur, and, good monsieur, have a care the
honey-bag break not; I would be loth
to have you over-flown with a honey-bag,
Signior.—Where's monsieur Mustard-seed?

[*right*]
Must. Ready.
Bot. Give me your nief, monsieur Mustard-
seed. Pray you, leave your courtesy,good
Monsieur.
Must. What's your will?
Bot. Nothing, good monsieur, but to help
Cavalero Cobweb to scratch.
I must to the barber's; monsieur; for methinks I
am marvellously hairy about the
face: and I am such a tender ass, if my hair do
but tickle me, I must scratch.
Dimensions: ■ 44.0 x 59.0 cm | 17⁵/16" x 23³/16"
(Bodleian Sutherland 172)

Other locations: Essick; Folger Art Flat b1 c.1;
Folger Art Flat b1-2 c.2; Folger Art Flat b1-2
c.3; Huntington 21148; LC NE1713.B6 fol.;
YCBA L 198.212 (fB)
Plate only: Basel 1938.79; BM Dd 6 No. 21;
DHW; KHZ 1917/2
Lacking plate: LC NE1713.B7 fol.
Lit.: Schiff 753; Schiff, *Sommernachtstraum*,
1961, 12ff.; Schiff-Viotto 1977, no. 80; Boydell,
Catalogue of Plates (1803), p. xx, 20; *Letters*,
45-46
Exh.: Chicago 1978 (6); Kansas City 1982 (22).

Variants

I. Unfinished proof (etched state) before letters:
Folger Art Flat b1 c.4
Dimensions: 43.6 x 58.6 cm
Other locations: Essick; Folger Art Flat b1-2
c.2
II. Proof before letters: YCBA B1977.14.11600
Other locations: KHZ 1940/121
III. Proof before all letters (lacking verse) (open
letters) (Folger Art Flat b1 c.4)

IV. Reworked and reissued (1852) with plate
number ('22') added bottom left: Folger Art
Flat b10 c.1
Other locations: Birmingham 386911; Folger
Art Flat b10 c.2; Folger Art Flat b10 c.3 (43.0
x 59.1 cm); Folger Art Flat b3 (Rice); LC
NE1713.B72 fol.; NYPL *NDC+++ 1852

Oberon and Titania, the king and queen of the
fairies, had quarrelled and Oberon cast a spell on
her, so that she would fall in love with the first
creature she sees on awaking. Fuseli's design
depicts Titania doting over Bottom, the object of
her involuntary passion, who is wearing an ass's
head. But even more strange and grotesque are
some of the creatures—such as the little bearded
philosopher being led on a leash, or the elf with
the head of a moth, or the changeling just formed
out of wax on the lap of a shrouded sibylline
figure—that Fuseli places on the fringes of
Titania's retinue. Fuseli was paid £294 (280
guineas) for his painting; the engraver's payment
was £367. 10s. (350 guineas).

118.

SHAKSPEARE.
Midsummer Nights Dream

119.

119. *Titania's Awakening*, 1803
(*A Midsummer Night's Dream*, IV, i)
(Vol. I, Plate XXI)

Stipple engraving by Thomas Ryder (1746-1810) and Thomas Ryder, Jr. after Fuseli's painting No. 3 in the Shakspeare Gallery in the Kunstmuseum Winterthur ([1785-1790]); Schiff 754).
Imprint: Pub. Decr. 1. 1803, by J. & J. BOYDELL, at the Shakspeare Gallery, Pall Mall; & at N°. 90, Cheapside, London.
Inscription: Painted by Henry Fuseli R.A. | | Engraved by Thos. Ryder & Thos. Ryder Junr. | SHAKSPEARE. | **Midsummer-Night's Dream.** | ACT IV. SCENE I. | Oberon, Queen of the Fairies, Puck, Bottom, and Fairies attending, &c. |

[*left*]
Queen. My Oberon! what visions have I seen
Methought, I was enamour'd of an ass.
Ob. There lies your love.

[*right*]
Queen. How came these things to pass?
O, how mine eyes do loath his visage now!

Ob. Silence, a while.—Robin, take off this
head.—

Dimensions: ■ 44.2 x 59.7 cm | 17^5/16" x 23^7/16" (Bodleian Sutherland 172)
Other locations: Essick; Essick; Folger Art Flat b1 c.1; Folger Art Flat b1-2 c.2; Folger Art Flat b1-2 c.3; Huntington 21148; LC NE1713.B7 fol.; National Gallery of Victoria; Newberry Case +YS 65.11; YCBA L 198.212 (fB)
Plate only: Basel 1938.78; BM Dd 6 No. 26; DHW; KHZ 1917/1; YCBA 1977.14.11601 (not seen)
Lit.: Schiff 754; Boydell, *Catalogue of Plates* (1803), xx, 21; Schiff, *Sommernachtstraum*, 1961, 15-19, pl.8;Schiff-Viotto 1977,no. 81; *Letters*, 47
Exh.: Florence 1979 (41); Kansas City 1982 (24).

Variants:
I. Unfinished proof (etched state) before letters: Folger Art Flat b1 c.4
Other locations: Essick; YCBA B1977.14.19982
II. Proof before all letters (lacking verse): LC NE1713.B6 fol.
Imprint (etched letters): Pub. Decr. 1. 1803 by J. & J. BOYDELL at the Shakspeare Gallery

Pall Mall & at N°. 90 Cheapside London
Inscription (open capitals): Painted by Henry
Fuseli R.A. | | Engraved by Tho⁶. Ryder & Tho⁶.
Ryder Jun'. | SHAKSPEARE | Midsummer
Night's Dream | ACT IV SCENE I | Oberon,
Queen of the Fairies, Puck, Bottom, and Fairies
attending &c
III. Coloured impression: Folger Art Flat b1 c.1
(sheet inlaid, covering imprint)
IV. Reworked and reissued (1852) with plate
number ('23') added bottom left: LC
NE1713.B7 fol.
Other locations: Birmingham 386911; Folger
Art Flat b3 (Rice); Folger Art Flat b10 c.2;
Folger Art Flat b10 c.3; NYPL *NDC+++
1852

120. *The Witches Appear to Macbeth and
Banquo*, 1798
(*Macbeth*, I, iii)
(Vol. I, Plate XXXVII)

Stipple engraving by James Caldwall (1739-1819?)
with preliminary etching by Thomas Trotter

(1756-1803) after Fuseli's lost painting No. 4 in
the Shakspeare Gallery ([1785-1790]; Schiff 737).
Imprint: Pub. April 23, 1798, by J & J.
BOYDELL, at the Shakspeare Gallery, Pall Mall,
& N°. 90, Cheapside.
Inscription: Painted by H. Fuseli R.A. | | Engraved
by Ja⁶. Caldwall. | SHAKSPEARE. | **Macbeth.** |
ACT I. SCENE III. | A Heath.—Macbeth, Banquo,
& three Witches. |

[*left*]
Macb.—Say, from whence
You owe this strange intelligence? or why

[*right*]
Upon this blasted heath you stop our way
With such prophetic greeting?—Speak, I charge
you.

Dimensions: ■ 44.5 x 59.9 cm | 17½" x 23⁹/₁₆"
(Bodleian Sutherland 172)
Other locations: Essick; Folger Art Flat b1 c.1;
Folger Art Flat b1-2 c.2; Folger Art Flat b1-2
c.3; Huntington 21148; LC NE 1713.B7 fol.;
Newberry Case +YS 11.65; YCBA L 198.212
(fB)

120.

Plate only: Basel 1938.77; BM Dd 6 No. 42; DHW; ETH 1420

Lit.: Schiff 737 (44.7 x ?53.0 cm); Boydell, *Catalogue of Plates* (1803), xxi, 37; Schiff-Viotto 1977, no. 59; Friedman 1976, 222-223

Exh.: Chicago 1978 (5); Kansas City 1982 (25); London, Heim, 1991 (77).

Variants:

I. Unfinished proof (untouched etching) by Thomas Trotter (1756-1803): Folger Art Box F993 no. 5

II. Unfinished proof (2nd etched state) before all letters (1790): BM 1922-4-28-67

Inscription (etched letters): Painted by H. Fuseli. || Publish'd Jany. 1. 1790. by J. & J. Boydell, Cheapside & at the Shakspeare Gallery, Pall Mall London. || Aqua fortis by Trotter. | SHAKSPEARE. [open letters]

Other locations: Folger Art Box F993 no. 9; LC NE1713.B6 fol.; YCBA B1977.14.19997

III. Unfinished proof (3rd etched state): Folger Art Box F993 no. 4

IV. Unfinished proof (4th etched state): Folger Art Box F993 no. 8

V. Proof marked by the artist (?inscription cropped): Folger Art Box F993 no. 6

VI. Proof before letters: LC NE1713.B6 fol.

VII. Proof before all letters (lacking verse): KHZ B43

Imprint: Pub April 23 1798 by J & J BOYDELL at the Shakspeare Gallery Pall Mall & N° 90 Cheapside

Inscription (scratched letters): Painted by H Fuseli RA || Engraved by Ja^s Caldwall | SHAKSPEARE. | Macbeth | ACT I. SCENE 3. | A Heath—Macbeth Banquo & three Witches

VIII. Reworked and reissued (1852) with plate number ('46') added bottom left: Folger Art Flat b10 c.1

Other locations: Birmingham 386911; Folger Art Flat b10 c.2; Folger Art Flat b11 c.3 (43.8 x 60.1 cm); NYPL *NDC+++ 1852

Plate only: DHW

David Alexander suggests that Thomas Trotter may have passed on the unfinished plate to Caldwall due to illness, since it was about this time that a falling flower-pot injured Trotter's eyes, ending his engraving career (see

Gentleman's Magazine, LXXIII, Feb. 1803, 198f.). If so, he would have had to return part of his remuneration of £252, thereby increasing the recorded sum of £131.5.0 paid to Caldwall. Fuseli had received £210 (200 guineas).

Fuseli's illustration represents Macbeth's first encounter with the three weird sisters upon the blasted heath. Incited by their predictions and urged on by his wife, Macbeth will hereafter give free rein to his 'o'erleaping' ambition. The skulls and bones at his feet bespeak his future path.

Fuseli's criticism of Sir Joshua Reynolds' painting of Macbeth and the witches for Boydell highlights his own treatment here:

> It is not by the accumulation of infernal or magic machinery, distinctly seen, by the introduction of Hecate and a chorus of female demons and witches, by surrounding him with successive apparitions at once, and a range of shadows moving above or before him, that Macbeth can be made an object of terror,—to render him so you must place him on a ridge, his downdashed eye absorbed by the murky abyss; surround the horrid vision with darkness, exclude its limits, and shear its light to glimpses (Lecture IV; Knowles, II, 225-226).

121.

122.

121. *Prince Hal and Poins Surprise Falstaff with Doll Tearsheet*, 1795
(*King Henry the Fourth*, Part 2, II, iv)
(Vol. II, Plate IV)

Stipple engraving by William Satchwell Leney
(1769-1831) after Fuseli's lost painting No. 5 in
the Shakspeare Gallery ([1785-1790]; Schiff 724).
Imprint: Published March 25ᵗʰ. 1795, by JOHN &
JOSIAH BOYDELL, at the Shakspeare Gallery,
Pall Mall, & at Nº. 90. Cheapside, LONDON.
Inscription: Painted by Henry Fuseli R.A. | |
Engraved by Wᵐ. Leney. | SHAKSPEARE. |
Second Part of| **King Henry the Fourth.** | ACT II.
SCENE IV. | Doll Tearsheet, Falstaff, Henry, &
Poins. |

  [*left*]
Dol. I' faith, and thou followd'st him like a
  church.
Thou whoreson little tidy Bartholomew boar-
  pig,
  [*right*]
when will thou leave fighting o' days, & foining
 'o nights,
& begin to patch up thine old body for heaven.

Dimensions: ■ 49.2 x 36.2 cm | 19⁶/16" x 14⁵/16"
(Bodleian Sutherland 173)
Other locations: Essick; Folger Art Flat b1-2 c.2
(cut down to platemark); Folger Art Flat b1-2 c.3;
Folger Art Flat b2 c.1; Huntington 21148; LC
NE1713.B6 fol.; LC NE1713.B7 fol.; Newberry
Case +YS 65.11; YCBA L 198.212 (fB)
Plate only: Basel 1938.73 (badly creased); BM Dd
6 No. 10; Browne; KHZ 1940/130
Lit.: Schiff 724 (49.1 x 36.2 cm); Boydell,
Catalogue of Plates (1803), xxii, 8; Schiff-Viotto
1977, no. 43; Friedman 1976, 222
Exh.: Kansas City 1982 (35); London, Heim,
1991 (78).

Variants:
I. Unfinished proof (etched state) before all
letters (signatures and imprint only): YCBA
B1977.14.20014
Imprint (etched letters): Pub. Jan. 29. 1793, by
J. & J. Boydell, Shakspeare Gallʸ. Pall Mall, &
Cheapside.
Inscription (etched letters): Painted by H.
Fuseli. | | Aqua-fortis by W. Leney. |
SHAKSPEARE.

Other locations: Essick; Folger Art Flat b2 c.4
II. Proof before all letters (lacks verse): KHZ
B43
Inscription: Painted by Henry Fuseli, R.A.||
Engraved by W^m. Leney.|SHAKSPEARE.|
Second Part of|**King Henry the Fourth.**|ACT
II. SCENE IV.|Doll Tearsheet, Falstaff,
Henry, & Poins.
Other locations: Folger Art Flat b1 c.4
III. Reworked and reissued (1852) with plate
number ('62') added bottom left: Folger Art
Flat b11 c.1
Other locations: Birmingham 386911; Folger
Art Flat b11 c.2; Folger Art Flat b11 c.3;
Folger Art Flat b4 (Rice); LC NE1713.B72
fol.; NYPL *NDC+++ 1852
Plate only: DHW

For this painting Fuseli received £102.10s; the
engraver was paid £105 (100 guineas).

Fuseli has given Falstaff the features of a noted
actor in this role—John Henderson (1747-1785).

122. *King Henry Condemning Cambridge, Scroop and Northumberland*, 1798
(*King Henry the Fifth*, II, ii)
(Vol. II, Plate XII)

Stipple engraving by Robert Thew (1758-1802)
after Fuseli's lost painting No. 6 in the
Shakspeare Gallery ([1785-1790]; Schiff 737), of
which a finished study is in the Royal Shakespeare
Theatre Picture Gallery, Stratford-upon-Avon
([1786-1789]; Schiff 725).
Imprint: Pub^d. Decr. 1. 1798, by J. & J.
BOYDELL, at the Shakspeare Gallery, Pall Mall;
& N°. 90, Cheapside.
Inscription: Painted by H Fuseli R.A.||Engraved
by Robt. Thew.|Hist^l. Engraver to H.R.H. the P.
of Wales.|SHAKSPEARE.|**King Henry the
Fifth**|ACT II. SCENE II.|Southampton.—The
King, Scroop, Cambridge, Grey, & attendants.|

[*left*]
K. Hen.—Why, how now, Gentlemen?
What see you in those papers, that you lose
So much complexion?—look ye, how they
  change!
Their cheeks are paper.—Why, what read you
  there,

[*right*]
That hath so cowarded & chas'd your blood
Out of appearance?

Cam. I do confess my fault;
And do submit me to your highness' mercy.

Dimensions:■ 44.1 x 59.5 cm | 17^5/16" x 23^7/16"
(Bodleian Sutherland 173)
Other locations: Essick; Folger Art Flat b2 c.1;
Folger Art Flat b1-2 c.3; Huntington 21148; LC
NE1713.B7 fol.; Newberry Case +YS 11.65;
YCBA L 198.212 (fB)
Plate only: Basel 1938.71; BM Dd6 No. 14;
DHW; KHZ 1940/122
Lacking plate: LC NE1713.B6 fol.
Lit.: Schiff 725; Boydell, *Catalogue of Plates*
(1803), xxii, 12; Tomory 1972, pl. 82; Friedman
1976, 222; Schiff-Viotto 1977, no. 44
Exh.: Kansas City 1982 (36); London, Heim,
1991 (79)

Variants:
I. Unfinished proof (etched state) before all
letters (signatures and imprint only) (1789):
YCBA B1977.14.20017
Imprint: Aquafortis Publish'd March 25. 1789,
by John & Josiah Boydell, N°. 90, Cheapside
London.
Inscription: Fuseli. Pinxit.||Thew. Sculpsit.
Other locations: Essick; Folger Art Flat b2 c.4
II. Proof before all letters (lacking verse): KHZ
B43
Imprint: Pub^d Decr 1 1798 by J & J BOYDELL
at the Shakspeare Gallery Pall Mall & N 90
Cheapside
Inscription (open letters): Painted by H Fuseli
RA||Engraved by Robt. Thew|Hist Engraver to
HRH the P of Wales|SHAKSPEARE|King
Henry the Fifth|ACT II SC II|Southampton—
The King Scroop Cambridge Grey & attendants
Other locations: Folger Art Flat b1 c.4
III. Coloured impression: Folger Art Flat b2 c.1
Other locations: DHW
IV. Reworked and reissued (1852) with plate
number ('66') added bottom left: Folger Art
Flat b11 c.1
Other locations: Birmingham 386911; Folger
Art Flat b4 (Rice); Folger Art Flat b11 c.2;
Folger Art Flat b11 c.3; LC NE1713.B72 fol.;
NYPL *NDC+++ 1852

Fuseli depicts the moment when the plotters
receive warrants for their execution.

Fuseli was paid £63 (60 guineas) for his
painting, while for his labours Thew received
£315 (300 guineas)—five times as much.

123.

123. *Lear Casting out his Daughter Cordelia*,
1792
(*King Lear*, I, i)
(Vol. II, Plate XXXVIII)
(Issued in Part No. III)

Stipple engraving by Richard Earlom (1742?-
1822) after Fuseli's painting No. 7 in the
Shakspeare Gallery ([1785-1790]; Schiff 739)
Imprint: Published Augᵗ. 1, 1792, by JOHN &
JOSIAH BOYDELL, at the Shakspeare Gallery
Pall Mall, & N°. 90. Cheapside London.
Inscription: Painted by Hʸ. Fuseli. | | Engrav'd by
Rᵈ. Earlom. | SHAKSPEARE. | **King Lear,** | ACT
I. SCENE I. |

[*left*]

Lear. Let it be so,—Thy truth then be thy
  dower:
For, by the sacred radiance of the sun;
The mysteries of Hecate, and the night;
By all the operations of the orbs,
From whom we do exist, and cease to be;
[*right*]
Here I disclaim all my paternal care,

Propinquity and property of blood,
And as a stranger to my heart and me
Hold thee, from this, for ever.

Dimensions: ■ 44.6 x 59.6 cm | 17⁹/16" x 23½"
(Bodleian Sutherland 173)
Other locations: Essick; Folger Art Flat b1-2 c.2;
Folger Art Flat b1-2 c.3; Folger Art Flat b2 c.1;
Huntington 21148; LC NE1713.B7 fol.; Newberry
Case +YS 65.11; YCBA L 198.212 (fB)
Plate only: Basel 1938.75; BM Dd 6 No. 40;
DHW; KHZ 1940/129; KHZ B43
Lit.: Boydell, *Catalogue of Plates* (1803), xxiv,
38; Friedman 1976, 222; *Letters*, 24
Exh.: Chicago 1978 (4); Florence 1979 (39);
Kansas City 1982 (34); London, Heim, 1991 (80)

Variants:
I. Unfinished proof (etched state) before all
letters (signatures and imprint only): Folger Art
Flat b2 c.4
Imprint (etched letters): Aquafortis: Publish'd
April 23ᵈ. 1788, by John & Josiah Boydell.
Cheapside London.

Inscription (etched letters): Painted. by
Fuseli. | | Engraved. in Aquafortis. by R Earlom.
Other locations: LC NE1713.B6 fol.
II. Proof before all letters (lacking verse) (open
letters): Folger Art Flat b1 c.4
III. Coloured impression: DHW
IV. Reworked and reissued (1852) (in Vol. I)
with plate number ('49') added bottom left:
Folger Art Flat b10 c.1
Other locations: Birmingham 386911; Folger
Art Flat b10 c.2; Folger Art Flat b10 c.3;
Folger Art Flat b3 (Rice) (44.0 x 59.6 cm); LC
NE1713.B72 fol.NYPL *NDC + + + 1852
Plate only: DHW; MMA 42.119.540

Fuseli's sense of the dramatic is powerfully
exemplified in his illustration of this scene, the
fulcrum on which the whole play turns, showing
Lear rejecting Cordelia, his only truly loving and
devoted daughter. The design typifies Fuseli's
ability to create figures that are the embodiment
of their passions. But Lear's expressive force and
theatricality of gesture is also intrinsic to the
deliberately centripetal principle of the
composition in his Shakespeare pictures, with

their dark backgrounds and strongly foreshortened
figures thrusting powerfully against the pictorial
plane.

Fuseli was paid £262. 10s. (250 guineas) for his
painting, while Earlom received £420 (400
guineas) for engraving it.

124. *Hamlet, Horatio, Marcellus and the Ghost*,
1796
(*Hamlet*, I, iv)
(Vol. II, Plate XLIV)

Stipple engraving by Robert Thew (1758-1802)
after Fuseli's lost painting No. 8 in the
Shakspeare Gallery formerly in the Earle
collection, Liverpool (1788-1789; Schiff 731).
Imprint: Published Sept. 29. 1796, by J. & J.
BOYDELL, at the Shakspeare Gallery, Pall Mall,
& at N. 90, Cheapside, London.
Inscription: Painted by H. Fuseli R.A. | | Engraved
by R. Thew. | Hist. Engraver to H.R.H. the P. of
Wales. | SHAKSPEARE. | **Hamlet,** | **Prince of
Denmark.** | ACT I. SCENE IV. | The Platform
before the Palace of Elsineur.—Hamlet, Horatio,
Marcellus and the Ghost. |

124.

[*left*]

Ham. Still am I call'd.—unhand me, gentlemen;
        [Breaking from them.

[*right*]

By heaven, I'll make a Ghost of him that lets
        me:—
I say, away:—Go on,—I'll follow thee.

Dimensions: ■ 44.1 x 59.6 cm | 17⁶/16" x 23½"
(Bodleian Sutherland 172)
Other locations: Folger Art Flat b1-2 c.2; Folger
Art Flat b1-2 c.3; Folger Art Flat b2 c.1;
Huntington 21148; LC NE1713.B7 fol.;
Newberry Case +YS 65.11; YCBA L 198.212
(fB)
Plate only: Basel 1938.76; BM Dd 6 No. 46;
DHW; KHZ 1940/132; LC P&P XVIII.T419 01
(not seen); MMA 42.119.545; V & A Dyce 2909
Lacking plate: LC NE1713.B6 fol.
Lit.: Schiff 731 (44.4 x 59.5 cm); Boydell,
Catalogue of Plates (1803), xxiv, 44; Todd 1947,
75-76; Tomory 1972, pl. 221; Friedman 1976,
222; Schiff-Viotto 1977, 51¹; Boime 1987, 297
('depicting an electrically charged apparition ...
surrounded by a dazzling array of meteoric
effects'), pl. 4.11.
Exh.: Kansas City 1982 (33); London, Heim,
1991 (81).

Variants:

I. Unfinished proof (etched state) before all
letters (1793): Essick
Imprint: Publish'd June 24. 1793. by J. & J.
Boydell, Cheapside. & at the Shakspeare
Gallery Pall Mall.
Inscription: Painted by H. Fuseli. | | Etched by
R. Thew. | (open letters): SHAKSPEARE.
Other locations: Folger Art Flat b1 c.4
II. Proof before all letters lacking verse: KHZ
B43
Imprint: Published Sept. 29. 1796 by J. & J.
BOYDELL at the Shakspeare Gallery Pall Mall
& at N. 90 Cheapsid[e] London
Inscription: Painted by H Fuseli R.A. | |
Engraved by R. Thew. | Hist Engraver to
H.R.H. the P. of Wales. | SHAKSPEARE.
(open letters) | Hamlet, Prince of Denmark. |
ACT I. Scene IV. | The platform before the
Palace of Elsineur.—Hamlet, Horatio,
Marcellus and the Ghost.
III. Reworked and reissued (1852) with plate
number ('96') added bottom left (Folger Art
Flat b11 c.1) (43.5 x 59.8 cm)

Other locations: Birmingham 386911; Folger
Art Flat b11 c.2; Folger Art Flat b11 c.3;
Folger Art Flat b4 (Rice); LC NE1713.B72
fol.; NYPL *NDC+++ 1852
Plate only: KHZ B43
IV. Proof before all letters (lacking verse):
MMA 42.119.545 (1852)

As usually happened, Fuseli was paid less for
this painting (£210 or 200 guineas) than the
engraver, who received £315 (300 guineas).

Fuseli's illustration of the ghost in *Hamlet* was
outstripped in popularity only by his *Nightmare*.
Benjamin Robert Haydon considered it 'The finest
conception of a ghost that ever was painted':

> There it quivered with martial stride, pointing
> to a place of meeting with Hamlet; and round its
> visored head was a halo of light that looked
> sulphureous, and made one feel as if one
> actually smelt hell, burning cinder, and
> suffocating. The dim moon glittered behind; the
> sea roared in the distance as if agitated by the
> presence of a supernatural spirit; and the ghost
> looked at Hamlet, with eyes that glared like the
> light in the eyes of a lion, which is savagely
> growling over his bloody food. But still it was a
> German ghost, and not the ghost of Shakespeare.
> There was nothing in it to touch human
> sympathies combined with the infernal; there
> was nothing at all of 'his sable, silvered beard,'
> or his countenance more 'in sorrow than in
> anger;' it was a fierce demonical, armed fiend
> reeking from hell, who had not yet expiated
> 'the crimes done in his days of nature,' to
> 'qualify him for heaven.'

******

No. 125.
THE | DRAMATIC WORKS | OF | SHAKSPEARE
| REVISED | BY GEORGE STEEVENS. | VOL. I
[-VOL. IX]. | LONDON: | PRINTED BY W.
BULMER AND CO. | SHAKSPEARE
PRINTING = OFFICE, | FOR JOHN AND
JOSIAH BOYDELL, GEORGE AND W.
NICOL: | FROM THE TYPES OF W. MARTIN. |
MDCCCII [1802] (1/95(?) illus.).

BOYDELL'S | GRAPHIC ILLUSTRATIONS | OF
THE | DRAMATIC WORKS, | OF |
SHAKSPEARE; | CONSISTING OF | A | SERIES
OF PRINTS | FORMING AN ELEGANT AND

USEFUL COMPANION TO THE|VARIOUS EDITIONS OF HIS WORKS,|ENGRAVED FROM PICTURES, PURPOSELY PAINTED| BY THE VERY FIRST ARTISTS, AND LATELY EXHIBITED AT|THE SHAKSPEARE GALLERY.|=| LONDON:|PUBLISHED BY MESS^{RS}. BOYDELL & CO. CHEAPSIDE| Tomkins scrip^t. & Halliwell Sculp^t. [?1803] (1/99 illus. + 1 portrait).

THE|DRAMATIC WORKS|OF|WILLIAM SHAKSPEARE:|WITH GLOSSARIAL NOTES,| A SKETCH OF HIS LIFE, AND AN ESTIMATE OF HIS WRITINGS;|NEWLY ARRANGED AND EDITED [*by Charles Henry Wheeler*].|[Vignette]| *View of an Ancient Building in Henley-street, Stratford-on-Avon, the Birth-place of Shakspeare;* |*With a Representation of THE JUBILEE PROCESSION, SEPTEMBER 6, 1769*| LONDON:| MOON, BOYS, & GRAVES, PRINTSELLERS TO THE KING, PALL MALL.|1832.

For a caricature version see No. **125A** below.

ADVERTISEMENT
[TO *GRAPHIC ILLUSTRATIONS*]
[Ashmolean]
=

PORTRAIT OF THE LATE
ALDERMAN JOHN BOYDELL.

The Engravings that ornament the truly magnificent Edition of Shakspeare, projected by Mr. Nicol, edited by Mr. Steevens, and printed by Mr. Bulmer, were undertaken and completed by the late Alderman John Boydell, and are so well known to the public, and have been so highly patronised, that in prefixing his Portrait to the present Collection of them, the publishers have no apprehension of being accused of vanity or partiality.

To the visitors of the late Shakspeare Gallery, or the possessors of this National Edition of Shakspeare, it need not be mentioned, that the present volume consists of *one part* of the embellishments attached to that grand design.* The vast expense of reprinting the Text of so great a work has induced the proprietors to avail themselves of the opportunity offered, to publish such a Selection of the Prints belonging to it, *separately*, as from their uniform size, and style of engraving, might form an elegant

accompaniment to all other editions of Shakspeare; and the present Collection is respectfully submitted to the public as the result.

In presenting a series of ONE HUNDRED FINE ENGRAVINGS, copied from the pencils of Sir Joshua Reynolds, Romney, Opie, Smirke, Northcote, Fuseli, Hamilton, Tresham, Westall, and other first-rate British Artists, panegyric seems superfluous; the publishers, however, beg leave to observe, 'that it should always be remembered, that our great Dramatic Bard possessed powers which no pencil can reach: for such was the force of his creative imagination, that though he frequently goes beyond Nature, he still continues to be natural; and seems only to do that which Nature would have done had she o'erstepp'd her usual limits.—It must not then be expected that the art of the painter can ever equal the sublimity of our poet. The strength of Michael Angelo united to the grace of Raphael would have laboured in vain;—for what pencil can give to his airy beings 'a local habitation and a name?'—+

Viewing the Prints here collected with this regard, it may without presumption be affirmed, that such a varied combination of talent united in the embellishment of a single author, is not elsewhere to be found. This volume is therefore confidently offered, not only as an ornament to any edition of Shakspeare, but as a valuable Specimen of the Fine Arts of the Country.

It need only be added, that in binding up the collection, the engravings have been placed strictly conformable to the order in which the Plays are arranged in the edition of JOHNSON and STEEVENS; an Alphabetical List of them also is given, with the Scenes to which they respectively refer; and they are further prefaced

*[Original footnote]: The Collection of the *Large* Plates which ornament this grand National Edition of Shakspear, above referred to, consists of
—Two Volumes Atlas,
containing Ninety-three Plates,—
the whole of which are engraven from the Originals by the same Artists, and were lately exhibited in the Shakspeare Gallery. Of this magnificent Publication, for the honour of our Nation, it may be truly said, that no country, nor age, has yet produced an edition of any author's works of such exquisite taste and beauty. It surpasses in splendour, all former publications, as far as the genius of Shakspeare surpasses that of all other Dramatic Poets.

by an Explanatory Index, containing a concise account of the subject of each plate, and the *Dramatis Personae* introduced in it. The several passages in the different Dramas which they elucidate are thus rendered immediately obvious on inspection.

The Monument, and the fine *Alto-relievo* from the front of the Shakspeare Gallery in Pall-Mall, will, it is presumed, be found additional illustrations to the works of our immortal Bard.

The *Dramatic Works* (1802) in nine folio volumes, George Steevens's elegantly printed edition of Shakespeare's complete plays (usually referred to as the 'small Boydell'), are not to be confused with the Atlas-folio-size *Collection of Prints* (1803) (without text), illustrating Shakespeare's plays (commonly known as the 'large Boydell'). The price of the *Dramatic Works*, 'with Ninety-five Plates of a proper size to bind with the work' is given in Boydell's *Alphabetical Catalogue of Plates* (1803) as £42. The *Graphic Illustrations* are not mentioned, however, in the *Catalogue*, and thus seem to have been collected and issued in this form only later.

125.

125. *Robin Goodfellow-Puck*, 1799
(*A Midsummer Night's Dream*, II, i)
(Vol. II [1802], facing p. 15)

Engraved by James Parker (1757-1805) after Fuseli's untraced painting No. 9 in Boydell's Shakspeare Gallery ([1787-1790]; Schiff 750)
Imprint: Pub^d. Septr. 29. 1799 by J. & J. Boydell, N°. 90, Cheapside; & at the Shakspear Gallery, Pall Mall.
Inscription: Painted by H. Fuseli R.A. | | Engraved by Ja^s. Parker. | MIDSUMMER=NIGHT'S DREAM. | Act 2. Scene 1. | **A Wood.—Puck** | (tiny etched letters below panel): Painted by H Fuseli R.A. | Engraved by J. Parker.
Dimensions (excl. lower panel): ■ 21.6 x 15.5 cm | 8½" x 6²/16"; ■ 22.0 x 16.5 cm | 8¹⁰/16" x 6½" (BL 1870.c.10)
Other locations: Ashmolean fol. 928.6 Boy; Bodleian M.adds.51.c.7; Dörrbecker; Folger Art Vol.f.88 (XXV); Folger Art Vol. f.87 (XXV); Folger PR2752.1802 c.1; Folger PR2752.1832h c.2 (between pp. 607-609); Huntington 27435; LC PR2752.S8 1802; Princeton Ex 3925.1802f; Princeton Ex 3925.1802.11f

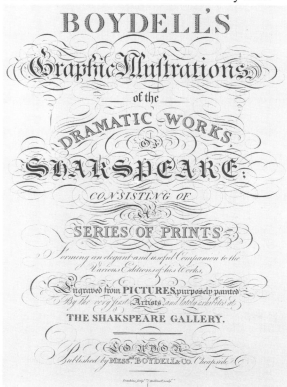

Fig. 6. *Graphic Illustrations*, [?1803]. Title page.

Plate only: BM J.29. No. 10; Fitzwilliam 32K6; Folger PR2572.1807c c.4 (Vol. I, facing p. 25)
Lacking plate: DHW; Folger PR2752.1802 c.5
Lit.: Tomory 1972, pl. 169; Friedman 1976, pl. 270

Variants:

I. Unfinished proof (etched state) (no lower panel) (signatures only): Huntington 181067, XIII, 44
Other locations: Folger PR2752.1802 c.3 (Vol. II, between pp. 14-15)
Plate only: Folger Art File S528m5 no. 8
Inscription (etched letters): Painted by H Fuseli R.A. | | Etched by J Parker
II. Proof (incompletely lined lower panel) (open letter capitals): Folger PR2752.1802 c.2
Other locations: Folger Art Vol. f.89 (Boydell's own copy); Folger PR2752.1802 c.3; Folger PR2752.1802 c.4

The design shows Robin Goodfellow-Puck, the 'merry wanderer of the night', drawing a circle of little orbs, moon and stars around his head as he prepares to 'put a girdle round about the earth in forty minutes'. We also see the 'shrewd and knavish sprite' plying his mischief by 'beguiling' the bean-fed horse (lower right): it is so startled that it throws its rider. Meanwhile Queen Mab, aided by one of the bizarre denizens of her realm (lower left) 'misleads' the panic-stricken monkish night-wanderer. Both the fairy figures are drawn much larger than the humans they are tormenting.

******

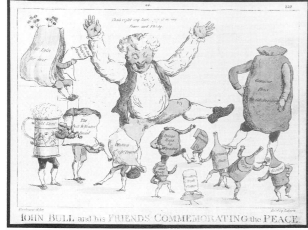

125A.

125A. *John Bull and his Friends Commemorating the Peace of Amiens*, [?March 1802]

A pastiche of Fuseli's design etched by P. Roberts after George Moutard Woodward (1760?-1809).
Imprint: London Pub^d by P. Roberts 28, Middle-Row, Holborn.
Inscription: IOHN BULL AND HIS FRIENDS COMMEMORATING THE PEACE. | Woodward Delin | | Etch^d by Roberts.
Dimensions: ■ 23.5 x 33.0 cm | 9¼" x 13" (BM ?)
Other locations: Lewis Walpole Library 8023.01
Lit.: George 9850; F.D. Klingender, *Hogarth and English Caricature* (1944), no. 107.

The Peace of Amiens in 1802 represented the first real break in hostilities with France since 1794. This political cartoon based on Fuseli's Shakespeare illustration depicts Robin Goodfellow as John Bull in a bottom wig, dancing to celebrate the return of 'Peace and Plenty'. His friends are cavorting figures with human arms and legs but with bodies composed of 'Mutton 3^d ½ P^r. Pound', 'Double Gloucester', 'Mealy Potatoes', and 'Excellent Fresh Butter', or of bottles of Port and 'Coniac'.

******

Nos. 117A, 120A - 121A, 123A.
THE | PLAYS | OF | WILLIAM SHAKSPEARE. | WITH THE | CORRECTIONS AND ILLUSTRATIONS | OF | VARIOUS COMMENTATORS. | TO WHICH ARE ADDED, | NOTES | BY | SAMUEL JOHNSON AND GEORGE STEEVENS. | A NEW EDITION. | REVISED AND AUGMENTED | (WITH A GLOSSARIAL INDEX). | BY THE EDITOR OF DODSLEY'S COLLECTION OF | OLD PLAYS [*i.e. Isaac Reed*]. | ΤΙΣ ΦΥΣΕΩΣ ΓΡΑΜΜΑΤΕΥΣ ΗΝ, ΤΟΝ ΚΑ ΛΑΜΟΝ | ΑΠΟΒΡΕΧΩΝ ΕΙΣ ΝΟΥΝ. | *Vet. Auct. apud. Suidam.* | *MULTA DIES, VARIUSQUE LABOR MUTABILIS AEVI* | *RETULIT IN MELIUS, MULTOS ALTERNA REVISENS* | *LUSIT, ET IN SOLIDO RURSUS FORTUNA LOCAVIT.* | *Virgil.* | — | BASIL: | PRINTED AND SOLD BY J. J. TOURNEISEN. | M.DCCC. [1800, *rectè* 1799-1802] (4/60 illus.).

ADVERTISEMENT
(Princeton)
(Vol. 23)

...Several Subscribers having manifested a wish to see the present edition embellished with engravings, the proprietor of the Collection of English Classics, ever ready to meet the wishes of the public, has been at a considerable expense to get the plates of that monument to the glory of the British nation, the *Shakspeare-Gallery* copied in a smaller size, by eminent engravers in France and Germany. Sixty of these plates are now on sale, and the remaining are already in great forwardness, and will be ready for delivery in the course of next summer.

117A. *Prospero, Miranda, Caliban and Ariel*, 1799
(*The Tempest*, I, ii, 325
(Vol. 4, facing p. 10)

Re-engraved in reduced format by Wolf
Inscription: H. Fuseli inv:│ │Wolf sculpsit.│ SHAKSPEARE.│**Tempest**│ACT. I. SCEN. II.│

[*left*]
Pro. For this, be sure, to-night thou shalt have cramps,
Side-stitches that shall pen thy breath up; urchins
Shall, for that vast of night that they may work,
[*right*]
All exercise on thee: thou shalt be pinch'd
As thick as honey-combs, each pinch more stinging
Than bees that made them.│

The inchanted Island: before the Cell of Prospero. —Prospero, Miranda, Caliban, & Ariel.
Dimensions: ■ 9.3 x 13.1 cm │ 3⁶/16" x 5³/16"
(Princeton 3925.1799)
Other locations: Bern L9.554 (facing p. 36)
Plate only: Folger Art File S528t2 no. 20; KHZ 1940/107
Lacking plate: UB Basel A.0.V.4; BL Gal.9.S.g.; Bodleian Vet.D5.e.368; Folger PR2752.1799-1802; Geneva 13/6087; Lausanne M2750; Lucerne Bb1
Lit.: Lonchamp 1920, no. 676; Bircher & Straumann 1971, 176, 178

120A. *The Witches Appear to Macbeth and Banquo*, 1801
(*Macbeth*, I, iii)
(Vol. 11, facing p. 23)

Re-engraved in reduced format by Johann Jakob von Mechel (1764-1816)
Inscription: Painted by H. Fuseli R.A.│ │Engraved in Lörach by J.J. Mechel.│ SHAKSPEAR.│ **Macbeth.**│ACT I. SCENE III.│

[*left*]
Macb— Say, from whence
You owe this strange intelligence? or why
[*right*]
Ypon this blasted heath you stop our way
With such prophetic greeting?—Speack, I charge you.│

A Heath.—Macbeth Banquo, & three Witches
Dimensions: ■ 9.4 x 12.4 cm │ 3¹¹/16" x 4¹⁴/16"
(Princeton 3925.1799)
Other locations: Bern L9.554 (facing p. 35)
Plate only: Basel 1941.351; Folger Art File S528m1 no. 6
Lacking plate: UB Basel A.0.V.11; BL Gal.9.S.g.; Bodleian Vet.D5.e.371; Folger PR2752.1799-1802; Geneva 13/6087; Lausanne M2750; Lucerne Bb1
Lit.: Lonchamp 1920, no. 676; Bircher & Straumann 1971, 177-178

121A. *Falstaff and Doll Tearsheet Surprised by Prince Hal and Poins*, [1802]
(*King Henry the Fourth*, Part 2, II, 4)
(Vol. 13, facing p. 74)

Re-engraved in reduced format by Johann Jakob von Mechel (1764-1816)
Inscription: Painted by Henry Fuseli R.A.│ │gestochen in Lörrach von J.J. Mechel. Junger.│ SHAKSPEARE│Second Part of│King Henry the Fourth│ACT II.Scene IV.│

[*left*]
Dol. I' faith and thou followdst him like a church.
Thou whoreson little tidy Bartholomew boar pig,
[*right*]
when wilt thou leave fighting o' days, & foining o' nights
& begin to patch up thine old body for heaven.│

Doll Tearsheet, Falstaff, Henry & Poins.
Dimensions: ■ 12.2 x 9.1 cm | 4¹³/16" x 3⁹/16"
(Princeton 3925.1799)
Plate only: Folger Art File S528.k1b no. 11 c.2
Lacking plate: Bern L9.554
Lit.: Lonchamp 1920, no. 676; not noted in
Bircher & Straumann 1971

123A. *Lear Casting out his Daughter Cordelia*,
1802
(*King Lear*, I, i)
(Vol. 20, facing p. 265)

Re-engraved in reduced format by C. Lepine (d.
1808)
Inscription: Painted by Hʸ. Fuseli | | L'Epine,
Dir. | SHAKSPEARE. | King Lear. | ACT. I.
SCENE I. |

[*left*]
Let it be so.—Thy truth then be thy dower:
For, by the sacred radiance of the sun;
The mysteries of Hecate, and the night;
By all the operations of the orbs,
From whom we do exist, and cease to be;

[*right*]
Here I disclaim all my paternal care,
Propinquity and property of blood,
And as a stranger to my heart and me
Hold thee, from this, for ever.

Dimensions: ■ 8.9 x 13.4 cm | 3½" x 5¼"
(Princeton 3925.1799)
Other locations (plate only): Folger Art File
S528??
Lacking plate: UB Basel A.0.V.20; BL
Gal.9.S.g.; Bodleian Vet.D5.e.376; Folger
PR2752.1799-1802; Geneva 13/6087; Lausanne
M2750, Lucerne Bb1
Lit.: Lonchamp 1920, no. 676; Bircher &
Straumann 1971, 177-178

Variants:
I. Before all letters (lacking verse) (facing p.
274): Bern L9.554

******

Nos. 120B - 122B.
SHAKSPEARE'S | DRAMATISCHE WERKE, |
ÜBERSETZT | VON | A.W. SCHLEGEL UND
J.J. ESCHENBURG. | — | ERSTER BAND.
[-ACHTZEHNTER BAND]. | — | — | [*Contents per*

volume] | | — | WIEN, | BEY ANTON PICHLER. |
1810-1812 (2/18 illus.).

SUPPLEMENTE | ZU | SHAKSPEARE'S |
DRAMATISCHEN WERKEN, | NACH | A.W.
SCHLEGEL UND J.J. ESCHENBURG. | — |
ERSTER BAND. [-ZWEYTER BAND (*i.e. vols.*
19-20)] | [*Contents per volume*] | — | — | WIEN, |
BEY ANTON PICHLER. | 1812 (1 illus. + portr.
frontis.).

120B. *Macbeth, Banquo, and the Witches*, 1811
(*Macbeth*, I, iii)
(Vol. IX, facing title page)

Re-engraving in reduced format by Martin Pöltzel
(1776-1814)
Inscription (bottom right): M Pölzel sc |
Macbeth. | Act. I. Scene III.
Dimensions: ■ 11.5 x 7.0 cm | 4½" x 2¾" (BL
11762.df.2)
Other locations: Birmingham 387-9; Illinois
822.33.Ns 1811

121B. *Falstaff with Doll Tearsheet*, 1812
(*King Henry the Fourth*, Part 2, II, iv)
(Vol. VI, facing title page)

Re-engraving in reduced format by Martin Pöltzel
(1776-1814)
Inscription (bottom): König Heinrich IV. | Act. II.
Scen. IV.
Dimensions: ■ 11.8 x 7.3 cm | 4¹⁰/16" x 2¹⁴/16"
(BL 11762.df.2)
Other locations: Birmingham 384-6; Illinois
822.33.Ns 1811

122B. *King Henry Condemning Cambridge,*
Scroop, and Northumberland, 1812
(*King Henry the Fifth*, II, ii)
(Vol. VII, facing title page)

Re-engraved in reduced format by Martin Pöltzel
(1776-1814)
Inscription (bottom): König Heinrich V. | Act. II.
Scen II.
Dimensions: ■ 11.8 x 7.3 cm | 4¹⁰/16" x 2¹⁴/16"
(BL 11762.df.2)
Other locations: Birmingham 387-9; Illinois
822.33.Ns 1811

******

No. 125B.

THE | WORKS | OF | SHAKSPEARE; | FROM THE
TEXT OF | JOHNSON, STEEVENS, AND
REED: | — | WITH A | BIOGRAPHICAL
MEMOIR, | AND A VARIETY OF
INTERESTING MATTER, ILLUSTRATIVE OF
HIS | LIFE AND WRITINGS. | BY W. HARVEY,
ESQ. | — | EMBELLISHED WITH A PORTRAIT
OF SHAKSPEARE; | EIGHT PORTRAITS OF
EMINENT PERFORMERS OF HIS
CHARACTERS; | VIEW OF HIS BIRTH-PLACE
AT STRATFORD-ON-AVON; | HIS RESIDENCE
AT NEW PLACE; | HIS MONUMENT IN
STRATFORD-ON-AVON CHURCH, AND |
WESTMINSTER ABBEY; | A VIEW OF THE
GLOBE THEATRE; | THE INSIDE OF THE
RED BULL PLAYHOUSE, CLERKENWELL; |
THE FALCON TAVERN, BANKSIDE; | AND
ILLUSTRATIONS OF HIS PLAYS AND
POEMS. | — | [LONDON:] PUBLISHED FOR
THE PROPRIETORS OF THE | 'LONDON
STAGE', BY SHERWOOD, JONES & CO. |
PATERNOSTER ROW. | [1825] (1/51 illus. +
portr. frontisp.).

...EMBELLISHED WITH A PORTRAIT OF
SHAKSPEARE; | EIGHT PORTRAITS OF
EMINENT PERFORMERS OF HIS
CHARACTERS; | VIEW OF HIS BIRTH-PLACE
AT STRATFORD-ON-AVON; | HIS RESIDENCE
AT NEW PLACE; | HIS MONUMENT IN
STRATFORD-ON-AVON CHURCH, AND |
WESTMINSTER ABBEY; | AND
ILLUSTRATIONS OF HIS PLAYS AND
POEMS. | — | [LONDON:] PUBLISHED FOR
THE PROPRIETORS OF THE | 'LONDON
STAGE', BY SHERWOOD & CO. |
PATERNOSTER ROW. | [1825] (1/51 illus. +
portr. frontisp.).

ADDRESS
[First three paras. omitted]

...There are fifty-one Embellishments, engraved
by the best artists. Those which accompany the
Prolegomena [*8*] cannot fail to prove
interesting, and the Illustrations to the Plays
[*37*] and Poems [*5*] of Shakspeare, and the very
novel feature of the Eight Portraits of eminent
by-gone Performers [*on 1 engraved plate*], who
have been distinguished for personating his
characters. But the main point, on which the

real value of their labours must inevitably
depend, is, the extreme cheapness of their
volume, which presents the entire Works of our
immortal Poet, adorned by the talents of the
critic, the antiquary, and the engraver, at the
very low price usually charged for a common
and incorrect edition of his his PLAYS
ALONE, without either Poems, Illustrative
Matter, or Embellishments; and the Proprietors
cannot but feel they have attained an object of
no mean importance, in thus placing within the
reach of the humblest Reader, the cheapest and
most complete Edition of the Works of
Shakspeare that has ever yet been published....
JUNE, 1825.

Fuseli provided nine paintings for Boydell's
Shakespeare Gallery, none of which were used in
the 'small Boydell', for which, however, Fuseli
did one new design to *A Midsummer-Night's
Dream* (see No. **125**). Apart from the illustrations
to the *Tempest, Twelfth Night, King John* and
Pericles, the wood engravings in this cheap
edition, were recut in wood from the line
engravings accompanying the plays in the 1802
edition. Hence the single illustration by Fuseli.
Neither these nor the five others Sherwood & Co.
provided to accompany the Poems in their edition
had ever formed any part of the Boydell
Shakespeare. The engravers responsible for the
woodcuts accompanying the plays were I. Byfield
(11), Mary Byfield (13) and George Wilmot
Bonner (3); the remaining ten cuts are unsigned.

MIDSUMMER-NIGHT'S DREAM.

Act IV. Scene 1.

125B.

125B. *Robin Goodfellow-Puck*, 1825
(*A Midsummer Night's Dream*, II, i)
(top of page 111)

Woodcut by George Wilmot Bonner (1796-1836)
Inscription (top): MIDSUMMER-NIGHT'S
DREAM. | (lower left-hand side of design): G.
Bonner Sc. | (bottom right): Act IV. Scene 1.
Dimensions: 6.9 x 10.0 cm | 2^{11}/16" x 3^{15}/16" (BL
642.f.21)
Other locations: Birmingham 16278; Cambridge
Nn.14.17; Folger PR2754.1yv2 c.1; Folger
PR2754.1yv c.1 (Sherwood, Jones); Folger
PR2754.1yv2 c.2; Folger PR2754.1yv2 c.3;
Folger PR2754.1yv2 c.4; Folger PR2754.1yv2
c.5; Princeton 3925.1825.3 (Sherwood, Jones)

******

No. 125C.
THE | DRAMATIC WORKS | OF | WILLIAM
SHAKSPEARE, | ACCURATELY PRINTED |
FROM THE TEXT OF THE CORRECTED
COPY | LEFT BY THE LATE | GEORGE
STEEVENS, ESQ. | WITH A | GLOSSARY, AND
NOTES, | AND A SKETCH OF | THE LIFE OF
SHAKSPEARE. | — | IN TWO VOLUMES. |
VOL. I [-VOL. II]. | — | NEW-YORK: | W.
BORRADAILE, 118 FULTON-STREET. |
STEREOTYPED BY A. CHANDLER. | — | 1828.
(1/37 illus. + 2 frontisp.).

[Added engraved title page]: THE | DRAMATIC
WORKS, | OF | WILLIAM SHAKSPEARE, |
ACCURATELY PRINTED FROM | THE TEXT
OF THE CORRECTED COPY LEFT BY THE |
LATE | GEORGE STEEVENS, ESQ, | WITH A |
GLOSSARY AND NOTES. | [Vignette] | Tempest.
[Merchant of Venice.] | NEW YORK, W
BORRADAILE. | 1828.

...HARTFORD: | PUBLISHED BY SILAS
ANDRUS. | — | 1829.

...NEW = YORK: | PRINTED AND PUBLISHED
BY J. & J. HARPER, | NO. 82 CLIFF-STREET. |
— | 1829. [With added engraved t.p. with
vignette.]

...HARTFORD, CT. | PUBLISHED BY SILAS
ANDRUS. | — | 1831.

...HARTFORD: | PUBLISHED BY SILAS
ANDRUS. | SOLD ALSO BY THE BOOK-
SELLERS GENERALLY. | — | 1831. [With added
engraved t.p. with vignette.]

...HARTFORD, CT. | PUBLISHED BY SILAS
ANDRUS. | — | 1832. [With added engraved t.p.
with vignette.]

...HARTFORD, CT. | PUBLISHED BY ANDRUS
AND JUDD | — | 1833 [With added engraved t.p.
with vignette.]

...HARTFORD, CON. | PUBLISHED BY
ANDRUS & JUDD, | LEE STREET. [n.d.]

...HARTFORD: | PUBLISHED BY JUDD,
LOOMIS & CO. | 1836, 1837

...HARTFORD, CON.: | ANDRUS, JUDD, &
FRANKLIN. | 1836, 1837. ['AJF']

...PHILADELPHIA: | THOMAS,
COWPERTHWAIT & CO. | 1842.

...PHILADELPHIA: | PUBLISHED BY THOMAS
DAVIS | 171 MARKET STREET | — | 1849.

THE | DRAMATIC WORKS | OF | WILLIAM
SHAKSPEARE, | ACCURATELY PRINTED
FROM | THE TEXT OF THE CORRECTED
COPY LEFT BY THE LATE | GEORGE
STEEVENS, ESQ. | WITH | GLOSSARIAL
NOTES, | AND | A SKETCH OF THE LIFE OF
SHAKSPEARE. | VOL. I. [-VOL II.] | — |
PHILADELPHIA: | PUBLISHED BY THOMAS
DAVIS. | — | 1850.

THE | DRAMATIC WORKS | OF | WILLIAM
SHAKSPEARE, | ACCURATELY PRINTED |
FROM THE TEXT OF THE CORRECTED
COPY | LEFT BY THE LATE | GEORGE
STEVENS, ESQ. | WITH A | GLOSSARY AND
NOTES, | AND A SKETCH OF | THE LIFE OF
THE POET | WITH FORTY ILLUSTRATIONS. |
— | IN TWO VOLUMES. | VOL.I. [-VOL. II.] |
BOSTON: | PHILLIPS, SAMPSON, AND
COMPANY, | IN WASHINGTON STREET. |
1851, 1852.

WILLIAM SHAKSPEARE'S | COMPLETE
WORKS, | DRAMATIC AND POETIC: | THE
TEXT FROM THE | CORRECTED COPY OF
THE LATE GEORGE STEEVENS, ESQ. |
WITH | GLOSSARIAL NOTES AND A SKETCH
OF THE AUTHOR'S LIFE, | COPIOUSLY
ILLUSTRATED. | IN TWO VOLUMES | VOL. I.
[-VOL. II.] | HARTFORD: | SILAS ANDRUS
AND SON. | — | 1852, 1853, 1854 (1/37 illus. +
portr. frontis.)

As is the case with the Sherwood edition (125B), from which the Andrus series of woodcuts were re-engraved, the designs are based on the illustrations engraved for the small Boydell, except that in the Andrus and related editions *six*, rather than four, of these illustrations (*Tempest, Twelfth Night, King John, King Richard III, Antony and Cleopatra*, and *Pericles*) are derived from sources other than Boydell.

125C. *Robin Goodfellow-Puck*, 1828
(*A Midsummer Night's Dream*, II, i)
(Vol. I, facing p.140)

Woodcut re-engraved perhaps by William D. Smith (1800?-*post* 1860).
Inscription: MIDSUMMER NIGHT'S DREAM.|
Act IV.—Scene 1.
Dimensions: 6.9 x 9.9 cm | 2³/16" x 3¹⁴/16"
(Princeton 3925.1828)
Other locations: Birmingham 89645 (1832); Birmingham 141880 (n.d.); Folger PR2752.1828c (37 woodcuts bound in at front of Vol. I, 2 cuts per page); Folger PR2752.1829a; Folger PR2752.1829b c.2 (facing p. 152); Folger PR2752.1849d; Folger PR2752.1831a c.1 (facing p. 141); Georgia PR2752.S8 (1829) (facing p. 153); Harvard 13436.11 (1831) (facing p. 141); Huntington 371170 (1837); LC PR2752.S8 1833 (facing p. 141); LC PR2752.S8 1849; NYPL *NCM (Steevens) 1829; NYPL *NCM (Steevens) (1830); NYPL *NCM (Steevens) 1831 (vol. 1 lacking); Princeton 3925.1829.2 (facing p. 141); Princeton 3925.1836.2; Princeton 3925.1837.4 (AJF); Southern California PR2752.S8 (1832) (facing p. 141); St. Louis 822.33 Lst (1833) (facing p. 141); Virginia PR2752.S8 1829; Virginia PR2752.S8 (1836); Virginia PR2752.S8 (n.d.) (facing p. 141); Virginia PR2752.S8 1850 (facing p. [141]); Yale Ig.18.31bb (1837)
Plate only: DHW
Lacking plate: Princeton 3925.1849.5

Variants:
I. Reissued (1852) with Volume, page and plate nos. added) (Vol. I, facing p. 141): Folger PR2752.1852d c.1
Inscription: MIDSUMMER NIGHT'S DREAM. Act IV.—Scene 1.|Vol. I.—p. 141.| (bottom of page): (4.)
Other locations: Folger PR2752.1852d c.2;

NYPL *NCM Stevens 1851-1852 (Boston); Folger PR2752.1853c; Yale Ig18.31c (1854)

******

Nos. 117D - 119D, 123D.
G. Hamilton.
THE|ENGLISH SCHOOL|A SERIES OF|THE MOST APPROVED PRODUCTIONS|IN| PAINTING AND SCULPTURE;|EXECUTED BY BRITISH ARTISTS|FROM THE DAYS OF HOGARTH TO THE PRESENT TIME;| SELECTED, ARRANGED, AND ACCOMPANIED WITH DESCRIPTIVE AND| EXPLANATORY NOTICES IN ENGLISH AND FRENCH,|BY G. HAMILTON.|ENGRAVED IN OUTLINE UPON STEEL.|—|VOL. 1. [-VOL. 4.]|—| LONDON.|CHARLES TILT, 86, FLEET STREET.|—|1831 [-1832]. (10/288 illus.)

[ÉCOLE|ANGLAISE,|RECUEIL|DE TABLEAUX, STATUES ET BAS-RELIEFS| DES PLUS CÉLÈBRES ARTISTES ANGLAIS,| DEPUIS LE TEMPS D'HOGARTH JUSQU'À NOS JOURS,|GRAVÉ A L'EAU-FORTE SUR ACIER;|ACCOMPAGNÉ|DE NOTICES DESCRIPTIVES ET HISTORIQUES,|EN FRANÇAIS ET EN ANGLAIS,|PAR G. HAMILTON,|ET PUBLIÉ SOUS SA DIRECTION.|—|VOL. 1 [-TOME 4]|—|À PARIS.|CHEZ M. HAMILTON, GRANDE RUE DES BATIGNOLLES, N° 50,|PRÈS LA BARRIÈRE DE CLICHY;|ET CHEZ AUDOT, LIBRAIRE, RUE DES MAÇONS-SORBONNE, N° 11.|—|1831].

SELECT SPECIMENS|OF|BRITISH ARTISTS, |FROM THE DAYS|OF HOGARTH TO THE PRESENT TIME;|OR|SERIES OF 72 ENGRAVINGS OF THEIR MOST|APPROVED PRODUCTIONS.|EXECUTED ON STEEL IN THE FIRST STYLE OF OUTLINE,| SELECTED, ARRANGED, AND ACCOMPANIED WITH DESCRIPTIVE AND EXPLANATORY|NOTICES IN ENGLISH AND FRENCH,|BY G. HAMILTON.| PARIS:| BAUDRY'S EUROPEAN LIBRARY,|9, RUE DU COQ, NEAR THE LOUVRE.|—|1837 (2/72 illus.).

[CHEFS-D'OEUVRE|DES|ARTISTES ANGLAIS,|DEPUIS|HOGARTH JUSQU'A NOS

JOURS,|OU|SUITE DE 72 GRAVURES DE LEURS PRODUCTIONS|LES PLUS ESTIMÉES,|SOIGNEUSEMENT GRAVEES AU TRAIT SUR ACIER,|CHOISIS, MIS EN ORDRE ET ACCOMPAGNÉ DE NOTES DESCRIPTIVES ET EXPLICATIVES|EN ANGLAIS ET EN FRANÇAIS,|PAR G. HAMILTON.| PARIS,|BAUDRY, LIBRAIRIE EUROPEENNE,|9, RUE DU COQ, PRÈS LE LOUVRE.|—|1837].

GALLERY|OF|BRITISH ARTISTS,|FROM THE DAYS|OF HOGARTH TO THE PRESENT TIME,|OR|SERIES OF 288 ENGRAVINGS OF THEIR MOST|APPROVED PRODUCTIONS.| EXECUTED ON STEEL IN THE FIRST STYLE OF OUTLINE,|SELECTED, ARRANGED, AND ACCOMPANIED WITH DESCRIPTIVE AND EXPLANATORY NOTICES|IN ENGLISH AND FRENCH,|BY G. HAMILTON.|—|IN FOUR VOLUMES.|—|VOL. I. [-VOL.IV.]| PARIS,|BAUDRY'S EUROPEAN LIBRARY,|9, RUE DU COQ, NEAR THE LOUVRE.|1837, 1839.

[GALERIE|DES|ARTISTES ANGLAIS,| DEPUIS|HOGARTH JUSQU'À NOS JOURS,| OU|SUITE DE 288 GRAVURES DE LEURS PRODUCTIONS|LES PLUS ESTIMÉES,| SOIGNEUSEMENT GRAVÉES AU TRAIT SUR ACIER,|CHOISIE, MISE EN ORDRE ET ACCOMPAGNÉE DE NOTES DESCRIPTIVES ET EXPLICATIVES|EN ANGLAIS ET EN FRANÇAIS,|PAR G. HAMILTON.|EN QUATRE VOLUMES.|VOL. I. [-VOL. IV.]| PARIS,|BAUDRY, LIBRAIRIE EUROPEENNE, 9, RUE DU COQ, PRÈS LE LOUVRE.|—| 1837, 1839.]

William Shakespeare.
THE|COMPLETE WORKS|OF|WILLIAM SHAKSPEARE,|WITH EXPLANATORY & HISTORICAL NOTES|BY THE MOST EMINENT COMMENTATORS.| ACCURATELY PRINTED FROM THE CORRECT AND ESTEEMED EDITION OF| ALEXANDER CHALMERS, F.S.A.|—|IN TWO VOLUMES.|WITH WOOD AND STEEL ILLUSTRATIONS.|VOL. I [-VOL. II.]| [Vignette]|*The Globe Theatre, where Shakspeare acted.*| PARIS,|BAUDRY'S EUROPEAN LIBRARY,|9, RUE DU COQ, NEAR THE LOUVRE.|—|1838.

ILLUSTRATIONS|OF|SHAKSPEARE'S WORKS,|CONTAINING|ONE HUNDRED AND FIFTY ENGRAVINGS|ON STEEL AND WOOD,|ADAPTED TO ALL EDITIONS.| [Vignette]| PARIS,|BAUDRY'S EUROPEAN LIBRARY,|9, RUE DU COQ, NEAR THE LOUVRE.|—|1839.

For the other illustrations in these work see also Nos. **226A, 263B, 285A, 288A, 293A, 298A, 299B**.

The English School appeared in 48 numbers. Its scope is indicated in the following review from *The Gentleman's Magazine* (n.s. 26, Pt. I, February 1833, 156):

At the very moderate price of three pence a print, it conveys in delicate and expressive outlines, an acquaintance with the best works of the most eminent painters and sculptors of England. The whole number of prints is 288; comprising specimens of the works of ninety artists; of the most eminent there are several pieces; of West's pictures so many as eighteen; of Wilkie's fifteen; of Reynolds's fourteen; of Fuseli's ten; of Stothard's nine; of Lawrence's seven; the whole sets of Hogarth's Marriage à-la-Mode, and Rake's Progress; of Smirke's Seven Ages; and of Barry's paintings at the Society of Arts. Then, in Sculpture, of Flaxman's works eleven; of Westmacott's ten; of Chantrey's five, &c. &c. Altogether two [*sic*] charming little volumes. The descriptive notices in English and French, are judicious and satisfactory. We believe other European Schools of Art are published at Paris on a uniform plan.

The prints were originally spread arbitrarily throughout the different numbers in which they appeared in *The English School* (1831-1834). In the *Gallery of British Artists* (1837, 1839) they were instead gathered together in alphabetical order under the names of the individual artists.

117D. *Prospero, Miranda, Caliban and Ariel,* 1831
(*The Tempest*, I, ii, 325)
(Not in Hamilton; in Shakespeare 1838 only)
(Vol. I, facing p. 4)

Unsigned outline engraving perhaps by Normand fils, i.e., Louis-Marie Normand (1789-1874)

Inscription (bottom left): Fuseli del| TEMPEST | Prospero, Miranda, Caliban & Ariel| Act I. Scene II
Dimensions: ■ 7.2 x 10.0 cm | 2¹⁴/16" x 3¹⁵/16";
◪ 7.5 x 10.3 cm | 2¹⁵/16" x 4¹/16" (BL 7812.a.19)
Other locations: Folger PR2752.1838e; Folger Art Vol. e.50 (1839) (Plate 19); Princeton 3925.1838 (Vol. I, facing p.4); YCBA N6764.H35

118D. *Titania and Bottom with the Ass's Head*, 1831
(*A Midsummer Night's Dream*, IV, i)
(Vol. I, Plate No. 8)

Outline engraving on steel by Normand fils, i.e., Louis-Marie Normand (1789-1874)
Inscription: Fuseli.| |Normand fils.|TITANIA & BOTTOM.
Dimensions: ■ 8.5 x 11.5 cm | 3⁶/16" x 4⁹/16;
◪ 8.9 x 12.0 cm | 3½" x 4¹¹/16" (BL 7812.a.19)
Other locations: SB Bern Litt.LI 3162 (1839) (Vol. 2, pl. 8); BL 1422.a.25; BL 1267.a.19 (Gallery 1837); DHW; Essick; Lausanne AVA 3356; NYPL 3-MCT 1831 (not seen) (Vol. I missing); NYPL 3-MAMR (Gallery 1837); Princeton 3925.1838 (Vol. I, facing p. 173); YCBA N6764.H35
Plate only: Huntington 181067, XIII, 147

119D. *Oberon, Titania and Bottom*, 1831
(*A Midsummer Night's Dream*, IV, i)
(Vol. I, Plate No. 51)

Outline engraving on steel by Normand fils, i.e., Louis-Marie Normand (1789-1874)
Inscription: Fuseli.| |Normand fils.|OBERON, TITANIA & BOTTOM.
Dimensions: ■ 8.2 x 10.9 cm | 3¼" x 4⁵/16";
◪ 8.4 x 11.2 cm | 3⁵/16" x 4⁶/16" (BL 7812.a.19)
Other locations: BL 1422.a.25; BL 1267.a.19 (Gallery 1837); DHW (1839); Essick; Folger PR2752.1838e; Folger Art Vol. e.50 (Plate 37); NYPL 3-MCT 1831 (not seen) (Vol. I missing); NYPL 3-MAMR (Gallery 1837); YCBA N6764.H35

123D. *Lear Casting Out his Daughter Cordelia*, 1831
(King Lear, I, i)
(Vol. II; Plate No. 95)

Outline engraving on steel by Normand fils, i.e., Louis-Marie Normand (1789-1874)
Inscription: Fuseli.| |Normand fils.|SCENE FROM KING LEAR.|LE ROI LEAR.
Dimensions: ■ 8.2 x 11.2 cm | 3¼" x 4⁷/16";
◪ 8.5 x 11.6 cm | 3⁵/16" x 4⁹/16" (BL 7812.a.19)
Other locations: SB Bern Litt.LI 3162 (1839); BL 1422.a.25; BL 1267.a.19 (Gallery 1837); DHW (1839); Essick; Folger Art Vol. e.50 (1839) (Pl. 99); Folger PR2752.1838e (Vol. II, facing p. 515); ah.102b; Lausanne AVA 3356; NYPL 3-MCT 1831; NYPL 3-MAMR (Gallery 1837); Princeton 3925.1838 (Vol. II, facing p. 515); YCBA N6764.H35; ZBZ AQ 645 (1837)
Plate only: Folger Art File S528k6 no. 3

******

Nos. 117E - 125E.
William Shakespeare
THE|PLAYS AND POEMS|OF| SHAKSPEARE,|WITH A LIFE, GLOSSARIAL NOTES,|AND ONE HUNDRED AND SEVENTY ILLUSTRATIONS|FROM THE PLATES IN BOYDELL'S EDITION.|EDITED BY A.J. VALPY, M.A.|LATE FELLOW OF PEMB. COLL., OXFORD.|—|IN FIFTEEN VOLUMES.|VOL. I [-VOL. XV].|—| LONDON PRINTED AND PUBLISHED BY A.J. VALPY, RED LION COURT, FLEET STREET; AND SOLD BY ALL BOOK[-] SELLERS, 1832-1834 (10/170 illus. + 2 portr. frontis.).

THE|PLAYS AND POEMS|OF| SHAKSPEARE,|ACCORDING TO THE| IMPROVED TEXT OF EDMUND MALONE,| INCLUDING THE LATEST REVISIONS,| WITH,|A LIFE GLOSSARIAL NOTES, AN INDEX,|AND|ONE HUNDRED AND SEVENTY ILLUSTRATIONS,|FROM DESIGNS BY ENGLISH ARTISTS.|EDITED BY|A.J. VALPY, A.M.|FELLOW OF PEMBROKE COLLEGE, OXFORD.|IN FIFTEEN VOLUMES.|VOL. I. [-VOL. XV.]| LONDON:| HENRY G. BOHN, YORK STREET, COVENT GARDEN.|1842, 1844, 1848, 1853.

[Title on spine]: SHAKSPEARE|WITH 170| ILLUSTRATIONS|VALPY'S|PICTORIAL| EDITION (1848).

THE|PLAYS AND POEMS|OF SHAKESPEARE.|WITH|ONE HUNDRED AND

SEVENTY ILLUSTRATIONS, | FROM DESIGNS BY ENGLISH ARTISTS. | EDITED BY | A.J. VALPY, A.M. | FELLOW OF PEMBROKE COLLEGE OXFORD. | IN FIFTEEN VOLUMES. | VOL. I. [VOL. XV.] | LONDON: | BELL & DALDY, YORK STREET, COVENT GARDEN. | 1870.

...FIFTEEN VOLUMES IN EIGHT. | VOL. I. [-VOL. VIII.] | PHILADELPHIA: | GEBBIE & BARRIE, 615 SANSOM STREET. | 1878.

CABINET BOYDELL EDITION. | — | THE | WORKS | OF | SHAKESPEARE | COMPLETE AND UNABRIDGED | EDITED BY | A.J. VALPY, A.M., | FELLOW OF PEMBROKE COLLEGE, OXFORD. | WITH | NEARLY FOUR HUNDRED ENGRAVINGS. | FROM DESIGNS BY EMINENT ARTISTS. | IN FIFTEEN VOLUMES. | VOL. I. [-VOL. XV.] | PHILADELPHIA | GEBBIE & BARRIE | 1876-1877.

THE WORKS | OF | WILLIAM | SHAKESPEARE | EDITED BY | WILLIAM GEORGE CLARK, M.A., | AND | WILLIAM ALDIS WRIGHT, M.A. | WITH 171 ENGRAVINGS ON STEEL AFTER THE BOYDELL | ILLUSTRATIONS. | IN SEVEN VOLUMES. | VOLUME ONE. [-VOLUME SEVEN.] | NEW YORK: | DODD, MEAD, & COMPANY, PUBLISHERS. | [1887].

ILLUSTRATIONS | TO | SHAKSPEARE, | FROM THE PLATES IN | BOYDELL'S EDITION, | AS PUBLISHED IN THE EDITION RECENTLY EDITED AND | PRINTED IN FIFTEEN VOLUMES, | BY | A.J. VALPY, M.A. | — | LONDON: | 1834 (169 illus. + 1 frontis. portr.).

THE SHAKSPEARE GALLERY [n.d.] (Portfolio of illustrations).

PUBLICATION ANNOUNCEMENT
(Bound in at the front of Vol. I)

On the First of November, 1832, was published, Price 5s. bound in cloth, uniformly with the new Editions of Byron and Scott, | VOL. I. OF | THE PLAYS AND POEMS OF SHAKSPEARE, | WITH A LIFE, GLOSSARIAL NOTES, | AND ONE HUNDRED AND SEVENTY ILLUSTRATIONS | FROM THE PLATES IN |

BOYDELL'S EDITION. | Edited by A.J. Valpy, M.A., Late Fellow of Pemb. Coll., Oxford. |

Numerous and varied as are the forms in which the Works of SHAKSPEARE have appeared, it will be readily acknowleged that an improved edition, printed in the same form as the most popular productions of the present day, is still a desideratum.

The text of MALONE, as published in 1821, in twenty-one volumes 8vo, will be adopted; GLOSSARIAL NOTES on all obsolete words will be given; and a brief HISTORICAL DIGEST prefixed to each Play.

In addition to the many advantages offered in the present edition, it will be embellished with ONE HUNDRED AND SEVENTY ILLUSTRATIONS, executed on steel in the first style of outline engraving, designed from the Plates in BOYDELL'S SHAKSPEARE, which was originally published at £95, and large paper at £190.

The attention of the youthful reader will be directed to the MOST STRIKING AND BRILLIANT PASSAGES by an INDEX, which will be printed at the end of the work, and which will form a complete reference to the BEAUTIES OF SHAKSPEARE.

The number and excellence of the illustrations, and the style of the letter-press, will render the present edition superior to any yet published; while the convenience and portability of the form adopted, and the moderate terms on which it may be purchased, will merit the approbation of every admirer of the Bard of Avon.

The Work will be handsomely printed, hot-pressed, and bound in cloth, price 5s. per volume.

The immediate re-issue of 'VALPY'S SHAKSPEARE' announced at the end of Vol. XV appeared in January 1834:

This edition of the Works of our great Dramatist, which has experienced the most favorable reception during the course of publication, may now be had complete, in fifteen volumes, price £3.15s. The plates may be purchased in one volume, handsomely bound for the Drawing-Room, price £1.11s.6d.
For the accommodation of **New Subscribers**, the Publisher will commence a RE-ISSUE IN 15 MONTHLY VOLUMES,

Price 5s. each, on the First of February next [1834].

The distinguishing features of this edition are—the text of MALONE; GLOSSARIAL NOTES on all obsolete words; and an HISTORICAL DIGEST and ARGUMENT prefixed to each Play.

117E. *Prospero, Miranda, Caliban and Ariel,* 1832
(*The Tempest*, I, ii, 325)
(Vol. I, facing p. 19)

Outline engraving on steel in reduced format by William Francis Starling (fl. 1832-1883).
Printed on tinted paper.
Inscription: Fuseli del. | | Starling sc. | TEMPEST | Prospero, Miranda, Caliban & Ariel. | Act I. Scene II.
Dimensions: ■ 7.3 x 10.2 cm | 2^{14}/16" x 4"; ▣ 7.7 x 10.5 cm | 3" x 4¼" (Yale Ig.18.32c)
Other locations: BL 11765.A.53 (1834)(*Illus.*); DHW; Folger PR2752.1876-1877a c.1 (facing p. 18); Princeton 3925.1832; Princeton 3925.1851; Virginia PR2753.C6.1887 (Vol. I, facing p. 16)
Plate only: Folger Art File S528t2 no. 19 c.1 (perhaps from *SG*); Folger Art File S528t2 no. 19 c.2

118E. *Titania and Bottom with the Ass's Head,* 1833
(*A Midsummer Night's Dream*, IV, i)
(Vol. III, facing p. 182)

Outline engraving on steel in reduced format by William Francis Starling (fl. 1832-1883).
Printed on tinted paper.
Inscription: Fuseli del. | | Starling sc. | MIDSUMMER NIGHT'S DREAM | Titania, Bottom, Fairies, &c. | Act IV. Scene I.
Dimensions: ■ 7.3 x 10.4 cm | 2^{14}/16" x 4^1/16"; ▣ 7.6 x 10.7 cm | 3" x 4^3/16" (Yale Ig.18.32c)
Other locations: BL 11765.A.53 (1834)(*Illus.*); DHW; Folger 1876-1877a c.1; Huntington 474366 (1848); Huntington PR3753.V3.1853; Princeton 3925.1832; Princeton 3925.1851; Virginia PR2753.C6.1887 (Vol. II, facing p. 44); Yale (1853)

119E. *Titania's Awakening*, 1833
(*A Midsummer Night's Dream*, IV, i)
(Vol. III, facing p. 184)

Outline engraving on steel in reduced format by William Francis Starling (fl. 1832-1883).
Printed on tinted paper.
Inscription: Fuseli del. | | Starling sc. | MID[-] SUMMER NIGHT'S DREAM | Oberon, Titania, Puck, Bottom, Fairies, &c | Act IV. Scene I.
Dimensions: ■ 7.0 x 10.5 cm | 2¾" x 4^2/16"; ▣ 7.3 x 10.9 cm | 2^{14}/16" x 4^5/16" (Yale Ig.18.32c.)
Other locations: BL 11765.A.53 (1834) (*Illus.* 35/169); DHW; Huntington 141943 (*SG*); Huntington 474366 (1848); Huntington PR3753.V3.1853; Folger PR2752.1876-1877a c.1; Princeton 3925.1832; Princeton 3925.1851; Virginia PR2753.C6.1887 (Vol. II, facing p. 47)

120E. *The Witches Appear to Macbeth and Banquo*, 1833
(*Macbeth*, I,iii)
(Vol. VI, facing p. 13)

Outline engraving on steel in reduced format by William Francis Starling (fl. 1832-1883).
Printed on tinted paper.
Inscription: Fuseli del. | | Starling sc. | MACBETH | A Heath. Macbeth, Banquo and Witches | Act I. Scene III
Dimensions: ■ 7.6 x 10.7 cm | 3" x 4^2/16"; ▣ 7.9 x 10.9 cm | 3^1/16" x 4^5/16" (Yale Ig.18.32c)
Other locations: BL 11765.A.53 (1834) (*Illus.* 71/169); DHW; Huntington 141943 (*SG*); Huntington 474366 (1848); Huntington PR3753.V3.1853; Folger PR2752.1876-1877a c.1; Princeton 3925.1832; Princeton 3925.1851; Virginia PR2753.C61.1887 (Vol. VI, facing p. 84)
Plate only: Folger Art File S528m1 no. 7 (perhaps from *SG*)

121E. *Prince Hal and Poins Surprise Falstaff with Doll Tearsheet*, 1833
(*King Henry the Fourth*, Part 2, II, iv)
(Vol. VII, facing p. 196)

Outline engraving on steel in reduced format by William Francis Starling (fl. 1832-1883)
Printed on tinted paper.
Inscription: Fuseli del. | | Starling sc. | KING HENRY 4th. (SECOND PART) | Doll Tearsheet, Falstaff, Henry & Poins | Act II. Scene IV.

Dimensions: ■ 10.5 x 7.1 cm | 4²/16" x 2¹³/16";
■ 10.9 x 7.5 cm | 4⁵/16" x 3" (Yale Ig.18.32c)
Other locations: BL 11765.A.53 (1834) (*Illus.*
90/169); Folger PR2752.1876-1877a c.1; Harvard
(1844); Huntington 141943 (*SG*); Huntington
474366 (1848); Huntington PR3753.V3.1853;
Illinois (1842); Iowa (1870); Southern Illinois;
Princeton 3925.1832; Princeton 3925.1851;
Virginia PR2753.C6.1887 (Vol. III, facing p.
378); Yale (1853)
Plate only: Folger Art File S528k1b no. 11 c.1

**122E. *King Henry Condemning Cambridge,
Scroop and Northumberland*, 1833**
(*King Henry the Fifth*, II, ii)
(Vol. VII, facing p. 316)

Outline engraving on steel in reduced format by
William Francis Starling (fl. 1832-1883).
Printed on tinted paper.
Inscription: Fuseli del.||Starling. sc.|KING
HENRY 5ᵗʰ.|King, Scroop, Cambridge &c.|Act
II. Scene II.
Dimensions: ■ 7.1 x 10.0 cm | 2¾" x 4";
■ 7.5 x 10.5 cm | 3" x 4²/16" (Yale Ig.18.32c)
Other locations: BL 11765.A.53 (1834) (*Illus.*
96/169); DHW; Huntington 141943 (*SG*);
Huntington 474366 (1848); Huntington PR
3753.V3.1853; Folger PR2752.1876-1877a c.1;
Princeton 3925.1832; Princeton 3925.1851;
Virginia PR2753.C61.1887 (Vol. III, facing p.
462)

**123E. *Lear Casting out his Daughter Cordelia*,
1833**
(*King Lear*, I, i)
(Vol. XIII, facing p. 14)

Outline engraving on steel in reduced format by
William Francis Starling (fl. 1832-1883).
Printed on tinted paper.
Inscription: Fuseli del.||Starling sc.|KING
LEAR.|Lear, Goneril, Regan, Cordelia, &c.|Act
I. Scene I.
Dimensions: ■ 7.4 x 9.9 cm | 2¹⁵/16" x 3¹⁴/16";
■ 7.8 x 10.2 cm | 3¹/16" x 4" (Yale Ig.18.32c)
Other locations: BL 11765.A.53 (1834) (*Illus.*
149/169); DHW; Folger PR2752.1876-1877a c.1;
Princeton 3925.1832; Virginia PR2753.C6.1887
(Vol. ? facing p. 270)

Plate only: Folger Art File S528k6 no. 4 (perhaps
from *Shakspeare Gallery*)

**124E. *Hamlet, Horatio, Marcellus and the
Ghost*, 1833**
(*Hamlet*, I, iv)
(Vol. XIV, facing p. 38)

Outline engraving on steel in reduced format by
William Francis Starling (fl. 1832-1883).
Printed on tinted paper.
Inscription: Fuseli del.||Starling sc.|HAMLET.|
Hamlet, Horatio & Ghost.|Act I. Scene IV.
Dimensions: ■ 7.1 x 10.2 cm | 2¾" x 4";
■ 7.4 x 10.5 cm | 2¹⁴/16" x 4²/16" (Yale
Ig.18.32c).
Other locations: BL 11765.53 (1834) (*Illus.*
159/169); DHW; Folger 2752.1876-1877a c.1;
Huntington 141943 (*SG*); Huntington 474366
(1848); Huntington PR3753.V3.1853; Princeton
3925.1832; Princeton 3925.1851; Virginia
PR2753.C6.1887 (Vol. VI, facing p. 84); Yale
1853

125E. *Robin Goodfellow-Puck*, 1833
(*A Midsummer Night's Dream*,
(Vol. III, facing p. 137)

Outline engraving on steel in reduced format by
William Francis Starling (fl. 1832-1883)
Inscription: Fuseli del.||Starling sc.|
MIDSUMMER NIGHT'S DREAM|A Wood.
Puck.|Act II. Scene I.
Dimensions: ■ 10.4 x 7.3 cm | 4²/16" x 2¹⁴/16";
■ 10.7 x 7.6 cm | 4¼" x 2¹⁵/16" (Yale
Ig.18.32c)
Other locations: BL 11765.A.53 (1834)(*Illus.*);
DHW; Folger PR2752.1876-1877a c.1; Princeton
3925.1832; Princeton 3925.1851; ?Virginia
PR2753.C6.1887?; Yale 1853?
Plate only: Folger Art File S528m5 no. 9

******

No. 117F.
THE|COMPLETE WORKS|OF|WILLIAM
SHAKSPEARE.|PRINTED|FROM THE TEXT|
OF THE MOST RENOWNED EDITORS,|WITH
NEARLY|270 ENGRAVINGS,|ACCOUNTS
HISTORICAL AND EXPLANATORY OF EACH

PLAY,|A COPIOUS AND ELABORATE GLOSSARY,|AND THE AUTHOR'S LIFE.| [Vignette].|LEIPZIG, 1837.|PRINTED FOR BAUMGÄRTNER (1/270 illus.)

W. SHAKESPEARE'S|SÄMMTLICHE WERKE |IN|EINEM BANDE.|IM|VEREIN MIT MEHREREN ÜBERSETZT,|UND HERAUS-GEGEBEN|VON|JULIUS KÖRNER.|MIT 40 HOLZSCHNITTEN VERMEHRTE AUSGABE.| [Vignette].| LEIPZIG,|BAUMGÄRTNER'S BUCHHANDLUNG.|1838.

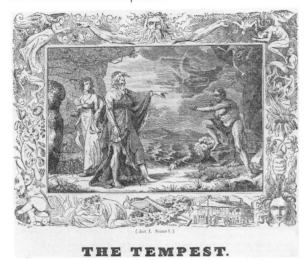

THE TEMPEST.

117F.

117F. *Prospero, Miranda, Caliban and Ariel*, 1837
(*The Tempest*, I, ii, 325)
(p. 3)

Wood engraving in reduced format by Adolf Menzel after the drawing by Albert Vogel
Inscription (bottom left within plate): Fuseli inv.| (bottom left edge of ornamental frame): A. MENZEL sc.||(bottom centre): A VOGEL gez.| (centre beneath frame): (Act I. Scene I)
Dimensions: ■ 7.1 x 10.1 cm | 2¹³/16" x 4"; ■ 10.4 x 13.2 cm | 4¹/16" x 5³/16" (BL 11766.d.8)
Other locations: Folger PR2752.1837b (not seen)

Variants:
I. Reissued (1838) with German inscription (facing p. [2]): Birmingham 43674
Inscription (bottom centre): Der Sturm. Act I. Scene I.
Other locations:Folger PR2796.GR1838 (not seen)

******

Nos. 117G - 118G, 122G - 124G.
THE|DRAMATIC WORKS|OF| SHAKESPEARE.|WITH|NUMEROUS ILLUSTRATIONS|ON|STEEL AND WOOD.| VOL. I.[-V].| LONDON:|I.J. CHIDLEY.|123, ALDERSGATE STREET,|—|1843 (5/37 illus. + 37 vignettes).
(Each play is individually paginated.)

117G. *Prospero, Miranda, Caliban and Ariel*, 1843
(*The Tempest*, I, ii)
(Vol. I, facing p. 7)

Re-engraved on steel in miniature format by William Home Lizars (1788-1859)
Inscription (top centre): Act I. Scene II.|(bottom left): Fuseli del.||TEMPEST||Lizars sc.
Dimensions: ■ 4.3 x 7.3 cm | 1¹¹/16" x 2¹⁴/16"
(Birmingham 365290)
Other locations: Folger PR2752.1843h (not seen)

118G. *Titania and Bottom with the Ass's Head*, 1843
(*A Midsummer Night's Dream*, IV, i)
(Vol. I, facing p. 37)

Re-engraved on steel in miniature format by William Home Lizars (1788-1859)
Inscription (top centre): Act IV Scene I|(bottom left): H. Fuseli R.A. del.||MIDSUMMER NIGHTS DREAM||Lizars sc.
Dimensions: ■ 4.3 x 7.3 cm | 1¹¹/16" x 2¹⁴/16"
(Birmingham 365290)
Other locations: Folger PR2752.1843h (not seen)

122G. *King Henry Condemning Cambridge, Scroop and Northumberland*, 1843
(*King Henry the Fifth*, II,ii)
(Vol. III, facing p. 19)

Re-engraved on steel in miniature format by William Home Lizars (1788-1859)
Inscription (top centre): Act II. Scene II.|(bottom left): Fuseli R.A. del.|KING HENRY THE FIFTH||Lizars sc.
Dimensions: ■ 4.3 x 7.2 cm | 1¹¹/16" x 2¹³/16"
(Birmingham 365292)
Other locations: Folger PR2752.1843h (not seen)

123G. *Lear Casting Out his Daughter Cordelia,* 1843

(*King Lear*, I, i)

(Vol. V, facing p. 6)

Re-engraved on steel in miniature format by William Home Lizars (1788-1859)
Inscription (top centre): Act I. Scene I; (bottom left): H. Fuseli R.A. del | | KING LEAR | | Lizars sc.
Dimensions: ■ 4.3 x 7.4 cm | 1^{11}/16" x 2^{14}/16"
(Birmingham 365294)
Other locations: Folger PR2752.1843h (not seen)

124G. *Hamlet, Horatio, Marcellus and the Ghost,* 1843

(*Hamlet*, I, iv)

(Vol. V, facing p. 19)

Re-engraved on steel in miniature format by William Home Lizars (1788-1859)
Inscription (top centre): Act I. Scene IV. | (bottom left): Fuseli R.A. del. | | HAMLET | | Lizars sc.
Dimensions: ■ 4.3 x 7.2 cm | 1^{11}/16" x 2^{13}/16"
(Birmingham 365294)
Other locations: Folger PR2752.1843h (not seen)

******

Nos. 117H, 119H.
Allan Cunningham.
PART 1 [-PART 24]. | | THE PEOPLE'S EDITION. | | PRICE 25 CENTS. | THE | DRAMATIC WORKS | OF | WILLIAM SHAKSPERE. | ILLUSTRATED | BY FORTY-EIGHT FINE STEEL PLATES, | AFTER SIR JOSHUA REYNOLDS, SMIRKE, STOTHARD, WESTALL, & OTHERS. | WITH A BIOGRAPHY. | THE TEXT ENRICHED BY MANY VALUABLE NOTES, AND A COPIOUS GLOSSARY, | ACCOMPANIED BY AN INQUIRY INTO THE AUTHENTICITY OF THE SHAKSPERE PORTRAITS, | BY A. WIVELL ESQ. | [Vignette] | COMPLETE IN TWENTY-FOUR SHILLING PARTS, EACH CONTAINING TWO FINE STEEL PLATES. | — | LONDON: GEORGE VIRTUE, IVY LANE, AND 26, JOHN STREET, NEW YORK. | [1847-1848] (2/49 illus.).

THE | DRAMATIC WORKS | OF | WILLIAM SHAKSPERE. | WITH AN ORIGINAL

MEMOIR. | — | THE TEXT ENRICHED BY MANY VALUABLE NOTES, AND A COPIOUS GLOSSARY. | ALSO, | AN INQUIRY INTO THE AUTHENTICITY OF THE SHAKSPERE PORTRAITS, | BY A. WIVELL ESQ. | — | ILLUSTRATED BY FORTY-NINE ENGRAVINGS ON STEEL. | — | LONDON: | GEORGE VIRTUE. | [1848?] (2/49 illus.).

[Added engraved title page]: THE | DRAMATIC WORKS | OF | WILLIAM SHAKSPERE. | ILLUSTRATED. | [Vignette] | *The birthplace of Shakspere.* | *With Garrick's Jubilee Procession.* | LONDON. GEORGE VIRTUE, IVY LANE.

DRAMATIC WORKS... | ILLUSTRATED WITH FIFTY-ONE ENGRAVINGS. | GEORGE VIRTUE, LONDON & NEW YORK.

THE | GALLERY OF PICTURES | BY | THE FIRST MASTERS | OF | THE ENGLISH AND FOREIGN SCHOOLS, | WITH | BIOGRAPHICAL AND CRITICAL DISSERTATIONS | BY | A. CUNNINGHAM. | VOL. I. [-VOL. II.] | — | LONDON: | GEORGE VIRTUE, IVY LANE. [*post* 1847-1848] (1/96 illus.).

[Added engraved title page]: ALLAN CUNNINGHAM'S | GALLERY | OF | PICTURES | BY THE FIRST MASTERS | OF THE | ENGLISH AND FOREIGN SCHOOLS. | LONDON | GEORGE VIRTUE: IVY LANE.

When first published in 1834 the *Cabinet Gallery* comprised 72 line engravings after some 50 painters, of which the Italian and Dutch schools were particularly strongly represented. No less than 20 of the 24 plates added in subsequent editions were after paintings from Boydell's Shakespeare Gallery; these had obviously been prepared for Virtue's Shakespeare edition but could thus be made to serve double duty. Only one of Fuseli's Boydell illustrations from the [1847-1848] Shakespeare edition was selected for inclusion in the enlarged *Gallery of Pictures.* Allan Cunningham (1784-1842) was the author of *Lives of the Painters.* For an account of George Virtue, see Eugene C. Worman, Jr.'s articles in *AB Bookman's Weekly*: 'George Virtue's New York Connection, 1836-1879', 30 March 1987, 1350-1363; and 'George Virtue and the British "Numbers" Game', 15 June 1987, 2646-2657.

117H. *Prospero, Miranda, Caliban, and Ariel,*
[n.d.]
(*The Tempest*, I, ii)
(Vol. II, facing p. 85)

Unsigned re-engraving in reduced format on steel
by anonymous engraver
Imprint: LONDON: GEORGE VIRTUE.
Inscription: Fuseli, R.A. | PROSPERO AND
CALIBAN.
Dimensions: ■ 11.2 x 15.0 cm | 4⁷/16" x 5¹⁴/16"
(Yale WE 3060)
Other locations: Folger PR2754.1t2 c.1 ('51')
(facing p. 6); Harvard 13435.27 [1848] (facing p.
49)
Plate only: Folger Art File S528t2 no. 21 c.2;
Folger Art File S528t2 c.3 (imprint cropped?)
Lacking plate: LC PR2753.V5 [1847-1848] (Part
1/24 not present)

Variants:
I. With new imprint and inscription (plate only):
DHW
Imprint: JOHN Mᶜ. GOWAN LONDON.
Inscription (bottom centre): Fuseli R.A. | THE
TEMPEST. | ACT I. SCENE II.
Other locations: Folger Art File S528t2 no. 21
c.1 (imprint cropped); Lucerne

119H. *Titania's Awakening* [n.d.]
(*A Midsummer Night's Dream*, IV, i)
(Vol. I, between pp. 576-577)
(Part 13/24)

Unsigned re-engraving on steel in reduced format
by anonymous engraver from the Boydell plate
Inscription: Fuseli, R.A. | [*signature illegible*] |
MIDSUMMER NIGHT'S DREAM. | ACT 4,
SCENE 1.
Dimensions: ■ 11.1 x 15.2 cm | 3¹⁴/16" x 5¹⁵/16"
(LC PR2753.V5)
Other locations: Harvard 13435.27 [1848] (facing
p. [621]); ??Yale WE 3060

Variants:
I. With new imprint and inscription (plate only):
DHW
Imprint: MᶜGOWAN & Cᵒ. LONDON.

******

No. 125I.
THE | COMPLETE WORKS | OF |
SHAKESPEARE. | WITH | LIFE BY
ALEXANDER CHALMERS, A.M. | AND
FORTY STEEL ENGRAVINGS. | LONDON:
I.J. CHIDLEY, 123, ALDERSGATE
STREET. | — | 1845 (1/40 illus.).

125I. *Robin Goodfellow-Puck*, [1845]

Engraved in outline on steel by Alexander T.
Aikman (fl. 1843-1845)
Inscription: MIDSUMMER NIGHT'S DREAM. |

Puck.   I am that merry wanderer of the night.

(bottom right): Act I. Scene. I. | Fuseli | | p.32. | |
A.T. Aikman.
Dimensions (excl. inscribed panel): 11.4 x 8.6 cm
| 4½" x 3⁶/16"; (incl. panel): 13.3 x 8.6 cm |
5¼" x 3⁶/16" (Birmingham 174413)
Plate only: Folger Art File S528m5 no. 10

******

Nos. 117J - 118J.
NEW SERIES. | VOLUME VII. | THE | ART
JOURNAL. | [Title illustration.] | 1861. | JAMES S.
VIRTUE, LONDON; AND 26, JOHN STREET,
NEW YORK. (3/3 illus. = essay only).

For the other illustration in this work see also No.
67F.

117J. *Prospero, Miranda, Caliban*, 1861
(*The Tempest*, I, ii, 325)
(James Dafforne, 'British Artists: ... No.
LVII.—Henry Fuseli, R.A.', p. 326)

Steel engraving [perhaps by James Dafforne (d.
1880)
Inscription: MIRANDA, PROSPERO, AND
CALIBAN.
Dimensions: ■ 10.6 x 14.5 cm | 4³/16" x 5¹¹/16"
(DHW)

118J. *Titania and Bottom*, 1861
(*A Midsummer Night's Dream*, IV, i)
(p. 327)

Steel engraving [perhaps by James Dafforne (d.
1880)]
Inscription: TITANIA.
Dimensions: ■ 13.1 x 17.5 cm | 5²/16" x 6¹⁴/16"
(DHW)

The little demon suckling at the breast of the young woman at the right leading an old hermit on a leash has been omitted, presumably for propriety's sake.

******

Nos. 117K - 118K, 124K.
[Theophile Etienne Joseph Thoré].
HISTOIRE|DES PEINTRES|DE TOUTES LES ÉCOLES|ÉCOLE ANGLAISE|PAR|M.W. BÜRGER.|[Medallion].| PARIS:|V^{VE} JULES RENOUARD, LIBRAIRE-EDITEUR| DIRECTEUR-GÉRANT: G ÉTIENNE-PERON| RUE DE TOURNON, N° 6, FAUBOURG SAINT-GERMAIN|—|MDCCCLXIII [1863]. (4/5 illus. + portr. = Fuseli essay [pp. 1-12] only).

Each section is individually paged. For the other illustration to this work see No. **67G**.

Proposed Order of Publication
(BL 2262.G1)

—Numéro d'ordre de la Publication.

Histoire|Des Peintres|De Toutes Les Écoles/Depuis La Renaissance Jusqu'à Nos Jours|Avec Notes, Recherches et Indications| —|Textes Par M. Charles Blanc, Ancien Directeur Des Beaux-Arts|Et Par Divers Écrivains Spéciaux|Illustrations Par Les Plus Habiles Artistes Dessinateurs et Graveurs| Accompagnée Du Portrait Des Peintres|De La Reproduction De Leurs Plus Beaux Tableaux|et du Fac-simile de leurs signatures, Marques et Monogrammes|Avec Notes, Recherches Et Indications[:]|École Anglaise|H. Fuseli|Une feuille et demie|T. Stothard|Demi-feuille|Par W. Burger|On Souscrit à Paris|Chez V^E Jules Renouard, Libraire-Éditeur|6, Rue De Tournon, Faubourg Saint-Germain.|18-19.-Numero d'ordre de l'École.|En vertu des traités internationaux, toute traduction ou contrefaçon de l'HISTOIRE DES PEINTRES sera poursuivie par l'Éditeur-Propriétaire.

117K. *Prospero, Ariel, Miranda and Caliban*, 1863
(2. série. *Les peintres anglais*)
(p. 3)

Steel engraving by Jean-Baptiste-Charles

Carbonneau (1815-*post* 1869) from the drawing by Louis-Alexandre-Eustache Lorsay (b. 1822)
Inscription: E. LORSAY. D||FUSELI.P.|| CARBONNEAU|LA TEMPÊTE
Dimensions: ■ 10.8 x 14.7 cm | 4½" x 5⁹/16" (BL 2262.G1)
Other locations: Basel A204

118K. *Titania and Bottom*, 1863
(2. série. *Les peintres anglais*)
(p. 9)

Steel engraving by Adolphe Gusmand (1821-1905)
Inscription: H. FUSELI. PINX.||N. CARASSON. DEL.||A. GUSMAND. SC.| TITANIA ET BOTTOM.
Dimensions: ■ 13.2 x 17.6 cm | 5³/16" x 6¹⁵/16" (BL 2262.G1)
Other locations: Basel A204
Plate only: DHW

124K. *Hamlet and the Ghost*, 1863
(2. série. *Les peintres anglais*)
(p. 7)

Steel engraving by Adolphe-François Pannemaker (b. 1822)
Inscription (bottom right): PANNEMAKER| HAMLET ET LE SPECTRE.
Dimensions: ■ 10.4 x 14.0 cm | 4¹/16" x 5½" (BL 2262.G1)
Other locations: Basel A204
Plate only: DHW

******

Nos. 126 - 130.
BELL'S|BRITISH THEATRE.|=|CONSISTING OF|THE MOST ESTEEMED| ENGLISH PLAYS.|=|VOL. I. [-VOL. XXII.]|=|BEING THE FIRST VOLUME OF [TRAGEDIES].|=| CONTAINING|[*Contents per volume*]|=| LONDON:|=|PRINTED BY| JOHN BELL, BRITISH=LIBRARY, STRAND,| BOOKSELLER TO HIS ROYAL HIGHNESS THE PRINCE OF WALES.| |—|MDCCXCI. [1791-1793] (5/140 pictorial title pages + 140 full length portraits of actors in costumes).

BELL'S|BRITISH THEATRE.|=|CONSISTING OF|THE MOST ESTEEMED|ENGLISH PLAYS.|=|VOL. I [-VOL. XXXV.]|=| CONTAINING|[*Contents per volume*]|=|

LONDON: | = | PRINTED FOR, AND UNDER
THE DIRECTION OF, | GEORGE CAWTHORN,
BRITISH LIBRARY, STRAND. | — | 1797.

For the re-engravings of 1795, and 1805 -1827,
see **Nos. 126A - 127A, 126B - 127B, 129B.**

The individual volumes of Cawthorn's 1797
edition have **an** added general title page with a
new imprint and date, but each of the plays in any
particular volume also retains its separate title
page with Bell's imprint and earlier date.
Likewise, the imprint and date on the prints,
whether collected in volumes under Bell's or
Cawthorn's name, remain the same; large
numbers of impressions were printed from the
original copper plates, as is reflected in the
uneven quality of prints that one encounters. This
would explain why Charles Cooke would have
decided to use the illustrations from *Bell's British
Theatre* in re-engraved form in his collection in
fourteen volumes of the so-called *Cooke's British
Drama* series (see Nos. **126B-127B, 129B** below).

126.

127.

126. *Lady Alicia Finds Jane Shore Perishing for
Want at her Door*, 1791
(Nicholas Rowe, *Jane Shore*, V, i)
(Vol. III)

Engraved by Thomas Holloway (1748-1827) after
Fuseli's untraced painting (1791)
Imprint: London. Printed for J. Bell, British
Library, Strand, Septr. 2. 1791.
Inscription: BRI[*TISH TH*]EATRE | (bottom
panel): JANE SHORE. |

Alic —Thou art that fatal fair, that cursed she
    That set my brain a madding.
                Act 5. |

(below): Fuseli pinx^t. | | Holloway sculp.
Dimensions: 12.8 x 7.5 cm | 5^1/16" x 2^{15}/16" (BL
2304.c.3) (H = 19.4 cm)
Other locations: DHW; Dörrbecker; Folger
PR1241.B46 (Vol. VIII); Huntington 112533
(facing p. 66); Huntington PR1241.B4 (facing p.
64); Illinois 822.08 B41b 1797 (facing p. 63);
Illinois x822.08 B41b; Newberry Y134.08

Plate only: BM 1875-7-10-3379 (Sheet=18.7 cm);
BM 1863-5-9-58; Pierpoint Morgan 6300.E-2.76B
Lit.: Schiff 940 (12.8 x 7.5 cm), 1034 (the
preliminary drawing of the frame and cartouche,
V & A); Hammelmann 1975, 35; *Letters*, 599
Exh.: Kansas City 1982 (62)

Variants:
I. Proof before all letters: BM 1849-5-12-298
Inscription: Fuseli RA | | Holloway | Jane Shore

Once 'the first and fairest of our English
dames', Jane Shore has been reduced since the
death of Edward IV to beggary and is here being
reviled by Alicia, her former friend and 'partner
of her heart,' as the cause of Alicia's misfortunes
and madness: it was on account of his defence of
Jane Shore's interests that Alicia's beloved,
Hastings, had been executed.

127. *Mathew Complains to Bobadill that He is
Almost out of Money*, 1791
(Ben Jonson, *Every Man in his Humour* [1616],
I, v)
(Vol. IV)

Engraved by Charles Grignion (1721-1810) after
Fuseli's painting in the von Albertini collection,
Zurich (1791; Schiff 886)
Imprint: London, Printed for J. Bell, British
Library, Strand Septr. 24. 1791.
Inscription (top left): Act I. | BRIT[*ISH
THEATRE*] | (bottom panel): EVERY MAN IN
HIS HUMOUR. |

> Bob.   What Money ha' you about you, M^r.
>   Mathew?
> Mat.   Faith, I ha' not past a two shillings, or
>   so. |

(below): Fuseli pinx^t | | Grignion sculp
Dimensions: 12.5 x 7.5 cm | 4^{15}/16" x 2^{15}/16" (BL
2304.c.4) (H=19.4 cm)
Other locations: DHW; Dörrbecker; Folger
PR1241.B46 (Vol. V); Huntington 112533 (facing
p. [9]); Huntington PR1241.B4 (between pp. 22-
23); Illinois 822.08 B41b; Illinois x822.08 B41b;
Newberry Y134.08
Plate only: BM 1849-5-12-299
Lit.: Schiff 941 (12.5 x 7.5 cm); Hammelmann
1975, 35
Exh.: Kansas City 1982 (63)

Variants:
I. Unfinished proof before letters (faces in
etched state): Ashmolean

Master Mathew and Captain Bobadill are
preparing to go out to the tavern. While Bobadill
gets dressed, Mathew checks the state of his
finances.

128.

128. *Oedipus Implores the Gods*, 1792
(John Dryden & Nathaniel Lee, *Oedipus*, II, i)
(Vol. XV, frontispiece to play)

Engraved by Thomas Holloway (1748-1827) after
Fuseli's lost painting
Imprint: London. Printed for J Bell, British
Library, Strand, Feby. 11. 1792.
Inscription (top): Act II. | | Scene I. | BRI[TISH
THE]ATRE | (bottom panel): OEDIPUS |

> Oedip   — hear me, hear me gods! |

(bottom): Fuseli pinx^t. | | Holloway sc.
Dimensions (including panel below): ■ 13.3 x 8.0
cm | 5¼" x 3^2/16" (BL 2304.c.15) (H=19.4 cm)
Other locations: DHW; Dörrbecker; Folger

PR1241.B46 (Vol.XII); Huntington 112533
(imprint trimmed); Huntington PR1241.B4 (facing
p. 33); Illinois 822.08 B41b.1797; Illinois 822.08
B41b; Newberry Y134.08
Plate only: BM 1863-5-9-26 (Sheet=20.5 cm)
Lit.: Schiff 944 (13.2 x 8.0 cm); Hammelmann
1975, 35
Exh.: Kansas City 1982 (64)

Variants:
I. Proof before all letters: BM 1849-5-12-297
Inscription: Fuseli RA | | Holloway | [*verse*]

Sophocles' tragedy is the model for this version
by Dryden and Lee. Unaware that he is the cause
of the portents and plagues that beset Thebes,
Oedipus offers himself in 'expiation for murder'd
Laius' if the gods will spare his kingdom. The
two figures in the sky are thereupon crowned with
the names of Oedipus and Jocasta, written in
characters of gold.

129.

129. *Dying Osmond Stabs Sigismunda as She
Throws Herself Upon Him*, 1792
(James Thomson, *Tancred and Sigismunda*, V, ii)
(Vol. XIV)

Engraved by Francis Legat (1755-1809) after
Fuseli's lost original
Imprint: London. Printed for J. Bell, British
Library, Strand, April 28. 1792.
Inscription: Act V. | | Scene II. | B[R]ITIS[H
THEA]TRE | (bottom panel): TANCRED AND
SIGISMUNDA |

Osm.   — Perfidious Woman, die!

(below): Fuseli pinx^t. | | Legat sculp.
Dimensions (including bottom panel): ■ 13.1 x
7.9 cm | 5²/16" x 3²/16" (BL 2304.c.14) (H=19.4
cm)
Other locations: DHW; Dörrbecker; Folger
PR1241.B46 (Vol. XIX) (imprint and top line
trimmed); Huntington 112533 (facing p. 88) (top
line trimmed); Newberry Y134.08
Plate only: BM 1863-5-9-60
Lit.: Schiff 943 (13.0 x 8.0 cm); Tomory 1972,
pl. 185; Hammelmann 1975, 35
Exh.: Kansas City 1982 (65)

Variants:
I. Proof before all letters (lacking 'Act'/
'Scene'): Huntington PR1241.B4 (facing p. 83)
Other locations: Illinois 822.08 B41b.1797

Tancred's beloved, Sigismunda, has been
trapped into marrying the villainous Osmond by
her father, Siffredi, in order to secure the
succession to the throne of Sicily. The old king
also designates Tancred as heir to the throne, on
condition that he marry Constantia, the king's
sister. Tancred becomes king but rejects this
condition; instead, he proclaims Sigismunda's
(unconsummated) marriage to Osmond annulled.
In the last act Tancred mortally wounds Osmond.
While attempting to tend to her dying husband, he
stabs her to death, thus bringing Thomson's
murky plot to a morally edifying and tear-
brimming conclusion.

130. *Leonora Discovers the Dagger Alonzo has
Dropped*, 1793
(Edward Young, *The Revenge*, V, ii)
(Vol. VIII)

Engraved by William Satchwell Leney (1769-
1831) after Fuseli's painting in the Miller
collection, London (1793; Schiff 887)
Imprint: London. Printed for J. Bell, British
Library, Strand, March 9. 1793

Inscription: Act V. | | Scene II. | [*BRITISH THEATRE*] | (bottom panel): THE REVENGE. |

Leon.   I am sinking in my fears
    Alonzo dropp'd this dagger. |

(below): Fuseli pinx^t. | | Leney sculp.
Dimensions: 12.9 x 7.7 cm | 5^1/16" x 3^1/16" (BL 2304.c.8) (H = 19.4 cm)
Other locations: DHW; Dörrbecker; Folger PR1241.B46 (Vol. XVI); Huntington 112533 (facing p. 70) (top line cropped); Huntington PR1241.B4 (facing p. 65); Newberry Y134.08
Plate only: Huntington 110136, pt. 2, 365 (13.1 x 7.6 cm) (13.0 x 7.4 cm)
Lit.: Schiff 942 (13.0 x 7.7 cm) (imprint date given as 'March 1793'), 887.

Variants:
I. Proof before letters: BM 1863-5-9-59

130.

******

Nos. 126A - 127A.
JONES'S | BRITISH THEATRE. | = | VOL. I [-VOL. X]. | CONTAINING, | [*Contents*] | = |

DUBLIN: | PRINTED BY JOHN CHAMBERS, | FOR WILLIAM JONES, NO. 86, DAME STREET. | = | 1795 (2/? illus.).

I am informed by Vincent Kinane that there is also an 8-vol. edition of this work in Trinity College Library, Dublin. I have not seen this. The emphasis in Jones's *British Theatre*, in contrast to Bell's, seems to be on comedies.

126A. *Lady Alicia Finds Jane Shore Perishing for Want at her Door*, 1795
(Nicholas Rowe, *Jane Shore*, V, i)
(Vol. IV, before p. [167])

Frontispiece re-engraved (1795) by H. Houston (fl. 1791-1795) (image reversed)
Inscription: BRITI[*SH THE*]ATRE | (bottom panel): JANE SHORE. |

Thou art that fatal fair that cursed she
That set my brain a madding.
        Act 5. |
(below): Fuseli pinx^t. | | Houston sculp.
Dimensions: 12.6 x 7.3 | 4^{15}/16" x 2^{14}/16" (BL 11784.g.8/4) (H = 17.1 cm)
Other locations: DHW; Huntington 136020 (between pp. 166-[167])

127A. *Mathew Complains to Bobadill that He is Almost Out of Money*, 1795
(Ben Jonson, *Every Man in his Humour* [1616], I, v)
(Vol. III)

Frontispiece re-engraved (1795) by Henry Brocas (1762-1837) from Grignion's plate of 1791 (image reversed)
Imprint: Dublin, Published by W^m. Jones N°. 86 Dame street.
Inscription (top left): Act I. | BRITI[*SH THEATRE*] | (bottom panel): EVERY MAN IN HIS HUMOUR. |

Bob.   What Money ha' you about you M^r. Mathew?
Mat.   Faith, I ha' not past a two shillings or so. |

(below): Fusile pinx^t. | | H. Brocas sc.
Dimensions: 12.3 x 7.4 cm. | 4^{13}/16" x 2^{14}/16" (BL 11784.g.8/3) (H = 17.1 cm)

Other locations: BL 1474.aaa.20.4; DHW; Huntington 136020 (before t.p. to play)

******

No. 126B-127B, 129B.

[General title]: THE | BRITISH DRAMA, | A COLLECTION OF THE MOST | ESTEEMED DRAMATIC PRODUCTIONS, | WITH | BIOGRAPHY | OF THE RESPECTIVE AUTHORS; | AND | CRITIQUE ON EACH PLAY, | BY R. CUMBERLAND, ESQ. | IN FOURTEEN VOLUMES. | — | VOL. I [-XIV]. | = | CONTAINING | [*Contents*] | = | LONDON; | PRINTED FOR C. COOKE, | No. 17, PATERNOSTER ROW; | *And Sold by all Booksellers in the United Kingdom.* | 1817 (1/58? illus.).

[Title and author of individual work:] | ADAPTED FOR THEATRICAL REPRESENTATION, | *As performed at the Theatres-Royal,* | COVENT-GARDEN AND DRURY-LANE. | REGULATED FROM THE PROMPT BOOKS, | BY PERMISSION OF THE MANAGERS. | WITH A CRITIQUE, | BY R. CUMBERLAND, ESQ. | The Lines distinguished by Inverted Commas are omitted | in the Reproductions. | = | **COOKE'S EDITION.** | = | [Vignette] | = | SUPERBLY EMBELLISHED. | = | LONDON: | PRINTED FOR C.COOKE, PATERNOSTER-ROW, | BY R. M'DONALD, 13, GREEN ARBOUR COURT, AND | SOLD BY ALL THE BOOKSELLERS IN THE | UNITED KINGDOM. | [1806-1807] (3/58? illus.).

COOKE'S ILLUSTRATIONS TO THE BRITISH THEATRE. | [LONDON, PRINTED FOR C. COOKE, 1821?, 1828?].

Publication of the series was announced in the *Times* of 28 May 1806. The edition comprised 125 weekly numbers, each of one play, the first to appear being *Every Man in His Humour*. The 'cheap' edition, with one role-portrait, cost 1s. per number. The 'superior' edition, printed on 'wove vellum paper' and containing an additional vignette, cost 1s.6d. Complete sets ('intitled the British Theatre') were immediately available at 6d. and 9d. respectively per play.

126B. *Lady Alicia Finds Jane Shore Perishing for Want at her Door*, 1807
(Nicholas Rowe, *Jane Shore*, V, i)
(frontispiece to Vol. I)

Re-engraved with new cartouche and ornamental swags by Thomas Holloway (1748-1827)
Imprint: Printed for C. Cooke, May 16. 1807.
Inscription (in swag): JANE SHORE |
    Alicia. Thou art that fatal fair that
    cursed she, That set my soul [*sic*] a madding. |
Painted by Fuseli, Engrav'd by Holloway. | Act V Scene 1.
Dimensions (oval): 7.8 x 6.8 cm | 3^{1}/16" x 2^{11}/16" (Illinois 822.08 B773)
Other locations: BL 11785.a.1 (not seen); Harvard (not seen); Illinois 792.C774 (*Illus.*) (missing)

127B. *Mathew Complains to Bobadill that He is Almost out of Money*, 1806
(Ben Jonson, *Every Man in His Humour*, I, v)
(Vol. IX)

Re-engraved with new cartouche and swag by Charles Grignion (1721-1810)
Imprint (in swag): Printed for | C. Cooke, May 24. | 1806
Imprint (in swag top left): EVERY MAN IN HIS HUMOUR. | Painted by Fuseli R.A. | | Engraved by Grignon. |
    Bob What money ha' you about you M^r. Mathew?
    Mat. Faith I ha' not past a two shillings, or so.
                                    Act I. Scene 4.
Dimensions (oval): 8.0 x 7.0 cm | 3^{2}/16" x 2¾" (Illinois 822.08 B773)
Other locations: BL 11785.a.1 (not seen); Harvard (not seen); Illinois 792.C774 (*Illus.*) (missing)

129B. *Dying Osmond Stabs Sigismunda as She Throws Herself Upon Him*, 1807
(James Thomson, *Tancred and Sigismunda*, V, ii)
(Vol. XII)

Re-engraved by unknown engraver from the 1792 plate by Francis Legat (1755-1809)
Imprint (at knot of swag at left): Printed for | C. Cooke. | Sept. 19. 1827.
Inscription (in swag across bottom of plate): TANCRED AND SIGISMUNDA. |
    Osmond. Perfidious Woman, die. |
                Vide Act V. Scene 2.
Dimensions: 8.7 x 6.5 cm | 3^{7}/16" x 2^{10}/16" (Illinois 822.08 B773)
Other locations: BL 11785.a.1 (not seen); Harvard (not seen); Illinois 792.C774 (*Illus.*) (missing); Peter Tomory, Melbourne

******

131.

131. *Caractacus at the Tribunal*, 1792
(Tacitus, *Annals*, XII, 37)

Engraved by A. Birrell after Fuseli's since-dismembered painting, now extant only in the form of three separate fragments in the collections of Richard L. Feigen (New York), A. & F. Kirchheimer-Bollag (Küsnacht, Zurich) and Carl Laszlo (Basel) ([1792]; Schiff 762, 877, 1760) Imprint: Publish'd June 1. 1792, by R. Pollard, Engraver, & Printseller, Spa-fields London. Inscription: H. Fuseli, R.A. Pinᵗ. | | A. Birrell. sculpᵗ. | CARACTACUS at the TRIBUNAL of CLAUDIUS at ROME. |

[*left*]
This British Prince for 9 years having successfully defeated the attempts of the Romans to subdue his native country was at last vanquished | & taken, who with his wife & family were sent prisoners to Rome to grace the triumph of the victor—on his entering the Imperial presence he boldly | approached the Tribunal with a countenance fixed & undaunted thus addressing the Emperor—'Had my moderation in prosperity been equal to my | birth & fortune, I had come to this City as a friend

rather than a captive nor would you [*have*] disdain'd to have received me as an ally since I am by birth | a Prince & by fortune the chief of many free & warlike nations—my present state is as humiliating to me as it is glorious to you. with these chains you can confine
[*right*]
my person but heaven has given me a mind out of the reach of human power to enslave. I once had horses, men, arms, & riches, was it strange I should be unwilling to | part with them? If your ambition aims at universal sway mankind are not all obliged to submit to the yoke—had I fallen in battle or sooner been betrayed neither my | misfortune nor your success would at this time have been so renowned—if to defend my life my liberty & my country be a crime punish me with death & my misfortunes | will end with it. if I am suffered to live then to future ages I shall remain a monument of your clemency' — Claudius was astonished at so spirited a speech delivᵈ. by a Prince | in captivity. it raised his wonder created his esteem & moved with generosity & the friendly interposition of the Empress [*Claudius*] order'd his chains to be taken off & the captives to be liberated

Dimensions: ■42.8 x 58.1 cm | 16¹³/16" x 22¹³/16"
(BM 1873-8-9-237).
Other locations: YCBA B1978.43.231; ETH 403
Lit.:Schiff 876 (42.5 x ?51.8 cm), 762, 877, 1760

Variants:

I. Proof before all letters (lacking inscription):
BM 1861-5-18-152

David Alexander informs me that Pollard, after
buying *Edgar and Elfrida*, 1786, from Ryland's
widow, had *Caractacus* engraved as a pendant
(see Pollard's sale, 10 December 1810, lot 148).

Fuseli's model for Caractacus may have been
the figure of 'A Britaine' on the title page of John
Speed's *History of Great Britain*, 1611.

******

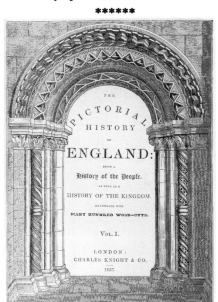

Fig. 7. [G.L. Craik.] *Pictorial History of England*,
1837. Title page.

No. 131A.
[George Lillie Craik].
[Engraved title page]: THE | PICTORIAL |
HISTORY | OF | ENGLAND: | BEING A |
HISTORY OF THE PEOPLE, | AS WELL AS A |
HISTORY OF THE KINGDOM. |
ILLUSTRATED WITH | MANY HUNDRED
WOOD-CUTS. | VOL. I. [-VOL. IV.] |
LONDON: | CHARLES KNIGHT & CO. | — |
1837, 1846 (1/524 illus.).

THE | PICTORIAL | HISTORY OF ENGLAND: |
BEING | A HISTORY OF THE PEOPLE, | AS
WELL AS A HISTORY OF THE KINGDOM. |

ILLUSTRATED WITH | MANY HUNDRED
WOOD-CUTS | OF | MONUMENTAL RECORDS;
COINS; CIVIL AND MILITARY COSTUME;
DOMESTIC BUILDINGS, FURNITURE, AND |
ORNAMENTS; CATHEDRALS AND OTHER
GREAT WORKS OF ARCHITECTURE;SPORTS
AND OTHER | ILLUSTRATIONS OF
MANNERS; MECHANICAL INVENTIONS;
PORTRAITS OF THE KINGS | AND QUEENS;
AND REMARKABLE HISTORICAL SCENES. |
— | VOLUME I.[-VOLUME VI.] | — | LONDON: |
CHARLES KNIGHT AND CO., 22, LUDGATE-
STREET. | — | MDCCCXXXVIII [1838]

...BY | GEORGE L. CRAIK AND CHARLES
MACFARLANE, | ASSISTED BY OTHER
CONTRIBUTORS. | IN SIX VOLUMES. | —
VOLUME I. [-VOLUME VI.] | — | LONDON: |
CHARLES KNIGHT AND CO., 22, LUDGATE
STREET. | — | MDCCCXLI [1841].

STANDARD EDITION. | — | THE | PICTORIAL |
HISTORY OF ENGLAND: | BEING | A HISTORY
OF THE PEOPLE, | AS WELL AS A HISTORY
OF THE KINGDOM. | ILLUSTRATED WITH |
MANY HUNDRED WOOD-CUTS; | AND | ONE
HUNDRED AND FOUR ILLUSTRATIVE
PORTRAITS, ENGRAVED ON STEEL. | BY |
GEORGE L. CRAIK AND CHARLES
MACFARLANE, | ASSISTED BY OTHER
CONTRIBUTORS. | IN EIGHT VOLUMES. |
VOLUME I. [-VOLUME VIII.] | LONDON: |
CHARLES KNIGHT, 22, LUDGATE STREET. |
— | 1847.

...LONDON: | CHARLES KNIGHT, 90, FLEET
STREET. | — | 1849

131A.

131A. *Caractacus at Rome*, 1837
(Vol. I, p. 42)

Wood engraving by unknown engraver.
Inscription: CARACTACUS AT ROME.—Fuseli.
Dimensions: ■ 10.3 x 12.5 cm │ 4^1/16" x 4^{15}/16"
(BL 806.f5)
Other locations: BL 09504.1.2 (1846) (with added title page from 1849); DHW (with added title pages from 1838 and 1841); Northern Iowa DA30.C887. 1838; Northern Iowa DA30.C887.1841; Virginia DA30.C75 (1846); Princeton 1426.272.2 (1847); Vanderbilt DA30.C887 (1849); Virginia DA30.C75 (1849); Yale ?
Lit.: Schiff 876 (citing only '1840' edition)

The work appears to have been issued in fortnightly numbers. In DHW's copy the first owner has noted in ink in Vol. I at the head of the 1837 title page: '*Commenced this work 17th July 1840*│to take one Number every fortnight'. For the later edition in numbers, see the Prospectus preceding No. **131C**.

No. 131B.
THE│PICTORIAL│HISTORY│OF│ENGLAND:│ BEING A│HISTORY OF THE PEOPLE,│AS WELL AS A│HISTORY OF THE KINGDOM.│ ILLUSTRATED WITH│SEVERAL HUNDRED WOOD-CUTS.│VOL. I. [-VOL. IV.]│ NEW YORK:│HARPER & BROTHERS.│1846 (1/1259 illus.).

131B. *Caractacus at Rome*, 1846
(Vol. I, p. 38)

Newly engraved on wood by unknown engraver for the first American edition
Inscription: CARACTACUS AT ROME.—Fuseli.
Dimensions: 10.4 x 12.8 cm │ 4^2/16" x 5^1/16"
(Wisconsin—Milwaukee).
Other locations: Virginia DA30.C887.1846; Virginia Polytechnic DA30.C887.1846

The four volumes, published in 44 numbers between May 1846 and 10 March 1848, contained 1259 engravings, for which Harpers paid a total of $4375 (an average of $3.47 per engraving).

✱✱✱✱✱✱

No. 131C.
THE│PICTORIAL│HISTORY OF ENGLAND│ BEING│A HISTORY OF THE PEOPLE│AS WELL AS A HISTORY OF THE KINGDOM│ ILLUSTRATED WITH│MANY HUNDRED WOOD-ENGRAVINGS│A NEW EDITION, REVISED AND EXTENDED│IN TEN VOLUMES│VOL. I [-VOL. VI]│ LONDON│W. AND R. CHAMBERS 47 PATERNOSTER ROW │AND HIGH STREET EDINBURGH│—│ MDCCCLV [1855]

PROSPECTUS
(BL 09504.1.2)

W. and R. Chambers's New and Revised Editions of Standard Works.
RE-ISSUE, commencing on the 4th NOVEMBER, 1854.

No. I., price 6d.; also, Part I., price 2s.:│

THE│PICTORIAL HISTORY OF ENGLAND.│ ILLUSTRATED BY UPWARDS OF SIXTEEN HUNDRED WOODCUTS.│A NEW AND IMPROVED ISSUE,│CARRIED DOWN TO THE COMMENCEMENT OF THE RUSSIAN WAR.│=│

THE PICTORIAL HISTORY OF ENGLAND —one of the many admirable books planned by Mr. CHARLES KNIGHT—has long established itself in public esteem, as a history, not merely of political events (to which character most histories are limited), but of the PEOPLE, *in their common life and social progress*. The *Edinburgh Review* bore testimony to its merits in the following passage:
"'The Pictorial History of England,' now before us, seems to be the very thing required by the popular taste of the present day; adding to the advantage of a clear historical narrative, all the varied illustrations of which the subject is capable. After the fashion, first introduced by Dr. Henry, the authors have divided their subjects into periods; the narrative of civil and military events in each being followed by chapters on the history of religion, the constitution and laws, the condition of the people, national industry, manners and customs; and almost every page in the earlier volumes is enriched with appropriate woodcuts, generally

of able execution—dresses, arms, industrial employments, sports, copied from illuminated manuscripts of the periods to which they belong —views of scenes rendered famous by historical events, taken from drawings or prints as near the period as could be obtained—ample illustrations of architecture and sculpture; portraits and fac-similes—and here and there cuts from historical pictures."

It is proposed to re-issue the work, in its original form, and with all its original Illustrations—forming Eight Volumes, and terminating with the year 1815. To this series will be added a New Edition of the HISTORY OF THE PEACE, extended, under the care of MESSRS. CHAMBERS, to March 1854, printed uniformly with the above, including a COMPLETE CHRONOLOGICAL INDEX based on that prepared by H.C. HAMILTON, Esq., of the State Paper Office. Thus the entire work will be

A PICTORIAL HISTORY OF ENGLAND
TO THE COMMENCEMENT OF THE
RUSSIAN WAR.
IN TEN VOLUMES.

This Edition will be carefully printed, on good paper, and will form the most complete and highly illustrated work of the kind ever published.

A NUMBER, consisting of 32 pages, super royal 8vo, price 6*d*., in a coloured paper Cover, will appear every *Saturday*; and a PART, consisting of 128 pages, price 2*s*., will appear every Month with the Magazines. The work will comprise about 60 Parts.

The First Number and First Part will be issued on the First Saturday in November.

₊ Orders executed by all Booksellers. | —|W. & R. CHAMBERS,|BRIDE'S-PASSAGE, FLEET-STREET, LONDON; AND HIGH-STREET, EDINBURGH:|H. CAMPBELL, GLASGOW: J. M'GLASHAN, DUBLIN:|C.S. FRANCIS AND CO., NEW YORK: LIPPINCOTT, GRAMBO, AND CO., PHILADELPHIA: HEW RAMSAY,| MONTREAL: AND ALL BOOKSELLERS.

131C. *Caractacus at Rome*, 1854
(Vol. I, p. 42)

Re-engraved on wood by Edward Whymper (1840-1911)

Inscription (right-hand corner of plate): E WHIMPER. SC.|CARACTACUS AT ROME.—Fuseli.
Dimensions: 10.5 x 12.5 cm | 4²/16" x 4¹⁵/16" (BL 9505.f.2)
Other locations: Newberry F45.467

******

Nos. 132 - 134.
SEVENTEEN|ENGRAVINGS,|TO ILLUSTRATE|SHAKSPEARE,|FROM| PICTURES BY EMINENT BRITISH ARTISTS.| =|ENGRAVED BY|[*col. 1*] *HALL,*|*SOW,*| *FITTLER,*||[*col. 2*] *SHARPE,*|*BROMLEY,*| *RHODES,*|—| LONDON:|PUBLISHED BY A. WOODMASON, EASING LANE CHEAPSIDE: AND TO BE HAD AT MESSRS BOYDELL & CO.'S|NO 90 CHEAPSIDE: AND OF ALL PRINT AND BOOK-SELLERS.|—|MAY 17, 1817 (3/17 illus.). [=‘1817¹’]
Contains a 'List of the Engravings'.

A|SERIES|OF|ENGRAVINGS|TO ILLUSTRATE THE|WORKS OF SHAKSPEARE,|BY HEATH, HALL, RHODES, FITLER, &C.| =| LONDON:|PUBLISHED BY JOHN MURRAY, ALBEMARLE-STREET; J. HEATH, RUSSELL PLACE, FITZROY-| SQUARE; AND W. WOODMASON, LEADENHALL-STREET.|1817 (2/37 illus.). [=‘1817²’]

[Printed Label]: A SERIES OF|MAGNIFICENT ENGRAVINGS.|TO ILLUSTRATE THE| WORKS OF SHAKSPEARE.|BY HEATH, HALL, RHODES, FITLER, &C.|PRICE £8:8S.

A SERIES OF ENGRAVINGS BY HEATH AND BARTOLOZZI, FROM PAINTINGS BY STOTHARD TO ILLUSTRATE THE WORKS OF SHAKSPEARE AND MILTON; FORMING AN ELEGANT LIBRARY ACCOMPANIMENT TO THE VARIOUS EDITIONS OF THOSE AUTHORS| =|price £9:9S.| =| LONDON, PRINTED FOR H. M'LEAN. 1818 (2/34 illus.). [=‘1818¹’]

...LONDON:|PRINTED AT THE COLUMBIAN PRESS, BY HOWLETT AND BRIMMER, 10, FRITH STREET, SOHO,|FOR H. M'LEAN, 16, SALISBURY STREET, STRAND.|—|1818 (2/22 illus.). [=‘1818²’]

A|SERIES|OF|MAGNIFICENT|ENGRAVINGS |TO|ILLUSTRATE THE VARIOUS|FOLIO OR

QUARTO EDITIONS|OF|THE WORKS|OF| SHAKESPEARE AND MILTON;|OR, BOUND UP, TO FORM|A LIBRARY ACCOMPANIMENT|TO ANY OF THE| SMALLER EDITIONS OF THOSE AUTHORS.| =|PRICE £9 :9s.|=| LONDON:|PRINTED BY J. BARFIELD, WARDOUR-STREET,|FOR H. M'LEAN, NO. 8, SOHO-SQUARE.|—|1818 (5/51 illus.). [='1818³')

For the other illustrations in this volume see also Nos. **182-183**.

PROSPECTUS
(Birmingham Shakespeare Library 95841)

NEW SHAKSPEARE GALLERY,
N° 88, PALL MALL.
=
PROSPECTUS.
=
SUBSCRIPTION
FOR PROOF-PRINTS ONLY.
=

The late Proprietor's avocations obliging him to relinquish all personal attention to this undertaking, he has disposed of the greatest part of his interest to Gentlemen who propose having Prints engraved *in Stroke* from the several Pictures here exhibited, and to take off only a small number from each, *all Proof-Prints*. They have accordingly appointed Mr. JOSEPH KIRTON, N° 16, Great Marlborough Street, their sole agent.

The Proprietors are aware, that in thus asking Subscriptions for Prints they have much to combat. The prejudices against Subscription Prints are many, and with abundant justice. Some Publishers, it is notorious, have held half-subscriptions for near *ten years*, and no Print yet delivered; others, after keeping the money subscribed for many years, have been dishonourable enough to obtrude *bad Impressions* on their earliest Subscribers, even touched up with Indian ink to conceal the fraud, reserving to themselves a great number of Proofs and first Impressions.

Stroke *engraving*, too, has been promised and subscribed for; and stip[p]ling, or chalk, or some other illegitimate branch of the art, unblushingly produced as a substitute.

In addition to these flagrant deceptions, after a *stated number* from a Plate has been promised, more numerous Impressions have been taken off than were either agreed or subscribed for, and far better Prints than those delivered to the Subscribers, sold singly to individuals in open shops.

All these ignominious practices the present Proprietors are resolutely determined to avoid. *They will produce all that they promise*: and, to obviate every possible suspicion, accompanied by such testimonies as cannot fail to prove perfectly satisfactory.

In the first place, the *name* and *residence* of each Subscriber, is all that will be required at the time of subscribing, as *no money* will be received till the *delivery* of the respective Proof-Prints.

No Artists, but such as are of eminence in *Stroke engraving*, will be engaged: their names will demonstrate this fact; and, for their own reputation, it may reasonably be presumed, they will not finish an indifferent Plate. Indeed, as it is meant to obtain the highest execution that the first Artists in this country can produce, unless each Plate actually does equal the best performances of the respective arts, it will not be used. The decision of this shall be confided to the judgment of Three known independent Gentlemen, Subscribers; who shall approve the execution of each Plate, and testify such their approbation, by signing a certificate to that purport, before a single Impression is delivered.

Only *Five Hundred* of each Print are to be subscribed for. The size, 9¾ by 8 Inches; the price, Half-a-Guinea a Print; the present number, Twenty-seven.

The following Pictures are already in the hands of the Engravers, and most of them nearly finished—

Engravers		Numb.	Painted by
HALL.	King John	XVII.	OPIE.
SHARP.	Macbeth	XI.	FUSELI.
SHARP.	Macbeth	XII.	FUSELI.
BROMLEY.	Tempest	XXVI.	PETERS.
FITLER.	Measure for Measure	XVI.	HAMILTON.
STOWE.	Timon of Athens	XIX.	NORTHCOTE.
RHODES,	Mid. Night's Dream	XXI.	FUSELI.

The grand object which the Proprietors propose, is to *secure* to the Subscribers, *without a possibility* of fraud, the first 500 Proof-Prints.

For this purpose, no Plate will be permitted to remain, after it is finished, in the hands of any single individual whatever; not even the Copper-plate Printer, who will be constantly attended by a trusty person, *sworn* to see compleat justice done to the Subscribers. The Copper-plate Printer is also to make *oath*, that no more than the agreed number are taken from each Plate.

As it is proposed to print only 500 Proofs, the possessor of the *last* or 500th Impression, will have a *superior* Print to the very *first* Subscribers to other Subscription Prints, as they are usually managed.

A STROKE-engraved Plate, it is sufficiently known, when well executed, is capable of producing at least *Two Thousand* good Prints; and the Proprietors will demonstrate by the following unprecedented, advantageous, and liberal Plan, that they do not aim at making a *large* profit—they only seek honourably to secure a small one.

As, after the 500 Proofs are printed off, each Plate will afford 1500 more *good* common Impressions, the Proprietors mean to present, to each Subscriber, *Three* of these Prints from every Plate, without any farther additional expence, than the very trivial price of paper and printing, which cannot exceed Half-a-Crown for the Three Prints.

Every Subscriber must immediately perceive the advantage of this offer; as he will become not only possessed, with certainty, of a *real* Proof-Print of intrinsic value, but will obtain it, in fact, for nothing: the three *common* Prints, which must necessarily be all *good impressions*, being worth far more, on the most moderate computation, than the entire sum advanced. In fact, every Subscriber may safely count on putting something in his pocket; more, or less, according to the celebrity of the work, which cannot well fail to be great.

In order to prevent, as far as possible, *this* work from interfering with any other undertaking, it is intended, that the subjects shall in future be such as have not been painted for any work of the kind. SHAKSPEARE'S known fertility, and inexhaustible variety, will render this an easy task, the greatest number of his most striking scenes being yet untouched.

=

The PROPRIETORS are so determined to keep strictly to their engagements, that they will thankfully receive any additional hint or advice that can be given them, to secure to the SUBSCRIBERS still stronger, if possible, the certainty that not a single PROOF shall be taken off, beyond the 500.

=

A Book is in the Room, for the purpose of receiving the Names and Residence of SUBSCRIBERS.

Engravings were made after seventeen of the twenty-seven paintings in Woodmason's Irish Shakspeare Gallery (Dublin) and New Shakspeare Gallery (London), of which eleven were published by Woodmason in 1794; the remaining six had to await publication until 1817, when they appeared under Murray's imprint. Only three out of Fuseli's five contributions eventually appeared as prints. *Gertrude, Hamlet and the Ghost of his Father* (1793; Schiff 1747) was never engraved. *Macbeth and the Armed Head* (1794; Schiff 881) 'was chosen by [*William*] Sharpe, and some progress made by him in the engraving of it, when [*Woodmason's*] scheme was abandoned' (Knowles, I, 189), although Sharpe's working drawing for the never-completed engraving has survived (BM 1853-12-10-481) (see Susan Lambert, *The Image Multiplied: Five centuries of printed reproductions of painting and drawings*, 1987, pl. 36).

The problems involved for an outsider like Alfred Woodmason in undertaking such a publication may be gauged from two letters preserved in the archives of Messrs. John Murray. In the first, dated 11 March 1816, Woodmason asks for advice about matters such as the trade allowance, since the 'Booksellers' ... 28½ per cent, ... with the 10 per cent for publishing & other expences, would so reduce the proceeds, as not to repay the expences, that is if the work is sold at 4 & 2 Gui[*nea*]s'. On 30 December 1816, now that 'the Shakespeare prints are nearly finished & worked off, & will be ready for publication in about 6 weeks or 2 months', he wishes to know from Murray, who has agreed to be the publisher, how he should announce the forthcoming publication to the trade and the public. He proposes 'to have the [*seventeen*] Plates stitched in very thin Boards, covered with a buff or brown wrapper with ornaments & title &ᶜ.

printed on it, & to have a fly leaf between each print, containing an extract from the Scene described therein & a title page', although he is not sure whether any sort of preface will be necessary. (The 'extracts' and the preface were omitted from the *Seventeen Engravings*, as published—undoubtedly on Murray's advice.) Woodmason's suggested price was 5 Guineas for Proofs, 2½ Guineas 'for common impressions', although it is not clear whether purchasers were offered this choice. In subsequent editions the number of engravings was increased (from 17 to 51) and the price raised to 9 guineas. The prints were worked off by Dixon of Tottenham Street.

132.

132. *Oberon Squeezing the Flower on Titania's Eyelids*, 1794
(*A Midsummer Night's Dream*, II,ii)
(Plate no. 5/17)

Engraved by Richard Rhodes (1765-1838) after Fuseli's painting No. 10 in 'Woodmason's Shakspeare Gallery' now in the Frey collection, Wangen bei Olten, Switzerland (1793; Schiff 884).

Imprint: Publish'd Augt. 1st. 1794. by M^r. Woodmason Leadenhall Street London.
Inscription: Painted by H. Fuseli R.A. | | Engraved by Rhodes. | MIDSUMMER-NIGHT'S DREAM. | Act 2. Scene 3. | A Wood. | Oberon, Queen, Puck, and Fairies.
Dimensions: ■ 24.8 x 20.0 cm | 9^{13}/16" x 7^1/16"; ■ 24.9 x 20.2 cm | 9^{14}/16" x 7^{15}/16" (Birmingham 223602) (1817^1)
Other locations: Birmingham 551749 (1817^2)(pl. 7/37); Birmingham 515585 (1818^1) (no t.p., pl. 6/31); Birmingham 242279 (1818^2); DHW (1818^3) (H=49.5 cm); Illinois (1818); LC PR 2883.S7 (1818^1); Yale (1818^1)
Plate only: BM 1870-5-14-1708; Folger Art File S528m5 no. 28; Folger PR3004.B4 ex-ill. (imprint cropped) (facing p. 51)
Lacking plate: Folger Art Vol. f79 (34 plates)
Lit.: Schiff 884A (24.1 x 20.3 cm); R. Hamlyn, 'An Irish Shakespeare Gallery', *Burlington*, August 1978, 515-529, pl. 30.
Exh.: Kansas City 1982 (21).

Variants:
I. Proof before all letters (lacking stage instructions), open capitals: KHZ 1931/43
Other locations: Essick; Huntington 181067, XIII, 75; Huntington 181067, XIII, 114

Titania, queen of the fairies, has angered Oberon by refusing to let him have her beautiful changeling boy to be his page. To 'torment her for this injury,' Oberon seeks out Titania asleep in a moonlit glade and squeezes on her eyelids the juice of a magic flower ('love-in-idleness'), which will make her a slave of love to the first creature (animal or human) she lays eyes upon when she awakens.

> What thou seest when thou dost wake,
> Do it for thy true-love take,
> Love and languish for his sake.
> Be it ounce, or cat, or bear,
> Pard, or boar with bristled hair,
> In thy eye that shall appear
> When thou wak'st, it is thy dear.
> Wake when some vile thing is near.

At Titania's feet, the fairy attendant who is supposed to be standing sentinel has also fallen asleep, while Puck peers mischievously over Oberon's shoulder at the scene.

133.

133A.

Lit.: Schiff 885; Robin Hamlyn, 'An Irish Shakespeare Gallery', *Burlington*, August 1978, 515-529; John Updike, 'A Case of Overestimation', *Just Looking*, 1989, 30-32.
Exh.: Kansas City 1982 (23)

******

133A. *The Grasshopper Man* [n.d.]

Enlarged detail from *Titania Embracing Bottom* etched by Theodor Mathias von Holst (1810-1844) from the plate by Rhodes
Inscription: H. Fuseli inv^t. et Del—||T M. von Holst fecit
Dimensions (sheet): 23.0 x 18.9 cm | 9" x 7^7/16" (Courtauld, Witt 933/27.6)
Lit.: Todd 1947, repr. 82

******

134. *The Witches Appear to Macbeth and Banquo*, 1817
(*Macbeth*, I, iii)
(Plate no. 9/17)

Engraved by William Bromley (1769-1842) after Fuseli's painting No. 11 in 'Woodmason's Shakspeare Gallery'.
Imprint: Published Jany. 1, 1817, by John Murray, Albemarle Street, London.
Inscription: H. Fuseli pinxit.||W. Bromley Sculp. |MACBETH.|Act I. Scene 3.|

133. *Titania Embracing Bottom*, 1794
(*A Midsummer Night's Dream*, III, i)
(Plate no. 6/17)
Engraved by Richard Rhodes (1765-1838) after Fuseli's painting No. 21 in 'Woodmason's Shakspeare Gallery' now in the Kunsthaus, Zurich (1793; Schiff 885).
Imprint: Published Augt. 1. 1794, by Mr Woodmason, Leadenhall Street, London.
Inscription: Painted by H. Fuseli.||Engraved by R. Rhodes.|MIDSUMMER NIGHT'S DREAM.| Act 3. Scene 1.|A Wood.|Quince, Bottom with with an Ass's Head, Queen, Fairies|Pyramus, Thisbe, Puck, and Snout.
Dimensions: ■ 25.1 x 20.4 cm | 9^{14}/16" x 8"; ▣ 25.2 x 20.5 cm | 9^{15}/16" x 8^1/16" (Birmingham 223602) (1817^1)
Other locations: Birmingham 551749 (1817^2) (pl. 8/37); Birmingham 515585 (1818^1) (no t.p., pl. 7/31); DHW (1818^3) (H=49.5 cm)
Plate only: BM 1870.5.14.1709; Folger Art File S528m5 no. 48; Folger PR3004.B4 Ex-ill. (imprint cropped) (facing p. 12)
Lacking plate: Folger Art Vol. f79 (34 plates)

Banquo.   ____What are these
        So wither'd and so wild in their attire;
        That look not like the inhabitants o' the
           earth,
        And yet are on't?____

Dimensions: ■ 24.5 x 20.2 cm | 9¹¹/16" x 7¹⁵/16"
(Birmingham 223602) (1817¹)
Other locations: Birmingham 551749 (1817²) (pl.
11/37); Birmingham 515585 (1818¹) (no t.p., pl.
10/31); DHW (1818³) (H=49.5 cm)
Plate only: BM 1870-5-14-1712; Essick;
Huntington 181067, XX, 44; KHZ
Lacking plate: Folger Art Vol. f79 (34 plates)
Lit.: Schiff 880; Robin Hamlyn, 'An Irish
Shakespeare Gallery', *Burlington*, August 1978,
521, pl. 32; *Letters*, 161, 175
Exh.: Kansas City 1982 (27).

  Hamlyn points out that Fuseli's narrow canvas
'forced the action to the edges of the composition,
an unusual feature in Fuseli's work'. Thus,
despite a certain 'unearthliness', 'the breadth of
the elemental powers of nature and barrenness of
landscape ... captured so successfully by Fuseli in
his Boydell work [*are*] here absent'.

134.

135.

135. *An Incubus Leaving Two Sleeping Young Women*, [*post* 1794]

Engraved by Theodor Falckeisen (1765-1814) after his own drawing in the Oeffentliche Kunstsammlung, Basel, from Fuseli's painting in the Muraltengut, Zurich (1794; Schiff 929). Proof before letters.
Inscription (in pencil): Fuesli inv: | Falkeysen sc:
Dimensions: ■ 18.9 x 23.0 cm | 7⁷/₁₆" x 9¹/₁₆"
(Basel J34.VIII.Bi5)
Other locations: Basel 1927.121
Lit.: Schiff 929; *Helvetisches Journal* (1802), I, 169-171; *Letters*, 127; Weinglass 1988, 68; Andersen 1989, 280, repr. 203.

Variants:
I. Modern pull (1926): KHZ 1926/89

'Incubus' was the standard eighteenth-century term for nightmare, although in modern usage this refers rather to the male spirit or demon said to lie upon sleeping women in the night.

Theodor Falkeisen of Basel purchased Fuseli's picture from him for 30 guineas in 1794, and transferred it to copper at an undetermined date after his return to Switzerland. We may view the image as a counterpart to Fuseli's *Nightmare* (see No. **67**), although it depicts two female figures instead of a single one, and the persuasive details of the bedroom furnishings which could identify scene and subject as contemporary have been eliminated. While both engravings (like the original paintings) evoke the terror and suffocating oppression experienced during a nightmare, as well as the fusion of natural and supernatural elements which commonly occurs in the nocturnal world of the dreamer, this later version clearly lacks the dark sublimity and atavistic force of the erotic obsession Fuseli invested in the *Nightmare*.

However, if we see in the *Nightmare*, 'the incubus demon taking the place of the artist himself' (Horst W. Janson, 'Fuseli's *Nightmare*', *Sixteen Studies*, 1973, 75-88), we are likely to agree with Gert Schiff that the young woman's release from the thrall of the incubus would also represent the artist's liberation through art from a hopeless but obsessive passion. It would not be fully exorcised until Fuseli's reworking of the image in his drawing of 1810 (Schiff 1445).

✶✶✶✶✶✶

UNDE UNDE EXTRICAT

London Published Feb.2.1795 by T.Cadell Strand.

136.

Nos. 136 - 138.
[William Seward].
ANECDOTES | OF SOME | DISTINGUISHED PERSONS, | CHIEFLY OF | THE PRESENT AND TWO PRECEDING | CENTURIES. | — | ADORNED WITH SCULPTURES. | — | VOL. I [-VOL. III]. | — | LONDON: | PRINTED FOR T. CADELL, JUN. AND W. DAVIES, | SUCCESSORS TO MR. CADELL, IN THE STRAND. | 1795 (2/9 illus. + 2 facs.).

...THE SECOND EDITION, | WITH ADDITIONS AND CORRECTIONS. | = | VOL. I. [-VOL. IV.] | LONDON: | PRINTED FOR T. CADELL, JUN. AND W. DAVIES, | SUCCESSORS TO MR. CADELL, IN THE STRAND. | 1795 (3/9 illus. + 2 facs.).

...THE THIRD EDITION. | — | VOL. I. [-VOL. IV.] | — | LONDON: | PRINTED FOR T. CADELL, JUN. AND W. DAVIES, | SUCCESSORS TO MR. CADELL, IN THE STRAND. | 1796.

ANECDOTES | OF | DISTINGUISHED PERSONS, | CHIEFLY OF THE | PRESENT AND

TWO PRECEDING | CENTURIES. |
ILLUSTRATED BY ENGRAVINGS. | *Indocti
Discant, Et Ament Meminisse Periti.* | THE
FOURTH EDITION: | CONSIDERABLY
ENLARGED, | AND | NEWLY ARRANGED
AND DIGESTED. | IN FOUR VOLUMES. | VOL.
I. [-VOL. IV.] | LONDON: | PRINTED FOR T.
CADELL JUN. AND W. DAVIES, | IN THE
STRAND. | 1798.

...THE FIFTH EDITION. | IN FOUR
VOLUMES. | —VOL. I. [-VOL. IV.] | — |
LONDON PRINTED FOR T. CADELL, AND
W. DAVIES, | IN THE STRAND. | = | 1804. | W.
FLINT, PRINTER, OLD BAILEY.

136. *Allegorical Figure of Erichtho*, 1795
(Horace, *Satires*, I, iii, 87-88)
(Vol. I, facing title page)

Frontispiece engraved by William Sharp (1749-
1824)
Imprint: London, Published Feby. 1. 1795, by T.
Cadell, Strand.
Inscription (in lower panel): UNDÊ UNDÊ
EXTRICAT | (bottom right): W Sharp sculp.
Dimensions: ■ 8.7 x 7.1 cm | 3^6/16" x 2^{13}/16"
(BL 1087.a.1)
Other locations: BL 1509/4308 (2d ed.); Bodleian
III-H-77 (2d ed.); Brandeis CT102.S4 (3rd ed.);
Cambridge 7450.d.104 (2nd ed.); Cambridge
7450.d.135 (3rd ed.); DHW (2nd ed.); Essick;
Folger PN6260.S4 1796 (3rd ed.) (Vol. III,
facing t.p.); Huntington D106.S4 (3rd ed.);
Huntington 21974 (3rd ed.)
Plate only: BM 1849-5-12-840.(3); BM 1868-8-
22-1837.(2); BM 1875-2-13-251; Huntington Pr.
Box 786/20
Lit.: Schiff 977 (8.7 x 7.0); Baker 1875, no. 168;
Tomory 1972, pl. 109; Hammelmann 1975, 35.
Exh.: Kansas City 1982 (80).

Variants:
I. Before all letters (panel inscribed): BM 1863-
5-9-80.
Other locations: BM 1853-12-10-341
II. Reissued (1798) with page and Volume nos.
added: BL 123.d.8
Other locations: Newberry E3.808
Inscription (top right): Frontispiece to Vol. I. |
(lower panel): UNDÊ UNDÊ EXTRICAT |
(bottom right): W Sharp sculp.

Other locations: BL 10601.ee.12 (5th ed.);
Huntington 21544 (5th ed.); Huntington 286646
(5th ed.); LC PN6260.S4 1798
Plate only: Huntington Pr. Box 786/20

The motto is taken from Horace (*'nisi, cum
tristes misero venere Kalendae, mercedem aut
nummos UNDÊ UNDÊ EXTRICAT'*) (tr. H.R.
Fairclough): 'If at the coming of the sad Kalends
he cannot *scrape up from some quarter* either
interest or principal....' In this case what Seward
must scrape up are anecdotes!

Although Fuseli was now 51 tears old, in his
'Advertisement' Seward attributes the frontispiece
to 'a YOUNG FRIEND of the COMPILER, "who...
requires only the mediocrity of RAFFAELLE, with
respect to rank and to fortune, to enable him to
become the rival of that great master in the
noblest efforts of his genius and of his
knowledge."'

DIES PRÆTERITOS!

137.

137. *Allegorical Figure of a Woman
Representing Past Days*, 1795
(Martial, *Epigrams*, X, xxiii, 3)
(Vol. III, facing title page)

Frontispiece engraved by William Sharp (1749-
1824)

Imprint: Published Novr. 1. 1795. by Cadell & Davies, Strand.

Inscription (bottom right): Sharp sc. | DIES PRAETERITOS!

Dimensions: ■ 9.6 x 6.0 | 3¹³/16" x 2⁶/16" (?? Location)

Plate only: BM 1863-5-9-78; BM 45-7-24-130, BM T.13; Huntington Pr. Box 786/19

Lacking plate: Bodleian III-H-79 (3rd ed.); Cambridge 7450.d.135 (3rd ed.)

Lit.: Schiff 978 (9.6 x 6.0 cm); Baker 1875, no. 166 (3⁸/10" x 2³/10"); Hammelmann 1975, 35.

Variants:

I. Before letters: BM 1853-12-10-350

II. Before all letters (lacking imprint): BL 1087.a.3

Other locations: BL 1509/4308 (2d ed.); DHW; Essick; Folger PN6260.S4 1796 (3rd ed.) (Vol. I, facing t.p.); Huntington D10654 (3d ed.); Huntington 21974 (3rd ed.)

III. Reissued (1798) with page and Volume nos. added: BL 123.d.10

Inscription: (top right): Frontispiece to Vol. III | (bottom right): Sharp sc. | DIES PRAETERITOS!

Other locations: BL 10601.ee.12; Huntington 21544 (5th ed.); Huntington 286646 (5th ed.); Newberry E3.808

Lacking plate: LC PN6260.S4 1798 (4th ed.)

The motto comes from Martial ('*PRAETERITOSque DIES et totos respicit annos*') (tr. Walter C.A. Ker): 'He looks back upon *past days* and the vista of his years.' The last line of the epigram sums up the moral: 'He lives twice who can find delight in life bygone.'

138. *Allegorical Figure of Discretion*, 1795
(Horace, *Odes*, IV, 1, 35-36)
(Vol. IV, facing title page)

Frontispiece engraved by William Sharp (1749-1824)

Imprint: Published Feb. 1. 1796, by Cadell & Davies, Strand.

Inscription (bottom right): Sharp sc. | DECORO INTER VERBA SILENTIO.

Dimensions: ■ 9.3 x 5.9 cm | 3¾" x 2¼" (BL 1087.a.4)

Other locations: BL 1509/4308 (2d ed.); BL 10601.ee.12 (5th ed.) (1804); Cambridge

7450.d.107 (2nd ed.); Folger PN6260.S4 1796; Huntington 21974 (3rd ed.)

Plate only: BM 1863-5-9-79; BM 45-5-13-488; BM E-e-2-13-252

Lacking volume: Cambridge 7450.d.135 (3rd ed.)

Lit.: Schiff 979 (9.4 x 5.8 cm); Baker 1875, no. 167; Hammelmann 1975, 35.

Variants:

I. Reissued (1798) with page and Vol. nos. added: BL 123.d.11

Inscription (top right): Frontispiece to Vol. IV. | (bottom right): Sharp sc. | DECORO INTER VERBA SILENTIO.

Other locations: Huntington 286646; Newberry E3.808

Plate only: BM 1875-2-13-252; Huntington 786/19

Lacking plate: LC PN6260.S4 1798

DECORO INTER VERBA SILENTIO.

Published Feb.1.1796, by Cadell & Davies, Strand.

138.

The motto comes from Horace ('*cur facunda parum DECORO INTER VERBA cadit lingua SILENTIO*') (tr. C.E. Bennett): 'Why halts my tongue *with unbecoming silence midst my speech?*' The omission of '*parum*' ('*un*becoming') implies that there are anecdotes about distinguished persons that are better *not* related.

'The figure of DISCRETION ... was furnished by the same kind Pencil that supplied the former

FRONTISPIECES; by that Pencil which, in the opinion of one long conversant in the contemplation of the *beauties* both of forms and of ideas, "unites the playfulness of CORREGIO with the chastity of the ANTIQUE"' ('Advertisement', Vol. IV).

******

139.

No. 139.
[Sir Brooke Boothby].
SORROWS.|SACRED TO THE MEMORY|OF| PENELOPE.|=|*—ipso sese solatio cruciabat—.*| =| LONDON:|PRINTED BY W. BULMER AND CO.|AND SOLD BY MESSRS. CADELL AND DAVIES, STRAND;|EDWARDS, PALL-MALL; AND JOHNSON, ST. PAUL'S| CHURCH-YARD. 1796 (1/6 illus. + 4 tailpieces).

139. *The Apotheosis of Penelope Boothby*, 1796
(Frontispiece)
(Facing title page)

Frontispiece engraved in stipple by Michele Benedetti (1745-1810) after Fuseli's painting in

the Wolverhampton Art Gallery ([1792-1794]; Schiff 980).
Inscription: Painted by H. Fuseli.||Engravd by M. Benedetti.
Dimensions: ■ 29.6 x 17.6 cm|11^{10}/16" x 6^{15}/16"; ■ 29.8 x 17.8 cm | 11¾" x 7" (V & A E.1208-1886) (plate only)
Other locations (plate only): Essick
Lacking plate: Cambridge Nn.10.3
Lit.: Schiff 980 (29.9 x 17.6 cm); Hammelmann 1975, 35; *Letters*, 14, 25
Exh.: Kansas City 1982 (52).

Variants:
I. Proof before all letters: BL 75.h.19 (H=35.2 cm)
Inscription (bottom centre): Fuseli pinx^t.
Other locations: Bodleian 280.C.259; Cambridge Lib.3.79.5; DHW; DHW; Dörrbecker; Huntington 449263; Library Company *O Ger Buer 561.F; Newberry Wing fZP45.B8705; Princeton Ex 3633.938.386q
Plate only: BM 1853-5-9-45; Huntington 49000, 4379 (inscribed in pencil: 'Artist's proof')

Fuseli's picture (painted on a tall canvas and resembling an altarpiece) was conceived as a memorial to Sir Brooke Boothby's daughter, Penelope, who died in 1791 at the age of five. Boothby describes the painting in admiring terms in his Sonnet XVI, contained in the slender collection of undistinguished verse to which Benedetti's print serves as frontispiece:

My Fuseli! before thy ken of thought,
Imagination's world expanded lies;
And to ideal shapes, in orient dies,
To give a breathing form thy art has taught.
Witness yon bright illusion thou hast wrought,
With pictured bliss, to cheat these weary eyes,
And raise my drooping spirit to the skies,
On Fancy's wing to scenes celestial brought.
'Tis Immortality that sounds the call!
Lo, the mild angel to receive her bends!
From the dark disk of this terraqueous ball,
The spotless shade to her own heaven ascends.
The towering Day-star, smiling, points the way
To glorious regions, bright with cloudless ray!

Boothby (1743-1824), whom Joseph Wright of Derby has immortalised in his celebrated portrait (1781), showing him meditating in the woods upon the works of Jean-Jacques Rousseau, was one of the members of the Lichfield literary circle, which included Erasmus Darwin, through whom Fuseli may have got to know him.

The overturned pitcher at the bottom of the illustration symbolises death, while the butterfly, normally used by Fuseli as an image of eros and dreams, serves here as a reference to ephemerality.

*****

140.

140. *Konrad Baumgarten Slays Governor Wolfenschiessen in his Bath*, [1795-1800] (Johannes von Müller, *Geschichten schweizerischer Eidgenossenschaft*)

Soft ground etching by Henry Fuseli
Inscription (in pencil, bottom, outside platemark): H. Fuseli inv. f. Only 2 impressions taken.
Dimensions: 24.0 x 30.0 cm | 9⁷/₁₆" x 11¾"
(BM 1882-5-13-533).
Lit.: Schiff 981 (24.2 x 30.0 cm)

No. 140A.
HISTORISCH MERKWÜRDIGE|SCHWEIZER-SZENEN.|NACH ZEICHNUNGEN|VON|H. LIPS, F. HEGI, U.A.|ERSTES HEFT. [SECHSTES HEFT.]|—| ZÜRICH,|BEY FUESSLI UND COMP. 1812 [-1822] (1/24 illus.).

SCÈNES TIRÉES DE L'HISTOIRE DES SUISSES, GRAVÉES D'APRÈS LES DESSEINS DE H. LIPS, F. HEGI, ETC. PREMIER CAHIER. [-SIXIÈME CAHIER.]| ZURIC,| CHEZ FUESSLI ET COMP. 1812.

Baumgartner erschlägt den Wolfenschiefs im Baade.

140A.

140A. *Konrad Baumgarten Slays Governor Wolfenschiessen in his Bath*, [1795-1800]
(Johannes von Müller, *Geschichten schweizerischer Eidgenossenschaft*)
(Plate No. IV, facing p. 11)

Aquatint by Johann Heinrich Lips (1758-1817)
Inscription: Heinrich Fuessli del. | | H. Lips sculp. | Baumgartner erschlägt den Wolfenschiess im Baade.
Dimensions: ■ 17.0 x 13.4 cm | 6¹¹/₁₆" x 5¼" (KHZ C82/65).
Other locations (plate only): KHZ C4/IIIB, 1345
Lit.: Schiff 265 (17.0 x 13.4 cm)

Variants:
I. Coloured impression: Basel K 1957.44
II. Uncoloured, before letters: BL 9304.ee.29

The subject is taken from an incident that occurred in 1306, exemplifing the Swiss people's love of freedom and their resistance to tyranny and injustice under the Austrian yoke. Smitten by the beauty of Baumgarten's wife, Wolfenschiessen, the Governor of Unterwalden, forces his attentions upon her during her husband's absence. Trapped in her own house, she must prepare a bath for him, but manages to slip out of the back door just as her husband returns home.

Fuseli's dramatic illustration depicts the moment of retribution as the husband grapples with the would-be ravisher, sprawled naked in the tub, his wine cup dangling from his hand. Wolfenschiessen struggles futilely as Baumgarten grasps him by the hair and pins him with his knee, his axe upraised to deliver the fatal blow. In striking contrast to the scene of violence she is observing, the woman stands calmly at the door, clothed in all the respectability of everyday dress, including a hat.

As the editor explains in his introduction to this series of patriotic illustrations, the 'unfamiliar' new renditions of Swiss mediaeval costume were actually far more accurate than the supposedly 'traditional' representations; for these had been based on sixteenth century dress, as perpetuated in the engravings of that period. They were thus mere anachronisms, if not pure figments of earlier artists' imagination. Having made this point, the editor immediately expresses the hope that no matter how blatantly Fuseli also sins against this principle, 'the genius of his drawing will make up for this error' (p. iv).

******

No. 141.

[THE | HOLY BIBLE. | VOLUME I. (-VOLUME VI.)] | THE | OLD TESTAMENT, [NEW TESTAMENT,] | EMBELLISHED WITH | ENGRAVINGS, | FROM | PICTURES AND DESIGNS | BY THE MOST EMINENT | ENGLISH ARTISTS. | LONDON. | PRINTED FOR THOMAS MACKLIN, | BY | THOMAS BENSLEY. | 1800 (1/71 pls. + 111 head and tail pieces).

PROPOSALS
FOR
MACKLIN'S BIBLE
(from *Catalogue of the Third Exhibition of Pictures, Painted for Mr. Macklin by the Artists of Britain, Illustrative of The British Poets, and the Bible*, April 2, 1790, pp. 38-40)
(National Library of Wales)

I.
Sixty Pictures shall be painted, from the most interesting passages, by the first artists; and engraved, in the manner of WOLFE, BY Mr. BARTOLOZZI, Mr. SHARPE, &c. &c.

II.
The work will be published, as nearly as can be computed, in SIXTY numbers, making THREE magnificent volumes. Each number to contain ONE capital historical print. The size TWELVE by TEN inches.

III.
EVERY book will be enriched with VIGNETTTES, as head and tail pieces, exclusive of the large prints.

IV.
SUBSCRIBERS to pay ONE GUINEA as a security for completing their set, for which a receipt will be given by the proprietor. The receipt may be transferred, and the holder entitled to its advantages, according as it stands in the list.

[Page] *(39)*
V.
No proofs will be taken off the plates, the proprietor being determined that the subscribers shall have them in the order they are subscribed for.

VI.
The price to subscribers will be FIFTEEN SHILLINGS each number, and to non-subscribers

ONE GUINEA; to be paid on delivery.

VII.

The first number will be published in MAY 1790; and, if possible, one number the first of each succeeding month, till the work is completed.

VIII.

The names of subscribers will be published.

IX.

A VOLUME OF NOTES, by the *most learned men* of the age, will be published as a SUPPLEMENT. The subscribers will be at liberty to receive or reject this volume, as it may or may not meet their approbation: the price will be announced as soon as possible.

X.

The work will be executed on a TYPE CAST, and a PAPER manufactured, on purpose, and the whole finished in a style of elegance, which from the specimens already exhibited, the best judges have assured the Proprietor is hitherto unparalleled.

———

(40)

☞ *Those who wish to become subscribers are requested to recollect, that the proprietor has given up every advantage arising from proof impressions, consequently early subscribers will be in possession of those prints which would constitute the proofs, and every subscriber indiscriminately sure of fine impressions.*

By the liberal assistance which he is promised from the first artists, and his own determination that no expense or pains shall be wanting, he feels himself emboldened to assure the public, that this Publication will, in every part of it, be the most perfect and magnificent ever yet offered to the public in any country.

He cannot help observing, that it will cost him upwards of THIRTY THOUSAND POUNDS.

———

SUBSCRIPTIONS received by the proprietor, THOMAS MACKLIN, at Poets' Gallery, Fleet-street, and his Gallery of Poets, Pall-mall; Messrs. EDWARDS and SONS, Booksellers, of Pall-mall and Halifax; and Mr. DILLY, Bookseller, in the Poultry: where specimens of the PAPER and TYPE may be seen.

141.

141. *St. John's Vision of the Seven Lights*, 1797
(*Revelations*, 1: 12-17)
(Vol. VI, facing sig. [8H2])
Engraved by James Thomson (1788 or 1789-1850) after Fuseli's lost original
Imprint: London, Published 14th. Jan[y]. 1797, by Tho[s]. Macklin, Poets Gallery, Fleet Street.
Inscription: H. Fuseli R.A. pinx[t]. | | Jo[s]. Thomson sculp[t]. | S[T]. JOHN'S VISION. | Vide Rev[s]. Ch. 1. ve. 12 to 17.
Dimensions: ■ 30.8 x 25.6 cm | 12²/16" x 10³/16"; ■ 31.2 x 26.1 cm | 12¼" x 10⁵/16" (BL 681.K. 1-7)
Other locations: Bodleian Mason BB.173 (no page signatures); DHW; Huntington 112962; Newberry +C223.8; NYPL *YCD++ (not seen)
Plate only: BM 1859-3-12-179; Essick (64/65 plates bound without text)
Lit.: Schiff 931 (30.8 x 25.8 cm); Schiff 1963, 17, 18, pl. 1; Boase 1963, 168, pl. 24e; Hammelmann 1975, 36, 60; *Letters*, 147-150, 160-161

Variants:

I. Proof before all letters: Huntington 49000, 10913

Inscription (scratched letters and open capitals):
Hᵧ Fusile Pinx | | Josʰ Thomson Sculpᵗ | VISION
of Sᵗ. JOHN. REV: CHAP: I
II. Before all letters (lacking chapter and verse):
V & A E.1197-1886
Inscription: H. Fuseli R.A. pinxᵗ. | | Jos.
Thomson sculpᵗ. | Sᵀ. JOHN's VISION.
III. Proof with earlier imprint, lacking title:
KHZ 1931/45
Imprint: Published as the Act directs 1 [*open
space*] 1796 by Thomas Macklin Poets Gallery
Fleet Street.

Fuseli resented the way Macklin had 'gorged'
other painters while unfairly overlooking him. He
only received this commission through the
intervention of William Roscoe, whose friend,
Edward Rogers, was a silent partner in Macklin's
project. Fuseli's alternative subject, the 'three
unclean spirits' that come out of the mouths of the
dragon, the beast, and the false prophet
(*Revelation*, 16: 13), was never executed.

Fuseli also felt slighted because the work was
given to the precocious James Thomson to
engrave rather than to William Bromley as he had
been promised.

✶✶✶✶✶✶

Nos. 142 - 145.
Charles Allen.
A NEW AND IMPROVED | ROMAN HISTORY,
| FROM THE | FOUNDATION OF THE CITY
OF ROME, | TO ITS FINAL | DISSOLUTION AS
THE SEAT OF EMPIRE, | IN THE | YEAR OF
CHRIST 476, | INCLUDING A PERIOD OF
ABOUT 1228 YEARS | FROM ITS |
COMMENCEMENT UNDER ROMULUS. | — |
BY CHARLES ALLEN, A.M. | AUTHOR OF
THE HISTORY OF ENGLAND, &C. | — | THE
SECOND EDITION. | EMBELLISHED WITH
FOUR COPPER PLATES. | = | LONDON: |
PRINTED FOR J. JOHNSON, NO. 72, ST.
PAUL'S | CHURCH-YARD. | — | 1798 (4/4 illus.).

In Robert Essick's copy the four plates are still
on one folded sheet showing a continuous platemark top and bottom, indicating the plates were
all engraved on a single copperplate and printed in
one pull.

In the Huntington copy the two sheets on which
the plates are printed may also originally have
been a single sheet (see Essick 1985, 204).

Mars and Rhea Silvia.

London, Published Decʳ 1, 1797 by J.Johnson, Sᵗ Paul's Church Yard.

142.

142. *Mars and Rhea Silvia*, 1797
(facing p. 2)

Engraved by William Blake (1757-1827)
Imprint: London, Published Decʳ. 1, 1797 by, J.
Johnson, Sᵗ. Paul's Church Yard.
Inscription (top right): P. 2 | (bottom right): Blake:
s. | **Mars and Rhea Silvia**.
Dimensions: ■ 14.3 x 8.1 cm | 5¹⁰/16" x 3³/16"
(BL 9041.aa.3.)
Other locations: Essick (bound as 1/4 facing t.p.);
Huntington 108270 (bound as 1/4 before title
page); LC DG210.A5; Princeton 1426.119
Plate only: DHW; Fitzwilliam P.538.1985; LC
Rosenwald 1838.23 (i); LC Rosenwald 1838.23
(ii); LC Rosenwald 1838.23 (iii) (imprint partially
trimmed)
Lit.: Schiff 932 (14.3 x 8.0 cm); Essick 1991, no.
XXXVII/1

　　Numitor, the last king [*of Rome*] ... was
dethroned by Amulius, his younger brother; and
in order to secure himself in his ill-got power,
the usurper put to death his brother's son,

Ægestus, and deprived his only daughter, Ilia, or Rhea Silvia, of all hopes of having posterity by appointing her one of the vestal virgins; an office, which obliged her to observe a perpetual virginity, or, in case of violating it, to undergo a cruel and ignominous death, no less that of being buried alive. His barbarous policy, however, failed of its effect. Rhea Silvia proved with child, by the god Mars, as she gave out, whom she met, she said, in the sacred grove, as she was going to fetch water for one of the sacred offices of her religion, and who there forced her; though the general opinion was, that it was some young lover of her own, whom she met by appointment; and there were not even wanting some who alledged, that Amulius himself had been guilty of this double crime, of violating a vestal, and deflowering his own niece; a supposition, which his vicious life in other respects rendered the less improbable.

Whoever was the father, certain it is, that in due time Rhea Silvia was delivered of twins, who were afterwards known by the names of Romulus and Remus. Her own life was saved at the intercession of her cousin, the daughter of Amulius; but she was put in chains, and condemned to perpetual imprisonment. As to the infants themselves, they were ordered to be thrown into the Tyber. (pp. 2-3)

143. *The Death of Lucretia*, 1797
(facing p. 33)

Engraved by William Blake (1757-1827)
Imprint: London, Published Dec`r`. 1, 1797, by J. Johnson, S`t`. Paul's Church Yard.
Inscription (top right): P. 33. | (bottom right): Blake: sc | **The Death of Lucretia**.
Dimensions: ■ 15.0 x 8.2 cm | 5`14`/16" x 3¼" (BL 9041.aa.3)
Other locations: Essick (facing p. viii);
Huntington 108270 (bound as 1/2 before t.p.); LC DG210.A5;
Plate only: DHW; Fitzwilliam P.539.1985 (imprint partially trimmed); MMA 40.52.117;
Princeton (Art Museum); LC Rosenwald 1838.23 (i); LC Rosenwald 1838.23 (ii)
Lit.: Schiff 933 (15.0 x 8.2 cm); Essick 1991, no. XXXVII/2
Exh.: Princeton 1969-1970 (58)

The Death of Lucretia.
London, Published Dec`r`. 1, 1797, by J. Johnson, S`t`. Paul's Church Yard.

143.

Lucretia relates to her husband Collatinus, her father Lucretius, her kinsman Valerius (omitted from the illustration), and Junius Brutus, how she was raped by Tarquin:

['] Collatinus, thy bed has been defiled by a stranger; but my body only is polluted; my mind is innocent, as my death shall testify. Promise me only, that you will not suffer the adulterer to go unpunished.' ... They all promised to avenge her cause. ... [*Lucretia replied*]: 'No immodest woman hereafter shall plead Lucretia's example for outliving the loss of her honour.' So saying, she drew a dagger from under her robe, and ... plunged it in her bosom. ... Brutus, without spending time in useless lamentations, drew out the dagger all bloody from Lucretia's wound, and holding it up towards heaven, exclaimed, 'I swear by this blood, ... and I call you, O ye gods, to witness, that I will pursue with fire and sword the tyrant, his wife, and all his guilty race; nor will I ever suffer any king [*in*] future to sway the sceptre in Rome.' He then presented the dagger to the rest of the company and exacted from them the same oath. (pp. 32-33)

144.

his troops to the gates of the city, and entering it sword in hand, threatened immediately to set it on fire if he met with the least opposition. Marius at first endeavoured to oppose him; but finding it impossible to do so effectually, he quitted Rome, and a price being afterwards set upon his head, he was exposed to a variety of adverse fortune. He was obliged to conceal himself in the marshes of Minturnum, where he spent a whole night up to his neck in mud. He was then seized, and conducted to prison, and a Cimbrian slave was sent to dispatch him. But the barbarian had no sooner entered the prison for this purpose, than he was so struck with the awful look of the fallen general, that he threw down his sword, exclaiming, at the same time, that he found himself incapable of executing his orders.

144. *C. Marius at Minturnum*, 1797
(facing p. 174)

Engraved by William Blake (1757-1827)
Imprint: London, Published Dec^r, 1, 1797, by Johnson, S^t. Paul's Church Yard.
Inscription (top right): P. 174 | (bottom right): Blake: sc | **C. Marius at Minturnum**.
Dimensions: ■ 14.5 x 8.4 cm | 5^{11}/16" x 3^5/16" (BL 9041.aa.3)
Other locations: Essick (after p. 158); Huntington 108270 (bound as 3/4 before t.p.); LC DG210.A5
Plate only: DHW; Fitzwilliam P.540.1985 (imprint damaged); Princeton (Art Museum); LC Rosenwald 1838.23 (i);LC Rosenwald 1838.23 (ii)
Lit.: Schiff 934 (14.4 x 8.3 cm); Essick 1991, no. XXXVII/3
Exh.: Princeton 1969-1970 (58)

145.

The people hav[ing] reversed the decree [of the senate appointing Cinna to conduct the war against Mithridates], and transferred the command to Marius ... Cinna ... was so enraged at this affront, that he advanced with

145. *The Death of Cleopatra*, 1797
(facing p. 292)

Engraved by William Blake (1757-1827)
Imprint: London. Published Dec^r, 1, 1797, by J, Johnson, St Paul's Church Yard.

Inscription (top right): P. 292. | (bottom right):
Blake: s|**The Death of Cleopatra.**
Dimensions: ■ 14.7 x 8.2 cm | 5¹³/₁₆" x 3³/₁₆"
(BL 9041.aa.3).
Other locations: Essick (facing p. 159);
Huntington 108270 (bound as 4/4 before t.p.); LC
DG210.A5
Plate only: DHW; Fitzwilliam P.541.1985;
Princeton (Art Museum); LC Rosenwald 1838.23
(i); LC Rosenwald 1838.23 (ii)
Lit.: Schiff 935 (14.6 x 8.1 cm); Essick 1991, no.
XXXVII/4
Exh.: Princeton 1969-1970 (58)

Octavius's desire to parade Cleopatra through
Rome is disappointed. When his men enter the
chamber, they find the queen already dead, and
all 'counter-poisons' and other attempts to revive
her prove futile. The narrator's uncertainty about
the cause of death is not shared by Fuseli, whose
illustration shows the asp still attached to
Cleopatra's breast.

> Of the two women who attended her ... Iris
> lay dead at her mistress's feet, and ...
> Charmion, already staggering, and hardly able
> to support herself, was putting the diadem on
> Cleopatra's head. ... '[*S*]uch a death [*she said*]
> becomes a queen descended from a race of
> glorious ancestors.' On pronouncing these
> words, she fell down and expired. (p. 292)

******

Nos. 146 - 149.
Charles Allen.
A NEW AND IMPROVED|HISTORY OF
ENGLAND,|FROM|THE INVASION OF
JULIUS CAESAR TO THE END OF THE|
THIRTY-SEVENTH YEAR OF THE REIGN|OF
KING GEORGE THE THIRD.|—|BY
CHARLES ALLEN, A.M.|AUTHOR OF THE
ROMAN HISTORY, &C.|—|THE SECOND
EDITION,|EMBELLISHED WITH FOUR
COPPER PLATES, AND A CHRONOLO-|
GICAL CHART OF THE REVOLUTIONS IN
GREAT BRITAIN.|—|CONCLUDING WITH A
SHORT BUT COMPREHENSIVE HISTORICAL
VIEW|OF EUROPE, FROM THE ABOLITION
OF THE MONARCHICAL FORM OF|
GOVERNMENT IN FRANCE; THE MILITARY
AND NAVAL OPERATIONS,|WITH THE
CONQUESTS AND REVOLUTIONS IN ITALY

TO THE|PEACE OF UDINA. THE CHANGES
AND REVOLUTIONS IN THE|POLITICAL
STATE OF THE FRENCH REPUBLIC, AND A
MORE PARTI-|CULAR DETAIL OF THE
BRITISH HISTORY DURING THAT PERIOD.|
=| LONDON:|PRINTED FOR J. JOHNSON,
NO. 72, ST. PAUL'S|CHURCH-YARD. |—|
1798 (4/4 illus.).

Allen's text is essentially an abridgement of
Hume's *History of England*. Indeed, the passages
on which Fuseli based these illustrations appear to
have been lifted almost directly from Hume's text.

Alfred and the Neat-herd's Wife.

London, Published Dec*. 1. 1797 by J.Johnson, S*Paul's Church Yard.

146.

146. *King Alfred Burns the Cakes,* 1797
(facing p. 15)

Engraved by William Blake (1757-1827)
Imprint: London Published Dec*. 1, 1797, by, J.
Johnson, S*. Paul's Church Yard.
Inscription (top right): P. 15; (bottom right):
Blake: s.|**Alfred and the Neat-herd's Wife.**
Dimensions: ■ 14.5 x 8.0 cm | 5¾" x 3²/₁₆"
(Princeton Ex 1426.119)

Other locations: Essick (facing p. 13) (imprint
trimmed)
Plate only: Essick; LC Rosenwald 1838.22
Lit.: Schiff 936 (14.5 x 8.0 cm); Hammelmann
1975, 35; Essick 1991, no. XXXVI/1
Exh.: Princeton 1969 (57); London 1992 (29)

Fuseli here illustrates the famous story of King
Alfred, who after being defeated by the Danish
invaders and abandoned by his troops is forced to

[*lay*] aside all the ensigns of royalty, and
conceal himself in the house of a neat-herd. ...
One day ... the neat-herd's wife, who was
ignorant of his quality, desired him to take care
of some cakes that were toasting ... But
Alfred[*'s*] thoughts were otherwise engaged ...
and the good woman, on her return, finding her
cakes all burnt, rated him very severely, and
said that he seemed always very ready to eat her
warm cakes, though he was thus negligent in
toasting them. (pp. 14-15)

147. *King John Absolved by The Cardinal Pandulph*, 1797
(facing p. 78)

Engraved by William Blake (1757-1828)
Imprint: London, Published Decr. 1. 1797 by, J.
Johnson, S^t. Paul's Church Yard.
Inscription (top right): P. 78. | (bottom right):
Blake: sc | **King John absolved by Pandulph.**
Dimensions: ■ 14.4 x 8.2 cm | 5^{11}/16" x 3¼"
(Princeton Ex 1426.119)
Other locations: Essick; LC Rosenwald 1838.22
Plate only: DHW; Essick
Lit.: Schiff 938 (14.5 x 8.0 cm); Antal 1956, 125,
130, pl. 33a; Essick 1991, no. XXXVI/2
Exh.: Princeton 1969 (57); London 1992 (30)

Fuseli's illustration shows King John,
excommunicated by Pope Innocent, abasing
himself before Pandolf, the pope's legate, and
swearing fealty to the pope.
Antal argues that 'the realistic aspect' of this
scene is largely attributable to Blake's engraving.

King John absolved by Pandulph.

London, Published Dec. 1. 1797 by J. Johnson, St Paul's Church Yard.

147.

Wat Tyler and the Tax-gatherer.

London Published Dec. 1.1797 by J.Johnson , St Paul's Church Yard.

148.

148. *Wat Tyler and the Tax Gatherer*, 1797
(facing p. 128)

Engraved by William Blake (1757-1827)
Imprint: London Published Dec[r]. 1, 1797, by J.
Johnson, S[t]. Paul's Church Yard.
Inscription (top right): P. 128. | (bottom right):
Blake: s. | **Wat Tyler and the Tax-gatherer**.
Dimensions: 14.6 x 8.1 cm | 5¾" x 3³/16"
(Princeton Ex 1426.119)
Other locations: Essick; Fitzwilliam (formerly Sir
Geoffrey Keynes) (cropped inside frame)
Plate only: Essick (imprint cropped); LC
Rosenwald 1838.22 (imprint cropped)
Lit.: Schiff 937 (14.5 x 8.0 cm); Hammelmann
1875, 35; Essick 1991, no. XXXVI/3.
Exh.: Princeton 1969 (57); London 1992 (31)

Fuseli depicts Wat Tyler, one of the leaders of
the Peasants' Revolt, knocking out the brains of
the tax gatherer who molested his daughter while
attempting to collect the poll tax, that Richard
imposed in 1377 in order to fund his wars.

149.

149. *Queen Elizabeth and Essex*, 1797
(facing p. 224)

Engraved by William Blake (1757-1827)
Imprint: London, Published Dec[r]. 1. 1797, by J.
Johnson, S[t]. Paul's Church Yard.
Inscription (top right): P. 224. | (bottom right):
Blake: s. | **Queen Elizabeth and Essex**.
Dimensions: ■ 14.4 x 8.0 cm | 5¾" x 3²/16"
(Princeton Ex 1426.119)
Other locations: Essick
Plate only: DHW; Essick (imprint cropped);
Fitzwilliam P.537.1985 (cropped) (Keynes copy);
LC Rosenwald 1838.22 (imprint partially cropped)
Lit.: Schiff 939 (14.5 x 8.0 cm); Hammelmann
1975, 35; Essick 1991, no. XXXVI/4
Exh.: Princeton 1969 (57); London 1992 (32)

Fuseli here illustrates Elizabeth's favourite, the
earl of Essex, affronting his sovereign by failing
to control his temper.

Being once engaged in a dispute with her ...
he was so heated in the argument, that he
entirely forgot the rules both of duty and
civility; and turned his back upon her in a
contemptuous manner. Her anger, naturally
prompt and violent, rose at this provocation;
and she gave him a box on the ear. ... Instead
of recollecting himself ... he clapped his hand to
his sword, and swore, that he would not bear
such treatment, were it from Henry VIII
himself; and he immediately withdrew from
court.

Egerton, the chancellor ... exhorted him to
repair his indiscretion. ... But Essex was deeply
stung with the dishonour he had received; and
seemed to think, that an insult, which might be
pardoned in a woman, was ... a mortal affront
when it came from his sovereign. (p.224)

******

150. *The Nurse*, 1798

Engraved proof in stipple and line by Moses
Haughton (1772 or 1774-1848) after Fuseli's pen
and wash drawing in the Liverpool City Libraries
(1798; Schiff 1040)
Inscription: H. Fuseli R.A. inv[t]. | | M. Haughton
fecit 1798

Dimensions: ■ 27.5 x 21.0 cm | 10¹³/16" x 8¼"
(Hornby Library, Liverpool City Libraries)
Lit.: Schiff 1039 (23.8 x 17.8 cm), 1040; Schiff
1963, 22, pl. 3; *Letters*, 178, 179, 182, 187,
189f., 191, 192.

150.

This illustration was intended to illustrate
William Roscoe's translation of Luigi Tansillo's
poem in praise of mothers' breastfeeding their
children, but was not used in the published work
(*The Nurse*, 1798) since Fuseli felt that Moses
Haughton's engraving 'travestied his figures'

(4 January 1799), which required 'more of the
graver than of the Needle' (31 August 1798).
Haughton's proof had been 'done with more
freedom than taste, and with more assurance than
penetration or *Amore*'; 'the Anubis' (No. **115**)
would provide 'a Clue' for a young engraver (17
August 1798), for whom 'Freedom' must be 'the
result of diligence' (4 January 1799). Yet when
Haughton moved to London, he soon established a
close personal and professional relationship with
Fuseli, who now praised him for 'the most
Valuable [*qualifications*] in an Engraver, fidelity,
diligence and taste' (20 August 1802). In 1803, as
part of the two men's agreement jointly to publish
Fuseli's prints, Haughton became Fuseli's resident
engraver and subsequently accompanied the new
Keeper to the Royal Academy, where he remained
with him in the same capacity until 1819.

The original composition shows the mother
dandling an infant on her knee, while a second
infant stands besides her and seems to want to
clamber up into her lap. In the engraving, the
standing infant is omitted, and the other is now
shown supported in a lying rather than a sitting
position, suckling at his mother's breast.

151. *William Tell Shooting Gessler*, 1798

Soft ground etching by Fuseli after his pen and
ink drawing in the Reinhart Collection, Winterthur
(1798; Schiff 1001)
Inscription (bottom right in the plate, reversed):
Jan. 1. 1798
Dimensions: 19.6 x 27.0 cm | 7¹¹/16" x 10¹⁰/16"
(BM 1856-12-13-143)
Lit.: Schiff 982 (19.6 x 27.0 cm)

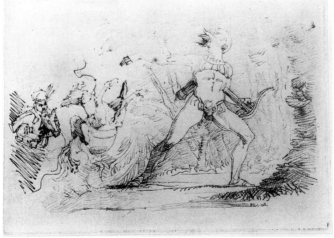

151.

152.

152. *Naked Man Carrying a Clothed Woman on his Shoulder Up a Rocky Slope*, [1796-1800]
(John Milton, *Paradise Lost*, XI, 742-756)

Etching on pale brown paper by Henry Fuseli after his drawing in the Reinhart Collection, Winterthur ([1796-1800]; Schiff 1026)
Dimensions: 24.1 x 16.7 | 9½" x 6⁹/16" (BM 1863-5-9-5)
Lit.: Schiff 983 (24.1 x 16.7 cm), 1026

This is a reversed version of an unused preliminary study for Fuseli's lost painting, *The Vision of the Deluge*, No. XXV of the Milton Gallery, preserved in the form of the outline engraving by Normand fils (see Nos. **301** and **301A**). A second version of the painting (Schiff 901) with various divergences in composition from the engraving is in the Kunstmuseum, Winterthur.

The *Vision of the Deluge* depicts the first of the series of dreadful images of death and suffering shown to Adam by the Archangel Michael, that await Adam and Eve in the fallen world as a result of their eating of the fruit of the Forbidden Tree. This engraved detail shows a couple attempting to escape the rising waters of the flood that will overwhelm most of mankind.

******

No. 153.
Alexander Pope.
THE | RAPE OF THE LOCK, | AN | HEROI-COMICAL POEM, | BY | A. POPE. | = | ADORNED WITH PLATES. | = | LONDON: | PRINTED BY T. BENSLEY | FOR F.J. DU ROVERAY, GREAT ST. HELENS; | AND SOLD BY J. AND A. ARCH, GRACECHURCH- | STREET; AND J. WRIGHT, PICCADILLY. | — | 1798 (1/5 illus. + frontis.)

...LONDON: | PRINTED BY W. BULMER AND CO. | FOR F.J. DU ROVERAY [*i.e. J. Wright*], GREAT ST. HELENS; | AND SOLD BY J. WRIGHT, PICCADILLY. | 1801.

For the re-engraving of 1809 see No. **153A** below.

The Rape of the Lock was the second of the nine titles published by Francis Isaac Du Roveray (1772-1849) between 1796 and 1806 (see Du Roveray I-IV), of which Fuseli provided designs for seven. There were no illustrations after Fuseli in either the first book in the series, Glover's *Leonidas* (1798), or the fourth, Goldsmith's *Poems* (1800). Although dated 1798 on the title page, the *Rape* was not actually published until January 1799 (see *Monthly Epitome and Catalogue of New Publications*, III, 34). Cadell & Davies considered this edition 'a very admirable Proof of what may be done on a small Scale, from a Picture of Mr. Fuseli's' (*Letters* 1982, 191).

On 16 December 1798, Du Roveray informed Farington that he had 500 subscribers and could thus count on clearing his expenses (III, 1113). 950 copies of the work were printed (probably 750 small, 200 large), of which he had disposed of 650 by the 4th March 1799 (J. Neagle, Philadelphia Free P.L.) Ordinary copies in boards were 10s.6d. each; for those in the trade, the 'Subscription price' was 8s.0d., on which FID was prepared to grant '6 Months credit'. The large-paper copies, 'with Proof Impressions of the

Plates' sold for one guinea. A set of proofs was 4s.6d. (to Thomas Palser, 28 November 1809). The total cost of the edition (including payments to artists and engravers) was probably about £340 (G.E. Bentley's estimate of £352+ was for 1250? copies; Du Roveray II, 79). A small number of copies were printed on vellum.

Du Roveray afterwards sold the rights in the *Rape* and Gray's *Poems* (1800), together with the copper-plates, to John Wright, who in 1801 took the 'unwarrantable liberty' of publishing new editions of these under Du Roveray's imprint without his authorisation. Du Roveray complained that the copies were not only 'passed off as [*his*] editions, and sold at reduced prices' but were printed 'on inferior paper, and with the Plates completely worn out' (Du Roveray II, 74-77).

Du Roveray first approached Fuseli on 1 March 1798 to request a drawing in water colours approximately the same size as the intended plate. By 4 April Fuseli had negotiated an increase in size to '24 inches or upwards, upright, with a proportionate width' at a price of thirty guineas (rather than the ten guineas Du Roveray had at first reckoned upon). The medium agreed on was 'Oil colour on *Strained paper*, as uniting with all the advantages of Watercolours those of warmth and durability' (31 March 1798). The picture was finished and ready for inspection by May 5th (to Du Roveray, unpublished, collection DHW). The six designs for the illustrations were 'already in the hands of the different engravers' before Du Roveray requested Dr. John Aikin, 23 June 1798 (Bodleian, Montagu.d.11) to write a prefatory essay to the edition. (When Aikin declined, Du Roveray wrote it himself but submitted it before publication to Fuseli's opinion.)

The following is the earliest of Du Roveray's prospectuses found to date; it is bound in at the end of one of DHW's copies of *Leonidas*.

PROSPECTUS
(D.H. Weinglass)

PROPOSALS
FOR
A NEW AND ELEGANT EDITION
OF
POPE'S
RAPE OF THE LOCK.
=

To be printed by T. BENSLEY in the same form

as LEONIDAS, but with some improvements; and adorned with a Plate of a similar size to each Canto, besides a Frontispiece; making together Six Engravings, two of which Mr. BARTOLOZZI has kindly undertaken to do in the same finished manner as the "Parting of Leonidas and his Wife;" the others will be executed by Messrs. HOLLOWAY, BROMLEY, A. SMITH, and NEAGLE; the whole will be from Pictures and Drawings by Messrs. FUSELI, HAMILTON, STOTHARD, and BURNEY.

Price TEN SHILLINGS AND SIX PENCE to Subscribers, and ONE GUINEA for a few copies, which will be taken off on Royal Octavo, with Proof Impressions of the Plates.

The Books will be delivered in the order they are subscribed for, which will secure the best Impressions of the Plates to the earliest patronizers of the work.

Subscribers [*sic*] names will be received by addressing a line to F.J. DU ROVERAY, No. 14, Great St. Helens, and for him by J. and A. ARCH, Gracechurch Street; and J. WRIGHT, Piccadilly; but no money will be required till the work is published.

Description of the Subjects for the Plates.

	Painters.	Engravers.
Frontispiece, from the following lines of Parnell, alluding to the Poem, "The Graces stand in sight; a satyr train "Peeps o'er their head, and laughs behind the scene."	HAMILTON	BARTOLOZZI.
Belinda at her toilet...Canto I.	BURNEY.	BARTOLOZZI.
Belinda sailing down the Thames with the Sylphs playing about the vessel, ... Canto II.	STOTHARD.	A. SMITH.
The Baron cutting off Belinda's Lock, ... Canto III.	STOTHARD.	NEAGLE.
The Cave of Spleen, with Umbriel receiving from the Goddess the Bag and Vial ... Canto IV.	FUSELI.	HOLLOWAY.
The Fight ... Canto V.	STOTHARD.	BROMLEY.

=

Whilst so many inferior productions of our literature have been published with all the decorations of fine printing and elegant engravings, to many it will doubtless appear

strange that equal honours should not have been bestowed on that most attractive and excellent of all comi-heroick poems, the "RAPE OF THE LOCK." Perhaps a reason for it may be found in the intrinsic, and universally acknowledged, merit of the work, which needs not the aid of any borrowed ornament to set it off: yet, since decorations of the most expensive kind have been lavished on other works of equal celebrity, no apology will, it is presumed, be thought necessary for the present edition of one so well adapted to display the progress made by this Country in the Arts of Painting and Engraving. The names of the Artists employed to embellish it will sufficiently evince that no expense has been spared to render the external appearance of the work equal to its intrinsic merit. To promise more would be to promise what could not be performed. The Editor has only, therefore, to add that it will be published with all the dispatch consistent with a due attention to the finishing of the Plates.
JULY 1798.

The gnome rejoicing bears her gifts away.
Spreads his black wings, and slowly mounts to day.

153.

153. *The Cave of Spleen, with Umbriel Receiving from the Goddess the Bag and Vial*, 1798
(Canto IV, 79-88)
(facing p. 41)

Engraved by Thomas Holloway (1748-1827) after Fuseli's lost 'Oil colour on Strained paper' exhibited at the Royal Academy (1799/157)
Imprint: Publish'd 1ˢᵗ. Novʳ. 1798. by F.I. Du Roveray. London.
Inscription (top right): Canto. IV. | (bottom): Hʸ. Fuseli R.A. pinxit. | | Thoˢ. Holloway sculpᵗ. |

The gnome rejoicing bears her gifts away,
Spreads his black wings, and slowly mounts to day.

Dimensions: ■ 10.4 x 7.8 cm | 4¹/16" x 3¹/16"; ■ 10.8 x 8.2 cm | 4¼" x 3¼" (BL 1163.b.40)
Other locations: BL 11632.bb.36 (1801); Bodleian Vet.A6.e.512 (1801) (not seen); Bodleian 2799.e.585 (1801) (facing p. 46); Cambridge 7720.d.266; DHW (1801) (facing p. 46); Library Company O Eng Pope Rape 1798; Library Company O Eng Pope Rape 1801; NYPL NCL 1798; NYPL NCL (1801); ZBZ BB 1559 (1801)
Lit.: Schiff 945 (10.8 x 8.2 cm); Hammelmann 1975, 35; Halsband 1980, 44-53, pl. 23; *Letters*, 180-185, 193-194; Du Roveray I, 1-19; II, 72-79; III, 137-139, pl. 15; IV, 168.
Exh.: Kansas City 1982 (53).

Variants:
I. Proof before letters (India paper): BM 1853-12-10-563
Other locations: Huntington 133026 (between pp. [40-41])
II. Proof before all letters (lacking Canto number and verse): LC PR3629.A1 1798
Other locations: DHW (H=23.9 cm); DHW (H=24.8 cm); Dörrbecker; Essick (H=22.8 cm); Huntington 133026; Newberry Y185.P8373

Of Fuseli's three illustrations to Pope, two are taken from *The Rape of the Lock*, the only work, Fuseli maintained, in which Pope ever showed true poetic genius: 'A poet is an inventor; and what has Pope invented except the Sylphs?' (Knowles I, 359). The subject was specifically chosen by Du Roveray; the title is also his.
Fuseli's design shows listless, discontented Spleen throned on her 'pensive bed,' surrounded

by her various handmaids: Pain, with drawn features, cowled like a nun; Megrim, supporting her aching head in her hands; Ill-Nature, dressed 'like an ancient Maid,' showing only her back and reading her prayer book, is based on a drawing of Mrs. Fuseli reading the newspaper, 1791, Schiff 1095); Affectation, at Spleen's left hand, 'languishes with Pride,' holding her fan and fondling her lap-dog. The 'unnumber'd throngs' of transformed bodies, include a 'Snake on rolling spires,' a talking 'Goose-pye,' and a living teapot. Winged Umbriel is reminiscent more of the angel with the flaming sword in *The Expulsion from Paradise* (**No. 170**) than of the supposedly 'dusky melancholy Spright'. He carries in one hand a bag swollen with 'Sighs, Sobs, and Passions, and the War of Tongues', in the other, the vial full of 'fainting Fears, | Soft Sorrows, melting Griefs, and flowing Tears.'

******

No. 153A.
[Unidentified edition.]
Alexander Pope.
[THE RAPE OF THE LOCK.]

153A. *The Cave of Spleen*, 1809
(Alexander Pope, *The Rape of the Lock*, IV, 79-88)

Re-engraved in reduced format by William Bromley (1769-1842)
Imprint: London: Published by W. Suttaby, Nov 1 1809.
Inscription: Painted by H. Fuseli, RA. | | Engraved by W. Bromley. |

> Here in a grotto, shelter'd close from air,
> And screen'd in shades from day's detested glare,
> She sighs for ever on her pensive bed,
> Pain at her side, and Megrim at her head.
> Rape of the Lock. page 14.

Dimensions: ■ 8.3 x 5.4 cm | 3¼" x 2²/16"; ■ 8.6 x 5.6 cm | 3⁶/16" x 2¼" (V & A 1212-1886)

Variants:
I. Proof before letters (India paper): BM 1853-12-10-567

******

154.

154. *Chrysogone Conceives in a Ray of Sunshine Amoretta and Belphoebe*, [1800-1810]
(Edmund Spenser, *The Faerie Queene*, III, vi,)

Etching by Henry Fuseli
Inscription (bottom right, in the plate): [Greek: illegible]; (in pencil): Nature Germinating
Dimensions (to platemark): 19.8 x 27.1 cm | 7^{13}/16" x 10^{11}/16" (BM 1878-5-11-1229)
Other locations: MMA 55.565.122 (sheet= 22.8 x 30 cm); McGill Blake 5.2 F8C57 18ooz
Lit.: Schiff 1347 (19.6 x 27.0 cm)

Chrysogone, the virgin mother of Amoretta and Belphoebe, was the daughter of Amphisa, of the race of Fairy Land. While resting naked after bathing in a fountain ('far from all men's view'), she was miraculously made pregnant by the rays of 'Titan' (*sic*), the Sun God. Although she had no reason to reproach herself, she fled in shame into the depths of the forest, where she gave birth in her sleep to twin daughters. 'Unawares she them conceived, unawares she bore | ... withouten paine, that she conceived | Withouten pleasure'. Still asleep, she was found with her babies by Venus (who was searching for runaway Cupid) and Diana. Without awaking the mother, each goddess took away one of the babies to rear, thus separating the sisters: Amoret would be raised by Venus, Belphoebe by Diana.

Naked Chrysogone lies in a half-reclining position, in the attitude of Leda. The nude figure of the Sun God hovers before her, clasping a bow, one of his traditional attributes, sunbeams radiating towards her body. The illustration thus represents simultaneously the act of impregnation and the birth of the twins: one of the newborns is visible on Chrysogone's stomach, the other on the ground between her legs.

※※※※※

Nos. 155 - 157.
Thomas Gray.
THE | POEMS | OF | GRAY. | A NEW EDITION. | = | ADORNED WITH PLATES. | = | LONDON: | PRINTED BY T. BENSLEY, | BOLT COURT, FLEET STREET, | FOR F.J. DU ROVERAY, GREAT ST. HELENS; | AND SOLD BY J. WRIGHT, PICCADILLY; | AND T. HURST, PATERNOSTER-ROW. | — | 1800 (3/6 illus. + portr. frontis.).

...LONDON: | = | PRINTED BY W. BULMER AND CO. | FOR F.J. DU ROVERAY [*i.e. J. Wright*], GREAT ST. HELENS; | AND SOLD BY J. WRIGHT, PICCADILLY. | 1801.

For the re-engraving of 1821 see No. **155A** below.

ADVERTISEMENT
(Essick)

[...] *speedily will be published,*
A NEW EDITION | OF | GRAY'S POEMS, | UNIFORM WITH THE [*RAPE OF THE LOCK*], | And adorned with SIX PLATES, to be engraved by the | First Artists, | From Pictures and Drawings by H. FUSELI, R.A. | and W. HAMILTON, R.A. |
After stating his belief that the RAPE OF THE LOCK is entirely free from typographical errors, the Editor thinks he may venture to promise that his Edition of GRAY shall be found equally correct.

PRINTED NOTICE IN 'GOLDSMITH'S POEMS'
(D.H. Weinglass)

GRAY'S POEMS,
Complete, from the Text of Mr. Mason's Edition,
With 6 Plates; Price 10s.6d. Boards.
N.B. A few copies ... remain, printed on large Paper, and containing Proof Impressions of the Plates; Price 1£.1s. in Boards.

Bentley estimates the total cost of the edition, comprising 1000 small and 250 large copies (including payments to artists and engravers) to be £495.19s. (Du Roveray II, 69, 79). Three copies, priced at £8.8s. each, were printed on vellum (Du Roveray II, 72-73). These have been praised by Thomas Lange for their 'magical luminescence' (*Huntington Library Quarterly*, 54, 1991, 88). John Wright, who had earlier published a new edition of the *Rape* under Du Roveray's imprint without his authorisation (Du Roveray II, 74-77), did the same in 1801 with Gray's *Poems*.

Thomas Holloway, who had played such a large role in the publication of the English edition of Lavater's *Essays on Physiognomy*, not only enthusiastically agreed to engrave *The Bard* and *The Descent of Odin* for Du Roveray (February 1799), but also offered to take 15 to 20 copies of *Gray's Poems* to sell, suggesting such activities were more than a casual sideline for him.

Fuseli had looked over Du Roveray's preface to the *Rape* before publication; for the *Poems of Gray*, Du Roveray prevailed upon him to contribute some remarks on the poems that Gray had imitated from Welsh poetry and from the nordic epic, the *Edda* (printed pp. xviii, xxiii-xxv; MS. in the Archives of the History of Art of the Getty Center for the History of Art and the Humanities). Another unpublished letter of 19 February [i.e., October] 1799 indicates how seriously Fuseli took this task, albeit he referred to the illustrations as 'trifles' (to Roscoe, 2 April 1800).

But there were also disagreements: Du Roveray appears to have blamed Fuseli for some of the delays in completing the engravings. Fuseli's response reflects a widely-held view of the engraver's role as being that of a mere artisan:

if the Engravers do their duty [—] Considering the Comparative facility of their task which has nothing of the precariousness of the Painter[']s, who is often obliged to wait for happy moments [—] if he deserve to be employed at all, the Etchings might even now be finished.

155.

155. *The Last Bard Cursing Edward I*, 1800
(Pts. I, 2 - I, 3)
(Facing p. 29)

Engraved by Thomas Holloway (1748-1827) after the lost painting exhibited at the Royal Academy (1800/48); a preliminary pen and ink drawing is now in the Reinhart collection, Winterthur ([1799]; Schiff 1037)
Imprint: Published 1st. January 1800. by F.J. Du Roveray. London.
Inscription (top right): Page 29. | (bottom): H^y. Fuseli R.A. pinx^t. | | Thos. Holloway sculp^t. |

With me in dreadful harmony they join,
And weave with bloody hands the tissue of thy line

The Bard.

Dimensions: ■ 10.3 x 7.8 cm | 4^1/16" x 3^1/16"; ■ 10.6 x 8.1 cm | 4^3/16" x 3^3/16" (Bodleian 2799.E.300)
Other locations: BL 11633.c.25 (1801); Bodleian 2799.e.446 (1801) (facing p. 33); DHW; DHW; Essick; Essick (1801); LC PR3500.A2 1801 (facing p. 33); Princeton Ex 3761.1800.2; Princeton 3761.1.1801; ZBZ AX939 (1801)
Lacking plate: Library Company O Eng Gray Poems 1800
Lit.: Schiff 1313 (10.6 x 8.1 cm), 1037; F.I. McCarthy, '*The Bard* ... and its Use by Painters', *National Library of Wales Journal*, XIV, Summer 1965, 1, 105-113; Hammelmann 1975,36; *Letters*, 194, 210; Du Roveray III, 139-140, pl. 16.

Variants:
I. Proof before all letters (signatures only): V & A E.1206-C-86
Inscription (scratched letters): H Fuseli RA Pinx^t. | | T Holloway Sculp
II. Proof before all letters (lacking verse): BL C.43.d.27 (H=25.6 cm)
Other locations: DHW (H=24.2 cm); Dörrbecker (H=24.2 cm); Essick (H=24.5 cm); Huntington 108770 (H=24.4 cm) (between pp. 28-29); Newberry Y185.G798
Plate only: BM 1849-5-12-247 (Sheet=24.8 cm)
III. Printed on vellum: Huntington 491714

William Cowper praised Gray as 'the only poet since Shakespeare entitled to the character of sublime'; other contemporaries also saw *The Bard* as the epitome of the sublime. According to F.I. McCarthy (1965), the poem 'highlights the importance of primitivist attitudes to poetry in the 1750s [*which elevated*] the ... Welsh Bard [*into*] the champion of liberty and independence' (105).

Fuseli's treatment of the Bard cursing Edward I for the suffering and misery he has brought on the Welsh, marks the introduction of the motif of the 'superhuman bard' into English art (111).

Fuseli's remarks, incorporated in Du Roveray's preface, will later be repeated almost verbatim in his twelfth Lecture (Knowles, III, 34).

It is ... somewhat strange that, in characterising the figure of his Bard, Mr. Gray should have had, as he tells us, an eye to Raphael's design of the Supreme Being in the vision of Ezekiel; whilst he informed Mr. Mason that the figure of Moses breaking the tables of the law by Parmegiano 'came still nearer to his meaning'; figures than whom, no two more dissimilar to each other in conception, can be found in the whole series of Painting: the figure of Raphael, rather dignified and calm than sublime, is wrapt in contemplation: that of Parmegiano has more of passion than of energy, and loses the legislator in the savage.

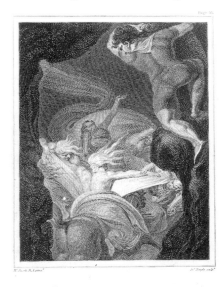

Mortal, thou that hear'st the tale,
Learn the tenor of our song.

The Fatal Sisters.

156.

156. *The Fatal Sisters*, 1800
(ll. 57-58)
(Facing p. 53)

Engraved by James Neagle (1760?-1822) after the

lost original exhibited at the Royal Academy (1800/172)
Imprint: Published 1ˢᵗ. January 1800. by F.I. Du Roveray London.
Inscription (top right): Page 53. | (bottom): Hʸ. Fuseli R.A. pinxᵗ. | | Jaˢ. Neagle sculpᵗ. |

Mortal, thou that hear'st the tale,
Learn the tenor of our song.
The Fatal Sisters.

Dimensions: ■ 10.1 x 7.6 cm | 4" x 3";
■ 10.6 x 8.1 cm | 4³/16" x 3³/16" (Bodleian 2799.E.300)
Other locations: BL 11633.c.25 (1801); Bodleian 2799.e.446 (1801) (facing p. 57); DHW; DHW; Essick; Essick (1801); LC PR3500.A2 1801 (facing p. 57); Library Company O Eng Gray Poems 1800; Princeton Ex 3761.1.1800.2; Princeton 3761.1.1801ZBZ AX 939 (1801)
Lit.: Schiff 1312 (10.6 x 8.1 cm); Hammelmann 1975, 36; *Letters*, 209-210;
Exh.: Kansas City 1982 (57).

Variants:
I. Proof before all letters (signatures only): Huntington 108770 (H=24.4 cm)
Inscription (scratched letters): H. Fuseli RA Pinxt. | | J. Neagle Scᵗ.
Other locations: Essick (H=24.5 cm); Huntington 108770 (H=24.4 cm) (between pp. 52-53)
Plate only: BM 1863-5-9-20 (Sheet=22.7 cm); DHW
II. Proof before verse: BL C.43.d.27 (H=25.6 cm) (facing p. 57)
Other locations: DHW (H=24.2 cm); Dörrbecker (H=24.2cm); Newberry Y185.G798
III. Printed on vellum: Huntington 491714

Fuseli's illustration shows the 'native of Caithness' observing the Valkyries or 'Choosers of the Slain' at their loom, selecting the heroes, destined for Valhalla, who will fall in the battle of Clontarf (A.D. 1014). As Fuseli notes, the poem furnishes 'a striking instance of the unequal power of images addressed to the ear, and to the eye.' If imitated by painting, the 'grisly texture' woven of human entrails would have inspired equal loathing for the artist and for the work (xxiv).

For Fuseli's own translation of the *Edda* of Saemundus, see *The Analytical Review* II (Nov.-Dec. 1788), 337-344, 461-471.

157.

157. *The Descent of Odin*, 1800
(ll. 75-76)
(Facing p. 59)

Engraved by Thomas Holloway (1748-1827) after
the drawing exhibited at the Royal Academy
(1800/85), now in the Oeffentliche
Kunstsammlung, Basel ([1799]; Schiff 1416)
Imprint: Published 1st. January 1800. by F.J. Du
Roveray, London.
Inscription (top right): Page 59. | (bottom): H^y.
Fuseli R.A. pinx^t. | Thos. Holloway sculp^t. |

> What virgins these, in speechless woe,
> That bend to earth their solemn brow?
> Descent of Odin.

Dimensions: ■ 10.5 x 8.0 cm | 4^2/16" x 3^2/16";
■ 10.7 x 8.2 cm | 4^3/16" x 3^3/16" (Bodleian
2799.E.300)
Other locations: BL 11633.c.25 (1801); Bodleian
2799.e.446 (1801) (facing p. 64); DHW; DHW;
Essick; Essick (1801); LC PR3500.A2 1801
(facing p. 64); Library Company O Eng Gray
Poems 1800; Princeton Ex 3761.1.1800.2;
Princeton 3761.1.1801; ZBZ AX 939 (1801)
Plate only: V & A E.1206-A-1886
Lit.: Schiff 1314 (10.2 x 8.2 cm); Hammelmann
1975, 36

Variants:
I. Proof before all letters (signatures only):
Huntington 108770 (H=24.4 cm)
Inscription (scratched letters): H Fuseli RA
Pinx^t. | | T. Holloway Sculp
II. Proof before all letters (lacking verse): BL
C.43.d.27 (H=25.6 cm)
Other locations: Dörrbecker (H=24.2 cm);
Essick (H=24.5 cm); Huntington 108770
(H=24.4 cm) (between pp. 58-59); Newberry
Y185.G798 (facing p. 64)
Plate only: BM 1849-5-12-246 (Sheet=24.4 cm)
III. Printed on vellum: Huntington 491714

Odin is depicted seated at the entrance to the
underworld, to which he has descended in order to
learn the fate of his son, Balder. He is pointing to
the vision of Balder being mourned by the Norns.
The evil deity, Lok, had placed a bough of
mistletoe in the hand of blind Hoder and directed
his arm so that it struck and killed Balder. (When
she exacted an oath from all other things that they
would not harm her son, Frigga had overlooked
the mistletoe.)

Fuseli notes that the *Descent of Odin* owes some
of its sublimity 'to its being a fragment', Gray
having omitted the five introductory stanzas
containing the 'debates of the celestial synod on
the impending fate of Balder':

> The abruptness with which [*Gray*] hurries into
> the midst of his subject, forcibly seizes the
> reader, and ensures restless curiosity; he has
> not, however, always reached the mysterious
> grandeur of the original tale, and, by his metre,
> sometimes counteracts the awful simplicity of its
> language.

The hands emerging from the earth are a
favourite motif of Fuseli's (see Nos. **114** and
256).

✶✶✶✶✶✶

No. 155A.
Thomas Gray.
THE | POETICAL WORKS | OF | THOMAS
GRAY, | WITH | AN ACCOUNT | OF | THE LIFE
AND WRITINGS | OF | THE AUTHOR. | — |
LONDON: | PRINTED FOR SUTTABY,
EVANCE, AND FOX, | STATIONERS'-COURT;
| AND BALDWIN, CRADOCK, AND JOY, |
PATERNOSTER-ROW. | — | 1821 (1/1 illus.).

155A. *The Bard*, 1821
(facing title page)

Frontispiece re-engraved in smaller format by
Charles Fox (1794-1849).
Imprint: Published by Suttaby. Evance & Fox.
July 2. 1821.
Inscription: Fuseli del.||Fox. sculp.|GRAY.|

> Ruin Seize thee, ruthless King!
> Confusion on thy banners wait.
> The Bard. Page, 42.

Dimensions: ■ 7.2 x 5.5 cm | 2¹⁴/₁₆" x 2³/₁₆";
■ 7.6 x 5.9 cm | 3" x 2⁵/₁₆" (BL 11658.de.4)
Other locations: Bodleian 2799.g.31
Plate only: BM 1866-11-10-1268

Variant:

I. Proof (India paper) (facing p. 32):
Huntington 108770

******

No. 158 - 160.
Vincent Xavier Boiste.
L'UNIVERS,|POÈME EN PROSE,|EN DOUZE
CHANTS;|SUIVI|DE NOTES ET
D'OBSERVATIONS|SUR LE SYSTÈME DE
NEWTON|ET LA THÉORIE PHYSIQUE DE
LA TERRE.|ORNÉ DE FIGURES|D'APRÈS
RAPHAEL, LE POUSSIN, FUESLY, LE
BARBIER;|AVEC VIGNETTES D'APRÈS
MONNET ET LEJEUNE.|*Pictoribus atque*
poetis|*Quidlibet audendi semper fuit aequa*
potestas.|*HORAT.*|—| À PARIS,|CHEZ|
BOISTE, IMPRIMEUR, RUE HAUTE-
FEUILLE, Nᵒ. 21.|AGASSE, IMPRIMEUR-
LIBRAIRE, RUE DES POITE-|VINS, Nᵒ. 18.|
DETERVILLE, LIBRAIRE, RUE DU
BATTOIR, Nᵒ. 16.|AN IX (1801) (3/6 illus. +
vign.).

L'UNIVERS,|NARRATION EPIQUE;|SUIVIE
DE NOTES ET D'OBSERVATIONS|SUR LE
SYSTÈME DE NEWTON|ET LA THÉORIE
PHYSIQUE DE LA TERRE, ETC.|PAR P.C.V.
BOISTE,|AUTEUR DU DICTIONNAIRE DE
LA LANGUE FRANÇOISE AVEC LE LATIN.|
DEUXIÈME EDITION.|AVEC FIGURES.|—|
L'Univers est une pensée de l'Eternel.|—|TOME
PREMIER.[-TOME SECONDE.]|—| À PARIS,|
DE L'IMPRIMERIE DE L'AUTEUR,|RUE
HAUTEFEUILLE, Nᵒ. 21.|—|AN XII. 1804.

158.

158. *Head of Satan*, 1801
(Facing titlepage)

Pastiche, perhaps by Charles Monnet or Nicolas
Lejeune, in the form of an unsigned vignette
below illustration after Raphael
Dimensions: 2.2 x 6.5 cm | 1¼" x 2½" (BL
11482.g.11)
Other locations: Bodleian 8° A.313.BS; LC
PQ2198.B33U5 1801; LC PQ2198.B33U5 1804;
MMA 65.562.4; ZBZ WC 350

159.

**159. *Allegory of Superstition (La Sybille, ou*
Apparition), 1801**
(Chant VIII)
(Facing p. 214)

Engraved pastiche by an anonymous engraver
after Fuseli's Lavater illustration ([1779], 1791;
Schiff 774, 957)
Inscription: H. Fuessli inv.
Dimensions (excluding vignette): ■ 7.8 x 12.5 cm|
3¹/₁₆" x 4¹⁴/₁₆" (BL 11482.g.11)
Other locations: Bodleian 8° A.313.BS; LC
PQ2198.B33U5 1801; LC PQ2198.B33U5 1804
(Vol.II, facing p. 72); MMA 65.562.4; ZBZ WC
350
Plate only: BM 1863-5-9-33
Lit.: Schiff 1344 (11.4 x 14.3 cm)

Fuseli's illustration of the witch of Endor (nos. **48, 94**) has here been deftly converted into an Allegory of Superstition. A fainting young woman supported in the arms of blindfolded Ignorance, summons up her dead lover through the medium of a sybilline figure of 'a woman raddled by Time and Remorse ... now a minister of Fate, who was once Priestess of Venus' (p. 214).

160.

160. *Tubal Contemplating the Corpse of his Brother, Adul, whom he has Murdered* (*Meurtre*), 1801
(Chant X)
(Facing p. 270)

Engraved pastiche by an anonymous engraver after Fuseli's two Lavater illustrations (1779, 1791; Schiff 770, 953; 781, 965)
Inscription: H. Fuessli inv.
Dimensions: ■ 8.0 x 12.5 cm | 3²/16" x 4¹⁵/16" (BL 11482.g.11)
Other locations: Bodleian 8° A.313.BS; LC PQ2198.B33U5 1801; LC PQ2198.B33U5 1804 (Vol. I, facing p. 338); MMA 65.562.4; ZBZ WC 350 (facing p. 264)
Lit.: Schiff 1345 (8.0 x 12.4 cm)

This pastiche of Fuseli's *Death of Abel* shows Tubal stricken with remorse after murdering his brother Adul out of jealousy and desire for Adul's wife, Zulma.

✶✶✶✶✶

Nos. 161 - 162.
Henry Fuseli.
LECTURES|ON|PAINTING,|DELIVERED AT THE ROYAL ACADEMY|MARCH 1801,|BY HENRY FUSELI, P.P.|WITH ADDITIONAL OBSERVATIONS AND NOTES.|[Vignette]|

LONDON:|PRINTED FOR J. JOHNSON, ST. PAUL'S CHURCH-YARD.|1801.|—|LUKE HANSARD, PRINTER, NEAR LINCOLN'S-INN FIELDS (2/2 illus.).

For the re-engravings of 1820 see **161A - 162A** below.

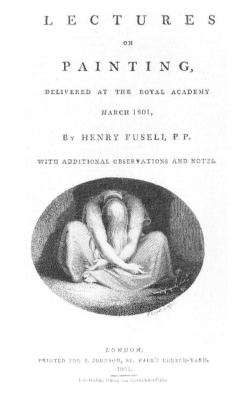

161.

LECTURES
ON
PAINTING,
DELIVERED AT THE ROYAL ACADEMY
MARCH 1801,
BY HENRY FUSELI, P.P.
WITH ADDITIONAL OBSERVATIONS AND NOTES.

LONDON:
PRINTED FOR J. JOHNSON, ST. PAUL'S CHURCH-YARD.
1801.
Luke Hansard, Printer, near Lincoln's-Inn Fields

161. *Silence*, 1801
(title page)

Oval vignette engraved by Francis Legat (1750-1809) after Fuseli's painting formerly in the Ganz collection, Oberhofen, and now in the Kunsthaus, Zurich ([1799-1801]; Schiff 908).
Inscription (in the composition, left): ΣΙΓΑ| (bottom right): F. Legat sculp‘.
Dimensions: ■ 7.5 x 9.0 cm | 3" x 3½" (BL 59.b.11) (H=27.5 cm)
Other locations: Bodleian 170.n.184; Cambridge Nn.24.7; DHW (H=29.0 cm); ETH A.146; Essick; Huntington 292894; Illinois x750.4.f9861; Library Company Is Fues 903.2; NYPL MC 1801; Pierpont Morgan E2.66.E; University College 310 (Quartos) C10 FUE; University College R310.MG.19[R] FÜS; YBCA ND1150.+F9

Lit.: Schiff 908 (engraver given as 'J. Burnet'); Hammelmann 1975, 36; Schiff-Viotto 1977, repr. 84, bottom right

Variants:

I. Proof (India paper) before all letters (signatures only): BM 1849-5-12-248
Inscription (bottom right): H. Fuseli, Pinx^t.—|F. Legat sculp^t.

Ancora imparo.
M: Angelo Bonarroti.

162.

162. *Fantasy Portrait of Michelangelo Before the Roman Coliseum*, [1801]
(page 151)

Engraved vignette by William Blake (1757-1827) after Fuseli's pen-and-ink preliminary sketch ([1785-1790]; Schiff 873) in the Essick collection.
Inscription (bottom right): Blake: sc|Ancora imparo.|M: Angelo Bonarroti.
Dimensions: ■ 11.9 x 7.4 cm | 4^{11}/16" x 2^{15}/16" (BL 59.b.11) (H=27.5 cm)
Other locations: Bodleian 170.n.184; Cambridge Nn.24.7; DHW (H=29.0 cm); Essick; ETH A.146; Huntington 292894; Illinois x750.4.F986l; Library Company Is Fues 903.2; NYPL MC 1801; Pierpont Morgan E2.66.E; University

College R310 MG19 [R] FÜS; University College 310 (Quartos) C10.FUE; YCBA ND1150.+F9
Plate only: BM 1864-5-14-245; Dörrbecker
Lit.: Schiff 873; Todd 1971-1972, 173-181; Tomory 1972, pl. 155; Hammelmann 1975, 36; Essick 1991, no. XL

Variants:

I. Proof before all letters (signature only): LC Rosenwald 1823.24 (watermarked 1799)
Other locations: Essick

Fuseli's preliminary drawing omits Michelangelo's feet and the wall of the Colosseum. Given the 'trusting relationship' (Essick) between the two men, it is possible that Fuseli may have left it up to Blake, after giving him oral instructions, to develop a more detailed drawing from which to engrave, as was apparently also the case in No. **115**. Todd has speculated that both the drawing and the engraving of Michelangelo were executed c. 1788 for the Ur-version of Fuseli's 'Aphorisms on Art' (the sheets of which were destroyed in a fire).

✶✶✶✶✶✶

Nos. 161A - 162A.
Henry Fuseli.
LECTURES|ON|PAINTING,|DELIVERED AT THE ROYAL ACADEMY,|BY HENRY FUSELI, P.P.|WITH ADDITIONAL OBSERVATIONS AND NOTES.|[Vignette]|LONDON:|PRINTED FOR T. CADELL AND W. DAVIES, IN THE STRAND,|BOOK[-]SELLERS TO THE ROYAL ACADEMY;|AND W. BLACKWOOD, EDINGBURGH. [*sic*]|1820 (2/2 illus.).

...A NEW EDITION.|[Vignette]| LONDON:| PRINTED FOR T. CADELL, IN THE STRAND, BOOKSELLERS TO THE ROYAL ACADEMY; |AND W. BLACKWOOD, EDINBURGH.|1829.

...FIRST SERIES.|—|A NEW EDITION.| [Vignette]| LONDON:|HENRY COLBURN AND RICHARD BENTLEY,|NEW BURLINGTON STREET.|1830.
(Lectures 1 - 6).

LECTURES|ON|PAINTING,|DELIVERED AT THE ROYAL ACADEMY,|BY HENRY FUSELI, P.P.|NOW FIRST PRINTED FROM THE ORIGINAL MANUSCRIPTS.|—|SECOND SERIES.|—|[Vignette]| LONDON:|HENRY

COLBURN AND RICHARD BENTLEY, | NEW
BURLINGTON STREET. | 1830.
(Lectures 7 - 12).

Vol. II of the 1820 edition contains no
illustrations. There is a title page dated 1829
issued by Cadell & Blackwood in Anderdon's
'Collectanea Biographica' (BM 38.175), but no
copy of the book has been located.

On 22 May 1830, Henry Colburn and Richard
Bentley paid Thomas Cadell eighty-five pounds
for the copyright of Fuseli's *Lectures*. For this
sum they also acquired 'one Hundred and Fifty
Eight copies of the Work and the Copper plates of
two Vignettes and Portrait' (see the Agreement
Memorandum Books 1827-1833, Bentley
Archives, British Library; Chadwyck-Healy, reel
25, L52, 147). The published price of the two
volumes of the 1830 edition was apparently
£1.10s.

161A. *Silence*, 1820
(Title page)

Re-engraved by John Burnet (1784-1868) for the
second (enlarged) edition of the *Lectures*.
Inscription: ΣΙΓΑ; (bottom right): J. Burnet
Sculp'.
Dimensions: 7.5 x 9.0 cm | 3" x 3⁹/16"
(Newberry W6.315)
Other locations: Bern L.5.520 (1830/2); BL
561*.d.14 (1830/2); Cambridge Nn.24.7; DHW
(H=27.0 cm); Essick; Essick (1830/2); Folger
ND1150.F9; ZBZ AQ 122 (1830)
Plate only: BM 1853-12-10-569; V & A E.1210-
1886 (cut out; engraver's name cropped)
Lit.: Hammelmann 1957, repr. (1830) facing p.
350; Hammelmann 1975, 36; *Letters*, 242.
Exh.: Kansas City 1982 (50).

Variants:
I. Proof (India paper) (1830): BM 1853-12-10-
569 (Sheet=26.5 cm)

162A. *Fantasy Portrait of Michelangelo Before the Roman Coliseum*, 1820
(page 257)

Re-engraved by Francis Engleheart (1775-1849)
for the second (enlarged) edition of the *Lectures*.
Inscription: F: Engleheart Sculp: 1820:

Dimensions: 11.8 x 7.5 cm | 4¹¹/16" x 3¹⁵/16"
(Newberry W6.315)
Other locations: Bern L.5.520 (1830); DHW
(H=27.0 cm); Essick (1830); Folger ND1150.F9;
ZBZ AQ 122 (1830)
Plate only: BM 1885-3-14-297
Lacking plate: Cambridge Nn.24.7
Lit.: Hammelmann 1975, 36; *Catalogue of the ...
Blake Collection ... McGill University*, 1983, 151-
153.

Engleheart was paid 22 guineas by Cadell &
Davies for engraving this plate (Receipt, 13 May
1820; McGill University, Blake 6 E53R42 1820).

******

Nos. 163 - 164.
James Thomson.
THE | SEASONS, | BY | JAMES THOMSON. | A
NEW EDITION. | = | ADORNED WITH
PLATES. | = | LONDON: | PRINTED BY T.
BENSLEY, BOLT-COURT, FLEET-STREET, |
FOR F.J. DU ROVERAY; | AND SOLD BY W.
MILLER, E. LLOYD, R. DUTTON, | AND B.
CROSBY AND CO. | — | 1802 (2/6 illus. +
frontis.).

PRINTED NOTICE IN 'GOLDSMITH'S POEMS'
(D.H. Weinglass)

Speedily will be published,
A NEW AND HIGHLY DECORATED EDITION
OF
THOMSON'S SEASONS.
=

There is reason to believe that the present
Volume [*Goldsmith's Poems*] does not contain
one typographical error. As the Editor proceeds,
it will be his aim to render each succeeding
Publication superior, if possible to the preceding
one. He has only to add, that *Thomson's
Seasons* will be printed with the same degree of
accuracy as *Gray* and *Goldsmith*; and that
several improvements will be made in the
exterior embellishments of it.

Du Roveray appears to have begun to make his
preparations for this new edition in September or
October 1800. One of the 'exterior
embellishments' was the new type that Bensley
used to print the work, which was designed and
cast by the distinguished typefounder Vincent
Figgins. Du Roveray also considered printing the

Thomson in a quarto format, but was deterred by the price ('ab¹. £534') and settled for 1000 copies in octavo and 250 on large paper. A few copies were printed on India paper, which were notable for the 'very clear & beautiful ... impression of the type' (Du Roveray II, 70-72). According to the lot description, Robert Hoe's copy (sold by Anderson, New York, 18 November 1912; Part IV - L-Z, lot 3125), was one of only three 'large and thick paper copies ... printed'. The source of this statement is not known.

Bentley estimates the total cost of the edition, including designs and engravings, at £697.15s. (II, 79). In 1803, when he needed to capitalise his Homer editions, Du Roveray sold the rights and plates to Thomson's *Seasons*, Glover's *Leonidas*, and probably Goldsmith's *Poems*, to E. Lloyd.

163.

163. *Celadon and Amelia*, 1801
(III, *Summer*, 1159-1212)
(Facing p. 113)

Engraved by William Bromley (1769-1842) after the painting exhibited at the Royal Academy (1801/41) and now in the Staatliche Kunsthalle, Karlsruhe (1801; Schiff 1218).

Imprint: Published 1ˢᵗ. December 1801, by F.J. Du Roveray, London.
Inscription: Painted by H. Fuseli R.A. | | Engraved by W. Bromley. |

    'Tis safety to be near thee sure, and thus
    To clasp perfection! -
          Summer.

Dimensions: ■ 10.9 x 8.1 cm | 4¼" x 3³/16";
■ 11.1 x 8.4 cm | 4⁶/16" x 3¼" (Bodleian 280.o.275)
Other locations: DHW; Essick; NYPL NCL; Dörrbecker
Lacking plate: DHW
Lit.: Schiff 1316 (11.1 x 8.4 cm); Tomory 1972, pl. 108; Hammelmann 1975, 36; *Letters*, 242-245; R.D. Stock, *The Holy and the Daemonic*, 1982, 186, pl. 4; Du Roveray III, 140.

Variants:
I. Proof before letters: BM 1849-5-12-245 (Sheet=28.6 cm)
Other locations: V & A E.1206-E-1886
II. Proof before all letters (lacking verse): BL 1490.de.44 (H=23.3 cm)
Other locations: DHW (H=23.6 cm); Huntington 21982 (H=23.5 cm)

Fuseli illustrates Thomson's tale of the innocent pastoral lovers caught by the storm on 'the tender walk'. At the very moment that Celadon is reassuring Amelia that the selfsame God who summons up the tempest also protects and guards the innocent, the guiless maiden, depicted by Fuseli in the attitude of the 'Dying Bacchante', is incinerated by lightning.

Du Roveray's correspondence with his engravers shows he had unexpected problems with *Celadon and Amelia*. It was first assigned to Francis Legat who was, however, forced to withdraw from the task after 'fixing the Drawing and form', for which he declined any payment 'as a small Mitigation of not being able to perform his promise'. The engraving was finally completed after considerable delays by William Bromley, who complained (13 January 1802) that if he 'had known the time, that the subject ... has taken up [*he*] wou'd not have engaged to have done it for less than 20 guineas' (he may have received 15 or 18 guineas). No copies have been located of the 12 unfinished proofs in the etched state that Du Roveray usually requested, which Bromley seems to be referring to in his letter of 22 March 1802.

164.

164. *The Dying Shepherd*, 1801
(*Winter*, IV, 294ff)
(facing p. 220)

Engraved by William Bromley (1769-1842) after
Fuseli's lost original.
Imprint: Published 1ˢᵗ. December 1801, by F.J.
Du Roveray, London.
Inscription: Painted by H. Fuseli R.A. | | Engraved
by W. Bromley. |

_____ down he sinks
Beneath the shelter of the shapeless drift,
Thinking o'er all the bitterness of death.
                    Winter.

Dimensions: ■ 10.6 x 8.0 cm | 4³/16" x 3¹³/16";
■ 11.0 x 8.4 cm | 4⁵/16" x 3⁵/16" (Bodleian
280.o.275)
Other locations: DHW; DHW (facing p. [205]);
Dörrbecker; Essick; NYPL NCL
Lit.: Schiff 1315 (10.5 x 8.1 cm); Cohen 1964,
277, pl. 21; Tomory 1972, pl. 144 (as 'The Lost
Shepherd'); Hammelmann 1975, 36.
Exh.: Kansas City 1982 (55).

Variants:
I. Proof before letters: BM 1849-5-12-244

Other locations (plate only): NYPL MEM
R153re (facing p. 50); V & A E.1205-B-1886
II. Proof before all letters (lacking verse): BL
1490.de.44 (H=23.3 cm)
Other locations: DHW (H=23.6 cm);
Huntington 21982 (H=23.5 cm)
Plate only: DHW

Fuseli's choice of subject for his only other
illustration from Thomson is equally pessimistic,
representing the despair and horror of the
'disaster'd' shepherd, lost in a snow storm as
night falls and the storm blots out all his familiar
landmarks. His death from the 'creeping cold'
serves as a suitably bleak transition to the poet's
'reflections on the wants and miseries of human
life' in *Winter*.

Ralph Cohen sees 'Fuseli's closed, confined,
circular view of the smallness of man [*and*] the
triviality of his effort at safety' as representing
Fuseli's ironic attitude towards the sublime. This
irony was 'supported by the protruding tail and
rear of the dog side by side with the face of the
shepherd, whose safety consisted [*in*] hiding under
a cloak' (277).

******

Nos. 165 - 170.
John Milton.
MILTON'S | PARADISE LOST. | A NEW
EDITION. | = | ADORNED WITH PLATES. | = |
VOL. I. [-VOL. II.] | LONDON: | PRINTED BY
T. BENSLEY, BOLT COURT, FLEET STREET;
| FOR F.J. DU ROVERAY. | SOLD BY R.
DUTTON, B. CROSBY AND CO. | E. LLOYD,
AND J. BELL, 1802 (6/12 illus. + frontis.).

For the re-engravings of 1807 and 1808 see Nos.
165B - 168B, 170B and **165C - 170C** below.

PRINTED NOTICE IN 'THOMSON'S SEASONS'
(DHW)

Speedily will be published,
A NEW EDITION
of
MILTON'S PARADISE LOST,
In Twelve Numbers, adorned with Twelve
highly finished Engravings (exclusive of a
Portrait engraving by SHARP, after an original
Miniature by the celebrated S. COOPER) by
Mr. BARTOLOZZI, &c. from the Designs of
H. FUSELI, R.A. and the late W.

HAMILTON, R.A. Price 3s. § Number, and 5s. for the large paper copies.

PUBLICATION ANNOUNCEMENT
(*Monthly Epitome*, n.s. II, January 1803, 50)

A New Edition of Milton's Paradise Lost; with the Letter-press executed by Mr. Bensley, and each Book adorned with an highly-finished Engraving by the first Artists, from the Designs of H. Fuseli, R.A. and the late Wm. Hamilton, R.A. besides a new Portrait engraved by Sharp after a Miniature by the celebrated S. Cooper. In twelve Numbers, 3s. each, and on large Paper, Proof Impressions, 5s. each. Du Roveray.

It should be noted that the above portrait after Cooper does not represent Milton but the Puritan mathematician and cryptographer Noah Bridges (fl. 1661-1662) (Du Roveray I, 10, 15, note 60).

Fuseli's six paintings for *Paradise Lost* were ready for the engraver by 25 Sept 1801 (*Letters*, 242f.). The engravings after them are dated '1st. July 1802', but most were ready only later; some were still in the proof stage in late September. The book appeared in twelve numbers; publication was not announced until January 1803 (*Monthly Epitome*, n.s. II, 50): ordinary copies cost £1.16s; while Large Paper copies were £3.

Bentley (Du Roveray II, 79) calculates that total production costs for an estimated 1,000 ordinary and 250 Large-Paper copies amounted to just under £1,300, of which about £700 represented the cost of illustrations. But Bentley erroneously gives seven illustrations to Fuseli (Du Roveray III, 105; IV, 170)—led astray perhaps by the misnumbering of *Uriel Observing Satan* (Book III) in all the Large-Paper copies as 'Book VI'.

There are some puzzling elements with regard to the engravers and their chosen subjects. Thus, although only *Satan Summoning Up his Legions* appears in all the copies of the 1802 edition, Bromley may have originally engraved as many as three plates after Fuseli. Plates by Bromley of *Uriel Observing Satan's Flight* (**167A**) are found as variants in a few copies of the 1802 edition, but Charles Warren's plate is the standard. In contrast, all the 1808 copies contain Bromley's plate (**167C**). Fuseli treats *Satan Starting at the Touch of Ithuriel's Spear* as by Bromley (27 September 1802), even though the published plate is signed by Anker Smith. A year earlier (25

September 1801) Smith had agreed to 'undertake to produce the best plates [*he*] possibly could for 40 Guineas [*for*] the two of the size you mention', notwithstanding *Ithuriel* was too 'heavy [*a*] subject [*to*] undertake for 20 Guineas' and the *Expulsion* (No. **170**) was also not a light subject.

These illustrations, despite their 'puny' dimensions, allowed Fuseli to reprise with great effect many of the scenes he had already treated on a far grander scale in his Milton Gallery. But as Mary Ravenhall argues in Chapter VIII of her *Illustrations of* 'Paradise Lost' *in England, 1688-1802* (UMI: 1980), Fuseli's Milton illustrations for Du Roveray 'represent the culmination of a developing tradition rather than a radical departure into new modes of seeing Milton's epic' (p. 589).

165.

165. *Satan Calling Up His Legions*, 1802
(Book I, 330 ff.)
(Vol. I, facing p. [3])

Engraved by William Bromley (1769-1842) after Fuseli's painting in the Kunsthaus, Zurich (1802; Schiff 1209).
Imprint: Published 1st. July 1802, by F.J. Du Roveray, London.

Inscription (top right): Book I. | (bottom): Painted by H. Fuseli R.A. | | Engraved by W. Bromley. |
    Awake, arise, or be for ever fall'n!
Dimensions: ■ 11.4 x 8.8 cm | 4½" x 3½"; ▣ 11.6 x 9.0 cm | 4⁹/16" x 3⁹/16" (Birmingham 835293)
Other locations: Huntington 183052 (facing p. 18)
Plate only: V & A E.1205-D-1886
Lacking plate: NYPL *NCH 1802
Lit.: Schiff 1298 (11.8 x 9.0 cm); Schiff 1963, 45, pl. 8; Collins Baker 1948, 102; Pointon 1970, 116, pl. 105; Allentuck 1974, 214; Hammelmann 1975, 36; Ravenhall 1980, 537-540; *Letters*, 245, 252-253; Du Roveray III, 140-141, pl. 19.
Exh.: Kansas City 1982 (39);Kansas City 1989 (5)

    Variants:
I. Proof before letters (plate only): DHW (Sheet=25.7 cm)
II. Proof before all letters (lacking verse): BL C.109.bb.11 (H=22.9 cm)
Other locations: DHW (H=23.6 cm); DHW (H=23.6 cm) (facing p. [1]); Huntington 69888 (facing p. [3])
Plate only: BM 1849-5-12-243 (Sheet=26.5 cm)
Lacking plate: Princeton Ex 3859.369.23 (H=22.5)

Fuseli criticised Bromley's proof as 'a very inadequate transcript': Satan's and Beelzebub's limbs lacked precision; sky, rocks and ridges were not sufficiently discriminated. Satan's stance and gestures of command are the same used by Gray's Prophet-Bard (No. **155**),cursing Edward I.

166. *Satan Encountering Death at Hell's Gate, Sin Interposing*, 1802
(Book II, 727 ff.)
(Vol. I, facing p. [41])

Engraved by James Neagle (1760?-1822) after Fuseli's painting in the Bayerische Staatsgemäldesammlungen (1802; Schiff 1210).
Imprint: Published 1st. July 1802, by F.J. Du Roveray, London.
Inscription (top right): Book II. | (bottom): Painted by H. Fuseli R.A. | | Engraved by Jas. Neagle. |
    'O father, what intends thy hand,' she cried, 'Against thy only son?[']—
Dimensions: ■ 11.4 x 8.7 cm | 4½ x 3⁷/16"; ▣ 11.6 x 8.9 cm | 4⁹/16" x 3½" (Birmingham 835293)

Other locations: Huntington 183052 (facing p. 75)
Plate only: V & A E.1205-C-1886
Lacking plate: NYPL *NCH 1802
Lit.: Schiff 1299 (11.9 x 9.1 cm), 1210; Collins Baker 1948, 102, pl. VI; Schiff 1963, 51, pl. 15; Hammelmann 1975, 36; Ravenhall 1980, 540-545, pl. 157; Du Roveray III, 141, pl. 21
Exh.: Kansas City 1982 (39);Kansas City 1989 (9)

    Variants:
I. Proof before all letters (lacking verse): BL C.109.bb.11 (H=22.9 cm)
Other locations: DHW (H=23.6 cm); DHW (H=23.6 cm); Huntington 69888; Princeton Ex 3859.369.23 (H=22.5) (facing p.75)
Plate only: BM 1849-5-12-242 (Sheet=26.1 cm)

The scene at Hellgate, when Sin intervenes between her father (Satan) and his incestuously begotten son (Death), is one of the most dramatic in *Paradise Lost*. With the complicity of Sin and Death, Satan proceeds to Earth to seduce God's new creation. Fuseli's Sin is the embodiment of the Eternal Feminine: while Milton dwells on Sin's nether deformities, Fuseli gives her an inconspicuous serpent tail, but also legs and feet.

"O father, what intends thy hand," she cried,
"Against thy only son?"

166.

167.

168.

167. *Uriel Observing Satan's Flight*, 1802
(Book III, 740 ff.)
(Vol. I, facing p. [93])
Engraved by Charles Warren (1766-1823) after
Fuseli's painting in the Ulrich collection, Zurich
(1802; Schiff 1211).
Imprint: Published 1st. July 1802, by F.J. Du
Roveray, London.
Inscription (top right): Book III. | (bottom):
Painted by H. Fuseli R.A. | | Engraved by C.
Warren. |

   Down from th'ecliptic, sped with hop'd success,
   Throws his steep flight in many an airy wheel.
Dimensions: ■ 11.5 x 8.8 cm | 4^{1}/16" x 3^{7}/16";
■ 11.7 x 9.0 cm | 4^{9}/16" x 3½" (Birmingham
835293)
Other locations: Huntington 183052 (facing p.
126)
Plate only: V & A 23711-14 (cut within frame)
Lit.: Schiff 1300 (11.6 x 9.0), 1211; Collins
Baker 1948, 102; Tomory 1972, pl. 90 (as 'The
Fall of Satan'); Hammelmann 1975, 36;
Ravenhall 1980, 545-548, pl. 158; *Letters*, 245,
253; Boime 1987, 301f., pl. 4.13.

Variants:
I. Proof before letters (plate only): V & A
E.1205-Y-1886 (torn across)
Other locations: DHW (Sheet=25.8 cm)
II. Proof before all letters (lacking verse) (mis-
lettered Book no.) (between 220-[221]): BL
C.109.bb.11 (H=23.6 cm)
Inscription (top right): Book VI. | Painted by H.
Fuseli R.A. | | Engraved by C. Warren
Other locations: DHW (H=23.6 cm) (facing p.
[223]); DHW (H=23.6 cm) (facing p. [221]);
Huntington 69888 (facing p. 263); Princeton Ex
3859.369.23 (H=22.5) (facing p. 126)
Plate only: BM 1849-5-12-241 (Sheet=26.6 cm)
Lit.: Collins Baker 1948, 102
Exh.: Kansas City 1982 (40)

167A. 1802.
Re-engraved by William Bromley (1769-1842)
Imprint: Published 1st. July 1802, by F.J. Du
Roveray, London.
Inscription (top right): Book III. | Painted by H.
Fuseli R.A. | | Engraved by W. Bromley. |

   Down from th'ecliptic, sped with hop'd success,
   Throws his steep flight in many an airy wheel.

Dimensions: ■ 11.5 x 8.8 cm | 4½" x 3⁷/16";
■ 11.7 x 8.9 cm | 4¹⁰/16" x 3½" (NYPL *NCH 1802)
Other locations: Birmingham 835293; Huntington 183052 (Vol. I, facing p. 126)

Emerging unscathed from the perils of Chaos, Satan disguises himself as a 'stripling Cherub', and after receiving directions from Uriel, cartwheels downwards to earth, already confident of his success.

168. *Satan Starting from the Touch of Ithuriel's Spear*, 1802
(Book IV, 813-822)
(Vol. I, facing p. [127])

Engraved by Anker Smith (1759-1819) after Fuseli's painting in the Ulrich collection, Zurich (1802; Schiff 1212).
Imprint: Published 1ˢᵗ. July 1802, by F.J. Du Roveray, London.
Inscription (top right): Book IV. | (bottom): Painted by H. Fuseli R.A. | | Engraved by A. Smith A. |

_____Up he starts
Discover'd and surpris'd._____

Dimensions: ■ 11.8 X 8.9 cm | 4¹⁰/16" x 3½";
■ 2.0 X 9.1 | 4¹¹/16" x 3⁹/16" (Birmingham 835293)
Other locations: Huntington 183052 (facing p. 165); NYPL *NCH 1802
Plate only: BM 1849-5-12-238 (Sheet=25.9 cm);
V & A E.309-1941; V & A E.1205-F-1886; V&A 23711.11 (cut to frame)
Lit.: Schiff 1301 (11.9 x 9.1 cm), 1212; Collins Baker 1948, 102; Pointon 1970, 90, pl. 88; Hammelmann 1975, 36; Ravenhall 1980, 548-551, pl. 159; *Letters*, 243, 253; Du Roveray III, 141, pl. 20

Variants:
I. Proof before all letters (signatures only): BM 1868-8-22-2911
Inscription (scratched letters): H. Fuseli R.A. Pinxᵗ. | | A. Smith. A.R.A. Sculpᵗ.
Other locations: BM 1849-5-12-237; DHW
Exh.: Kansas City 1989 (11)
II. Proof before all letters (lacking verse): BL C.109.bb.11 (H=22.9 cm)
Other locations: DHW (H=23.6 cm); DHW (H=23.6 cm); Huntington 69888 (facing p.

[129]); Princeton Ex 3859.369.23 (facing p. 165)
Exh.: Kansas City 1982 (41)

Having gained entry to Paradise, Satan takes the form of a toad and creeps up on Adam and Eve as they sleep. Fuseli shows him as he is intercepted by Ithuriel and revealed in his true guise.

Fuseli's interest in this traditional subject dated back to his Roman period (Schiff nos. 482-483, 483a).

According to Ravenhall, 'Because Fuseli seeks to capture the dramatic action of the episode rather than the moral implications ... [t]he two good angels [are] placed slightly lower in the composition [and] shown as less than the equivalent of Satan's single figure' (550f.).

No copy has been found of Bromley's putative plate. Fuseli received a proof in late September and considered it 'too much of one depth', lacking 'Strength', 'grandeur and truth'. In contrast, Anker Smith's published plate was praised by Du Roveray's knowledgeable clients as 'a most exquisite specimen of genius & art in both painter & engraver' (Bryan Troughton to FID, 19 March 1805).

169.

169. *The Triumphant Messiah*, 1802
(Book VI, 824-866)
(Vol. I, facing p. [223])

Engraved by Charles Warren (1766-1823) after
the painting in the Schlatter collection, Zurich
(1802; Schiff 1213)
Imprint: Published 1st. July 1802, by F.J. Du
Roveray, London.
Inscription (top right): Book VI. | Painted by H.
Fuseli R.A. | | Engraved by C. Warren. |

_____ Headlong themselves they threw
Down from the verge of heaven.

Dimensions: ■ 11.3 x 8.6 cm | 4⁷/16" x 3⁶/16";
■ 11.6 x 9.0 cm | 4⁹/16" x 3⁹/16" (Birmingham
835293)
Other locations: Huntington 183052 (facing p.
262); NYPL *NCH 1802
Plate only: V & A 23711.16 (cut to frame)
Lit.: Schiff 1302 (11.7 x 9.1 cm); Collins Baker
1948, 102 (as 'Battle of the Angels');
Hammelmann 1975, 36; Ravenhall 1980, 556-
560, pl. 161 (as 'The Fall of Satan'); Behrendt
1983, 151, pl. 47 (as 'Rout of the Rebel Angels'

Variants:
I. Proof before all letters (scratched signatures
only): BM 1849-5-12-236 (Sheet=26.1 cm)
Inscription (scratched letters): H. Fuseli
Pinxt. | | C Warren. Sculpt.
II. Proof before all letters (lacking verse)
(between p. 220-[221]): BL C.109.bb.11
(H=22.9 cm)
Other locations: DHW (H=23.6 cm) (facing p.
91, i.e. before Book III); DHW (H=23.6 cm)
(Vol. II, facing p. [5], i.e. before Book VII);
Huntington 69888; Princeton Ex 3859.369.23
(facing p. 262)

Fuseli here sees the overthrow in terms of an
underlying symbolic act; the illustration portrays
'the rout as the result not so much of an external
military action as of a verbal (perhaps even
mental) command by the Son. Not armed for
battle, the Son merely extends his arm, and the
issue is resolved' (Behrendt). For Ravenhall, the
central theme of the illustration is Satan's fall,
exemplified by the rebel angels throwing
themselves over the wall of Heaven (558).

170.

170. *The Expulsion from Paradise*, 1802
(Book XII, 645-649)
(Vol. II, facing p. [221])

Engraved by Anker Smith (1759-1819) after
Fuseli's painting in the Dreyfus collection, Basel
(1802; Schiff 1214).
Imprint: Published 1st. July 1802, by F.J. Du
Roveray, London.
Inscription (top right): Book XII. | (bottom):
Painted by H. Fuseli R.A. | | Engraved by A.
Smith A. |

Some natural tears they dropt, but wip'd them
soon;
The world was all before them.

Dimensions: ■ 11.8 x 9.0 cm | 4¹⁰/16" x 3⁹/16";
■ 12.0 x 9.1 cm | 4¹¹/16" x 3⁹/16" (Birmingham
835294)
Other locations: DHW; Huntington (facing p.
250); NYPL *NCH 1802
Plate only: V & A 307-1941; V & A E.308-1941;
V & A 23711.17
Lit.: Schiff 1303 (11.9 x 9.1 cm), 1214; Collins
Baker 1948, 102; Pointon 1970, 199, pl. 179;
Ravenhall 1980, 577-584, pl. 167 (as 'Adam and
Eve Outside Paradise'); Behrendt 1983, 174, pl.52.

Variants:

I. Proof before letters (India paper): V & A
E.306-1941
Other locations: Huntington 49000, 474
II. Proof before all letters (signatures only): BM
1849-5-12-239
Inscription (scratched letters): A. Smith. ARA.
Sculp^t. | | H. Fuseli. R.A. Pinx^t.
Other locations: DHW; Huntington 69888
Exh.: Kansas City 1989 (19)
III. Proof before all letters (lacking verse): BL
C.109.bb.11 (facing p. 219) (H=23.6 cm)
Other locations: Bodleian Vet.A6.d.15/2; DHW
(H=23.6 cm); Princeton Ex 3859.369.23
(H=22.5)
Plate only: BM 1849-5-12-240 (Sheet=26.8 cm)
Lacking plate: DHW

******

Nos. 165A - 166A, 168A - 170A.
John Milton.
MILTON'S | PARADISE LOST. | A NEW
EDITION. | — | ADORNED WITH BEAUTIFUL
PLATES. | — | VOLUME I. [-VOLUME II.] |
[Vignette] | — | EDINBURGH | PRINTED FOR W
& J. DEA[N]S | BOOKSELLERS HIGH STREET
| — 1807. – (5/5 illus.).

165A. *Satan Risen from the Flood*, 1807
(Book I, 330 ff.)
(Vol. I, facing p. 12)

Re-engraved by Daniel Lizars (d. 1812)
Inscription: D. Lizars Sculp^t | —Book 1st. Line
330.—
Dimensions: ■ 11.4 x 7.5 cm | 4^7/16" x 2^{15}/16";
■ 11.7 x 7.7 cm | 4^{10}/16" x 3^1/16" (BL
11630.aaa.22)
Other locations: Illinois x821M64 1807
Lit.: Schiff 1298; Collins Baker 1948, 106.

166A. *Satan, Sin and Death*, 1807
(Book II, 727 ff.)
(Vol. I, facing p. 49)

Re-engraved by Daniel Lizars (d. 1812)
Inscription: D. Lizars Sculp^t | —Book II^d. Line
727.—
Dimensions: ■ 11.7 x 7.9 cm | 4^{10}/16" x 3^1/16"
(Illinois x821M64.M1.1807)
Lacking plate: BL 11630.aaa.22.
Lit.: Collins Baker 1948, 106 (omitted)

168A. *Satan Starting from the Touch of
Ithuriel's Spear*, 1807
(Book IV, 813-822)
(Vol. I, facing p. 108)

Re-engraved by Daniel Lizars (d. 1812)
Inscription: D Lizars Sculp^t | —Book IVth. Line
813.—
Dimensions: ■ 11.3 x 7.3 cm | 4^7/16" x 2^{13}/16";
■ 11.6 x 8.0 cm | 4^9/16" x 3^2/16" (BL
11630.aaa.22)
Other locations: Illinois x821M64 1807
Lit.: Schiff 1298; Collins Baker 1948, 106.

169A. *The Triumphant Messiah*, 1807
(Book VI, 824-866)
(Vol. II, facing p. 27)

Re-engraved by Daniel Lizars (d. 1812)
Inscription: D Lizars Sculp^t. | —Book VIth. Line
864.—
Dimensions: 11.6 x 7.8 cm | 4^9/16" x 3^1/16" (BL
11630.aaa.22).
Other locations: Illinois x821M64M1 1807 (facing
p. [1]).
Lit.: Schiff 1298; Collins Baker 1948, 106 (as
'Battle of the Angels').

170A. *The Expulsion from Paradise*, 1807
(Book XII, 645-649)
(Vol. II, facing p. 183)

Re-engraved by Daniel Lizars (d. 1812).
Inscription: D. Lizars Sculp^t. | —Book XII. Line
645.—.
Dimensions: 12.0 x 7.8 cm | 4^{11}/16" x 3^1/16" (BL
11630.aaa.22)
Other locations: Illinois x821.M64.M1 1807
(facing p. 175)
Lit.: Collins Baker 1948, 106 (as 'Adam and Eve
Leave Paradise')

******

Nos. 165B - 170B.
John Milton.
PARADISE LOST. | A | POEM. | IN | TWELVE
BOOKS. | — | BY JOHN MILTON. | — | PRINTED
FROM THE | TEXT OF TONSON'S CORRECT
EDITION OF 1711. | — | A NEW EDITION,
WITH PLATES. | = | LONDON: | PRINTED
FOR J. JOHNSON; W.J. AND J.
RICHARDSON; | OTRIDGE AND SON; R.
BALDWIN; VERNOR, HOOD, AND | SHARPE;
CUTHELL AND MARTIN; J. WALKER; F.
AND C. | RIVINGTON; SCATCHERD AND

LETTERMAN; WILKIE|AND ROBINSON; J. NUNN; R. LEA; LONGMAN, HURST,|REES AND ORME; CADELL AND DAVIES; T. PAYNE; W.|LOWNDES; LACKINGTON, ALLEN, AND CO.; CLARKE AND|SONS; J. TAYLOR; E. JEFFERY; J. MAWMAN; MATHEWS AND LEIGH; J. CARPENTER; AND J. BOOKER;|AT THE UNION PRINTING OFFICE, ST. JOHN'S SQUARE, BY W. WILSON.|—|1808 (6/12 illus. + frontis.)

[Added engraved t.p.]: PARADISE LOST|BY| JOHN MILTON.|[Title vignette by E.F.Burney]| *Outstretch'd he lay, on the cold ground, and oft*| *Curs'd his creation.Book X.line 851.*|LONDON.| PRINTED FOR THE PROPRIETORS.|1808.

165B. *Satan Risen from the Flood*, 1808 (Book I, 330ff.) (facing p. [3])

Re-issue with new imprint of the 1802 plate engraved by William Bromley (1769-1842). Imprint: London: Publish'd by Vernor, Hood & Sharpe, Poultry, 1808. Inscription (top right): Book I.|(bottom): Painted by H. Fuseli R.A.||Engraved by W. Bromley.| Awake, arise or be for ever fall'n!

Dimensions: ■ 11.4 x 8.8 cm | 4½" x 3⁷/16"; ▣ 11.5 x 9.0 cm | 4⁹/16" x 3⁹/16" (BL 11626.bb.35) Other locations: Birmingham 84095; Bodleian 280j.727; Cambridge 8700.d.998; DHW; DHW; Essick (facing p. [1]); Folger PR3560.1808 (facing p. 13); Huntington 183055; Princeton Ex 3859.369.122; ZBZ AL 6404 Lit.: Collins Baker 1948, 106f.; Hammelmann 1975, 36

166B. *Satan, Sin and Death*, 1808 (Book II, 727 ff.) (facing p. [31])

Re-issue with new imprint of the 1802 plate by James Neagle (1760?-1822) Imprint: London: Publish'd by Vernor, Hood & Sharpe, Poultry, 1808. Inscription (top right): Book II.|(bottom): Painted by H. Fuseli R.A.||Engraved by Jaˢ. Neagle.| 'O father, what intends thy hand,' she cried, 'Against thy only son?['}—-

Dimensions: ■ 11.4 x 8.7 cm; | 4½" x 3⁷/16"; ▣ 11.6 x 8.9 cm | 4⁹/16" x 3½" (BL 11626.bb.35) Other locations: Birmingham 840495; Bodleian

280j.727; Cambridge 8700.d.998; DHW; DHW; Essick (facing p. [29]); Folger PR3560.1808 (facing p. 54); Huntington 183055 (facing p. [30]); Princeton Ex 3859.369.122; ZBZ AL 6404 Lit.: Schiff 1299; Collins Baker 1948, 106f.; Hammelmann 1975, 36.

167B. *Uriel Observing Satan's Flight*, 1808 (Book III, 740 ff.) (facing p. [67])

Re-engraved by William Bromley (1769-1842) Imprint: London: Publish'd by Vernor, Hood & Sharpe, Poultry, 1808. Inscription (top right): Book III.|(bottom): Painted by H. Fuseli R.A.||Engraved by W. Bromley.| Down from th'ecliptic, sped with hop'd success, Throws his steep flight in many an airy wheel.

Dimensions: ■ 11.4 x 8.7 cm | 4½" x 3⁷/16"; ▣ 11.7 x 8.9 cm | 4¹/16" x 3⁹/16" (BL 11626.bb.35) Other locations: Birmingham 840495; Bodleian 280j.727; Cambridge 8700.d.998; DHW; DHW; Essick (facing p. 65); Folger PR3560.1808 (facing p. 90); Huntington 183055; Princeton Ex 3859.369.122; ZBZ AL 6404 Lit.: Collins Baker 1948, 106f.; Hammelmann 1975, 36

168B. *Satan Starting from the Touch of Ithuriel's Spear*, 1808 (Book IV, 813-822) (facing p. [93])

Re-issue with new imprint of the 1802 plate engraved by Anker Smith (1759-1819) Imprint: London: Publish'd by Vernor, Hood & Sharpe, Poultry, 1808. Inscription (top right): Book IV.|(bottom): Painted by H. Fuseli R.A.||Engraved by A. Smith A.| _____Up he starts Discover'd and surpris'd._____

Dimensions: ■ 11.7 x 8.9 cm | 4¹⁰/16" x 3½"; ▣ 11.9 x 9.1 cm | 4¹¹/16" x 3⁹/16" (BL 11626.bb.35) Other locations: Birmingham 840495; Bodleian 280j.727; Cambridge 8700.d.998; DHW; Essick (facing p. [91]); Folger PR3560.1808 (facing p. 118); Huntington 183055; Princeton Ex 3859.369.122; ZBZ AL 6404 Lit.: Collins Baker 1948, 106f.; Hammelmann 1975, 36

169B. *The Triumphant Messiah*, 1808
(Book VI, 824-866)
(facing p. [161])

Re-issue with new imprint of the 1802 plate engraved by Charles Warren (1766-1823).
Imprint: London: Publish'd by Vernor, Hood & Sharpe, Poultry, 1808.
Inscription (top right): Book VI. | Painted by H. Fuseli R.A. | | Engraved by C. Warren. |

_____Headlong themselves they threw
Down from the verge of heaven.

Dimensions: ■ 11.2 x 8.6 cm | 4^7/16" x 3^6/16";
◼ 11.6 x 9.0 cm | 4^9/16" x 3^9/16" (BL 11626.bb.35)
Other locations: Birmingham 840495; Bodleian 280j.727; Cambridge 8700.d.998; DHW; DHW; Essick (facing p. [159]); Folger PR3560.1808 (facing p. 188); Huntington 183055; ZBZ AL 6404
Lit.: Collins Baker 1948, 106f.; Hammelmann 1975, 36.

170B. *The Expulsion from Paradise*, 1808
(Book XII, 645-649)
(facing p. [351])

Re-issue with new imprint of the 1802 plate engraved by Anker Smith (1759-1819)
Imprint: London: Publish'd by Vernor, Hood & Sharpe, Poultry, 1808.
Inscription (top right): Book XII. | (bottom):

Painted by H. Fuseli R.A. | | Engraved by A. Smith A. |
   Some natural tears they dropt, but wip'd them soon;
   The world was all before them.
Dimensions: ■ 11.8 x 8.9 cm | 4^{10}/16" x 3½";
◼ 11.9 x 9.1 cm. | 4^{11}/16" x 3^9/16" (BL 11626.bb.35)
Other locations: Birmingham 840495; Bodleian 280j.727; Cambridge 8700.d.998 (facing p. 349); DHW; DHW; Essick (facing p. [349]); Folger PR3560.1808 (facing p. 372); Princeton Ex 3859.369.122; ZBZ AL 6404
Lit.: Collins Baker 1948, 106f.; Hammelmann 1975, 36

✶✶✶✶✶

No. 170C.
[Unidentified edition.]
[John Milton.]
[*PARADISE LOST*, N.d.]

170C. *The Expulsion from Paradise*, [n.d.]
(Book XII, 645-649)

Re-engraved by S. Watts
Proof on India paper before all letters
Inscription (bottom centre, within frame): S. Watts. Sculp.
Dimensions: ■ 11.6 x 8.7 cm | 4^9/16" x 3^7/16";
◼ 11.9 x 9.1 cm | 4^{11}/16" x 3^9/16" (V & A E.1205-E-1886)

✶✶✶✶✶

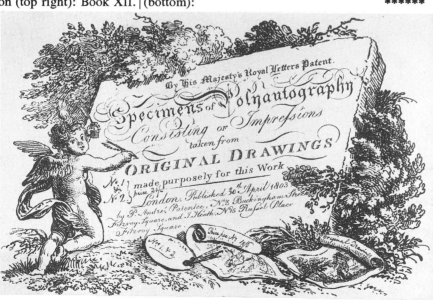

Fig. 8. Title page, *Specimens of Polyautography* (P. André), 1803.

Nos. 171 - 172.
BY HIS MAJESTY'S ROYAL LETTERS
PATENT. | SPECIMENS OF
POLYAUTOGRAPHY | CONSISTING OF
IMPRESSIONS | TAKEN FROM | ORIGINAL
DRAWINGS | MADE PURPOSELY FOR THIS
WORK. | — | N°. 1 | & | N° 2. | PRICE 21/- |
LONDON. PUBLISHED 30th APRIL 1803. | BY
P. ANDRÉ, PATENTEE, N° 15 BUCKINGHAM
STREET | FITZROY-SQUARE, AND J. HEATH,
N° 15 RUSSEL PLACE | FITZROY
SQUARE. | [*on palette*] N°s. 1. & 2. | [*on rolled
sheet*] PRICE PER N° 10/6 | [*on rolled sheet*]
ORIGINAL DRAWINGS (2/12 illus.).

BY HIS MAJESTY'S ROYAL LETTER
PATENT, | AND | UNDER THE PATRONAGE
OF HER MAJESTY | AND THEIR ROYAL
HIGHNESSES THE PRINCESSES. |
SPECIMENS OF POLYAUTOGRAPHY |
CONSISTING OF IMPRESSIONS | TAKEN
FROM | ORIGINAL DRAWINGS | MADE ON
STONE PURPOSELY FOR THIS WORK. |
PRICE 10/6. | LONDON | PUBLISHED BY G.J.
VOLLWEILER, PATENTEE, SUCCESSOR TO
MR. ANDRE, | N°. 9, BUCKINGHAM-PLACE,
FITZROY SQUARE), [1806].

ADVERTISEMENT
(BM 190* b.1, fol. 24)

Just published by G.J. Vollweiler, N°. 9
Buckingham Place, | Fitzroy-Square and sold by
the principal printsellers. |
N°. 4, Specimens of Polyautography
Price 10s.6d.

This work consisting of impressions taken
from original drawings made on stone is
published in numbers containing six subjects
each, and claims the attention of the lovers of
this art in a twofold degree; in the first place it
furnishes very excellent studies by the best
artists of this country of every kind and in every
style; secondly it shows the true and unmixed
style of the most distinguished artists; the
impressions being taken from the drawings
themselves, they are but multiplied originals.

The present fourth number is designed by
Mssrs. H. Singleton, W.H. Pyne, E.V. Utterson
(amateur), T. Barker, R.L. West, and W.
Havell.

The three preceding numbers are designed by
Mssrs. B. West, P.R.A. R. Ker Porter, T.
Stothard, R.A. R. Cooper, R. Corbould, H.
Fuseli, R.A. T. Hearne, J. Barry, T. Barker,
C. Gessner, W. Delamotte, Ch. Heath, J.T.
Serres, H.W. Chalon, Wm..

This invention cannot but be very acceptable to
the lovers of drawing the Artists, as they may
themselves multiply their own designs without
any knowledge of the art of engraving as the
stone is prepared so as to admit of being drawn
upon with the same facility as paper.

Amateurs and artists who wish to multiply
their drawings, may have them printed by Mr.
Vollweiler, who furnishes a stone and the
necessary materials for drawing, and of whom
further particulars may be had.

Printed from stone by G.J. Vollweiler, at the
polyautographic office, N°. 9 Buckingham
Place, | Fitzroy Square.

Lithography was invented by Aloys Senefelder
who called his process 'polyautography' because
of its capability to 'multiply originals', i.e.,
reproduce exact copies of whatever was drawn on
the stone. However, for a very long time
Senefelder 'regarded lithography primarily as a
mere technical extension of the printer's trade'
(Weber 1966, 75): the new invention's artistic
potential was not explored until Philipp André,
who acquired Senefelder's English and Scottish
patents in 1801, established the first lithographic
press in London and encouraged experiments by
artists such as Barry, West, Stothard, and Fuseli
in the medium. In 1803 André published his
Specimens of Polyautography, comprising twelve
artist's lithographs in pen and ink, together with a
separate title page (fig. 8), issued in two sets
('Numbers') of six each. The price was 10s.6d.
per set. Three years later André's successor G.J.
Vollweiler issued an enlarged album of thirty-six
prints both in crayon and in pen and ink in six
Numbers. These included the twelve prints
previously published.

As Lynn M. Gould reminds us, 'The earliest
lithographers, unsure of the new medium's
capacities, depended on established drawing
techniques', particularly those of pen and ink
drawing as well as intaglio printmaking (2).

171.

171. *Evening Thou Bringest All*, [1802]
(Issued in Part II, no. VII)

Pen and tusche lithograph by the artist derived from both his drawing at Dresden (1800; Schiff 1433) and his painting in the Goethe-Museum, Frankfurt am Main ([1800-1805]; Schiff 1240). Copies are found on white or cream paper. Inscription (on the divan, at the left-hand edge of the composition, but not reversed): H Fuseli del; (below, Greek letters reversed): Εσπερε Παντα Φερειϭ

Dimensions: ■ 21.5 x 31.7 cm | 8½" x 12½"; (YCBA L 194.65 (fB)) (Sheet=22.9 x 32.6 cm)
Other locations (white paper): YCBA IR 73/695; Basel Bi.247; Basel; Essick; ETH 524; (cream paper): BM 1862-10-11-246; BM 1867-12-14-419; BM 1874-7-11-908; V & A E.1193-1886 (Robert Balmanno's copy); V & A E.1107-1899; YCBA L 272.8

Lit.: Schiff 1434 (?31.5 x 20 cm); Glaser 1922, repr. 183; Man 1962, no. 64, repr. 101; Weber 1966, 41f., repr. 42 (reversed)

Exh.: Zurich 1926 (361); Cleveland 1948 (175); Florence 1979 (42); Washington 1988 (no number)

Variants:
I. With imprint: Yale Art Gallery 1962.9.22
(sheet: 23.0 x 33.3 cm)
Imprint: LONDON printed from a Pen & Ink drawing on stone at the polyautographic office, N°. 9 Buckingham Place, Fitzroy Square.— Inscription (within composition, left): H Fuseli del—; (below, Greek letters reversed): Εσπερε Παντα Φερειϭ

The woman seated on the divan looking out of the window can now be identified as Fuseli's wife, Sophia (1763?-1832), whom he frequently portrayed.

As evidence of Fuseli's reliance on 'traditional drafting techniques', Gould points to his use of receding diagonals to indicate depth, and closely spaced parallel lines to indicate shade. She finds the spontaneity and freshness of the print particularly impressive, given the other two versions of the subject by Fuseli in different media from which it is derived (2).

172.

172. *Heavenly Ganymede*, [1804]
(Issued in Part V, no. XXV)
(Homer, *Iliad*, XX, 234)

Crayon lithograph by Henry Fuseli
Inscription (top right): HF | (bottom right): TON
ΚΑΙ ΑΝΡΗΡΕΙΨΑΝΤΟ ΘΕΟΙ
Dimensions: ■ 30.9 x 23.6 cm | 12³/16" x 9⁵/16"
(YCBA L 194.65 (fB))
Other locations: BM 1852-2-14-21) (sheet=33.9 x
26.4 cm); Chicago 1982.496; BM 1874.7.11.926;
MMA 31.69.1, f. 24; V & A E.1106-1899;
YCBA IR 53/Z;
Lit.: Schiff 1346 (33.7 x 26.4 cm); Man 1962,
no. 65; Weber 1966, repr. 145 (as 'The Rape of
Ganymede').
Exh.: Zurich 1941 (358) (as 'The Rape of
Ganymede');Washington 1988 (unnum.)(as 1941).

The line of Greek in the lower right-hand
corner is quoted from the *Iliad*. (The English
equivalent is italicised in the longer quotation

below). Ganymede was one of the three sons of
Tros, king of Troy. As Homer tells us (*Iliad*, XX,
232-235), he 'was born the fairest of mortal men;
wherefore the gods caught him up on high to be
cupbearer to Zeus by reason of his beauty, that
he might dwell with the immortals' (trans. A.T.
Murray).

The most frequently represented version of the
story ('The Rape of Ganymede') shows Zeus in
the form of an eagle bearing away the beautiful
boy. Fuseli has chosen instead to depict hovering
Ganymede, already installed on Mount Olympia, a
cup in his right hand, being greeted by an Apollo-
like god. On the left a jealous Hebe observes the
scene.

Fuseli was left handed but since the image was
reversed when the plate was printed, his
characteristic hatching, from upper left to lower
right is also inverted and appears as if done by a
right-hander.

******

Nos. 173 - 176.
Erasmus Darwin.
THE|TEMPLE OF NATURE;|OR, THE|
ORIGIN OF SOCIETY:|A POEM,|WITH
PHILOSOPHICAL NOTES.|BY|ERASMUS
DARWIN, M.D. F.R.S.|AUTHOR OF THE
BOTANIC GARDEN, OF ZOONOMIA, AND
OF|PHYTOLOGIA.|*Unde hominum pecudumque
genus, vitaeque volantum,*|*Et quae marmoreo fert
monstra sub aequore pontus?*|*Igneus est illis
vigor, & caelestis origo. VIRG. AEn. VI. 728.*|
LONDON:|PRINTED FOR J. JOHNSON, ST.
PAUL'S CHURCHYARD,|BY T. BENSLEY,
BOLT COURT, FLEET STREET.|1803 (4/4
illus.).

For the re-engravings of 1804 and 1807 see Nos.
173A - 176A and **173B - 176B** below.

Although announced in the *Monthly Magazine*
for December 1802 as *The Origins of Society*, the
work was not published until April 1803, when it
appeared under the title *The Temple of Nature*. It
was issued in both quarto and royal quarto format
(H=30.0 cm) at £1.5s. and £1.15s. respectively
(*Monthly Epitome*, n.s. II, 225-233).

The Preface is dated 'Jan. 1, 1802' but as
Darwin remarks in the very last lines he ever
wrote, 'My bookseller, Mr. Johnson, will not
begin to print the Temple of Nature [Origin of
Society?], till the price of paper is fixed by
Parliament' (to Richard Edgeworth, 17 April
1802, *Letters of Erasmus Darwin*, ed. D. King-
Hele, 338, 339 note 7).

The edition of 1825 (Jones & Company)
(Bodleian 280.e.3909) is not illustrated with
plates.

Much of the renewed interest in Erasmus
Darwin (1731-1802) is due to the numerous
apparent anticipations in his writings of his
grandson Charles Darwin's theory of evolution.
The aim of *The Temple of Nature* is, as the poet
notes in his Preface, to bring in poetical form
'distinctly to the imagination the beautiful and
sublime images of the [*progressive*] operations of
Nature' from the beginnings of microscopic life to
the development of society. The structure of the
poem corresponds to the gradual initiation of the
neophyte ('muse') into the philosophy of the
Temple via the 'allegoric scenery' of the
Eleusinean mysteries, explained by the Hierophant
(priestess).

173.

173. *The Priestess Unveiling the Statue of the
Goddess of Nature*, 1803
(Canto I, 129-136, 167-172; IV, 517-524)
(facing title page)

Frontispiece engraved in stipple by Moses
Haughton (1772 or 1774-1848) after the drawing
in the Kunsthaus Zurich (1803; Schiff 1421)
Imprint: Pub^d. Feby. 1st. 1803, by I. Iohnson,
London.
Inscription (top centre): FRONTISPIECE.|
(bottom): Fuseli del^t.||Houghton sculp.|THE
TEMPLE OF NATURE.
Dimensions: ■ 20.9 x 16.8 cm | 8¼" x 6^{10}/16"
(BL 642.1.17)
Other locations: Cambridge Bury.22.13;
Cambridge CCA.24.63; Cambridge CCA.24.64;
DHW (H=30.0 cm); DHW; Dr. Williams's;
Essick; Huntington 347104; LC PR3396.A77
1803; Princeton Ex 3706.5.389.1803
Plate only:BM 1866-11-10-1147 (Sheet=29.2 cm)
Lacking plate: Bodleian 3974.d.344(1)
Lit.: Schiff 1338 (?12.5 x 8.7 cm), 1421

Variants:
I. Before letters:BM 1863-5-9-43(hand coloured)

The illustration is not limited to a single scene in the first Canto. Rather, it telescopes the whole process of revelation, showing the final rites of the initiation ceremony as the Hierophant withdraws the veil from the Goddess of Nature, while the awe-struck muse kneels and 'Lifts her ecstatic eyes to TRUTH DIVINE' (IV, 524). The Goddess is represented in Fuseli's illustration without the hyperbolic physical attributes Darwin ascribes to her. Fuseli dispenses with the towers 'crest[*ing*] ... her beamy forehead' and with her hundred hands, reducing her hundred breasts to three and omitting the 'unnumber'd births' suckling upon them (I, 129-132). The figures on the left probably represent the couples thronging 'Pair after Pair, in bright procession|With flower-fill'd baskets round the altar' (I, 159-161).

174.

174. *The Creation of Eve*, 1803
(Canto II, 135-142)
(facing p. 55)

Stipple engraving by Moses Haughton (1772 or 1774-1848) after the drawing in the Kunsthaus Zurich (1803; Schiff 1422)

Imprint: Pub^d. Feby. 1st. 1803, by I. Iohnson London.
Inscription (top right): p. 55 | (bottom): Fuseli del^t. | | Houghton sculp. | THE CREATION OF EVE. |

So erst in Paradise creation's Lord,

Form'd a new sex, the Mother of Mankind.
_____Buoyed on light step the Beauty seem'd to swim,
And stretch'd alternate every pliant limb.

Dimensions: ■ 21.5 x 15.3 cm | 8^7/16" x 6" (BL 642.1.17)
Other locations: Cambridge Bury.22.13; Cambridge CCA.24.63 (imprint trimmed); Cambridge CCA.24.64; DHW (H=30.0 cm); DHW (imprint cropped); Dr. Williams's 1009.S.21; Huntington 34107; LC PR3396.A77 1803; Princeton Ex 3706.5.389.1803
Plate only: BM 1866-11-10-1148; Huntington 4900, 181; V & A E.1305-1941
Lacking plate: Bodleian 3974.d.344(1)
Lit.: Schiff 1339 (?12.5 x 8.5 cm), 1422; Collins Baker 1948, 102; Pointon 1970, pl. 100
Exh.: Kansas City 1989 (13)

Variants:
I. Unfinished proof (etched state): V & A E.303-1941

Canto II once again reflects the way in which Darwin's concern with mythology also dictates the content of his poetry. Here he enumerates nature's methods for reproducing the species, progressing from the production of such 'orphan babes of solitary love' (106) as the tape-worm, to the perfection and delight of sexual love that 'gives ... the vital breath, | And parries ... the shafts of death' (259-260).

Typical of Darwin's procedure throughout the work, in this canto his investigation of nature is simultaneously conceived as a branch of moral philosophy and as such allows him to plunge into an extended exploration of the biblical account of the creation of Eve from the rib of Adam. For Darwin the creation of Eve, whose description he borrows from Milton (*Paradise Lost*, VIII, 460-478), exemplifies the realisation of 'the fond wish to form a softer sex ... | Whose mingling virtues interweave at length | The mother's beauty with the father's strength' (114, 123-124).

175.

176.

175. *Eros and Dione*, 1803
(Canto III, 187-196)
(facing p. 99)

Stipple engraving by Moses Haughton (1772 or
1774-1848)
Imprint: Pub^d. Feby. 1st. 1803, by I. Iohnson,
London.
Inscription (top right): p. 99 | Fuseli del^t. | |
Houghton sculp. | EROS & DIONE. |

> Warm as the sun-beam, pure as driven snows,
> The enamour'd God for young Dione glows.

Dimensions: ■ 21.7 x 15.7 cm | 8^9/16" x 6^3/16"
(BL 642.1.17)
Other locations: Cambridge Bury 22.13;
Cambridge CCA.24.63 (facing p. 98); Cambridge
CCA; DHW (H=30.0 cm); DHW; Dr. Williams'
1009.S.21; Essick; Huntington 347104; LC
PR3396.A77 1803; Princeton Ex 3706.5.389.1803
Plate only: BM 1866-11-10-1149(Sheet=29.8 cm)
Lacking plate: Bodleian 3974.d.344(1)
Lit.: Schiff 1340 (?22.8 x 15.8 cm), 1164

Dione and Eros are an allegory of the power of
love 'bind[*ing*] Society in silken chains' (III, 206).

176. *The Power of Fancy in Dreams*, 1803
(Canto IV, 201-204)
(facing p. 146)

Stipple engraving by Moses Haughton (1772 or
1774-1848) after the drawing in an English private
collection (1803; Schiff 1423)
Imprint: Pub^d. Feby. 1st. 1803, by I. Iohnson,
London.
Inscription (top right): p. 146 | (bottom): Fuseli
del^t. | | Houghton sculp. | THE POWER OF
FANCY IN DREAMS. |

> So holy transports in the cloister's shade
> Play round thy toilet, visionary maid!
> Charm'd o'er thy bed celestial voices sing,
> And Seraphs hover on enamour'd wing.

Dimensions: ■ 22.0 x 15.6 cm | 8^10/16" x 6^2/16"
(BL 642.1.17)
Other locations: Cambridge Bury.22.13;
Cambridge CCA.24.63; Cambridge CCA.24.64;
DHW (H=30.0 cm); DHW; Dr. Williams'
1009.S.21 (facing p. 147); Essick; Huntington
347104; LC PR3396.A77 1803; Princeton Ex
3706.5.389.1803
Plate only: BM 1863-5-9-36; BM 1866-11-10-
1150 (Sheet=29.8 cm)

Lacking plate: Bodleian 3974.d.344(1)
Lit.: Schiff 1341 (22.1 x 15.7 cm), 1423;
Exh.: Kansas City 1982 (5).

'One of the most unexplored regions of art is
dreams,' so asserted Fuseli in his Aphorism 231
(Knowles, III, 145). Yet this illustration is but one
among many that bears out the curious fact that
after *The Nightmare* Fuseli reverted to traditional
formulae whenever he needed to depict a dream
state (cf. *Prince Arthur's Vision*).

******

Nos. 173A - 176A.
Erasmus Darwin.
THE|TEMPLE OF NATURE;|OR, THE|
ORIGIN OF SOCIETY.|A POEM,|WITH
PHILOSOPHICAL NOTES.|BY|ERASMUS
DARWIN, M.D. F.R.S.|AUTHOR OF THE
BOTANIC GARDEN, OF ZOONOMIA,|AND
OF PHYTOLOGIA.|*Unde hominum pecudumque
genus, vitaeque volantum,|Et quae marmoreo fert
monstra sub aequore pontus?|Igneus est illis
vigor, and* [sic] *caelestis origo. VIRG. Aen. VI.
728.*|=| BALTIMORE.|PRINTED BY JOHN
W. BUTLER, AND BONSAL & NILES,|FOR
BONSAL & NILES, SAMUEL BUTLER, AND|
M. AND J. CONRAD & CO.|=|1804. (4/4
illus.).

There is another American edition in this year
by T.J. Swords but it does not contain Fuseli's
illustrations.

173A. *The Priestess Unveiling the Statue of the
Goddess of Nature*, 1804
(Frontispiece)
(facing title page)

Re-engraved in stipple by Benjamin Tanner (1775-
1848) as frontispiece to the American edition.
Inscription (top centre): FRONTISPIECE.|
(bottom): Fuseli, del.||Tanner, sc.|THE
TEMPLE OF NATURE.
Dimensions: ■ 14.4 x 10.1 cm | 5^{11}/16" x 4";
■ 4.8 x 10.5 cm | 5^{13}/16" x 4^2/16" (LC
PR3396.A77 1804 Toner)
Other locations: Huntington 73378; Kentucky
821.D259t; Library Company Am 1804 Dar;
Newberry Y185.D255; NYPL NCL; Tampa
PR3396.A77 1804; Old Dominion

Plate only: LC P&P (PAGA 3—AA—1921:R1)
Lacking Plate: LC PR3396.A77 1804 c.2

174A. *The Creation of Eve*, 1804
(Canto II, 135-142)
(Facing p. 70)

Re-engraved in stipple by David Edwin (1776-
1841) for the American edition.
Inscription (bottom right): D. Edwin sc|THE
CREATION OF EVE.
Dimensions: ■ 14.6 x 9.8 cm | 5¾" x 3^{14}/16"
(LC PR3396.A77 1804 Toner)
Other locations: Huntington 73378; Kentucky
821.D259t; Library Company Am 1804 Dar;
Newberry Y185.D255; NYPL NCL (facing p.
69); Tampa PR3396.A77 1804; Old Dominion
(facing p. 69)
Plate only: LC P&P (PAGA 3—AA—1921:R1)
Lacking plate: LC PR3396.A77 1804 c.2
Lit.: Mantle Fielding, *Catalogue of the Engraved
Work of David Edwin* (1905), no. 224.

175A. *Eros and Dione*, 1804
(Canto III, 187-196)
(Facing p. 121)

Re-engraved in stipple by Cornelius Tiebout
(1777-1830?) for the American edition.
Inscription (bottom right): Tiebout Sc|EROS &
DIONE.
Dimensions: ■ 13.9 x 10.0 cm | 5½" x 3^{15}/16"
(LC PR3396.A77 1804 Toner) (facing p. 120)
Other locations: Huntington 73378; Newberry
Y185.D255; Library Company Am 1804 Dar;
NYPL NCL (facing p. 120); Tampa PR3396.A77
1804; Old Dominion (facing p. 120)
Plate only: LC P&P (PAGA 3—A—1921:R1);
NYPL MDGZ
Lacking plate: Kentucky 821.D259t; LC
PR3396.A77 1804 c.2

176A. *The Power of Fancy in Dreams*, 1804
(Canto IV, 201-204)
(facing p. 173)

Re-engraved in stipple by Samuel Seymour (fl.
1797-1822) for the American edition.
Inscription (bottom right): S. Seymour sc.|THE
POWER OF FANCY IN DREAMS.
Dimensions: ■ 14.4 x 9.8 cm | 5^{10}/16" x 3^{14}/16"
(LC PR3396.A77 1804 Toner)

Other locations: Huntington 73378; Kentucky 821.D259t; Library Company Am 1804 Dar; NYPL NCL (facing p. 172); Tampa PR3396.A77 1804

Plate only: LC P&P (PAGA 3—AA—1921:R1) Lacking plate: LC PR3396.A77 1804 c.2; Old Dominion

******

Nos. 173B - 176B.
Erasmus Darwin.
THE | POETICAL WORKS | OF | ERASMUS DARWIN, | M.D. F.R.S. | CONTAINING THE BOTANIC GARDEN, IN TWO PARTS, | AND THE TEMPLE OF NATURE. | WITH | PHILOSOPHICAL NOTES AND PLATES. | IN THREE VOLUMES. | VOL. III. | CONTAINING THE TEMPLE OF NATURE. | LONDON: | PRINTED FOR J. JOHNSON, ST. PAUL'S CHURCH-YARD, | BY T. BENSLEY, BOLT COURT, FLEET STREET. | 1806. (4/4 illus.).

173B. *The Priestess Unveiling the Statue of the Goddess of Nature*, 1807
(Frontispiece)
(Facing title page)

Re-engraved in line and stipple by John Dadley (1767-*post* 1807)
Imprint: London, Published May 1. 1807 by J. Johnson, S^t. Paul's Church Yard.
Inscription (top right): Frontispiece: V. III. | H. Fuseli Esqr. R.A. inv^t. | | J. Dadley, sculp^t. | **The Temple of Nature.**
Dimensions: ■ 14.0 x 9.5 cm; | 5^8/16" x 3¾"; ▣ 14.2 x 9.7 cm | 5^9/16" x 3^{13}/16" (BL 11641.dd.11)
Other locations: Dr. Williams's 1110.H.11; Essick; Fribourg ANT 9847; Huntington 421361; Newberry Y185.D25; Yale Im D259e

174B. *The Creation of Eve*, 1807
(Canto II, 135-142)
(Facing p. 61)

Re-engraved in line and stipple by John Dadley (1767-*post* 1807).
Imprint: London Published May 1. 1807 by J. Johnson S^t. Paul's Church Yard.
Inscription (top right): V. III. P. 61. | (bottom): H Fuseli Esqr. R.A. inv^t. | | J. Dadley sculp^t. | **The Creation of Eve.**

Dimensions: ■ 13.9 x 8.8 cm | 5^7/16" x 3^7/16"; ▣ 14.2 x 9.1 cm | 5^9/16" x 3^9/16" (BL 11641.dd.11)
Other locations: Dr. Williams's 1110.H.11; Essick; Fribourg ANT 9847; Huntington 421361 Newberry Y185.D25; Yale Im D259e
Plate only: BM 1863-5-9-8; DHW; RA Anderdon XIII, 130.

Variants:
I. Perhaps before imprint: V & A E.304-1941

175B. *Eros and Dione*, 1807
(Facing p. 109)

Re-engraved in line and stipple by John Dadley (1767-*post* 1807)
Imprint: London, Published May 1. 1807 by J. Johnson, S^t. Paul's Churh [*sic*] Yard.
Inscription (top right): V. III. P. 109. | (bottom): H. Fuseli Esqr. R.A. inv^t. | | J. Dadley sculp^t. | **Eros and Dione.**
Dimensions: ■ 14.2 x 9.1 cm | 5^9/16" x 3^9/16"; ▣ 14.4 x 9.3 cm | 5^{10}/16" x 3^{10}/16" (BL 11641.dd.11)
Other locations: Dr. Williams's 1110.H.11; Essick; Fribourg ANT 9847; Huntington 421361; Newberry Y185.D25; Yale Im D259e
Plate only: BM 1863-5-9-67 (cropped); Essick

176B. *The Power of Fancy in Dreams*, 1807
(Facing p. 160)

Re-engraved in line and stipple by John Dadley (1767-*post* 1807).
Imprint: London. Published May 1. 1807 by J. Johnson, S^t. Paul's Church Yard.
Inscription (top right): V. III. P. 160. | (bottom): H. Fuseli Esqr. R.A. inv^t. | | J. Dadley, sculp^t. | **The Power of Fancy in Dreams.**
Dimensions: ■ 13.9 x 9.4 cm | 5½" x 3^7/16"; ▣ 14.1 x 9.6 cm | 5^{10}/16" x 3^{13}/16" (BL 11641.dd.11)
Other locations: Dr. Williams's 1110.H.11; Essick; Huntington 421361; Fribourg ANT 9847; Newberry Y185.D25; Yale I D259e
Plate only: BM 1863-5-9-37
Lit.: Tomory 1972, 182, pl. 152

******

No. 177.
David Hume.
THE | HISTORY | OF | ENGLAND, | FROM THE | INVASION OF JULIUS CAESAR | TO THE |

REVOLUTION IN 1688, | BY | DAVID HUME. |
LONDON | PRINTED BY T. BENSLEY, BOLT-
COURT, FLEET-STREET, | FOR | ROBERT
BOWYER, PALL-MALL. 1806 (1/70 full-page
illus. + 122 engr. title pages, portraits, etc.).

For the re-engraving of [1852] see No. **178A**.
below.

PROSPECTUS
(American Philosophical Society
Pam. 1108 No. 14)
DEDICATED
by Permission
TO HIS MAJESTY
COMPLETE | HISTORY OF ENGLAND, |
from | THE INVASION OF JULIUS CÆSAR |
TO THE REVOLUTION IN 1688, | BY DAVID
HUME; | FROM | THE REVOLUTION to the
PRESENT TIME | BY | DAVID WILLIAMS. | —
GENERAL DESIGN
FOR A COMPLETE
HISTORY OF ENGLAND,
SUPERBLY ORNAMENTED.

=

History is the school of the moralist and
politician: and the fluctuations of governments,
so interesting to the world, render the study and
composition of it the most important
occupations of literature.

The merit of HUME, like that of LIVY, is a
circumstance not inconsiderable in the
reputation of his country. The little blemishes of
his style; the supposed petulance of his
philosophy; and his partiality to the House of
Stuart—are foils only to the great beauties of a
composition, the produce of profound
knowledge, under the direction of a vigorous
and elegant imagination.

(2)

When Miltiades had rendered Greece immortal
by the victory at Marathon, the pencil of
Polygnotus delineated the action on the walls of
the Pæcile; and the Arts gave their aid to the
genius of the Historian, in cherishing patriotic
virtue and the genuine love of glory. In modern
times, Historic Painting has been employed on
detached subjects; sometimes selected by
caprice, and generally modified by poetic fancy.

To combine the effect of the Arts with that of
Historic Eloquence, in a connected series of
those events which have formed the political

government, the religion, the manners, and the
character, of a great nation, is an undertaking
that may deserve public notice; and if the
abilities of the projectors be competent, may
claim public encouragement.

It is proposed, therefore to print a New
Edition of HUME'S HISTORY OF ENGLAND;
illustrated by HISTORIC PRINTS; ornamented with
VIGNETTES, Impressions of MEDALS and COINS;
Views of the present, and of the ruins of
ancient, PALACES, CASTLES, and PUBLIC
BUILDINGS; PORTRAITS and MONUMENTS of
Kings, Queens, Princes, and of those eminent
Personages in the Senate, the Church, the
Army, the Navy, in Literature, Philosophy, and
the Arts, whose talents, characters, and
reputations, have influenced the various events
of the kingdom, from the earliest periods of it's
annals to the present time.

But, as the History of Mr. HUME terminates at
the Revolution; and the government originating
in that period has given the English [*p.* (3)]
nation a new character; as no historic
production appears to the Proprietors, or to
those persons of learning and knowledge they
have the honor to consult, to be a proper and
satisfactory continuation of the work of Mr.
HUME; they have determined to procure an
original composition;—and Mr. WILLIAMS has
undertaken to continue the HISTORY OF
ENGLAND from the Revolution to the present
time: and his production being illustrated and
ornamented like that of Mr. HUME—the whole
will form a Magnificent Work; highly
interesting to the reputation, and it is hoped
highly deserving the patronage of a great and
opulent Nation.

The Public is in possession of considerable
specimens of the abilities and knowledge of Mr.
WILLIAMS; and on the opinion of those specimens
the Proprietors must rely. The species of
independence he has ever displayed; his peculiar
indifference to all political parties, and to the
general motives of ambition—are pledges of his
impartiality and candor: and the Public may
expect a History, not so much of Persons, as of
Facts, of Principles, and of Causes.

The Illustrations and Embellishments from the
Arts will be under the direction of Mr.
BOWYER, Miniature Painter to His MAJESTY,
one of the proprietors; in conjunction with Mr.

FITTLER; whose applications to the most eminent Artists of the age have been received with an enthusiasm, which must ensure every exertion of Genius to perfect a National Work.

When all the Engravings are made, the Paintings will be presented by the Proprietors to the NATION, and deposited at the [*p.* (4)] discretion and command of the LEGISLATURE; to whom the work will be respectfully inscribed.

The manner in which this Magnificent Undertaking will be executed is specified in the following

PARTICULARS.

SIXTY PICTURES will be painted from the most interesting events in the British History.

The Engravings from those Pictures will be in the manner of the celebrated prints of 'General Wolfe' and 'The Death of Lord Chatham'.

The whole History will be published, as nearly as can be computed, in Sixty Numbers; making Five Magnificent Volumes in Imperial Quarto: each Number containing One Capital HISTORIC PRINT; with One or more VIGNETTES, PORTRAITS, Views of NAVAL ENGAGEMENTS, MONUMENTS, or RUINS, as the subject may require.

When a sufficient number of Pictures are finished for the purpose, they will form and Exhibition.

Subscribers are to deposit ONE GUINEA; for which a receipt will be given, entitling them to fine impressions of the Prints, [*p.* [5]) and to Tickets of Admission to the Exhibition. The receipt will be transferable; and the holder be possessed of it's advantages as it stands in the list. Such an Engagement will be given on the receipt as will preclude all doubt or suspicion respecting the fair and proper delivery of the impressions.

The price to SUBSCRIBERS will be ONE GUINEA each Number, to be paid for on delivery: and, when the Subscription is full, the price will be considerably advanced. The Names of Subscribers will be printed.

As the Proprietors mean to give up the advantage arising from Proof Prints, they think it necessary to inform those, who would wish to become Subscribers, that, by inserting their names early, they will ensure to themselves the possession of the Prints which would constitute Proofs; and that every Subscriber will have an equal chance of fine impressions. They intend, however, to take off Three Sets of Proofs, and no more. One copy will be deposited with the Pictures for the NATION; one presented to His MAJESTY, under whose Patronage the Arts and Artists of this country have been raised to the rank and estimation they hold in the Schools of Europe; and one to HIS ROYAL HIGHNESS THE PRINCE OF WALES.

It is intended to publish the First Number in the ensuing Summer; and the following numbers as early in succession as the Nature and Splendor of the undertaking will admit. The Proprietors are aware of the delays which have and do attend the publication of large works; and, though they humbly conceive a [*p.* (6)] more extensive or magnificent undertaking has not distinguished or adorned the literary annals of this country; yet, from arrangements already made, and which they are pursuing with the utmost vigor, they presume to assure the patrons of the work, that it will be completed in much less time than (considering the delays which have attended other publications) they may have reason to expect.

They are happy in being able to assure the Public that the following Artists have undertaken to exert their abilities in the embellishments of it.

PAINTERS OF THE HISTORIC SUBJECTS

J. BARRY, R.A. Professor of Painting to the Royal Academy	G. ROMNEY.
J.S. COPLEY, R.A.	J.F. RIGAUD, R.A.
R. COSWAY, R.A. Principal Painter to his Royal Highness the PRINCE OF WALES.	R. SMIRKE, A.
	T. STOTHARD, A.
	H. TRESHAM, A.
	J. WRIGHT, of Derby, A.
Mrs. COSWAY.	F. WHEATLEY, R.A.
H. FUSELI, R.A.	R.L. WEST, and
W. HAMILTON, R.A.	BENJAMIN WEST, R.A. Historical Painter to HIS MAJESTY.
J. NORTHCOTE, R.A.	
J. OPIE, R.A.	

(7)

ENGRAVERS.

F. BARTOLOZZI, R.A. Engraver to His MAJESTY.	J. HALL, Historical Engraver to His MAJESTY.
W. BYRNE.	J. LANDSEER.
T. BROMLEY	T. MEDLAND.
W. BLAKE.	P. NEAGLE.
J. COLLIER, A. Engraver to Her MAJESTY.	T. POUNCY.
	W. SHARP.
J. DELATRE.	W. SKELTON.

J. EMES.

W. ELLIS

J. FITTLER, Engraver to His
  MAJESTY.

A. SMITH.

S. SMITH.

J. STOWE.

The DRAWINGS for the VIGNETTES will be made
        by E. BURNEY and C.R. RYLEY.
The MARINE DEPARTMENT is undertaken by J.T.
SERRES, Marine Painter to His Royal Highness
        the Duke of CLARENCE.
The DRAWINGS OF ANCIENT PALACES and RUINS
                by
        P. SANDBY, R.A. and T. HEARNE.
And the PUBLIC EDIFICES, &c. by T. MALTON.
                (8)
The plan of this comprehensive and
magnificent Work requiring the Portraits of
eminent personages, from the earliest periods to
the present time, it will necessarily be enriched
by the productions of REUBENS,[*sic*] VANDYKE,
JANSSEN, LELY, KNELLER, Sir JOSHUA
REYNOLDS, GAINSBOROUGH, &c.—And the

Prints of admired Monuments, Statues and
Relievos, shall be from the exquisite Works of
ROUBILIAC, CIBBER, SCHEEMACKER, BACON,
BANKS, NOLLEKENS, &c. &c.

The LETTER-PRESS will be executed by T.
BENSLEY; from a Type cutting, on purpose for
this Work by J. JACKSON; and upon a Paper of
peculiar beauty and excellence, manufacturing at
the Mills of LEPARD, SMITH, and LEPARD.

The Proprietors presume to flatter themselves,
from the very great Patronage bestowed on
other works, that an undertaking so interesting
as a complete HISTORY of ENGLAND, adorned
with the masterly productions of the first Artists
of the age, will be patronized and encouraged in
proportion to it's magnitude and importance.

Subscribers' Names are entered, and
specimens of the work may be seen, at Mr.
BOWYER'S, No. 68, Berner's Street.

LONDON,

JANUARY 1792.

THE DEATH OF CARDINAL BEAUFORT

177.

177. *The Death of Cardinal Beaufort*, 1803
(Shakespeare, *King Henry VI*, Part 2, III, iii)
(Vol. II/5 = III/10, facing p. 338)

Engraved by William Bromley (1769-1842) after
Fuseli's lost painting
Imprint: London Published by R. Bowyer,
Historic Gallery, Pall Mall, July 1803.
Inscription: THE DEATH OF CARDINAL
BEAUFORT | (bottom): H. Fuseli pinx^t. | | W.
Bromley sculp^t.
Dimensions (excluding lower panel): ■ 28.3 x
20.9 cm | 11^3/16" x 8^5/16"; ■ 29.0 x 22.2 cm |
11^7/16" x 8¾" (Pierpont Morgan)
Other locations: BL 749.f.1; Huntington 128912
Plate only: BM 1858-10-9-105; DHW; Essick
Lit.: Schiff 1260 (28.4 x 21.2 cm); Irwin 1966,
96; Bentley 1980, 74-76.
Exh.: Kansas City 1982 (37).

The first work that Fuseli ever submitted for
exhibition to the Royal Academy was a large wash
drawing representing the death of Beaufort done
at Rome (1772; Schiff 440). This rather wooden
rendition was one of the four painted versions he
prepared in the first decade of the new century.

The death of Beaufort was a popular and
traditional passage. The agony of Beaufort
contrasted with the sympathetic attitude of the
young king was supposed to demonstrate the basic
qualities of tragedy, fear and compassion. Fuseli
captures the moment when Henry urges the dying
Cardinal to make his peace with heaven. The
lines illustrated are:

Lord Cardinal, if thou thinks't on heaven's
  bliss,
Hold up thy hand, make signal of thy hope.—
He dies, and makes no sign. O God forgive
  him!

This was Fuseli's sole contribution to Bowyer's
project. As Farington noted in his diary (17 July
1793), Bowyer was 'afraid to employ Fuseli on
acct of the great inequality of his works'
(*Farington Diary*, I, 215).

******

No. 177A.
David Hume.
THE | HISTORY OF ENGLAND: | FROM THE
TEXT OF | HUME AND SMOLLETT | TO THE |
REIGN OF GEORGE THE THIRD; | AND
THENCE CONTINUED TO INCLUDE THE |
RESTORATION OF THE EMPIRE IN

FRANCE, | THE | GREAT EXHIBITION OF THE
INDUSTRY OF ALL NATIONS, | AND
THE | DEATH OF THE DUKE OF
WELLINGTON. | — | BY THOMAS GASPEY,
ESQ. | — | VOL. I. [-VOL. VIII.] | PRINTED AND
PUBLISHED BY | THE LONDON PRINTING
AND PUBLISHING COMPANY, | 97 AND 100,
ST. JOHN STREET; 1 AND 2, BLUECOAT
BUILDINGS, CHRIST'S HOSPITAL, LONDON;
AND | 55, DEY STREET, NEW YORK. | [1852].

[*Added engraved title page*]: THE | HISTORY OF
ENGLAND: | FROM THE TEXT OF | HUME
AND SMOLLETT: | CONTINUED TO THE
PRESENT TIME | BY THOMAS GASPEY,
ESQ. | AUTHOR OF 'THE PICTORIAL
HISTORY OF FRANCE,' &C. | [Vignette] |
PAINTED BY BURNEY. | | *ENGRAVED BY J.
ROGERS.* | *Death of William Rufus.* | JOHN
TALLIS & COMPANY, LONDON & NEW
YORK [1852].

...J. & F. TALLIS, LONDON, EDINBURGH &
DUBLIN. [1852]

177A. *The Death of Beaufort*, [1852]
(Vol. I, facing p. 484)

Re-engraved on steel by John Rogers (1808?-
1888)
Imprint: THE LONDON PRINTING AND
PUBLISHING COMPANY
Inscription: Painted by H. Fuseli. | | Engraved by
J. Rogers | [Vignette medallion]: JOAN OF ARC
BEFORE THE ECCLESIASTICAL COURT AT
ROUEN. | THE DEATH OF CARDINAL
BEAUFORT | KING HENRY VI. | Part 2. Act 3.
Sc.3.
Dimensions: ■ 15.0 x 10.9 cm | 5^{14}/16" x 4^5/16"
(Browne) (plate only)

Variants:
I. Imprint changed (facing p. 484): BL 9505.f.1
Imprint: JOHN TALLIS & COMPANY
LONDON & NEW YORK
Other locations (plate only): Essick (all below
signatures cropped); Huntington 265806.I.434;
NYPL MCT+ S.B. 11
II. Imprint changed (facing p. 484): DHW
(H=29.5 cm)
Imprint: J. & F. TALLIS, LONDON,
EDINBURGH & DUBLIN.
Other locations: Dartmouth DA 30.q.H95.1852

******

178.

178. *Solitude. Twilight*, 1803
(*Lycidas*, ll. 26, 28)

Stipple engraving by Moses Haughton (1772 or
1774-1748) with aquatint by Frederick Christian
Lewis (1779-1856) after the lost painting No.
XXXVII in The Milton Gallery.
Inscription: Painted by H. Fuseli R.A.—Engraved
by M. Haughton, & Publish'd Sep'. 13, 1803, N°.
13 Berners S'. London.||Aquatinta by F.C.
Lewis|**Lycidas.**|

> Under the opening eye-lids of the morn,
> What time the gray-fly winds her sultry horn.

Dimensions: ■ 29.3 x 24.3 cm | 11½" x 9⁹/16"
(BM 1880-6-12-352) (Sheet=39.1 cm).
Other locations: DHW; Essick; NG 1980.45.960
Lit.: Schiff 903 (29.3 x 24.3 cm) ('Berwin S'.'
for 'Berners S'.'); *Monthly Magazine* (April
1804), 268; *Litteratur und Kunst* (1806), II, 372;
Schiff-Viotto 1977, no. 166; *Letters*, 294;
Farington, VI, 2255.

Variants:
I. Imprint on separate line: BM 1979.u.1247
Imprint: Publish'd Sep'. 13th. 1803, by M.
Haughton, N°. 13. Berners Street, Oxford
Street, London.
Inscription: Fuseli. pinx'.||Lewis, Aquatinta.||
M. Haughton. Sculp'.| **Lycidas.**|[Verses]
Other locations: Geneva (Cabinet d'Estampes)
E71/77
II. Lacking name of Lewis: V & A E.1190-
1886 (imprint cropped?)
Inscription: Fuseli. pinx'.||M. Haughton.
Sculp'.|**Lycidas.**|[Verses]

The price of the print was 10s.6d.
In spring 1803, Moses Haughton moved into the
large house in Berners Street that Fuseli had
recently taken, to become Fuseli's resident
engraver. *Lycidas* was the first of an intended
series of prints 'from Milton, Shakespeare and
Dante after Paintings by Fuseli' to be engraved by
Haughton, announced in a prospectus (now lost),

published in German translation in the Zurich *Journal für Litteratur und Kunst*, II, 1806, 378-380. Incredibly, twenty-seven of the plates were announced as 'already finished' in a summary notice in the January 1805 issue of *The Monthly Magazine* (XVIII, 539). In reality, the fourteen large stipple plates Haughton had engraved by 1813 would never again be mentioned in any such context, although Haughton told Farington (27 February 1804) that 'He expects to be able to print out about four prints in a year,—that the prices will vary from half a guinea to a guinea and a very few something more than a guinea. The whole expence of the *50 prints* proposed to be published He concludes will be abt. £35'.

Lycidas and *The Dream of Eve*, were rather harshly reviewed in the *Monthly Magazine* for April 1804 (268):

> [*The Milton Gallery*] was the production of a mind fraught with peculiar energy, of a man who was perfectly acquainted with the anatomy of the human figure, but who, ... sometimes soared into the regions of absurdity. To copy his style demands a portion of his feeling,—and ... [*in*] attempt[*ing*] to transfer his figures from the canvas to the copper ...[*there*] is some danger of rendering what was *character* in the picture, *caricature* in the print; of *out Heroding Herod!* and rendering that which was high art in the original, ridiculous in the copy: the picture of *Lycidas* was a chaste and beautiful performance; ... almost every thing which gave value to the painting is lost in the engraving. ... The manner of engraving is extremely singular.

******

No. 178A.
[Charles Knight].
UNDER THE SUPERINTENDENCE OF THE SOCIETY FOR THE DIFFUSION OF | USEFUL KNOWLEDGE. | THE | GALLERY OF PORTRAITS: | WITH | MEMOIRS. | — | VOLUME I. [-VOLUME VII.]— | LONDON: CHARLES KNIGHT, [22, LUDGATE ST, | AND 13,] PALL-MALL EAST. | — | 1833 [-1837]. | — | PRICE ONE GUINEA, BOUND IN CLOTH. (1/144 pls. + 107 vignettes & medallions).

THE | PENNY MAGAZINE | OF | THE SOCIETY | FOR THE | DIFFUSION OF USEFUL KNOWLEDGE. | — | 1832. | — | LONDON: CHARLES KNIGHT 1832-1834.

The illustration in *The Penny Magazine* is taken from 'a Memoir of Milton in *The Gallery of Portraits*'. It is not included in the list of illustrations in Vol. I of *The Penny Magazine*. The illustration does not appear in the American edition (published by B.F. and J.J. Greenough, Boston), although the quotation from *Lycidas* is present (I, 164).

178A.

178A. *Lycidas*, 1832.
(*The Gallery of Portraits*)
('Life of Milton', I, 54)

Woodcut vignette by John Jackson (1801-1848) after a drawing by Fuseli.
Inscription (lower left of design): JACKSON.
Dimensions: 6.7 x 6.5 cm / 3^{10}/16" x 3½" (BL 10803.1.3)

Variants:
I. Reissued as illustration in (*The Penny Magazine*, 14 July 1832, I, 152) with added inscription
Inscription (lower left of design): JACKSON. | (bottom right): [Lycidas. From a design by Fuseli.] [*brackets in the original*] (BL P.P. 6000.bb.)
Other locations: NYPL *DA 1832

******

No. 178B.
DAS | PFENNIG-MAGAZIN | DER | GESELLSCHAFT | ZUR | VERBREITUNG

GEMEINNÜTZIGER KENNTNISSE | — |
ERSTER BAND. [-ZEHNTER BAND.]. |
LEIPZIG [VERLAG VON BOSSANGE
VATER]. 1834-

178B. *Lycidas*, 1834
(*Das Pfennig-Magazin*, II, 440)
(17 May 1834)

Woodcut vignette by John Jackson (1801-1848)
reissued 1834

Inscription (lower left of design): JACKSON | Der
schlafende Schäfer, nach einer Zeichnung v
Füssli.
Dimensions: ■ 6.6 x 6.2 cm | 2¾ " x 2¹⁵/₁₆"
(UB Basel Z4.61)
Other locations: SB Bern S.M.Q32; Indiana
AP30.P45; Lucerne B50 fol.
Lit.: Federmann 1927, p. 178

******

179. *The Dream of Eve*, 1804
(*Paradise Lost*, V, 86-91)

Stipple engraving by Moses Haughton (1772 or
1774-1848) with aquatint by Frederick Christian
Lewis (1779-1856) after Fuseli's lost painting No.
XVI in the Milton Gallery
Inscription: Painted by H. Fuseli R.A. Engraved
by M. Haughton. & Publish'd as the Act directs.
Janʸ. 26ᵗʰ. 1804. Nᵒ. 13. Berners Street.
London. | | Aquatinta by F.C. Lewis. | The Dream
of Eve |

179.

_____Forthwith up to the clouds
with him I flew, and underneath beheld
The earth outstretch'd immense,___

_____

_____suddenly
My guide was gone, and I, methought, sunk
down.

Dimensions: ■ 49.0 x 42.8 cm | 19⁵/₁₆" x 16¹³/₁₆"
(BM 1861-5-18-156) (formerly Moses Haughton)
Other locations: BM T.16.15
Lit.: *Litteratur und Kunst* (1806), 370-371

Variants:

I. Proof before letters: BM 1852-11-16-550
(48.2 x 42.3 cm)

II. Proof before all letters (lacking imprint):
KHZ 1940/142

Incription: H. FUSELI. R.A. PINX^T. | | M.
HAUGHTON. SCULP^T.

Other locations: Essick; V & A E.1199-B-1886

III. Proof before all letters (lacking verse): BM
1927-2-18-67

Lit.: Schiff 896A; *Monthly Mag.* (April 1804),
268; Schiff 1963,66, pl.29; Warner 1984, pl.82

******

Nos. 180 - 181.

John Milton.

PARADISE LOST: | A POEM, | IN TWELVE
BOOKS. | THE AUTHOR, | JOHN MILTON. | — |
COLLATED WITH THE BEST EDITIONS: |
BY | THOMAS PARK, ESQ. F.S.A. | — | VOL. I.
[-VOL. II.] | — | LONDON | PRINTED AT THE
STANHOPE PRESS, BY CHARLES
WHITTINGHAM, UNION BUILDINGS,
LEATHER LANE; FOR JOHN SHARPE,
OPPOSITE YORK-HOUSE, PICCADILLY. 1805
(2/5 illus.).

[General title]: THE | WORKS | OF THE | BRITISH
POETS, | COLLATED WITH THE BEST
EDITIONS: | BY | THOMAS PARK, F.S.A. | — |
VOL. I. [-VOL. II.] | — | CONTAINING | THE
FIRST AND SECOND VOLUMES [THE THIRD
AND FOURTH VOLUMES] | OF | MILTON. | = |
LONDON: | PRINTED FOR J. SHARPE,
OPPOSITE ALBANY, PICCADILLY; AND
SOLD BY W. SUTTABY, STATIONERS'
COURT, LUDGATE STREET. | 1808.

[Added title]: THE | POETICAL WORKS | OF |
JOHN MILTON. | — | COLLATED WITH THE
BEST EDITIONS: | BY | THOMAS PARK, F.S.A.
| — | VOL. I. [-VOL. IV.] | = | LONDON: |
PRINTED AT THE STANHOPE PRESS, | BY
WHITTINGHAM AND ROWLAND, |
GOSWELL STREET; | FOR SUTTABY,
EVANCE, AND FOX, STATIONER'S
COURT; | SHARPE AND HAILES, MUSEUM,
PICCADILLY; TAYLOR AND | HESSEY,
FLEET-STREET; AND R. JENNINGS,
POULTRY. | — | 1814.

PARADISE LOST: | A POEM, | IN TWELVE
BOOKS. | THE AUTHOR, | JOHN MILTON. | — |
COLLATED WITH THE BEST EDITIONS: |

BY | THOMAS PARK, F.S.A. | — | VOL. II. | = |
LONDON: | PRINTED AT THE STANHOPE
PRESS, | BY WHITTINGHAM AND
ROWLAND, | GOSWELL STREET; | FOR
SUTTABY, EVANCE, AND FOX,
STATIONERS' COURT; | SHARPE AND
HAILES, MUSEUM, PICCADILLY; TAYLOR
AND | HESSEY, FLEET STREET; AND R.
JENNINGS, POULTRY. | — | 1814.

[General title]: THE | WORKS | OF | THE BRITISH
POETS. | INCLUDING | TRANSLATIONS |
FROM THE GREEK AND ROMAN
AUTHORS. | COLLATED WITH THE BEST
EDITIONS, | BY THOMAS PARK, F.S.A. | — | IN
THIRTY-SIX VOLUMES. | I. | THE POEMS OF
MILTON, VOL. I. AND II. [VOL. III. AND
IV.] | = | LONDON: | PRINTED FOR JOHN
SHARPE, PICCADILLY; | AND SUTTABY,
FOX, AND SUTTABY, STATIONERS'
COURT, | LUDGATE STREET. | — | 1828 (72
illus.).

[General title]: THE | BRITISH POETS: | WITH
THE MOST | APPROVED TRANSLATIONS | OF
THE | GREEK AND ROMAN POETS, | WITH |
DISSERTATIONS, NOTES, &C. | = | THE
TEXT COLLATED WITH THE BEST
EDITIONS, | BY THOMAS PARK, ESQ. F.S.A.
| — | ILLUSTRATED BY A SERIES OF
ENGRAVINGS, BY THE | MOST EMINENT
ARTISTS. | — | IN ONE HUNDRED
VOLUMES. | VOL. XXIII. XXIV. |
CONTAINING THE POETICAL WORKS OF |
COLLINS. | MILTON. IN 3 VOLUMES. VOLS.
1. 2. | = | PRINTED FOR J. SHARPE. | — | 1810-
1824.

...VOL. XXIII. [VOL. XXIV.] | CONTAINING
THE POETICAL WORKS OF | MILTON. VOL.
1. [-VOL. 2.] | PARADISE LOST. BOOKS I-VI.
[BOOKS VII-XII.] | = | LONDON: | PRINTED
FOR J. SHARPE. | — | 1810-1824.

For the other illustration in this series see No. **294**
below.

The issue in one hundred volumes appears to be
very rare. I have come across only one partial set,
lacking many plates. Another series, *The British
Poets. Including Translations. In One Hundred
Volumes* (Newberry Y184.I21), printed by C.
Whittingham in 1822 for a group of fourteen
booksellers, headed by J. Carpenter, is apparently
a competing set.

180.

180. *Satan Rousing his Legions*, 1803
(*Paradise Lost*, I, 130)
(Vol. I, facing p. [14])

Engraved by Peltro W. Tomkins (1760-1840)
Imprint: Published 1st. Jany. 1805, by John
Sharpe,| Piccadilly.
Inscription (lower panel): MILTON.|

  Awake, arise or be for ever fall'n.
    Vol. I. Par. Lost. B. 1. L 330.|

(bottom): Painted by Hy. Fuseli R.A.||Engraved
by P.W. Tomkins.
Dimensions (excluding bottom panel): ■ 7.5 x 6.0
cm | 2¹⁵/16" x 2⁶/16"; ■ 7.9 x 6.3 cm | 3²/16" x
2½" (BL 1066.c.13).
Other locations: SB Bern Litt XVII 194; DHW
(1814/1828) (Vol. I, facing title page); Harvard
10487.38 (1805/1808) (facing p. [14]); Harvard
10487.40 (1814/1828) (facing p. [170]); LC
PR1173.B6 (1805/1828) (Vol. I, facing title page)
Plate only: Huntington 108370 (bound vols. of
plates) (Vol. I, f 25); V & A E.1204-1886
Lacking plate: DHW (1810/1824)
Lit.: Schiff 1304 (7.6 x 6.0 cm); Collins Baker
1948, 104; Pointon 1970, 120, pl. 119.

Variants:
I. Proof before all letters (imprint only): BM
1865-10-14-135 (Sheet=22.5 cm)
Imprint (scratched letters): Published as the Act
directs Decr. 1803 by J. Sharpe Piccadilly.
II. Proof before all letters (lacking signatures):
BM 1864-12-10-117 (Sheet=22.1 cm)

181.

181. *The Temptation of Eve*, 1805
(*Paradise Lost*, IX, 527)
(Vol. II, facing p. 64)

Engraved by Peltro W. Tomkins (1760-1840) after
Fuseli's painting in the City of Auckland Art
Gallery (1804; Schiff 1215)
Imprint: Published 1st. Jany. 1805, by John
Sharpe,| Piccadilly.
Inscription (bottom panel): MILTON.|

  His gentle dumb expression turn'd at length,
  The eye of Eve—
      Vol. II. Par. Lost, B. 9. L. 527.

(bottom): Painted by Hy. Fuseli R.A.||Engraved
by P.W. Tomkins.
Dimensions (excl. bottom panel): ■ 7.5 x 6.0 cm |
2¹⁵/16" x 2⁵/16";■ 7.8 x 6.3 cm | 3¹/16" x 2⁷/16"
(BL 1066.c.13).

Other locations: SB Bern (facing p. [2]); DHW (1814/1828) (Vol. II, facing t.p.); Harvard 10487.38 (Vol. II facing t.p.); Harvard 10487.40 (1814/1828) (Vol. II, facing p. 49); Huntington 108370 (bound vols. of plates)(Vol. I, f. 27); LC PR1173.B62 (1814/1828) (Vol. II, facing t.p.)
Lacking plate: DHW (1810/1824)
Lit.: Schiff 1305 (7.6 x 6.0 cm); Collins Baker 1948, 104; Pointon 1970, 111, pl. 96; Behrendt 1983, 106, 160, pl. 29.
Exh.: Kansas City 1989 (18)

Variants:
I. Proof before all letters (lacking imprint): BM 1863-5-9-9
II. Proof before all letters (imprint only): V & A E.347-1941
Imprint (scratched letters): Published as the Act directs Decr. 1803 by J. Sharpe Piccadilly.
III. Unfinished proof, before frame & lower panel: V & A E.346-1941
Imprint (scratched letters): Published as the Act directs Decr. 1803, by J. Sharpe Piccadilly.

The action has been telescoped: textually this is only the preliminary stage of the temptation. Having 'ambushed' Eve among her flowers Satan attempts to catch her eye. The serpent must still lead Eve to the Tree of Knowledge to eat the apple. The 'visual beams' the serpent directs at Eve are not found in the painting.

******

No. 181A.
John Milton.
THE | POETICAL WORKS | OF | JOHN MILTON. | WITH THE LIFE OF THE AUTHOR. | IN TWO VOLUMES. | VOL. I. [-VOL. II.] | — | PHILADELPHIA: | PUBLISHED BY JOHN STEVENSON. | ANDERSON & MEEHAN, PRINTERS. | — | 1821 (1/3 illus.).

181A. *The Temptation of Eve*, 1821
(*Paradise Lost*, IX, 527)
(Vol. I, facing p. 234)

Re-engraved by William Kneass (1780-1840)
Inscription (bottom panel): MILTON. |
His gentle dumb expression turn'd at length,
The eye of Eve——
          Vol II Par. Lost ?? 527
(bottom): Painted by H. Fuseli R.A. | | Kneass Young & Co.
Dimensions (excl. bottom panel): ■ 7.5 x 5.9 cm | 2^15/16" x 2¼"; ■ 7.8 x 6.1 cm | 3^1/16" x 2½";

(incl. bottom panel): ■ 9.8 x 5.9 cm | 3^13/16" x 2^6/16"; ■ 10.1 x 6.1 cm | 4" x 2^6/16" (American Antiquarian Society).
Other locations: Illinois 821.M64.K1821(not seen)

Variants:
I. Proof? (facing p. 233): Rice PR3350.E21
Inscription: [Verse in panel]; (bottom right) (scratched signature): Young & Kneass Sc!
The accompanying illustrations ('Milton Composing Paradise Lost' and 'The Mower Whetting his Scythe', both after Westall) are also taken from Sharpe's edition. The first of these is lacking in my 36-volume set, but is found as frontispiece to Vol. XXV of the 100-vol. edition.

******

Nos. 182 - 183.
William Shakespeare.
THE | PLAYS | OF | WILLIAM SHAKESPEARE. | FROM | THE CORRECTED TEXT | OF | JOHNSON AND STEEVENS, | — | EMBELLISHED WITH PLATES. | — | IN SIX VOLUMES | VOL. I. [-VOL. VI. | = | LONDON: | PRINTED FOR JOHN STOCKDALE, PICCADILLY. | 1807 (2/22 illus.).
SEVENTEEN | ENGRAVINGS, | TO ILLUSTRATE | SHAKSPEARE, | FROM | PICTURES BY EMINENT BRITISH ARTISTS. | = | ENGRAVED BY | [*col. 1*] HALL, | SOW, | FITTLER, | | [*col. 2*] SHARPE, | BROMLEY, | RHODES, | — | LONDON: | PUBLISHED BY A. WOODMASON, EASING LANE CHEAPSIDE: AND TO BE HAD AT MESSRS BOYDELL & CO.'S | NO 90 CHEAPSIDE: AND OF ALL PRINT AND BOOK-SELLERS. | — | MAY 17, 1817 (3/17 illus.).
Contains a 'List of the Engravings'.
A | SERIES | OF | ENGRAVINGS | TO ILLUSTRATE THE | WORKS OF SHAKSPEARE, | BY HEATH, HALL, RHODES, FITLER, &C. | = | LONDON: | PUBLISHED BY JOHN MURRAY, ALBEMARLE-STREET; J. HEATH, RUSSELL PLACE, FITZROY- | SQUARE; AND W. WOODMASON, LEADENHALL-STREET. | 1817 (2/37 illus.).
[Printed Label]: A SERIES OF | MAGNIFICENT ENGRAVINGS. | TO ILLUSTRATE THE | WORKS OF SHAKSPEARE. | BY HEATH, HALL, RHODES, FITLER, &C. | PRICE £8:8S.
A SERIES OF ENGRAVINGS BY HEATH AND

BARTOLOZZI, FROM PAINTINGS BY STOTHARD TO ILLUSTRATE THE WORKS OF SHAKSPEARE AND MILTON; FORMING AN ELEGANT LIBRARY ACCOMPANIMENT TO THE VARIOUS EDITIONS OF THOSE AUTHORS| =|price £9:9S.| =| LONDON, PRINTED FOR H. M'LEAN. 1818 (2/34 illus.).

...LONDON:|PRINTED AT THE COLUMBIAN PRESS, BY HOWLETT AND BRIMMER, 10, FRITH STREET, SOHO,|FOR H. M'LEAN, 16, SALISBURY STREET, STRAND.|—|1818 (2/21 illus.).

A|SERIES|OF|MAGNIFICENT|ENGRAVINGS|TO|ILLUSTRATE THE VARIOUS|FOLIO OR QUARTO EDITIONS|OF|THE WORKS|OF|SHAKESPEARE AND MILTON;|OR, BOUND UP, TO FORM|A LIBRARY ACCOMPANIMENT|TO ANY OF THE|SMALLER EDITIONS OF THOSE AUTHORS.| =|PRICE £9 :9s.| =| LONDON:|PRINTED BY J. BARFIELD, WARDOUR-STREET,|FOR H. M'LEAN, NO. 8, SOHO-SQUARE.|—|1813 (5/51 illus.).

A|SERIES|OF|ENGRAVINGS,|TO|ILLUSTRATE THE WORKS|OF|SHAKSPEARE,|FORMING|AN ELEGANT LIBRARY ACCOMPANIMENT|TO THE|VARIOUS EDITIONS OF THAT AUTHOR.| =| LONDON:|PRINTED BY HOWLETT AND BRIMMER, FRITH STREET, SOHO SQUARE,|FOR HECTOR M'LEAN, NO. 113, STRAND. 1822 (2/21 illus.).

[Cover title]: GRAPHIC ILLUSTRATIONS|OF|SHAKSPEARE|ENGRAVED BY HEATH,|FROM PAINTINGS BY STOTHARD.|—|Price *£3.13s.6d.*

For the other illustrations in this volume see Nos. **132-134**.

PROSPECTUS
(BL 644.m.6)

SHAKSPEARE.
=

MESSRS. HEATH AND ROBINSON| Respectfully inform the Admirers of Shakspeare and the Fine Arts,|That on FRIDAY, JANUARY 1, 1802, will be published,|THE FIRST NUMBER OF|**A NEW EDITION**|OF|**SHAKSPEARE'S PLAYS,**| From the Corrected Text of|JOHNSON AND

STEEVENS;|To be Embellished with| **PRINTS** ENGRAVED BY MR. **HEATH,**| Historical Engraver to His Majesty &c.|After Pictures Painted for this Purpose By|

B. WEST, President of the Royal Academy, and Historical Painter to the King

J.S. COPLEY, R.A.	T. STOTHARD, R.A.
H. FUSELI, R.A.	H. TRESHAM, R.A.
W. HAMILTON, R.A.	F. WHEATLEY, R.A.
J. OPIE, R.A.	R. COURBOULD &C.

The Letter-Press will be executed with every Advantage of Paper and Type,
by T.BENSLEY.
=

This Work will be printed in Imperial Quarto, and comprized in Thirty-six Numbers, each containing ONE PLAY, With Two appropriate ENGRAVINGS, at ONE GUINEA a Number, to be Paid on delivery

A Number of this Work will be published every two months, till completed.

A few Copies will be printed on a Superior Paper, with Proof Impressions of the Plates, Price ONE GUINEA AND A HALF the Number.

The Impressions will be delivered in the exact order subscribed for.

Annexed to the Plays will be given a LIFE and PORTRAIT of the AUTHOR.

Specimens of the PAINTINGS and ENGRAVINGS may be seen at Mr. HEATH'S, No. 15, Russell Place, Fitzroy Square, where Books are opened to receive Subscriptions; and at Messrs. ROBINSON'S, Paternoster Row; BELL and BRADFUTE'S, Edinburgh; BRASH and REID'S, Glasgow; and J. ARCHER'S, Dublin.

LONDON, November 1801.

T. Bensley, Printer, Bolt Court, Fleet Street London.

Preparations for this edition, for which originally 'Stothard was intended to make all the designs' were already well in hand by December 1796, when it was 'thought more prudent to add other artists.' These included West, Hamilton and Fuseli. Westall had at first 'without reflecting on it engaged to paint six pictures in 6 years.' But on hearing of Smirke's hesitation, lest the Boydells' 'expensive undertakings' should be 'injured by Proposals including so many names of persons who have been employed by them,' he also declined to take part (*Farington Diary*, III, 720).

The four small pictures from *Hamlet* and *Macbeth* that 'Heath bespoke of Fuseli' in February 1797 (*Farington Diary*, III, 764) represented, as Fuseli reported to Roscoe, 'all the work I Could produce this Year....Smaller than anything I ever painted before, at 15 guineas a piece' (5 December 1797, *Letters*, 175). Of these only the two below appear to have been engraved for this edition. Once the paintings had served their immediate purpose, Heath sold them at auction. (John Sharpe had similarly disposed of his commissioned paintings in order to recapitalise.) (See under 'Owners' in Burton B. Fredericksen, *Index of Paintings*, 1806-1810, II/2, 1333 and 1367).

182.

182. *Macbeth and Banquo meet the Witches on the Heath*, 1804
(*Macbeth*, I, iii)
(Vol. III, facing p. 9)

Engraved by James Heath (1757-1834) after the lost original

Imprint: Published April 1. 1804, by J. Heath, 15, Russell Place, Fitzroy Square; and G. & J. Robinson, Pater noster Row.
Inscription: MACBETH|

 Banquo. what are these
 So wither'd and so wild in their attire?
 That look not like th' inhabitants o' th' earth,
 And yet are on't? Live you, or are you aught
 That man may question? you seem to
  understand me,
 By each at once her choppy finger laying
 Upon her skinny lips.
                              Act I Sc. 4.|
Painted by H. Fuseli R.A.||Engraved by J. Heath, Historical Engraver to his Majesty, and A.R.A.
Dimensions: ■ 21.0 x 14.8 cm | 8½" x 5^{13}/16";
■ 22.0 x 15.7 cm | 8^{10}/16" x 6^{3}/16" (Huntington 406915)
Other locations: BL 644.m.6 (2/6 vols. only); DHW (1818) (H=49.5 cm); Folger Art Vol. f79 (1818) (19/34 plates); Folger PR2752.1807c c.1; Folger PR2752.1807c c.2; Folger PR2752.1807c c.3; Folger PR2752.1807c c.4); Huntington 350598 (1818) (18/33 plates); LC PR2752.S8 1807; Michigan (1822);NYPL *NCM+ Johnson; YCBA PR2752.+S8 1807 (not seen)
Plate only: BM 1863-5-9-54; BM 1870-5-14-1712; Essick (imprint cropped); Folger PR2752.1823c c.1 (signatures and imprint cropped) (facing p. 321); Huntington 181067, XX, 51; KHZ 1940/148; V & A 1203-A-1886 (cropped?)
Lit.: Schiff 1258; *Letters*, 175, 176; *Farington Diary*, III, 720, 764; Fredericksen 1988-, II/1, 378.
Exh.: Kansas City 1982 (28).

Variants:
 I. Etched proof (1803) (oval in etched state; open capitals in title and scratched letters in panel) (bound in an extra-illustrated copy of Mrs. Bray's *Life of Thomas Stothard, R.A.*): Essick
Imprint: Published Novr. 1. 1803, by J. Heath, 15, Russell Place, Fitzroy Square; and G. & J. Robinson, Pater noster Row.
Inscription (at bottom of frame): Painted by T. Stothard R.A. [*sic*]||Engraved by J. Heath, Historical Engraver to his Majesty, and A.R.A.
 II. Proof (open capitals in title and scratched letters in panel): Huntington 181067, XX, 50.

182A.

182A. *Macbeth and Banquo*, [n.d.]
(*Macbeth*, I, iii)

Enlarged detail etched by H. Fernell (fl. 1834-1835) from Heath's plate, perhaps intended as frontispiece for an unidentified edition
Inscription: Fuseli del||H Fernell Sc; (bottom, in pencil): Banquo & Macbeth.
Dimensions (to platemark): 10.6 x 7.4 cm | 4½" x 2¹⁴/16" (DHW)

******

183.

183. *'I've Done the Deed'*, 1804
(*Macbeth*, II, ii)
(Vol. III, facing p. 31)

Engraved by James Heath (1757-1834) after Fuseli's lost painting (perhaps before 1800; Schiff Lost Work 26)
Imprint: Published April 1804, by J. Heath, N°. 15, Russell Place, Fitzroy Square; and G. & J. Robinson, Paternoster Row.
Inscription: Painted by H. Fuseli R.A.||Engraved by J.Heath, Historical Engraver to his Majesty, and to his Royal Highness the Prince of Wales.| MACBETH.|

Mac   I have done the deed.
          Act. II. Scene II.

Dimensions: ■ 20.4 x 15.0 cm | 8" x 5¹³/16";
■ 21.5 x 16.0 cm | 8⁷/16" x 6⁵/16" (Huntington 406915)
Other locations: BL 644.m.6 (2 of 6 vols. only); DHW (1818) (H=49.5 cm); Folger Art Vol. f79 (1818) (17/34 plates); Folger PR2752.1807c c.1 (imprint cropped); Folger PR2752.1807c c.2; Folger PR2752.1807c c.3; Folger PR2752.1807c c.4 (between pp. 30-31); Huntington 350598 (1818) (17/33 plates); KHZ 1940/149; LC PR2752.S8 1807; Michigan (1822); NYPL *NCM + Johnson; YCBA PR2752.+S8 1807 (not seen)
Plate only: BM 1861-6-8-157; BM 1863-5-9-52; Huntington 181067, XX, 100; Huntington 265806, I, 304 (imprint cropped); V & A E1208-B-1886
Lit.: Schiff 1259 (20.4 x 15.0 cm);
Exh.: Kansas City 1982 (30).

Macbeth emerges after murdering Duncan, shaken and conscience-stricken. His wife dismisses such thoughts as 'brainsickly.'

Lady M. Go get some water,
And wash this filthy witness from your hand.
Why did you bring these daggers from the
    place?
They must lie there. Go carry them; and smear
The sleepy grooms with blood.
Macb.   I'll go no more.
I am afraid to think what I have done;
Look on't again I dare not.
Lady M. Infirm of purpose!
Give me the daggers.

The features and the gestures of Macbeth and Lady Macbeth are those of David Garrick and Mrs. Pritchard whose performance Fuseli had captured in a drawing he made from life c. 1766 (Schiff 341).

******

No. 184.
SHARPE'S | BRITISH THEATRE | VOLUME THE FIRST. [-VOLUME THE FOURTH.] | [VIGNETTE]. | LONDON. | PRINTED BY C. WHITTINGHAM, DEAN STREET. | PUBLISHED BY JOHN SHARPE, PICCADILLY. | 1804 (1/18 illus.).

184.

184. *Melancholy*, 1804
(*Il Penseroso*, 40)
(Vol. III, title page)

Oval vignette engraved by William Sharp (1749-1824) after Fuseli's lost painting, No. XLVI in the Milton Gallery ([1799-1800]; Schiff Lost Work 55)
Inscription: SHARPE'S | BRITISH THEATRE | VOLUME THE THIRD. | [Vignette]. | LONDON. | Printed by C. WHITTINGHAM, Dean Street. | Published by JOHN SHARPE, Piccadilly. | 1804. | (outside frame, bottom centre): H^y. Fuseli R.A. inv^t.
Dimensions (diameter):5.1 x 3.8 cm | 2" x 1^7/16"; (incl. top and bottom panel): ■ 9.0 x 5.0 cm |

3^7/16" x 1^15/16"; ■ 3^10/16" x 2^1/16" (BL 11784.ee.3)
Other locations: McGill
Lit.: Schiff 1306 (9.2 x 5.4 or 5.0 x 3.8 cm); Knowles, I, 234; Bain 1960; Schiff 1963, 94, 98, pl. 52; Schiff-Viotto 1977, no. 180

Variants:
I. Proof before all letters (imprint only) (upper and lower panels blank): BM 1863-5-9-32 Imprint (scratched letters): Published as the Act directs April 1804, by J. Sharpe Piccadilly London.

Fuseli's description of the lost original in the Milton Gallery, 1800, also applies to the engraved version:

MELANCHOLY, Reclining on her throne—*Her rapt soul sitting in her eyes*, with the attendant GENII of TERROR and GRIEF at her Feet, and behind her the Shadow of UGOLINO and his dead SON.—The Whole dimly illuminated by a Moon-beam.

******

Nos. 185 - 186.
[[General title]: THE BRITISH CLASSICS: EMBELLISHED WITH ENGRAVINGS FROM PAINTINGS (EXECUTED ON PURPOSE FOR THE WORK) BY THE MOST DISTINGUISHED ARTISTS OF THIS COUNTRY; AND ILLUSTRATED WITH BIOGRAPHICAL AND CRITICAL ESSAYS, BY NATHAN DRAKE, M.D. | LONDON: | PRINTED BY CHARLES WHITTINGHAM, | DEAN STREET; | FOR JOHN SHARPE, OPPOSITE YORK HOUSE, PICCADILLY. | 1804. (2/104 illus., incl. engr. title pages + 20 portraits).

[Vignette] | THE | TATLER | VOLUME THE FIRST [-VOLUME THE FOURTH.] | LONDON. | PRINTED BY C. WHITTINGHAM, DEAN STREET. | PUBLISHED BY JOHN SHARPE, PICCADILLY. | 1804 [1813] (1/? illus.).

THE | SPECTATOR. | — | VOLUME THE FIRST. [-VOLUME THE EIGHTH.] | — | LONDON: | PRINTED BY CHARLES WHITTINGHAM, | DEAN STREET; | FOR JOHN SHARPE, OPPOSITE YORK HOUSE, PICCADILLY. | — | 1803 [1812] (1/34 illus. incl. 8 engr. t.p. + 8 engr. portraits).

PROSPECTUS
(BL 11902.c.26 (12))

PROSPECTUS | OF A NEW AND | SUPERB EDITION | OF THE | BRITISH CLASSICS: | EMBELLISHED WITH | ENGRAVINGS FROM PAINTINGS | (EXECUTED ON PURPOSE FOR THE WORK) | BY THE MOST DISTINGUISHED | ARTISTS OF THIS COUNTRY; | AND ILLUSTRATED WITH | BIOGRAPHICAL AND CRITICAL ESSAYS, | BY NATHAN DRAKE M.D. | Author of 'Literary Hours,' &c. | = | LONDON: | PRINTED BY CHARLES WHITTINGHAM, | DEAN STREET, | FOR JOHN SHARPE, OPPOSITE YORK HOUSE, PICCADILLY. | 1803.

ADDRESS. [*Omitted*]

GENERAL PLAN.

This work will comprize correct and uniform editions of the Spectator [*Vols. 5-12*], Tatler [*Vols. 1-4*], Guardian [*Vols. 13-14*], Rambler [*Vols. 15-18*], Idler [*Vols. 23-24*], Adventurer [*Vols. 19-22*], World, Connoisseur, &c. &c. with biographical, critical, and other necessary illustrations, from the pen of NATHAN DRAKE, M.D. whose writings have honourably borne the sanction and testimony of the Public.

THE ENGRAVINGS WILL BE EXECUTED BY Messrs. BARTOLOZZI, R.A. *Lisbon*, SHARP, Armstrong, Bromley, Collyer, A.R.A. Cromek, Delatre, Evans, Fittler, A.R.A. Holl, Knight, Landseer, Neagle, Parker, Raimbach, Schiavonetti, Skelton, Smith, A.R.A. Tomkins, Warren.

FROM PAINTINGS BY

Artaud, Fuseli, Prof. R.A. Howard, A.R.A. De Loutherbourg, R.A. Northcote, R.A. Opie, R.A. Porter, Singleton, Stothard, R.A. Thomson, A.R.A. Tresham, R.A. Westall, R.A.

The GUARDIAN entirely from Paintings by SMIRKE, R.A.

Drawings by Burney, and Thurston. And Vignettes by Burney, Singleton, and Thurston.

In addition to the above splendid combination of talents, Mr. WEST, President of the Royal Academy, with a liberality highly honourable to himself and worthy of his official station, has kindly consented to contribute his assistance, independent of any pecuniary advantage; the produce of which will be (as the Proprietor feels it ought to be) conveyed to the Public in addition to the hereafter stipulated number of embellishments.

The republic of letters has long been accustomed to the incomparable engravings of Mr. BARTOLOZZI; and it is no small pleasure to the present Proprietor to be enabled to prolong their continuance, having, previous to Mr. BARTOLOZZI'S departure from this country (an event much to be lamented) formed arrangements with that gentleman, from which he anticipates the happiest results.

The PAPER will be found (even in the state of perfection which that manufacture has sometime been thought to have arrived) to possess new and valuable qualities; and in addition to its beauty as a fabric, to receive the impression from the type with a clearness and perspicuity hitherto unparalleled.

The TYPE is presumed to be formed upon those principles of science (rejecting some recent innovations) which ought to be rigidly adhered to; and the PRINTER'S efforts will be such throughout the work, as shall reflect honour on the British Press.

The PUBLISHER pledges himself not to depart from the liberal scale with which he commences; but that his exertions shall be vigorous and unabated, not only to prevent the deficiencies which too often occur in periodical works, but to excel, if possible, in its progression; for on this foundation he humbly hopes to build some fame. Should he be guilty of a violation of this pledge, as every Classic will be distinct, and complete in itself, the public will have an opportunity of effectually punishing him, by withdrawing their patronage.

MODE OF PUBLICATION.

It is intended to divide each volume into three parts, one of which will be published every fortnight, or oftener. It had been originally the intention to have undertaken a weekly publication; but finding, notwithstanding every effort, that the possibility of this, with due attention to the execution of the work, was problematical, the Publisher names a fortnight as the time (reserving to himself the freedom of making it as often WEEKLY as circumstances will permit) rather than risk the confidence of the Public, by an unseasonable delay, or deviation from the plan laid down at the commencement.

The First Part will make its appearance on SATURDAY, *March* 19, 1803.

Each part will contain, on the average, eight or nine sheets of letter-press, elegantly printed in small octavo, with Two highly finished ENGRAVINGS; that is to say, either an Historical Plate, and a Portrait of one of the principal Authors; and Historical Plate, and a Vignette Title Page; or two Historical Plates. The price of each part, thus richly embellished, will be *Three Shillings and Sixpence*, to be paid on the delivery of the books.

But for the gratification of the Amateur, and of those who wish to possess the most finished specimens of art, an edition of TWO HUNDRED AND FIFTY COPIES (which number will on no account be exceeded) will be printed on a larger paper; the size, a SMALL DEMY OCTAVO; and contain PROOF IMPRESSIONS of the embellishments; which, from the impossibility of their ever being reprinted, will, doubtless, rapidly increase in value. These copies will be published only in volumes (each volume in advance upon its publication in parts) the subscription to which will require a deposit of *One Guinea*, and the same price for every volume, excepting the last, which will be delivered free of expense, on producing the receipt that will be given at the time of subscribing.

And, to accommodate those to whom the above editions may be too expensive, or who are desirous of possessing the literary part only, an edition will be printed on an inferior paper, but with neatness and care, which will contain none of the embellishments, excepting the *Portraits* of the *Authors*. This edition will be charged at the low price of *One Shilling and Sixpence* each part; and, when formed into volumes, will rank in price with the cheapest productions of our Press.

Subscribers Names (to be printed at the conclusion of the work) will be entered in books already opened for the purpose, by the Proprietor, JOHN SHARPE, opposite York House, Piccadilly, where Specimens of the Paintings and Engravings may be seen; Messrs. BOYDELL, Cheapside; KNIGHT and TRIPHOOK, Booksellers to the KING, St. James's Street; HATCHARD, Bookseller to the QUEEN, Piccadilly; SYMONDS, Paternoster Row; MILLER, Old Bond Street; TOMKINS, New Bond Street; WESTLEY and BICKERSTAFF, Strand; WHITE, Fleet Street; ASPERNE, Cornhill; ARCH, Gracechurch Street; and BLACKS and PARRY, Leadenhall Street; also by Deighton, Cambridge; Hanwell and Parker, Oxford; Norton and Son, Bristol; Barratt, Bath; Jones, Liverpool; Clarke and Co. Manchester; Knott and Lloyd, Birmingham; Woolmer, Exeter; Collins, Salisbury; Merridew, Coventry; Knight, Windsor; Simmons and Kirby, Canterbury; Rackham, Bury St. Edwards; Beatnisse, Norwich; Todd, York; Sands, Newcastle; Bell and Bradfute, Edinburgh; Brash and Reid, Glasgow; Archer, Dublin; Magee, Belfast; White, Cork; Fush and Detervolle, Paris; and FRANCESCO BARTOLOZZI, Esq. R.A. Engraver to the Court at Lisbon; with whom those who are desirous of possessing early Impressions are requested to enter their names and address, which will be punctually transmitted to the Proprietor, and ensure the same respect and attention as those with which he may be personally favoured.

The following pages [9-16] exhibit a SPECIMEN of the WORK.

185. *Tiresias Appearing to Odysseus in the Underworld*, 1804
(*Odyssey*, XI, 90-98, cited in *The Tatler*, No. 152)
(Vol. III, facing p. 196)

Engraved by William Bromley (1769-1842) after Fuseli's painting (Private collection).
Imprint: Published 17th. Feby. 1804. by John Sharpe, | Picadilly.
Inscription (top): TATLER | (below): VOL. 3. N°. 152. | Painted by Hy. Fuseli, R.A. | | Engraved by Wm. Bromley.
Dimensions: 8.5 x 7.5 cm | 3^6/16" x 2^{14}/16" (BL 1456.h.3)
Other locations (plate only): BM 1868-8-22-3182
Lit.: Schiff 1309 (8.6 x 7.6 cm, resp. 12.6 x 7.9 cm); J. Pye, *Patronage of British Art*, 1845, 373.

Variants:
I. Proof before letters (India paper): BM 1863-5-9-24
II. Proof before all letters: BM 1868-8-22-3183
III. Proof before verses (India paper): BM 1875-7-10-3380 (Sheet=22.5 cm)

Bromley received 18 guineas for his plate (Pye).

185.

186.

186. *Rosicrusius's Sepulchre*, 1803
(*Spectator* No. 379)
(Vol. IX, facing p. 307)

Engraved by William Sharp (1749-1824) after
Fuseli's painting exhibited at the Royal Academy
(1804/90) and now in a private collection, Rome
(1803; Schiff 1217)
Imprint: Published 20th. Augt. 1803, by John
Sharpe; | Piccadilly.
Inscription (top panel): SPECTATOR; (bottom
panel): VOL. 5. No. 379. | Painted by Hy. Fuseli,
R.A. | | Engraved by Wm. Sharp.
Dimensions: ■ 12.1 x 7.3 cm | 4¹²/16" x 2¹⁴/16";
■ 12.5 x 7.7 cm | 4¹⁵/16" x 3¹/16"; (including
lettered panels): 8.6 x 7.3 cm | 5½" x 2¹⁴/16"
(BL 1456.h.9)
Other locations (plate only): BM 1868-8-22-3130;
BM 1843-5-13-504; V & A E.1211-1886
Lit.: Schiff 1310, 1217; Pye 1845, 373; Baker
1875, no. 174; Tomory 1972, pl. 233; Marie
Roberts, *Gothic Immortals*, 1990, 98f., repr. fpce.

Variants:
I. Proof before all letters: BM 1868-8-22-3131
(signed 'Robert Balmanno')
Inscription: H. Fuseli R.A. pinxt. | | Wm. Sharp
sculpt. | Pubd. 20th. Augt. 1803. by J. Sharpe.
II. [Unchecked Variants]:-BM 1848-5-13-502;
BM 1848-5-13-503; 1863-5-9-25

Pye records that Sharp was paid twenty guineas
for this plate.
The engraving illustrates the opening of the
tomb of Rosicrucius after the buried entrance is
uncovered. Upon forcing the door,

> ... [*the intruder*] was immediately surprized by
> a sudden blaze of Light, and discovered a very
> fair Vault: At the upper end of it was the Statue
> of a Man in Armour sitting by a Table, and
> leaning on his Left Arm. He held a Truncheon
> in his Right Hand, and had a Lamp burning
> before him. The Man had no sooner set one
> Foot within the Vault, than the Statue erecting it
> self from its leaning Posture, stood bolt upright;
> and upon the Fellow's advancing another Step,
> lifted up the Truncheon in its Right Hand. The
> Man still ventured a third Step, when the Statue
> with a furious Blow broke the Lamp in a
> thousand pieces, and left his Guest in a sudden
> Darkness (*Spectator*, ed. Bond, III, 425).

The Statue, which was made of brass, turns out to be 'nothing more than a piece of Clockwork' set in motion when the intruder entered by a system of springs underlying the floor of the Vault. Marie Roberts suggests that the inspiration for Fuseli's illustration may have been the mechanical man of Albertus Magnus, although the source she cites (William Godwin's *Lives of the Necromancers*, 1834) was not published until after Fuseli's death.

******

No. 187.
Alexander Pope.
THE | POETICAL WORKS | OF | ALEXANDER POPE. | A NEW EDITION. | = | ADORNED WITH PLATES. | = | VOL. I. [-VOL. VI.] | — | LONDON: | PRINTED FOR F.J. DU ROVERAY, | BY T. BENSLEY, | BOLT COURT; | AND SOLD BY J. AND A. ARCH, CORNHILL; AND | E. LLOYD, HARLEY STREET. | 1804 (1/19 illus. + portr. frontis.).

187.

187. *Isaiah's Vision of the Messiah*, 1804
('Messiah,' ll. 29-30)
(Vol. II, facing p. [53])

Engraved by Robert Shipster.
Imprint: Published 1st. October 1804, by F.J. Du Roveray, London.
Inscription: Drawn by Hy Fuseli R.A. | | Engraved by R. Shipster. |

> Hark! a glad voice the lonely desert Cheers;
> Prepare the way! a God, a God appears!
>   *Messiah.*

Dimensions: ■ 11.4 x 8.8 cm | 4½" x 3⁷/₁₆";
■ 11.5 x 9.0 cm | 4½" x 3½" (BL 11609.cc.20)
Other locations: BL 11609.d.17; DHW (orig. boards); DHW
Lit.: Schiff 1311 (11.5 x 9.0 cm); (on *Poetical Works*): Du Roveray II, 78-80; III, 103-105; IV, 172-173
Exh.: Kansas City 1982 (54).

Variants:
I. Proof before all letters (lacking verse): Bodleian Vet.A6.d.62/1-2 (H=26.0 cm)
Other locations: Huntington 134287 (H=27.5 cm); Newberry Y185.P818 (facing p. 55)
Plate only: BM 1863-5-9-13 (Sheet=21.2 cm)

Fuseli's single illustration to this edition, represented John the Baptist pointing to Christ (after Parmigianino). But Du Roveray's client, Bryan Troughton, considered it 'a disgrace to the Artist' and hoped it would be replaced (Du Roveray III, 104). Such subjects were handled more lightly by Thomas Stothard, Du Roveray's 'favorite Artist', who contributed seven very popular illustrations.

Bentley estimates the size of the edition at 1,000 ordinary and 250 large-paper sets, although according to Robert Hoe's catalogue (Pt.II—L-Z, no. 2775) only 50 royal 8vo copies were printed. Bentley calculates total production costs would have amounted to £2,296.17s.7d. (ordinary sets sold at £2, large-paper sets at £10.15s.0d.); he suggests it was to cover these huge expenses that Du Roveray, in February 1803, sold the plates of his editions of Glover's *Leonidas* and Thomson's *Seasons* (Du Roveray II, 79, 80). For Du Roveray the 'Works of Pope' designated combined sets of his editions of *The Poetical Works of Pope* and Pope's translation of the *Iliad* (Nos. **227-236**) and *Odyssey* (Nos. **237-243**) in 18 vols., which he was resolved not to sell separately. (Such 'Complete Works' appear to be traditional: e.g. my set of Warton's *Pope*, 1797, is bound uniformly with G. Wakefield's *Iliad* and *Odyssey*, 1796, in 18 vols.).

******

188.

188. *Sin Pursued by Death*, 1804
(J. Milton, *Paradise Lost*, II, 787, 790-792)

Stipple engraving and aquatint by Moses Haughton (1772 or 1774-1848) with background by Frederick Christian Lewis (1779-1856) after Fuseli's painting No. VII in the Milton Gallery now in the Kunsthaus Zurich ([1794-1796]; Schiff 892)

Inscription: H^y. Fuseli Pinx^t. R.A. Moses Haughton Sculp^t. and Published by them as the Act directs. N°. 13 Berners Street, London, Novr. 27th. 1804. | | The Back-Ground by F.C. Lewis. |
Sin Pursued by Death. |

——I fled, and cried out Death;
I fled, but he pursued——
——and swifter far
Me overtook——-Book 2. Ver. 787.

Dimensions: ■ 41.5 x 50.0 cm | 16⁵/16" x 19¹¹/16" (BM T.16.16)
Other locations: BM 1861-5-18-154; KHZ 1931/42; MMA 1970.603.2; V & A E1199-A-1886; Essick (imprint trimmed off)
Lit.: Schiff 892A (?35.0 x 50.0 cm); *Litteratur und Kunst* (1806), II, 369-70; Schiff 1963, 51, 55,

pl. 18; Pointon 1970, 133f., pl. 127; Hunt 1973, pl. 15; Behrendt 1983,106; Gill Saunders, *The Nude*, 1989, repr. 31.
Exh.: Zurich 1941 (137); Stockholm 1990 (63)

Variants:
I. Unfinished proof: BM 1872-5-11-975
Dimensions: 41.0 x 49.3 cm
II. Address changed in inscription/imprint (India paper): V & A E.112-1971
Inscription: H^y. Fuseli Pinx^t. R.A. Moses Haughton Sculp^t. and Published by them as the Act directs. Royal Academy, London, Novr. 27th. 1804. | | The Back-Ground by F.C. Lewis. |
Sin pursued by Death. | [Verses]
Other locations: Basel
III. Reissued (1867) with new imprint and inscription by Louis Brall: MMA 65.686.5
Imprint: LONDON: PUBLISHED MARCH 12TH.. 1867, BY LOUIS BRALL, 6 GREAET [*sic*] PRESCOT STREET.
Inscription: H. FUSELI. R.A. PINX^T. | | M. HAUGHTON, SCULP^T. | **Sin Pursued by Death.** | [Verses]

******

Fig. 9. Title page, *The Plays of William Shakspeare*, ed. A. Chalmers, 9 vols., 1805.

Nos. 189 - 225.

THE|PLAYS|OF|WILLIAM SHAKSPEARE,|
ACCURATELY PRINTED FROM THE TEXT
OF THE CORRECTED COPY LEFT BY THE
LATE|GEORGE STEEVENS, ESQ.|WITH|A
SERIES OF ENGRAVINGS,|FROM ORIGINAL
DESIGNS OF|HENRY FUSELI, ESQ. R.A.
PROFESSOR OF PAINTING:|AND A
SELECTION|OF EXPLANATORY AND
HISTORICAL NOTES,|FROM THE MOST
EMINENT COMMENTATORS;|A HISTORY
OF THE STAGE, A LIFE OF SHAKSPEARE,
&C.|BY ALEXANDER CHALMERS, A.M.|
=|IN TEN VOLUMES.|=| VOLUME I.
[-VOLUME X.]|CONTAINING|[*Contents per
volume*]|—| LONDON:|PRINTED FOR F.C.
AND J. RIVINGTON; J. JOHNSON; R.
BALDWIN; H.L.|GARDNER; W.J. AND J.
RICHARDSON; J. NICHOLS AND SON; T.
PAYNE; R.|FAULDER; G. AND J.
ROBINSON; W. LOWNDES; G. WILKIE;
SCATCHERD AND|LETTERMAN; T.
EGERTON; J. WALKER; W. CLARKE AND
SON; J. BARKER AND SON;|D. OGILVY
AND SON; CUTHELL AND MARTIN; R.
LEA; P. MACQUEEN; LACKINGTON,|
ALLEN AND CO.; T. KAY; J. DEIGHTON; J.
WHITE; W. MILLER; VERNOR AND|HOOD;
D. WALKER; C. LAW; B. CROSBY AND CO.;
R. PHENEY; LONGMAN, HURST,|REES,
AND ORME; CADELL AND DAVIES; J.
HARDING; R.H. EVANS; S. BAGSTER;|J.

MAWMAN; BLACKS AND PARRY;
J.BADCOCK; J. ASPERNE; AND T. OSTELL.|
—|1805 (37/37 illus. + portr. frontis.).

...IN NINE VOLUMES.| =|VOLUME I.
[VOLUME IX.]|[&C.]|1805.

...A NEW EDITION.| =|IN NINE VOLUMES.
| =|VOLUME I. [-VOLUME IX.]|
CONTAINING|[*Contents per volume*]|—|
LONDON:|PRINTED FOR J. NICHOLS AND
SON; F.C. AND J. RIVINGTON; J.
STOCKDALE;|W. LOWNDES; G. WILKIE
AND J. ROBINSON; T. EGERTON; J.
WALKER;|W. CLARKE AND SON; J.
BARKER; J. CUTHELL; R. LEA;
LACKINGTON AND|CO.; J. DEIGHTON; J.
WHITE AND CO.; B. CROSBY AND CO.; W.
EARLE;| J. GRAY AND SON; LONGMAN
AND CO.; CADELL AND DAVIES; J.
HARDING;|R.H. EVANS; J. BOOKER; S.
BAGSTER; J. MAWMAN; BLACK AND CO.;|
J. RICHARDSON; J. BOOTH; NEWMAN AND
CO; R. PHENEY; R. SCHOLEY;|J. ASPERNE;
J. FAULDER; R. BALDWIN; CRADOCK AND
JOY; J, MACKIN-|LAY; J. JOHNSON AND
CO.; GALE AND CURTIS; G. ROBINSON;
AND WILSON|AND SON, YORK.|—|1811.

[Paper label on spine]: SHAKSPEARE'S|
PLAYS|WITH SELECT NOTES, &C.|BY |A.
CHALMERS, A.M.|NEW EDITION,|IN NINE
VOLUMES|WITH PLATES| 1812.|£5.8s.|—|
VOL. I. [-VOL. IX.]|—|[*Contents per volume*]

PROSPECTUS
(Folger Shakespeare Library
AP4 G3 vol. 72 part 1)

[December 1, 1802.
PROSPECTUS
OF A NEW EDITION OF
SHAKSPEARE'S
PLAYS,

[Printed from the Text of the Corrected Edition
left|by the late Mr. STEEVENS, and now in the
Press.]|WITH A SERIES|OF ELEGANT
COPPERPLATE ENGRAVINGS,|FROM
ORIGINAL DESIGNS;|BY|HENRY FUSELI, ESQ.
R.A.|PROFESSOR OF PAINTING,|AND|A
SELECTION OF EXPLANATORY AND HISTORICAL
NOTES,|FROM THE MOST EMINENT
COMMENTATORS;|A HISTORY OF THE STAGE, A
LIFE OF SHAKSPEARE, &c.|BY|ALEXANDER

CHALMERS, A.M. London: Printed F. and C. Rivington, no. 62, St. Paul's│church-yard;│J. Johnson, R. Baldwin, H.L. Gardner, W.J. and J. Richardson, J. Nichols and Son, T. Payne, R. Faulder, G. and J. Robinson, W. Lowndes, G. Wilkie, J. Scatcherd, T. Egerton, J. Walker, W. Clarke and Son, J. Barker and Son, D. Ogilvie and Son, Cuthell and Martin, R. Lea, P. Macqueen, J. Nunn, Lackington, Allen and Co. T. Kay, J. Deighton; J. White, Vernor and Hood, D. Walker, Longman and Rees, Cadell and Davies, Murray and Highley, T. Hurst, J. Harding, R.H. Evans, J. Mawman, Black and Parry, and J. Sharpe.│
C. Baldwin, Printer,│New Bridge-street, London.│

[*p. ii*]
CONDITIONS.
=

1. It is proposed to publish this work in numbers, each number to contain ONE PLAY, and an ENGRAVING: and the whole to be comprised in about THIRTY-EIGHT, but not exceeding FORTY NUMBERS, making EIGHT VOLUMES, OCTAVO.

2. The First Number, containing the TEMPEST, will be published on the First of January 1803; and the succeeding numbers every fortnight.

3. At the close of the work will be given A LIFE OF SHAKSPEARE; to which will be prefixed a FINELY engraved Head, Dr. JOHNSON'S celebrated PREFACE, &c.

4. The work will be printed upon an ELEGANT NEW TYPE, and SUPERFINE WOVEN DEMY paper, at TWO SHILLINGS each number.—A superior edition will be printed on an EXTRA ROYAL wovenpaper, hot-pressed, with first impressions of the plates, and sold at FOUR SHILLINGS each number.

5. It is presumed that this Edition being undertaken by the PROPRIETORS of JOHNSON and STEEVENS' SHAKSPEARE, will be an acceptable pledge to the publick for the accuracy of its contents,and the certainty of its completion. It will also have the peculiar advantage of being printed from the Text of the CORRECTED COPY left by the late Mr. STEEVENS, now printing, and which will shortly be published,by the PROPRIETORS of this EDITION, in TWENTY-ONE volumes, medium octavo.

[*p. iii*]
ADDRESS.
=

NOTWITHSTANDING the variety of editions of SHAKSPEARE which have of late years been presented to the Public, and which have their respective merits, it has been thought that one upon the plan now offered would be highly acceptable to a great proportion of readers, without attempting to injure, or being liable to suffer by comparison.

While it is universally acknowledged that the voluminous edition of JOHNSON and STEEVENS affords a mass of information which seems to preclude all future labours, it cannot be denied that from the necessary circumstances of size and price, it is restricted in its circulation, and therefore limited in its utility. However copious in critical illustration, and fertile in authorities and references, such amplitude of comment, and such extension of inquiry, seem fitted rather to the congenial spirit of learned research, than to the more moderate expectations of the general reader.

Influenced by these considerations, the Proprietors have been induced to offer to the public an edition of our immortal Bard, illustrated by a SELECTION of the most IMPORTANT and INTERESTING NOTES which the labours of the various commentators have accumulated. In forming this SELECTION, the object will be to separate the conjectural from the decisive explanations and amendments, to leave the reader under no difficulty which investigation has removed, and to furnish every information that is necessary to a knowledge of the text, or of the history of the play.

Whatever regards questions of taste or emendation, will be retained, but the prescribed limits of an edition strictly useful, and easy to consulted, in which what is wanted may be found without effort, and comprehended without study, must necessarily exclude the elaborate contests of critics, and the prolix quotations from authorities in support of their opinions. These, although useful for occasional reference, and honourable to the industry and judgment ofthe gentlemen who have devoted their time to the [*p.* (iv)] purification of the text, are obstructions in the way of the general reader, until they can be brought to a decision which may in few words convey some useful information.

The proposed SELECTION, therefore, may, it is hoped, be made without derogating from the praise so justly due to the abilities and zeal of our commentators; and without lessening the reverence by which they were led to bestow so much pains on the works of an author who cannot be celebrated beyond reason, nor blamed without respect. It is honourable to the nation which gave him birth, that it has encouraged every LEGITIMATE and ACCURATE transmission of his works; and has patronized the most splendid forms in which they have been conveyed to posterity.

The TEXT of the present Edition will be that of the CORRECTED COPY left by the late Mr. STEEVENS, and now printing by the same Proprietors in twenty-one volumes medium octavo; and which, by repeated collations, and every mode of critical investigation, has been made to approach the nearest to its original state. It appears, indeed, from the many alterations and improvements in Mr. Steevens's corrected copy, to be now fixed beyond the hope, or at least the probability, that any future discoveries will be able to add much to its purity. The obscurities, however, which yet remain, and the doubts which have not yet been resolved, will be stated in the notes to prevent the reader from being ashamed of not understanding what the profoundest CRITICS have hitherto been unable to explain.

With these advantages of the present edition will be combined, besides the attractions of type and paper, the superior embellishments of a series of engravings from original drawings made by Mr. FUSELI, an artist who, with a critical knowledge of the text, has been justly celebrated for that originality of conception, and those bold and wild graces which seem best calculated to illustrate the various imagery and magic combinations of SHAKSPEARE.

C. Baldwin, Printer,
New Bridge-street, London.

Other copies of the prospectus, which 'accompanied every play' (Editor's Preface), are in the British Library (11902.c.26), the University of Illinois—Urbana and the Boston Public Library.

For the 'distressingly intricate' publication history of Chalmers' *Shakspeare*, see also G.E.

Bentley in *Blake Books*, 617-621, albeit the ledger sheets cited here and reproduced in the Appendix (pp. 357-359), do not support all his hypotheses.

The edition was intended to 'oppose that with wooden Cuts from the designs of Thurston' (*Farington Diary*, 3 January 1803; V, 1958). A notice in the *Monthly Epitome* for January 1803 (n.s. II, 49), announcing the issue of Numbers 1 and 2, price 2s. each, also confirms that the work was intended to appear in forty numbers (the prospectus had estimated 38-40). Blake sent William Hayley 'the concluding numbers' on 18 December 1804 (Blake's *Letters*, 1980, 105). Advertisements announcing completion and promising 'speedy' publication in book form appeared in the *Times* on 4th and 9th January 1805.

Of the 3,250 sets printed, dated 1805, 1,150 were issued in the form of 46,000 numbers! The edition (all sets in boards) consisted of 1,500 Demy octavo 'fine paper' sets in 9 vols. (at 10s.6d. per vol. or £4.14s.6d. for the set) and 1,000 on 'inferior paper' (at 7s. per vol. or £3.3s. the set), together with 500 'Royal octavo' and 250 'Super Royal octavo' sets in 10 vols. on finest paper, selling at £9.0s. and £10.10s. respectively. The *Times* advertisement specifically mentions copies 'without the copper-plates'. The lines in the title referring to Fuseli and the engravings after him are omitted from the title pages of the unillustrated copies of 1805 and 1811, although the appropriate title page is not always correctly assigned.

Total publication costs in 1805 amounted to £8,121. Fuseli was paid £3.3s. for each of his 37 drawings (£116.11s.) (it is not known when he completed these), receiving also a complimentary ten-volume 'Royal octavo' set. Excluding repair of the existing plate of Shakespeare's portrait (£7.17s.6d.), the overall cost of the 37 plates was £1,246.19s.3d. (£873.1s.6d. for engraving, £13.16s. for lettering, £182.10s. for printing, and £77.11s.9d. for paper). Blake was paid 25 gs. per plate, but other engravers clearly received less (£873 ÷ 37 pl. = £23.12s.). The 9-volume edition of 1811 was printed in 2,000 sets—'500 fine with plates, 500 fine without pl. 1000 Comm. no pl.', priced respectively at £5.8s., £4.14s. 6d., and £3.12s. in boards. Charles Heath was paid £47.15s.6d. to repair the badly worn plates.

Both editions were issued under the trade share system, whereby the partners in large bookselling projects shared the risk according to the number of books each subscribed for.

189.

189. *Prospero Summons Ariel*, 1803
(*The Tempest*, I, ii, 187-188)
(Vol. I/10, facing p. 17=sig. C)

Engraved by William Bromley (1769-1842) after
Fuseli's lost drawing
Imprint: Publish'd by F & C. Rivington London
Jan 1. 1803.
Inscription (top): Act 1.||TEMPEST.||Sc. 2.|
(bottom): Fuseli del||Bromley sculp.|

_____Miranda sleeps,
  Prosp. Come away, servant, come; I am ready
       now;
       approach, my Ariel; come.

Dimensions: ■ 15.8 x 8.7 cm | 6³/16" x 3⁷/16";
■ 16.0 x 8.9 cm | 6⁵/16" x 3½" (BL 80.f.8)
Other locations (**1805/10**): (**1.**) (as above):
Huntington 140092 (H=26.9 cm) (between pp.
16-17);—(**2.**). (facing p. [1]=sig. B): Birmingham
180.5 (H=23.8); Bodleian M.adds 51.d.43/1
(H=26.0 cm); Essick; Illinois 822.33 Ich Ed.
1805; Princeton Ex 3925.1805 (H=23.0 cm);
—(**3.**) (facing p. [5]=sig. [B3]): Dörrbecker
(H=26.8 cm); ZBZ AX 481 (H=22.7 cm);—(**4.**)
(facing p. 8=sig. [B4]): Folger PR2752.1805a1
c.1 (H=26.8 cm); Folger PR2752.1805a1 c.2
(H=23.3 cm)

(**1805/9**) (Vol. I/9):—(**1.**) (facing p. [1]=sig. B):
Browne; KHZ GB 38/I;—(**2.**) (facing p. 17=sig.
C): Bern A16.757; Illinois 822.33 Ich 1805 c.2.
(**1811/9**) (Vol. I/9):—(**1.**) (facing p. 8=sig. [B4]):
Illinois 822.33 Ich 1811;—(**2.**) (facing p. 17=sig.
C): Birmingham 16031; NYPL *NCM Chalmers
1811
(**1812/9**) (Vol. I/9) (facing p. [5]=sig. [B3]):
Folger PR2572.1805a1 c.2
Plate only: DHW; Folger PR2752.1807c c.4 (Vol.
IV, 15) (top line partially cropped); Huntington
112766 (between pp. 24-25); Huntington 181067,
VI, 51; V & A E.1202-H-1886
Lacking plate: Cambridge Bury.35.15 (1811/9);
NYPL *NCM Chalmers 1805 (1805/10)
Lit.: Schiff 1261 (16.0 x 8.8 cm); Powell 1972,
56, pl. 20; Hodnett 1982, 72
Exh.: New Haven 1981 (177a)

Variants:
I. Proof before letters (India paper) (1805/10)
(between pp. 16-17=sig.C): Huntington 140092
Other locations (plate only): BM 1868-8-22-
5578; BM 1868-8-22-5579

190.

190. *Julia Sends Away Lucetta*, 1803
(*Two Gentlemen of Verona*, I, i)
(Vol. I/10, facing p. 123=sig. [K8])

Engraved by William Bromley (1769-1842) after Fuseli's lost drawing

Imprint: Publish'd by F & C Rivington, London. Jan. 8. 1803.

Inscription (top): Act I.||TWO GENTLEMEN OF VERONA.||Sc. 1.|(bottom): Fuseli del.|| Bromley sculp.|

   Julia.   Go, get you gone; and let the papers lie:

Dimensions: ■ 15.8 x 8.6 cm | 6¼" x 3⁶/16";
■ 16.0 x 8.8 cm | 6⁵/16" x 3½" (BL 80.f.8).
Other locations (**1805/10**): (**1.**) (as above):
Huntington 140092 (H=26.9 cm);—(**2.**) (facing p.
[109]=sig. K): Birmingham 180.5 (H=23.8 cm);
Bodleian M.adds 51.d.43/1 (H=26.0 cm); Essick;
Illinois 822.33 Ich Ed. 1805; Princeton Ex
3925.1805 (H=23.0 cm);—(**3.**)(facing p.
[113]=sig. [K3]): Dörrbecker (H=26.8 cm);
Folger PR2752.1805a1 c.1 (H=26.8 cm); Folger
PR2752.1805a1 c.2 (H=23.3 cm); ZBZ AX 481
(H=22.7 cm)
(**1805/9**) (Vol. I/9):—(**1.**) (facing p. [109]=sig.
K): Browne; KHZ GB 38/I;—(**2.**) (facing p.
123=sig. [K8]): Bern A16.757; Illinois 822.33
Ich 1805 c. 2.
(**1811/9**) (Vol. I/9):—(**1.**) (facing p. [113]=sig.
[K3]: Illinois 822.33 Ich 1811;—(**2.**) (facing p.
123=[K8]): Birmingham 16031; Folger
PR2752.1811a c.3; NYPL *NCM Chalmers 1811
(**1812/9**) (Vol. I/9) (facing p. [113]=sig. [K3]:
Folger PR2752.1805b c.1
Plate only: DHW; Folger Art Vol. 655 (Vol. IV,
10); Folger 2752.1807c c.4 (Vol. II, 13);
Huntington 112766 (between pp. 200-201);
Huntington 181067, VII, 29;V&A E.1202-D-1886
Lacking plate: Cambridge Bury.35.15 (1811/9);
NYPL *NCM Chalmers 1805 (1805/10)
Lit.: Schiff 1262 (16.0 x 8.8 cm); Argan 1960,
repr. I, 576; Hodnett 1982, 73

Variants:

I. Proof before letters (India paper): BM 1868-8-22-5580.

Other locations: DHW; Folger Art File S528t7 no.3 c.2

Julia has been discussing her many suitors with her maid, Lucetta, who tells her mistress to 'cast her love' on Proteus. To advance his suit, Lucetta brings a letter from 'Poor forlorn, Proteus, passionate Proteus|To the sweet Julia'. This wins Julia over, although she throws it down pretending lack of interest in him.

191.

191. *Falstaff at Hearne's Oak*, 1803
(*Merry Wives of Windsor*, V, v)
(Vol. I/10, facing p. 300=sig. [X8])

Engraved by William Bromley (1769-1842) after Fuseli's lost drawing

Imprint: Publish'd by F & C Rivingtons Jan. 27. 1803.

Inscription (top): Act 5.||MERRY WIVES OF WINDSOR.||Sc. 5.|(bottom): Fuseli del.|| Bromley sc.|

   I think the devil will not have me damn'd,
   lest the Oil that is in me should set hell on fire.

Dimensions: ■ 15.9 x 8.7 cm | 6¼" x 3⁷/16";
■ 16.0 x 8.8 cm | 6⁵/16" x 3½" (BL 80.f.8).
Other locations: (**1805/10**) (**1.**) (as above): Folger
PR2752.1805a1 c.2 (H=23.3 cm); Huntington
140092 (H=26.9 cm);—(**2.**) (facing p. [195]=sig.
[P4]): Bodleian M.adds.51d.43/1 (H=26.0 cm);
—(**3.**) (facing p. [201]=sig. [P7]): Birmingham
180.5 (H=23.8cm); Illinois 822.33 Ich Ed. 1805;
Princeton Ex 3925.1805 (H=23.0 cm);—(**4.**)
(facing p. [205]=sig. Q): Dörrbecker (H=26.8
cm); Essick; ZBZ AX 481 (H=22.7 cm);—(**5.**)
(facing p. 295=sig. [X6]): Folger PR2752.1805a1
c.1 (H=26.8 cm);
(**1805/9**) (Vol. I/9):—(**1.**) (facing p. [201]=sig.

[P7]): Browne; KHZ GB 38/I;—(**2.**) (facing p. 205=sig. Q): Birmingham 22362;—(**3.**) (facing p. 300=sig. [X8]: Bern A16.757; Illinois 822.33 Ich 1805 c.2.;
(**1811/9**) (Vol. I/9) (facing p. 300=sig. [X8]): Birmingham 16031; Folger PR2752.1811a c.3; Illinois 822 33 Ich 1811; NYPL *NCM Chalmers 1811
(**1812/9**) (Vol. I/9) (facing p. [205]=sig. Q): Folger PR2752.1805b c.1
Plate only: DHW; Huntington 181067, VIII, 201; V & A E.1202-E-1886
Lacking plate: Cambridge Bury.35.15 (1811/9); NYPL *NCM Chalmers 1805 (1805/10)
Lit.: Schiff 1263 (16.0 x 8.8 cm); Argan 1960, repr. II, 576; Tomory 1972, 163, pl. 149; Hodnett 1982, 73

Variants:
I. Proof before letters: BM 1868-8-22-558.

The illustration conflates action described but not actually seen in Acts IV and V. Mistress Ford and Mistress Page prepare their final jest in revenge against Falstaff. The horned cap is Herne the Hunter's 'buck's head' that the knight will wear to meet them in the park at midnight. His words are spoken in the park.

Mal. *Sir Topas, Sir Topas.*
Sir To.. *My most exquisite Sir Topas!*
Publish'd by F.& C.Rivingtons Feb.1.1803.

192.

192. *Malvolio in the Dungeon*, 1803
(*Twelfth Night*, IV, ii)
(Vol. II/10, facing p. 78=sig. [G5])

Engraved by William Bromley (1769-1842) after Fuseli's lost drawing
Imprint: Publish'd by F. & C. Rivingtons Feb. 1. 1803.
Inscription (top): Act 4. | | TWELFTH NIGHT. | | Sc. 2. | (bottom): Fuseli del. | | Bromley sc. |

Mal.   Sir Topas, Sir Topas—
Sir To.   My most exquisite Sir Topas!

Dimensions: ■ 15.9 x 9.0 cm | 6³/16" x 3½";
■ 16.0 x 9.1 cm | 6¼" x 4⁵/16" (BL 80.f.9).
Other locations: (**1805/10**): (**1.**) (as above): Huntington 140092 (H=26.9 cm); NYPL *NCM Chalmers 1805;—(**2.**) (facing t.p.): Bodleian M.adds.51.d.43/2 (H=26.0 cm); Illinois 822.33 Ich Ed. 1805; Princeton Ex 3925.1805 (H=23.0 cm); ZBZ AX 482 (H=22.7 cm);—(**3.**) (facing p. [1]=sig. B): Birmingham 180.5 (H=23.8 cm); Essick;—(**4.**) (facing p. 76=sig. [G4]): Folger PR2752.1805a1 c.1 (H=26.8 cm); Folger PR2752.1805a1 c.2 (H=23.3 cm);—(**5.**) (facing p. XX=sig. [C]): (Dörrbecker (H=26.8 cm).
(**1805/9**) (Vol. II/9):—(**1.**) (facing title page): Browne; KHZ GB 38/II;—(**2.**) (facing p. 5=sig. C): Birmingham 22363;—(**3.**) (facing p. 76=sig. [G4]: Illinois 822.33 Ich 1805 c.2.;—(**4.**) (facing p. 78=sig. [G5]: Bern A16.757
(**1811/9**) (Vol. II/9):—(**1.**) (facing p. 76=sig. [G4]): Essick; Folger PR2752.1811a c.3; Illinois 822.33 Ich 1811;—(**2.**) (facing p. 78=sig. [G5]: Birmingham 16032; NYPL *NCM Chalmers 1811
(**1812/9**) (Vol. II/9) (facing p. [5]=sig. C): Folger PR2752.1805b c.1
Plate only: DHW; Folger PR2752.1807c c.4 (Vol. IV, facing p. 88) (imprint cropped); Huntington 112766 (facing p. 25); Huntington 181067, XVIII, 153
Lit.: Schiff 1264 (15.8 x 9.0 cm); Christie's, 14 April 1992, no. 24

Variants:
I. Proof before letters: BM 1868-8-22-559.

The figure of Maria in the drawing sold at Christie's, 14 April 1992, is identical with that in the engraving; it has also been indented for transfer.

Isab. *O, I do fear thee Claudio.*
— *Dar'st thou die?*
Publish'd by F.&C. Rivington London, Mar. 15. 1803.

193.

Urs. *She's lim'd, I warrant you:—*
Publish'd by F.&C. Rivington London, May 12. 1803.

194.

193. *Isabella Visiting Claudio in Prison*, 1803
(*Measure for Measure*, III, i)
(Vol. II/10, facing p. 146 = sig. [M7])

Engraved by William Bromley (1769-1842) after
Fuseli's lost drawing
Imprint: Publish'd by F. & C. Rivington London,
Mar. 15. 1803.
Inscription (top): Act III. | | MEASURE FOR
MEASURE. | Sc. I. | (bottom): Fuseli del. | |
Bromley sc. |

    Isab.   O, I do fear thee Claudio;
    _____Dar'st thou die?

Dimensions: ■ 15.7 x 8.5 cm | 5³/₁₆" x 3⁶/₁₆";
▣ 15.9 x 8.8 cm | 6½" x 3⁷/₁₆" (BL 80.f.9)
Other locations (**1805/10**): (**1.**) (as above):
Huntington 140092 (H=26.9 cm); NYPL *NCM
Chalmers 1805;—(**2.**) (facing p. [97]=sig. I):
Birmingham 180.5 (H=23.8 cm); Bodleian
M.adds 51.d.43/2 (H=26.0 cm); Illinois 822.33
Ich Ed. 1805; Princeton Ex 3925.1805 (H=23.0
cm);—(**3.**) facing p. [101]=sig. K): Dörrbecker
(H=26.8 cm); Essick; ZBZ AX 482 (H=22.7
cm);—(**4.**) (facing p. 143=sig. [M6]): Folger
PR2752.1805a1 c.1 (H=26.8 cm); Folger
PR2752.1805a1 c.2 (H=23.3 cm)

(**1805/9**) (Vol. II/9):—(**1.**) (facing p. [97]=sig. I):
Birmingham 22363; Browne; KHZ GB 38/II;
—(**2.**) (facing p. 146=[M7]): Bern A16.757;
Illinois 822.33 Ich 1805 c.2.
(**1811/9**) (Vol. II/9):—(**1.**) (facing p. 143=sig.
[M6]): Essick; Illinois 822.33 Ich 1811;—(**2.**)
(facing p. 146=sig. [M7]: Birmingham 16032;
Folger PR2752.1811a c.3; NYPL *NCM
Chalmers 1811
(**1812/9**) (II/9) (facing p. [101]=sig. K): Folger
PR2752.1805b c.1
Plate only: DHW; Folger PR2752.1807c c.4 (Vol.
IX, facing p. 56); Huntington 112766 (facing p.
194); Huntington 181067, IX, 73
Lit.: Schiff 1265 (15.9 x 8.8 cm) Argan 1960,
repr. III, 48; Tomory 1972, 72, pl. 17; Hodnett
1982, 72

Variants:
I. Proof before letters: BM 1868-8-22-5582.

    Claudio has been sentenced to death for getting
his betrothed with child. When Isabella intercedes
with Angelo, he demands her viginity as the price
of mercy. Fuseli's scene, showing Isabella fiercely
rejecting her brother's pleas to save him, 'has a
grimness new to English illustration' (Hodnett).

194. *Beatrice Eavesdropping on Hero and Ursula*, 1803
(*Much Ado About Nothing*, III, i)
(Vol. II/10, facing p. 249 = sig. [U3])

Engraved by Robert Hartley Cromek (1770-1812) after Fuseli's lost drawing
Imprint: Publish'd by F. & C. Rivington, London, May 12. 1803.
Inscription (top): Act 3. | |MUCH ADO ABOUT NOTHING. | |Sc. 1. |(bottom): Fuseli del. | | R.H. Cromek sc. |

Urs.   She's lim'd, I warrant you; _____

Dimensions: ■ 15.7 x 8.6 cm | 6²/16" x 3⁶/16";
■ 16.0 x 8.9 cm | 6¼" x 3½" (BL 80.f.9).
Other locations (**1805/10**): (**1.**) (as above): Huntington 140092 (H=26.9 cm); NYPL *NCM Chalmers 1805;—(**2.**) (facing p. [205] = sig. R): Birmingham 180.5 (H=23.8 cm); Bodleian M.adds 51.d.43/2 (H=26.0 cm); Essick; Illinois 822.33 Ich Ed. 1805; Princeton Ex 3925.1805 (H=23.0 cm);—(**3.**) (facing p. [XXX] = sig. [R2]: Dörrbecker (H=26.8 cm);—(**4.**) (facing p. [209] = sig. [R3]): ZBZ AX 482 (H=22.7 cm);—(**5.**) (facing p. 246 = sig. U): Folger PR2752.1805a1 c.1 (H=26.8 cm); Folger PR2752.1805a1 c.2 (H=23.3 cm)
(**1805/9**) (Vol. II/9):—(**1.**) (facing p. [205] = sig. R): Browne; KHZ GB 38/II;—(**2**) (facing p. [210] = sig. [R3]: Birmingham 22363;—(**3.**) (facing p. 249 = sig. [U3]): Bern A16.757; Illinois 822.33 Ich 1805 c.2.
(**1811/9**) (Vol. II/9):—(**1.**) (facing p. 246 = sig. [U]): Essick; Illinois 822.33 Ich 1811;—(**2.**) (facing p. 249 = [U3]): Birmingham 16032; Folger PR2752.1811a c.3; NYPL *NCM Chalmers 1811
(**1812/9**) (Vol. II/9) (facing p. [209] = sig. [R3]): Folger PR2752.1805b c.1
Plate only: Folger PR2752.1807c c.4 (Vol. I, between pp. 50-51); Huntington 181067, XI, 79
Lit.: Schiff 1266 (15.5 x 8.7 cm); Antal 1956, 118; Hammelmann 1957, repr. facing p. 355; Argan 1960, II, 288; Hodnett 1982, 73

Variants:
I. Proof before all letters (signatures only): BM 1868-8-22-5584.

As part of their plot to get Benedick and Beatrice to fall in love with each other, Hero and Ursula allow Beatrice to overhear them talking of Benedick's love for her. Don Pedro, Claudio and Leonato will treat Benedick in similar fashion.

195. *Titania Commending Bottom with the Ass's Head to the Care of her Serving Ladies*, 1803
(*A Midsummer Night's Dream*, III, i, 167 ff.)
(Vol. II/10, facing p. 342 = sig. EE)

Engraved by Richard Rhodes (1765-1838) after Fuseli's lost drawing
Imprint: Publish'd by F. & C. Rivington London.
Inscription (top): Act 3. | |MIDSUMMER NIGHT'S DREAM. |Sc.1. |(bottom): Fuseli del. | | Rhodes sculp. |

Titania.   Be kind and courteous to this gentleman.

Dimensions: ■ 16.0 x 9.4 cm | 6⁵/16" x 3¹¹/16";
■ 16.5 x 9.9 cm | 6½" x 3¹⁴/16" (BL 80.f.9)
Other locations (**1805/10**): (**1.**) (as above): Huntington 140092 (H=26.9 cm) (between pp. 342-343; NYPL *NCM Chalmers 1805;—(**2.**) (facing p. [302] = sig. BB): Birmingham 180.5 (H=23.8cm); Bodleian M.adds 51.d.43/2 (H=26.0 cm); Essick; Illinois 822.33 Ich Ed. 1805; Princeton Ex 3925.1805 (H=23.0 cm);—(**3.**) (facing p. [XXX] = sig. [BB3]): Dörrbecker (H=26.8 cm);—(**4.**) (facing p. [307] = sig. [BB8]): ZBZ AX 482 (H=22.7 cm);—(**5.**) (facing p. 336 = sig [DD6]): Folger PR2752.1805a c.1 (H=26.8 cm);—(**6.**) (facing p. 337 = sig [DD7]): Folger PR 2752.1805a1 c.2 (H=23.3 cm)
(**1805/9**) (Vol. II/9):—(**1.**) (facing p. [303] = sig. BB): Browne; KHZ GB 38/II;—(**2.**) (facing p. [307] = sig. BB3: Birmingham 22363;—(**3.**) (facing p. 342 = sig. EE): Bern A16.757;—(**4.**) (facing p. 343 = sig. EE2): Illinois 822.33 Ich 1805 c.2.
(**1811/9**) (Vol. II/9):—(**1.**) (facing p. 336 = sig. [DD6]): Essick; Illinois 822.33 Ich 1811;—(**2.**) (facing p. 342 = sig. EE): Birmingham 16032; Folger PR2752.1811a c.3; NYPL *NCM 1811
(**1812/9**) (Vol. II/9) (facing p. [307] = [BB3]): Folger PR2752.1805b c.1
Plate only: Folger PR2752.1807c c.4 (Vol. I, between pp. 42-43) (imprint cropped); Huntington 12766 (facing p. 15); Huntington 181067, XIII, 116
Lit.: Schiff 1267 (16.1 x 9.7 cm); Schiff 1961, 11, 20f.; Hodnett 1982, 73f.; Weinglass 1991, 300, pl. 4
Exh.: Berlin 1986 (16)

Variants:
I. Proof before letters: Huntington 181067 XIII, 115.

Act.3.   MIDSUMMER NIGHT'S DREAM.   Sc.1.

Fuseli del.   Rhodes sculp.
Titania. *Be kind and courteous to this gentleman.*
Publish'd by F. & C. Rivington London.

195.

Act.4.   LOVE'S LABOUR LOST.   Sc.3.

Fuseli, del.   Dadley Sculp.
King. *What, Longaville! and reading; listen ear.*
Publish'd by F. & C. Rivington London May 24. 1803.

196.

This illustration is a good example of the peculiar appositeness of Fuseli's pictorial eclecticism, which may, as here, also provide critical insight into an important aspect of Shakespeare's moral thought. The composition is derived from Veronese's painting *Mars and Venus United by Love* (Metropolitan Museum of Art) which exemplified for the Renaissance the opposing concepts of the 'concupiscible' and the 'irascible'.

196. *The King and Biron Watching Longaville Reading the Sonnet*, 1803
(*Love's Labour's Lost*, IV, iii, 44-76)
(Vol. III/10, facing p. 52 = sig. E2)

Engraved by John Dadley (1767-*post* 1807) after Fuseli's lost drawing
Imprint: Publishd by F. & C. Rivington London May 24. 1803.
Inscription (top): Act 4. | | LOVE'S LABOUR LOST. | | Sc. 3. | (bottom): Fuseli, del. | | Dadley, Sculp. |

King.   What, Longaville! and reading; listen ear.

Dimensions: ■ 15.8 x 9.3 cm | 6⁵/16" x 3¹¹/16"; ■ 16.0 x 9.5 cm | 6⁶/16" x 3¾" (BL 80.f.10)
Other locations (**1805/10**): (**1.**) (as above): Folger PR2752.1805a1 c.1 (H=26.8 cm); Folger PR2752.1805a1 c.2 (H=23.3 cm); Huntington 140092 (H=26.9 cm) (between pp. 52-53); NYPL *NCM Chalmers 1805;—(**2.**) (facing t.p.): Bodleian M.adds 51.d.43/3 (H=26.0 cm); Illinois 822.33 Ich Ed. 1805; Princeton Ex 3925.1805 (H=23.0 cm); ZBZ AX 483 (H=22.7 cm);—(**3.**) (facing p. [i]=sig. B): Essick;—(**4.**) (facing p. [5]=sig. [B3]): Dörrbecker (H=26.8 cm);—(**5.**) (facing p. [307]=sig. [BB3]: Birmingham 180.5 (H=23.8 cm)
(**1805/9**) (Vol. II/9):—(**1.**) (facing p. [389]=sig. HH): Browne; KHZ GB 38/II;—(**2.**) (facing p. [394]=sig. HH3): Birmingham 22363;—(**3.**) (facing p. 440=sig. LL2): Bern A16.757; Illinois 822.33 Ich 1805 c. 2.
(**1811/9**) (Vol. II/9) (facing p. 439/440=sig. LL2): Birmingham 16032; Essick; Folger PR2752.1811a c.3; Illinois 822.33 Ich 1811; NYPL *MCM Chalmers 1811
(**1812/9**) (Vol. II/9) (facing p. [393]=sig. [HH3]: Folger PR2752.1805b c.1

Plate only: DHW; Folger PR2752.1807c c.4 (Vol. V, facing p. 59) (imprint and all but signatures cropped); Folger Art File S528L1 no. 31; Huntington 181067, XII, 72
Lit.: Schiff 1268 (15.9 x 9.3 cm); Antal 1956, 101; Argan 1960, repr. I, 640; Hodnett 1982, 72.

Variants:

I. Proof before all letters (signatures only) **(1805/10)**: Huntington 140092 (H=26.9 cm)

The King has taken a solemn vow to go into seclusion for three years in order to study, forgoing all pleasures and the company of women. Biron, Dumain, Longaville, 'brave conquerors … |That war against [*their*] own affections' (I, i, 8-9) are forced to take the same vow. However, it is not long before all four men reveal themselves to each other as 'forsworn'. Here Longaville is caught reading love verses he has composed.

197.

197. *Shylock, Antonio and Portia Before the Doge*, 1803
(*The Merchant of Venice*, IV, i, 121-122)
(Vol. III/10, facing p. 180=sig. Q2)

Engraved by James Neagle (1769?-1822) after Fuseli's lost drawing

Imprint: Publish'd by F. & C. Rivington, May 10. 1803.
Inscription (top): Act 4.||MERCHANT OF VENICE.||Sc. 1.|(bottom): H Fuseli del||I Neagle Sc^t,|

Bass.	Why dost thou whet thy Knife so earnestly?
Shy.	To cut the forfeiture from that bankrupt thee

Dimensions: ■ 15.8 x 8.8 cm | 6³/₁₆" x 3⁷/₁₆"; ■ 15.9 x 8.9 cm | 6½" x 3½" (BL 80.f.10)
Other locations **(1805/10)**: **(1.)** (as above): Huntington 140092 (H=26.9 cm) (between pp. 180-181); NYPL *NCM Chalmers 1805;—**(2.)** (facing p. [107]=sig. K): Birmingham 180.5 (H=23.8 cm); Bodleian M.adds 51.d.43/3 (H=26.0 cm); Essick; Illinois 822.33 Ich Ed. 1805; Princeton Ex 3925.1805 (H=23.0 cm); —**(3.)** (facing p. [113]=sig. M): Dörrbecker (H=26.8 cm); ZBZ AX 482 (H=22.7 cm);—**(4.)** (facing p. 176=sig. [P8]): Folger PR2752.1805a1 c.1 (H=26.8 cm); Folger PR2752.1805a1 c.2 (H=23.3 cm)
(1805/9) (Vol. III/9):—**(1.)** (facing t.p.): ?Browne; KHZ GB 38/III;—**(2.)** (facing p. 74=sig. H2): Illinois 822.33 Ich 1805 c.2.
(1811/9) (Vol. III/9):—**(1.)** (facing p. 70=sig. [G8]): Illinois 822.33 Ich 1811;—**(2.)** (facing p. 180=sig. Q2): Folger PR2752.1811a c.3
Plate only: DHW; Huntington 181067, XIV, 162; Huntington 265806, I, 257 (imprint cropped)
Lacking plate: Cambridge Bury 35.16 (1811/9)
Lit.: Schiff 1269 (15.9 x 8.9 cm); Argan 1960, repr. II, 48; Hodnett 1982, 72.

Variants:

I. Proof before all letters (signatures only) **(1805/10)**: Huntington 140092 (H=26.9 cm)
Other locations: Essick
Plate only: BM 1868-8-22-5587; Huntington 181067, XIV, 161
II. Corrected inscription (line 2 of verse) **(1805/9)** (Vol. III/9) (facing p. [7]=sig. D): Birmingham 22364
(1812/9) (Vol. III/9) (facing p. [7]=sig. D): Folger PR2752.1805b c.1
Inscription (verse only, remainder as above):

Bass.	Why dost thou whet thy Knife so earnestly?
Shy.	To cut the forfeiture from that bankrupt there.

Other locations (**1811/9**): (**1.**) (facing p. 70=sig. [G8]): Essick; Illinois 822.33 Ich 1811; —(**2.**) (facing p. 74=sig. H2): Bern A16.757 (1805/9); Birmingham 16031; Folger PR2752.1811a c.3; NYPL *NCM Chalmers 1811

Plate only: Folger PR2752. 1807c c.4 (Vol. VI, facing p. 87) (imprint cropped)

198.

198. *Orlando Appears Before the Duke with Drawn Sword*, 1803

(*As You Like It*, II, vii, 88)
(Vol. III/10, facing p. 247=sig. [X4])

Engraved by Isaac Taylor Jr. (1759-1829) after Fuseli's lost drawing
Imprint: Publish'd by F. & C. Rivington London Ap. 2. 1803.
Inscription (top): Act 2.||AS YOU LIKE IT.|| Sc. 3.|(bottom): Fuseli del.||Taylor sculp.|

  Orlando.   Forbear and eat no more.

Dimensions: ■ 15.8 x 8.9 cm | 6³/16" x 3½"; ■ 16.0 x 9.2 cm | 6⁹/16" x 3²/16" (BL 80.f.10)
Other locations (**1805/10**): (**1.**) (as above): Huntington 140092 (H=26.9 cm); NYPL *NCM Chalmers 1805;—(**2.**) (facing p. [205]=sig. S): Birmingham 180.5 (H=23.8 cm); Bodleian

M.adds 51.d.43/3 (H=26.0 cm); Essick; Illinois 822.33 Ich Ed. 1805; Princeton Ex 3925.1805 (H=23.0 cm);—(**3.**) (facing p. [209]=sig. T): Dörrbecker (H=26.8 cm); ZBZ AX 483 (H=22.7 cm);—(**4.**) (facing p. 234=sig. [U5]): Folger PR2752.1805a1 c.1 (H=26.8 cm); Folger PR2752.1805a1 c.2 (H=23.3 cm); Folger PR2752.1805a1 c.2
(**1805/9**) (Vol. III/9):(**1.**) (facing p. [99]=sig. K): Browne; KHZ GB 38/III;—(**2.**) (facing p. [103]=sig. L): Birmingham 22364;—(**3.**) (facing p. 129=[M6]): Illinois 822.33 Ich 1805 c.2.; —(**4.**)(facing p. 141=sig. [N4]): Bern A16.757 (facing p. 141=sig. [N4])
(**1811/9**) (Vol. III/9):—(**1.**) (facing p. 128=sig. [M6]): Birmingham 16033; Essick;—(**2.**) (facing p. 141=sig. [N4]): Folger PR2752.1811a c.3; Illinois 822.33 Ich 1811; NYPL *NCM Chalmers 1811
(**1812/9**) (Vol. III/9) (facing p. [104]=sig. L): Folger PR2752.1805b c.1
Plate only: DHW; Folger PR2752.1807c c.4 (Vol. VII, facing p. 47); Folger Art Vol. 655 (Vol. III, facing p. 40); Huntington 112766 (between pp. 26-27)
Lacking plate: Cambridge Bury 35.16 (1811/9)
Lit.: Schiff 1270 (15.7 x 9.0 cm); Cunningham 1830, 289; Argan 1960, repr. II, 512; Mason 1964, 95; Hodnett 1982, 78.

Forced to flee by the treachery of his brother, Orlando and his old servant Adam wander through the Forest of Arden until Adam collapses from hunger. Encountering the exiled Duke and his band of outlaws at their meal, Orlando rushes upon them with his sword drawn and demands food. He is put to shame by the Duke's cordial invitation to share his hospitality.

The 'very curious capers' Fuseli cuts in his 'attempts to escape from the fetters of costume' (Cunningham) and other aspects of his treatment of this untraditional and inconsequential Shakespearean subject have been cited as typical of the deplorable extravagance of his style. Hodnett (who is generally hostile to Fuseli) calls it an 'example of an illustration losing its integrity when an artist puts the image before the text'. The composition and in particular the figure of Orlando resemble Blake's (less dynamic) illustration to 'Laughing Song' in *Songs of Innocence*.

199. *Helena Confesses Her Love for Bertram to his Mother the Countess*, 1803
(*All's Well That Ends Well*, I, iii, 192-193)
(Vol. III/10, facing p. 337=sig. EE)

Engraved by J[?ohn] G. Walker (b. 1760?) after
Fuseli's lost drawing
Imprint: Publish'd by F. & C. Rivington London
Ap^l. 30. 1803.
Inscription (top): Act. 1.||ALL'S WELL THAT
ENDS WELL.||Sc. 1.|(bottom): Fuseli del.||
J.G. Walker, sc,|

> Hel. _____Then I confess,
> Here on my knee before high heaven
> & you.

Dimensions: ■ 16.0 x 8.7 cm | 6^5/16" x 3^7/16";
■ 16.3 x 8.9 cm | 6^7/16" x 3½" (BL 80.f.10).
Other locations (**1805/10**): (**1.**) (as above):
Huntington 140092 (H=26.9 cm); NYPL *NCM
Chalmers 1805;—(**2.**) (facing p. [313]=sig. Cc):
Birmingham 180.5 (H=23.8 cm); Bodleian
M.adds 51.d.43/3 (H=26.0 cm); Essick; Illinois
822.33 Ich Ed. 1805; Princeton Ex 3925.1805
(H=23.0 cm);—(**3.**) (facing p. [317]=sig. [Cc3]):
Dörrbecker (H=26.8 cm); Folger PR2752.1805a1
c.2 (H=23.3 cm); ZBZ AX 483 (H=22.7 cm);
—(**4.**) (facing p. [319]=sig. [Cc4]: Folger
PR2752.1805a1 c.1 (H=26.8 cm)
(**1805/9**) (Vol. III/9):—(**1.**) (facing p. [207]=sig.
S): Browne; KHZ GB 38/III;—(**2.**) (facing p.
[211]=sig. [S3]): Birmingham 22364;—(**3.**)
(facing p. 213=[S4]): Illinois 822.33 Ich 1805
c.2.;—(**4.**) (facing p. 231=sig. U): Bern A16.757
(**1811/9**) (Vol. III/9):—(**1.**) (facing p. [211]=sig.
[S3]): Birmingham 16033; Essick; Illinois 822.33
Ich 1811;—(**2.**) (facing p. 231=sig. U): Folger
PR 1811a c.3; NYPL *NCM Chalmers 1811
(**1812/9**) (Vol. III/9) (facing p. [211]=sig. [S3]):
PR2752.1805b c.1
Plate only: DHW; Folger PR2752.1807c c.4
(between pp. 24-25) (imprint cropped);
Huntington 112766 (facing p. 34)
Lacking plate: Cambridge Bury 35.16 (1811/9)
Lit.: Schiff 1271 (16.0 x 8.7 cm); Boase 1959, 8,
pl. 4a; Argan 1960, repr. II, 960; Hodnett 1982,
73

Variants:
I. Proof before all letters (signatures only): BM
1868-8-22-5590.

199.

200.

200. *The Lord Finds Drunken Sly Asleep*, 1803
(*Taming of the Shrew*, Induction, i, 34-41)
(Vol. IV/10, facing p. 9=sig. [C4])

Engraved by Charles Warren (1766-1823) after
Fuseli's lost drawing
Imprint: Publish'd by F. & C. Rivington,
London, Aug. 2. 1803.
Inscription (top): Induction||TAMING OF THE
SHREW.||Sc. 1.|(bottom): Fuseli RA Del.||C.
Warren Scp.ᴸ.|

> Lord. O Monstrous beast! how like a swine
> he lies.

Dimensions: ■ 15.3 x 9.3 | 6' x 3¹¹/16";
■ 15.5 x 9.4 cm | 6²/16" x 3¾" (BL 80.f.11)
Other locations (**1805/10**): (**1.**) (as above):
Huntington 140092 (H=26.9 cm); NYPL *NCM
Chalmers 1805;—(**2.**) (facing t.p.): Bodleian
M.adds 51.d.43/4 (H=26.0 cm); Illinois 822.33
Ich Ed. 1805; Princeton Ex 3925.1805 (H=23.0
cm); ZBZ AX 482 (H=22.7 cm);—(**3.**) (facing p.
[1]=sig. B): Birmingham 180.5 (H=23.8 cm);
Essick;—(**4.**) (facing p. [7]=sig. [C3]:
Dörrbecker (H=26.8 cm); Folger PR2752.1805a1
c.2 (H=23.3 cm);—(**5.**) (facing p. [8]=sig.
[C4]): Folger PR2752.1805a c.1 (H=26.8 cm)
(**1805/9**) (Vol. III/9):—(**1.**) (facing p. [324]=sig.
Cc): KHZ GB 38/III;[?Browne 325=sig. Cc?]
—(**2.**) (facing p. [333]=sig. [DD3]): Birmingham
22364;—(**3.**) (facing p. 333=sig. [DD4]): Bern
A16.757; Illinois 822.33 Ich 1805 c.2.
(**1811/9**) (Vol. III/9):—(**1.**) (facing p. 331=sig.
[DD3]): Essick; Illinois 822.33 Ich 1811;—(**2.**)
(facing p. 333=sig. [DD4]): Birmingham 16033;
Folger PR2752.1811a c.3; NYPL *NCM
Chalmers 1811
(**1812/9**) (Vol. III/9) (facing p. [331]=sig.
[DD3]): PR2752.1805b c.1
Plate only: DHW; Folger PR2752.1807c c.4 (Vol.
I, facing p. 6)
Lacking plate: Cambridge Bury 35.16 (1811/9)
Lit.: Schiff 1272 (15.3 x 9.4 cm); Antal 1956,
10; Argan 1960, repr. I, 432; Tomory 1972, pl.
125; Keay 1974, pl. 34; Hodnett 1982, 74;
Weinglass 1991, 301, pl. 8

Variants:

I. Proof before letters: Essick
II. Proof before all letters (signatures only): BM
1868-8-22-5589.

201.

201. *The Old Shepherd Finds Perdita*, 1803
(*A Winter's Tale*, III, iii, 67-68)
(Vol. IV/10, facing p. 166=sig. O2)

Engraved by James Neagle (1769?-1822) after
Fuseli's lost drawing
Imprint: Publish'd by F. & C. Rivington, London
July 2. 1803.
Inscription (top): Act 3.||WINTER'S TALE.||
Sc. 3.|(bottom): H Fuseli del||I Neagle Sc|

> Old Shepherd.
> What have we here? Mercy on's, a barne;
> a very pretty barne!

Dimensions: ■ 15.7 x 9.3 cm | 6³/16" x 3¹¹/16";
■ 16.0 x 9.6 cm | 6½" x 3¾" (BL 80.f.11)
Other locations (**1805/10**): (**1.**) (as above):
Huntington 140092 (H=26.9 cm) (between pp.
166-167); NYPL *MCM Chalmers 1805;—(**2.**)
(facing p. [107]=sig. K): Birmingham 180.5
(H=23.8 cm); Bodleian M.adds 51.d.43/4
(H=26.0 cm); Essick; Illinois 822.33 Ich Ed.
1805; Princeton Ex 3925.1805 (H=23.0 cm);
—(**3.**) (facing p. [113]=sig. [K4]): Dörrbecker
(H=26.8 cm); ZBZ AX 482 (H=22.7 cm);—(**4.**)
(facing p. 164=sig. [O]): Folger PR2752.1805a1

c.1 (H=26.8 cm); Folger PR2752.1805a1 c.2
(H=23.3 cm)
(1805/9) (Vol. III/9)—**(1.)** (facing p. [431]=sig.
LL): Browne; KHZ GB 38/III;—**(2.)** (facing p.
[438]=sig. ?): Birmingham 22364;—**(3.)** (facing
p. 490=sig. [PP2]): Illinois 822.33 Ich 1805 c.2;
—**(4.)** (facing p. 491=[PP3]): Bern A16.757
(1811/9) (Vol. III/9)—**(1.)** (facing p. 488=sig.
PP): Illinois 822.33 Ich 1811;—**(2.)** (facing p.
490=sig. PP2):Birmingham 16033; Essick; Folger
PR2752.1811a c.3; NYPL *NCM Chalmers 1811
(1812/9) (Vol. III/9) (facing p. [437]=sig. [LL4]):
PR2752.1805b c.1 (signs of reworking)
Plate only: DHW; Folger PR2752.1807c c.4 (Vol.
II, between pp. 64-65) (imprint cropped);
Huntington 112766, 19
Lacking plate: Cambridge Bury 35.16 (1811/9)
Lit.: Schiff 1273 (15.7 x 9.3 cm); Argan 1960,
repr. III, 784; Keay 1974, pl. 19; Hodnett
1982, 72

Variants:

I. Proof before all letters (India paper)
(signatures only) **(1805/10)** (between pp. 166-
167): Huntington 140092 (H=26.9 cm)
Other locations: Essick
II. Proof before all letters (signatures only)
(between pp. 166-167): Huntington 140092
(H=26.9 cm)
Other locations (plate only): BM 1868-8-22-
5592.

202. *Antipholus of Syracuse Meets Adriana and Luciana in the Street*, 1804

(*Comedy of Errors*, II,ii, 148)
(Vol. IV/10, facing p. 254=sig. [U6])

Engraved by Thomas Milton (1743-1827) after
Fuseli's lost drawing
Imprint: Published Oct[r]. 19th. 1804, by F. & C.
Rivington, S[t]. Paul's Church Yard.
Inscription (top): Act II.||COMEDY of
ERRORS.||Sc. II.|(bottom): H. Fusili R.A.
del.||T. Milton sc.|

> Aut.S. Plead you to me, fair Dame? I know
> you not.

Dimensions: ■ 16.0 x 9.0 cm | 6¼" x 3½" (BL
80.f.11)
Other locations **(1805/10)**: **(1.)** (as above):
Huntington 140092 (H=26.9 cm) (between pp.

202.

203.

254-255);—(**2.**) (facing p. [231]=sig. T):
Birmingham 180.5 (H=23.8 cm); Bodleian
M.adds 51.d.43/4 (H=26.0 cm); Essick; Illinois
822.33 Ich Ed. 1805; Princeton Ex 3925.1805
(H=23.0 cm);—(**3.**) (facing p. [235]=sig. [T3]):
Dörrbecker (H=26.8 cm); ZBZ AX 484
(H=22.7 cm);—(**4.**) (facing p. 249=sig. [U4]):
Folger PR2752.1805a1 c.2 (H=23.3 cm); NYPL
*NCM Chalmers 1805
(**1805/9**) (Vol. IV/9): (**1.**) (facing t.p.): ?Browne;
KHZ GB 38/IV;—(**2.**) (facing p. [6]=sig. [B3]):
Birmingham 22365;—(**3.**) (facing p. 19=sig.
[C4]): Illinois 822.33 Ich 1805 c.2.;—(**4.**) (facing
p. 24=sig. [C6]): Bern A16.757
(**1811/9**) (Vol. IV/9) (**1.**) (facing p. 19=sig.
[C4]): Illinois 822.33 Ich 1811;—(**2.**) (facing p.
24=sig. [C6]): Birmingham 16034; Folger
PR2752.1811a c.3; NYPL *NCM Chalmers 1811
(**1812/9**) (Vol. IV/9) (facing p. [5]=sig. [B3]):
Folger PR2752.1805b c.1
Plate only: DHW; Folger PR2752.1807c c.4 (Vol.
III, facing p. 26) (imprint cropped); Huntington
112766 (between pp. 24-25); Huntington 181067,
X, 47
Lacking plate: Folger PR2752.1805a1 c.1 (Vol.
IV/10)
Lit.: Schiff 1274 (?15.0 x 9.3 cm); Keay 1974,
pl. 20; Hodnett 1982, 73

Antipholus of Syracuse, who has just arrived in
Ephesus, is unaware that he has an identical twin,
Antipholus of Ephesus. In this scene Antipholus
S. is mistaken by his lost twin's wife for her
husband and shows appropriate bafflement.

203. *Lady Macbeth Walking in her Sleep*, 1803
(*Macbeth*, V, i, 38)
(Vol. IV/10, facing p. 400=sig. [FF7])

Engraved by Charles Warren (1766-1823) after
Fuseli's lost drawing
Imprint: Publishd by F. & C. Rivington, London
Nov. 15. 1803.
Inscription (top): Act 5||MACBETH.||Sc. 1.|
(bottom): H. Fuseli R.A. Del.||C Warren Scp.|

Enter Lady Mackbeth with a taper.
L.M.　—One; Two; why, then 'tis
　　　time to do't:—Hell is murky!
Dimensions: ■ 15.1 x 9.2 cm | 5⁵/16" x 3¹⁰/16";
■ 15.3 x 9.4 cm | 6' x 3¹¹/16" (BL 80.f.11)
Other locations (**1805/10**): (**1.**) (as above):

Huntington 140092 (H=26.9 cm); NYPL *NCM
Chalmers 1805;—(**2.**) (facing p. [307]=sig. AA):
Birmingham 180.5 (H=23.8 cm); Bodleian
M.adds 51.d.43/4 (H=26.0 cm); Essick; Illinois
822.33 Ich Ed. 1805; Princeton Ex 3925.1805
(H=23.0 cm);—(**3.**) (facing p. [313]=sig. [AA4]):
Dörrbecker (H=26.8 cm); Folger PR2752.1805a1
c.2 (H=23.3 cm); ZBZ AX 484 (H=22.7 cm)
(**1805/9**) (Vol. IV/9) (**1.**) (facing p. 77=sig. G):
Browne; KHZ GB 38/IV;—(**2.**) (facing p.
[83]=sig. G4): Birmingham 22365;—(**3.**) (facing
p. 170=sig. [M7]): Bern A16.757; Illinois 822.33
Ich 1805 c.2.
(**1811/9**) (Vol. IV/9) (facing p. 170=sig. [M7]):
Birmingham 16034; Folger PR2752.1811a c.3;
Illinois 822.33 Ich 1811; NYPL *NCM Chalmers
1811
(**1812/9**) (Vol. IV/9) (facing p. [83]=sig. [G4]):
Folger PR2752.1805b c.1
Lacking plate: Folger PR2752.1805a1 c.1
Plate only: Folger PR2752.1807c c.4 (Vol. III,
between pp. 92-93) (imprint cropped); Huntington
112766 (facing p. 99); Huntington 181067, XX,
198; V & A E.1202-A-1886
Lit.: Schiff 1275 (15.0 x 9.3 cm); M. Balmanno,
Pen and Pencil, 1858, 199; Keay 1974, pl. 18

Variants:
I. Proof before all letters (signatures only): BM
1868-8-22-5611
Other locations: Essick.

Lady Macbeth, hitherto the stronger partner in
Macbeth's murderous rise to the kingship, but
now with her mind broken by the horror of her
deeds, is observed by the Doctor and the waiting
maid walking in her sleep, attempting to
'sweeten' her hands and wash them clean of
imagined blood, as she relives in her dreams
Duncan's assassination.

204.

205.

204. *Queen Constance, Arthur and Salisbury*,
1803
(*King John*, (III, i, 73)
(Vol. V/10, facing p. 41 = sig. [D5])

Engraved by Samuel Noble (1779-1853) after
Fuseli's lost drawing
Imprint: Publish'd by F. & C. Rivington London
July 22. 1803.
Inscription (top): Act 3. | | KING JOHN. | | Sc. 1. |
(bottom): Fuseli del. | | Noble sculp. |

　　Constance.

　　___here I and sorrow sit;

Dimensions: ■ 16.1 x 9.5 cm | 6⁶/16" x 3¹¹/16";
■ 16.6 x 10.0 cm | 6½" x 3¹⁵/16" (BL 80.f.12)
Other locations (**1805/10**): **(1.)** (as above):
Huntington 140092 (H=26.9 cm); NYPL *NCM
Chalmers 1805;—**(2.)** (facing t.p.): Bodleian
M.adds 51.d.43/5 (H=26.0 cm); Illinois 822.33
Ich Ed. 1805; Princeton Ex 3925.1805 (H=23.0
cm); ZBZ AX 485 (H=22.7 cm);—**(3.)** (facing p.
[1] = sig. B): Birmingham 180.5 (H=23.8 cm);
Essick;—**(4.)** (facing p. [5] = sig. [B3]:
Dörrbecker (H=26.8 cm); —**(5.)** (facing p.
38 = sig. [D3]): Folger PR2752.1805a1 c.1

(H=26.8 cm); Folger PR 2752.1805a1 c.2
(H=23.3 cm)
(**1805/9**) (Vol. IV/9):—**(1.)** (facing p. [180] = sig.
O): KHZ GB 38/IV; Browne 189 = sig. O;—**(2.)**
(facing p. [193] = sig. [O3]): Birmingham 22365;
—**(3.)** (facing p. 229 = sig. [Q5]): Bern A16.757;
Illinois 822.33 Ich 1805 c.2.
(**1811/9**) (Vol. IV/9):—**(1.)** (facing p. 226 = sig.
[Q3]): Illinois 822.33 Ich 1811;—**(2.)** (facing p.
229 = sig. [Q5]): Birmingham 16034; Folger
PR2752.1811a c.3; NYPL *NCM Chalmers 1811
(**1812/9**) (Vol. IV/9) (facing p. [193] = sig. [O3]):
Folger PR2752.1805b c.1 (heavy wear on knight's
leg)
Plate only: Folger PR2752.1807c c.4 (Vol. V,
facing p. 43) (imprint cropped); Huntington
112766 (facing p. 190); V & A E.1202-G-1886
Lit.: Schiff 1276 (16.0 x 9.5 cm); Argan 1960,
repr. I, 960.

Constance of Brittany, the widow of Geoffrey
Plantagenet, the brother of King John, is plunged
into an intemperate fit of grief when her royal
ambitions for her son Arthur are thwarted by the
proposed union of Blanch of Castile and the
Dauphin of France. Here we see her upon her
'throne of grief', nursing her 'proud sorrows'.

205. *Richard II in the Dungeon of Pomfret Castle*, 1803

(*King Richard the Second*, [V], v, 49-50)
(Vol. V/10, facing p. 206=sig. [P7])

Engraved by Robert Hartley Cromek (1770-1812)
after Fuseli's lost drawing
Imprint: Publish'd by F. & C. Rivington,
London, Aug. 15. 1803.
Inscription (top): Act 4.||RICHARD II.||Sc. 5.|
(bottom): H. Fuseli del.||R.H. Cromek sc.|

> Richard.
> I wasted Time and now doth Time waste me,
> For now hath Time made me his numb'ring
>   clock.

Dimensions: ■ 15.8 x 8.8 cm | 6³/16" x 3⁷/16";
▣ 16.2 x 9.2 cm | 6⁶/16" x 3¹⁰/16" (BL 80.f.12)
Other locations (**1805/10**): (**1.**) (as above):
Huntington 140092 (H=26.9 cm) (between pp.
254-255); NYPL *NCM Chalmers 1805;—(**2.**)
(facing p. [103]=sig. I): Birmingham 180.5
(H=23.8 cm); Bodleian M.adds 51.d.43/5
(H=26.0 cm); Essick; Illinois 822.33 Ich Ed.
1805; Princeton Ex 3925.1805 (H=23.0 cm);
—(**3.**) (facing p. [107]=sig. [I3]): Dörrbecker
(H=26.8 cm); ZBZ AX 485 (H=22.7 cm);—(**4.**)
facing p. 179=sig. O2): Folger PR2752.1805a1
c.2 (H=23.3 cm)
(**1805/9**) (Vol. IV/9):—(**1.**) (facing p. [291]=sig.
X): Browne; KHZ GB 38/IV;—(**2.**) (facing p.
[295]=sig. [X3]): Birmingham 22365;—(**3.**)
(facing p. 394=sig. [DD7]): Bern A16.757;
Illinois 822.33 Ich 1805 c.2
(**1811/9**) (Vol. IV/9):—(**1.**) (facing p. 373=sig.
[CC5]): NYPL *NCM Chalmers 1811;—(**2.**)
(facing p. 392=sig. [DD6]): Illinois 822.33 Ich
1811;—(**3.**) (facing p. 394=sig. [DD7]):
Birmingham 16034; Folger PR2752.1811a c.3
(**1812/9**) (Vol. IV/9) (facing p. [295]=sig. [X3]):
Folger PR2752.1805b c.1
Plate only: DHW; Folger PR2752.1807c c.4 (Vol.
IX, facing p. 122) (imprint cropped); Huntington
112766 (facing p. [170]); Huntington 181067,
XXIII, 138; V & A E.1202-F-1886 (verse and
imprint cropped)
Lacking plate: Cambridge Bury 35.16 (1811/9)
Lit.: Schiff 1277 (15.8 x 8.8 cm); Boase 1959,
109, pl. 30b; Tomory 1972, pl. 175.

Variants:
I. Proof before all letters (signatures only): BM
1868-8-22-5594.

206.

206. *Hotspur, Worcester, Mortimer and Glendower Dividing Up Trent*, 1803

(*King Henry the Fourth*, Part 1, III, i, 103-105)
(Vol. V/10, facing p. 276=sig. X2)

Engraved by Richard Rhodes (1765-1838) after
Fuseli's lost drawing, of which a fragmentary
study survives in the Kunsthaus, Zurich (1803;
Schiff 1405 verso)
Imprint: Publish'd by F & C. Rivington, London,
Octr. 29th. 1803.
Inscription (top): Act. 3.||HENRY IV.||Sc. 1.|
(bottom): Fuseli, del.||Rhodes, sculp.|

> Hotspur.
> Trent shall not wind with such a deep
>   indent.
> Glendow^r.
> Not wind? it shall, it must; you see, it doth.

Dimensions: ■ 15.8 x 8.7 cm | 6¼" x 3⁷/16";
▣ 16.2 x 9.2 cm | 6⁶/16" x 3¹⁰/16" (BL 80.f.12)
Other locations (**1805/10**): (**1.**) (as above):
Huntington 140092 (H=26.9 cm);—(**2.**) (facing p.
213]=sig. R): Birmingham 180.5 (H=23.8 cm);
Bodleian M.adds 51.d.43/5 (H=26.0 cm); Essick;
Illinois 822.33 Ich Ed. 1805; Princeton Ex
3925.1805 (H=23.0 cm);—(**3.**) (facing p.

207.

208.

[217]=sig. [R3]): Dörrbecker (H=26.8 cm); ZBZ AX 485 (H=22.7 cm);—(4.) (facing p. 273=sig. X): Folger PR2752.1805a1 c.1 (H=26.8 cm); Folger PR2752.1805a1 c.2 (H=23.3 cm);—(5.) (facing p. 277=sig. [X3]): NYPL *NCM Chalmers 1805
(1805/9) (Vol. IV/9):—(1.) Browne (facing p. [401]=sig. FF): KHZ GB 38/IV;—(2.) (facing p. [405]=sig. [FF3]): Birmingham 22365;—(3.) (facing p. 464=sig. KK2): Bern A16.757;—(4.) (facing p. 465=sig. [KK3]): Illinois 822.33 Ich 1805 c.2.
(1811/9) (Vol. IV/9):—(1.) (facing p. 461=sig. KK): Illinois 822.33 Ich 1811;—(2.) (facing p. 464=sig. KK2): Birmingham 16034; Folger PR2752.1811a1 c.3;NYPL *NCM Chalmers 1811
(1812/9) (Vol. IV/9) (facing p. [415]=sig. [FF5]): Folger PR2752.1805b c.1
Plate only: DHW; Folger PR2752.1807c c.4 (Vol. VI, facing p. 71) (imprint cropped); Huntington 112766, 21
Lit.: Schiff 1278 (15.8 x 8.7 cm), 1405

Variants:

I. Proof before letters: Essick (trimmed within platemark).

207. *Henry and Poins Surprise Falstaff and Doll Tearsheet*, 1803
(*King Henry the Fourth*, Part 2, II, iv, 264-265)
(Vol. V/10, facing p. 382=sig. [EE7])

Engraved by James Neagle (1769?-1822) after Fuseli's lost drawing
Imprint: Publish'd by F. & C. Rivington London Oct. 1. 1803.
Inscription (top): Act 2.||IIᵈ. PART OF HENRY IV.||Sc. 4.|(bottom): H Fuseli RA del,||I Neagle Sculp¹,|

    P. Hen.   Look, if the wither'd elder hath not
            his poll claw'd like a parrot.

Dimensions: ■ 16.3 x 9.5 cm | 6⁷/16" x 3¾";
■ 16.6 x 9.7 cm | 6½" x 3¹³/16" (BL 80.f.12)
Other locations **(1805/10): (1.)** (as above): Huntington 140092 (H=26.9 cm) (between pp. 382-383);—**(2.)** (facing p. [331]=sig. BB): Birmingham 180.5 (H=23.8 cm); Bodleian M.adds 51.d.43/5 (H=26.0 cm); Essick; Illinois 822.33 Ich Ed. 1805; Princeton Ex 3925.1805 (H=23.0 cm);—**(3).** (facing p. [337]=sig. CC): Dörrbecker (H=26.8 cm); ZBZ AX 485 (H=22.7 cm);—**(4.)** (facing p. 373=sig. [EE3]): Folger PR2752.1805a1 c.1 (H=26.8 cm);—**(5.)** (facing

p. 384=sig. [EE8]): Folger PR2752.1805a1 c.2
(H=23.3 cm)
(1805/9) (Vol. V/9):—**(1.)** (facing t.p.): Browne;
KHZ GB 38/V;—**(2.)** (facing p. [7]=sig. C):
Birmingham 22365;—**(3.)** (facing p. 52=sig.
[E7]): Bern A16.757; Illinois 822.33 Ich 1805
c.2. **(1811/9)** (Vol. V/9):—**(1.)** (facing p. 43=sig.
[E3]): Illinois 822.33 Ich 1811;—**(2.)** (facing p.
52=sig. [E7]): Birmingham 16035; Folger
PR2752.1811a1 c.3;NYPL *NCM Chalmers 1811
(1812/9) (Vol. V/9) (facing p. [7]=sig. [C]):
Folger PR2752.1805b c.1 (signs of reworking)
Plate only: DHW; Folger PR2752.1807c c.4 (Vol.
VI, between pp. 56-57) (imprint cropped);
Huntington 112766, 21; Huntington 181067,
XXIV, 78
Plate lacking: NYPL *NCM Chalmers 1805
(1805/10)
Lit.: Schiff 1279 (16.7 x 9.5 cm); Argan 1960,
repr. II, 208; Hodnett 1982, 73

Variants:
I. Proof before letters: Essick
II. Proof before all letters (India paper)
(signatures only) **(1805/10)**: Huntington 140092
(H=26.9 cm)
III. Proof before all letters (signatures only):
BM 1868-8-22-5596
Other locations (plate only): Huntington
181067, XXIV, 78

208. *The Death of Falstaff*, 1803
(*King Henry the Fifth*, II, iii, 22-24)
(Vol. VI/10, facing p. 38=sig. E)

Engraved by Samuel Noble (1779-1853) after
Fuseli's lost drawing
Imprint: Publish'd by C. & F. Rivington,
London. Dec. 31. 1803.
Inscription (top): Act 2.||HENRY V.||Sc. 3.|
(bottom): Fuseli del.||S. Noble sculp.|

M^{rs}. Quickly.
So a bade me lay more Clothes on his
feet: I put my hand into the bed & felt them,
and they were as cold as any stone.

Dimensions: ■ 15.9 x 9.3 cm | 6¼" x 3^{10}/16";
■ 16.4 x 9.8 cm | 6^{7}/16" x 3^{13}/16" (BL 80.f.13)
Other locations **(1805/10)**: **(1.)** (as above): Folger
PR2752.1805a1 c.1 (H=26.8 cm); Folger
PR2752.1805a1 c.2 (H=23.3 cm); Huntington
140092 (H=26.9 cm);—**(2.)** (facing t.p.):
Birmingham 180.5 (H=23.8 cm); Bodleian

M.adds 51.d.43/6 (H=26.0 cm); Illinois 822.33
Ich Ed. 1805; Princeton Ex 3925.1805 (H=23.0
cm); ZBZ AX 486 (H=22.7 cm);—**(3.)** (facing p.
[1]=sig. B): Essick;—**(4.)** (facing p. [9]=sig.
[C3]): Dörrbecker (H=26.8 cm);—**(5.)** (facing p.
39=sig. E2): NYPL *NCM Chalmers 1805
(1805/9) (Vol. V/9):—**(1.)** (facing p. [131]=sig.
L): Browne; KHZ GB 38/V;—**(2.)** (facing p.
[139]=sig [M3]): Birmingham 22365;—**(3.)**
(facing p. 168=sig. O): Bern A16.757; Illinois
822.33 Ich 1805 c.2.
(1811/9) (Vol. V/9) (facing p. 168=sig. O):
Birmingham 16035; Folger PR2752.1811a1 c.3;
Illinois 822.33 Ich 1811; NYPL *NCM Chalmers
1811
(1812/9) (Vol. V/9) (facing p. [139]=sig. [M3]):
PR2752.1805b c.1 (plate reworked upper right
and upper left)
Plate only: DHW; Folger PR2752.1807c c.4 (Vol.
III, facing p. 107) (imprint cropped); Folger
PR2752.1807c c.4 (Vol. VI, facing p. 39)
(imprint cropped); Huntington 112766 (facing p.
26); Huntington 181067, XXV, 72
Lit.: Schiff 1280 (15.8 x 9.3 cm); Tomory 1972,
48, 117, 163, pl. 132; Hodnett 1982, 73

209.

209. *Joan of Arc*, 1803
(*King Henry the Sixth*, Part 1, V, iii, 24)
(Vol. VI/10, facing p. 220=sig. [R4])

Engraved by [John?] Lee (d. 1804) after Fuseli's lost drawing
Imprint: Publish'd by C. & F. Rivington London Dec 15. 1803.
Inscription (top): Act 5.||1. K. HENRY VI.||Sc. 3.|(bottom): Fuseli RA del.||Lee, Sculp.|

Enter Fiends—
La Pucelle. See! they forsake me.—

Dimensions: ■ 16|0 x 8.7 cm | 6¼" x 3⁷/16";
■ 16.5 x 9.2 cm | 6½" x 3¹⁰/16" (BL 80.f.13)
Other locations (**1805/10**): (**1.**) (as above): Folger PR2752.1805a1 c.1 (H=26.8 cm); Folger PR2752.1805a1 c.2 (H=23.3 cm); Huntington 140092 (H=26.9 cm); NYPL *NCM Chalmers 1805;—(**2.**) (facing p. [129]=sig. L): Birmingham 180.5 (H=23.8 cm); Bodleian M.adds 51.d.43/3 (H=26.0 cm); Essick; Illinois 822.33 Ich Ed. 1805; Princeton Ex 3925.1805 (H=23.0 cm); —(**3.**) (facing p. [133]=sig. M): Dörrbecker (H=26.8 cm); ZBZ AX 486 (H=22.7 cm)
(**1805/9**) (Vol. V/9):—(**1.**) (facing p. [259]=sig. U): Browne; KHZ GB 38/V;—(**2.**) (facing p. [263]=sig. X): Birmingham 22365;—(**3.**) (facing p. 350=sig. [Cc4]): Bern A16.757; Illinois 822.33 Ich 1805 c.2.
(**1811/9**) (Vol. V/9):—(**1.**) (facing p. 350=sig. [Cc4]): Birmingham 16035; Folger PR2752.1811a1 c.3; NYPL *NCM Chalmers 1811;—(**2.**) (facing p. 353=sig. [Cc6]): Illinois 822.33 Ich 1811
(**1812/9**) (Vol. V/9) (facing p. [263]=sig. X): PR2752.1805b c.1 (signs of wear on plate)
Plate only: DHW; Folger PR2752.1807c c.4 (Vol. III, facing p. 107) (imprint cropped); Huntington 112766, 20; Huntington 181067, XXVI, 224
Lit.: Schiff 1281 (15.9 x 8.7 cm)

Variants:
I. Proof before letters and frame: Huntington 181067 (XXVI, 223).

As a truce nears, the English army, united for the first time, rallies and scatters the French forces. La Pucelle (Joan of Arc) conjures up the fiends to help her. But her 'ancient incantations are too weak,|And hell too strong' and despite her desperate offer of 'soul, body, soul and all', the fiends refuse to aid her and she is taken prisoner and will be burned at the stake.

210.

210. *King Henry at the Deathbed of Beaufort*, 1803
(*King Henry the Sixth*, Part 2, III, iii, 27-28)
(Vol. VI/10, facing p. 316=sig. [AA4])

Engraved by Robert Hartley Cromek (1770-1812) after the drawing in the Kunsthaus, Zurich (1803; on reverse of Schiff 1411).
Imprint: Publish'd by F. & C. Rivington London Sepʳ. 10. 1803.
Inscription (top): Act III.||IIⁿᵈ. PART HENRY VI.||Sc. III.|(bottom): H. Fuseli R.A del.||R. H. Cromek sc-|

K. Henry.
Lord Cardinal if thou thinks't on Heaven's bliss Hold up thy Hand._____

Dimensions: ■ 15.5 x 8.6 cm | 6²/16" x 3⁶/16";
■ 16.0 x 9.0 cm | 6⁵/16" x 3⁹/16" (BL 80.f.13)
Other locations (**1805/10**): (**1.**) (as above): Folger PR2752.1805a1 c.1 (H=26.8 cm); Folger PR2752.1805a1 c.2 (H=23.3 cm); Huntington 140092 (H=26.9 cm); NYPL *NCM Chalmers 1805;—(**2.**) (facing p. [239]=sig. T): Birmingham 180.5 (H=23.8 cm); Bodleian M.adds 51.d.43/6;

Essick; Illinois 822.33 Ich Ed. 1805; Princeton
Ex 3925.1805 (H=23.0 cm);—(3.): (facing p.
[243]=sig [T3]): Dörrbecker (H=26.8 cm); ZBZ
AX 486 (H=22.7 cm)
(1805/9) (Vol. V/9):—(1.) (facing p. [369]=sig.
EE): Browne; KHZ GB 38/V;—(2.) (facing p.
[373]=sig. EE3): Birmingham 22365;—(3.)
(facing p. 446=sig. [KK4]): Bern A16.757;
Illinois 822.33 Ich 1805 c.2. (1811/9) (Vol. V/9)
(facing p. 446=sig. [KK4]): Birmingham 16035;
Folger PR2752.1811a1 c.3; Illinois 822.33 Ich
1811; NYPL *NCM Chalmers 1811)
(1812/9) (Vol. V/9) (facing p. [373]=sig. [EE3]):
PR2752.1805b c.1
Plate only: DHW; Folger PR2752.1807c c.4 (Vol.
VII, facing p. 135) (imprint cropped); Folger
PR2752.1807c c.4 (Vol. III, facing p. 92)
(imprint cropped); Huntington 112766 (facing p.
23); V & A E.1202-B-1886
Lit.: Schiff 1282 (15.5 x 8.5 cm); Boase 1959,
103, pl. 26g; Tomory 1972, 208, pl. 131; Keay
1974, pl. 33

Variants:

I. Proof before all letters (signatures only): BM
1868-8-22-5599.

Act 5.   Ill. K. HENRY VI.   Sc.6.

Henry, the Lieutenant of the Tower:
Enter Gloster.   Good day, my Lord: What,
at your book so hard?

211.

211. *Gloucester Visits King Henry in the Tower*,
1803
(*King Henry the Sixth*, Part 3, V, vi, 1)
(Vol. VI/10, facing p. 472=sig. MM2)

Engraved by James Neagle (1769?-1822) after
Fuseli's lost drawing
Imprint: Publish'd by C. & F. Rivington, London,
Dec 1. 1803.
Inscription (top): Act 5. | | III. K. HENRY VI. | |
Sc.6. | (bottom):H Fuseli RA, del. | | J Neagle Sc^t, |
     Henry, the Lieutenant of the Tower;
 Enter Gloster.   Good day, my Lord! What,
        at your book so hard?
Dimensions: ■ 15.8 x 9.1 cm | 6^3/16" x 3^9/16";
■ 16.0 x 9.4 cm | 6^5/16" x 3^11/16" (BL 80.f.13)
Other locations (1805/10): (1.) (as above): Folger
PR2752.1805a1 c.1 (H=26.8 cm); Folger
PR2752.1805a1 c.2 (H=23.3 cm); Huntington
140092 (H=26.9 cm) (between pp. 472-473);
—(2.) (facing (p. [361]=sig. EE): Birmingham
180.5 (H=23.8 cm); Bodleian M.adds 51.d.43/6
(H=26.0 cm); Illinois 822.33 Ich Ed. 1805;
Princeton Ex 3925.1805 (H=23.0 cm);—(3.)
(facing p. [365]=sig. [EE3]): Dörrbecker
(H=26.8 cm); ZBZ AX 486 (H=22.7 cm);—(4.)
Essick (facing p. [373], i.e. sig. EE);—(5.) (facing
p. 473=sig.[MM3]):NYPL *NCM Chalmers 1805
(1805/9) (Vol. VI/9):—(1.) (facing t.p.): Browne;
KHZ GB 38/VI;—(2.) (facing p. [5]=sig. [B3]):
Birmingham 22366;—(3.) (facing p. [112]=sig.
I2): Bern A16.757;—(4.) (facing p. 113=sig [I3]):
Illinois 822.33 Ich 1805 c.2.
(1811/9) (Vol. VI/9):—(1.) (facing p. 112=sig.
I2): Birmingham 16036; Folger PR2752.1811a
c.3; Illinois 822.33 Ich 1811;—(2.) (facing p.
113=sig. [I3]): NYPL *NCM Chalmers 1811
(1812/9) (Vol. VI/9) (facing p. [5]=sig. [B3]):
Folger PR2752.1805b c.1
Plate only: DHW; Huntington 112766 (between
pp. 190-191); Huntington 181067, XXVIII, 172
Lit.: Schiff 1283 (15.8 x 9.0 cm)

Variants:

I. Proof before letters: Essick
II. Proof before all letters (India paper)
(signatures only) (1805/10): Huntington 140092
(H=26.9 cm)
III. Proof before all letters (signatures only):
BM 1868-8-22-5600
Other locations: Huntington 181067 (XXVIII,
172).

The Ghosts vanish. King Richard starts out of his Dream.
K. R. *Give me another horse* —
— *the lights burn blue.* —

212.

Katharine, Griffiths & Patience.
Kath. *Spirits of peace, where are ye? Are ye all gone?*

213.

212. *King Richard Beset in a Dream by the Ghosts of his Victims*, 1804
(*King Richard the Third*, V, iii, 178-181)
(Vol. VII/10, facing p. 133 = sig. L)

Engraved by James Neagle (1769?-1822) after Fuseli's lost drawing
Imprint: Publish'd by C & F. Rivington, London. Feb^y: 15th. 1804.
Inscription (top): Act. 5.||K. RICHARD. III.|| Sc. 3.|(bottom): H Fuseli RA, del||I Neagle Sc|
The Ghosts vanish.
King Richard starts out of his Dream.
K.R.   Give me another horse—
—the lights burn blue.—
Dimensions: ■ 16.2 x 9.6 cm | 6⁵/16" x 3¾";
■ 16.4 X 9.9 cm | 6½" X 3¹⁴/16" (BL 80.f.14)
Other locations (**1805/10**): (**1.**) (as above): Huntington 140092 (H=26.9 cm); NYPL *NCM Chalmers 1805;—(**2.**) (facing t.p.): Bodleian M.adds 51.d.43/7 (H=26.0 cm); Illinois 822.33 Ich Ed. 1805; Princeton Ex 3925.1805 (H=23.0 cm); ZBZ AX 487 (H=22.7 cm);—(**3.**) (facing p. [1] = sig. B): Birmingham 180.5 (H=23.8 cm); Essick;—(**4.**) (facing p.5=sig. C): Dörrbecker (H=26.8 cm);—(**5.**) (facing p. 124=sig. [K4]): Folger PR2752.1805a1 c.1 (H=26.8 cm);

—(**6.**) (facing p. 125=sig. [K5]): Folger PR2752.1805a1 c.2 (H=23.3 cm)
(**1805/9**) (Vol. VI/9):—(**1.**) (facing p. [121]=sig. K): Browne; KHZ GB 38/VI;—(**2.**) (facing p. [125]=sig. L): Birmingham 22366;—(**3.**) (facing p. 253=sig. T): Bern A16.757; Illinois 822.33 Ich 1805 c.2.
(**1811/9**) (Vol. VI/9):—(**1.**) (facing p. 245=sig. [S5]): Illinois 822.33 Ich 1811;—(**2.**) (facing p. 253=sig. T): Folger PR2752.1811a c.3; NYPL *NCM Chalmers 1811
(**1812/9**) (Vol. VI/9) (facing p. [125]=sig. L): Folger PR2752.1805b c.1
Plate only: DHW; Folger PR2752.1807c c.4 (Vol. IX, between pp. 158-159); Huntington 112766 (facing p. 100) (1 line of verse and imprint cropped); Huntington 181067, XXX, 121
Lit.: Schiff 1284 (16.2 x 9.7 cm); Argan 1960, repr. I, 304; Hodnett 1982, 72, pl. 9

Variants:
I. Proof before all letters (India paper) (signatures only) (**1805/10**) (between pp. 132-133): Huntington 140092 (H=26.9 cm)
II. Proof before all letters (signatures only): BM 1868-8-22-5601
Other locations:Huntington 181067 (XXX, 120).

213. *Queen Katharine's Dream*, 1804
(*King Henry the Eighth*, IV, ii)
(Vol. VII/10, facing p. 235 = sig. [S4])

Engraved by William Blake (1767-1827) after
Fuseli's lost drawing.
Imprint: Publish'd May 12. 1804, by F & C.
Rivington, S'. Paul's Church Yard.
Inscription (top):Act IV. | |KING HENRY VIII. | |
Sc. II. | (bottom): Fuseli. inv | |Blake. sculp|

Katharine, Griffiths & Patience.
Kath.   Spirits of Peace, where are ye? Are ye
all gone?

Dimensions: ■ 15.8 x 9.5 cm | 6³/16" x 3¾"
(BL 80.f.14)
Other locations (1805/10): (1.) (as above):
Huntington 140092 (H=26.9 cm) (between pp.
234-235); NYPL *NCM Chalmers 1805;—(2.)
(facing p. [143] = sig. M): Birmingham 180.5
(H=23.8 cm); Essick; Illinois 822.33 Ich Ed.
1805; Princeton Ex 3925.1805 (H=23.0 cm);
—(3.) (facing p. [145] = sig. M2): Bodleian
M.adds 51.d.43/7 (H=26.0 cm);—(4.) (facing p.
[149] = sig. N): Dörrbecker (H=26.8 cm); ZBZ
AX 487;—(5.) (facing p. 232 = sig. S2): Folger
PR2752.1805a1 c.1 (H=26.8 cm); Folger
PR2752.1805a1 c.2 (H=23.3 cm)
(1805/9) (Vol. VI/9):—(1.) (facing p. [263] = sig.
U): Browne; KHZ GB 38/VI;—(2.) (facing p.
[272] = sig. X): Birmingham 22366;—(3.) (facing
p. 357 = sig. [Cc4]): Bern A16.757; Illinois
822.33 Ich 1805 c.2.
(1811/9) (Vol. VI/9):—(1.) (facing p. 354 = sig.
Cc2): Illinois 822.33 Ich 1811;—(2.) (facing p.
357 = sig. [Cc4]): Folger PR2752.1811a c.3;
NYPL *NCM Chalmers 1811
(1812/9) (Vol. VI/9) (facing p. [271] = sig. X]):
Folger PR2752.1805b c.1 (plate worn)
Plate only: BM 1863-5-9-51; Fitzwilliam
P.586.1985 (15.9 x 9.6 cm); Folger Art File
S528k4 no. 40; Folger PR2752.1807c c.4 (Vol.
IV, between pp. 114-115) (imprint cropped);
Huntington 112766 (facing p. 13); Huntington
140091, 53, 376a; Huntington 181067, XXXII,
130; Rosenwald 1838.27 (37.135c); Rosenwald
1838.27 (37.135e)
Lit.: Schiff 1285 (15.8 x 9.6 cm); A. Gilchrist,
Life of Blake, 1863, II, 261; Russell 1912, no.
99. I; Keynes 1921, no. 128; Tomory 1972, 119,
pl. 127; Bentley 1977, no. 498; Essick 1991, no.
XLVII.1

Exh.: Florence 1979 (45)

Variants:
I. Proof before all letters (India paper)
signatures only): BM 1868-8-22-5602
Other locations: Rosenwald 1838 (37.135a);
Charles Ryskamp; Private collection, Melbourne

Blake had begun work on his Chalmers plates in
October 1803; he was paid 25 guineas per plate.
The squared drawing after Fuseli that Blake
prepared for this purpose is in the National
Gallery of Art, Washington, Inv. no. Rosenwald
B11063.

214.

214. *Diomedes Snatches the Glove from
Cressida*, 1804
(*Troilus and Cressida*, V, ii)
(Vol. VII/10, facing p. 381 = sig. [EE5])

Engraved by James Neagle (1769?-1822) after
Fuseli's lost drawing
Imprint: Publish'd by F & C Rivington London.
14 Apr'. 1804
Inscription (top): Act 5 | |TROILUS and
CRESSIDA | |Sc 2 | (bottom): H Fuseli RA. del, | |
I Neagle Sc|

Cressida.
_____O pretty pretty pledge!
_____nay do not snatch it from me;
He that takes that, must take my heart withal.

Dimensions: ■ 16.1 x 9.4 cm | 6⁶/16" x 3¹¹/16";
■ 16.3 x 9.6 cm | 6⁷/16" x 3¹³/16" (BL 80.f.14)
Other locations (**1805/10**): (**1.**) (as above):
Huntington 140092 (H=26.9 cm); NYPL *NCM
Chalmers 1805;—(**2.**) (facing p. [267]=sig. X):
Birmingham 180.5 (H=23.8 cm); Bodleian
M.adds 51.d.43/7 (H=26.0 cm); Essick;
Princeton Ex 3925.1805 (H=23.0 cm);—(**3.**)
(facing p. [275]=sig. [X5]): Dörrbecker (H=26.8
cm); ZBZ AX 487;—(**4.**) (facing p. 378=sig.
[EE3]): Folger PR2752.1805a1 c.1 (H=26.8 cm);
Folger PR2752.1805a1 c.2 (H=23.3 cm)
(**1805/9**) (Vol. VI/9):—(**1.**) (facing p. [389]=sig.
FF): Browne; KHZ GB 38/VI;—(**2.**) (facing p.
397=sig. FF5): Birmingham 22366;—(**3.**) (facing
p. 503=sig. [NN5]): Bern A16.757; Illinois
822.33 Ich 1805 c.2.
(**1811/9**) (Vol. VI/9):—(**1.**) (facing p. 500=sig.
[NN3]): Illinois 822.33 Ich 1811;—(**2.**) (facing p.
503=sig. [NN54]): Birmingham 16036; Folger
PR2752.1811a c.3; NYPL *NCM Chalmers 1811
(**1812/9**) (Vol. VI/9) (facing p. [397]=sig.
[FD5]): PR2752.1805b c.1
Plate only: Folger PR2752.1807c c.4 (Vol. V,
between pp. 134-135) (imprint cropped);
Huntington 112766 (facing p. 200) (imprint
cropped); Huntington 181067, XXXVIII, 146
Lacking plate: Illinois 822.33 Ich Ed. 1805
Lit.: Schiff 1286 (16.1 x 9.5 cm); Antal 1956;
Merchant 1959, 79; Argan 1960, repr. II, 720;
Tomory 1972, 117, 171, pl. 120; Hodnett 1982,
73

Variants:

I. Proof before all letters (India paper)
(signatures only) (**1805/10**) (between pp. 380-
381): Huntington 140092 (H=26.9 cm)
II. Proof before all letters (signatures only): BM
1868-8-22-5603
Other locations: Huntington 181067 (XXXVIII,
145).

215. *Timon Cursing Athens*, 1803
(*Timon of Athens*, IV, i, 1)
(Vol. VIII/10, facing p. 61=sig. [F6])

Engraved by Robert Hartley Cromek (1770-1812)
after the wash drawing in the Kunsthaus, Zurich
(1803; Schiff 1411).
Imprint: Publish'd by F. & C. Rivington London
Oct. 15 1803.
Inscription (top): Act 4.||TIMON OF
ATHENS.||Sc. 1.|(bottom): Fuseli R.A. del.||
R.H. Cromek sc-|

Timon.   Let me look back on thee,_____

Dimensions: ■ 15.6 x 8.9 cm | 6²/16" x 3½";
■ 16.1 x 9.3 cm | 6⁵/16" x 3¹¹/16" (BL 80.f.15).
Other locations (**1805/10**): (**1.**) (as above): Folger
PR2752.1805a1 c.1 (H=26.8 cm); ??Folger
PR2752.1805a1 c.2??]; Huntington 140092
(H=26.9 cm); NYPL *NCM Chalmers 1805;
ZBZ AX 488 (H=22.7 cm);—(**2.**) (facing t.p.):
Birmingham 180.5 (H=23.8 cm); Bodleian
M.adds 51.d.43/8 (H=26.0 cm); Illinois 822.33
Ich Ed. 1805; Princeton Ex 3925.1805 (H=23.0
cm);—(**3.**) (facing p. [1]=sig. B): Essick;—(**4.**)
(facing p. [5]=sig. C2): Dörrbecker (H=26.8 cm)
(**1805/9**) (Vol. VII/9):—(**1.**) (facing t.p.): Browne;
KHZ GB 38/VII;—(**2.**) (facing p. [5]=sig. C2):
Birmingham 22367;—(**3.**) (facing p. 61=sig.
[F6]): Bern A16.757; Illinois 822.33 Ich 1805 c.2.
(**1811/9**) (Vol. VII/9) (facing p. 61=sig. [F6]):
Birmingham 16037; Folger PR2752.1811a c.3;
Illinois 822.33 Ich 1811; NYPL *NCM Chalmers
1811
(**1812/9**) (Vol. VII/9) (facing p. [5]=sig. C2):
Folger PR2752.1805b c.1
Plate only: DHW; Folger PR2752.1807c c.4 (Vol.
VII, facing p. 68) (imprint cropped); Huntington
181067, XXXVI, 59
Lit.: Schiff 1287 (15.5 x 9.0 cm); Argan 1960,
repr. III, 544; Tomory 1972, 165, 206f., 215, pl.
171; Hodnett 1982, 73

Variants:
I. Proof before all letters: BM 1868-8-22-5608.

The illustration is at odds with the lines cited;
they seem more appropriate for Timon in his
Cave.

Timon. *Set me look back on thee—*

215.

A Hall in Aufidius's House. Coriolanus.
Aufidius. *Say, what's thy Name?*
Thou hast a grim appearance—

216.

216. *Coriolanus Before Aufidius*, 1804
(*Coriolanus*, IV, v, 63-64)
(Vol. VIII/10, facing p. 203 = sig. [Q5])

Engraved by Robert Hartley Cromek (1770-1812)
after the pen and wash drawing in the Kunsthaus,
Zurich (1804; Schiff 1407).
Imprint: London Pub. Aug. 18. 1804, by F. & C
Rivington S^t. Paul's Church Yard—
Inscription (top): Act IV.||CORIOLANUS.||Sc.
V.|Fuseli RA. del.||R.H. Cromek sc.|

    A Hall in Aufidius's House. Coriolanus.
Aufidius.   Say, what's thy Name?
      Thou hast a grim appearance—

Dimensions: ■ 15.9 x 9.6 cm | 6¼" x 3¾";
■ 16.2 x 9.9 cm | 6⁶/16" x 3¹⁴/16" (BL 80.f.15).
Other locations (**1805/10**): (**1.**) (as above):
Huntington 140092 (H=26.9 cm) (between pp.
202-203); NYPL *NCM Chalmers 1805;—(**2.**)
(facing p. [101] = sig. K): Birmingham 180.5
(H=23.8 cm); Bodleian M.adds 51.d.43/8
(H=26.0 cm); Essick; Illinois 822.33 Ich Ed.
1805; Princeton Ex 3925.1805 (H=23.0 cm);
—(**3.**) (facing p. [105] = sig. [K3]): Dörrbecker
(H=26.8 cm); ZBZ AX 488; —(**4.**) facing p.
299 = sig. [Q3]): Folger PR2752.1805a1 c.1
(H=26.8 cm); [?? Folger PR2752.1805a1 c.2??];
(**1805/9**) (Vol. VII/9):—(**1.**) (facing p. [101] = sig.
K): Browne; KHZ GB 38/VII;—(**2.**) (facing p.
[105] = sig. [K3]): Birmingham 22367;—(**3.**)
(facing p. 200 = sig. [Q3]): Illinois 822.33 Ich
1805 c.2.;—(**4.**) (facing p. 202 = sig. [Q4]): Bern
A16.757
(**1811/9**) (Vol. VII/9):—(**1.**) (facing p. 200 = sig.
[Q3]): Illinois 822.33 Ich 1811;—(**2.**) (facing p.
203 = sig. [Q5]): Birmingham 16037; Folger
PR2752.1811a c.3; NYPL *NCM Chalmers 1811
(**1812/9**) (Vol. VII/9) (facing p. [105] = sig. [K3]):
PR2752.1805b c.1
Plate only: DHW; Folger PR2752.1807c c.4 (Vol.
VII, between pp. 118-119) (imprint cropped);
Huntington 181067, XXXIII, 128
Lit.: Schiff 1288 (15.8 x 9.8 cm), 1407, 1543;
Hodnett 1982, 73

          Variants:
I. Proof before all letters (signatures only): BM
1868-8-22-5604
    Other locations: BM 1868-8-22-5605.

217.

218.

217. *The Ghost of Caesar Appears to Brutus*,
1804
(*Julius Caesar*, IV, iii, 279-280)
(Vol. VIII/10, facing p. 323 = sig. AA)

Engraved by Charles Warren (1766-1823) after
Fuseli's lost drawing
Imprint: Publish'd by F & C Rivington London
May 6- 1804.
Inscription (top): Act IV. | |JULIUS CAESAR.| |
Sc III.|(bottom): Fuseli Del.ᴸ.| |C. Warren Scpᴸ.. |

  Br.   _____Why com'st thou?

    Ghost. To tell thee, thou shalt see me at
            Phillippi.

Dimensions: ■ 15.1 x 8.7 cm | 5¹⁵/16" x 3⁷/16"
(BL 80.f.15)
Other locations (**1805/10**): (1.) (as above): Folger
PR2752.1805a1 c.1 (H=26.8 cm); [??Folger
PR2752.1805a1 c.2]; Huntington 140092
(H=26.9 cm)(between pp. 322-323); NYPL
*NCM Chalmers 1805;—(2.) (facing p.
[243] = sig. T): Birmingham 180.5 (H=23.8 cm);
Bodleian M.adds 51.d.43/8 (H=26.0 cm); Essick;
Illinois 822.33 Ich Ed. 1805; Princeton Ex
3925.1805 (H=23.0 cm);—(3.) (facing p.
[247] = sig. [T3]: Dörrbecker (H=26.8 cm); ZBZ
AX 488 (H=22.7 cm)

(**1805/9**) (Vol. VII/9):—(**1.**) (facing p. [243] = sig.
T): Browne; KHZ GB 38/VII;—(**2.**) (facing p.
[247] = sig. T3): Birmingham 22367;—(**3.**) (facing
p. 323 = sig. AA): Bern A16.757; Illinois 822.33
Ich 1805 c.2
(**1811/9**) (Vol. VII/9):—(**1.**) (facing p. 312 = sig.
[Z3]): Illinois 822.33 Ich 1811;—(**2.**) (facing p.
322/323 = sig. AA): Birmingham 16037; Folger
PR2752.1811a c.3; NYPL *NCM Chalmers 1811
(**1812/9**) (Vol. VII/9) (facing p. [247] = sig. [T3]):
Folger PR2752.1805b c.1
Plate only: DHW; Folger PR2752.1807c c.4 (Vol.
IV, facing p. 97) imprint cropped; Huntington
181067, XXXIV, 147
Lit.: Schiff 1289 (15.2 x 8.8 cm); Keay 1974, pl.
31; Hodnett 1982, 73; Tomory 1972, 117, 181,
pl. 220

Variants:

I. Proof before all letters (India paper)
(signatures only) (**1805/10**): Huntington 140092
(H=26.9 cm)
Other locations(plate only):BM 1868-8-22-5609;
BM 1868-8-22-5610; Huntington 181067
XXXIV, 146)

II. Proof before all letters (signatures only):
Essick.

218. *The Death of Cleopatra*, 1804
(*Antony and Cleopatra*, V, ii, 319-320)
(Vol. VIII/10, facing p. 477=sig. [Kκ6])

Engraved by Robert Hartley Cromek (1770-1812)
after Fuseli's lost drawing
Imprint: Publish'd by C & F. Rivington, London.
May 1. 1804.
Inscription (top centre): ANTONY and
CLEOPATRA.|(bottom): Fuseli RA. del.||R.H.
Cromek sc.|

> Act V. Sc. II. (a room in the Monument,
> enter guards rushing in.)
> 1. Guard.   —Where is the Queen?
> Charmian.   —Speak softly, wake her not.

Dimensions: ■ 15.8 x 9.5 cm |6¼" x 3¾";
▣ 16.2 X 9.9 cm | 6⁵/16" x 3¹⁴/16" (BL 80.f.15)
Other locations (**1805/10**): (**1.**) (as above): Folger
PR2752.1805a1 c.1 (H=26.8 cm); Huntington
140092 (H=26.9 cm); NYPL *NCM Chalmers
1805;—(**2.**) (facing p. [339]=sig. Bв):
Birmingham 180.5 (H=23.8 cm); Bodleian
M.adds 51.d.43/8 (H=26.0 cm); Essick; Illinois
822.33 Ich Ed. 1805; Princeton Ex 3925.1805
(H=23.0 cm); [??Folger PR2752.1805a1 c.2];
—(**3.**) (facing p. [343]=sig. [Bв3]): Dörrbecker
(H=26.8 cm); ZBZ AX 488 (H=22.7 cm)
(**1805/9**) (Vol. VII/9):—(**1.**) (facing p. [343]=sig.
[Bв2]): Birmingham 22367;—(**2.**) (facing p.
[339]=sig. [Bв3]): Browne; KHZ GB 38/VII;
—(**3.**) (facing p. 477=sig. [KK6]): Bern
A16.757; Illinois 822.33 Ich 1805 c.2
(**1811/9**) (Vol. VII/9):—(**1.**) (facing p. 463=sig.
[Iı7]: Illinois 822.33 Ich 1811;—(**2.**) (facing p.
477=sig. [Kκ6]): Birmingham 16037; Folger
PR2752.1811a c.3; NYPL *NCM Chalmers 1811
(**1812/9**) (Vol. VII/9) (facing p. [343]=sig.
[Bв3]): PR2752.1805b c.1
Plate only: Essick; Folger PR2752.1807c c.4
(Vol. VIII, facing p. 151) (imprint cropped);
Huntington 112766 (facing p. 24) (imprint
cropped); Huntington 181067, XXV, 188
Lit.: Schiff 1290 (15.8 x 9.8 cm); Argan 1960,
repr. III, 368; Keay 1974, pl. 22

> Variants:
> I. Proof before all letters (signatures only): BM
> 1868-8-22-5615.

219.

219. *Iachimo Emerging from the Chest*, 1804
(*Cymbeline*, II, ii, 15)
(Vol. IX/10, facing p. 37=sig. [D3])

Engraved by Robert Hartley Cromek (1770-1812)
after Fuseli's lost drawing
Imprint: London Pub. July 2-1804, by F. & C.
Rivington, Sᵗ. Paul's Church Yard.
Inscription (top): Act. II.||CYMBELINE.||Sc.
II.|(bottom): Fuseli R.A. del.||R.H. Cromek
sc.|

> Imogen sleeps. Jachimo, from the trunk.
> Jachimo. _____How bravely thou becom'st thy
> bed.—

Dimensions: ■ 15.9 x 9.8 cm | 6¼" x 3¹⁴/16";
▣ 16.2 x 10.1 cm | 6⁶/16" x 4" (BL 80.f.16)
Other locations (**1805/10**): (**1.**) (as above): Folger
PR2752.1805a1 c.2 (H=23.3 cm); NYPL *NCM
Chalmers 1805—(**2.**) (facing t.p.): Bodleian
M.adds 51.d.43/9 (H=26.0 cm); Illinois 822.33
Ich Ed. 1805; Princeton Ex 3925.1805 (H=23.0
cm); ZBZ AX 489 (H=22.7 cm);—(**3.**) (facing p.
[1]=sig. B): Birmingham 180.5 (H=23.8 cm);
Essick;—(**4.**) (facing p. 5=sig. [B3]): Dörrbecker
(H=26.8 cm);—(**5.**) (facing p. 36=sig. D2):
Folger PR2752.1805a1 c.1 (H=26.8 cm);
Huntington 140092 (H=26.9 cm)

(1805/9) (Vol. VIII/9):—**(1.)** (facing t.p.):
Browne; KHZ GB 38/VIII;—**(2.)** (facing p.
[5]=sig. [B3]): Birmingham 22368;—**(3.)** (facing
p. 36=sig. D2): Bern A16.757;—**(4.)** (facing p.
37=sig. [D3]): Illinois 822.33 Ich 1805 c.2
(1811/9) (Vol. VIII/9):—**(1.)** (facing p. 36=sig.
D2): Birmingham 16038; Illinois 822.33 Ich 1811;
—**(2.)** (facing p. 37=sig. [D3]): Folger
PR2752.1811a c.3; NYPL *NCM Chalmers 1811
(1812/9) (Vol. VIII/9): (facing p. [5]=sig. [B3])
(signs of reworking): Folger PR2752.1805b c.1
Plate only: DHW (16.3 x 10.2 cm); Folger
PR2752.1807c c.4 (Vol. VIII, facing p. 42)
(imprint cropped); Huntington 112766 (between
pp. 24-25); Huntington 181067, XXXIX, 41
Lit.: Schiff 1291 (15.8 x 9.8 cm); Argan 1960,
repr. III, 704

Variants:

I. Proof before all letters (signatures only): BM
1868-8-22-5616

**220. *Martius Finding the Body of Bassanius in
the Cave*,** 1804
(*Titus Andronicus*, II, iii, 222-230)
(Vol. IX/10, facing p. 176=sig. [N8])

Engraved by John Dadley (1767-*post* 1807) after
the drawing in the British Art Center, Yale (1804;
Schiff 1410)
Imprint: Publish'd by F & C. Rivington London
31st. March. 1804.
Inscription (top): Act II.||TITUS
ANDRONICUS.||Sc. IV.|(bottom): Fuseli,
del.||Dadley, sculp.|

Martius. Lord Bassanius lies embrewed here,
      All on a heap_____

Dimensions: ■ 15.8 x 9.3 cm | 6³/16" x 3¹¹/16";
■ 16.0 x 9.5 cm | 6¼" x 3¾" (BL 80.f.16)
Other locations **(1805/10)**: **(1.)** (as above): Folger
PR2752.1805a1 c.1 (H=26.8 cm); Folger
PR2752.1805a1 c.2 (H=23.3 cm); Huntington
140092 (H=26.9 cm);—**(2.)** (facing p. [139]=sig.
L): Birmingham 180.5 (H=23.8 cm); Bodleian
M.adds 51.d.43/9 (H=26.0 cm); Essick; Illinois
822.33 Ich Ed. 1805; Princeton Ex 3925.1805
(H=23.0 cm);—**(3.)** (facing p. [145]=sig. M):
Dörrbecker (H=26.8 cm); ZBZ AX 489;—**(5.)**
(facing p. 177=sig. O): NYPL *NCM Chalmers
1805
(1805/9) (Vol. VIII/9):—**(1.)** ?Browne 139=sig.
L] (facing p. [141]=sig. L): KHZ GB 38/VIII;

220.

221.

—(2.) (facing p. [145]=sig. M): Birmingham 22368;—(3.) (facing p. 176=sig. [N8]): Bern A16.757; Illinois 822.33 Ich 1805 c.2
(1811/9) (vol. VIII/9) (facing p. 176=sig. [N8]): Birmingham 16038; Folger PR2752.1811a c.3; Illinois 822.33 Ich 1811; NYPL *NCM Chalmers 1811
(1812/9) (Vol. VIII/9) (facing p. [145]=sig. M): Folger PR2752.1805b c.1
Plate only: DHW; Folger PR2752.1807c c.4 (Vol. V, facing p. 43) (imprint cropped); Huntington 181067, XXXVI, 72
Lit.: Schiff 1292 (?16.4 x 9.5 cm); Mason 1964, 89; Hodnett 1982, 74

221. *Marina Addresses Pericles*, 1804
(*Pericles*, V, 1, 85)
(Vol. IX/10, facing p. 321=sig. AA)

Engraved by Richard Rhodes (1765-1838)
Imprint: Publish'd by C & F. Rivington London 9th. Marh. 1804.
Inscription (top): Act. 5.||PERICLES.||Sc. 1.|
(bottom): Fuseli del.||Rhodes sc.|

Marina. Hail Sir! My Lord, Lend ear.—

Dimensions: ■ 15.7 x 9.1 cm | $6^3/16$" x $3^5/16$;
■ 16.1 x 9.6 cm | $5^6/16$" x $3^5/16$" (BL 80.f.16)
Other locations (1805/10): (1.) (as above): Huntington 140092 (H=26.9 cm) (between pp. 320-321); NYPL *NCM Chalmers 1805;—(2.) (facing p. [235]=sig. S): Birmingham 180.5 (H=23.8 cm); Bodleian M.adds 51.d.43/9; Illinois 822.33 Ich Ed. 1805; Princeton Ex 3925.1805 (H=23.0 cm);—(3.) (facing p. [241]=sig. T): Dörrbecker (H=26.8 cm); ZBZ AX 489 (H=22.7 cm);—(4.) (facing p. 317=sig. [Z7]): Folger PR2752.1805a1 c.1 (H=26.8 cm); Folger PR2752.1805a1 c.2 (H=23.3 cm)
(1805/9) (Vol. VIII/9):—(1.) (facing p. [235]=sig. S): Browne; KHZ GB 38/VIII (facing p. [235]=sig. S);—(2.) (facing p. [241]=sig. T): Birmingham 22368;—(3.) (facing p. 321=sig. AA): Bern A16.757 (16.2 x 9.6 cm) [15.7 x 9.2 cm]; Illinois 822.33 Ich 1805 c.2
(1811/9) (Vol. VIII/9):—(1.) (facing p. 317=sig. [Z7]): Illinois 822.33 Ich 1811;—(2.) (facing p. 321=sig. AA): Birmingham 16038; Folger PR2752.1811a c.3; NYPL *NCM Chalmers 1811
(1812/9) (Vol. VIII/9) (facing p. [242]=sig. T): Folger PR2752.1805b c.1
Plate only: DHW; Folger PR2752.1807c c.4 (Vol.

VIII, facing p. 101) (imprint cropped); Huntington 112766 (facing p. 19); Huntington 181067, XLIV, 103
Lit.: Schiff 1293 (15.7 x 9.1 cm); Antal 1956, 112, note 68; Argan 1960, repr. III, 624; Hagstrum 1964, 40, pl. XVIIc; Tomory 1972, 117, 167, pl. 123

Variants:
I. Proof before letters (India paper): Essick.

222.

222. *Lear Carrying the Body of Dead Cordelia*, 1804
(*King Lear*, V, iii)
(Vol. IX/10, facing p. 467=sig. LL2)

Engraved by Robert Hartley Cromek (1770-1812) after Fuseli's lost drawing
Imprint: Publish'd by C & F. Rivington, London, Feby. 1st. 1804.
Inscription (top): Act. 5.||KING LEAR.||Sc. 3.| H. Fuseli R.A. del.||R:H: Cromek sc-|

Enter King Lear supporting the Dead Body of his Daughter.
Lear.   Howl! Howl! Howl!

Dimensions: ■ 15.3 x 9.3 cm | 6' x $3^{10}/16$";
■ 15.6 x 9.6 cm | $6^2/16$" x $3^{13}/16$" (BL 80.f.16)

Other locations (**1805/10**): (**1.**) (as above):
Huntington 140092 (H=26.9 cm);NYPL *NCM
Chalmers 1805;—(**2.**) (facing p. [335]=sig. BB):
Birmingham 180.5 (H=23.8 cm); Bodleian
M.adds 51.d.43/9 (H=26.0 cm); Essick; Illinois
822.33 Ich Ed. 1805; Princeton Ex 3925.1805
(H=23.0 cm);—(**3.**) facing p. [339]=Cc2):
Dörrbecker (H=26.8 cm); ZBZ AX 489
(H=22.7 cm);—(**4.**) (facing p. 457=sig. [KK5]):
Folger PR2752.1805a1 c.1 (H=26.8 cm); Folger
PR2752.1805a1 c.2 (H=23.3 cm)
(**1805/9**) (Vol. VIII/9):—(**1.**) (facing p.
[335]=sig. BB): Browne; KHZ GB 38/VIII;—(**2.**)
(facing p. [339]=sig. Cc2): Birmingham 22368;
—(**3.**) (facing p. 467=sig. LL2): Bern A16.757;
Illinois 822.33 Ich 1805 c.2
(**1811/9**) (Vol. VIII/9):—(**1.**) Illinois 822.33 Ich
1811 (facing p. 457=sig. [KK5]);—(**2.**) (facing p.
467=sig. LL2): Birmingham 16038; Folger
PR2752.1811a c.3; NYPL *NCM Chalmers 1811
(**1812/9**) (Vol. VIII/9) (facing p. [339]=sig.
Cc2): Folger PR2752.1805b c.1 (signs of
reworking)
Plate only: DHW; Folger PR2752.1807c c.4 (Vol.
V, between pp. 154-155) (imprint cropped)
Lit.: Schiff 1294 (15.3 x 9.2 cm); Tomory 1972,
117, pl. 117; Hodnett 1982, 74

Variants:
I. Proof before all letters (signatures only): BM
1868-8-22-5613

223. *Romeo and the Apothecary*, 1804
(*Romeo and Juliet*, V, i, 58-59)
(Vol. X/10, facing p. 107=sig. [I4])

Engraved by William Blake (1757-1827) after
Fuseli's lost drawing
Imprint: Publish'd by C & F Rivington London
Jan 14. 1804.
Inscription (top):Act 1.||ROMEO and JULIET.||
Sc. 1.|(bottom): H. Fuseli. R.A. inv.||W. Blake.
sc|

Enter Apothecary.
Romeo.   Come hither Man.— I see, that thou
            art poor;
         Hold, there's forty ducats:—
Dimensions: ■ 17.1 x 9.3 cm | 6¾" x 3¹¹/₁₆"
(BL 80.f.17)
Other locations (**1805/10**): (**1.**) (as above):
Huntington 140092 (H=26.9 cm) (between pp.

223.

224.

106-107); NYPL *NCM Chalmers 1805;—(2.) (facing t.p.): Bodleian M.adds 51.d.43/10 (H=26.0 cm); Illinois 822.33 Ich Ed. 1805; Princeton Ex 3925.1805 (H=23.0 cm); ZBZ AX 490 (H=22.7 cm);—(3.) (facing p. [1]=sig. B): Birmingham 180.5 (H=23.8 cm); Essick;—(4.) (facing p. [7]=sig. C2): Dörrbecker (H=26.8 cm); Folger PR2752.1805a1 c.1 (H=26.8 cm); Folger PR2752.1805a1 c.2 (H=23.3 cm)
(1805/9) (Vol. IX/9):—**(1.)** (facing t.p.): Browne; KHZ GB 38/IX;—**(2.)** (facing p. [7]=sig. C2): Birmingham 22369; Illinois 822.33 Ich 1805 c.2;—**(3.)** (facing p. 107=sig. [I4]): Bern A16.757
(1811/9) (Vol. IX/9):—**(1.)** (facing p. [7]=C2): Illinois 822.33 Ich 1811;—**(2.)** (facing p. 107=sig. [I4]): Folger PR2752.1811a c.3; NYPL *NCM Chalmers 1811
(1812/9) (Vol. IX/9) (facing p. [7]=sig. C2): Folger PR2752.1805b c.1 (plate worn)
Plate only: Folger Art File S528r1 no. 85 c.1 (2 lines of verse and imprint cropped); Folger Art File S528r1 no. 85 c.41; Huntington 140091, 56, 68a (imprint cropped); Rosenwald 1838.27 (37.1350)
Lacking plate: Birmingham 16039 (1811)
Lit.: Schiff 1295 (17.0 x 9.3 cm); Russell 99. II; Keynes 1928, no. 128; Argan 1960, repr. I, 720; Keay 1974, pl. 21; Bentley 1977, no. 498B.2; Weinglass 1980, 666; Hodnett 1982, 74; Essick 1991, no. XLVII.2, pl. 213

Variants:

I. Proof before all letters (India paper) (signatures only) **(1805/10)**: Huntington 140092 (H=26.9 cm)
Other locations: Rosenwald 1838.27 (37.135D)
II. Proof before all letters (signatures only): BM 1868-8-22-5607.

Steevens comments on the apothecary's stuffed crocodile hanging from the ceiling:

> ... formerly, when an apothecary first engaged with his druggist, he was gratuitously furnished by him with these articles of show, which were then imported for that use only. I have met with the alligator, tortoise, &c. hanging up in the shop of an ancient apothecary at Limehouse. ...
> See Hogarth's *Marriage Alamode*, Plate III.

224. *Hamlet and the Ghost*, 1804
(*Hamlet*, I, iv, 84)
(Vol. X/10, facing p. 155=sig. [N4])

Engraved by Joseph Clarendon Smith (1778-1810) after Fuseli's lost drawing
Imprint: London Pub. Aug. 2. 1804, by F. & C. Rivington Sᵗ. Pauls Church Yard.
Inscription (top): Act I.||HAMLET.||Sc. IV.| (bottom): Fusili del. RA||Joseph Smith sculpᵗ.|

Ghost beckons.
Hamlet.   Still am I Called; Unhand me.—

Dimensions: ■ 15.7 x 9.4 cm | 6³/16" x 3¹¹/16"; ◼ 16.0 x 9.6 cm | 6⁵/16" x 3¹³/16" (BL 80.f.17)
Other locations **(1805/10)**: **(1.)** (as above): NYPL *NCM Chalmers 1805;—**(2.)** (facing p. [123]=sig. L): Birmingham 180.5 (H=23.8 cm); Bodleian M.adds 51.d.43/10 (H=26.0 cm); Essick; Illinois 822.33 Ich Ed. 1805; Princeton Ex 3925.1805 (H=23.0 cm);—**(3.)** (facing p. [127]=sig. [L3]): Dörrbecker (H=26.8 cm); ZBZ AX 490 (H=22.7 cm);—**(4.)** (facing p. 151=sig. N2): Folger PR2752.1805a1 c.2 (H=23.3 cm)
(1805/9) (Vol. IX/9):—**(1.)** (facing p. [123]=sig. L): Browne; KHZ GB 38/IX;—**(2.)** (facing p. [127]=sig. [L3]): Birmingham 22369;—**(3.)** (facing p. 155=sig. [N4]): Bern A16.757; Illinois 822.33 Ich 1805 c.2
(1811/9) (Vol. IX/9): Folger PR2752.1811a c.3;—**(1.)** (facing p. 151=sig. N2): Illinois 822.33 Ich 1811;—**(2.)** (facing p. 155=sig. [N4]): NYPL *NCM Chalmers 1811.
(1812/9) (Vol. IX/9) (facing p. [127]=sig. [L3]): Folger PR2752.1805b c.1
Plate only: Folger PR2752.1807c c.4 (Vol. II, between pp. 32-33) (imprint cropped)
Lacking plate: Birmingham 16039 (1811)
Lit.: Schiff 1296 (15.7 x 9.5 cm); Argan 1960, repr. III, 800; Tomory 1972, 117, pl. 130; Keay 1974, pl. 32; Hodnett, 1982, 74, pl. 10
Exh.: New Haven 1981 (177d)

Variants:

I. Date in imprint changed **(1805/10)** (between pp. 154-155): Huntington 140092 (H=26.9 cm)
Imprint: London Pub. July 18. 1804, by F. & C. Rivington Sᵗ. Pauls Church Yard
Other locations (facing p. 151=sig. N2): Folger PR2752.1805a1 c.1 (H=26.8 cm)

225.

c.1 (H=26.8 cm); Folger PR2752.1805a1 c.2 (H=23.3 cm);
(1805/9) (Vol. IX/9):—**(1.)** (facing p. [287]=sig. Y): Browne; KHZ GB 38/IX;—**(2.)** (facing p. [291]=sig. Y3): Birmingham 22369;—**(3.)** (facing p. 409=sig. [GG3]): Bern A16.757; Illinois 822.33 Ich 1805 c.2
(1811/9) (Vol. IX/9):—**(1.)** (facing p. 407=sig. GG2): Illinois 822.33 Ich 1811;—**(2.)** (facing p. 409=sig. [GG3]): Folger PR2752.1811a c.3; NYPL *NCM Chalmers 1811
(1812/9) (Vol. IX/9) (facing p. [286]=sig. Y): Folger PR2752.1805b c.1
Plate only: Folger PR2752.1807c c.4 (Vol. VIII, facing p. 139) (imprint cropped); Huntington 112766 (between pp. 192-193) (imprint cropped); Huntington 181067, XLIII, 158
Lacking plate: Birmingham 16039
Lit.: Schiff 1297 (15.5 x 9.1 cm); Argan 1960, repr. III, 128; Tomory 1972, 117, pl. 118; Keay 1974, pl. 17; Hodnett 1982, 74f.; Paul H.D. Kaplan, 'The Earliest Images of Othello', *Shakespeare Quarterly* 39 (1988), 171-186.
Exh.: New Haven 1981 (177d)

******

226. *The Dismission of Adam and Eve from Paradise*, 1805
(John Milton, *Paradise Lost*, XII, 637-645)

Stipple engraving by Moses Haughton (1772 or 1774-1848) after Fuseli's painting, No. XXVII in the Milton Gallery ([1796-1799]; Schiff, Lost Work 45), now in the Collection of the Sarah Campbell Blaffer Foundation
Inscription: H^y. Fuseli R.A. Pinx^t. Moses Haughton Sculp^t. and Published by them as the Act directs July 20th. 1805. Royal Academy, London. | **The dismission of ADAM and EVE from Paradise.** |

[*left*]
—-then disappear'd
They looking back, all the eastern side beheld
Of Paradise, so late their happy seat,
[*right*]
Wav'd over by that flaming brand, the gate
With dreadful faces throng'd and fiery arms:
Some natural tears they dropt. Par. Lost
     Book 12. v. 637.

Dimensions: ■ 53.5 x 39.2 cm | 21^1/16" x 15^7/16" (BM T.16.14) (formerly 'MH'=Moses Haughton)

225. *Othello and Desdemona*, 1804
(*Othello*, V, ii, 38-39)
(Vol. X/10, facing p. 409=sig. [GG3])

Engraved by Richard Rhodes (1765-1838) after Fuseli's lost drawing
Imprint: Publish'd by F. & C. Rivington S^t. Paul's Church Y^d. July 14= 1804.
Inscription (top): Act. V. | | OTHELLO. | | Sc. II. | (bottom): Fusili del. | | Rhodes sc. |

Des.   ___Why I should fear, I know not, since guiltiness I know not; but yet I feel, I fear.

Dimensions: ■ 15.5 x 9.2 cm | 6^1/16" x 3^{10}/16"; ■ 15.9 x 9.6 cm | 6^5/16" x 3¾" (BL 80.f.17)
Other locations **(1805/10)**: **(1.)** (as above): Huntington 140092 (H=26.9 cm); NYPL *NCM Chalmers 1805;—**(2.)** (facing p. [285]=sig. Y): Birmingham 180.5 (H=23.8 cm); Bodleian M.adds 51.d.43/10 (H=26.0 cm); Essick;—**(3.)** (facing p. [287]=sig. Y2): Illinois 822.33 Ich Ed. 1805; Princeton Ex 3925.1805 (H=23.0 cm); —**(4.)** (facing p. [291]=sig. [Y3]): Dörrbecker (H=26.8 cm); ZBZ AX 490 (H=22.7 cm);—**(5.)** (facing p. 407=sig. GG2): Folger PR2752.1805a1

Other locations: BM 1861-5-18-161 (formerly 'MH'=Moses Haughton); Fitzwilliam K.38; V & A Dyce 3126; V & A E.1199-D-1886 Lit.: Schiff Lost Work, 45 (painting); *Letters*, 346.

Variants

I. Misspelling ('direts') in the inscription (Fitzwilliam K.38)

Inscription: H^y. Fuseli R.A. Pinx^t. Moses Haughton Sculp^t. and Published by them as the Act direts July 20th. 1805. Royal Academy, London. | The dismission of ADAM and EVE from Paradise. [Verse]
Other locations: Huntington 4900, 473 (verses cropped)

226.

No. 226A.

G. Hamilton.

THE | ENGLISH SCHOOL | A SERIES OF | THE MOST APPROVED PRODUCTIONS | IN | PAINTING AND SCULPTURE; | EXECUTED BY BRITISH ARTISTS | FROM THE DAYS OF HOGARTH TO THE PRESENT TIME; | SELECTED, ARRANGED, AND ACCOMPANIED WITH DESCRIPTIVE AND | EXPLANATORY NOTICES IN ENGLISH AND FRENCH, | BY G. HAMILTON. | ENGRAVED IN OUTLINE UPON STEEL. | — | VOL. 1. [-VOL. 4.] | — | LONDON. | CHARLES TILT, 86, FLEET STREET. | — | 1831 [-1832](10/288 illus.).

[ÉCOLE | ANGLAISE, | RECUEIL | DE TABLEAUX, STATUES ET BAS-RELIEFS | DES PLUS CÉLÈBRES ARTISTES ANGLAIS, | DEPUIS LE TEMPS D'HOGARTH JUSQU'À NOS JOURS, | GRAVÉ A L'EAU-FORTE SUR ACIER; | ACCOMPAGNÉ | DE NOTICES DESCRIPTIVES ET HISTORIQUES, | EN FRANÇAIS ET EN ANGLAIS, | PAR G. HAMILTON, | ET PUBLIÉ SOUS SA DIRECTION. | — | VOL. 1 [-TOME 4] | — | À PARIS. | CHEZ M. HAMILTON, GRANDE RUE DES BATIGNOLLES, N° 50, | PRÈS LA BARRIÈRE DE CLICHY; | ET CHEZ AUDOT, LIBRAIRE, RUE DES MAÇONS-SORBONNE,

N° 11.|—|1831].

SELECT SPECIMENS|OF|BRITISH
ARTISTS,|FROM THE DAYS|OF HOGARTH
TO THE PRESENT TIME;|OR|SERIES OF 72
ENGRAVINGS OF THEIR MOST|APPROVED
PRODUCTIONS.|EXECUTED ON STEEL IN
THE FIRST STYLE OF OUTLINE,|
SELECTED, ARRANGED, AND
ACCOMPANIED WITH DESCRIPTIVE AND
EXPLANATORY|NOTICES IN ENGLISH AND
FRENCH,|BY G. HAMILTON.| PARIS:|
BAUDRY'S EUROPEAN LIBRARY,|9, RUE
DU COQ, NEAR THE LOUVRE.|—|1837
(?/72 illus.).

[CHEFS-D'OEUVRE|DES|ARTISTES
ANGLAIS,|DEPUIS|HOGARTH JUSQU'A
NOS JOURS,|OU|SUITE DE 72 GRAVURES
DE LEURS PRODUCTIONS|LES PLUS
ESTIMÉES,|SOIGNEUSEMENT GRAVEES AU
TRAIT SUR ACIER,|CHOISIS, MIS EN
ORDRE ET ACCOMPAGNÉ DE NOTES
DESCRIPTIVES ET EXPLICATIVES|EN
ANGLAIS ET EN FRANÇAIS,|PAR G.
HAMILTON.| PARIS,|BAUDRY, LIBRAIRIE
EUROPEENNE,|9, RUE DU COQ, PRÈS LE
LOUVRE.|—|1837].

GALLERY|OF|BRITISH ARTISTS,|FROM
THE DAYS|OF HOGARTH TO THE PRESENT
TIME,|OR|SERIES OF 288 ENGRAVINGS OF
THEIR MOST|APPROVED PRODUCTIONS.|
EXECUTED ON STEEL IN THE FIRST STYLE
OF OUTLINE,|SELECTED, ARRANGED,
AND ACCOMPANIED WITH DESCRIPTIVE
AND EXPLANATORY NOTICES|IN ENGLISH
AND FRENCH,|BY G. HAMILTON.|—|IN
FOUR VOLUMES.|—|VOL. I. [-VOL.IV.]|
PARIS,|BAUDRY'S EUROPEAN LIBRARY,|9,
RUE DU COQ, NEAR THE LOUVRE.|1837,
1839 (10/288 illus.).

[GALERIE|DES|ARTISTES ANGLAIS,|
DEPUIS|HOGARTH JUSQU'A NOS JOURS,|
OU|SUITE DE 288 GRAVURES DE LEURS
PRODUCTIONS|LES PLUS ESTIMÉES,|
SOIGNEUSEMENT GRAVÉES AU TRAIT SUR
ACIER,|CHOISIE, MISE EN ORDRE ET
ACCOMPAGNÉE DE NOTES DESCRIPTIVES
ET EXPLICATIVES|EN ANGLAIS ET EN
FRANÇAIS,|PAR G. HAMILTON.|EN
QUATRE VOLUMES.|VOL. I. [-VOL. IV.]|
PARIS,|BAUDRY, LIBRAIRIE EUROPEENNE,

9, RUE DU COQ, PRÈS LE LOUVRE.|—|
1837, 1839.

For the other illustrations in this work see also
Nos. **117D-119D, 123D, 263B, 285A, 288A,
293A, 298A, 299B**

The prints were originally spread arbitrarily
throughout the different numbers in which they
appeared in *The English School* (1831-1834). In
the *Gallery of British Artists* (1837, 1839) they
were instead gathered together in alphabetical
order under the names of the individual artists.
For other publication details, see the note to Nos.
117C-119C, 123C.

226A. *The Expulsion of Adam and Eve from
Paradise*, 1832.
(J. Milton, *Paradise Lost*, XII, 637-645)
(Vol. III, f. 208)

Outline engraving on steel by Normand fils, i.e.,
Louis-Marie Normand (1789-1874)
Inscription: Fuseli.||Normand fils.|THE
DESPAIR OF EVE.|DÉSESPOIR D'EVE.
Dimensions: ■ 11.4 x 8.3 cm | 4½" x 3¼";
■ 11.6 x 8.5 cm | 4⁹/₁₆" x 3⁵/₁₆" (BL 1267.a.19)
Other locations: SB Bern Litt.LI3162 (vol. II, f.
208); BL 1422.a.25; DHW (1839); Essick; KHZ
ah.102c; YCBA N67.H35

In keeping with the title he has assigned,
Hamilton gives as the source of the illustration the
tenth Book of *Paradise Lost*, where Eve, in an
agony of despair at the consequences of her
disobedience, proposes to Adam that they should
inflict death upon themselves:

She ended here, or vehement despair
Broke off the rest; so much of Death her
  thoughts
Had entertain'd, as dy'd her cheeks with pale.
But *Adam*, with such counsel nothing sway'd,
To better hopes his more attentive mind
Laboring had rais'd; and thus to *Eve* reply'd.
      (X, 1007-1012)

While 'The Despair of Eve' is not wholly
inappropriate to designate the subject, the presence
of the angel with the flaming sword moves the
emphasis from Eve and her despair, before God's
verdict, to the reality of the Expulsion.

******

Nos. 227 - 236.

THE|ILIAD OF HOMER,|TRANSLATED|BY A. POPE.|A NEW EDITION.| = |ADORNED WITH PLATES.| = |VOLUME I. [-VOLUME VI.]|—| LONDON: PRINTED FOR F.J. DU ROVERAY,|BY T. BENSLEY, BOLT COURT; |AND SOLD BY J. AND A. ARCH, CORNHILL, AND E. LLOYD, HARLEY STREET.|1805 (10/25 illus. + portr. frontis.).

...LONDON:|PRINTED FOR F.J. DU ROVERAY,|AND SUTTABY, EVANCE, AND FOX.|1813.

THE|ILIAD OF HOMER,|TRANSLATED INTO|ENGLISH BLANK VERSE,|BY| WILLIAM COWPER, ESQ.|WITH A PREFACE BY HIS KINSMAN,|J. JOHNSON, LL.B.|AND ILLUSTRATED WITH ENGRAVINGS,|FROM THE|PAINTINGS AND DESIGNS|OF FUSELI, HOWARD, SMIRKE,|STOTHARD, WESTALL, |&C. &C.|MEMBERS OF THE|ROYAL ACADEMY.|—|Τάδε δ᾽ ἀεὶ παρεσθ᾽ ὅμοια, διὰ δὲ τῶν αὐτῶν ἀεὶ.—EPICHARMUS.|—| VOL. I. [-VOL. II.]| = | LONDON.| PUBLISHED BY J. JOHNSON AND Cᵒ. ST. PAUL'S CHURCH YARD,|AND SHARPE AND HAILES, PICCADILLY.|PRINTED BY S. HAMILTON, WEYBRIDGE.| = |1810.

[Paper labels]: COWPER'S|HOMER.|4 VOLS.| LARGE PAPER, EARLY PROOFS.|£7.4S. BOARDS.|—|50 PLATES, FROM DESIGNS| BY|[*col. 1*]: *Fuseli, Howard, Smirke,*||[*col. 2*]: *Stothard, Westall, &c. &.*

[Plates only]: ILLUSTRATIONS|OF THE| ILIAD AND ODYSSEY OF HOMER;|FIFTY ENGRAVINGS,|FROM THE DESIGNS OF| FUSELI, HOWARD, SMIRKE, STOTHARD, WESTALL, &C.&C.|ROYAL ACADEMICIANS|ADAPTED TO THE TRANSLATIONS|OF THE LATE|WILLIAM COWPER, ESQ. ALEXANDER POPE, ESQ.| OR THE|VARIOUS EDITIONS OF THE ORIGINAL GREEK.| = |PRICE £3.3s.0d.|OR WITH COWPER'S TRANSLATION, 4 VOLS £4.16s.0d. IN BOARDS.| = |PUBLISHED BY J. JOHNSON AND CO. ST. PAUL'S CHURCH-YARD; AND|SHARPE AND HAILES, OPPOSITE ALBANY, PICCADILLY.|

A few Copies, *early Proofs*, on large Paper, with Cowper's Translation,|4 vols. royal 8vo. Price £7.4s. in Boards.|*Also, of Sharpe and Hailes may be had*, Westall's Illustrations of Mr. Scott's MARMION, and LAY OF THE|LAST MINSTREL, Price £1.4s. in Portfolio.

[Plates only]: A|SERIES OF ENGRAVINGS| ILLUSTRATIVE OF|POPE'S TRANSLATION| OF HOMER'S|ILIAD AND ODYSSEY,| ENGRAVED BY THE MOST EMINENT ARTISTS,|AFTER DESIGNS|BY STOTHARD, FUSELI, WESTALL, SMIRKE, &C.&C.| FORTY PLATES.| LONDON: PRINTED BY W. LEWIS, FINCH-LANE, CORNHILL.|[1819-1836] (10/39 illus. + 2 portrs.).

For the re-engravings of 1815 and 1818 see No. **227A** below.

Bentley estimates that perhaps 1000 ordinary sets and 250 on large paper were printed at a total cost of £2,723.3s.4d. (Du Roveray II, 79). The six-volume large-paper sets were priced at £9.9s. Du Roveray did not, however, intend to sell the *Iliad* or the *Odyssey* separately: they were to be sold as a unit with Pope's *Poetical Works*, forming 18-volume sets in either Imperial Octavo (£37.16s.0d.), Royal Octavo (£18.18s.0d.), or Crown Octavo (£9.9s.0d.) (Du Roveray to James Norton, 13 August 1807; collection DHW) (Du Roveray II, 83, note 22). Unfortunately most of these sets were destroyed in a fire at Bensley's warehouse on 5 November 1807, although the prints intended to be bound up with them survived (Du Roveray II, 80). Du Roveray sold some of the prints from this involuntary 'overstock' to Joseph Johnson who used them in his reissued edition of William Cowper's translation of Homer (1810), affixing a label to some copies, like that at Princeton (Ex 3693.7.347.1810), which reads as follows:

The Engravings which decorate this Copy of COWPER'S HOMER, were originally designed for a Splendid Edition of POPE'S TRANSLATION, lately published. But a limited number of PROOF IMPRESSIONS being taken from the Plates, in the state they came from the hands of the Engravers, *and even prior to the names of the Artists being affixed to their performances*, or if affixed, to their Autograph being changed by the writing Engraver; it has been thought proper to appropriate them to the Illustration of a select number of LARGE PAPER copies of COWPER'S VERSION, to which, as the quotations have not been added,

they are equally as applicable as to the
Translation of Pope.　　March 25. 1810.

Du Roveray's 'new and splendid edition …
highly ornamented with engravings' was
announced as 'nearly ready for publication' in the
February 1806 issue of the *Literary Magazine* (p.
118), but no firm publication date has been found:
the late date on plates Nos. **230, 232, and 235**—
'1st. October 1806' in contrast to '1st. October
1805' on the other seven—seems to indicate
considerable delays in finishing the engravings.

The 1813 edition is made up of 'portions of the
Letterpress' which Du Roveray sold Suttaby,
combined with a new title page and newly-printed
text (Du Roveray II, 81). Indeed, complete sets of
both the *Iliad* and the *Odyssey* with the 1813 title
page, as opposed to mixed sets where some
volumes have the title page of the 1805 edition,
are somewhat uncommon.

A portfolio of a complete set of the prints,
made up of such surplus copies, was issued by J.
Johnson and Co. in 1810 (£3.3s.0d.), who also
offered sets of '*early Proofs*, on large Paper', i.e.
royal octavo, priced at £7.4s. in boards. A single
complete copy of another, considerably later,
'illustrative' collection in bound form, containing
forty large-paper 'Proofs' with added inscriptions,
published by the printer William Lewis (for whom
see Todd's *Directory of Printers*, 1972, 119), has
been located (Yale Center for British Art,
PA4033.S4); there are also separate prints in
Lucerne and London. (For an analogous
compilation of print remainders, 'forming an
elegant Library Accompaniment to the Various
Editions' of Shakespeare and Milton, see Nos.
132-134, 182-183).

Not content with the commission Du Roveray
appears to have given him earlier in the autumn to
make six designs for the *Iliad* and six for the
Odyssey, on 27th December 1802 Fuseli requested
twelve designs for the *Iliad* alone. There must
have been considerable discussion before Du
Roveray finally agreed to allow him ten. Six
months later Fuseli would charge that he had been
unjustly deprived of his promised designs for the
Odyssey (Du Roveray III, 142-144, 146). In the
event Du Roveray, with considerable forbearance,
assigned him seven more, bringing the Homer
illustrations that Fuseli designed for him to
seventeen, more than half of the total of thirty.

THE

ILIAD OF HOMER,

TRANSLATED INTO

ENGLISH BLANK VERSE,

BY

WILLIAM COWPER, ESQ.

WITH A PREFACE BY HIS KINSMAN,

J. JOHNSON, L.L.B.

AND ILLUSTRATED WITH ENGRAVINGS,

FROM THE

PAINTINGS AND DESIGNS

OF

FUSELI, HOWARD, SMIRKE,

STOTHARD, WESTALL,

&c. &c.

MEMBERS OF THE

ROYAL ACADEMY.

Τάδε δ᾽ ἀεὶ παρεσθ᾽ ὅμοια, διὰ δὲ τῶν αὑτῶν ἀεὶ ... EPICHARMUS.

VOL. 1.

LONDON.

Published by J. JOHNSON and CO S.t Paul's Church Yard,
and SHARPE and HAILES. Piccadilly.
Printed by S. Hamilton, Weybridge.

1810.

Fig. 10. Title page of William Cowper's translation
of the *Iliad*, reissued, 1810, by J. Johnson & Co.
with Du Roveray's illustrations.

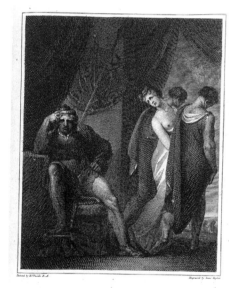

She, in soft sorrows, and in pensive thought,
Past silent, as the heralds held her hand,
And oft look'd back, slow moving o'er the strand.

Book I.

227.

227. *Briseis Led Away by the Heralds*, 1806
(Book I, 345-350)
(Vol. I, facing p. [131])

Engraved by Isaac Taylor, Jr. (1759-1829) after
Fuseli's lost painting
Imprint: Published 1ˢᵗ. October 1806, by F.J. Du
Roveray, London.
Inscription: Painted by Hʸ. Fuseli R.A. | |
Engraved by Isaac Taylor. |

> She, in soft sorrows, and in pensive thought,
> Past silent, as the heralds held her hand,
> And oft look'd back, slow moving o'er the
>   strand.   Book I.

Dimensions: ■ 12.0 x 8.9 cm | 4¾ " x 3½";
■ 12.4 x 9.2 cm | 4¹⁴/16" x 3⁹/16"
(NYPL 8-NRLP Pope 1805)
Other locations (**1813/I**): (**1.**) (as above): BL
11315.1.3 ; Yale Gfh91.Eg715Go;—(**2.**) (facing p.
[129]): Bodleian Monroe.e.67;—(**3.**) (facing p.
150): Huntington 321465
Plate only: DHW; V & A E.1205-U-1886
(imprint cropped)
Lit.: Schiff 1241 (11.9 x 8.9 cm); Schiff-Viotto
1977, no. 197; *Letters*, 272, 345; Du Roveray III,
142; IV, 174
Exh.: Kansas City 1982 (73).

Variants:

I. Unfinished proof (etched state before frame)
(**1805/I**) (between pp. 130-[131]): Huntington
143633 (H=26.5 cm)
II. Unfinished proof (etched state after frame)
(**1810/I**) (between pp. 22-23): Princeton Ex
3693.7.347.1810 (H=25.0 cm)
III. Proof (India paper) before all letters (before
imprint) (**1805/I**): Huntington 143633 (H=26.5
cm)
Inscription (scratched signatures): Painted by H.
Fuseli. | | Engraved by Isaac Taylor.
IV. Proof before all letters (before imprint)
(**1810/I**) (between pp. 22-23): Princeton Ex
3693.7.347.1810 (H=25.0cm)
Other locations (facing p. 22): Princeton Ex
3693.7.347.3.1810/I (H=24.8)
V. Proof before all letters (lacking verse)
(**1805/I**) (between pp. 130-[131]): Huntington
143633
Other locations (**1805/I**): (**1.**) DHW (H=23.4
cm);—(**2.**) (facing p. 150): Newberry
Y642.H918 (H=24 cm); (**1810/I**) (facing p. 2):

Dörrbecker; Huntington 321473; NYPL 8-
NRLP Cowper) 1810
Plate only: BM 1853-12-10-546; Huntington
78219 (1810 portf.)
VI. Reissued (1819-1836) with additional
inscription, but lacking imprint (H=26.1 cm):
YCBA PA4033.S4 (f.3)
Inscription (top of sheet): The anger of Achilles
on resigning Briseis|to the Heralds sent by
Agamemnon.|(bottom): Painted by Hʸ. Fuseli
R.A. | | Engraved by Isaac Taylor. |

> She in soft sorrows, and in pensive thought,
> Past silent, as the heralds held her hand,
> And oft look'd back, slow moving o'er the
>   strand.   Iliad. Book I.

The new inscription is not quite square with the
image and frame.

Briseis, the beautiful daughter of Chryses the
priest of Apollo, has been given among his share
of the other spoils to Achilles. But when
Agamemnon refuses to release her or accept the
ransom her father offers, Apollo sends down a
plague upon the Greeks. To placate the god,
Agamemnon, over the protests of Achilles, sends
her back to Chryses. She goes unwillingly, while
Achilles weeps to lose her.

Briseis was undoubtedly one of the two pictures
sent to Taylor at the beginning of July 1803; the
plate was probably begun shortly thereafter. Fuseli
wrote to Du Roveray on 22 November 1803
(collection DHW), objecting to the early proofs
submitted to him by the engraver:

> It is impossible for [*Mr. Fuseli*] to add in the
> present State of the plate any thing to the
> remarks Made on it by Mr. D[*u*] R[*overa*]y
> except with regard to the raised Leg of Achilles
> where, by the Line, the Lower Calf appears to
> go *behind* the upper. The double chin of
> Achilles will probably disappear, at present he
> Seems more fit to hold a Living than a Spear.
> The Mouth of the Briseis *must* be false; at
> present her hair appears rugged: but the greatest
> danger Seems to Lie in the Lower part of
> Achilles, which is undoubtedly too puny for the
> upper, he Seems too Little and the Legates and
> Briseis too big. Mr. F. Can only recommend to
> Mr. T[*aylo*]r a Careful examination of the Lines
> of the Picture; if the Eye fail, there is Little to
> be hoped from the Ear in a thing of this Kind.

Monarch, awake! 'tis Jove's command I bear
Book II.

Published 1st. October 1805, by F.J. Du Roveray London.

228.

228. *Nestor Appearing in a Dream to Agamemnon*, 1805
(Book II, 26-34)
(Vol. I, facing p [179])

Engraved by James Heath (1757-1834) after Fuseli's lost painting
Imprint: Published 1st. October 1805, by F.J. Du Roveray, London.
Inscription: Painted by Hy. Fuseli R.A. | |
Engraved by Jas. Heath, A. |

　　Monarch, awake! 'tis Jove's command I bear.
　　　　　　　Book II.
Dimensions: ■ 11.9 x 8.8 cm | 4¹¹/16" x 3⁶/16";
■ 12.3 x 9.1 cm | 4¹³/16" x 3⁹/16"
(NYPL 8-NRLP Pope 1805)
Other locations (**1813/I**): (**1.**) (as above): BL 11315.l.3; Yale Gfh91.Eg715Go;—(**2.**) (facing p. [177]): Bodleian Monroe.e.67;—(**3.**) (facing p. 180): Huntington 321465
Plate only: V & A E.1205-P-1886
Lit.: Schiff 1242 (11.7 x 8.7); Schiff-Viotto 1977, no. 198; Du Roveray III, 104

　　　　　Variants:
I. Unfinished proof (etched state before frame)

(**1805/I**) (between pp. 178-[179]): Huntington 143633 (H=26.5 cm)
Other locations (**1810/I**) (between pp. 38-39): Princeton Ex 3693.7.347.1810 (H=25.0 cm)
Inscription (lettered in pencil): H. Fuseli del. | | J. Heath sc.
Plate only: V & A E.613.87
II. Proof before letters and before frame: BM 1853-12-10-559
III. Proof before letters (India paper) (with frame) (**1805/I**) (facing p. [179]): Huntington 143633 (S=26.5 cm)
IV. Proof before letters (**1810/I**)(between pp. 38-39): Princeton Ex 3693.7.347.1810 (H=25.0 cm)
V. Proof before all letters (signatures only) (**1810/I**) (facing p. 38): Princeton Ex 3693.7.347.3.1810/I (H=24.8 cm)
Inscription (scratched letters): H. Fuseli del. | | J. Heath sc.
VI. Proof before all letters (lacking verse) (**1805/I**) (between pp. [178-179]): Huntington 143633 (H=26.5 cm)
Other locations (**1805/I**) (facing p. [179]): DHW (H=23.4 cm); (facing p. 180): Newberry Y642.H918 (H=24 cm); (**1810/I**) (facing p. 38): Dörrbecker; Huntington 321473; NYPL 8-NRLP (Cowper) 1810
Plate only: Huntington 78219 (1810 portf.)
Lit.: Heath 1992, no. 1805(2).1
VII. Reissued (1819-1836) with additional inscription, but lacking imprint (H=26.1 cm): YCBA PA4033.S4 (f. 4)
Inscription (top of sheet): Agamemnon deluded by the Vision appearing under | the form of Nestor. | (bottom): Painted by Hy. Fuseli R.A. | | Engraved by Jas. Heath A. |

　　Monarch, awake! 'tis Jove's command I bear.
　　　　　　　Iliad Book II.
Dimensions (to platemark): 26.4 x 17.7 cm | 10⁷/16" x 7"
Plate only: V & A 612.87

Zeus, in order to fulfil his promise to Thetis that he will help the Trojans, sends Agamemnon a delusory dream. To make it more convincing, Zeus's dream-herald appears in the likeness of Nestor, whom Agamemnon particularly admired. The ruse succeeds in inspiring the king with false hopes that the Greeks will defeat the Trojans in an all-out battle the next day.

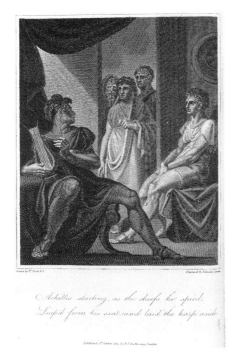

229.

229. *Achilles in his Tent with Patroclus is Visited by a Delegation from the Greek Leaders*, 1805
(Book IX, 182-196)
(Vol. III, facing p. [85])

Engraved by Edward Smith (fl. 1805-1851) after Fuseli's lost painting exhibited (1812/?) at the Liverpool Academy.
Imprint: Published 1st. October 1805, by F.J. Du Roveray, London.
Inscription: Drawn by H^y. Fuseli RA.||Engraved by Edward Smith.|

   Achilles starting, as the chiefs he spied,
   Leap'd from his seat, and laid the harp aside.

Dimensions: ■ 11.9 x 9.2 cm | 4^{11}/16" x 3^{10}/16";
▣ 12.2 x 9.5 cm | 4^{13}/16" x 3¾" (NYPL 8-NRLP Pope 1805)
Other locations (**1805/III**): (**1.**) (facing p. [135]): Yale Gfh91eg715gj; (**1813/III**): (**2.**) (facing p. [85]): BL 11315.l.3; Bodleian Monro.e.69; Yale Gfh91.Eg715Go;—(**3.**) (facing p. 95): Huntington 321465
Plate only: V & A E.1205-N-1886
Lit.: Schiff 1243 (11.9 x 9.1); Schiff-Viotto 1977, no. 199

Variants:
I. Unfinished proof (etched state) (framed)

(**1805/III**) (between pp. [84-85]): Huntington 143633 (H=26.5 cm)
Other locations (**1810/III**) (between pp. 270-271): Princeton Ex 3693.7.347.1810 (H=25.0 cm)
Inscription (lettered in pencil): H. Fuseli del.|| E. Smith sc.
II. Proof before letters (India paper) (**1805/III**): Huntington 143633 (H=26.5 cm)
III. Proof before letters (**1810/I**) (between pp. 270-271): Princeton Ex 3693.7.347.1810 (H=25.0 cm)
Other locations (facing p. 210): Princeton Ex 3693.7.347.3.1810/I (H=24.8 cm)
IV. Proof before all letters (lacking verse) (**1805/III**) (between pp. [84-85]): Huntington 143633 (H=26.5 cm)
Other locations (**1805/III**) (facing p. 95): Newberry Y642.H918 (H=24.0 cm); (facing p. [85]): DHW (H=23.4 cm); (**1810/I**) (facing p. 270): Dörrbecker; Huntington 321473; NYPL 8-NRLP (Cowper) 1810
Plate only: BM 1853-12-10-550; Huntington 78219 (1810 portf.); V & A E.1205-x-1886
V. Reissued (1819-1836) with additional inscription, but lacking imprint: YCBA PA4033.S4 (H=26.1 cm) (f. 9)
Inscription (top of sheet): Achilles and the Grecian Delegates.|(bottom): Drawn by H^y. Fuseli R.A.||Engraved by Edward Smith.|

   Achilles starting as the chiefs he spied,
   Leap'd from his seat, and laid the harp aside.

Dimensions: ■ 11.7 x 9.0 cm | 4^{10}/16" x 3^5/16";
▣ 12.1 x 9.3 cm | 4¾" x 3^{11}/16"

When Hector routs the demoralised Greeks and drives them back to their ships, Nestor suggests that a delegation be sent to lure sulking Achilles back to the battlefield. The envoys led by Odysseus find Achilles in his tent 'delighting his soul with a clear-toned lyre'. Despite the return of Briseis and other gifts offered him in recompense, Achilles cannot forgive the public insult and adamantly refuses to rejoin the battle.

Edward Smith is probably the 'Liverpool' engraver employed by William Roscoe and often mentioned in his letters during the 1820s.

Though the plate he had sent to Du Roveray on 26 April 1804 was still in an 'unfinish'd state', Smith hoped 'in a few days' to deliver 'a Proof sufficiently advanc'd' for Du Roveray's and Fuseli's observations.

While unresolv'd the son of Tydeus stands.
Pallas appears, and thus her chief commands.

Book X

Published 1st October 1806, by F.J. Du Roveray, London.

230.

230. *Pallas Appears to Diomedes in the Tent of Rhesus*, 1806
(Book X, 503-511)
(Vol. III, facing p. [135])

Engraved by Isaac Taylor Jr. (1759-1829) after Fuseli's lost painting
Imprint: Published 1st. October 1806, by F.J. Du Roveray, London.
Inscription: Painted by Hy. Fuseli R.A. | |
Engraved by Isaac Taylor. |

> While unresolv'd the son of Tydeus stands,
> Pallas appears, and thus her chief commands.
> Book X.

Dimensions: ■ 11.9 x 8.8 cm | 4^{11}/16" x 3^7/16";
■ 12.3 x 9.2 cm | 4^{14}/16" x 3^{11}/16" (NYPL 8-NRLP Pope 1805)
Other locations (1813/III): (1.) (as above): BL 11315.l.3; Bodleian Monro.e.69; Yale Gfh91.Eg715Go (1813) (imprint cropped);—(2.) (facing p. 159): Huntington 321465
Plate only: V & A E.1205-L-1886
Lit.: Schiff 1244 (11.9 x 8.8 cm); Schiff-Viotto 1977, no. 200, pl. 200^1; *Letters*, 272, 280, 313
Exh.: Kansas City 1982 (74)

Variants:
I. Unfinished proof (etched state before frame)

(1805/III) (between pp. [134-135]): Huntington 143633 (H=26.5 cm)
Other locations (1810/I): Princeton Ex 3693.7.347.1810 (H=25.0 cm) (between pp. 326-327)
II. Proof before all letters (India paper) (signatures only) (framed) (1805/III) (facing p. [135]): Huntington 143633 (H=26.5 cm)
Inscription (scratched letters): Painted by H. Fuseli | |Engraved by Isaac Taylor.
III. Proof before all letters (signatures only) (1810/I) (between pp. 326-327): Princeton Ex 3693.7.347.1810 (H=25.0 cm)
Other locations (facing p. 326): Princeton Ex 3693.7.347. 3.1810/I (H=24.8 cm)
IV. Proof before all letters (lacks verse) (1805/III) (facing p. 159): Newberry Y642.H918 (H=24.0 cm)
Other locations (1805/III) (facing p. [135]): DHW (H=23.4 cm); (1810/I) (as above): Dörrbecker; Huntington 321473; NYPL 8-NRLP (Cowper) 1810 (facing p. 326)
Plate only: BM 1853.12.10.553; Huntington 78219 (1810 portf.); NYPL MEM R153rm (facing p. 108)
V. Reissued (1819-1836) with additional inscription, but lacking imprint: YCBA PA 4033.S4 (H= 26.1 cm) (f. 10)
Inscription (top of sheet): Diomedes, having slain Rhesus, counselled by Minerva | to return to the grecian army. | (bottom): Painted by Hy. Fuseli R.A. | |Engraved by Isaac Taylor. |

> While unresolv'd the son of Tydeus stands,
> Pallas appears and thus her chief commands.
> Iliad Book X.

Ulysses and Diomedes have penetrated the camp of the Thracians under the cover of darkness and slain King Rhesus and twelve of his warriors in order to steal his famed white horses. While Ulysses waits, Diomedes tarries undecided whether to carry off the chariot or to kill more Thracians, until the goddess Athene appears to him and commands him to leave forthwith.

Fuseli's original was apparently one of the two pictures received by Taylor on 4 July 1803. On 5th November 1803, Taylor sent Du Roveray an 'Etching proof', although as he notes, 'So much of it being Drapery and fit only for the graver there is little to See'. Since James Gravel took final proofs in mid-April 1805, it is not clear why publication was delayed until '1st. October 1806'.

Hear this, remember, and our fury dread.
Book XV.

231.

231. *Zeus Awakens on Mount Ida After Being Distracted from the Battle by Hera*, 1805
(Book XV, 4 ff.)
(Vol. IV, facing p. [141])

Engraved by James Stow (1770?-*post* 1820) after Fuseli's lost painting, exhibited (1812/13) at the Liverpool Academy.
Imprint: Published Octr. 1st. 1805, by F.J. Du Roveray, London.
Inscription: Painted by H^y. Fuseli R.A.||
Engraved by Ja^s. Stow.|

Hear this, remember, and our fury dread.
Book XV.

Dimensions: ■ 11.9 x 9.1 cm | 4^{11}/16" x 3^{10}/16";
■ 12.4 x 9.5 cm | 4^{14}/16" x 3¾ " (NYPL 8-NRLP Pope 1805)
Other locations (1813/IV): (1.) (as above): BL 11315.l.3; Bodleian Monro.e.70; Yale Gfh91.Eg715Go;—(2.) (facing p. 142): Huntington 321465
Plate only: V & A E.1205-K-1886; V & A E.1215-L-1886 (cut to frame, imprint and verse lacking)
Lit.: Schiff 1245 (11.9 x 9.1 cm); Schiff-Viotto 1977, no. 201, pl. 201[1]

Exh.: Kansas City 1982 (75)
Variants:
I. Unfinished proof (etched state before frame) (**1805/IV**) (between pp. [140-141]): Huntington 143633 (H=26.5 cm)
Other locations (**1810/II**) (facing p. 80): Princeton Ex 3693.7.347.1810 (H=25.0 cm)
II. Proof before letters (India paper) (**1805/IV**) (facing p. [141]): Huntington 143633 (H=26.5 cm)
III. Proof before letters (**1810/II**) (between pp. 80-81): Princeton Ex 3693.7.347.1810 (H=25.0 cm)
Other locations (facing p. 80): Princeton Ex 3693.7.347.3.1810 (H=24.8 cm)
IV. Proof before all letters (lacking verse) (**1805/IV**) (facing p. 142): Newberry Y642.H918 (H=24.0 cm)
Other locations (**1805/IV**) (facing p. [141]): DHW (H=23.4 cm); Huntington 143633 (H=26.5 cm) (between pp. [140-141]);
(**1810/II**) (facing p. 80): Dörrbecker; Huntington 321473; NYPL 8-NRLP (Cowper) 1810
Plate only: BM 1853.12.10.556; Huntington 78219 (1810 portf.); V & A E.1205-Z-1886
V. Reissued (1819-1836) with additional inscription but lacking imprint: YCBA PA4033.S4 (H=26.1 cm) (f. 14)
Inscription (top of sheet): The Anger of Jupiter on finding himself deceived by Juno.|(bottom): Painted by H^y. Fuseli R.A.||Engraved by Ja^s. Stow.|

Hear this, remember, and our fury dread.
Iliad. Book XV.

With Zeus swaying the balance on their behalf, the Trojans seize the advantage and drive the Greeks back to their ships. But Hera distracts Zeus with her charms and turns the tide of battle in favour of the Greeks. Upon awakening, Zeus sees the Trojans in headlong flight. He immediately recognises how he has been tricked and warns Hera, who trembles at his fury, that she will pay for her treachery.

Fuseli would have known Pope's footnote to this passage: 'Adam, in *Paradise Lost* [IX, 1059 ff.], awakes from the Embrace of Eve, in much the same Humour with Jupiter in this Place.' Significantly, he was never inclined to pick up on the hint.

They to his friends the mournful charge shall bear

Book XVI.

232.

Fig. 11. Etched version of No. **232.** Variant I.

232. *Sleep and Death Bear the Body of Sarpedon Away to Lycia,* 1806
(Book XVI, 679-683)
(Vol. V, facing p. [7])

Engraved by James Stow (1770?-*post* 1820) after Fuseli's painting exhibited at the Royal Academy (1811/27) and now in the Haus zum Rechberg, Zurich (1803; Schiff 1190).
Imprint: Published October 1st. 1806, by F.J. Du Roveray, London.
Inscription: Painted by Hy. Fuseli R.A. | |
Engraved by Jas. Stow. |

> They to his friends the mournful charge shall
> bear.   Book XVI.

Dimensions: ■ 12.0 x 9.0 cm | 4¾ " x 3⁹/16";
▣ 12.5 x 9.5 cm | 4¹⁵/16" x 3¾ " (NYPL 8-NRLP Pope 1805)
Other locations (**1813/V**): (**1.**) (facing t.p.): BL 11315.l.3; Bodleian Monro.e.71; Yale Gfh91.Eg715Go;—(**2.**) (facing p. 41): Huntington 321456
Plate only: BM 1863-5-9-21 (cropped to frame)
Lit.: Schiff 1246 (12.3 x 9.0 cm); Schiff-Viotto 1977, no. 202, pl. 202¹
Exh.: Kansas City 1982 (76).

Variants:
I. Unfinished proof (etched state before frame) (**1805/V**) (between pp. [6-7]): Huntington 143633 (H=26.5 cm)
Other locations (**1810/II**) (facing p. 158): Princeton Ex 3693.7.347.1810 (H=25.0 cm) (lettered in pencil: H. Fuseli del. | | Stow sc.)
II. Proof before letters (India paper) (**1805/V**) (facing p. [7]): Huntington 143633 (H=26.5 cm)
Other locations (**1810/II**): Princeton Ex 3693.7.347.1810 (H=25.0 cm) (between pp. 158-159); Princeton Ex 3693.7.347.3.1810 (H=24.8 cm) (facing p. 158)
III. Proof before all letters (lacking verse) (**1805/V**) (between pp. [6-7]): Huntington 143633) (H=26.5 cm)
Other locations (**1805/V**) (facing p. [7]): DHW (H=23.4 cm); (facing p. 41): Newberry Y642.H918 (H=24.0 cm); (**1810/II**) (facing p. 158): Dörrbecker; Huntington 321473; NYPL 8-NRLP (Cowper) 1810
Plate only: Huntington 78219 (1810 portf.)
IV. Reissued (1819-1836) with additional inscription, but lacking imprint: YCBA PA4033.S4 (H=26.1 cm) (f. 15)
Inscription (top of sheet): Sleep & Death

conveying the dead body of Sarpedon│from the field of battle to Lycia.│(bottom): Painted by H^y. Fuseli R.A.│ │Engraved by Ja^s. Stow.│

They to his friends the mournful charge shall bear.   Iliad. Book XVI.

Zeus sends Apollo to carry off the body of his son, Sarpedon, from the battlefield. The illustration, with its obvious similarities to the Deposition, shows Apollo hovering at Sarpedon's head as he is conveyed to Lycia, borne up by Sleep (head averted and lower body enveloped in a dark cloud) and Death (invisible but for his dangling legs and the suggested triangle formed by his supporting arms beneath the shroud).

233.

233. *Thetis Entreats Hephaestus, who is Supported on Two Artificial Golden Handmaids, to Provide Achilles with Armour*, 1805
(Book XVIII, 410-420)
(Vol. V, facing p. [113])

Engraved by Edward Smith (fl. 1805-1851) after Fuseli's painting exhibited (1812/185) in the Liverpool Academy and now in the Kunsthaus, Zurich (1803; Schiff 1191)
Imprint: Published 1st. October 1805, by F.J. Du Roveray, London.

Inscription: Painted by H^y. Fuseli R.A.│ │Engraved by Edwd. Smith.│

On these supported, with unequal gait, He reach'd the throne where pensive Thetis sat.   Book XVIII.

Dimensions: ■ 11.8 x 8.6 cm │ 4^10/16" x 3^7/16"; ▣ 12.1 x 9.0 cm │ 4^13/16" x 3^5/16" (NYPL 8-NRLP Pope 1805)
Other locations (**1813/V**): (**1.**) (as above): BL 11315.l.3; Bodleian Monro.e.71(imprint cropped); Yale Gfh91.Eg715Go;—(**2.**) (facing p. 133): Huntington 321465
Plate only: V & A E.1205-M-1886
Lit.: Schiff 1247 (11.6 x 8.5 cm); Schiff-Viotto 1977, no. 203, pl. 203^1

Variants:
I. Unfinished proof (etched state) (framed) (**1805/V**) (between pp. [112-113]): Huntington 143633 (H=26.5 cm)
Other locations (**1810/II**) (facing p. 236): Princeton Ex 3693.7.347.1810 (H=25.0 cm)
II. Proof before letters (India paper) (**1805/V**): Huntington 143633 (H=26.5 cm)
III. Proof before letters (**1810/II**) (between pp. 236-237): Princeton Ex 3693.7.347.1810 (H=25.0 cm)
Other locations (facing p. 236): Princeton Ex 3693.7.347.3. 1810/II (H=24.8 cm)
Plate only: BM 1849-5-12-230
IV. Proof before all letters (lacking verse) (**1805/V**) (between pp. [112-113]): Huntington 143633 (H=26.5 cm)
Other locations (**1805/V**) (facing p. 113): DHW (H=23.4);(facing p. 133):Newberry Y642.H918 (H=24.0 cm); (**1810/II**)(facing p. 236): Dörrbecker; Huntington 321473; NYPL 8-NRLP (Cowper) 1810
Plate only: Huntington 78219 (1810 portf.) (12.1 x 9.0 cm)
V. Reissued (1819-1836) with additional inscription, but lacking imprint: YCBA PA4033.S4 (H=26.1 cm) (f. 17)
Inscription (top of sheet): Thetis entreating Vulcan to supply Achilles│with armour.│ (bottom): Painted by H^y. Fuseli R.A.│ │Engraved by Edwd. Smith.│

On these supported with unequal gait, He reach'd the throne where pensive Thetis sat.   Iliad. Book XVIII.

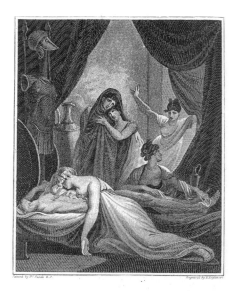

Prone on the body fell the heav'nly fair,
At her sad breast, and tore her golden hair.

Book XIX.

234.

234. *Briseis Throws Herself Upon the Body of Patroclus*, 1805
(Book XIX, 282 ff.)
(Vol. V, facing p. [153])

Engraved by Francis Engleheart (1775-1849) after Fuseli's lost painting exhibited (1812/187) at the Liverpool Academy.
Imprint: Published 1st. October 1805, by F.J. Du Roveray, London.
Inscription: Painted by Hy. Fuseli R.A.||
Engraved by F. Engleheart.|
  Prone on the body fell the heav'nly fair,
  Beat her sad breast, and tore her golden hair.
                                        Book XIX.
Dimensions: ■ 11.8 x 9.1 cm |4^{10}/16" x 3^9/16";
■ 12.0 x 9.4 cm | 4¾" x 3^{11}/16" (NYPL 8-NRLP Pope 1805)
Other locations (**1813/V**): (**1.**) (as above): 11315.l.3; Bodleian Monro.e.72; Yale Gfh91.Eg715Go;—(**2.**) (facing p. 165): Huntington 3214653
Plate only: V & A E.1205-J-1886
Lit.: Schiff 1248 (11.7 x 8.5); Schiff-Viotto 1977, no. 204, pl. 204[1]

Variants:
  I. Unfinished proof (etched state) (framed)

(**1805/V**) (between pp. [152-153]): Huntington 143633 (H=26.5 cm)
Other locations (**1810/II**) (facing p. 264): Princeton Ex 3693.7.347.1810 (H=25.0 cm)
II. Proof before letters (India paper) (**1805/V**): Huntington 143633 (H=26.5 cm)
Plate only: BM 1853.12.10.558
III. Proof before letters (**1810/II**) (between pp. 264-265): Princeton Ex 3693.7.347.1810 (H=25.0 cm)
Other locations (facing p. 264): Princeton Ex 3693.7.347.3. 1810/II (H=24.8 cm)
Plate only: BM 1853.12.10.588
IV. Proof before all letters (lacking verse) (**1805/V**) (between pp. [152-153]): Huntington 143633 (H=26.5 cm)
Other locations (**1805/V**) (facing p. [153]): DHW (H=23.4 cm); (facing p. 165): Newberry Y642.H918 (H=24.0 cm); (**1810/II**) (facing p. 264): Dörrbecker; Huntington 321473; NYPL 8-NRLP (Cowper) 1810
Plate only: Huntington 78219 (1810 portf.)
V. Reissued (1819-1836) with additional inscription, but lacking imprint: YCBA PA4033.S4 (H=26.1 cm) (f. 18)
Inscription (top of sheet): Briseis lamenting the death of Patroclus.|(bottom): Painted by Hy. Fuseli R.A.||Engraved by F. Engleheart.|
  Prone on the body fell the heav'nly fair,
  Beat her sad breast, and tore her golden hair.
                              Iliad. Book XIX.
Other locations (plate only): Browne

235. *Achilles Grasping at the Shade of Patroclus*, 1806
(Book XXIII, 99 ff.)
(Vol. VI, facing p. [89])

Engraved by James Heath (1757-1834) after Fuseli's painting exhibited (1812/12) at the Liverpool Academy and now in the Kunsthaus, Zurich (1803; Schiff 1192)
Imprint: Publish'd 1st. October 1806, by F.J. Du Roveray, London.
Inscription: Painted by Hy. Fuseli R.A.||
Engraved by Jas. Heath A.|
  He said, and with his longing arms essay'd
  In vain to grasp the visionary shade.
                                        Book XXIII.
Dimensions: ■ 12.2 x 8.8 cm| 4¾" x 3½";
■ 12.5 x 9.2 cm | 4^{15}/16" x 3^{10}/16" (NYPL 8-NRLP Pope 1805)

235.

He said, and with his longing arms essay'd
In vain to grasp the visionary shade.

Book XXIII.

Fig. 12. Etched version of No. **235.** Variant I.

Other locations (**1813/VI**): (**1.**) (as above): BL
11315.l.3; Bodleian Monro.e.72; Yale
Gfh91.Eg715Go;—(**2.**) (facing p. 93): Huntington
321465
Plate only: V & A E.1205-G-1886
Lit.: Schiff 1249 (12.1 x 8.8 cm); Schiff-Viotto
1977, no. 205, pl. 205[1];Du Roveray III,142,pl.23
Exh.: Kansas City 1982 (77)

Variants:
I. Unfinished proof (etched state before frame)
(**1805/VI**) (between pp. [88-89]): Huntington
143633 (H=26.5 cm)
Other locations (**1810/II**) (facing p. 378):
Princeton Ex 3693.7.347.1810 (H=25.0 cm)
Plate only: V & A E.610-87 (lettered in pencil:
a good promethius)
II. Proof before letters (India paper) (**1805/VI**)
(facing p. [89]): Huntington 143633 (H=26.5
cm)
III. Proof before letters (**1810/II**) (between pp.
378-379): Princeton Ex 3693.7.347.1810
(H=25.0 cm)
Other locations (**1810/II**) (facing p. 370):
Princeton Ex 3693.7.347.3.1810 (H=24.8 cm)
Plate only: V & A E.658.87
IV. Proof before all letters (lacking verse)
(**1805/VI**) (between pp. [88-89]): Huntington
143633) (H=26.5 cm)
Other locations (**1805/VI**) (facing p. [89]):
DHW (H=23.4 cm); (facing p. 93): Newberry
Y642.H918 (H=24.0 cm); (**1810/II**) (facing p.
370): Dörrbecker; Huntington 321473; NYPL
8-NRLP (Cowper) 1810
Plate only: Huntington 78219 (1810 portf.);
V & A E.1205-A-1886 (?imprint cropped)
V. Reissued (1819-1836) with additional
inscription but lacking imprint: YCBA
PA4033.S4 (H=26.1 cm) (f. 22)
Inscription (top of sheet): The Shade of
Patroclus entreating Achilles to|perform the
rites of burial to his remains.|(bottom): Painted
by H[y]. Fuseli R.A.||Engraved by Ja[s]. Heath
A.|

He said, and with his longing arms essay'd
In vain to grasp the visionary shade.
                                    Iliad Book XXIII.

Dimensions (to platemark): 26.2 x 17.7 cm |
10⁶/16" x 7"
Other locations (plate only): V & A 611.87

The spirit of Patroclus appears to Achilles as he sleeps on the sea shore and begs him to bury his body immediately so that he may pass through the gates of Hades. Warning that Achilles too is fated to die beneath the walls of Troy, he asks that they be buried together. Achilles attempts to clasp the spirit ... but it eludes him.

236.

236. *Priam Begs the Body of Hector*, 1805
(Book XXIV, 477)
(Vol. VI, facing p. [147])

Engraved by Louis Schiavonetti (1765-1810) after Fuseli's lost painting
Imprint: Published 1st. October 1805, by F.J. Du Roveray, London.
Inscription: Painted by Hy. Fuseli R.A.||
Engraved by Ls. Schiavonetti.|

Sudden (a venerable sight!) appears;
Embrac'd his knees, and bath'd his hands in
 tears.   Book XXIV.
Dimensions: ■ 12.1 x 9.1 | 4¾" x 3⁹/16";
■ 12.5 x 9.4 cm | 4¹⁵/16" x 3¹¹/16" (NYPL 8-NLRP Pope 1805)
Other locations (**1813/VI**): **(1.)** (as above): BL 11315.l.3; Yale Gfh91.Eg715Go (imprint

cropped);—**(2.)** (facing p. [145]): Bodleian Monro.e.72;—**(3.)** (facing p. 171): Huntington 321465; (**1810/II**) (facing p. 442): NYPL 8-NRLP (1810)
Plate only: V & A E.1205-H-1886
Lit.: Schiff 1250 (12.0 x 9.0 cm); Schiff-Viotto 1977, no. 206, pl. 206[1]

Variants:
I. Unfinished proof (etched state before frame) (**1805/VI**) (between pp. [146-147]): Huntington 143633 (H=26.5 cm)
Other locations (**1810/II**) (facing p. 442): Princeton Ex 3693.7.347.1810 (H=25.0 cm)
II. Proof before letters (India paper) (**1805/VI**) (facing p. [147]): Huntington 143633 (H=26.5 cm)
III. Proof before letters (**1810/II**) (between pp. 442-443): Princeton Ex 3693.7.347.1810 (H=25.0 cm)
Other locations (**1810/II**) (facing p. 442): Princeton Ex 3693.7.347.3.1810 (H=24.8 cm)
IV. Proof before all letters (lacking verse) (**1805/VI**) (between pp. [146-147]): Huntington 143633) (H=26.5 cm)
Other locations (**1805/VI**) (facing p. [147]): DHW (H=23.4 cm); (facing p. 171): Newberry Y642.H918 (H=24.0 cm); (**1810/II**) (facing p. 442): Dörrbecker; Huntington 321473; NYPL 8-NRLP (Cowper) 1810
Plate only: BM 1853.12.10.554; Huntington 78219 (1810 portf.)
V. Reissued (1819-1836) with additional inscription, but lacking imprint: YCBA PA4033.S4 (H=26.1 cm) (f. 23)
Inscription (top of sheet): Priam, king of Troy, supplicating Achilles|to deliver to him the body of his son Hector.|(bottom): Painted by Hy. Fuseli R.A.||Engraved by Ls. Schiavonetti.|

Sudden (a venerable sight!) appears;
Embrac'd his knees, and bath'd his hands in
 tears.   Iliad Book XXIV.

******

No. 227A.
THE|ILIAD OF HOMER,|TRANSLATED|BY|ALEXANDER POPE.|[Vignette by Cipriani].|LONDON,|PUBLISHED BY SUTTABY, EVANCE & FOX, AND CROSBY & CO.|STATIONERS COURT.|1815.|CORRALL PRINTER. (1/1 illus.).

...LONDON.|PUBLISHED BY SUTTABY, EVANCE & FOX,|STATIONERS COURT, AND|BALDWIN, CRADOCK & JOY, PATERNOSTER ROW.|1818.|CORRALL, PRINTER. (1/1 illus.).

227A. *Briseis Led Away by the Heralds*, 1815
(Book I, 345-350)
(facing title page)

Frontispiece re-engraved (1815) in reduced form by Abraham Raimbach (1776-1843) from the plate by Isaac Taylor Jr. (1759-1829)
Imprint: Published by Suttaby, Evance & Fox, Stationer's Court, Jany. 3, 1815
Inscription: Painted by H. Fuseli, R.A.||
Engraved by A. Raimbach.|

'She, in soft sorrows, and in pensive thought,
Past silent, as the heralds held her hand,
And oft look'd back, slow moving o'er the
    strand.'   Book I.

Dimensions: ■ 7.9 x 5.6 cm | 3²/16" x 2³/16";
■ 8.3 x 5.9 cm | 3¼" x 2⁵/16"(V&A 1205-1886)
Other locations (plate and t.p. only): NYPL R153re (p. 16)

Variants:
I. Proof before letters: NYPL MEM.R153re (p. 17)
II. Reissued (1818) with changed imprint: BL 11315.a.14
Imprint: Published by Suttaby, Evance & Fox, April 4. 1818

******

Nos. 237 - 243.
THE|ODYSSEY|OF|HOMER,|TRANSLATED BY A. POPE.|A NEW EDITION.|=|
ADORNED WITH PLATES.|=|VOLUME I. [-VOLUME VI.]|—| LONDON:|PRINTED FOR F.J. DU ROVERAY,|BY T. BENSLEY, BOLT COURT;|AND SOLD BY J. AND A. ARCH, CORNHILL, AND|E. LLOYD, HARLEY STREET.|1806 [1807] (7/24 illus. + frontis.).
...LONDON:|PRINTED FOR F.J. DU ROVERAY,|AND SUTTABY, EVANCE, AND FOX.|1813.
THE|ODYSSEY OF HOMER,|TRANSLATED INTO|ENGLISH BLANK VERSE,|BY|WILLIAM COWPER, ESQ.|WITH A PREFACE

BY HIS KINSMAN,|J. JOHNSON, LL.B.|AND ILLUSTRATED WITH ENGRAVINGS,|FROM THE|PAINTINGS AND DESIGNS|OF FUSELI, HOWARD, SMIRKE,|STOTHARD, WESTALL, |&C.&C.|MEMBERS OF THE|ROYAL ACADEMY.|—|Τάδε δ'ἀεὶ παρεσϑ' ὅμοια, διὰ δὲ τῶν αὐτῶν ἀεί.—EPICHARMUS.|—| VOL. I. [-VOL. II.]| =| LONDON.| PUBLISHED BY J. JOHNSON AND C⁰. ST. PAUL'S CHURCH YARD,|AND SHARPE AND HAILES, PICCADILLY.|PRINTED BY S. HAMILTON, WEYBRIDGE.| =|1810.

[Plates only]: ILLUSTRATIONS|OF THE| ILIAD AND ODYSSEY OF HOMER;|FIFTY ENGRAVINGS,|FROM THE DESIGNS OF| FUSELI, HOWARD, SMIRKE, STOTHARD, WESTALL, &C.&C.|ROYAL ACADEMICIANS|ADAPTED TO THE TRANSLATIONS|OF THE LATE|WILLIAM COWPER, ESQ. ALEXANDER POPE, ESQ.| OR THE|VARIOUS EDITIONS OF THE ORIGINAL GREEK.| =|PRICE £3.3s.0d.|OR WITH COWPER'S TRANSLATION, 4 VOLS £4.16s.0d.IN BOARDS.| =|PUBLISHED BY J. JOHNSON AND CO. ST. PAUL'S CHURCH-YARD; AND|SHARPE AND HAILES, OPPOSITE ALBANY, PICCADILLY.|
A few Copies, *early Proofs*, on large Paper, with Cowper's Translation,|4 vols. royal 8vo. Price £7.4s. in Boards.|*Also, of Sharpe and Hailes* may be had, Westall's Illustrations of Mr. Scott's MARMION, and LAY OF THE|LAST MINSTREL, Price £1.4s. in Portfolio.

[Plates only]: A|SERIES OF ENGRAVINGS| ILLUSTRATIVE OF|POPE'S TRANSLATION| OF HOMER'S|ILIAD AND ODYSSEY,| ENGRAVED BY THE MOST EMINENT ARTISTS,|AFTER DESIGNS|BY STOTHARD, FUSELI, WESTALL, SMIRKE, &C.&C.| FORTY PLATES.| LONDON: PRINTED BY W. LEWIS, FINCH-LANE, CORNHILL.|[1819-1836] (10/39 illus. + 2 portrs.).

Publication of the work was delayed until at least late May 1807 while Du Roveray waited upon a dilatory engraver. 'I still want One plate to publish the Odyssey, which, however, is to be delivered to me [about the middle of (*del.*)] next week' (to T. Bensley, 18 May [1807]; Huntington, Du Roveray Collection).

With that, her hand the sacred veil bestows.
Book V.

237.

The master came at last approached the gate.
Charged with his wool, and with Ulysses' fate.
Book IX

238.

237. *Odysseus on the Raft Receives the Sacred Veil from the Goddess Leucothea*, 1806
(Book V, 333-353)
(Vol. II, facing p. [81])

Engraved by William Bromley (1769-1842) after Fuseli's painting, formerly owned by Robert Balmanno, and now in the Dreyfus collection, Basel ([1805]; Schiff 1193)
Imprint: Published 1st. October 1806, by F.J. Du Roveray, London.
Inscription: Painted by Hy. Fuseli R.A. | |
Engraved by Wm. Bromley. |

With that, her hand the sacred veil bestows.
Book V.

Dimensions: ■ 12.1 x 8.9 cm | 4¾" x 3⁹/16";
■ 12.5 x 9.2 cm | 4¹⁵/16" x 3¹⁰/16" (NYPL 8-NRMH Pope 1806)
Other locations (**1806/II**): (as above): Yale Gfh91.fg725gb; Yale Gfh91Fg813B
(**1813/II**):—(**1.**) (as above) BL 11315.1.2;—(**2.**) (facing p. 101): Huntington 324021
Plate only: V & A E.1205-S-1886 (imprint cropped)
Lit.: Schiff 1251 (12.0 x 8.9 cm); Tomory 1972, pl. 106; Schiff-Viotto 1977, no. 207, pl. 207¹; Du Roveray III, 144; IV, 174

Variants:
I. Unfinished proof (etched state before frame) (**1806/II**) (between pp. [80-81]): Huntington 143632 (H=26.5 cm)
Other locations (facing p. 146): Princeton 3693.7.347.1810a/I (H=25.0 cm)
II. Proof before letters (India paper) (**1806/II**) (facing p. [81]): Huntington 143632 (H=26.5 cm)
III. Proof before letters (between pp. 146-147): Princeton 3693.7.347.1810a/I (H=25.0 cm)
Other locations (facing p. 146): Princeton Ex 3693.7.347.3.1810/I (H=24.8 cm)
IV. Proof before all letters (lacking verse) (**1806/II**) (between pp. [80-81]): Huntington 143632) (H=26.5 cm
Other locations: (**1806/II**) (facing p. [81]): DHW (23.4 cm); (facing p. 99): Newberry *Y642.H958 (H=24.0 cm); (**1810/I**) (facing p. 146): Bodleian Vet.A6.e.784/1; Dörrbecker
Plate only: BM 1853.12.10.551; Huntington 78219/III (1810 portf.)

This is not among the five subjects Du Roveray offered Fuseli in his letter of 30 June 1803, replying to the 'illiberal insinuations' in Fuseli's (untraced) letter about their agreement. The fact that *Odysseus and Leucothea* and *Ulysses Slaying the Suitors* were subsequently given to Fuseli gives the lie to his complaints about Du Roveray's treatment of him.

After holding Odysseus captive for nine years, Calypso relents and allows him to depart on the raft she helps him build. But Odysseus's old persecutor, Poseidon, seeing him still afloat, stirs up a fearsome storm and capsizes his vessel. In these straits, the goddess Leucothea comes to Odysseus's rescue, binding the veil around him that brings him after many perils to the shore.

238. *Blinded Polyphemus Checks the Sheep as They Leave the Cave*, 1806
(Book IX, 440-446)
(Vol. III, facing p. [55])

Engraved by J.G. Walker after Fuseli's painting in the Ulrich collection, Zurich (1803; Schiff 1194)
Imprint: Published 1st. October 1806, by F.J. Du Roveray. London.
Inscription: Painted by Hy. Fuseli R.A. | |
Engraved by I.G. Walker. |

> The master ram at last approach'd the gate,
> Charg'd with his wool, and with Ulysses' fate.
> Book IX.

Dimensions: ■ 12.1 x 8.9 cm | 4¾" x 3½";
■ 12.4 x 9.2 cm | 4¹⁴/16" x 3¹⁰/16" (NYPL 8-NRMH Pope 1806) (imprint cropped)
Other locations (**1806/III**): (as above): Huntington 324021; Yale Gfh91.fg725gb; Yale Gfh91.Fg813B (1806); (**1813/III**) (as above): BL 11315.1.2
Lit.: Schiff 1252 (12.1 x 8.8 cm); Schiff-Viotto 1977, no. 208, pl. 208¹; Du Roveray III, 144, pl. 24

Variants:
I. Unfinished proof (etched state before frame) (**1806/III**) (between pp. [55-56]): Huntington 143632 (H=26.5 cm)
Other locations (facing p. 254): Princeton Ex 3693.7.347.1810a/I (H=25.0 cm)
II. Proof before letters (India paper) (**1806/III**) (facing p.[55]): Huntington 143632 (H=26.5 cm)
III. Proof before letters (between pp. 254-255): Princeton Ex 3693.7.347.1810a/I (H=25.0 cm)
Other locations (**1806/III**)) (between pp. [54-55]): Huntington 143632 (H=26.5 cm);

(**1810/I**) (facing p. 254): Princeton Ex 3693.7.347.3.1810 (H=24.8 cm)
Plate only (India paper): BM 1863-5-9-30
IV. Proof before all letters (lacking verse) (**1806/III**) (between pp. [54-55]): Huntington 143632
Other locations (**1806/III**) (facing p. [55]): DHW (23.4 cm); (facing p. 77): Newberry *Y642.H958 (H=24.0 cm); (**1810/I**) (facing p. 254): Bodleian Vet.A6.e.784/1; Dörrbecker
Plate only: Huntington 78219 (1810/III portf.)

239.

239. *Odysseus Addressing the Shade of Ajax in Tartarus*, 1806 — (see also **Addenda**)
(Book XI, 543 ff.)
(Vol. III, facing p. [153])

Engraved by Isaac Taylor Jr. (1759-1829) after Fuseli's painting (1803-1804) in the Richard L. Feigen collection, New York, exhibited at the Royal Academy (1812/134)
Imprint: Published 1st. October 1806, by F.J. Du Roveray, London.
Inscription: Painted by Hy. Fuseli R.A. | |
Engraved by Isaac Taylor |

> While yet I speak, the shade disdains to stay,
> In silence turns, and sullen stalks away.
> Book XI.

Dimensions: ■ 12.0 x 8.8 cm | 4¾" x 3½";

■ 12.4 x 9.2 cm | 4^{14}/16" x 3^{10}/16" (NYPL
8-NRMH Pope 1806)
Other locations (**1806/III**): Huntington 324021;
Yale Gfh91.fg725gb; Yale Gfh91.Fg813B;
(**1813/III**): BL 11315.1.2
Plate only: V & A E.1205-V-1886 (imprint
cropped?)
Lit.: Schiff 1253 (12.0 x 8.8 cm); Schiff-Viotto
1977, no. 209, pl. 209^1; *Letters*, 265, 344-345;
Du Roveray III, 143
Exh.: Kansas City 1982 (78)

Variants:
I. Unfinished proof (etched state before frame)
(**1806/III**) (between pp. [152-153]): Huntington
143632 (H=26.5 cm)
Other locations (facing p. 324): Princeton Ex
3693.7.347.1810a/I (H=25.0 cm)
II. Proof before all letters (India paper)
(signatures only) (**1806/III**) (facing p. [153]):
Huntington 143632 (H=26.5 cm)
Inscription (scratched letters): Painted by H.
Fuseli||Engraved by Isaac Taylor
III. Proof before all letters (signatures only)
(between pp. 324-325): Princeton Ex
3693.7.347.1810a/II (H=24.8 cm)
IV. Proof before all letters (lacking verse)
(**1806/III**)(between pp. [152-153]): Huntington
143632 (H=26.5 cm)
Other locations (**1806/III**) (facing p. 153):
DHW (H=23.4 cm); (facing p. 182): Newberry
*Y642.H958 (H=24.0 cm); (**1810/I**) (facing p.
324): Bodleian Vet.A6.e.784/1; Dörrbecker;
Princeton Ex 3693.7.347.3.1810 (H=24.8 cm)
Plate only: BM 1853.12.10.548; Huntington
78219 (1810 portf.)

Odysseus narrates how he descends into the
underworld to consult Tiresias:

'And other spirits of those dead and gone
stood sorrowing, and each asked of those dear
to him. Alone of them all the spirit of Aias
[*Ajax*], son of Telamon, stood apart, still full of
wrath for the victory that I had won over him in
the contest by the ships for the arms of
Achilles. ... To him I spoke with soothing
words ... but he answered me not a word, but
went his way to Erebus to join the other spirits
of those dead and gone' (tr. A.T. Murray).

Fig. 13. Etched version of No. **239.** Variant I.

All unsustain'd between the wave and sky,
Beneath my feet the whirling billows fly.

Book XII.

240.

Regarding this plate, Isaac Taylor wrote to Du Roveray on 24 June 1806:

> ...the delivery proofs were taken off I believe three months ago...but I wished You to see the finished proof first as I have adopted a novel method of representing the Spectre which I flatter myself will both Surprize and please as it gives to the engraving all that aerial insubstantiality which the painter Secures by his blue and green tints[.] I have had a Stroke laid by the instrument (whose accuracy you cannot but be aware of) over the Sky and the ghost [*see Fig. 12.*] also uniting him hereby to the Air itself and have made out his Shape and effect by delicate Strokes on him the way of the drawing[—]this contrasted with all the force and richness I can put into the living figure of Ulysses will I hope appear both appropriate and Striking.

240. *Odysseus Between Scylla and Charybdis*, 1806 — (see also **Addenda**)
(Book XII, 429-518)
(Vol. IV, facing p. 7)

Engraved by William Bromley (1769-1842) after Fuseli's watercolour in the Kunsthaus, Zurich ([1803]; Schiff 1362)
Imprint: Published 1ˢᵗ. October 1806, by F.J. Du Roveray, London.
Inscription: Painted by Hʸ. Fuseli R.A. | |
Engraved by Wᵐ. Bromley. |

All unsustain'd between the wave and sky,
Beneath my feet the whirling billows fly.
           Book XII.

Dimensions: ■ 11.8 x 8.8 cm | 4¹⁰/16" x 3½";
■ 12.2 x 9.2 cm | 4¾" x 3¹⁰/16" (NYPL 8-NRMH Pope 1806)
Other locations (**1806/IV**): (**1.**) (facing t.p.): Yale Gfh91.fg725gb; Yale Gfh91.Fg.813B —(**2.**) (facing p. 29): Huntington 324021; (**1813/IV**) (facing t.p.): BL 11315.1.2
Plate only: V & A E.1205-O-1886
Lit.: Schiff 1254 (11.8 x 8.8 cm); Schiff-Viotto 1977, no. 210, pl. 210¹; *Letters*, 155, 297; Du Roveray III, 99, 143
Exh.: Kansas City 1982 (79)

Variants:
I. Unfinished proof (etched state before frame)

(**1806/IV**) (between pp. [6-7]): Huntington 143632 (H=26.5 cm)
Other locations (facing p. 350): Princeton Ex 3693.7.347.1810a/I (H=25.0 cm)
II. Proof before letters (India paper) (**1806/III**): Huntington 143632) (H=26.5 cm)
III. Proof before letters (between pp. 350-351): Princeton Ex 3693.7.347.1810a/I (H=25.0 cm)
Other locations (plate only):BM 1853-12-10-557
IV. Proof before all letters (lacking verse) (**1806/IV**) (between pp. [6-7]): Huntington 143632
Other locations (**1806/IV**) (facing p. [7]): DHW (H=23.4 cm); (facing p. 29): Newberry *Y642.H958 (H=24.0 cm); (**1810/I**) (facing p. 350): Bodleian Vet.A6.e.784/1; Princeton Ex 3693.7.347.3.1810 (H=24.8 cm)
Plate only: Huntington 78219 (1810 portf.)
Lacking plate: Dörrbecker (1810)

When Zeus sinks Odysseus's ship in retribution for the destruction of the Oxen of the Sun by his crew, Ulysses alone survives by clinging to the mast and broken keel, but is carried back towards the cave of the voracious sea monster Scylla and the irresistible whirlpool Charybdis. Odysseus relates how forewarned by the goddess, he is able to save himself:

> 'Charybdis ... verily sucked down the salt water of the sea, but I, springing up to the tall fig-tree, laid hold of it, and clung to it like a bat. Yet I could in no wise plant my feet firmly or climb upon the tree, for its roots spread far below and its branches hung out of reach above, long and great, and overshadowed Charybdis. There I clung steadfastly until she should vomit forth mast and keel again, and to my joy ... at length those spars appeared from out Charybdis' (trans. A.T. Murray).

Bromley's price for engraving the plate was 20 guineas (to Du Roveray, 11 May 1804).

240A. [n.d.]
Aquatint by an anonymous engraver
Dimensions: ■ 25.4 x 20.0 cm | 9¹⁵/16" x 7¹⁴/16" (BM 1863-5-9-88)

240B. [n.d.]
Lithograph by an anonymous engraver
Dimensions: ■ 66.4 x 45.5 cm | 26¼" x 17¹⁴/16" (BM 1870-10-8-2799)

Across her knees she laid the well-known bow,
And pensive sat, and tears began to flow.
                                        Book XXI.

Published 1st October 1806, by F.J. Du Roveray, London.

241.

The dreadful aegis blazes in their eye;
Amazed they see, they tremble, and they fly.
                                        Book XXII.

242.

241. *Penelope Holding the Bow of Odysseus*, 1806
(Book XXI, 55-60)
(Vol. VI, facing p. [7])

Engraved by Robert Hartley Cromek (1770-1812) after Fuseli's painting in the Röttinger collection, Zurich (1803; Schiff 1195).
Imprint: Published 1st. October 1806, by F.J. Du Roveray, London.
Inscription: Painted by H^y. Fuseli R.A.||
Engraved by R.H. Cromek|

  Across her knees she laid the well-known bow,
  And pensive sat, and tears began to flow.
                                        Book XXI.
Dimensions: ■ 11.9 x 8.8 cm | 4^{11}/16" x 3^{7}/16";
■ 12.2 x 9.1 cm | 4^{13}/16" x 3^{6}/16" (NYPL 8-NRMH Pope 1806)
Other locations (**1806/VI**) (facing t.p.): Yale Gfh91.fg 725gb; (**1813/VI**)—(**1.**) (facing t.p.): BL 11315.1.2; Yale Gfh91.Fg813B;—(**2.**) (facing p. 9): Huntington 324021
Plate only: Ashmolean (trimmed to frame); V & A E.1205-I-1886
Lit.: Schiff 1255 (11.8 x 8.8); Schiff-Viotto 1977, no. 211, pl. 211^{1}; Du Roveray III, 144

Variants:
I. Unfinished proof (etched state) before frame (**1806/VI**) (between pp. [6-7]): Huntington 143632 (H=26.5 cm)
Other locations (**1810/II**) (facing p. 225): Princeton Ex 3693.7.347.1810a (H=25.0 cm)
II. Proof before all letters (India paper) (signatures only) (**1806/VI**): Huntington 143632 (H=26.5 cm)
Inscription (scratched letters): H. Fuseli RA. pinxit.||Cromek sculp.
III. Proof before all letters (signatures only) (between pp. 224-225): Princeton Ex 3693.7.347.1810a/II (H=25.0 cm)
Inscription: H. Fuseli RA. pinxit.||Cromek sculp.
Other locations (**1810a/II**) (facing p. 226): Princeton Ex 3693.7.347.3.1810/II (H=24.8 cm); (**1806/VI**) (facing p. 9): Newberry *Y642.H958 (H=24.0 cm)
Plate only: BM 1853-12-10-552
IV. Proof before all letters (lacking verse) (**1806/VI**)(between pp.[6-7]):Huntington 143632
Other locations (**1806/VI**) (facing p. [7]): DHW (H-23.4); (**1810/II**) (facing p. 226): Bodleian Vet.A6.e.784/2; Dörrbecker

Plate only: Huntington 78219 (1810 portf.);
V & A E.1205-W-1886

Penelope is going to announce that she will marry the suitor who is able to string Odysseus's bow and shoot an arrow through the twelve axes with it. But Athena has fated that the contest will bring death to the contenders.

242. *Odysseus Slaying the Suitors*, 1806
(Book XXII, 297-309)
(Vol. VI, facing p. [47])

Engraved by Louis Schiavonetti (1765-1810) after Fuseli's lost painting exhibited (1812/) at the Liverpool Academy.
Imprint: Published 1st. October 1806, by F.J. Du Roveray London.
Inscription: Painted by Hy. Fuseli R.A. | |
Engraved by Ls. Schiavonetti. |

> The dreadful aegis blazes in their eye;
> Amaz'd they see, they tremble, and they fly.
> > Book XXII.

Dimensions: ■ 12.2 x 9.1 cm | 4¹³/16" x 3⁹/16"; ▣ 12.6 x 9.5 cm | 5" x 3¾" (NYPL 8-NRMH Pope 1806)
Other locations (**1806/III**) (as above): Yale Gfh91.fg725gb; (**1813/VI**):—(**1.**) (as above): BL 11315.1.2; Yale Gfh91.fg813B;—(**2.**) (facing p. 60): Huntington 324021
Plate only: V & A E.1205-Q-1886
Lit.: Schiff 1256 (12.2 x 9.1 cm); Schiff-Viotto 1977, no. 212, pl. 212¹; Du Roveray III, 144

Variants:
I. Unfinished proof (etched state before frame) (**1806/VI**) (between pp. [44-45]): Huntington 143632 (H=26.5 cm)
Other locations (**1810/II**) (facing p. 202): Princeton Ex 3693.7.347.1810a (H=25.0 cm)
II. Proof before all letters (India paper) (signatures only) (**1806/VI**) (facing p. [45]): Huntington 143632 (H=26.5 cm)
Inscription (scratched letters): Painted by H, Fuseli RA | | Engraved by L Schiavonetti
III. Proof before all letters (signatures only) (between pp. 202-203): Princeton Ex 3693.7.347.1810a/II (H=25.0 cm)
Other locations (**1810/II**) (facing p. 262): Princeton Ex 3693.7.347.1810 (H=24.8 cm)
IV. Proof before all letters (lacking verse) (**1806/VI**) (facing p. 61): Newberry

*Y642.H958 (H=24.0 cm)
Other locations (**1806/VI**) (facing p. 47): DHW (H=23.4 cm); (**1810/II**) (facing p. 262): Bodleian Vet.A6.e.784/2; Dörrbecker
Plate only: BM 1853-12-10-549; Huntington 78219 (1810 portf.)
IV. Reissued (1819-1836) with additional inscription but lacking imprint: YCBA PA4033.S4 (H=26.1 cm) (f. 40)
Inscription (top of the sheet): Minerva assisting Ulysses in the destruction of the Suitors. | (bottom of frame): Painted by Hy. Fuseli R.A. | | Engraved by Ls. Schiavonetti. |

> The dreadful aegis blazes in their eye;
> Amaz'd they see, they tremble, and they fly.
> > Odyssey, Book XXII.

Other locations (plate only): Lucerne

Athena stands beside Odysseus as he begins to slay the suitors. Her aegis, 'the bane of mortals', is seen above her in the form of a Medusa-head.

                                                    243.

243. *Penelope Reunited with Odysseus*, 1806
(Book XXIII, 168 ff.)
(Vol. VI, facing p. [91])

Engraved by Isaac Taylor Jr. (1759-1829) after Fuseli's painting (not in Schiff) in the Feigen collection, New York, exhibited (1812/186) at the Liverpool Academy.

Imprint: Published 1ˢᵗ. October 1806, by F.J. Du Roveray, London.

Inscription: Painted by Hʸ. Fuseli R.A. | | Engraved by Isaac Taylor. |

_____ to his arms she flew,
  And strained him close, as to his breast she
    grew.   Book XXIII.

Dimensions: ■ 12.1 x 8.6 cm | 4¾ " x 3⁶/16";
■ 12.4 x 9.0 cm | 5" x 3⁹/16" (NYPL 8-NRMH Pope 1806)
Other locations (1813/VI): (1.) (as above): BL 11315.1.2; Yale Gfh91.fg725gb; Yale Gfh91.Fg813B;—(2.) (facing p. 100): Huntington 324021
Lit.: Schiff 1257 (12.1 x 8.6 cm); Tomory 1972, pl. 213; Schiff-Viotto 1977, no. 213; *Letters*, 345, 355; Du Roveray III, 144, pl. 25

Variants:

I. Unfinished proof (etched state before frame) (1806/VI) (between pp. [90-91]): Huntington 143632 (H=26.5 cm)
Other locations (1810/II) (facing p. 284): Princeton 3693.7.347.1810a (H=25.0 cm)
II. Proof before letters (India paper) (1806/VI) (facing p. [91]): Huntington 143632 (H=26.5 cm)
III. Proof before letters (between pp. 284-285): Princeton Ex 3693.7.347.1810a/II (H=25.0 cm)
Other locations (1810/II) (facing p. 284): Princeton Ex 3693.7.347.3.1810 (H=24.8 cm)
IV. Proof before all letters (lacking verse) (1806/VI) (between pp. [90-91]): Huntington 143632 (H=26.5 cm)
Other locations (1806/VI) (facing p. 91): DHW (H=23.4 cm); (facing p. 99): Newberry *Y642.H958 (H=24.0 cm); (1810/II) (facing p. 284): Bodleian Vet.A6.e.784/2; Dörrbecker
Plate only: BM 1853-12-10-547; Huntington 78219 (1810 portf.)

The plate was still in the etching stage on 24 June 1806, but Taylor assured Du Roveray that he could 'complete [*his*] engagement within the Year as ... specif[*ied*]'. On 6 December 1806 he sent Du Roveray a proof, although he could 'hardly tell whether it is Yet fit to show Fuseli'.

******

Nos. 244 - 255.
Christoph Martin Wieland.
OBERON, | A POEM. | FROM THE GERMAN OF WIELAND. | BY WILLIAM SOTHEBY, ESQ. | IN TWO VOLUMES. | THE SECOND EDITION. | = | VOL. I. [-VOL. II.] | = | LONDON: | = | PRINTED BY W BULMER AND CO. | CLEVELAND-ROW, ST. JAMES'S; | FOR T. CADELL AND W. DAVIES, STRAND. | — | 1805 (12/12 illus.).

For the pastiches of 1858 see Nos. **244A** and **248A** below.

Apart from some 'finishing of the detail', Fuseli had 'Composed the whole ... [*of*] the [*twelve*] Little pictures for Mr. Sotheby's ex-wielanded *Oberon*' by the end of December 1804 (*Letters*, 312). The price agreed with Cadell & Davies was 120 guineas (£126) (*Farington Diary*, VI, 2454), although he felt this was not a 'very advantageous bargain' (He had been paid £116.11s./111 guineas for his 37 drawings for Chalmers's *Shakespeare*).

The poem was published on 14 August 1806. The notice in the *Times* described it as 'elegantly printed ... and illustrated with Engravings, price 15s. in boards'. The 'very few Copies on large paper, with first impressions of the Plates' cost £1.4s. in boards.

Drawn from such diverse (and 'un-German') sources as the chivalric romance *Huon de Bordeaux*, Chaucer's *The Merchant's Tale*, Shakespeare's *A Midsummer NIght's Dream*, and *The Thousand-and-One Nights*, C.M. Wieland's fanciful verse epic, *Oberon* (1780), earned him the title of 'the German Ariosto'. The 1st and 3rd English editions (1798, 1826) are unillustrated.

As noted by Werner W. Beyer in his *Keats and the Daemon King* (1947),

the prime mover of Wieland's tale is a composite figure [*with*] marked affinities with the daemons and angels of antiquity ... In this daemonic strain ... lay the reason for [*the English romanticists'*] profound interest ... in *Oberon*—pre-eminently by John Keats (p. 17).

The poem recounts the adventures of Huon of Bordeaux, sent by Charlemagne to Baghdad, where he must kill the knight seated to the left of the Caliph, rob the Caliph of four of his molars and a handful of his whiskers, and claim his daughter, Rezia, as his bride.

244.

James Heath received 72 guineas (£75.12s) for engraving four plates to *Oberon* (18 guineas each). The receipt in the Philadelphia Free Library, dated 4 September 1805, provides a terminus ad quem for completion of his plates.

The illustration shows Huon, who is seeking shelter from the storm, being challenged in the cave by a wild man, dressed in tatters and catskins. This proves to be Sherasmin, servant to Huon's father, Duke Siegewin of Guyenne, who had died in the Holy Land. Roused to new life by the opportunity to serve his old master's son, Sherasmin pledges his undying loyalty to Huon on his journey.

245.

244. *Huon Encounters Sherasmin in the Cave on Mount Lebanon*, 1806
(Canto I, xviii-xix)
(Vol. I, facing p. 10)

Engraved by James Heath (1757-1834) after the painting in the Reinhart collection, Winterthur, Switzerland (1804-1805; Schiff 1219)
Imprint: Published March 1st. 1806, by Cadell & Davies, Strand.
Inscription (top centre): OBERON, CANTO I. | (top right) Vol. I. Page 10. | (Bottom) H. Fuseli R.A. Pinxit | | I. Heath Sculpt. |
Dimensions: ■ 10.8 x 7.6 cm | 4¼" x 3';
■ 11.2 x 8.0 cm | 4⁷/16" x 3³/16" (BL 11526.bbb.54) (facing t.p.)
Other locations: **(1.)** (as above): Bodleian Douce W197; Cambridge 8746.d.97; DHW; DHW (H=22.3 cm); Folger PT2568 .A3027; NYPL NFW Wieland 1805;—**(2.)** (facing t.p.): Essick; Huntington 432405; LC PR2568.A3O27 1805 c.2
Lit.: Schiff 1317 (10.8 x 7.6 cm); Heath 1992, 1805(3).1

Variants:
I. Proof before letters: BM 1863-5-9-22

245. *Sherasmin and Huon Flee from Oberon*, 1806
(Canto II, xxix-xxx)
(Vol. I, facing p. 54)

Engraved by Francis Engleheart (1775-1849) after the painting in the Muraltengut, Zurich (1804-1805; Schiff 1220).
Imprint: Published March 1st. 1806, by Cadell & Davies, Strand.

Inscription (top centre): OBERON, CANTO II. |
(top right): Vol. 1. Page 54. | (bottom): H. Fuseli
RA. pinx'. | | F. Engleheart Sculp'.
Dimensions: ■ 10.7 x 7.7 cm | 4³/16" x 3";
■ 11.0 x 8.0 cm | 4⁵/16" x 3³/16" (BL
11526.bbb.54)
Other locations: **(1.)** (as above): Bodleian Douce
W197; DHW; DHW (H=22.3 cm);Essick; Folger
PT2568.A3O27; Huntington 432405;LC
PR2568.A3O27 1805 c.2; NYPL NFW Wieland
1806;—**(2.)** (facing p. 55): Cambridge 8746.d.97
Lit.: Schiff 1318 (10.8 x 7.7 cm)

Variants:

I. Proof before all letters (signatures only): BM
1849-5-12-254

According to a receipt, dated 8 November 1805
(Philadelphia Free Library), Engleheart was paid
16 guineas (£16.16s.) for one plate for *Oberon*—
presumably his second plate was the same price.

Seeking the shortest path to Baghdad, Huon
leads Sherasmin through the enchanted forest. The
illustration shows the storm unleashed by Oberon,
king of the elves, swirling around the riders: the
terror-stricken Sherasmin rides on madly,
dragging Huon's steed after him, while Huon
fixes his eyes on the pursuing spirit, entranced by
his beauty. But Oberon means them no harm;
instead, after demonstrating their purpose, he will
present Huon with a magic horn and cup.

246. *Huon Removes the Ring from the Giant
Angulaffer's Finger and Liberates Angela*, 1806
(Canto III, xxvii-xxix)
(Vol. I, facing p. 81)

Engraved by Francis Engleheart (1775-1849) after
the painting in the Hafter-Reinhart collection,
Zurich (1804-1805; Schiff 1221).
Imprint: Published March 1ˢᵗ. 1806, by Cadell &
Davies, Strand.
Inscription (top centre): OBERON, CANTO III. |
Vol. 1. Page 81. | (Bottom): H Fuseli RA. pinx. | |
F. Engleheart Sculp'.
Dimensions: ■ 10.8 x 7.7 cm | 4¼" x 3';
■ 11.0 x 8.0 cm | 4⁵/16" x 3²/16" (BL
11526.bbb.54)
Other locations: Bodleian Douce W197;
Cambridge 8746.d.97; DHW; DHW (H=22.3
cm); Essick; Folger PR2568.A3O27; Huntington
432405; LC PR2568.A3O27 1805; LC
PR2568.A3O27 1805 c.2; NYPL NFW Wieland
1806

246.

247.

Lit.: Schiff 1319 (10.8 x 7.7 cm)

Variants:

I. Proof before all letters (signatures only) (India paper): BM 1849-5-12-253 (Sheet=28.0 cm)

II. Proof before all letters (signatures only): BM 1849-5-12-252

Other locations (plate only): V & A E.1206-D-1886

Engleheart was probably paid at the same rate he received for his previous engraving—£16.16s.

Huon undertakes to free Angela, the Prince of Lebanon's bride, from the clutches of the giant Angulaffer, who has been made invincible by virtue of a ring he had stolen from Oberon. Entering the castle, Huon finds the giant in a leaden sleep which overcame him whenever he attempted to ravish the damsel. At Angela's urging Huon removes the ring from the giant's finger (thereby unwittingly acquiring its powers), but honour forbids him to kill a defenceless enemy, as Angela demands. Instead he awakens the giant and slays him in fair combat, after which, disdaining Angela's charms, he returns her to the prince and continues on his way.

247. *Huon Freeing Babekan Attacked by a Lion*, 1806

(Canto IV, xxiii-xxv)

(Vol. I, facing p. 113)

Engraved by Charles Warren (1766-1823) after the painting in the Schulthess-Bodmer collection, Zurich (1804-1805; Schiff 1222).

Imprint: Published March 1st. 1806, by Cadell & Davies, Strand.

Inscription (top centre): OBERON, CANTO IV.| Vol. I. page 113.|(bottom): H Fuseli R.A. pinxt.||C. Warren sculp.

Dimensions: ■ 10.8 x 7.8 cm | 4¼" x 3²/16"; ■ 11.1 x 8.1 cm | 4⁶/16" x 3³/16" (BL 11526.bbb.54)

Other locations (as above): Bodleian Douce W197; Cambridge 8746.d.97; DHW; DHW (H=22.3 cm); Essick; Folger PR2568.A3O27; Huntington 432405; LC PR2568.A3O27 1805; LC PR2568.A3O27 1805 c.2; NYPL NFW Wieland 1806

Lit.: Schiff 1320 (10.8 x 7.7 cm); *Letters*, 357.

Exh.: Kansas City 1982 (66)

Variants:

I. Proof before all letters (signatures only) (India paper): BM 1849-5-12-255 (Sheet=34.2 cm)

Inscription (scratched letters): H. Fuseli RA Pinxt. C. Warren Scᴸ..

Warren received 18 guineas (£18.18s.0d.) for engraving this plate. Since Warren had been paid for his finished plates on 4 June 1806 (receipt in the Philadelphia Free Library), 'the promised proofs from *Oberon*' that Fuseli still had not received by 20 January 1807 were probably intended for the artist's portfolio rather than for his improvements before publication.

Babekan, the haughty and guileful Saracen knight, whom Huon is here seen rescuing from the lion, requites the gift of his life by blaspheming the Christian God when the magic cup scorches his lips, and then by stealing Huon's horse. He will not, however, escape unscathed, for Huon is destined to encounter him again very soon in Baghdad at the court of the Caliph.

248.

248. *Huon and Rezia Embrace*, 1806
(Canto V, lxix-lxxv)
(Vol. I, facing p. 172)

Engraved by James Heath (1757-1834) after the painting in the Blattmann-Roth collection, Wädenswil, Kt. Zurich (1804-1805; Schiff 1223)
Imprint: Published March 1st. 1806, by Cadell & Davies, Strand.
Inscription (top centre): OBERON, CANTO V. | Vol. 1. Page 172. | (bottom): H. Fuseli, R.A. Pinxit. | | J. Heath Sculpt.
Dimensions: ■ 10.8 x 7.8 cm | 4¼" x 3¹/16";
■ 11.1 x 8.1 cm | 4⁶/16" x 3³/16" (BL 11526.bbb.54)
Other locations (as above): Bodleian Douce W197; Cambridge 9746.d.97; DHW; DHW (H=22.3 cm); Essick; Folger PR2568.A3O27; Huntington 432405; LC PR2568.A3O27 1805; LC PR2568.A3O27 1805 c.2; NYPL NFW Wieland 1805
Lit.: Schiff 1321 (10.8 x 7.9 cm); Heath 1992, no. 1805(3).2

Variants:
I. Proof before letters (India paper): V & A E.659.87

Heath was paid 18 guineas for engraving this plate (cp. No. **244**).

In Baghdad Huon and Sherasmin find lodging with the old mother of Princess Rezia's nurse, Fatma, from whom they learn that the Princess is to be married to Babekan. Huon is unaware that Rezia, like himself, has seen her true lover in a dream, and no longer wishes to marry Babekan. On the wedding day, Huon goes to the Caliph's palace garbed as an emir, where he lops off Babekan's head, who is sitting to the left of the Caliph. In the ensuing uproar, Huon and Rezia recognise each other as the promised lover of their dreams. They embrace and Huon slips the talisman on Rezia's finger, proclaiming her his bride.

However, the illustration depicts the later moment after the magic horn has wrapped the Sultan and his retainers in a deathlike slumber, when Oberon appears to ask Rezia if she truly wishes to accompany Huon. She answers in the affirmative and the lovers together with Sherasmin and Fatma are wafted away in Oberon's chariot.

249. *Sherasmin while en route to Lepanto Relates to Fatma, Huon and Rezia the Tale of Oberon and Titania Observing Gandolf and Rosetta in the Garden*, 1806
(Canto VI, xvi-xvii)
(Vol. I, facing p 187)

Engraved by John Dadley (1767-*post* 1807)
Imprint: Published March 1st. 1806, by Cadell & Davies, Strand.
Inscription (top): OBERON, CANTO VI. | Vol. I. page 187. | (bottom): H. Fuseli R.A. pinxt | | J. Dadley Sculpt
Dimensions: ■ 10.8 x 7.8 cm | 4¼" x 3¹/16";
■ 11.1 x 8.1 cm | 4⁶/16" x 3³/16" (BL 11526.bbb.54)
Other locations: (**1.**) (as above): Bodleian Douce W197; Cambridge 8746.d.97; DHW; DHW (H=22.3 cm); Essick; Folger PT2568.A3O27; Huntington 432405; LC PT2568.A3O27 (1805); LC PT 2568.A3O27 1805 c.2—(**2.**) (facing p. 186): NYPL NFW Wieland 1805
Lit.: Schiff 1322 (10.8 x 7.7 cm); Schiff-Viotto 1977, no. 254, pl. 254¹

Variants:
I. Proof before all letters (signatures only) (before frame): BM 1849-5-12-253

When Oberon puts Huon and Rezia on the boat that will carry them to Italy, he commands them to maintain their fidelity and chastity until their formal betrothal by the Pope. During the voyage, Rezia is baptised as a Christian and given the name Amanda. But the two lovers find it hard to curb their passion. To distract them, Sherasmin relates the story of Gandolf, the former roué, now old and blind, and his frisky young wife, Rosetta. Oberon and Titania, are witnesses one day to Rosetta's cleverness in finding a way to meet her young lover in the branches of a pear tree. Angered by this treachery, Oberon restores the husband's sight so that he can catch Rosetta in the arms of her lover. But Titania defends the wife and attacks the hypocrisy of 'liberty' for men and 'patience' for women. Oberon is enraged, and swearing an oath not to forgive Titania until a pair of lovers 'By innocence absolve this ... wanton shame', he disappears. Since then he had not been seen in his own guise and had made it 'His ceaseless pleasure, and his sole employ | To torture lovers, and their bliss destroy'.

249.

250.

250. *Amanda-Rezia Throws Herself After Huon Into the Sea*, 1806
(Canto VII, xxiv-xxv)
(Vol. II, facing p. 13)

Engraved by James Neagle (1760-1822) after the painting in the Blattmann-Ziegler collection, Wädenswil, Kt. Zurich (1804-1805; Schiff 1224)
Imprint: Published March 1st. 1806, by Cadell & Davies, Strand.
Inscription (top): OBERON, CANTO VII. | Vol. 2. Page 13. | (bottom): H. Fuseli RA. pinxt. | | I. Neagle Sc.
Dimensions: ■ 10.8 x 8.0 cm | 4¼" x 3²/16";
◨ 11.0 x 8.1 cm | 4¼" x 3²/16" (BL 11526.bbb.54) (facing title page)
Other locations: **(1.)** (as above): Bodleian Douce W198; Cambridge 8746.d.98; DHW; DHW (H=22.3 cm); Essick; Folger PT2568.A3027; Huntington 432405; LC PT2568.A3027 1805 c.2; NFW Wieland 1805;—**(2.)** (facing title page): LC PT2568.A3027 1805
Lit.: Schiff 1323 (18 x 8.0 cm), 1224; Tomory 1972, 116, 120, pl. 186
Exh.: Kansas City 1982 (67)

Variants:
I. Proof before all letters (signatures only) (India paper): BM 1849-5-12-249

James Neagle was assigned only one plate from *Oberon*, for which he was paid 18 guineas. The receipt, dated 3 July 1805, is in the Lande Collection at McGill University.

During their long sea journey Huon tries to comply with Oberon's edict by avoiding Amanda, who cannot understand his motives. Inevitably, the lovers give way to their desire, provoking a fearful storm. Huon accepts his guilt (although he does not repent—'Is love a sin?'), and is cast overboard to save the imperilled ship. Wild with woe, Amanda throws herself into the waves with him.

> Loose, like a lion's mane, her ringlets sweep
> Before the blast! With eyes that cannot weep,
> With love to frenzy wrought, with high-swoln breast,
> And circling arms round Huon closely prest,
> She hurls him with herself amid the swallowing deep!

Fatma watches 'their clasping forms | Entwin'd like tendrils,' disappear among the billows.

251. *Titania Shows Amanda her New-born Son in the Grotto*, 1806
(Canto VIII, xxiv)
(Vol. II, facing p. 86)

Engraved by Charles Warren (1766-1823) after
Fuseli's painting in the Muraltengut, Zurich
(1804-1805; Schiff 1225)
Imprint: Published March 1st. 1806, by Cadell &
Davies, Strand.
Inscription (top): OBERON, CANTO VIII. | Vol.
2. page 86. | (bottom): H. Fuseli R.A. pinx. | | C.
Warren sculp.
Dimensions: ■ 10.8 x 7.6 cm | 4¼" x 3";
■ 11.1 x 7.9 cm | 4⁶/16" x 3²/16" (BL
11526.bbb.54)
Other locations (as above): Bodleian Douce
W198; Cambridge 8746.d.98; DHW; DHW
(H=22.3 cm); Essick; Folger PT2568.A3027;
Huntington 432405; LC PT2568.A3O37 1805; LC
PT2568. A3027 1805 c.2.; NYPL NFW Wieland
1805
Lit.: Schiff 1324 (10.8 x 7.7 cm), 1225; Schiff-
Viotto 1977, no. 256; *Letters*, pp.312, 318, 357
Exh.: Kansas City 1982 (68)

Variants:
 I. Proof before all letters (signatures only)
 (before frame) (India paper): BM 1849-5-12-250
 (Sheet=33.2 cm)
 Inscription (scratched letters): H. Fuseli RA
 Pinx C Warren Sculpt
 Other locations: BM 1863-5-9-27

Warren received £18.18s.0d. for engraving this
(cp. No. **247**).
Saved from the storm by the power of the
magic ring that Huon had given Amanda, the
lovers are cast up on a desert island, where they
meet Alphonso, the saintly hermit, who welcomes
them to his idyllic valley and becomes their
spiritual mentor. He inspires Huon to make up for
his sin by voluntarily choosing to live the life of
chastity.
Unbeknown to them Titania had also chosen the
island for her secret refuge; she becomes
convinced that the young lovers are destined to
bring about her reconciliation with Oberon. When
Amanda's time approaches she is guided to
Titania's magic grotto and in the mystic presence
of the elfin queen gives birth to her son.

251.

252.

252. *Huon and Amanda Find Alphonso Dead*,
1806
(Canto IX, xxxvii-xxxix)
(Vol. II, facing p. 108)

Engraved by Robert Hartley Cromek (1770-1812)
after Fuseli's painting in the Laszlo collection,
Basel (1804-1805; Schiff 1788).
Imprint: Published March 1st. 1806, by Cadell &
Davies, Strand.
Inscription (top): OBERON, CANTO IX. Vol. 2.
page 108.|(bottom): Fuseli RA. pinxit.||R.H.
Cromek, sc
Dimensions: ■ 11.0 x 7.9 cm | 4^5/16" x 3^2/16";
■ 11.2 x 8.2 cm | 4^7/16" x 3¼" (BL
11526.bbb.54)
Other locations (as above): Bodleian Douce
W198; Cambridge 8746.d.98; DHW; DHW
(H=22.3 cm); Essick; Folger PT2568.A3027;
Huntington 432405; LC PT2568.A3O27 1805;
LC PT2568.A3O27 1805 c.2; NYPL NFW
Wieland 1805
Lit.: Schiff 1325 (11.0 x 7.9), 1788; *Letters*, 316.

Variants:
I. Proof before letters: BM 1849-5-12-251

It is not clear why Cromek's engraving, for
which he was paid 18 guineas, was not published
until 'March 1st. 1806', since the receipt is dated
31 May 1805 and it is to be assumed that payment
indicates completion of the assignment.

Remembering how Alphonso had spoken the
previous evening of passing beyond the dream
into real existence, Huon and Amanda anxiously
come at dawn to the hermit's 'hallow'd cell'
(whose depiction, however, suggests almost
palatial proportions) and find their mentor's
premonition of his death fulfilled. But even as
Huon and Amanda grieve for his passing, fate is
preparing to test their love: Titania too has had
forebodings and has acted on them—with her
departure the blooming valley she had created
reverts to its original rocky wilderness. Titania
has also stolen away Huonet from his parents.
While they search for him, Amanda is separated
from Huon and captured by pirates, and when
Huon comes to her rescue, he is secured to a tree
and left to die. (He will be released only by the
intervention of Oberon, and magically transported
to Sherasmin's hut in Tunis.)

253.

253. *Titania Finds the Magic Ring on the Shore*,
1806
(Canto X, ii-iii)
(Vol. II, facing p. 122)

Engraved by James Heath (1757-1834) after
Fuseli's painting in the Kunsthaus, Zurich (1804-
1805; Schiff 1226)
Imprint: Published March 1st. 1806, by Cadell &
Davies, Strand.
Inscription (top): OBERON, CANTO X.|Vol. 2.
page 122.|(bottom): H. Fuseli R.A. pinx^t.||J.
Heath sculp^t.
Dimensions: ■ 10.6 x 7.6 cm | 4^2/16" x 3';
■ 10.9 x 7.9 cm | 4¼" x 3^2/16" (BL
11526.bbb.54)
Other locations (as above): Bodleian Douce
W178; Cambridge 8746.d.98; DHW; DHW
(H=22.3 cm); Essick; Folger PT2568.A3027;
Huntington 432405; LC PT2568.A3O27; LC
PT2568.A3O27 1805; LC PT2568.A3O27 1805
c.2; NYPL NFW Wieland 1805
Lit.: Schiff 1326 (10.6 x 7.6 cm), 1226; Tomory
1972, 116, pl. 111; Heath 1992, no. 1805(3).3
Exh.: Kansas City 1982 (69)

Variants:
I. Proof before letters (India paper):
BM 1863-5-9-23

The engraver was paid 18 guineas (cp. No. **244**).

Fuseli has borrowed the falling and foreshortened figure of Titania from Blake's illustration to Edward Young's *Night Thoughts*, V, 246 ('I dive for precious pearls in Sorrow's Stream'), depicting a pearl diver seizing two pearls from the bottom of the sea—one of a limited number of examples in Fuseli's work of such borrowings from Blake, despite his reported remark that Blake was 'd---d good to steal from'.

As night falls, Titania hears Huon's cries of distress but is prevented from going to his aid. Looking down, she sees the ring that Amanda had dropped while struggling with the pirates, and rejoices to have found the talisman that will reunite her with Oberon and Amanda with Huon.

254. *Huon Disguised as a Gardener is Seen by the Sultana Almansaris and Nadine*, 1806
(Canto XI, xii-xiii)
(Vol. II, facing p. 155)

Engraved by Robert Hartley Cromek (1770-1812) after the painting in the Blattmann-Roth collection, Wädenswil, Kt. Zurich (1804-1805; Schiff 1227)
Imprint: Published March 1st. 1806, by Cadell & Davies, Strand.
Inscription (top): OBERON, CANTO XI. | (top right): Vol. 2. Page 155. | (bottom): Fuseli pinxit. | | Cromek sculp.
Dimensions: ■ 10.8 x 7.6 cm | 3¼" x 3';
■ 11.0 x 7.8 cm | 4⁵/16" x 3²/16" (BL 11526.bbb.54)
Other locations: (**1.**) (as above): Bodleian Douce W198; Cambridge 9746.d.98; DHW; DHW (H=22.3 cm); Essick; Folger PT2568.A3O27; LC PT2568.A3O27 1805; LC PT2568.A3O27 1805 c.2; NYPL NFW Wieland 1805;—(**2.**) (facing p. 154): Huntington 432405
Lit.: Schiff 1327 (10.6 x 7.6), 1227 259

Cromek was probably paid at the same rate for this engraving as for No. **252**.

Learning that Amanda has been brought to the Sultan's court after the sinking of the pirate ship by a thunderbolt, Huon finds employment in the gardens of the seraglio, and spends his nights

254.

255.

roaming the grounds in hope of seeing Amanda. On the fourth night, Huon is seen and questioned by Almansaris, the sultana. The illustration shows Huon at Almansaris' feet pleading, in mitigation of his presence, his misplaced zeal to gather a floral offering for her Majesty. Overcome with desire for the handsome gardener, Almansaris forgives his presumption—and since the Sultan now has eyes only for Amanda, makes plans to lure Huon 'within her amorous net'. Meanwhile, Huon's attempt to send a message to Amanda using the language of flowers leads instead to an assignation with Almansaris, from which Huon emerges with his virtue intact, while 'love's wildest fire' rages unabated in Almansaris' breast.

255. *Almansaris Visits Huon in Prison*, 1806
(Canto XII, xxxi-xxxviii)
(Vol. II, facing p. 198)

Engraved by James Heath (1757-1834) after the painting in the Kunsthaus, Zurich (1804-1805; Schiff 1228)
Imprint: Published March 1ˢᵗ. 1806, by Cadell & Davies, Strand.
Inscription (top): OBERON, CANTO XII. | (top right) Vol. 2. page 198. | (bottom): H. Fuseli R.A. pinxᵗ. | | J. Heath sculpᵗ.
Dimensions: ■ 10.6 x 7.7 cm | 4³/16" x 3¹/16"; ■ 11.0 x 7.9 cm | 4⁶/16" x 3²/16" (BL 11526.bbb.54)
Other locations: **(1.)** (as above): Bodleian Douce W198; DHW; DHW (H=22.3 cm); Essick; Folger PT2568.A3O27; Huntington 432405; LC PT2568.A3O27 1805; LC PT2568.A3O27 1805 c.2; NYPL NFW Wieland 1805;—**(2.)** (facing p. 188): Cambridge 8746.d.98
Lit.: Schiff 1328 (10.8 x 7.6 cm), 1228; Schiff-Viotto 1977, no. 260; Heath 1992, no. 1805(3).4

Failing for a second time to seduce Huon, the sultana accuses him of attempted rape; as a result he is condemned to be burned alive. That night Almansaris visits Huon in prison to offer him her hand and the sultan's throne. Meanwhile, Amanda rejects the sultan's conditions for sparing Huon's life; enraged, he condemns her also to the flames. But Oberon saves the lovers, whose constancy has brought about his reconciliation with Titania, and conveys them to France, where Huon regains his lands and the emperor's favour.

******

Nos. 244A, 248A.
Mary Balmanno.
LINES | ADDRESSED TO | THOMAS CROFTON CROKER, ESQ., F.S.A., | PRESIDENT OF THE ANTIQUARIAN SOCIETY OF NOVIOMAGUS, | BY MRS. BALMANNO, | ON HIS ACQUISITION OF | SHAKSPEARE'S GIMMEL RING. | [Vignette] | PRIVATELY PRINTED FOR THE PRESIDENT AND MEMBERS OF THE SOCIETY OF NOVIO-MAGUS, | BY J.D. TORREY, 18 SPRUCE STREET, NEW YORK, FEBRUARY 1857 (1/3 illus.).

PEN AND PENCIL. | BY | MRS. BALMANNO. | [Vignette] | NEW YORK: | D. APPLETON & CO., 348 BROADWAY. | — | 1858 (2/68 illus.).

The details below regarding the publishing history of Mary Balmanno's *Pen and Pencil* have been culled from the letters of her husband, Robert Balmanno, to his friend John Sartain of Philadelphia (Duyckinck collection, Manuscript Division, New York Public Library). Mary was 'So perfectly indifferent' to everything beyond the actual writing, that Balmanno handled all other matters pertaining to the publication of her book.

He initially expected the book 'to be out in 1855. 60 *cuts*!' (to Evart A. Duyckinck, 30 December 1854), but it was not until 14 March 1856 that Balmanno could report to Sartain that the book was to be published by 'Mʳ Russell Smith, Soho Sqʳᵉ.' and would 'very soon, if not already, be under the press'. On 22 September 1856, 'The long agony is over'. The book was to be printed by 'the best printer in NY *on his own hook* ... for bringing out the woodcuts ... he has an artist ... brought up by Viztelly of Fleet Street'. However, not long afterwards, printing had to be suspended due to 'the news of an expected Commercial Crisis in France & England' (19 November 1856). It was perhaps about this time that 'Putnam was obliged to abandon [*Pen and Pencil*], & other works'. While 'the Aˢ are to pay all expenses & one dollar per vol: Putnam was only to pay 75 cents' (3 September 1857).

Balmanno commented that the 300 pages of the book had cost him 'six or eight hundred *miles* of walking up stairs to Engravers ... and about Twelve hundred dollars hard cash for drawing & Engraving'. Although Balmanno did not expect the book to appear until at least April, the verso of page 299 is dated '1st JANUARY, 1858'.

244A. *Sir Huldbrand Beset by Spectres in the Enchanted Forest*, 1858
(Mary Balmanno, 'Undine,' Stanzas I-II)
(facing p. 231)

Wood engraving by James H. Richardson (fl. 1848-1880) and Thomas Cox Jr. (1831?-*post* 1860) of the firm of Richardson & Cox (1853-1859) from a drawing by Mary Balmanno derived from Fuseli's engraved illustration to *Oberon*
Inscription (bottom left): RICHARDSON = COX. SC.
Dimensions: ■ 11.8 x 6.2 cm | 4^{10}/16" x 2^7/16" (BL 12350.h.16) (1858)
Other locations: Cambridge Lib.5.88.257; DHW; Essick; Folger PS1059.B76P4;LC PS1059.B76P4; Newberry Y245.B21; NYPL NBG

Mary Balmanno has adapted one of Fuseli's illustrations for C.M. Wieland's *Oberon* and transferred it to *Undine* another romance by a different author (Friedrich de la Motte-Fouqué), to which Fuseli devoted eight drawings and two paintings, none of which were engraved (Schiff 1499, 1599-1565, 1822 + 2 not in Schiff).

Mary Balmanno's poem, describing Huldbrand's meeting with the 'wilful foster-child' of the old forester and his wife and telling how he rescues the maiden, while the hermit observes and smiles 'as in approval', is a very tame and truncated version (9 stanzas) of an episode in *Undine*.

This reversed version of *Huon and Sherasmin in the Cave on Mount Lebanon*, represents Sir Huldbrand, 'Ringstetten's youthful lord|A soldier from the stirrup to the crest,' making his way 'on milk-white courser|To an enchanted wood.' The figure of Sherasmin with his club has been replaced by phantom shapes among the branches of the trees. Stanza II continues:

> Amidst the leaves from morn till noon he rode,
> When sounds unearthly murmured on his ear,
> And phantom shapes, of wild and evil bode,
> Amongst the haunted boughs began to peer;
> Whereat the steed, oppressed with sudden fear,
> Across the forest with his rider flew;
> And soon had made a deep abyss his bier,
> But that a hermit old, all white of hue,
> His palely mantled form athwart the pathway
>   threw.

Mrs. Balmanno's poem closes with the celebration of Undine's marriage to the knight.

244A.

248A.

248A. *Shakespeare Embracing his Bride*, 1858
(Mary Balmanno, 'Shakespeare's Gimmel Ring,'
Stanza IX)
(p. 168)

Wood engraving by James H. Richardson (fl.
1848-1880) and Thomas Cox Jr. (1831?-*post*
1860) of the firm of Richardson & Son (1853-
1859) from a drawing by Mary Balmanno derived
from the engraving after Fuseli, illustrating her
poem 'Shakespeare's Gimmel-Ring'
Inscription (bottom left): RICHARDSON =
COX. SC.
Dimensions: ■ 12.0 x 5.3 cm | 4¾" x 2²/16" (BL
12350.h.16) (1858)
Other locations: Cambridge Lib.5.88.257; DHW;
Essick; Folger PS1059.B76P4; Newberry
Y245.B21; NYPL NBG

Variations:
I. Frame and signatures added: Folger (1857)
Inscription: RICHARDSON = COX. SC. |
(lower left): Fuseli invt.—M.B. delt.
Dimensions: ■ 15.4 x 5.5 cm | 6" x 2²/16"

This adaptation of Fuseli's *Huon Embraces
Rezia* retains only the two central figures and
provides a background of leafy trees. It represents
Shakespeare being reunited with his beloved
described in the poem's last stanza:

From such sweet musing see him start,
The boughs are drawn aside;
He clasps the maiden of his heart,
His long-loved promised bride.

✱✱✱✱✱

Nos. 256 - 259.
Joel Barlow.
THE COLUMBIAD, [1806] (4/4 unpublished
illus.).

The circumstances under which Fuseli's four
illustrations were solicited (1803) are unclear.
Fuseli had completed his assigned compositions
before Joel Barlow (1764-1812), the American
poet and diplomat, returned to the United States in
1804. The remaining subjects were to be
undertaken by another American, John Vanderlyn.
Vanderlyn, however, withdrew from the project
and the sumptuously printed *Columbiad*, published
in 1807 was embellished instead with ten
engravings after Robert Smirke.

The work had evolved (through 5 previous
editions) from Barlow's more modest
philosophical poem, *The Vision of Columbus*
(Hartford, Connecticut: 1787), which the poet
extensively revised in order to give it greater epic
elevation, reduce the religious element, and
sharpen his criticism of 'the mask of priesthood
and the mace of kings' which he condemned as
the 'agents of the woes of man'.

None of the engraved images is reversed from
the known originals.

256.

256. *The Inquisition, or Religious Fanaticism
Trampling Upon Truth*, [1806]
(IV, 201-224)

Unsigned stipple engraving by Moses Haughton
(1772 or 1774-1848) after the sketch in gouache at
the Art Institute of Chicago ([1806]; Schiff 1803)
Dimensions: 21.6 x 18.6 cm | 8½" x 7⁶/16" (BM
1863-5-9-39)
Other locations: V & A E.1200-A-1886
Lit.: Schiff 1342A (21.3 x ?16.3 cm), 1803; Antal
1956, 93, pl. 39B ('Religious Fanaticism attended
by Folly, Trampling upon Truth'); Boime 1987,
286, pl. 4.5

The illustration shows 'Gaunt Inquisition' (203) triumphantly raising over her head her 'flaming brand ... tipt with Sulphur' (208), while she plants her foot upon the breast of a woman lying in the same attitude as the sleeper in the *Nightmare*. This single figure, thus, becomes a powerful emblem of all the Inquisition's victims, whether 'Jews, Moors and Christians ... Dragg'd from a thousand jails' (215-216). In keeping with his stated rejection of 'horror and loathsomeness', Fuseli has deliberately omitted from his illustration the 'blood-nursed vulture' (204) and all the other 'various tools of torment' (205), except the crosses, listed by Barlow, i.e., 'Racks, wheels and ... faggots, stakes and strings' (206). As Fuseli tells us in his review of Roscoe's *Lorenzo de' Medici*, 'If you see only blood-tipped arrows, brain-dashed stones, excoriating knives, the artist, not the subject is detestable' (*Analytical Review*, XXIV, December 1796, 148-149). The face peering out from behind her skirts is to be seen as one of the Inquisition's 'spies with eye askance' (210) or as one of her "sly confessors with their secret scroll" (212).

257. *Caesar Crossing the Rubicon*, [1806]
(V, 385-404)

Unsigned stipple engraving by Moses Haughton (1772 or 1774-1848) after the painting in the Rust collection, Washington D.C. ([1806]; Schiff 1238)
Proof before letters
Dimensions: 21.0 x 16.0 cm | 8³/16" x 6⁵/16"
(BM 1863-5-9-41)
Other locations: V & A E.1200-C-1886
Lit.: Schiff 1342B (21.0 x 16.1 cm)

This passage, like the illustration from Book Eight, is representative of Barlow's attempt to achieve sublimity in his recast poem through the use of Homeric or epic similes. Fuseli's representations of such moral and metaphorical analogies to the main action are a staple of his Milton Gallery paintings (e.g. *Odysseus Between Scylla and Charybdis* or *Lapland Witches*)— although these were not translated to copper.

Fuseli illustrates the comparison drawn by Barlow between the endeavours of the American Congress to stem the violence of England and those of 'Rome's hoary Genius' to dissuade Caesar from passing the Rubicon. Fuseli's

257.

258.

illustration is dominated by the imposing figure of the god in the left foreground, standing in an attitude similar to that of Satan rallying his fallen angels 'with outstretcht arm and awful look'. The Miltonic overtones are reinforced by Barlow's reference to his 'stern brow ... worn by cares of state'. Undeterred by the warning, Caesar is shown waving his mounted legions across the river in defiance of Pompey and of the Roman senate, thereby unleashing the civil wars.

258. *Cruelty Reigning over the Prison Ship*, [1806]
(VI, 1-78)

Unsigned stipple engraving by Moses Haughton (1772 or 1774-1848) after the lost original
Dimensions: 21.2 x 16.2 cm | 8⁵/16" x 6²/16" (BM 1863-5-9-40)
Other locations: V & A E.1200-D-1886
Lit.: Schiff 1343A (21.3 x 16.3 cm); Boime 1987, 287

Book Six with its greatly expanded treatment of the American Revolution is the only new book of the revised poem; Barlow also portrays the British here in far harsher terms than anywhere else in the original versions. The passage illustrated by Fuseli is emblematic of 'the systematic and inflexible ... cruelties' of the British in the American Revolutionary war towards American prisoners, confined in unspeakable conditions on prison ships anchored off New York. However, Fuseli's more universalised representation of Cruelty, while tempering Barlow's specificity, is perhaps more powerful in its effect than his author's verses. In customary fashion, Fuseli eschews all overt depiction of 'loathsome' details in favour of a starker allegorical representation; a single scourge and a single length of chain draped over the bow replace Barlow's long list of instruments of torture. The '*eleven thousand*' American prisoners alleged to have died on one ship over a period of eighteen months are here metaphorized into a pair of imploring hands emerging from the 'tomb' of the ship's 'womb', while the Medusa-like female with great dugs and 'wings like thunder-clouds', attended by two grotesquely masked fiends, 'keeps with joy the register of death' and 'drinks every groan and treasures every sigh'.

259.

259. *Jason Stealing the Golden Fleece*, [1806]
(VIII, 94-130)

Unsigned stipple engraving by Moses Haughton (1772 or 1774-1848) after Fuseli's painting on millboard in the Department of Prints and Drawings of the British Museum ([1806]; Schiff 1239)
Dimensions: 21.3 x 16.6 cm | 8⁶/16" x 6½" (BM 1863-5-9-42)
Other locations: Private Collection, Melbourne; V&A E.1200-B-1886
Lit.: Schiff 1343B (21.1 x 16.6 cm)
Exh.: Florence 1979 (44)

Barlow's uses the theft of the golden fleece as a simile to illustrate how Freedom in the United States could also be lost by 'inattention'. See also Books Four (271-280) and Five (691-700).
    The Argonauts, led by Jason, have come to Colchis to win the legendary golden fleece. Jason will be helped by Medea, the king's daughter, who is shown administering a sleeping potion to the dragon, while Orpheus plays soothing music on his harp, and Jason seizes the fleece.

THE SPIRIT OF PLATO.

260.

260. *The Spirit of Plato*
(J. Milton, *Il Penseroso*, ll. 85-92)

Stipple engraving by Moses Haughton (1772 or
1774-1848) after Fuseli's lost original [1799-1800]
Inscription: Hʸ. Fuseli, Esqʳ. R.A. Pinxᵗ. | | Moses
Haughton sc. | THE SPIRIT OF PLATO. |

> Where I may. . . . . unsphere
> The spirit of Plato to unfold
> What worlds or what vast regions hold
> The immortal mind.
>
>   Il Penseroso.

Dimensions: ■ 41.4 x 50.2 cm | 16¼" x 19¾"
(BM 1850-10-14-883) (formerly collection of the
Earl of Harrowby)
Other locations: KHZ 1931/40 ('sc.' cropped
from right corner)
Lit.: Schiff 914 (41.0 x 50.2 cm); Schiff-Viotto
1977, no. 160, pl. 160¹; Hahn 1982, 194 (dated
as 'c. 1800'); *Letters*, 596

Variants:
I. Proof before letters: BM 1867.12.14.204

The engraving is listed in the catalogue of
Fuseli's 1827 sale (lot 24) as an 'unpublished
plate'. The passage it illustrates reads in full:

> Or let my Lamp at midnight hour,
> Be seen in some high lonely Tow'r
> Where I may oft outwatch the *Bear*,
> With thrice great *Hermes*, or unsphere
> The spirit of *Plato* to unfold
> What Worlds, or what vast Regions hold
> The immortal mind that hath forsook
> His mansion in this fleshly nook ...

The 'Tow'r' is Plato's 'acropolis of the soul'
and Isaiah's 'watchtower'. From here Milton
contemplates the constellation of the Great Bear
that never sets, which '*Hermes*' taught was a
symbol of perfection (M.Y. Hughes, 74, note).

******

No. 261.
THE | POETICAL WORKS | OF JOHN MILTON, | COMPLETE | IN TWO VOLUMES. | VOL. 1. [-VOL. II]. | = | PARADISE LOST. | [Vignette portrait] | MILTON. | LONDON. | PUBLISH'D BY W. SUTTABY, & B. CROSBY & Cº. STATIONERS COURT; | AND C. CORRALL, CHARING CROSS. | 1806. | CORRALL PRINTER (1/2 illus.).

[Cover]: THE | POETICAL WORKS | OF | JOHN MILTON, | COMPLETE IN TWO VOLUMES. | = | EMBELLISHED FROM PAINTINGS OF H. FUSELI, | ESQ. R.A. AND J. STOTHARD, ESQ. R.A. | ENGRAVED BY MR. A. RAIMBACH, AND | MR. F. ENGLEHEART. | — | VOL. I. [-VOL. II.] | — | LONDON: PUBLISHED BY W. SUTTABY, B. CROSBY | AND CO. SCATCHERD AND LETTER- | MAN, STATIONERS'-COURT; AND C. | CORRALL, CHARING CROSS. | 1806.

Paradise Lost was one of Suttaby's series of small-format volumes with engraved frontispiece and vignette title. A two-page list of titles bound in each vol., shows prices ranging from 8d. each for the Poetical Works of Gray and Goldsmith, to 4s. for Homer's *Iliad* or *Odyssey*. The Milton cost 2s.6d. per vol. The British Library copy has printed front and back covers.

261.

261. *The Birth of Sin*, 1806
(*Paradise Lost*, II, 746-758)
(Vol. I, facing title page)

Frontispiece engraved by Abraham Raimbach (1776-1843) after painting No. VI in the Milton Gallery ([1796-1799]; Schiff, Lost Work 34) (now Private Collection, London)
Imprint: Publish'd by W. Suttaby Aug. 1. 1806.
Inscription:

  All on a sudden miserable pain
  Surpris'd thee—

          page 46. |
Painted by Henry Fuseli RA. | | Engrav'd by Ab. Raimbach.
Dimensions (excl. lower panel): ■ 7.8 x 5.0 cm | $3^1/16$" x $1^{15}/16$"; ■ 7.9 x 5.1 cm | $3^2/16$" x 2"; (incl. lower panel): ■ 9.4 x 5.2 cm (BL 11626.a.31)
Other locations: DHW; Geneva Ariana 4696
Plate only: NYPL MEM.R.153re (p. 25)
Lit.: Schiff 1307 (7.6 x 5.0 cm); Collins Baker 1948, 105; Schiff 1963, 51, pl. 16
Exh.: Kansas City 1989 (7)

Sin intervenes to prevent Satan and Death from doing battle at Hell Gate, reminding Satan how, while he was still in heaven hatching his plots against God, she sprang fully formed out of his head, the crystallisation of Satan's festering lust and ambition. The revelation of Satan's incestuous relationship with Sin is part of Milton's carefully orchestrated scheme to undercut Satan's seeming heroism and show him in his true colours. In contrast, Fuseli and the Romantics prefer to see Satan as the Promethean hero of *Paradise Lost*.

No. 261A.
[Unidentified edition.]
[John Milton.]
[*PARADISE LOST*, n.d.]

261A. *The Birth of Sin*, 1821
(*Paradise Lost*, II, 746-758)

Re-issued engraving (1821) by Abraham Raimbach (1776-1843)
Imprint: Published March 1, 1821, by Suttaby & Cº. London.
Inscription:

  All on a sudden miserable pain
  Surpris'd thee_____

          page 46. |

Painted by Henry Fuseli RA||Engrav'd by Ab. Raimbach
Dimensions (excl.lettered panel): ■ 8.0 x 5.0 cm | 3²/16" x 2" (cut down inside frame) (DHW) (plate only)

******

No. 261B.
[Unidentified edition.]
[John Milton.]
[*PARADISE LOST*, n.d.]

261B.

261B. *The Birth of Sin*, [n.d.]
(*Paradise Lost*, II, 752-753)

Unsigned re-engraving perhaps by Abraham Raimbach (1776-1843) (design reversed)
Proof before letters
Dimensions: ■ 7.6 x 3.3 cm | 3" x 1⁷/16" (BM 1863-5-9-49)

******

Nos. 261C - 262.
John Milton.
PARADISE LOST|A POEM,|IN|TWELVE BOOKS,|BY| JOHN MILTON.|[Vignette]|
___*fairy elves,|Whose midnight revels, by a forest side|Or fountain, some belated peasant sees,|Or dreams he sees,*___|Book 1, pa. 23.|LONDON:|
PUBLISHED BY SUTTABY, EVANCE, AND FOX,|STATIONERS COURT, AND|

BALDWIN, CRADOCK & JOY, PATERNOSTER ROW.|1821.|CORRALL PRINTER (2/2 illus.).

261C. *The Birth of Sin*, 1821
(*Paradise Lost*, II, 752-753)
(facing the title page)

Frontispiece re-engraved by Andrew Duncan (1795-*post* 1849)
Imprint: Published by Suttaby & C°. London.| March 1. 1821.
Inscription: Painted by H. Fuseli R.A.||Engraved by A. Duncan.|THE BIRTH OF SIN.|

All on a sudden miserable pain
Surpris'd thee_____Book 2.pa.26.

Dimensions: ■ 7.9 x 5.0 cm | 3²/16" x 1¹⁵/16"; ▣ 8.3 x 5.5 cm | 3¼" x 2²/16" (Bodleian 2799.f.571)
Other locations: Cambridge 8700.e.200; Illinois 821.M64.M1⁵

Variant:
I. Proof before letters (conjointly with No. **262** below): BM 1863-5-9-28

262.

262. *The Shepherd's Dream*, 1821
(*Paradise Lost*, I, 781-784)
(title page)

Title vignette engraved by Andrew Duncan (1795-*post* 1849)

Imprint: London. | Published by Suttaby, Evance and Fox, | Stationers Court, and | Baldwin, Cradock & Joy, Paternoster Row. | 1821. | Corrall Printer.

Inscription: Painted by H, Fuseli R.A. | | Engraved by A. Duncan. |

> —fairy elves,
> Whose midnight revels, by a forest side
> Or fountain, some belated peasant sees,
> Or dreams he sees,— Book 1, pa. 23.

Dimensions: ■ 5.0 x 6.0 cm | 1¹⁵/₁₆" x 2⁵/₁₆" (Bodleian 2799.f.571)

Other locations: Cambridge 8700.e.200; Illinois 821M64.M1.1821⁵

Variants:

I. Proof before letters (conjointly with No. **261B**): BM 1863-5-9-28 (Sheet=13.0 cm)
Inscription (at bottom right, in pencil): 20 Janʸ 1821
Lit.: Schiff 1308 (9.0 x 6.5 cm) (engraver given as 'Abraham Raimbach')

******

263.

263. *Adam Resolved to Share the Fate of Eve*, 1806
(J. Milton, *Paradise Lost*, IX, 953-954, 958-960)

Engraved in stipple by Moses Haughton (1772 or 1774-1848), with aquatint by Frederick Christian Lewis (1779-1856) after Fuseli's lost painting No. XX in the Milton Gallery

Inscription: Henry Fuseli RA Pinxᵗ. Moses Haughton Sculpᵗ. and Published by them as the Act directs Janʸ. 20. 1806, Somerset House, Strand, London. | | Aquatinta by F.C. Lewis. |

ADAM resolved to share the fate of EVE; | (the
Guardian Angels leaving the Garden) |

    —--if death
    Consort with thee, death is to me as life;
    Our state cannot be sever'd, we are one,
    One flesh; to lose thee were to lose myself.
    So Adam————Par. Lost. Book 9. v. 953-8.

Dimensions: ■ 52.3 x 38.6 cm | 20⁹/16" x 15²/16"
(BM 1861-5-18-159)
Other locations: BM 1979.u.1248; ETH 417 (all
but 1st line of inscription cropped); Fitzwilliam
K.37; V & A E.1199-C-1886
Lit.: Schiff 898 (52.5 x 38.5 cm); Schiff 1963,
74, pl. 33; Hofstätter 1965, 192, pl. 74; Schiff-
Viotto 1977, no. 140, pl. 140¹; *Letters*, 346;
Weinglass 1991, 302
Exh.: Zurich 1941 (139); Florence 1979 (43)

Variants:

I. Before letters: BM 1852-11-16-549
II. Before all letters (lacking imprint): BM
1931-5-11-60
Inscription: H. FUSELI. R.A. PINXᵀ. | | M.
HAUGHTON. SCULPᵀ.
Other locations: Essick; KHZ 1931/39

Despairing at the thought of losing Eve after she
has eaten the apple, Adam 'scrupl'd not to eat, |
Against his better knowledge, not deceiv'd, | But
fondly overcome with Female charm' (997-999).

Fuseli considered that he had 'Contrived ... to
give Sentiment and modesty to passion', and that
the Guardian Angels 'in the airy distance' added
something sublime (to Roscoe, 5 June 1797). The
illustration also typifies (in Jeffery Daniels'
phrase) Fuseli's frequent 'Sado-Mannerist'
representations, drawn from history, literature and
mythology, of men in thrall to cruel tormentresses
(e.g. Huon and Almansaris, Nos. **254-255**).

263A. *Adam Resolved to Share the Fate of Eve*,
[n.d.]

Re-engraved on steel in reduced form from
Haughton's print by an unknown engraver
Proof (India paper) before all letters (imprint
only)
Imprint: Published by J. Hogarth, New Road, Sᵗ.
Pancras.
Dimensions: ■ 12.0 x 9.0 cm | 4¾" x 3½"
(V & A E.329-1941)

******

No. 263B.
G. Hamilton.
THE | ENGLISH SCHOOL | A SERIES OF | THE
MOST APPROVED PRODUCTIONS | IN |
PAINTING AND SCULPTURE; | EXECUTED
BY BRITISH ARTISTS | FROM THE DAYS OF
HOGARTH TO THE PRESENT TIME; |
SELECTED, ARRANGED, AND
ACCOMPANIED WITH DESCRIPTIVE AND |
EXPLANATORY NOTICES IN ENGLISH AND
FRENCH, | BY G. HAMILTON. | ENGRAVED
IN OUTLINE UPON STEEL. | — | VOL. 1.
[-VOL. 4.] | — | LONDON. | CHARLES TILT, 86,
FLEET STREET. | — | 1831 [-1832]. (10/288
illus.).

[ÉCOLE | ANGLAISE, | RECUEIL | DE
TABLEAUX, STATUES ET BAS-RELIEFS |
DES PLUS CÉLÈBRES ARTISTES ANGLAIS, |
DEPUIS LE TEMPS D'HOGARTH JUSQU'À
NOS JOURS, | GRAVÉ A L'EAU-FORTE SUR
ACIER; | ACCOMPAGNÉ | DE NOTICES
DESCRIPTIVES ET HISTORIQUES, | EN
FRANÇAIS ET EN ANGLAIS, | PAR G.
HAMILTON, | ET PUBLIÉ SOUS SA
DIRECTION. | — | VOL. 1 [-TOME 4] | — | À
PARIS. | CHEZ M. HAMILTON, GRANDE RUE
DES BATIGNOLLES, N° 50, | PRÈS LA
BARRIÈRE DE CLICHY; | ET CHEZ AUDOT,
LIBRAIRE, RUE DES MAÇONS-SORBONNE,
N° 11. | — | 1831].

SELECT SPECIMENS | OF | BRITISH
ARTISTS, | FROM THE DAYS | OF HOGARTH
TO THE PRESENT TIME; | OR | SERIES OF 72
ENGRAVINGS OF THEIR MOST | APPROVED
PRODUCTIONS. | EXECUTED ON STEEL IN
THE FIRST STYLE OF OUTLINE, |
SELECTED, ARRANGED, AND
ACCOMPANIED WITH DESCRIPTIVE AND
EXPLANATORY | NOTICES IN ENGLISH AND
FRENCH, | BY G. HAMILTON. | PARIS: |
BAUDRY'S EUROPEAN LIBRARY, | 9, RUE
DU COQ, NEAR THE LOUVRE. | — | 1837
(?/72 illus.).

[CHEFS-D'OEUVRE | DES | ARTISTES
ANGLAIS, | DEPUIS | HOGARTH JUSQU'A NOS
JOURS, | OU | SUITE DE 72 GRAVURES DE
LEURS PRODUCTIONS | LES PLUS
ESTIMÉES, | SOIGNEUSEMENT GRAVEES AU
TRAIT SUR ACIER, | CHOISIS, MIS EN
ORDRE ET ACCOMPAGNÉ DE NOTES
DESCRIPTIVES ET EXPLICATIVES | EN

ANGLAIS ET EN FRANÇAIS, | PAR G. HAMILTON. | PARIS, | BAUDRY, LIBRAIRIE EUROPEENNE, | 9, RUE DU COQ, PRÈS LE LOUVRE. | — | 1837].
GALLERY | OF | BRITISH ARTISTS, | FROM THE DAYS | OF HOGARTH TO THE PRESENT TIME, | OR | SERIES OF 288 ENGRAVINGS OF THEIR MOST | APPROVED PRODUCTIONS. | EXECUTED ON STEEL IN THE FIRST STYLE OF OUTLINE, | SELECTED, ARRANGED, AND ACCOMPANIED WITH DESCRIPTIVE AND EXPLANATORY NOTICES | IN ENGLISH AND FRENCH, | BY G. HAMILTON. | — | IN FOUR VOLUMES. | — | VOL. I. [-VOL.IV.] | PARIS, | BAUDRY'S EUROPEAN LIBRARY, | 9, RUE DU COQ, NEAR THE LOUVRE. | 1837, 1839 (10/288 illus.).

[GALERIE | DES | ARTISTES ANGLAIS, |

DEPUIS | HOGARTH JUSQU'A NOS JOURS, | OU | SUITE DE 288 GRAVURES DE LEURS PRODUCTIONS | LES PLUS ESTIMÉES, | SOIGNEUSEMENT GRAVÉES AU TRAIT SUR ACIER, | CHOISIE, MISE EN ORDRE ET ACCOMPAGNÉE DE NOTES DESCRIPTIVES ET EXPLICATIVES | EN ANGLAIS ET EN FRANÇAIS, | PAR G. HAMILTON. | EN QUATRE VOLUMES. | VOL. I. [-VOL. IV.] | PARIS, | BAUDRY, LIBRAIRIE EUROPEENNE, 9, RUE DU COQ, PRÈS LE LOUVRE. | — | 1837, 1839.

For the other illustrations in this work, see also Nos. **117D-119D, 123D, 226A, 285A, 288A, 293A, 298A, 299B**

For further publication details, see Nos. **117D-119D, 226A**.

264.

265.

263B. *Adam Resolved to Share the Fate of Eve*, 1832

(John Milton, *Paradise Lost*, IX, 953-960)
(Vol. IV, Plate No. 261)

Outline engraving on steel by Normand fils, i.e., Louis-Marie Normand (1789-1874)
Inscription: Fuseli. | | Normand fils. | ADAM RESOLVED TO SHARE THE FATE OF EVE. | ADAM PROMET A EVE DE PARTAGER SON SORT.
Dimensions: ■ 11.2 x 8.2 cm | 4⁷/16" x 3¼";
■ 11.5 x 8.6 cm | 4⁹/16" x 3⁶/16" (BL 7812.a.19)
Other locations: BL 1422.a.25; BL 1267.a.19(Gallery 1837);SB Bern Litt.LI.3162 (Gallery 1837) (Vol. II); DHW (1839); Essick; Lausanne AVA 3356; NYPL 3-MAMR (Gallery 1837); YCBA N6764.H35

******

264. *Milton Dictating to his Daughter*, 1806

Stipple engraving by Moses Haughton (1772 or 1774-1848) after a lost version of painting No. XL in the Milton Gallery ([1793-1796]; Schiff 922)
Inscription: Painted by Henʸ. Fuseli R.A. Engraved by Moses Haughton & Published by them as the Act directs Dec. 7. 1806. Somerset House. Strand, London. | MILTON DICTATING TO HIS DAUGHTER. [*open letters*] |

[*left*]
Τὸν πέρι Μουσ᾽ ἐφίλησε, δίδου δ᾽ἀγαθόν τε, κακόν τε,
Ὀφθαλμῶν μὲν ἄμερσε, δίδου δ᾽ἡδεῖαν ἀοιδήν. Page 257. lines 9 & 10. |
[*right*]
Dear to the Muse! who gave his days to flow With mighty blessings, mix'd with mighty woe:

With clouds of darkness quench'd his visual
  ray,
But gave him skill to raise the lofty lay.

Dimensions: ■ 51.5 x 41.8 cm | 20⁵/16" x 16⁷/16"
(BM 1861-5-18-157)
Other locations: Ashmolean (inscription trimmed);
BM T.16.9; Essick; Fitzwilliam K.36
Lit.: Schiff 922 (51.6 x 41.8); Schiff 1963, 110f.,
pl. 61; Schiff-Viotto 1977, no. 174, pl. 174¹

The quotation is from the *Odyssey*, VIII, 63-64,
and refers to blind Demodocus. It was frequently
applied to Milton (see *The Odyssey*, trans. A.
Pope, ed. Gilbert Wakefield, 1796, II, 176).

******

265. *Friar Puck (The Friar's Lantern)*, 1806
(J. Milton, *L'Allegro*, 104; *Paradise Lost*, IX,
634, 638-42)

Stipple engraving by Moses Haughton (1772 or
1774-1848) after painting No. XXXI in the Milton
Gallery (1794-1796; Schiff 912), now Victoria
University, Manchester
Inscription: Painted by Hʸ. Fuseli R.A. Engraved
by Moˢ. Haughton, and Published by them as the
Act directs. Decʳ. 23. 1806. Royal Academy,
London. | **Frier Puck.** | **L'Allegro.** |
  —as when a wand'ring sire [*sic*]
  Which oft, they say, some evil Spirit attends,
  Hovering and blazing with delusive light,
  Misleads th' amaz'd night-wand'rer from his
    way
  To bogs and mires, and oft through pond or
    pool,
  There swallow'd up and lost, from succour far.
      Vid. P. Lost, Book IX, v. 634.

Dimensions: ■ 29.5 x 24.0 cm | 11⁹/16" x 9⁹/16"
(BM 1861-5-18-155)
Other locations: BM 1979.u.1246; KHZ 1931/41;
KHZ 1940/120; V & A E.272-1889
Lit.: Schiff 913 (?51.6 x 41.8 cm); Schiff 1963,
94, pl. 51; Tomory 1972, pl. 81; Schiff-Viotto
1977, no. 155

Fuseli's quotation comes from *Paradise Lost*,
but the illustration is more in keeping with the
Allegro, his given source: here the will-o'-the
wisp is merely another mischievous country spirit;
in *Paradise Lost* he is used to demonstrate how
Satan exploits reason's 'delusive Light' to seduce
'credulous' Eve. A similar comparison occurs in
Lord Rochester's *Satire Against Mankind* (11-30).

No. 265A.
John Young.
A | CATALOGUE | OF | PICTURES BY BRITISH
ARTISTS, | IN THE POSSESSION OF | SIR
JOHN FLEMING LEICESTER, BART. | WITH
ETCHINGS FROM THE WHOLE
COLLECTION. | INCLUDING THE | PICTURES
IN HIS GALLERY AT TABLEY HOUSE,
CHESHIRE; | EXECUTED BY PERMISSION OF
THE PROPRIETOR; | AND ACCOMPANIED |
WITH HISTORICAL AND BIOGRAPHICAL
NOTICES. | — | BY | JOHN YOUNG, |
ENGRAVER IN MEZZOTINTO TO HIS
MAJESTY, | AND | KEEPER OF THE BRITISH
INSTITUTION. | = | LONDON: | = | PRINTED BY
W. BULMER AND W. NICOL, CLEVELAND-
ROW, ST. JAMES'S. | PUBLISHED BY THE
PROPRIETOR, NO. 65, UPPER CHARLOTTE-
STREET, FITZROY-SQUARE; | AND SOLD
ALSO BY R. JENNINGS, BOOKSELLER IN
THE POULTRY; | G. AND W. NICOL, PALL-
MALL; MOLTENO, PALL-MALL; CARPENTER,
BOND-STREET; | ACKERMAN, STRAND;
COLNAGHI, | COCKSPUR STREET; AND
LLOYDS, HARLEY STREET. | — | APRIL 2,
1821 (2/69 illus.).
For the other illustration in this work, see No.
298. For the edition of 1825, see also **Addenda**.

265A. *Friar Tuck*, 1821
(J. Milton, *Paradise Lost*, IX, 634, 638-42)
(facing p. 6; Plate No. 13)

Unsigned outline engraving by Normand fils, i.e.,
Louis-Marie Normand (1789-1874)
Inscription (top centre): N°. 13. | (bottom):
FUSELI.
Dimensions: ■ 8.9 x 7.5 cm | 3½" x 2¹⁵/16";
■ 9.1 x 7.7 cm | 3⁹/16" x 3" (BL 561.d.12/2)
Other locations: Ashmolean 908.2 Lei; DHW;
Newberry W111.D48; Witt

Variants:
I. Proof (India paper): BL 59.e.3
Other locations: DHW (H=38.6 cm)
II. Title line added: BM 1859-12-10-30
Inscription (top centre): N°. 13. | (bottom):
FUSELI. | LEICESTER GALLERY

Young notes that while this 'ideal being' is
known from both Shakespeare and Milton (hence
'Friar Puck; or Robin Goodfellow'), in Fuseli's
delineation he is closer to Shakespeare's sprite.

266.

266. *Puck Basking Asleep Before the Country Hearth (The Lubber Fiend)*, [n.d.]
(J. Milton, *L'Allegro*, 11. 101-112)

Unsigned stipple engraving (Proof) by Moses Haughton (1772 or 1774-1848) after Fuseli's lost painting No. XXXII in the Milton Gallery [1795]
Dimensions: ■ 23.6 x 29.4 cm │ 9⁶/16" x 11⁹/16"
(BM 1849-5-12-258)
Lit.: Schiff 911 (?29.3 x 29.7); Schiff 1963, 91, 94, pl. 48; Schiff-Viotto 1977, no. 156, pl. 156¹; *Letters*, 127, 141, 142;
Exh.: Hamburg 1974 (103); London 1975 (105); Paris 1975 (121)

The illustration shows the 'Lubber Fiend' or nocturnal household drudge of folklore, referred to by Fuseli as '*Robin Goodfellow from the Allegro*' (cp. note to No. **265A** above),

'… stretch'd out all the Chimney's length, Bask[*ing*] at the fire his hairy strength',

after earning the bowl of cream traditionally set out by the householder to reward him for his labours. Fuseli's endeavour in this representation was to express 'an Ideal nature of Child and Man at once' (to Roscoe, 29 October 1795).

✳✳✳✳✳✳

Nos. 267 - 274.
William Cowper.
POEMS, │ BY │ WILLIAM COWPER, │ OF THE INNER TEMPLE, ESQ. │ IN TWO VOLUMES. │ VOL. I. [VOL. II.] │ *Sicut aquae tremulum labris ubi lumen ahenis │ Sole repercussum, aut radiantis imagine lunae, │ Omnia pervolitat late loca, jamque sub auras │ Erigitur, summique ferit laquearia tecti. │ VIRG. Æn. viii. │ So water, trembling in a polish'd vase, │ Reflects the beam that plays upon its face; │ The sportive light, uncertain where it falls, │ Now strikes the roof, now flashes on the walls.* │ = │ A NEW EDITION. │ = │ LONDON: │ PRINTED FOR J. JOHNSON, IN ST. PAUL'S CHURCHYARD, │ BY T. BENSLEY, BOLT COURT, FLEET STREET. │ 1806 (8/8 illus.).

…LONDON: │ PRINTED FOR J. JOHNSON, IN ST. PAUL'S CHURCHYARD, │ BY T. BENSLEY, BOLT COURT, FLEET STREET. │ 1808.

… │ — │ A NEW EDITION. │ — │ LONDON: │ PRINTED FOR J. JOHNSON AND CO. │ ST. PAUL'S CHURCH-YARD. │ 1811.

[Title on spine]: COWPER'S │ POEMS, │ WITH │ FUSELI'S DESIGNS. │ = │ Demy Paper, │ Price 1l.6s. │ Volume I.

The edition was advertised as 'Printing' in November 1806, but was not published until July 1807 (Russell 1963, 76). Both large-paper and demy copies were available with (32s./24s.) and without plates (24s./18s.).

Fuseli thought 'Cowper the best of all the Poets of his period; above Hayley &c. & even Darwin. He had imagery and his stile was more perfect and pure' (*Farington,* VI, 2040; 28 May 1803).

William Cowper (1731-1800) shared Fuseli's fascination with Homer and Milton. Although the two men never met or communicated directly, Fuseli thoroughly revised Cowper's translation of the *Iliad* and part of the *Odyssey.* Fuseli's Milton Gallery was at one stage linked with plans for a splendid edition of Milton, to be published by Joseph Johnson, edited by Cowper and illustrated by Fuseli, but the scheme was undercut by the recurrence of Cowper's insanity, and in 1794 Boydell published just such an edition with illustrations by Richard Westall. Albeit Fuseli admired Cowper, his illustrations, with their 'twist towards the voluptuous' (Antal), often reflect a different perspective on the world than Cowper intended.

267. *The Poet's Vision*, 1807
(Vol. I, facing the title page)

Frontispiece engraved by Abraham Raimbach (1776-1843) after Fuseli's painting in the Senn collection, Basel (1806-1807; Schiff 1229).
Imprint: Pub. by J. Johnson London March 1. 1807.
Inscription (top centre): **The Poet's vision.** |
(right): Frontispiece Vol. I. | (bottom): H. Fuseli RA. pinx^t. | | Raimbach sculp^t. | **Sing the Sofa.**
Dimensions: ■ 12.6 x 9.0 cm | 4^{15}/16" x 3^1/16" (BL G.12944) (H=24.4 cm)
Other locations: BL 78.f.18 (1811) (H=24.5 cm); DHW (1808) (H=21.9 cm); DHW (1808) (H=22.2 cm); Dörrbecker (1808); Essick; KHZ 1940/119; NYPL NCL; Princeton Ex 3693.7.1811 c.2; Yale 1978.1002 (1808); ZBZ 1220 (not seen)
Plate only: V & A E.1201-G-1886
Lacking plate: Huntington 425904; Princeton Ex 3693.7.1806a
Lit.: Schiff 1329 (12.6 x 9.0 cm); Russell 1963, nos. 96, 99, 105; Schiff-Viotto 1977, no. 261; Weinglass 1978, 80; *Letters,* 354.

267.

267A.

Variants:

I. Proof before all letters (scratched signatures only) (India paper): BM 1853-12-10-544
Inscription (scratched letters): H. Fuseli R.A. pinx.||A. Raimbach sculp

Raimbach was paid 25 guineas for each of the two plates he engraved for this work (Joseph Johnson to Raimbach, 8 November 1806).

The illustration shows Cowper, sleeping on his sofa, being summoned to his 'Task' by the hovering muse and the smiling figure personifying 'Phantasy'. A copy of the *Iliad* stands at the foot of the sofa, open at the first word of the Greek text: 'MHNIN' (Wrath). The crouching mouse is emblematic of Smintheus-Apollo, the 'Mouse-god', and refers back to the *Iliad*.

******

267A. *The Poet's Vision (Unused design)*, [1807]

Proof (India paper) by anonymous engraver.
Perhaps unused design for frontispiece.
Dimensions: ■ 10.7 x 7.6 cm | 4³/16" x 3" (BM 1865-10-14-136)
Lit.: Schiff 1337 (10.8 x 7.6 cm)

******

268. *Virtue Reclaiming Youth from the Arms of Vice*, 1807
(*The Progress of Error*, ll. 71-72)
(Vol. I, facing p. 44)

Engraved by William Bromley (1769-1842) after the painting in the Ulrich collection, Zurich (1806-1807: Schiff 1230).
Imprint: Pub. by J. Johnson London March 1. 1807.
Inscription (top centre): Virtue reclaiming Youth &c.|(right): Vol. I P. 44|(bottom): H. Fuseli R.A. pinx'.||Bromley sculp'.|

    Is this the rugged path, the steep ascent,
    That virtue points to?_____

Dimensions: ■ 12.6 x 8.6 cm | 5⁷/16" x 3⁶/16" (BL G. 12944)
Other locations: BL 78.f.18 (1811) (H=24.5 cm); DHW (1808) (H=21.9 cm); DHW (1808) (H=22.2 cm); Dörrbecker (1808); Essick; NYPL NCL; Princeton Ex 3693.7.1811 c.2; Yale 1978.1002 (1808); ZBZ 1220 (not seen)
Plate only: V & A E.1201-A-1886

Is this the rugged path, the steep ascent,
That virtue points to?

268.

— folly ever has a vacant stare,
A simpering countenance, and a trifling air,
But innocence sedate, serene, erect,
Delights us, by engaging our respect.

269.

Lacking plate: Huntington 425904; Princeton Ex3693.7.1806a

Lit.: Schiff 1330 (12.6 x 8.6 cm); Russell 1963, nos. 96, 99, 105; Tomory 1972, pl. 142; Schiff-Viotto 1977, no. 262; Boerlin-Brodbeck 1981, 66; *Letters*, 354

Exh.: Kansas City 1982 (58).

Variants:

I. Proof before letters (India paper): BM 1849-5-12-232

Bromley was paid 25 guineas for each of the two plates he engraved (Joseph Johnson to Abraham Raimbach, 8 November 1806).

Schiff points out that in this illustration, modelled on the allegory of 'Hercules at the Crossroads', the features of the young man comfortably ensconced in the arms of Vice and waving away Virtue, bear a remarkable (coincidental and prescient) resemblance to Lord Byron, soon to establish his reputation throughout Europe as the 'genial immoralist'.

269. *A Dressing Room*, 1807
(*The Progress of Error*, 11. 205-208)
(Vol. I, facing p. 51)

Engraved by Richard Rhodes (1765-1838) after Fuseli's painting in the Ganz collection, Chicago (1806-1807; Schiff 1231).
Imprint: Pub. by J. Johnson London March 1. 1807.
Inscription (top centre): A Dressing room. |
(right): Vol. I. P. 51 | (bottom): H. Fuseli R.A. pinxᵗ. | | Rhodes sculpᵗ. |

    _____folly ever has a vacant stare,
  A simpering countenance, and a trifling air;
  But innocence, sedate, serene erect,
  Delights us, by engaging our respect.

Dimensions: ■ 12.4 x 8.7 cm | 5¹⁴/16" x 3⁷/16" (BL G. 12944)
Other locations: BL 78.f.18 (1811) (H=24.5 cm); DHW (1808) (H=21.9 cm); DHW (1808) (H=22.2 cm); Dörrbecker; Essick; NYPL NCL; Princeton Ex 3693.7.1811 c.2; Yale 1978.1002 (1808); ZBZ 1220
Lacking plate: Huntington 425904; Princeton Ex 3693.7.1806a
Lit.: Schiff 1331 (12.4 x 8.7 cm); Russell 1963, nos. 96, 99, 105; Hagstrum 1964, 68, pl. XLIB Schiff-Viotto 1977, no. 263; Weinglass 1991, 307

Variants:

I. Proof before letters (India paper): BM 1853.12.10.545
II. Before all letters (lacking Vol. and page no.): V & A E.1201-H-1886

The illustration juxtaposes the two simpering society ladies with their 'trifling air', representing 'Folly', and the 'serene' and 'erect' young woman in her simple dress, representing 'Innocence', who 'engag[es] our respect'.

A Mother with her Family in the Country.

The fruits that hang on pleasures flow'ry stem
Whate'er enchants them are no snares to them.

Pub. by J. Johnson London March 1807.

270.

270. *A Mother With Her Family In the Country*, 1807
(*Retirement*, ll. 179-180)
(Vol. I, facing p. 276)

Engraved by Richard Rhodes (1765-1835) after the painting in the Hanhart collection, Zurich (1806-1807; Schiff 1232).
Imprint: Pub. by J. Johnson London March 1. 1807.
Inscription (top): A Mother with her Family in the Country. | | (top right): Vol. I. P. 276. | (bottom): H. Fuseli R.A. Pinxᵗ. | | R. Rhodes Sculpᵗ. |
  The fruits that hang on pleasures flow'ry stem
  Whate'er enchants them, are no snares to them.

271.   **272.**

Dimensions: ■ 12.7 x 8.6 cm | 5' x 3⁶/16"
(BL G. 12944)
Other locations: BL 78.f.18 (1811)(H=24.5 cm);
DHW (1808) (H=21.9 cm); DHW (1808)
(H=22.3 cm); Dörrbecker; Essick; NYPL NCL;
Princeton Ex 3693.7.1811 c2; Yale 1978.1002
(1808); ZBZ 1220
Lacking plate: Huntington 425904; Princeton Ex
3693.7.1806a
Lit.: Schiff 1332 (12.7 x 8.6 cm); Schiff-Viotto
1977, no. 264; Weinglass 1991, 307

Variants:
I. Proof before all letters (signatures only)
(India paper): BM 1853.12.10.562
II. Proof before all letters (lacking Vol. and
page no.): V & A E.1201-E-1886

271. *The Negro Revenged*, 1807
(*The Negro's Complaint*, ll. 33-36)
(Vol. I, facing p. 375)

Engraved by Abraham Raimbach (1776-1843)
after Fuseli's painting formerly in the Hürlimann
collection, and now in the Kunsthaus Zurich
(1806-1807; Schiff 1233)
Imprint:Pub.by J.Johnson London March 1. 1807.

Inscription (top centre): The Negro revenged|
(right): Vol. I. P. 375.|(bottom): H. Fuseli R.A.
pinxᵗ.||Raimbach sculpᵗ.|

   Hark! he answers___Wild tornadoes,
   Strewing yonder sea with wrecks;
   Wasting towns, plantations, meadows,
   Are the voice, with which he speaks.

Dimensions: ■ 12.7 x 9.1 cm | 5' x 3⁹/16" (BL
G. 12944)
Other locations: BL 78.f.18 (1811)(H=24.5);
DHW (1808)(H=21.9 cm); DHW (1808)(H=22.2
cm); Essick; Dörrbecker; NYPL NCL; Princeton
Ex 3693.7.1811 c.2; Yale 1978.1002; ZBZ 1220
Plate only: BM 1847-2-4-7; Huntington 131211;
Lucerne; NYPL R153re, p. 53; V & A E.1201-B-
1886
Lacking plate: Huntington 425904; Princeton Ex
3693.7.1806a
Lit.: Schiff 1333 (12.7 x 9.1 cm); Antal 1956,
124; Russell 1963, nos. 96, 99, 105; Schiff-Viotto
1977, no. 265; *Letters*, 354; Boime 1987, 304-
306, pl. 4.15

Variants:
I. Proof before all letters (signatures only):
NYPL R153re, p. 52

Inscription: H. Fuseli R.A. pinx.||A: Raimbach sculp

Other locations: NYPL MEM.R153rm (facing p. 30)

Joseph Johnson asked Raimbach to engrave 'the remaining picture for Cowper' on 8 November 1806. He was paid 25 guineas.

Fuseli shows the African slave and his wife, 'magnified ... to the superhuman stature ... previously reserved for his mythical heroes' (Boime), watching the slave-ship go down, sunk as an act of divine retribution against the evils of the slave trade.

272. *Mad Kate*, 1807
(*The Task*, I, 534-556)
(Vol. II, facing the title page)

Frontispiece engraved by William Bromley (1769-1842) after Fuseli's painting in the Goethe-Museum, Frankfurt a/M (1806-1807; Schiff 1234).
Imprint: Pub. by J. Johnson London March 1. 1807.
Inscription (top centre): Kate.|(right): Frontispiece Vol. II.|H. Fuseli R.A. pinx^t.|| Bromley sculp^t.|

_____Kate is crazed.

Dimensions: ■ 12.5 x 8.6 cm | 4^{15}/16" x 3^6/16" (BL g. 12945)
Other locations: BL 78.f.19 (1811) (H=24.5 cm); DHW (1808)(H=21.9 cm);DHW (1808)(H=22.2 cm); Dörrbecker; Essick; NYPL NCL; Princeton Ex 3693.7.1811 c.2; Yale 1978.1002 (1808); ZBZ 1221
Plate only: V & A E.1201-C-1886
Lacking plate: Huntington 425904; Princeton Ex 3693.7.1806a
Lit.: Schiff 1334 (12.5 x 8.7 cm); Russell 1963, nos. 96, 99, 105; Tomory 1972, 178; Schiff-Viotto 1977, no. 266; Altick 1986, 413; P. Martin, *Mad Women in Romantic Writing*, 1987, 19-20

Variants:
I. Proof before letters (India paper): BM 1849-5-12-233
II. Proof before all letters (lacking Vol. and page nos.): V & A E.1201-I-1886
Inscription (top): Kate.|(bottom): H. Fuseli R.A. pinx^t.||Bromley sculp^t. (cropped?)

One of the most important and popular examples of the Romantic sentimentalised madwoman, the tale of Cowper's Mad Kate, the serving maid, whose lover had abandoned her and then died at sea, is told in the following lines:

Her fancy follow'd him through foaming waves
To distant shores; and she would sit and weep
At what a sailor suffers; fancy too,
Delusive most where warmest wishes are,
Would oft anticipate his glad return,
And dream of transports she was not to know.
She heard the doleful tidings of his death—
And never smil'd again! and now she roams
The dreary waste, there spends the livelong day,
And there, unless when charity forbids,
The livelong night. A tatter'd apron hides
Worn as a cloak, and hardly hides, a gown
More tatter'd still; and both but ill conceal
A bosom heav'd with never-ceasing sighs.
She begs an idle pin of all she meets,
And hoards them in her sleeve; but needful food,
Though press'd with hunger oft, or comelier clothes,
Though pinch'd with cold, asks never.—Kate is craz'd.

273.

273. *The Newspaper in the Country*, 1807
(*The Task*, IV, 30-33)
(Vol. II, facing p. 140)

Engraved by James Neagle (1769?-1822) after the painting in the Benzinger collection, Geneva (1806-1807; Schiff 1235).
Imprint: Pub. by J. Johnson London, March 1. 1807.
Inscription (top centre): The Newspaper in the Country. | (right): Vol. II P. 140. | (bottom): H. Fuseli R.A. pinx^t. | | Neagle Sculp^t. |

_____The grand debate,
The popular harrangue, the tart reply,
The logic and the wisdom and the wit,
And the loud laugh_____I long to know them all;

Dimensions: ■ 12.5 x 8.5 cm | 4^{14}/16" x 3^6/16" (BL G.12945)
Other locations: BL 78.f.19 (1811) (H=24.5 cm); DHW (1808) (H=21.9 cm); DHW (1808) (H=22.2 cm); Dörrbecker (1808); Essick; NYPL NCL (Cowper); Princeton Ex 3693.7.1811 c.2; Yale 1978.1002 (1808); ZBZ 1221 (not seen)
Plate only: V & A 1201-D-1886
Lacking plate: Huntington 425904; Princeton Ex 3693.7.1806a
Lit.: Schiff 1335 (12.5 x 8.5 cm); Leigh Hunt, *Autobiography*, 1872, I, 224; Antal 1956, p. 124; Russell 1963, nos. 96, 99, 105; Tomory 1972, pl. 212; Schiff-Viotto 1977, no. 267; Altick 1986, 412
Exh.: Kansas City 1982 (60)

Variants:
I. Proof before all letters (scratched signatures only) (India paper): BM 1849-5-12-231
Inscription (scratched letters): H. Fuseli pinxit | | I Neagle Sc.

The following supplement the inscription:

Now stir the fire, and close the shutters fast,
Let fall the curtains, wheel the sofa round,
And while the bubbling and loud hissing urn
Throws up a steamy column, and the cups,
That cheer but not inebriate, wait on each,
So let us welcome peaceful ev'ning in.

Commenting on the illustrations for Cowper, Leigh Hunt asserts that Fuseli 'endeavoured to bring Michael Angelo's apostles and prophets, with their super-human ponderousness of intention, into the commonplaces of modern life'. Of the illustration to *The Newspaper in the Country*, Hunt says:

> … the quiet tea-table scene in Cowper, [*Fuseli*] has turned into a preposterous conspiracy of huge men and women, all bent upon showing their thews and postures, with dresses as fantastical as their minds. One gentleman, of the existence of whose trowsers you are not aware till you see the terminating line at the ankle, is sitting and looking grim on a sofa, with his hat on and no waistcoat.

The Prison.

The oppressor holds
His body bound but knows not what a range
His spirit takes.

274.

274. *The Prison*, 1807
(*The Task*, VI, 774-776)
(Vol. II, facing p. 223)

Engraved by Charles Warren (1766-1823) after Fuseli's painting formerly in the Ganz collection and now in the Kunsthaus, Zurich (1806-1807; Schiff 1236).
Imprint: Pub. by J. Johnson London March 1. 1807.
Inscription (top centre): The Prison. | (right): Vol. II. P. 223. | (bottom): H. Fuseli R.A. pinx^t. | | Warren sculp^t. |

The oppressor holds
His body bound; but knows not what a range
His spirit takes,

Dimensions: ■ 12.5 x 9.1 cm |4¹⁵/₁₆" x 3⁹/₁₆"
(BL G. 12945)
Other locations: BL 78.f.18 (1811)(H=24.5 cm);
DHW (1808)(H=21.9 cm); DHW (1808)(H=22.2
cm); Dörrbecker (1808); Essick; NYPL NCL;
Princeton Ex 3693.7.1811 c.2; Yale; ZBZ 1221
Plate only: Lucerne; V & A E.1201-F-1886
Lacking plate: Huntington 425904; Princeton Ex
3693.7.1806a
Lit.: Schiff 1336 (12.5 x 8.2 cm); Russell 1963,
nos. 96, 99, 105; Schiff-Viotto 1977, no. 268;
Letters, 357;
Exh.: Kansas City 1982 (61).

Variants:

I. Proof before letters (India paper): BM 1849-
5-12-235
II. Before all letters (lacking Vol. and page
nos.) (plate only): DHW

Fuseli urged Warren on 20th January 1807 'to
give some dispatch to the plate from Cowper'.
Fuseli's design illustrates the personification of
the inner freedom of the believer, which has been
the subject of much of this book of the *Task*.

******

Fig. 14. H. Füssli, J.J. Horner, & F. Nüscheler,
Heinrich Fuessli's Sæmmtliche Werke, 1807. Title
page.

Nos. 275 - 283.
**[Heinrich Füssli, Johann Jakob Horner, &
Felix Nüscheler].**
[Overall title]: HEINRICH FUESSLI'S
SÄMMTLICHE WERKE,|NEBST EINEM

VERSUCH SEINER BIOGRAPHIE.|—|
ZÜRICH, 1807. [1809.]|IN DER
KUNSTHANDLUNG VON FUESSLI UND
COMPAGNIE.

[Wrappers]: HEINRICH FUESSLI'S|
SÆMMTLICHE WERKE|—|ERSTES HEFT.
[ZWEYTES HEFT.]| ZÜRICH, 1807. [1809]|IN
DER KUNSTHANDLUNG VON FUESSLI UND
COMPAGNIE (16/16 illus.).

For the other illustrations in this work see also
Nos. **13A, 70A-71A, 72C, 73E, 74A, and 93B
(Addenda).**

Although usually considered the editor of this
work, Nüscheler provided only the account of
Fuseli's early life. The explanations of the designs
were written by J.J. Horner (1779-1831) (see
Friedrich Horner, *Briefe des ... Prof. Joh. Jakob
Horner*, in the *Zürcher Taschenbuch*, 1917, 255).
The driving force behind the publication was
Fuseli's cousin, the painter and art dealer,
Heinrich Füssli (1751-1829), who bore the brunt
of finding suitable illustrations and getting them
engraved. Some interesting details concerning his
search for drawings may be gleaned from the
correspondence with Ulrich Hegner, and from
Hegner's diary (Zentralbibliothek Zürich and
Stadtbibliothek Winterthur). The work failed to
sell and publication was suspended after only two
issues (*Leben des Malers J.H. Füessli*, 1826, 9).
   Füssli outlined his plans in a letter to his cousin
(now lost). I quote from Fuseli's reply (8 August
1805; Zentralbibliothek, Zurich). His idiosyncratic
capitalisation and spelling of the original German
have been retained.

Ihr project blosse umrisse von meinen Werken
in freund Flaxmans Manier zu liefern, wenn es
vorzüge für den Student hat welches nur die
Linie & den Styl des Künstlers zu kennen
wünschet, hat wenig befriedigendes für den[,]
welchem die Wirkung der Composition & Licht
u[n]ᵈ Schatten das wichtigste Sind; auch
Zeichnen Mahler u[n]ᵈ Bildhauer, obgleich
Correctheit beyden wesentlich ist oder Seyn
Sollte, nicht auf *eine* art: nicht dass ich kalt auf
ihren plan blasen wollte; wer sich's Zum
hauptpunkte macht[,] die geschichte des
Vorwurfs Zu erzählen, den character Zu
Zeichnen, u[n]ᵈ die Leidenschaft
auszudrü[c]ken, der kann auch im blossen
Umrisse erkannt werden.

Sie Sehen also dass ich nichts dawider habe Ihnen auf die art wie Sie es verlangen behülflich Zu seyn: was von kupfern nach mir heraus ist, will ich Ihnen entweder unetgeltlich[,] wenn ich eines selbst publicirt habe oder mehr als einmal besi[t]ze, oder um was es mich kosten wird anzukaufen Zukoṁen Lassen. Zeichnungen nach mir, von guter hand unter meinem auge, stehen Ihnen nach Maass der Arbeit ŭ. Composition, von *einer* Guinee bis auf *fünfe* zu dienste: Sie müssen mich aber wissen Lassen *was* Sie von mir Schon kennen[,] besi[t]zen oder Zu bekoṁen wissen. die Abscheulichkeiten welche Lavater in seinen physiognomieen für Copien nach mir ausgiebt, hüten Sie Sich Zu republiciren; die Ideen welche Ich anerkenne habe ich in den Umrissen der Englischen Physiognomie verbessert gegeben.

[Your plan to publish plain outlines of my work in Friend Flaxman's manner, although it has advantages for the student who wishes merely to become acquainted with the artist's style, is not very satisfactory for those who consider the effect of the composition and light and shade to be the most important elements. Moreover, although correctness is essential, or should be, to both painters and sculptors, they do not draw in any given *single* way: not that I want to throw cold water on your plan; any artist that makes it his main task to use his picture to tell a story, to draw character and to express passion, will communicate this even through a simple outline.

As you see, I don't have anything against assisting you in the way you request: as for plates that have appeared after me, I will let you have copies of any that I published myself, or that I have duplicates of, free of charge. I will send you any others at the same price they cost me. Drawings after me, done by a decent artist under my supervision, are at your disposal for between *one* to *five* guineas each, depending on the size of the work and the composition. But you must let me know *what* you've already seen of mine, or own or can lay your hands on. But be careful not to republish those disgusting things in Lavater's *Physiognomies* that he claims are copies after me; the designs I acknowledge as mine are the ones I reworked and used in the English edition of the *Physiognomy*.]

Fuessli and Bodmer

275.

275. *Fuseli and Bodmer in Conversation*, 1806 (Part I, No. 1, facing p. XVIII)

Unsigned outline engraving by Johann Heinrich Lips (1758-1817) after Fuseli's painting in the Kunsthaus, Zurich ([1778-1781]; Schiff 366). Inscription (bottom centre): **Fuessli und Bodmer.** Dimensions: ■ 24.6 x 22.1 cm | 9¹¹/₁₆" x 8¹¹/₁₆" (KHZ D33)
Other locations: **(1.)** (as above): DHW; ETH 1524a; ETH 545/127; Lucerne H.36 gr.fol;—**(2.)** (facing t.p.): Bern A16.441;—**(3.)** (facing p. X): ZBZ KK 307; YCBA folio B.N.29 (not seen)
Plate only: MMA 55.526.3
Lit.: Schiff 366; Weinglass 1991a, 67
Exh.: Zurich 1926 (p. 30); Coburg 1989 (298)
Variants:
I. Proof before letters: KHZ C4/IIIA, 1188

Fuseli's painting was an act of homage to his intellectual mentor, Johann Jakob Bodmer (1698-1783), who had introduced the young student to the great poets down the ages, the source of much of the subject matter of his mature art. But the lack of humility and the arrogant detachment of Fuseli's self-portrait seem to suggest a reversal of the earlier roles of student and teacher. The bust between the two men appears to be that of Homer.

Joseph erklärt dem Beker und Mundschenk ihre Träume.

276.

276. *Joseph Interprets the Dream of the Baker and Butler*, 1806
(Genesis, 40: 1-23)
(Part I, No. 3, facing p. 2)

Unsigned outline engraving by Johann Heinrich Lips (1758-1817) after Fuseli's lost drawing
Inscription: **Joseph erklärt dem Beker und Mundschenk ihre Träume.**
Dimensions: ■ 25.2 x 20.6 cm | 9¹⁵/16" x 8²/16" (KHZ D33)
Other locations: Bern A16.441; DHW; ETH 545/132; ETH 1524a; Lucerne H.36 gr.fol.; YCBA folio B.N.29 (not seen); ZBZ KK 307
Lit.: Schiff 290

Variants:
I. Proof before letters: KHZ C4/IIIA, 1204

The original of this engraving was one of several Fuseli drawings owned by Ulrich Hegner (Füssli to Hegner, 21 July 1806; Winterthur), whose collections also included a series of wash drawings, comprising thirty-one (imaginary) portraits of Swiss painters from Henry Fuseli's juvenile period (now untraced, although perhaps related to Schiff 130-141), presented to Hegner by Füssli in 1805 (see Hegner's diary entry for 26 January 1805, Winterthur, UH 27; and Hegner to

Füssli, 3 February 1805, ZBZ).

Pharaoh's butler and baker, imprisoned in the same house as Joseph, relate to him their dreams. To the butler Joseph predicts that within three days he will be restored to the Pharaoh's favour. As for the baker, it is his fate to be hanged. The illustration shows a raven pecking at the heel of the doomed and despairing baker.

Wie Till die Schneider durch Säue straft.

277.

277. *How Till Eulenspiegel Punished the Tailors*, 1806
(*Hystorien Till Eulenspiegels* [Hamburg, 1641])
(Part I, No. 5, facing p. 4)

Unsigned outline engraving by Johann Heinrich Lips (1758-1817) after Fuseli's pen-and-wash drawing in the Kunsthaus, Zurich ([1758-1760]; Schiff 274).
Inscription: **Wie Till die Schneider durch Säue straft.**
Dimensions: ■ 25.5 x 19.5 cm | 10¹/16" x 7¹¹/16" (KHZ D33)
Other locations: (**1.**) (as above): A16.441; ETH 545/139; DHW; ETH 1524a; Lucerne H.36 gr.fol.;—(**2.**) (facing p. 3): ZBZ KK 307; YCBA folio B.N.29 (not seen)
Plate only: MMA 55.526.9
Lit.: Schiff 274

Variants:
I. Proof before letters: KHZ C4/IIIA, 1205
Exh.: Zurich 1926 (unnumbered; p. 31)

The satirical tales of Till Eulenspiegel's knavish escapades were based upon the life of the historical German prankster who died in 1350 at Mölln. Written c. 1480 in Low German, but first published in High German in 1519, the collection enjoyed enormous popularity, appearing in numerous translations, including English.

Here Eulenspiegel takes revenge on the tailors' apprentices who had mocked him, by secretly sawing through the posts of the wooden platform on which they sat. The pigs he drives through the shop, bring down the weakened posts and dislodge his tormentors from their perch.

Wie Till zum Barbier durch's Fenster kömt.

278.

278. *How Till Eulenspiegel Came In Through the Barber's Window*, 1806
(*Hystorien Till Eulenspiegels* [Hamburg, 1641])
(Part I, No. 6, between pp. 4-5)

Unsigned outline engraving by Johann Heinrich Lips (1758-1817) after Fuseli's pen-and-wash drawing in the Kunsthaus, Zurich ([1758-1760]; Schiff 275).

Inscription: **Wie Till zum Barbier durch's Fenster kömt.**
Dimensions: ■ 24.3 x 20.0 cm | 9⁹/₁₆" x 7¹⁴/₁₆"
(KHZ D33)
Other locations: Bern A16.441; DHW; ETH 545/139; ETH 1524a; Lucerne H.36 gr.fol.; YCBA folio B.N.29 (not seen); ZBZ KK 307
Plate only: MMA 55.526.10
Lit.: Schiff 275

Variants:
I. Proof before letters: KHZ C4/IIIA, 1206
Exh.: Zurich 1926 (unnumbered; p. 31)

Till deliberately misunderstands the barber and enters the shop through the window. As in No. **277** Fuseli incorporates his emblematic signature of the little feet (Füssli) into the design. Among the unusual appurtenances of the shop are the stuffed dog with two heads and the advertisement for the 'Universal Recipe for the Elixir of Life.'

279.

279. *Hercules Slays Diomedes and his Flesh-Eating Mares*, 1806
(Apollodorus, II, 5, 8; Quintus Smyrnaeus, VI, 247-250)
(Part I, No. 7, facing p. 6)

Unsigned outline engraving (image not reversed) by Johann Heinrich Lips (1758-1817) after Fuseli's drawing in the Art Institute of Chicago ([1800-1805]; Schiff 1371).
Inscription: **Hercules und Diomedes.**
Dimensions: ■ 29.6 x 22.9 cm | 11¹⁰/16" x 9" (KHZ D33)
Other locations:Bern A16.441; DHW;ETH 1524a; ETH 545/138; Lucerne H.36 gr.fol.; YCBA folio B.N.29 (not seen); ZBZ KK 307
Plate only: MMA 55.526.12
Lit.: Schiff 989 (iconography and source), 1371; Todd 1947, repr. 85; Tomory 1972, 183, pl. 153

Variants:
I. Proof before letters: KHZ C4/IIIA, 1197
Exh.: Zurich 1926 (unnumbered; p. 31)

The illustration shows Hercules slaying Diomedes and his flesh-eating mares as he fulfills the eighth of his twelve labours. The recumbent figure at the right is Abderus, Hercules' young lover, killed in the battle. For Fuseli's divergences from the standard sources, see Schiff 989. Schiff comments that Fuseli's redrawn version of Schiff 1371 (Schiff 1372; not repr.) may have been done 'for the engraver'—although the variations noted do not seem applicable to Lips's outline.

Der Kronenräuber.

280.

280. *Claudio Murders His Brother, King Hamlet, by Pouring Poison into His Ear as He Lies Sleeping in the Garden*, 1806
(Shakespeare, *Hamlet*, I, v, 58-78)
(Part I, No. 8, between pp. 7-8)

Unsigned outline engraving by Johann Heinrich Lips (1758-1817) after Fuseli's drawing in the Eidgenössische Technische Hochschule, Zurich (1771; Schiff 445).
Inscription: **Der Kronenräuber.**
Dimensions: ■ 20.6 x 30.5 cm | 8²/16" x 12" (KHZ D33)

Other locations: Bern A16.441; DHW; ETH 545/134; ETH 1524a; Lucerne H.36 gr.fol.; YCBA folio B.N.29 (not seen); ZBZ KK 307
Plate only: MMA 55.526.6

Variants:
I. Proof before letters: KHZ C4/IIIA, 1194
Exh.: Zurich 1926 (unnumbered; p. 31)

Fuseli's drawings illustrating Shakespeare, such as the original of this outline engraving, constitute a remarkable counterpoint to his Shakespeare paintings with their dark backgrounds and strongly foreshortened figures thrusting powerfully against the pictorial plane. The drawings exemplify Fuseli's aphorism that 'Genius either discovers new materials of nature, or combines the known with novelty'. In this particular case, the composition imitates in almost exact detail a scene of homosexual seduction, depicted on a 4th century attic vase, while simultaneously explicating the light-darkness metaphor encased within Hamlet's reference to his father as 'Hyperion to a satyr'. However, it should be noted that the effect has been considerably weakened in the plate by the loss of the dark wash and the replacement of the drawing's indeterminate dark background, that created a cave-like enclosure, by the over-naturalistic trees and foliage.

Ǫ Marius.

281. *Caius Marius and the Cimbrian Soldier*,
1806
(Plutarch, *Marius*; Lucan, *Pharsalia*, XI, 75-86)
(Part II, No. 13, between pp. 12-13)

Outline engraving by Johann Heinrich Lips (1758-1817) after Fuseli's lost drawing ([1768-1770]; Schiff 331).
Inscription (bottom right): H. Lips. sc. | **Marius.**
Dimensions: ■ 21.2 x 27.8 cm | 8⁵/16" x 10¹⁵/16"
(ZBZ KK 307)
Other locations: DHW; ETH 545/124; ETH 1524a; Lucerne H.36 gr.fol.
Plate only: MMA 55.526.5
Lit.: Schiff 331 (21.1 x 28.0 cm)
Exh.: Coburg 1989 (299)

Variants:
I. Proof before letters: KHZ C4/IIIA, 1200

281.
II. Proof (lacking signature): KHZ D33
Other locations: Bern A16.441 (facing p. 13)
Exh.: Zurich 1926 (unnumbered; p. 31)

This early drawing (also in the collection of Ulrich Hegner) was 'remarkable as a first sketch for the simplicity and purity of treatment of the subject' (p. 14). Füssli was uncertain at first about having it engraved. It was too 'trifling' and had 'already been etched'—although he may have had the subject only in mind, previously engraved by Lips (1789) after Jean-Germain Drouais.

The illustration shows Marius in prison, awaiting execution, after being captured, 89 A.D., in the marshes of Minturnum. The Cimbrian soldier sent to kill him is seen throwing down his sword and about to flee, terrified by the general's demeanour as he confronts him.

Der Schweizerbund

282.

282. *The Oath on the Rütli*, [1807-1809]
(Part II, No. 14, facing p. 14)

Outline engraving (not reversed) by Franz Hegi (1774-1850) after Fuseli's painting in the Rathaus, Zurich ([1779-1781]; Schiff 359).
Inscription (bottom right): F. Hegi sc. | **Der Schweizerbund**
Dimensions: ■ 29.0 x 19.4 cm | 11⁶/16" x 7¹⁰/16" (KHZ D33)
Other locations: Bern A16.441; DHW; ETH 1524a; ZBZ KK 307
Plate only: MMA 55.526.8
Lit.: Appenzeller 1906, no. 603; Weinglass 1991a, 67

The Oath on the Rütli is an exemplary patriotic celebration of the legendary founders of the Confederation, Arnold von Melchtal, Walter Fürst (centre), and Werner Stauffacher. In the painting Fuseli imbues the historic scene with epic sublimity and conveys the Confederates' almost sacred sense of mission. But Fuseli's image was not widely diffused abroad (this is the very first engraved version of the work) and, hence,—albeit not exclusively for this reason—was destined to be overshadowed in the public's awareness by David's *Oath of the Horatii* (1784-1785). But then this rendering in outline is hardly the medium to bring out the painterly virtues of its original.

Adam und Eva

283.

283. *Satan Starting From the Touch of Ithuriel's Spear*, 1806
(John Milton, *Paradise Lost*, IV, 799-822)
(Part II, No. 15, between pp. 14-15)

Outline engraving by Johann Heinrich Lips (1758-1817) after Fuseli's lost preparatory drawing for the painting now Private Collection, Paris (1780; Schiff, Lost Work, no. 18)
Inscription (bottom right): H. Lips. sc. | **Adam und Eva**
Dimensions: ■ 22.6 x 29.8 cm | 8¹⁴/16" x 11¾"
(KHZ D33)
Other locations: Bern A16.441 (facing p. 15); DHW; ETH 545/128; ETH 1524a; Lucerne H.36 gr.fol.; ZBZ KK 307 (facing p. 15)
Lit.: Dwight C. Miller, 'Another Drawing ... for Milton's *Paradise Lost*', *Master Drawings*, 2 (1990), 28, repr. 184.

Variants:
I. Proof before letters: KHZ C4/IIIA, 1201

The painting, recently recovered, was exhibited at the Royal Academy in 1780 (no. 179), where it received short shrift from Anthony Pasquin, who described it as 'the most ill looking devil I ever saw painted', and Horace Walpole, who called it 'extravagant and ridiculous'. The painting was an important precursor to the 47 pictures of Fuseli's Milton Gallery of the 1790s. Like these later pictures, it depicts Satan as a strong, almost heroic, figure. The lost drawing may have formed part of Hegner's collection.

Satan, plotting the destruction of mankind, disguises himself as a toad and creeps up on Adam and Eve as they sleep. Ithuriel touches him with his spear and reveals him in his true guise.

✶✶✶✶✶✶

No. 275A.
AN DIE | LERNBEGIERIGE ZÜRCHERISCHE JUGEND | AUF DAS JAHR 1878. | ZUM BESTEN DES WAISEN-HAUSES VON EINER GESELLSCHAFT HERAUS-GEGEBEN. | — | EINUNDVIERZIGSTES STÜCK. | — | ALS FORTSETZUNG DER NEUJAHRSBLÄTTER DER CHORHERRENSTUBE. | NO. 100. | — | ZÜRICH IN DER ZWEITEN HÄLFTE DES ACHTZEHNTEN JAHR-HUNDERTS. | ERSTE ABTHEILUNG. | — | ZÜRICH. | DRUCK VON J.J. ULRICH. | 1878.

[Cover title:] XLI. | NEUJAHRSBLATT | ZUM BESTEN DES | WAISENHAUSES | IN ZÜRICH | FÜR | 1878. | — | ZÜRICH IN DER ZWEITEN HÄLFTE DES ACHTZEHNTEN JAHR[-] HUNDERTS. | ERSTE ABTHEILUNG. | — | ZÜRICH. |

275A. *Fuseli and Bodmer in Conversation*, 1878
(frontispiece, before title page)

Lithograph by Rudolf Rey (1814-1897)
Inscription (bottom right): Lith. v. R. Rey. | FUESSLI BEI BODMER.
Dimensions: ■ 17.4 x 15.7 cm | 6¹⁴/16" x 6³/16"
(ZBZ LSH 1011 W1a)
Other locations: UB Basel EM 109 (1871-1885); DHW

✶✶✶✶✶✶

No. 276A.
[Johann Jakob Horner.]
ZWEY UND ZWANZIGSTES NEUJAHRS[-] STÜCK, | HERAUSGEGEBEN | VON DER KUENSTLER-GESELLSCHAFT IN ZÜRICH | AUF DAS JAHR 1826. | — | ENTHALTEND | DAS LEBEN DES MALERS JOHANN HEINRICH FÜESSLI | VON ZÜRICH. | Zurich, 1826. (1/1 illus. + portr. vignette).

Joseph erklärt dem Beker und Mundschenk ihre Träume.

276A.

276A. *Joseph Interprets the Dreams of the Baker and the Butler*, 1826
(*Genesis* 40: 1-23)
(facing p. [2])

Aquatint (coloured impression) by Franz Hegi (1774-1850) after Fuseli's lost drawing
Inscription: H. Fuseli del. | | F. Hegi sc. | Joseph erklärt dem Beker und Mundschenk ihre Träume.
Dimensions: ■ 16.8 x 13.6 cm | 16¹⁰/₁₆" x 5⁶/₁₆" (KHZ Per 309:1/24: 1805/1840)
Other locations: Basel Z120; SB Bern H.Z.Q28; Lucerne 114 4°
Lit.: Schiff 290 (14.2 x 11.5 cm); Appenzeller 1906, no. 1060

Variants:
I. Coloured aquatint before letters (NYPL 3-MAA 1826) (between pp. 304-305)

Other locations: Basel 1956.172.2; UB Basel EM 102 1805/1840; ZBZ KK 568a (facing p. [2])
II. Printed in brown (KHZ C64/A 1060)
Other locations: DHW
Plate only: DHW; ZBZ Ms. Lind. 73

The now-lost drawing, after which the aquatint was engraved, was in Ulrich Hegner's collection. It had previously served in the preparation of the outline engraving, No. **276**. Füssli wrote to Hegner on 1st October 1825 to request the loan of it for the engraver, asking also to borrow Hegner's other Fuseli drawings, apparently to show at a memorial ceremony for the artist ('für die Ausstattung am [?]Bechtoldstag') (Stadtbibliothek, Winterthur, UHBr 83/13).

******

284.

284. *Silence (A Mother With her Two Children)*, 1808
(John Milton, *Il Penseroso*, 78-84)

Stipple engraving by Moses Haughton (1772 or

1774-1848) after painting No. XXXIII in the Milton Gallery in the Senn collection, Basel ([1796-1799]; Schiff 915)
Inscription: Painted by H. Fuseli, R.A. Engraved by Moses Haughton, and Published by them as

the Act directs, Royal Academy, Somerset House, London, Jan.ʸ 6. 1808.|SILENCE.|

> Where glowing embers through the room
> Teach light to counterfeit a gloom
>   Il Penseroso.

Dimensions: ■ 42.0 x 50.6 cm | 16½" x 19¹⁵/₁₆" (MMA 62.600.686).
Lit.: Schiff 915A; Schiff 1963, 98; Tomory 1972, 179, pl. 215; *Letters*, 224, 364

Variants:

I. Proof (India paper) (open letter title): V & A E.114-1971

The lines illustrated are the following:

Or, if the Air will not permit,
Some still removed place will fit,
Where glowing Embers through the room
Teach light to counterfeit a gloom,
Far from all resort of mirth
Save the Cricket on the hearth,
Or the Bellman's drowsy charm,
To bless the doors from nightly harm.

Schiff suggests that the sculpture on the mantelpiece, a frontal variation on Menelaus and dying Patroclus, serves as an emblematic allusion to the fate that awaits the youth, perhaps an early death in the war, and as such introduces a note of menace into the otherwise peaceful scene.

******

No. 284A.
John Milton.

THE|POETICAL WORKS|OF|JOHN MILTON;|WITH|A MEMOIR;|AND SIX EMBELLISH[-]MENTS,|BY|FUSELI, WESTALL, AND MARTIN.| LONDON:|EDWARD CHURTON, 26, HOLLES STREET.|—|1836, 1838 (1/6 illus. + portr. frontis.).
[Half-title (1836): CHURTON'S BRITISH POETS.|—|FIRST SERIES.|—|THE|POETICAL WORKS|OF|JOHN MILTON.]
[On spine (1838): MILTON'S POETICAL WORKS.|NEW EDITION.]
...WITH|A MEMOIR;|AND SEVEN EMBEL-LISHMENTS,|BY|FUSELI, WESTALL, AND MARTIN.| LONDON:|EDWARD CHURTON, 26, HOLLES STREET.|—|1840 (1/7 illus. + portr. frontis.).
...LONDON:|J.J.CHIDLEY,123,ALDERSGATE STREET.|—|1841, 1842,1844, 1845.

...NEW EDITION.| LONDON:|J.J. CHIDLEY, 123, ALDERSGATE STREET.|—|1847.
...THE|POETICAL WORKS|OF|JOHN MILTON;|WITH |A MEMOIR;|EMBELLISHED WITH ENGRAVINGS AFTER DESIGNS|BY FUSELI, WESTALL, AND MARTIN.| LONDON:|H.G. BOHN, YORK STREET, COVENT GARDEN.|1848, 1852.

'Churton's Annual Catalogue' for 1840 (DHW) lists 'just published' copies at 10s. The 1842 cat. (DHW) offers new (?1840-1842) copies at 6s.0d.

284A. *Silence,* 1836
(John Milton, *Il Penseroso*, ll. 78-84)
(facing p. 417)

Re-engraving on steel in reduced format by John Rogers (1808?-1888)
Imprint: London, Published Jan.ʸ 23 1836 by Edw.ᵈ Churton 26, Holles Street.
Inscription: Fuseli, R.A. pinx.ᵗ.||J. Rogers sc.|
Silence.|Il Penseroso. L. 80.|Printed by J. Yates
Dimensions: ■ 7.1 x 9.2 cm | 2¾" x 3¹⁰/₁₆" (Illinois x821.M64.K1836)
Lit.: Schiff 915a; Schiff 1963, 98, pl. 54; Tomory 1973, 203; Schiff-Viotto 1977, 158
Exh.:Kansas City 1982 (48);Kansas City 1989(25)

Variants:

I. Reissued (1838) with printer's imprint added but without date: Birmingham 43225
Imprint: Printed by J. Yates.|London, Edward Churton, 26, Holles Street
Other locations: Geneva T9308; Harvard 14483.14.35 (1841); Huntington 440242; North Carolina PR3552.C5.1838; St. Mary of the Lake Seminary PR3550.E40 (1840)
II. Reissued (1842) without imprint of publisher and printer: Birmingham 809589 (1842)
Other locations: Birmingham 585691 (1844); Birmingham 809318 (1845); DHW (1842); DHW (1842); DHW (1844) (H=23.2 cm); DHW (1844); Dörrbecker (1842); Essick (1852); Harvard (1844); Huntington 71070 (1844); Illinois 821.M64.K1844 (1844); ZBZ (1844); Harvard 14483.15.12 (1847); Cambridge Syn. 6.84.60 (1848); LC PR3550.E52 (1852); USC 820.M662.rp.2
Lit.: Schiff 915A (1844) (7.0 x 9.1 cm)

******

285.

285. *Ugolino and his Sons Starving to Death in the Tower*, 1809
(Dante, *Inferno*, XXXIII, 22-51)

Stipple engraving by Moses Haughton (1772 or 1774-1848) after Fuseli's lost painting,
of which a preparatory drawing survives in the Art Institute of Chicago (1806; Schiff 1799A)
Inscription: Painted by H. Fusile, R.A. Engraved by M. Haughton, and Published by them at the Royal Academy. as the Act directs, Feby. 20. 1809. | VGOLINO (open letters) |
  [*left*]
Io non piangeva, si dentro impetrai.
  [*right*]
Bereft of tears, I inward turn'd to stone.
        Dante. Inferno. C.33.
Dimensions: ■ 51.3 x 37.8 cm | 20¼" x 14^{14}/16" (BM 1863-5-18-162)
Other locations: BM 16.T.10; Essick; KHZ
Lit.: Schiff 1200 (51.2 x 37.7 cm); Hartmann 1969, no. 12; Tomory 1972, pl. 147; Schiff-

Viotto 1977, no. 224, pl. 224[1]
Exh.: Zurich 1941 (131); Pescara 1985 (7)

The story of Ugolino, count of Donoratico, is 'second only to that of Francesca da Rimini in its appeal to popular sympathy' (*La Divina Commedia*, ed. C.H. Grandgent, 1972, 289). Ugolino relates his tale of horror to Dante, while gnawing at the skull and brain of Archbishop Ruggieri, who had brought about Ugolino's death and that of his sons. The scene depicted in Fuseli's illustration is summarised in the title given the painting when exhibited (R.A., 1806/19).

Count Vgolino, chief of the Guelphs at Pisa, locked up ·jy the opposite party with his four sons, and starved to death in the tower, which from that event acquired the name of *torre della fame*.

For No. **285A** see the combined entry for *The English School* following Nos. **299A-301A**.

287.

286.

286. *Death of Cardinal Beaufort*, 1809
(Shakespeare, *King Henry the Sixth*, Pt. 2, III, iii)

Stipple engraving by Moses Haughton (1772 or 1774-1848) after Fuseli's painting exhibited (1808/67) at the Royal Academy and now with Sabin Galleries, London (1808; Schiff 1787).
Inscription: Painted by H^y. Fuseli, R.A. Engraved by Moses Haughton, & Publish'd by them as the Act directs July 5, 1809. at the R^l. Academy Somerset House. | CARDINAL BEAUFORT'S BEDCHAMBER, HENRY, SALISBURY, WARWICK & ATTENDANTS. |

> Card.
> He hath no eyes the dust hath blinded them,
> Comb down his hair; look! look! it stands upright,
> Like Lime-twigs set to catch my winged Soul!
> Henry VI. Part II. Act III. Scene 3.

Dimensions: ■ 54.5 x 66.2 cm | 21^7/16" x 26^1/16" (BM Dd 6 no 10)
Other locations: BM 1861-5-18-163; BM T.16.17; KHZ 1940/135
Lit.: Schiff 1204 (54.5 x 66.2 cm)

Variants:
I. Title in open letters (India paper): V & A E.113-1971
II. Title in open letters: Essick

Soon after Gloucester's death, Cardinal Beaufort is taken by 'a grievous sickness'. The king is present at the cardinal's deathbed and hears him confess his part in the murder of Gloucester. Although the king urges him to 'make signal of [*his*] hope' of heaven, he dies without giving any sign of repentance.

******

287. *Two Nude Heroic Studies: ?'Hercules' and 'Satan'*, 1809

Etched by Robert Balmanno (1780-1861) after a lost drawing ([1790-1800]; Schiff 1140)
Inscription (left): Etching by Robert Balmanno | after Henry Fuseli R.A. | 1809 | (centre): Hercules | (bottom right): Satan; (in pencil on reverse): Etched by R Balmanno from H Fuseli
Dimensions: 19.2 x 30.1 cm | 7^9/16" x 11^{14}/16"; (to platemark): 20.8 x 31 cm | 8^3/16" x 12^9/16" (BM 1863-5-9-85)
Other locations: BM 1858-4-17-298

Lit.: Schiff 1140 (as 'Two Male Nudes') (not reproduced)

Schiff describes this sheet as 'an anonymous facsimile reproduction'. Whereas Balmanno identifies the two figures as Hercules and Satan, Schiff sees them merely as nude studies: the one on the left is in the attitude of an archer drawing his bow; while the other on the right, wearing a helmet, is reaching back over his shoulder as though pulling an arrow from his quiver. We might note that Fuseli's Hercules adopts a similar attitude, albeit likewise sans bow and arrow, both in the painting, *Hercules Saves Prometheus from the Eagle* (1781-1785; Schiff 711) and the pen-and-ink study for it (1781; Schiff 800). Schiff considers that the omission of the weapon in the painting may be a 'somewhat mannered borrowing from Michelangelo'.

******

288. *The Nursery of Shakespeare*, 1810

Stipple engraving by Moses Haughton (1772 or 1774-1848) after Fuseli's original painting which survives in fragmentary form in the Courtauld Institute, London (1805-1806; Schiff 1202)
Inscription: Painted by H. Fuseli, R.A. P.P. Engraved by Moses Haughton. & Publish'd as the Act directs. May 15, 1810. by them at the Royal Academy Somerset House. | NURSERY OF SHAKESPEAR (title in open letters)
Dimensions: ■ 51.8 x 40.3 cm | 20^6/16" x 15^{14}/16" (BM 1861-5-18-162)
Other locations: BM 16.T.12; Essick
Lit.: Schiff 1202A (51.8 x 40.5 cm); Cunningham 1830 (2nd ed.), 292-293; Schiff-Viotto 1977, no. 227, pl. 227^1

Variants:
I. Proof before letters: Max Browne
II. On India paper: V & A E.115-1971
III. Coloured impression: Art Institute of Chicago Box 455.

The subject is a traditional one: 'The Infant Nursed by Tragedy, Caressed by Comedy, and Surrounded by some of the most Striking Characters' (cp. Romney's painting for Boydell). The design evinces Fuseli's usual eclecticism in finding unexpected pictorial sources to adapt to his purposes: the central group is derived from Giulio Cesare Procaccini's *Holy Family* (c. 1616-1618; Nelson-Atkins Museum, Kansas City, Missouri).

288.

The original oil painting survives only in cut-down and fragmentary form and its full imaginative panoply is thus preserved only in Moses Haughton's engraving.

The following description of the spirited scene depicted in the painting was among the new materials Allan Cunningham added to his account of the artist in the second edition of his *Lives of the ... British Painters*:

Tragedy is represented, a beautiful and mournful dame, nursing in her bosom the young dramatist; she seems exhausted by her maternal indulgence, and the child—his lips moist with milk and his eyes beaming with inspiration and health—appears anxious to quit her bosom for that of Comedy—a more youthful and gladsome lady, who with loose looks and looser attire—with laughing eyes and feet made to do nothing but dance, has begun to toy and talk with him. Around this group the painter has summoned the various characters which the poet afterwards created. Lady Constance is there with her settled sorrow—Lady Macbeth exhibits herself in that sleeping scene to which a Siddons has added terrors all her own; the three weird sisters—those black and midnight hags—appear dim but well defined. Falstaff too is there, a hogshead of a man with a tun of wit: and Caliban, a strange creation—a connecting link between man and brute—comes grovelling forward to look at his creator. Over the whole glares Hamlet's Ghost, throwing a sort of supernatural halo upon all around. The mask of Othello lies in the robe of Tragedy, and Queen Mab and one of her merriest comrades are sporting in Shakespeare's cradle.

******

For No. **288A** see the combined entry for *The English School* following Nos. **299A-301A**.

******

I. CASP. LAVATER, FELIX HESS UND HEINRICH FÜESSLI BEY SPALDING ZU BARTH IN SCHWEDISCH POMMERN IM IAHR 1763

289.

289. *Fuseli, Lavater and Hess While Visiting the Rev. Spalding at Barth, 1763*, 1810

Etching by Eberhard Siegfried Henne (1759-1828) after Fuseli's lost grisaille painting (1763); Henne's drawing is in the Kunsthaus, Zurich. Imprint: Zu finden in Berlin im Verlag von Simon Schropp & Comp^e = und bey Schiavonetti und Gasp. Weiss Kunstverlegern unter den Linden. In Basel bey Wilhelm Haas zu St. Leonhard. Inscription: Grau in grau gemalt von Heinrich Fuessli 1763. | | Herausgegeben von Chr. von Mechel, Mitglied der Königl. Akademie. | I. CASP. LAVATER, FELIX HESS UND HEINRICH FÜESSLI BEY SPALDING ZU BARTH IN SCHWEDISCH POMMERN IM IAHR 1763. |

Es war im Frühling des gemeldeten Jahres, da diese nachmals so berühmt gewordenen drey schweizerischen Jünglinge (Lavater war 21 Jahr alt) den ehrwürdigen Spalding besuchten, und sind dieselben hier nebst dessen | Kindern und dem Herrn von Arnim auf Suckow, Spaldings Freunde, beym Frühstuck vorgestellt. Fuessli

malte dies Bild zum dankbaren Angedenken auf die Rückwand einer Sommerlaube in Spaldings | Garten zu Barth, von wo es bey dessen Berufung nach Berlin dahin gebracht wurde, und bis jetzt (1810) in der Probstey der Nicolai-Kirche, oder dem jetzigen Louisen-Stifte, aufbehalten wird.

[*Translation*: JOHANN CASPAR LAVATER, FELIX HESS AND HEINRICH FUSELI WHILE VISITING SPALDING IN BARTH IN SWEDISH POMERANIA IN 1763.

It was in spring of the above year when these three young Swiss, who would afterwards become so famous (Lavater was 21 years old), visited the worthy Rev. Spalding. They are shown here with Spalding's children and his friend, Herr von Arnim auf Suckow, together at breakfast. This picture was painted by Fuseli as a grateful memento of this visit on the back wall of a summer house in Spalding's garden at Barth; the painting accompanied Spalding to Berlin when he became Provost of St. Nicholas Church, where it now (1810) hangs in the present Louisenstiftung.]

Dimensions: ■ 34.9 x 50.7 cm | 13¾" x 19¹⁵/₁₆"
(Basel X.533).
Other locations: KHZ; ETH
Lit.: Schiff 288 (?46.0 x 63.0 cm); Wüthrich
1956, 299; Wüthrich 1959, no. 42; J.H. Füssli,
Sämtliche Gedichte, ed. M. Bircher & K. Guthke,
1973, repr. facing p. 32; Schiff-Viotto 1977, no.
2, pl. 2¹; Jaton 1988, repr. 20-21
Exh.: Frankfurt 1988 (231)

Variants
I. Proof before all letters (lacking imprint):
ETH 548a
III. Artist's name only without Mechel's
address: Basel 1916.101
Other locations: Stuttgart
IV. Imprint consolidated with artist's name:
Bern K41,206 Hz

In the wake of their denunciation of the corrupt
magistrate von Grebel, in their bold pamphlet,
Der ungerechte Landvogt (The Unjust Magistrate),
Lavater, Fuseli and Felix Hess were advised to
absent themselves from the country for a time.
Early in March 1763 they set out for Germany.
They spent that summer as guests of the
theologian Johann Joachim Spalding in Barth,
Pomerania. This design is one of three paintings
(now lost) with which Fuseli decorated the walls
of Spalding's garden house.

The plate shows Fuseli (right) sketching his
friends and members of Spalding's family. The
men round the breakfast table are (from left to
right) Spalding, von Arnim, Hess (standing) and
Lavater. A sheet of paper attached to the back
wall contains in slightly modified form the last
two stanzas of Klopstock's ode, *The Lake of
Zurich*. These may be rendered thus in English:

O, that you were here in this spot, you who
still love us, though wide distances separate us
from you in the bosom of the homeland; you to
whom in happier times our longing souls would
turn. Here would we build the abode of
friendship and dwell for ever. This peaceable
forest should be to us a Tempe, and this
dwelling an Elysium.

Spalding took Fuseli's grisaille painting with
him when he moved to Berlin about 1800. There
it ended up in the Luisenstiftung, a foundation for
the education of young women, and later, young
teachers. It was discovered by Mechel, who
commissioned Henne to make a drawing of it and
to undertake the engraving; to do the lettering
Mechel engaged Karl Friedrich von Klöden (1786-
1856), who later became an eminent geographer.

290.

290. *Night with her Children Aether and Hemera*, [1810-1815]
(Hesiod, *Theogony*, 124f.)

Unsigned etching in unfinished state by Henry Fuseli.
Inscription (false attribution, in pencil, bottom right within platemark): W Blake
Dimensions (to platemark): 31.0 x 29.3 cm | 12²/16" x 11⁹/16" (MMA 63.517.4)
Lit.: Schiff 1508 (31.0 x 29.5 cm) (not repr.)

The print shows slumbering Night with her arms around her two children, Aether (Sky), and Hemera (Day), begotten by her brother, Erebus. Aether, on the left, sleeps with his head resting in his mother's lap. In contrast, 'Cheerful Day', the child on the right, is smiling and wakeful. The dark shape at Night's side, with the vague suggestion of a face, represents Erebus, although at first glance it might almost be taken for her shadow—an appropriate correlative of the dialectical relationship between the pair. M.L. West in his edition of the *Theogony* (Oxford, 1966, 197) points out that the children 'are the antitheses of their parents, Hemera corresponding to Night and Aether to Erebus. The essential thing is not that they are opposites, but that they are naturally related: incompatible in nature, yet inseparable in thought'.

✶✶✶✶✶✶

291.

291. *The Witch and the Mandrake*, [1812]
(Ben Jonson, 'Witch's Song,' *Masque of Queens*)

Soft-ground etching (reversed) by Henry Fuseli after his working drawing in the Ashmolean Museum.
Dimensions (excl. panel): ■ 42.5 x 55.5 cm | 16¾" x 21¹⁴/16" (BM 1907-11-7-6)
Other locations: MMA 53.535.25
Lit.: Schiff 1510 (45.7 x 56.0 cm), 1497; Tomory 1972, pl. 159; Keay 1974, pl. 53; D. Brown, 'Fuseli's Drawings for Jonson's *Masque of Queenes*', *Burlington,* February 1979, 111-113; Stock 1989, pl.5('the witch as Mountain Mother')

Based upon Fuseli's two paintings (Schiff 1752 and 1497) and the recently rediscovered studies after them in the Ashmolean Museum, the two soft-ground etchings, No. **291** and its companion **292**, illustrating Ben Jonson's 'Witch's Song' in his *Masque of Queens*, represent different moments of the same episode, described in the following lines:

> I, last night, lay all alone
> O' the ground, to heare the Mandrake grone;
> And pluck'd him up, though he grew full low,
> And as I had done, the cock did crow.

In this first etching, the squatting witch is reminiscent of the old hooded crone in the *Seller of Cupids* (c. 1775-1776; Schiff 655). Her breasts are bared, for she has been suckling the blossom-headed mandrake she is about to destroy.

Both Tomory and Brown emphasise the strong influence of Guercino's *Night* (Villa Ludovisi) on the etching, with its 'rocky setting and skies shot with moonlight behind barred clouds'.

Brown comments on the etching technique:

> The initial composition drawing was evidently done in red chalk outline; on laying the paper on the waxed copper, Fuseli then built up the design, as the soft-ground technique demanded, by drawing heavily into the paper with the lead pencil.

292.

292. *The Mandrake: A Charm*, [1812]
(Ben Jonson, 'Witch's Song,' *Masque of Queens*)

Soft ground etching (reversed) by Henry Fuseli after his working drawing in the Ashmolean.
Dimensions: 42.8 x 55.1 cm | 16¹³/16" x 21¾"
(Hunterian Add. 1697)
Lit.: Schiff 1511 (42.7 x 55.2 cm); D. Brown, 'Fuseli's Drawings for Jonson's Masque of Queenes', *Burlington*, February 1979, 111-113.
Exh.: Glasgow 1990 (67)

A hooded witch is seen 'grubbing at the ground ... crouching so low that the mandrake itself is not to be seen' (Brown). As Schiff notes, explicit indications in the painting of ritual grave-robbery have been taken out, although such traditional demonological concepts remain as the 'young witch, just initiated and still afraid of the practices' (Schiff 1752). The owl, like the incubus on the witch's back, has disappeared, while background and sky have been reworked to enhance the Guercino-like effect.

293.

293. *The Vision of the Lazar House*, 1813
(J. Milton, *Paradise Lost*, XI, 477-490)

Stipple engraving by Moses Haughton (1772 or
1774-1848) after Fuseli's lost painting, No. XXIV
in the Milton Gallery, formerly in the collection
of Thomas Coutts ([1791-1795]; Schiff Lost Work
44)
Inscription: Painted by H. Fuseli, R.A. Engraved
by Moses Haughton, & Published by them as the
Act directs, Oct. 10th. 1813, at the Royal
Academy, Somerset House.│THE VISION of the
LAZAR-HOUSE. (open letters)│

 [*left*]
   immediately a place
Before his eyes appeard, sad, noisome, dark,
A lazar house it seem'd wherein were laid
Numbers of all diseas'd, all maladies.
Demoniac phrenzy, moping melancholy,
 [*right*]
And moon-struck madness, pining atrophy,
Marasmus
Dire was the tossing, deep the groans;

And over them triumphant Death his dart
Shook, but delayd to strike, though oft invok'd.
   Milton's P.L. Book XI. Verse 477.

Dimensions: 54.0 x 66.0 cm │ 21¼" x 26"
(BM 1861-5-18-160)
Other locations: Essick
Lit.: *Letters*, 250, 384, 398, 540
Exh.: San Marino 1987 (45)

   Variants:
I. On India paper: V & A 19954
Exh.: London 1989 (157)

Adam and Eve having eaten of the Forbidden
Tree, the Archangel Michael shows Adam what
the future holds for mankind. The Lazar House is
the second series of dreadful visions of death and
suffering that Adam is forced to observe.
 Bindman (exh. 1989) sees this 'grim scene of
self-laceration under an unseeing deity' as an
image of France under the Terror early in 1793.
In support of his argument he cites the close
proximity of the 'delivery' date of the Milton
Gallery painting ('16 February 1793') and the

publication of 'Fuseli's own renunciation of the Revolution' in the *Analytical Review* of November 1793. Bindman's dating of the painting is, however, erroneous: the letter to William Roscoe that he cites was written not in 1793 but in *1795* (see *Letters*, 126). The picture is therefore not so closely linked in time with events in France at the beginning of 1793; nor is the overlap between the 'renunciation' and work on the painting so easily determined. It is not clear to what extent these details affect Bindman's thesis.

******

For No. **293A** see the combined entry for *The English School* following Nos. **299A-301A**.

******

No. 294.
THE|ODES, EPODES, [SATIRES, EPISTLES,] &C.|OF|HORACE.|TRANSLATED FROM THE LATIN,|BY|PHILIP FRANCIS, D.D.| AND REVISED BY|H.J. PYE,|POET LAUREATE.|WITH OCCASIONAL NOTES.| —|VOL. I. [VOL. II.]|—|=| LONDON:| PRINTED AT THE STANHOPE PRESS,|BY WHITTINGHAM AND ROWLAND,| GOSWELL STREET;|PUBLISHED BY SUTTABY, EVANCE, AND FOX, STATIONERS'|COURT, LUDGATE STREET; SHARPE AND HAILES, PICCA-|DILLY; AND TAYLOR AND HESSEY, FLEET STREET.|—| 1812.

(*collective title*): THE|WORKS|OF|THE GREEK AND ROMAN|POETS,| TRANSLATED INTO ENGLISH VERSE.|—| VOL. I [VOL. XVIII.]|—CONTAINING| FRANCIS AND PYE'S VERSION OF HORACE.|=| LONDON:|PRINTED FOR SUTTABY, EVANCE, AND FOX, STATIONERS'|COURT; SHARPE AND HAILES, MUSEUM, PICCADILLY;|TAYLOR AND HESSEY, FLEET STREET; AND R. JENNINGS|POULTRY.|—|1813 (1/26 illus.).
THE|ODES, SATIRES, EPISTLES, &C.|OF| HORACE.|TRANSLATED BY PHILIP FRANCIS, D.D.|WITH| OCCASIONAL NOTES,|BY H.J. PYE, P.L.|—|VOL. III.|=| CHISWICK:|FROM THE PRESS OF C. WHITTINGHAM,|COLLEGE HOUSE.
THE|WORKS|OF|THE BRITISH POETS.|

INCLUDING|TRANSLATIONS|FROM THE GREEK AND ROMAN AUTHORS.| COLLATED WITH THE BEST EDITIONS,|BY THOMAS PARK, F.S.A.|—|IN THIRTY-SIX VOLUMES.|XXXI.|HORACE,TRANSLATED BY FRANCIS AND PYE.|=| LONDON:| PRINTED FOR JOHN SHARPE, PICCADILLY; |AND SUTTABY, FOX, AND SUTTABY, STATIONERS' COURT,|LUDGATE STREET.| —|1828 (1/71 illus.)

ILLUSTRATIONS TO SHARPE'S EDITION OF THE BRITISH POETS [n.d.]

[Binder's title]: POETICAL|ILLUSTRATIONS.

For the other works in this combined series see Nos. **180-181**.

294.

294. *The Poet Observing Neaera with Her New Lover in Her Grotto*, 1813
(Horace, *Epodes*, XV)
(Vol. XII, facing p. 172)

Engraved by Anker Smith (1759-1819) after Fuseli's lost painting
Imprint: Published by Suttaby, Evance & Fox,| Jan.ʸ. 30. 1813.

Inscription: HORACE. |
  —soon thy pride her wandering love shall
    mourn,
  While I shall laugh, exulting in my turn.
        Epode 15 to Neaera.
Painted by H. Fuseli, R.A. | | Engraved by A.
Smith, A.R.A.
Dimensions (excl. panel): ■ 7.8 x 6.1 cm |
3¹/16" x 2¹³/16"; ▣ 8.0 x 6.4 cm | 3³/16" x 2½";
(incl. panel): ■ 10.3 x 6.4 cm | 4" x 2½" (BL
1066.d.28.12).
Other locations: DHW (1828) (*Satires*, facing
t.p.); NYPL NCI (British) (Vol. 98, facing p. 45)
Plate only: BM 1864-12-10-114
Lit.: Schiff 1507 (7.9 x 6.2 cm/10.5 x 6.5 cm)

            Variants:
  I. Proof before letters: BM 1863-5-9-29
  II. Proof before all letters (lacking verse):
  Huntington 108370 (Vol. I, f.11)

            ✳✳✳✳✳✳

**295. *Dante Swooning Before the Soaring Souls
of Paolo and Francesca*, [1818]**
(Dante, *Inferno*, V, 80-142)

Etching and Aquatint by Henry Fuseli after the
sketch exhibited (1818/16) in the Royal Academy,
and now in the Oeffentliche Kunstsammlung Basel
(1815; Schiff 1537).
Inscription (handwritten): H. Fuseli inv'. | Dante
sees Paolo & Francesca amongst | the unhappy
Spirits v. Dante's Inferno C. | (outside platemark,
bottom right): private plate.
Dimensions: ■ 47.0 x 30.1 cm | 18⁷/16" x 11¹⁵/16"
(BM 1850-11-14-884)
Other locations: Art Institute of Chicago 1991.618
(Sheet=50 cm); ETH 572B; V & A E.1196-1886
(Sheet=49.5 cm); V & A HH25 (Sheet=60.0 cm)
Lit.: Schiff 1509 (47.0 x 35.0 cm)
Exh.: New York 1981 (4)

  Among the sinners in the second circle,
perpetually blown around and buffeted by the
whirlwind, typifying the storms of passion, Dante
meets the lovers Francesca and Paolo, whose love
for each other never forsakes them even amid the
sufferings and hatred of hell. Dante weeps for
them and 'out of pity, | I felt myself diminish, as
if I were dying, | And fell down, as a dead body
falls' (trans. C.H. Sisson, 1980).

            ✳✳✳✳✳✳

295.

296.

No. 296.
AN | DIE ZÜRCHERISCHE JUGEND | AUF DAS
JAHR 1819. | VON DER | NATUR[-]
FORSCHENDEN GESELLSCHAFT. | XXI.
STÜCK. [ZÜRICH]: 1819. (1/1 illus.)

296. *Portrait of Conrad Gessner (1516-1565),*
1819
(*Neujahrsblatt der Naturforschenden Gesellschaft
zu Zürich auf das Jahr 1819*)
(Before p. [1])

Engraved frontispiece by Franz Hegi (1774-1850)
after Fuseli's juvenile drawing ([1754-1756];
Schiff 156)
Inscr. (bottom left): H. Füessli composuit.
Dimensions: ■ 14.9 x 12.5 cm | 5^{14}/16" x 4^{15}/16"
(Michigan Q67.Z963 v.21)
Lit.: Schiff 156; Schiff, 'J.H. Füssli in Zürich',

Librarium, 1964, 132, pl. 4.

The original drawing of this portrait of Gessner,
the Renaissance polymath and naturalist, known as
'the German Pliny', forms part of an album of 46
imaginary portraits of Zurich humanists done c.
1754-1756 when Fuseli was about 14 years old.
Schiff points out that in most cases Fuseli based
his likenesses on authentic portraits,
superimposing the individual's facial features on
full-length figures shown in invented
surroundings. In this illustration, Gessner is seen
working in his museum. But his botanical and
zoological studies have been given a somewhat
esoteric cast by the presence of an alembic, a
specific attribute of the alchemist rather than the
naturalist. The lion in the foreground and
Gessner's pose suggest Fuseli's familiarity with
Durer's *Melencolia* and *St. Jerome*.

******

297.

297. *The Dream*, 1820

Engraved in stipple by Robert William Sievier
(1794-1865) after a miniature by Moses Haughton
(1772 or 1774-1848) of a sleeping young girl seen
from the back, based on Fuseli's painting, *Fairy
Mab Appearing to Two Sleeping Girls,* in the

Sandoz collection, La Tour-de-Peilz, Vaud ([1810-
1820]; Schiff 1504)
Imprint: London, Published Octr. 1, 1820, by
W.J. White, Brownlow Street, Holborn.
Inscription: ENGRAVED BY ROB^T. W^M.
SIEVIER, FROM A MINIATURE PAINTED BY
MOSES HAUGHTON. |

[*left*]

THE DREAM.
LOVE SPORTING IN THE MORNING BEAMS,
WAKES IN THEIR SOULS DELICIOUS DREAMS.
Talysen, Od. XV.v.10.

[*right*]

LE SONGE
L'AMOUR, ATTEND LE MATIN RADIEUX,
POUR INSPIRER DES SONGES AMOUREUX.
Talysen, Od. XV.v.10.

Dimensions: ■ 17.3 x 23.7 cm | 6¹³/16" x 9⁵/16";
■ 18.1 x 24.5 cm | 7²/16" x 9¹⁰/16" (BM
1867-12-14-239)
Other locations: DHW
Lit.: Schiff 1504

Variants:

I. Proof (India paper): BM 1867-3-9-1719

'Talysen' and the source of the verses in the
inscription have not been identified.

******

No. 298.
John Young.
A | CATALOGUE | OF | PICTURES BY BRITISH
ARTISTS, | IN THE POSSESSION OF | SIR
JOHN FLEMING LEICESTER, BART. | WITH
ETCHINGS FROM THE WHOLE
COLLECTION. | INCLUDING THE | PICTURES
IN HIS GALLERY AT TABLEY HOUSE,
CHESHIRE; | EXECUTED BY PERMISSION OF
THE PROPRIETOR; | AND ACCOMPANIED |
WITH HISTORICAL AND BIOGRAPHICAL
NOTICES. | — | BY JOHN YOUNG, |
ENGRAVER IN MEZZOTINTO TO HIS
MAJESTY, | AND | KEEPER OF THE BRITISH
INSTITUTION. | = | LONDON: | PRINTED BY
W. BULMER AND W. NICOL, CLEVELAND-
ROW, ST. JAMES'S. | PUBLISHED BY THE
PROPRIETOR, NO. 65, UPPER CHARLOTTE-
STREET, FITZROY SQUARE; | AND SOLD
ALSO BY R. JENNINGS, BOOKSELLER IN
THE POULTRY; | G. AND W. NICOL, PALL-
MALL; MOLTENO, PALL-MALL;
CARPENTER, BOND-STREET; |
ACKERMANN, STRAND; COLNAGHI, |
COCKSPUR STREET; AND LLOYDS,
HARLEY-STREET. | — | APRIL 2, 1821 (2/69
illus.).

For the other illustration in this work see also No.
265A. For the edition of 1825 see **Addenda.**

298.

298. *Theodore in the Haunted Wood, Deterred
from Rescuing a Female Chased by an Infernal
Knight*, 1821
(John Dryden, *Fables* VII, *Theodore and Honoria*)
(facing p. 14, Plate No. 31)

Outline engraving by Normand fils, i.e., Louis-
Marie Normand (1765-1840) after Fuseli's
painting exhibited (1817/99) at the Royal
Academy and now at the National Museum of
Western Art Tokyo (1817; Schiff, Lost Work 84).
Inscription (top centre): N°. 31. | (bottom centre):
FUSELI.
Dimensions: ■ 9.1 x 10 cm | 3⁹/16" x 4";
■ 9.5 x 10.3 cm | 3¹¹/16" x 4" (BL 561*.d.12.2)
Other locations: Ashmolean 908.2 Lei; DHW;
Newberry W111.D48; Witt; YCBA N5247. +D4
Plate only: BM 1859-12-10-302
Lit.: Schiff 1557; *Letters*, 21, 439
Exh.: Kansas City 1982 (70).

Variants:

I. Proof (India paper): BL 59.e.3 (H=36.5 cm)
Other locations: DHW (H=38.6 cm)

The 'proof for an unpublished plate' noted by
Mason (*Remarks*, 1962, p. 50, note a) is almost
certainly nothing more than the unidentified
orphan copy of this outline in BM. The scene is
summarized by Dryden in the following lines:

He rais'd his Head, and saw a beauteous Maid,
With Hair dishevell'd, issuing through the
  Shade;
Stripp'd of her Cloaths, and e'en those Parts
  reveal'd,
Which modest Nature keeps from Sight
  conceal'd.
Her Face, her Hands, her naked Limbs were
  torn
With passing through the Brakes, and prickly
  Thorn:
Two Mastiffs gaunt and grim, her flight
  pursu'd,
And oft their fasten'd Fangs in Blood embru'd:
Oft they came up and pinch'd her tender Side,
Mercy, O Mercy, Heav'n, she ran, and cry'd;
When Heav'n was nam'd they loos'd their Hold
  again,
Then sprung she forth, they follow'd her amain.
Not far behind, a Knight of swarthy Face,
High on a Coal-Black Steed pursu'd the Chace;
With flashing Flames his ardent eyes were
  fill'd,
And in his Hands a naked Sword he held:
He chear'd the Dogs to follow her who fled,
And vow'd Revenge on her devoted Head.
As *Theodore* was born of noble Kind,
The brutal Action rowz'd his manly Mind:
Mov'd with unworthy Usage of the Maid,
He, though unarm'd, resolved to give her Aid.
A Saplin Pine he wrench'd from out the
  Ground,
The readiest Weapon that his Fury found.

The spectral knight identifies himself as
Theodore's ancestor, Guido Cavalcanti, who had
been driven to suicide out of unrequited love for
the same Maid he now endlessly pursues, feeding
her 'harden'd heart' to his dogs.

******

For No. **298A** see the combined entry for *The
English School* following Nos. **299A-301A**.

******

Nos. **299 - 301**.
John Young.
A|CATALOGUE|OF THE|CELEBRATED
COLLECTION OF PICTURES|OF THE LATE|
JOHN JULIUS ANGERSTEIN, ESQ.|
CONTAINING|A FINISHED ETCHING OF

FUSELI.

299.

FUSELI.

300.

EVERY PICTURE, | AND ACCOMPANIED WITH | HISTORICAL AND BIOGRAPHICAL NOTICES | BY | JOHN YOUNG, | ENGRAVER IN MEZZOTINTO TO HIS MAJESTY, | AND | KEEPER OF THE BRITISH INSTITUTION. | = | LONDON: | = | PRINTED BY W. NICOL, CLEVELAND-ROW, ST. JAMES'S. | PUBLISHED BY JOHN YOUNG, NO. 65, UPPER CHARLOTTE STREET, FITZROY-SQUARE; | AND BY MESSRS. HURST, ROBINSON, AND CO., NO. 90, CHEAPSIDE, | AND NO. 8, PALL-MALL. | JULY, 1823.

[CATALOGUE | DE LA | COLLECTION CÉLÈBRE DE TABLEAUX | DE FEU | M. JEAN JULES ANGERSTEIN, | CONTENANT | UNE GRAVURE FINIE A L'EAU FORTE DE CHAQUE TABLEAU, | ET ACCOMPAGNÉE DE | NOTICES HISTORIQUES ET BIOGRAPHIQUES | PAR | JEAN YOUNG, | GRAVEUR EN MEZZOTINTO A SA MAJESTÉ | ET | CONSERVATEUR DE L'INSTITUTION BRITANNIQUE. | = | À LONDRES: | DE L'IMPRIMERIE DE W. NICOL, CLEVELAND-ROW, ST. JAMES'S. | CHEZ J. YOUNG, NO. 65, UPPER CHARLOTTE STREET, FITZROY-SQUARE; | ET CHEZ MESSRS. HURST, ROBINSON, ET CO., NO. 90, CHEAPSIDE, | ET NO. 8, PALL-MALL. | JUILLET, 1823 (3/43 illus.).

For the re-engravings of 1830 and 1832 see Nos. **299A-301A** and **299B-301B** below.

299. *Satan Starting from the Touch of Ithuriel's Spear*, 1823
(John Milton, *Paradise Lost*, IV, 810-814)
(facing p. 94, Plate No. 40)

Outline engraving on steel by Normand fils, i.e., Louis-Marie Normand (1789-1874) after Fuseli's lost painting No. XIV in the Milton Gallery, formerly in the collection of John Julius Angerstein (1795-1796; Schiff 895)
Imprint: London, March 20, 1823, Published by J. Young, 65, Upper Charlotte Street, Fitzroy Square; | and by | Messrs. Hurst, Robinson & Co. 90 Cheapside.
Inscription: ANGERSTEIN GALLERY. | FUSELI.
Dimensions: ■ 18.9 x 17.5 cm | 7^7/16" x 6^{14}/16" (BL 560.f.1)
Plate only: BM 1860-12-8-121 (Sheet=29.8 cm)

Lit.: Schiff 895 (19.0 x 17.5 cm)

Variants:
I. Proof before all letters (India paper) (Gallery name omitted): BL 1562/49
Imprint: London, March 20, 1823, Published by J. Young, 65, Upper Charlotte Street, Fitzroy Square, | and by | Messrs. Hurst, Robinson & Co. 90 Cheapside.
Inscription: FUSELI.
Other locations: Cambridge Eb.11.33; Cambridge Lib.2.82.3; DHW (H=38.6 cm); KHZ 1926/85
Plate only: V & A E.310-1941

300. *Birth of Eve*, 1823
(John Milton, *Paradise Lost*, VIII, 452-477)
(facing p. 96, Plate No. 41)

Outline engraving on steel by Normand fils, i.e., Louis-Marie Normand (1789-1874) after Fuseli's painting No. XVII in the Milton Gallery, formerly in the John Julius Angerstein collection and now in the Kunsthalle, Hamburg (1795; Schiff 897).
Imprint: London, March 20, 1823, Published by J. Young, 65, Upper Charlotte Street, Fitzroy Square, and by | Messrs. Hurst, Robinson C^o. 90 Cheapside.
Inscription: ANGERSTEIN GALLERY. | FUSELI.
Dimensions: ■ 16.5 x 11.9 cm | 6^7/16" x 4^{11}/16" (BL 560.f.1)
Other locations (plate only): BM 1860.12.8.120; V & A E.311-1941
Lit.: Schiff 897; *Letters*, 117, 126, 136f., 138, 140, 155, 196, 201
Exh.: Kansas City 1989 (14)

Variants:
I. Proof before all letters (India paper) (Gallery name omitted): BL 1562/49
Imprint: London, March 20, 1823, Published by J. Young, 65, Upper Charlotte Street, Fitzroy Square, and by | Messrs. Hurst, Robinson, C^o. 90 Cheapside.
Inscription: FUSELI.
Dimensions: 16.7 x 12.0 cm | 6^9/16" x 4¾"
Other locations: Cambridge Eb.11.33 (facing p. 95); Cambridge Lib.2.82.3; DHW (H=38.6 cm); KHZ 1926/86

In a letter to Roscoe, 14 August 1795, Fuseli denied that 'the aerial figure' was

a representation of the Supreme Being: no Such

thought entered my head—for Believers, let it be the Son, the Visible agent for His Father; for others it is merely a Superiour Being entrusted with her Creation, and looking up for approbation of His work to the inspiring power above'.

In his next letter, he added: 'To Him who reads Milton there can exist no *Uncertainty* who it is; the expression of the figure, looking *upwards* for approbation, points to a Superiour Being'.

While Adam lies 'Abstract as in a trance', God removes a rib from his left side:

Under his forming hands a Creature grew,
Manlike, but different sex, so lovely fair,
That what seem'd fair in all the World, seem'd now
Mean, or in her summ'd up, in her contain'd
And in her looks, which from that time infus'd
Sweetness into my heart, unfelt before,
And into all things from her Air inspir'd
The spirit of love and amorous delight.

FUSELI

301.

301. *The Deluge*, 1823
(John Milton, *Paradise Lost*, XI, 742-754)
(facing p. 98, Plate No. 42)

Outline engraving on steel by Normand fils, i.e.

Louis-Marie Normand (1789-1874), after Fuseli's lost painting No. XXV in the Milton Gallery
Imprint: London, March 20, 1823, Published by J. Young, 65, Upper Charlotte Street, Fitzroy Square, | and by | Messʳˢ. Hurst, Robinson & Cº.90 Cheapside.
Inscription: ANGERSTEIN GALLERY. | FUSELI
Dimensions: ■ 16.5 x 11.9 cm | 6⁷/16" x 4¹¹/16" (BL 560.f.1)
Other locations (plate only): BM 1860-12-8-119; BM 1860-12-8-122
Lit.: Schiff 900; Schiff 1963, 151; Schiff-Viotto 1977, no. 146, pl. 146¹; *Letters*, 155, 196, 218
Exh.: Zurich 1941 (142) (as 'Adam and Eve Before the Judge', by 'an English engraver')

Variants:
I. Proof before all letters (India paper) (Gallery name omitted): BL 1562/49
Imprint: London, March 20, 1823, published by J. Young, 65, Upper Charlotte Street, Fitzroy Square, | and by | Messʳˢ. Hurst, Robinson & Cº. 90 Cheapside.
Inscription: FUSELI.
Dimensions: ■ 16.7 x 12.0 cm | 6⁹/16" x 4¾"
Other locations: Cambridge Eb.11.33 (facing p. 97); Cambridge Lib.2.82.3; DHW (H=38.6 cm); KHZ 1926/87

******

Nos. 299A - 301A.
John Young.
A | CATALOGUE | OF THE | CELEBRATED COLLECTION OF PICTURES | OF THE LATE | JOHN JULIUS ANGERSTEIN, ESQ. | CONTAINING | A FINISHED ETCHING OF EVERY PICTURE, | AND ACCOMPANIED WITH | HISTORICAL AND BIOGRAPHICAL NOTICES. | BY JOHN YOUNG, | ENGRAVER IN MEZZO-TINTO TO HIS MAJESTY, AND KEEPER OF THE BRITISH INSTITUTION. | — | LONDON: | PRINTED J. MOYES, TOOK'S COURT, CHANCERY LANE. | PUBLISHED BY MOON, BOYS, AND GRAVES, | 6, PALL MALL. | 1829 (3/41 illus.).

299A. *Satan Starting from the Touch of Ithuriel's Spear*, 1830
(John Milton, *Paradise Lost*, IV, 810-814)
(Plate No. 39, facing p. 46)

Unsigned outline engraving on steel by [Normand fils, i.e. Louis-Marie Normand (1789-1874)]

Imprint: London, Published Jany 1, 1830 by Moon, Boys & Graves, 6, Pall Mall.
Inscription: FUSELI|SATAN STARTING FROM THE TOUCH OF ITHURIEL'S SPEAR.
Dimensions: ■ 19.2 x 17.7 cm | 7^9/16" x 7"; ▣ 19.8 x 18.4 cm | 7^{13}/16" x 7¼" (Bodleian 1706.d.525) (?imprint cropped)

Variants:
I. Proof (India paper): BM 181-2-12
Imprint: London, Published Jany 1, 1830 by Moon, Boys & Graves, 6, Pall Mall.

300A. *The Birth of Eve*, 1830
(John Milton, *Paradise Lost*, VIII, 426-470)
(Plate No. 40)

Unsigned outline engraving on steel
Imprint: London, Published Jany 1, 1830 by Moon, Boys & Graves, 6, Pall Mall.
Inscription: THE BIRTH OF EVE.|FUSELI.
Dimensions: ■ 16.8 x 12.2 cm | 6^{10}/16" x 4^{13}/16"; ▣ 17.6 x 12.9 cm | 6^{14}/16" x 5^3/16" (Bodleian 1706.d.525) (imprint lacking)

Variants:
I. Proof (India paper): BM 181-2-12

301A. *The Deluge*, 1830
(John Milton, *Paradise Lost*, XI, 742-754)
(unnumbered plate, between pp. 46-47)

Unsigned outline engraving on steel
Imprint: London. Published Jany 1. 1830 by Moon, Boys & Graves, 6. Pall Mall.
Inscription: FUSELI|THE DELUGE.
Dimensions: ■ 16.8 x 12.0 cm | 6^{10}/16" x 4¾"; ▣ 17.5 x 12.9 cm | 7" x 5^1/16" (Bodleian 1706.d.525)

Variants:
I. Proof (India paper): BM 181.2.12
Imprint: London. Published Jan.^y.1. 1830 by Moon, Boys & Graves, 6, Pall Mall.

******

Nos. 285A, 288A, 293A, 298A, 299B.
MUSEUM|OF|PAINTING AND SCULPTURE,|OR|COLLECTION|OF THE PRINCIPAL PICTURES,|STATUES AND BAS-RELIEFS|IN THE PUBLIC AND PRIVATE GALLERIES OF EUROPE,|DRAWN AND ETCHED|BY RÉVEIL:|WITH DESCRIPTIVE, CRITICAL AND HISTORICAL NOTICES,|BY DUCHESNE SENIOR.|—|VOLUME I. [-VOLUME XVI].|—| LONDON:|TO BE HAD AT THE PRINCIPAL BOOKSELLERS|AND PRINTSHOPS.|—|1829 [-1834] (1/1008 illus.).

[Added title page]: MUSÉE|DE|PEINTURE ET DE SCULPTURE,|OU|RECUEIL|DES PRINCIPAUX TABLEAUX,|STATUES ET BAS-RELIEFS|DES COLLECTIONS PUBLIQUES ET PARTICULIÈRES DE L'EUROPE.|DESSINÉ ET GRAVÉ À L'EAU FORTE|PAR RÉVEIL;|AVEC DES NOTICES DESCRIPTIVES, CRITIQUES ET HISTORIQUES,|PAR DUCHESNE AÎNÉ.|—| VOLUME I.[-XVI].|—| PARIS|AUDOT, ÉDITEUR,|RUE DES MAÇONS-SORBONNE, N° II.|1829 [-1834].

...AVEC DES NOTICES DESCRIPTIVES, CRITIQUES ET HISTORIQUES|PAR LOUIS ET RÉNÉ MÉNARD|VOLUME PREMIER [VOLUME VI].| PARIS|V^E A. MOREL & CIE, LIBRAIRES-ÉDITEURS|13, RUE BONAPARTE|1872.

MUSEO|DI PITTURA E SCULTURA,|OSSIA RACCOLTA|DEI PRINCIPALI QUADRI, STATUE E BASSIRILIEVI|DELLE| GALLERIE PUBBLICHE E PRIVATA D'EUROPA,|DISEGNATI ED INCISI SULL'ACCIAIO|DA RÉVEIL;|CON LE NOTIZIE DESCRITTIVE, CRITICHE E STORICHE|DI DUCHESNE PRIMOGENITO.| —|PRIMA TRADUZIONE ITALIANA.| VOLUME I.[-IV]|[-APPENDICE.|VOLUME I.-XIII.]| FIRENZE,|PAOLO FUMAGALLI E C., EDITORI;|MDCCCXXVII. [-M,DCCCXLV.] [1837-1845]

G. Hamilton.
THE|ENGLISH SCHOOL|A SERIES OF|THE MOST APPROVED PRODUCTIONS|IN| PAINTING AND SCULPTURE;|EXECUTED BY BRITISH ARTISTS|FROM THE DAYS OF HOGARTH TO THE PRESENT TIME;| SELECTED, ARRANGED, AND ACCOMPANIED WITH DESCRIPTIVE AND| EXPLANATORY NOTICES IN ENGLISH AND FRENCH,|BY G. HAMILTON.|ENGRAVED IN OUTLINE UPON STEEL.|—|VOL. 1. [-VOL. 4.]|—| LONDON.|CHARLES TILT, 86, FLEET STREET.|—|1831 [-1832].

[ÉCOLE|ANGLAISE,|RECUEIL|DE
TABLEAUX, STATUES ET BAS-
RELIEFS|DES PLUS CÉLÈBRES ARTISTES
ANGLAIS,|DEPUIS LE TEMPS D'HOGARTH
JUSQU'À NOS JOURS,|GRAVÉ A L'EAU-
FORTE SUR ACIER;|ACCOMPAGNÉ|DE
NOTICES DESCRIPTIVES ET HISTORIQUES,|
EN FRANÇAIS ET EN ANGLAIS,|PAR G.
HAMILTON,|ET PUBLIÉ SOUS SA
DIRECTION.|—|VOL. 1 [-TOME 4]|—|À
PARIS.|CHEZ M. HAMILTON, GRANDE RUE
DES BATIGNOLLES, N° 50,|PRÈS LA
BARRIÈRE DE CLICHY;|ET CHEZ AUDOT,
LIBRAIRE, RUE DES MAÇONS-SORBONNE,
N° 11.|—|1831].

SELECT SPECIMENS|OF|BRITISH
ARTISTS,|FROM THE DAYS|OF HOGARTH
TO THE PRESENT TIME;|OR|SERIES OF 72
ENGRAVINGS OF THEIR MOST|APPROVED
PRODUCTIONS.|EXECUTED ON STEEL IN
THE FIRST STYLE OF OUTLINE,|
SELECTED, ARRANGED, AND
ACCOMPANIED WITH DESCRIPTIVE AND
EXPLANATORY|NOTICES IN ENGLISH AND
FRENCH,|BY G. HAMILTON.| PARIS:|
BAUDRY'S EUROPEAN LIBRARY,|9, RUE
DU COQ, NEAR THE LOUVRE.|—|1837
(?/72 illus.).

[CHEFS-D'OEUVRE|DES|ARTISTES
ANGLAIS,|DEPUIS|HOGARTH JUSQU'A
NOS JOURS,|OU|SUITE DE 72 GRAVURES
DE LEURS PRODUCTIONS|LES PLUS
ESTIMÉES,|SOIGNEUSEMENT GRAVEES AU
TRAIT SUR ACIER,|CHOISIS, MIS EN
ORDRE ET ACCOMPAGNÉ DE NOTES
DESCRIPTIVES ET EXPLICATIVES|EN
ANGLAIS ET EN FRANÇAIS,|PAR G.
HAMILTON.| PARIS,|BAUDRY, LIBRAIRIE
EUROPEENNE,|9, RUE DU COQ, PRÈS LE
LOUVRE.|—|1837].

GALLERY|OF|BRITISH ARTISTS,|FROM
THE DAYS|OF HOGARTH TO THE PRESENT
TIME,|OR|SERIES OF 288 ENGRAVINGS OF
THEIR MOST|APPROVED PRODUCTIONS.|
EXECUTED ON STEEL IN THE FIRST STYLE
OF OUTLINE,|SELECTED, ARRANGED,
AND ACCOMPANIED WITH DESCRIPTIVE
AND EXPLANATORY NOTICES|IN ENGLISH
AND FRENCH,|BY G. HAMILTON.|—|IN
FOUR VOLUMES.|—|VOL. I. [-VOL. IV.]|

PARIS,|BAUDRY'S EUROPEAN LIBRARY,|
9, RUE DU COQ, NEAR THE LOUVRE.|1837,
1839 (10/288 illus.).

[GALERIE|DES|ARTISTES ANGLAIS,|
DEPUIS| HOGARTH JUSQU'A NOS JOURS,|
OU|SUITE DE 288 GRAVURES DE LEURS
PRODUCTIONS|LES PLUS ESTIMÉES,|
SOIGNEUSEMENT GRAVÉES AU TRAIT SUR
ACIER,|CHOISIE, MISE EN ORDRE ET
ACCOMPAGNÉE DE NOTES DESCRIPTIVES
ET EXPLICATIVES|EN ANGLAIS ET EN
FRANÇAIS,|PAR G. HAMILTON.|EN
QUATRE VOLUMES.|VOL. I. [-VOL. IV.]|
PARIS,|BAUDRY, LIBRAIRIE EUROPEENNE,
9, RUE DU COQ, PRÈS LE LOUVRE.|—|
1837, 1839.]

William Shakespeare.
THE|COMPLETE WORKS|OF|WILLIAM
SHAKSPEARE,|WITH EXPLANATORY &
HISTORICAL NOTES|BY THE MOST
EMINENT COMMENTATORS.|
ACCURATELY PRINTED FROM THE
CORRECT AND ESTEEMED EDITION OF|
ALEXANDER CHALMERS, F.S.A.|—|IN
TWO VOLUMES.|WITH WOOD AND STEEL
ILLUSTRATIONS.|VOL. I [-VOL. II.]|
[Vignette]| *The Globe Theatre, where Shakspeare
acted.*| PARIS,|BAUDRY'S EUROPEAN
LIBRARY,|9, RUE DU COQ, NEAR THE
LOUVRE.|—|1838.

ILLUSTRATIONS|OF|SHAKSPEARE'S
WORKS,|CONTAINING|ONE HUNDRED
AND FIFTY ENGRAVINGS|ON STEEL AND
WOOD,|ADAPTED TO ALL EDITIONS.|
[Vignette]| PARIS,|BAUDRY'S EUROPEAN
LIBRARY,|9, RUE DU COQ, NEAR THE
LOUVRE.|—|1839.

For the other illustrations in these works see also
Nos. **117D - 119D, 123D, 263B**

285A. *Ugolino,* 1831
(Dante, Inferno, XXXIII)
(G. Hamilton, II, Plate 140)

Outline engraving on steel by Normand fils, i.e.
Louis-Marie Normand (1789-1874)
Inscription: Fuseli.| |Normand fils.|UGOLINO.
Dimensions: ■ 10.7 x 8.2 cm | 4³/16" x 3¼";
■ 11.0 x 8.4 cm | 4⁵/16" x 3⁵/16" (Essick)

Other locations: SB Bern Litt.LI 3162 (1837); BL 1422.a.25; BL 1267.a.19 (Gallery 1837); DHW (1839); KHZ 102c (1839) (Vol. III, plate 140); Lausanne AVA 3356; NYPL MCT 1832; Witt (1839); YCBA N6764.H35; ZBZ AQ645 (1837)

288A. *The Nursery of Shakespeare*, 1832
(G. Hamilton, III, Plate 154)

Outline engraving by Normand fils, i.e. Louis-Marie Normand (1789-1874)
Inscription: Fuseli. | | Normand fils. | NURSERY OF SHAKSPEARE. | EDUCATION DE SHAKSPEARE.
Dimensions: ■ 10.1 x 8.0 cm | $3^{15}/16$" x $3^3/16$";
▣ 10.4 x 8.4 cm | $4^1/16$" x $5^5/16$" (Essick)
Other locations: BL 1422.a.25; BL 1267.a.19 (Gallery 1837); DHW (1839); Folger PR2752.1838e (Vol. I, between pp. cxxiv-cxxv); Folger Art Vol. e.50 (Plate 9); NYPL 3-MCT 1832; NYPL 3-MAMR (Gallery 1837) (Vol. II); YCBA N6764.H35
Plate only: Folger Art File S527.4 no. 6

293A. *The Vision of the Lazar House*, 1832
(J. Milton, *Paradise Lost*, XI, 477-490)
(G. Hamilton, IV, Plate No. 283)

Outline engraving on steel by Étienne-Achille Réveil (1800-1851) after Fuseli's lost painting, No. XXIV in the Milton Gallery, formerly in the collection of Thomas Coutts ([1794-1795]; Schiff Lost Work 44)
Inscription (bottom right within the border): AR | 995. | (bottom left): Fuseli pinx. | VISION D'UN HOPITAL. | THE VISION OF THE LAZAR-HOUSE.
Dimensions: ■ 8.1 x 10.1 cm | $3^3/16$" x 4";
▣ 8.4 x 10.3 cm | $3^5/16$" x $4^1/16$" (Essick)
Other locations: SB Bern Litt.LI 3162 (1839) (Vol. II); BL 7812.a.19 (1831); BL 1422.a.25; BL 1267.a.19 (Gallery 1837); DHW (1839); Essick; KHZ ah 102c; NYPL 3-MCT (1832); NYPL 3-MAMR (Gallery 1837); YCBA N6764.H35;
Plate only: Witt
Exh.: Kansas City 1989 (22)

Variants:
I. Lacking title in English (*Museum*, XIV): Chicago N7520.R45

II. Reissued with added inscription in Italian (*Museo*, V): Chicago N7520.R456 Append
Inscription (top left): Tab. de G136 bis | | (centre): Tavola 549 | (bottom right, within the border): AR | 995. | (bottom left): Fuseli pinx. | VISION D'UN HOPITAL. | THE VISION OF THE LAZAR-HOUSE. | VISIONE D'UN OSPEDALE
III. Reissued with Italian inscription in top line replaced with French (1872): Chicago N7520.R455 1872
Inscription (top line): T.6 | | P. 100 | [etc.]

298A. *Theodore in the Haunted Wood, Deterred from Rescuing a Female Chased by an Infernal Knight*, 1832.
(John Dryden, *Fables* VII, *Theodore and Honoria*)
(G. Hamilton, III, Plate 164)

Outline engraving on steel by Normand fils, i.e. Louis-Marie Normand (1789-1874)
Inscription: Fuseli. | | Normand fils. | THEODORE & HONORIA.
Dimensions: ■ 9.1 x 10.2 cm | $3½$" x 4";
▣ 9.3 x 10.5 cm | $3^{10}/16$" x $4^2/16$" (BL 7812.a.19)
Other locations: SB Bern Litt.LI.3162 (1839) (Vol II); BL 1422.a.25; BL 1267.a.19 (Gallery 1837); DHW (1839) (Vol. II); KHZ ah102c; Lausanne AVA 3356; NYPL 3-MCT 1832; NYPL 3-MAMR (Gallery 1837); YCBA N6764.H35
Plate only: Witt

299B. *Satan Starting from the Touch of Ithuriel's Spear*, 1832
(John Milton, *Paradise Lost*, IV, 810-814)
(G. Hamilton, IV, Plate No. 255)

Outline engraving on steel by Normand fils, i.e. Louis-Marie Normand (1789-1874)
Inscription: Fuseli. | | Normand fils. | SATAN & ITHURIEL.
Dimensions: ■ 11.1 x 8.2 cm | $4^6/16$" x $3¼$";
▣ 11.4 x 8.5 cm | $4½$" x $3^5/16$" (BL 7812.a.19)
Other locations: SB Bern Litt.LI 3162 (Vol. II); BL 1422.a.25; BL 1267.a.19 (Gallery 1837); DHW (1839) (Vol. II); KHZ ah102d; Lausanne AVA 3356; NYPL 3-MCT (1832); NYPL 3-MAMR (Gallery 1837); YCBA N6764.H35

******

MILTON when a BOY instructed by his MOTHER.

303.

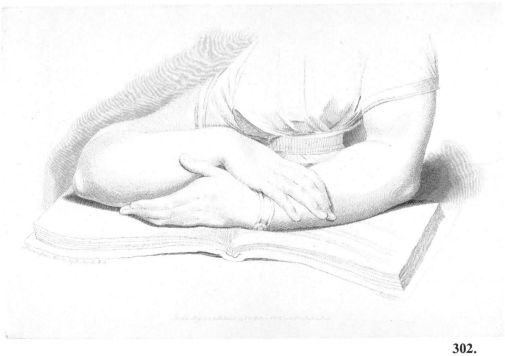

302.

302. *Woman's Bust and Folded Arms on Book*, 1825

Lithograph by J.G. Walker
Imprint: London, May 19, 1825, Publish'd by J.
G. Walker, N 6. Blizard Place Fulham Road.
Inscription: Drawn from Nature by H. Fuseli,
R.A.|J G Walker, sc.
Dimensions (sheet): ■ 22.3 32.5 cm |
8¹³/16" x 12¾" (BM 1863-5-9-87)

Neither William Todd's *Directory of Printers* nor Michael Twyman's *Lithographic Printers* lists Walker's name. I have not been able to determine whether he is related to the John Walker admitted at age 22 to the Royal Academy (10 March 1783) as an Engraver (Sidney C. Hutchinson, 'The Royal Academy Schools', no. 434).

The sitter shown in Walker's lithograph has not been identified. Apart from the known renderings of women's arms, prepared for Lavater (Nos. **62, 63, 109** and **110**; Schiff 505-508), there are two others previously unknown: an uncatalogued drawing of Mrs. Lavater's crossed hands at the Beinecke Library, Yale; and a study of a woman's gloved arms, showing also her bust as in this example, sold as lot 17 at Christie's Fuseli sale, 14 April 1992.

******

303. *Milton When a Boy Instructed by His Mother*, [n.d.]

Engraved in stipple by John Perry (n.d.) perhaps after a lost version of painting no. XXXVIII in the Milton Gallery ([1796-1799]; Schiff 916-916A)
Inscription: Henry Fusili Esqʳ. R.A. pinxᵗ.||J. Perry sculpᵗ.|MILTON when a BOY, instructed by his MOTHER.
Dimensions: 52.0 x 37.8 cm | 20⁷/16" x 14¹⁴/16" (BM 1907-11-66)
Lit.: Schiff 916-916A (50.0 x 40.2 cm); Altick 1985, pl. 34; Martyn Anglesea, *Portraits and Prospects*, 1989 (exh. cat.), no. 8, p. 16.

Martyn Anglesea thinks this engraving may be after a lost Milton Gallery painted version. Documentary evidence to support this view has in fact turned up in the form of an announcement, under the rubric, 'Monthly Retrospect of the Fine Arts', which appeared in the *Monthly Magazine* for August 1804 (XVIII, 62), describing a previously unknown engraving of '*Milton, when a Boy, instructed by his Mother.* H. Fuseli, R.A. pinxt. A[ntoine] Cardon [(1772-1813)] sculpt.':

The original from which this was copied was one of the sweetest pictures in the Milton Gallery, and is very well engraved in the chalk manner, but rather too violent in the effect; it wants somewhat of the half-tint, to produce a mellow and harmonious effect.

I have not yet located a copy of Cardon's plate. However, no evidence has yet been found to support Martyn Anglesea's suggestion that Moses Haughton rather than Perry engraved this plate.

******

304. *Oedipus Cursing His Son Polynices*, 1826
(Sophocles, *Oedipus in Colonus*, 1383-1389)

Engraved in stipple by John Perry (n.d.) after the painting exhibited (1786/84) in the Royal Academy and now in the National Gallery of Art, Washington ([1786]; Schiff, Lost Work 7)
Imprint (bottom left): London Pubᵈ. by H. Perry, 7. Hanover St. Hanover Sqʳᵉ. 1ˢᵗ. May 1826, and sold at Nᵒ. 747, facing the Print Gallery in the Bazaar, Soho Square—
Inscription (bottom left): Painted by H. Fuseli R.A.||Engrav'd by John Perry|(centre): OEDIPUS CURSING HIS SON POLYNICES (open caps)|

ΟΙΔ.
—σὺ δ᾽ ἔρρ᾽ ἀπόπτυστός τε, κἀπάτωρ ἐμοῦ,
κα κῶν κακιστε, τασδε συλλαβὼν ἄρὰς,
ἅς σοι καλοῦμαι, μήτε γῆς ἐμφυλίου
δόρει κρατῆσαι μήτε νοστῆσαι ποτε
τὸ κοῖλον Ἄργος, ἀλλὰ συγγενεῖ χερὶ
θανεῖν κτανεῖν Θ᾽ ὑφ᾽ οὗπερ ἐξελήλασαι.
τοιαῦτ ἀρῶμαι και καλῶ τὸ Ταρτάρου
Κ.Τ.Λ... Οἰδίπους ἐπὶ Κολωνῶ 1383 Ed
Brunck

Oed.
—Hence to thy doom, accursed! I disclaim
A fathers part in thee, thou scorn of men;
And with thee bear the curse I call to blast thee:
That thou may'st ne'er thy rightful throne regain;
And never to the Argive vales return;

But fall unpitied by a kindred hand,
Requiting first thine exile by his death.
Thus do I curse thee &c. |
Dales translation of the Tragedies of Sophocles,
    Vol. 1, p. 185.
Dimensions: ■ 30.0 x 35.5 cm | 11¾" x 14"
(BM 1870-10-8-2798)

Lit.: Schiff, Lost Work 7; Charlotte Haenlein, 'A
Fuseli "Oedipus", Lost and Now Found,' *Apollo*,
October 1974, 321, pl. 2

Variants:
I. Unfinished proof, before all letters (artist's
names only): V & A 186401

OEDIPUS CURSING HIS SON POLYNICES.

304.

305. *Fairy Mab*, 1834
(J. Milton, *L'Allegro*, l. 102)

Engraved by William Raddon (fl. 1816-1862)
after Fuseli's painting No. XXX in the Milton
Gallery in the Senn collection, Basel (1795; Schiff
909)
Imprint: London, Published for the Proprietor by
Messʳˢ Ackermann & Cᵒ Strand, & Moon, Boys &
Graves 6. Pall Mall. Febʸ 1, 1834.
Inscription: H. Fuseli R. A. Pinxᵗ. | | W. Raddon
sculpᵗ. | FAIRY MAB. | Engraved from the Original
Picture in the | | Collection of the Rᵗ. Honbᵉ. the
Countess of Guilford. | to whom by permission,
this Print is | | respectfully inscribed by her obliged
Servᵗ. W. Raddon.
Dimensions: ■ 18.5 x 22.8 cm | 7¼" x 9" (BM
1848-11-11-4)

Other locations: DHW; V & A E.1191-1886
Lit.: Schiff 909 A (18.3 x 22.8 cm); Schiff 1963,
94, pl. 49; *Letters*, 416, 417, 419
Exh.: Kansas City 1982 (47); Kansas City 1989(24)

Variants:
I. Proof (India paper) (Vol. III, between pp.
121-122): Folger Art Vol. 655

The reviewer in *Arnold's Magazine* for March
1834 (p. 489) found nothing 'wonderfully
captivating' in this print of Fuseli's
'extravaganza', which illustrates the line 'How
Faery Mab' the junkets eat'. This is the food
traditionally set out at night by country people for
the fairies.
    The figure behind Mab is her dwarfish
companion the Brownie.

305.

306.

306. *Portrait of Joseph Priestley*, 1836

Engraved in mezzotint by Charles Turner (1773-1857) after Moses Haughton's drawing from Fuseli's painting in Dr. Williams' Library, London (1783; Schiff 761)
Imprint: London, Published Octr 1836 by Richard Taylor, Red Lion Court, Fleet Street.
Inscription: Painted by — Fuseli, Esqr| |
Engraved by C. Turner, A.R.A.
Dimensions: ■ [28.6 x 22.0 cm | 11¼" x 8¾"]? (BM ??call no.)
Other locations: Dr. Williams's Library
Lit.: Alfred Whitman, *Charles Turner* (1907), no. 484.

Variants:
I. Proof before any letters: BM 1864-12-10-287

PUBLICATION NOTICE
[*The Christian Reformer*, XVIII (June 1835), II, 404-405]

PROPOSED ENGRAVING BY TURNER
IN MEZZOTINTO FROM A
PORTRAIT OF DR. PRIESTLEY BY FUSELI.

Several prints from portraits of Priestley have been published, some of which have possessed considerable merit as works of art. Yet they are contemplated with some feeling of disappointment. 'Where is that that fire and sensibility,' the spectator is disposed to exclaim, 'which I have been wont to attribute to Priestly? The writer of those deeply affecting letters from America, he whose friendship with Lindsey was one of the finest instances of fraternal union in modern history, must have been a man of more feeling than is legible in the lines of the countenance before me.'

The truth is, that the paintings from which these prints were copied were taken in later life and have too much the appearance of a countenance composed from a sitting; whereas that from which an engraving is now proposed to be made was taken when he was under fifty, and at a moment when engaged with the artist, a man of taste, warmly attached to civil and religious freedom and himself educated for the church, in conversation on some of those great topics which called forth the whole soul of each. It was in these favourable circumstances about the year 1780, in the parlour of the late

Mr. Johnson the bookseller, that Fuseli, nearly the first artist of his day, caught the image of the man. It extends nearly to the feet, and he is represented as seated with books and instruments before him. This painting stands at the head of the stairs at Dr. Williams's Library, Redcross Street, Cripplegate, where it may at any time be seen. When it becomes extensively known by means of an engraving in that superior style which is alone adapted to do it justice, when the master touches of the great Italian [*sic!*] shall have been faithfully copied by an accomplished professor of the sister art, it will throw fresh and more interesting light on the genius and character of one to whom posterity has not yet paid the full debt of justice. Such of his admirers as join in the sentiment of Coleridge respecting him,

'Whom that my fleshly eye hath ne'er beheld,
Still grieves my heart,'

will here recognize the Priestley they had always imagined to themselves, but of whom they had never yet seen a representation which came up to their own conception: while his few remaining *associates*, who must have known him chiefly in later life, will discover an identity of profile with the other paintings, united to the advantages of greater animation in the subject and superior skill in the artist. Should there be any in whose bosoms animosity towards him is not yet extinguished, they will say, 'Is this indeed the man of whom I have been so long speaking or thinking evil? He LOOKS the refutation of every unworthy design I had attributed to him.' No more appropriate present could be made to any young man who, as a Sunday-school teacher or otherwise, has made extraordinary and disinterested exertions for the temporal or spiritual improvement of his fellow-creatures; no more suitable ornament for that which was the scene of Priestley's most laborious and useful exertions, the fruits of which many still acknowledge with tears of gratitude,—the chapel vestry. His philosophical admirers, too, many of whom poured forth feeling and eloquent tributes to his memory on the centenary of his birth, may be expected to lend encouragement to any undertaking which contribute towards raising the name of the father of Pneumatic Chemistry, the great improver of our knowledge of the phenomena of light and colours, the accurate observer of the human mind and the philosophical defender of Revealed Religion, to that elevated pedestal in the sight of ages to which it is entitled.

A small committee of the earliest subscribers will attend to the execution of the design, and should more copies be subscribed for than are necessary to cover the expense, the writer begs leave to suggest that the surplus should be employed on a pencil lithograph for *cottage* use.

Hampstead, May 19, 1835.　　　GEORGE KENRICK.

ADDENDA

Der Besessene

93B.

No. 93B.
[Heinrich Füssli, Johann Jakob Horner, & Felix Nüscheler].
[Overall title]: HEINRICH FUESSLI'S SÄMMTLICHE WERKE, | NEBST EINEM VERSUCH SEINER BIOGRAPHIE. | — | ZÜRICH, 1807. [1809.] | IN DER KUNSTHANDLUNG VON FUESSLI UND COMPAGNIE.

[Wrappers]: HEINRICH FUESSLI'S | SÆMMTLICHE WERKE | — | ERSTES HEFT. [ZWEYTES HEFT.] | ZÜRICH, 1807. [1809] | IN DER KUNSTHANDLUNG VON FUESSLI UND COMPAGNIE (16/16 illus.).

For the other illustrations in this work see also Nos. **13A, 70A-71A, 72C, 73E, 74A, 275-283.**

93B. *The Escapee*, [1807-1809]
(Part II, No. 4, facing p. 12)

Outline engraving (not reversed) by Johann Heinrich Lips (1758-1817) after Fuseli's drawing in the British Museum ([1772]; Schiff 515)
Inscription (bottom right): H. Lips. sc. | **Der Besessene**
Dimensions: ■ 17.4 x 30.5 cm | 6¹³/₁₆" x 12"
Other locations: Bern A16.441; DHW; ETH 1524a; ZBZ KK 307

No. 178A.
[Charles Knight].
...THE GALLERY OF PORTRAITS [&c.]...
1833-1837 (for the original entry see *supra* p. 223).
Please insert after the titles:
　　　　PROSPECTUS
　　　　(BL 10803.1.3)

　　GALLERY OF PORTRAITS.

The Committee of the Society for the Diffusion of Useful Knowledge have directed their attention for more than a year, to the preparation of a series of engraved Portraits, of some of the most eminent men of every age and country. They have been led to undertake the publication of authentic and carefully, executed Portraits of those who have exercised the greatest influence on Science, Art, Literature, Politics, and Religion, from a belief that a large number of persons, whose knowledge has been cultivated by the reading of cheap books, may have their tast in the same way called forth and gratified by the possession of cheap, but well-engraved prints. A taste for the Fine Arts has been, to a certain extent, exclusive in this country; for the high price of *good* Engravings has prevented all but the more opulent from partaking of the improvement and gratification which they are calculated to afford. To place such engravings within the reach of the public at large is a novel experiment; but one which the Committee believe will not be unsuccessful. They have determined to make the experiment upon *Portraits*, in the first instance, because the associations connected with that branch of art are familiar to most persons. The short Biographical Memoir, also, which will be attached to each Engraving, will afford means of communicating information, which, although in some cases scanty, will be valuable to many readers, in connexion with faithful and spirited representations of those who have exercised a powerful influence upon the condition of mankind.

The "Gallery of Portraits" to be published by the Society, although similar in form, and not inferior in execution, to one or two series of Portraits now publishing, will be in a great degree different from any other, in the selection of those [ONE HUNDRED] illustrious persons whose likenesses it is thought desirable to make familiar to all...[*List of names omitted*]

The Committee have to acknowledge the ready assistance of many distinguished Personages and public bodies, in furthering their plan, by permitting copies to be made, for engraving, from original Pictures in their possession. Artists of ability have already finished many copies from the collections of His Majesty, of the King of the French, of the Royal Society, of the French Institute, of the Duke of Devonshire, the Duke of Marlborough, Lord Egremont, Lord Holland, and

Lord Dover. The execution of the Engravings from any of these Pictures has been confided to some of the most eminent engravers of the day.

Each Number will consist of THREE PORTRAITS, with accompanying biographical Memoirs, occupying upon an average twenty-four pages of letter-press. The size of the Work will be Super-royal Octavo, corresponding with the small-paper copies of Lodge's Portraits. The price of each Number will be HALF-A-CROWN. No large-paper copies will be printed.

The *First* Number will appear on the 31st of May, 1832, and the Work will be continued Monthly.

LONDON: CHARLES KNIGHT, PALL-MALL EAST.

Nos. 180-181.
John Milton.
PARADISE LOST [&c.]....1805 (for the original entry see *supra* p. 225).

Please insert before the 'Added title...1814':

SUPPLEMENT | TO THE | BRITISH POETS. | — | COLLATED WITH THE BEST EDITIONS: | BY | THOMAS PARK, F.S.A. | — | VOL. I. [-VOL. V] | = | LONDON: | PRINTED AT THE STANHOPE PRESS, | BY CHARLES WHITTINGHAM, | 103, GOSWELL STREET; | FOR J. SHARPE; AND SOLD BY W. SUTTABY, | STATIONERS' COURT, LUDGATE STREET. | — | 1808.

These contain 'ADDITIONAL POEMS, *Not inserted in the Works of the Poets*'.

Nos. 237-243.
THE | ODYSSEY | OF | HOMER, | TRANSLATED BY A. POPE [&c.]...1806 [1807]

239. *Odysseus Addressing the Shade of Ajax in Tartarus*, 1806
(Book XI, 543 ff.)

Engraved by Isaac Taylor Jr (1759-1829) (for the original entry see *supra* pp. 285-286)
Please add after Variant IV.:

V. Reissued 1819-1836 with additional inscription but lacking imprint: YCBA PA4033.S4 (H=26.1 cm) (f. 31)

Inscription (top of sheet): The Shade of Ajax indignantly refusing to commune | with Ulysses. | (bottom): Painted by H^y. Fuseli R.A. | | Engraved by Isaac Taylor |

　　While yet I speak the shade disdains to stay,
　　In silence turns, and sullen stalks away.
Odyssey, Book XI

Other locations: DHW (plate only)
(sheet = 29.3 cm)

240. *Odysseus Between Scylla and Charybdis,* 1806
(Book XII, 429-518)

Engraved by William Bromley (1769-1842) (for the original entry, see *supra* p. 287)
Please add after Variant IV.:

V. Reissued 1819-1836 with additional inscription but lacking imprint: YCBA PA4033.S4 (H = 26.1 cm) (f. 32)
Inscription (top of sheet): Ulysses after the destruction of his companions, escaping the | dangers of Scylla & Charybdis. |

　　All unsustained between the wave and sky
　　Beneath my feet the whirling billows fly.
Odyssey, Book XII.

Other locations: DHW (plate only)
(sheet = 28.5 cm)

Nos. 265A, 298.
John Young.
A | CATALOGUE | OF | PICTURES BY BRITISH ARTISTS, | IN THE POSSESSION OF | SIR JOHN FLEMING LEICESTER, BART. [&c.] …1821
Please add after last line of title (pp. 311, 341):

A | CATALOGUE | OF | PICTURES BY BRITISH ARTISTS, | IN THE POSSESSION OF | SIR JOHN FLEMING LEICESTER, BART. | WITH | ETCHINGS FROM THE WHOLE COLLECTION. | INCLUDING THE | PICTURES IN HIS GALLERY AT TABLEY HOUSE, CHESHIRE; | EXECUTED BY PERMISSION OF THE PROPRIETOR; | AND | ACCOMPANIED | WITH HISTORICAL AND BIOGRAPHICAL NOTICES. | — | BY JOHN YOUNG, | ENGRAVER IN MEZZOTINTO TO HIS MAJESTY, | AND | KEEPER OF THE BRITISH INSTITUTION. | — | LONDON: | PUBLISHED BY THE PROPRIETOR, NO. 65, UPPER CHARLOTTE-STREET, FITZROY-SQUARE; | AND SOLD ALSO BY HURST, ROBINSON AND CO. PALL-MALL; | R. JENNINGS, POULTRY; G. AND W. NICOL, PALL-MALL; MOLTENO, PALL-MALL; | COLNAGHI, COCKSPUR-STREET; AND LLOYD AND SON, HARLEY-STREET. | — | 1825. ['Printed by Robinson and Hernaman, | Leeds.'

Please add to 'Other locations' in entries No. **265A** and No. **298**: YCBA N5247. + D4 1825 (not seen)

303A. *Milton When a Boy Instructed by His Mother,* 1830

Mezzotint re-engraved on steel by Henry Edward Dawe (1790-1848)
Inscription: H Fuseli R·A· Pinx^t | | Pub^d April 1830 | | H Dawe Sculp
Dimensions: ■ 15.0 x 11.1 cm | 5^5/16" x 4^{11}/16" (DHW)

APPENDIX
PUBLICATION EXPENSES FOR 'CHALMERS' SHAKESPEARE', 1805, 1811
(Reading University)

[Page 1]
Shakspeare with Notes by
------ Chalmers ------

9 Vol* Demy 8°. fine paper N°*:	1500
9 do. inferior do	1000
10 Royal 8°	500
10 Super Royal 8°	250

Demy fine paper published in N°* 700 to divide

750 Ream Paper at 30/6 Longman		1143. 15. --
Interest on d°		22. -- --
130 Ream Paper at 32/ Longman & Co		208. -- --
11 d° &/s 32/6 d°		18. 5. 7.
17 d° d° 26 & 27 Morgan Wrapp*.		22. 4. --
Tissue paper for plates		2. 12. --
Patent blue for wrappers for demy & Royal paper of Cobb & C°		70. 8. 2.
Blue demy 11 q[uire]*		10. --
Printing	283 Sheets at £3.10/ @ Baldwins	1002. 7. --
	Reprinting N°. 1. 7 Sheets N° 600	17. 10. --
	do 4. 6 do 200	10. 10. --
	Wrappers, Prospectus, Labels &c. &c. &c. as per account	59. 11. --
	Sewing the Numbers	103. 14. 9.

Royal Ed. N° 500, 450 to divide

Paper	60 Ream at £3.14/ Hollingsworth & Co.	222. -- --
	124 do 4.4/ (do.)	520. 16. --
	104 do 4.7 (do)	452. 8. --
	9 do 7 q*. £1.6 Longman	19. 8. --
	Carr. Forward	3895. 19. 6.

Shakespear cont^d. [Page 2] Amount br^t. forw^d.		3895. 19. 6.
Printing	283 Sheets & ½ at 35/	496. 2. 6.
	Extra for 600 of Vol 1	14. 10. --
	d°. Title & Index	8. 17. 6.
	Reprinting N° 1 600	26. 19. 0.
	Hot pressing this & the Demy Edition	145. 12. --
	Sewing the Numbers	10. 3. --
	Paper for Wrappers	5. 9. 6.

Super Royal Edition N° 250

Paper	58 Ream at £3.3/ Hollingsworths	182. 14. --
	83½ do do 3.10.0 do	292. 5. --
Printing	283 Sheets & ½ at 21/	297. 13. 6.

Demy, Inferior Edition N° 1,000

Paper	500 Ream at 23/6 Morgan	587. 10. 0.
	66 do 27 do	89. 2. 0.
Printing	283 Sheets at 16/	226. 8. 0.
	Altering Titles	2. -- --
	The Editor Mr. Chalmers	105. -- --
	Mr. Fuseli for 37 Drawings at £3.3/	116. 11. --
	Engraving 37 Plates	865. 4. --
	d° writing on d°	13. 16. --
Head	Neagle Repairing	7. 17. 6.
	Richards printing the Plates	182. 10.
	Carr: Forwds.	7572.

	[Page 3] Shakspeare contd Amt brot. forwds	7572.
Paper for plates	2 Ream 8½ qu[ire]s Super Royal for Plates, Req	17. 15. --
	5 d° d°	23. 12. --
	14 ¾ d° Demy d°	53. 2. 3.
	Gravel printing the head for the demy Inf: Edit & Paper	5. 9. 6.
Incidents	Inserting Proposals, Advertisements, Sorting, and a set of the Royal paper for the Editor, & for Mr Fuseli	99. -- 3.
	Publishing at 4 Per Ct on £2001.12.0	80. -- --
	Purchase of Plates from Bunbury's designs of Marson[?]	160. -- --
	d° Mr. Ritson's MSS.	110. 16. --
		£8121. 12. --

Cr

By Sale of 26700 N°s on demy paper at £7.4/ Pr 100	1922. 8.		
d° 550 Royal d° 14.8/	79. 4	2001. 12. --	
2400 Sets divided at £2.11/ Per Ct		6120. -- --	
N° 1 of the demy Edit. sold & accounted for above	26700		
Divided this day 700 Sets of 40 N°s each	28000		
Remaining to be accounted for	6850		
Total Numbers printed	61550		

PUBLICATION EXPENSES FOR CHALMERS' SHAKESPEARE 1811

Jan 13	Chalmers Shakespear 9 Vols 8vo 500 fine with plates, 500 fine without pl. 1000 Com.[mon] no pl.		
	Paper 497 Reams fine demy 34/6 Key ---		857. 6. 6.
		Interest	8. 12. --
	566 Reams demy 31/6 Bowles & G.		891. 9. --
		Interest	14. 17. --
	for plates Bowles & G.		14. 17. 6.
	Print 6¾ Sh. Vol. 1 No. 750 @ 58/-		20. 6. --
	27¾ Sh. Notes to 1000 @ 65/-		890. 7. 6.
	2¼ Sh. Index @ 78/- with strong ink & extra press work		9. 15. 0
	Extra for Greek & altering title ---		1. 9. --
	283 Sh. No 1000 Com[mon] paper @ 9/- & Run extra press work		254. 14. --
	1000 Sets labels for each edition		5. -- --
	Underchd. on Royal 8vo Edition		11. -- --

Plates repairing by C. Heath from Fuseli		47. 15. 6.
Head d° by Collier		4. 14. 6.
Plates printing by Cox & Barnett		50. -- --
Advertising		19. 16. 6.
	31/-	3100. -- --

Fine 4.14.6 [?] Com[mon] 3.12.0
d° pl. 5.8.0 [?]

Aspern	17	Cradock	17	Lackington	100	Scholey	20
Bagster	33	Deighton	17	Mawman	50	Walker	117
Booth	17	Egerton	55	MacKinley		Wilkie	66
Baldwin	62	Earle	32	Lea	17	Longman	*250
Booker	25	Evans	33	Nichols	8	£387.10.0 at 6 Mos	
Barker	29	Faulder	116	Newman	48	15th. Jany. 18[12?]	
Black	48	Gray	32	Pheney	17	*63 Fine	
Cadell	11	Gale	37	Robinson	32	62 d° plates	
Crosby	33	Harding	8	Richardn.	33	125 Comn. no pl.	
Clarke	17	Johnston	83	Rivington	140	White	33
Cuthell	55	Lowndes	17	Stockdale	15	Wilson	50

[Page 2] Shakspeare contd

N° 1 of the Royal Edition sold and accounted for above   550
Divided this by 450 Sets of 40. N°s each   <u>1750</u>
                 Total Numbers <u>printed</u>   <u>20300</u>

It is proposed to sell
The super royal Edn @ 21/ per vol or £10.10.0 in Bds

Royal	18/	9. 0. 0	d°
Demy fine	10/6	4.14.6	d°
Demy inferior	7/-	3. 3. 0	d°

	Sup: Rl	Rl	Demy f.	Inf.		S Rl	R	DF	Inf
Asperne, Babcock, Black									
Clarke & Son, Crosby, Deighton}	2¹/12	3⁹/12	5⁵/12	8⁴/12	Payne	8	14²/5	23²/5	32
Gardner, Kay, Lea, D. Walker			Total 20 £50		Rivingtons	17½	31½	49	70
Bagster, Kent, Evans }					Richardsons	4¼	7¹⁰/20	11⁹/10	17
Lea, Ogilvy, White }	4¹/6	7³/6	11⁴/6	16⁴/6	Stockdale	2⁵/8	46²³/40	72⁸/20	143½
Baldwin	11⁵/10	20⁷/10	32²/10	46	Scatcherd	4²/3	8²/5	23¹/60	11½
Barker	3⁵/8	6²¹/40	10³/20	14½	Wilkie	8¹/3	15	23¹/3	33¹/3
Cadell & Co	14¹⁰/30	25⁸/10	40⁴/30	57¹⁰/30	John Walker	14²/3	26²/5	41⁹/15	58½
Cuthell & M Egerton	6¹⁷/18	12¹/3	19⁴/9	27⁷/9	Rems. 55/120				
Faulder, Hurst, Vernor	6¼	11¼	17½	25	60 £153				
Harding, Miller	1	1⁴/5	2⁴/5	4					
Johnson	10¹/3	18⁹/15	28⁴/16	41²/3					
Lowndes	2¹/48	3²/3	5³³/48	8¹/12					
Lackington	12½	22½	35	50					
Longman	20¹³/60	36²/5	56³⁷/60	80¹³/15	194 ⁶/60 £494.19.1				
Mc.Queen	2½	4½	7	10	⁷/60 SR	5.9.8			
Mawman	6¹/6	12¹/3	17⁷/60	24²/3	³/5 R	3.12.0			
Nichols	1¹/6	2¹/10	3⁴/15	4²/3	²³/60 D fine	1.8.0			
Ostell	2	5³/5	5³/5	8	⁵/8 Demy	5.4	Pd.....	<u>505.14.1</u>

ABBREVIATED REFERENCES AND BIBLIOGRAPHY
Compiled by M. Carbonell

I. MANUSCRIPT SOURCES

British Library.
Archives of Richard Bentley and Son, 1829-1898. Available in Chadwyck-Healey's series of microfilmed publishers' archives. See printed guides:

Michael L. Turner. *Index and Guide to the Lists of the publications of Richard Bentley & Son 1829-1898*. Bishops Stortford: Chadwyck-Healey Ltd.; Teaneck, N.J.: Somerset House, 1975.

Index to the archives of Richard Bentley & Son 1829-1898. Comp. Alison Ingram. Cambridge: Chadwyck-Healey; Teaneck, N.J.: Somerset House, 1977.

Huntington Library, San Marino, California.
Uncatalogued Du Roveray papers.

McGill University, McLennan Library
Lande Collection (publishers' and engravers' receipts; letters of H. Fuseli to Du Roveray).

New York Public Library, Manuscript Division.
Duyckinck Collection. Letters of Robert Balmanno to John Sartain of Philadelphia.

Philadelphia Free Library.
'Autograph Letters of Engravers' (mainly to Francis Isaac Du Roveray).

University of Reading.
Archives of Messrs. Longman. Available in Chadwyck-Healey's series of microfilmed publishers' archives. See printed guide:

Index to the archives of the House of Longman 1794-1914. Comp. Alison Ingram. Cambridge: Chadwyck-Healey; Teaneck, N.J.: Somerset House, 1981.

Schweizerische Landesbibliothek, Bern.
MS list of engravings by Johann Rudolf Schellenberg (Ms. 7361).

Collection of D.H. Weinglass & M. Carbonell.
Business letters, 1794-1810, to F.I. Du Roveray.

Winterthur, Kunstmuseum.
Account books of Johann Rudolf Schellenberg.

Winterthur, Stadtbibliothek.
Ulrich Hegner papers (incl. Hegner's MS. diary and letters from Johann Heinrich Füssli).

Zurich, Zentralbibliothek.
MS. Lind. (Johann Heinrich Füssli papers, incl. letters from Henry Fuseli and Ulrich Hegner).

II. GENERAL LIST

Allentuck 1974
ALLENTUCK, Marcia. 'Further Reflection on Henry Fuseli's *Nightmare* by Way of a New Inventory of Influence and Caricature'. *Humanities Association Review* (1974), 458-465.

Allentuck 1976
ALLENTUCK, Marcia. 'Henry Fuseli's "Queen Katherine's Vision" and Macklin's Poet's Gallery: A New Critique'. *Journal of the Warburg and Courtauld Institutes*, 39 (1976), 266-268.

Altick 1986
ALTICK, Richard. *Paintings from Books: Art and Literature in Britain, 1760-1900*. Columbus, OH: Ohio State University Press, 1986.

Analytical Review
The Analytical Review, or History of Literature Domestic and Foreign. Vols. I-XXVIII; n.s. Vol. I. London: 1788-1799.

Andersen 1989
ANDERSEN, Jørgen. *De År i Rom: Abilgaard, Sergel, Füssli*. Copenhagen: Christian Ejlers' Forlag, 1989.

Anglesea 1989
ANGLESEA, Martyn. *Portraits and Prospects. British and Irish Drawings and Watercolours from the Collection of the Ulster Museum*

Belfast. Belfast: Ulster Museum Belfast and the Smithsonian Institution Traveling Exhibition Service, 1989.

Antal 1956
ANTAL, Frederick. *Fuseli Studies*. London: Routledge & Kegan Paul, 1956.

Appenzeller 1906
APPENZELLER, Heinrich. *Der Kupferstecher Franz Hegi von Zürich 1774-1850. Sein Leben und Seine Werke. Beschreibendes Verzeichnis seiner sämtlichen Kupferstiche*. Zurich: Verlag von H. Appenzeller, 1906.

Argan 1960
ARGAN, Giulio Carlo. 'Fuseli, Shakespeare's Painter'. In *Il Teatro di William Shakespeare*. 3 vols. Milan: Giulio Einaudi, 1960, I, xxix-xli. (Reprinted: G.C. Argan. *Da Hogarth a Picasso, L'arte moderna in Europa*. Milan: Feltrinelli, 1983, 97-107).

Asiatic Researches
ASIATIC RESEARCHES. *Index to the First Eighteen Volumes of the Asiatic Researches, or Transactions of the Society, Instituted in Bengal for Enquiring into the History and Antiquities, the Arts, Sciences and Literature of Asia*. Calcutta: Printed at the Bengal Military Orphan Press, 1835.

Aubert & Roux 1921
AUBERT, Marcel & Marcel Roux. *Un siècle d'histoire de France par l'estampe. 1770-1871. Collection de Vinck*. Paris: Imprimerie nationale, 1921.

Baker 1875
BAKER, William Spohr. *William Sharp, Engraver, with a Descriptive Catalogue of His Works*. Philadelphia: Gebbie & Barrie, 1875.

Barlow
BARLOW, Joel. *The Works*. Ed. William K. Bottorff & Arthur L. Ford. 2 vols. Vol. I: Prose. Vol. II: Poetry. Gainesville, FL: Scholars' Facsimiles & Reprints, 1970.

Behrendt 1983
BEHRENDT, Stephen C. *The Moment of Explosion: Blake and the Illustration of Milton*. Lincoln: University of Nebraska Press, 1983

Bentley 1969
BENTLEY, G.E., Jr. *Blake Records*. Oxford: Clarendon Press, 1969.

Bentley 1977
——————. *Blake Books*. Oxford: Clarendon Press, 1977.

Bentley 1980
——————. 'The Great Illustrated Book Publishers of the 1790's and William Blake'. In *Editing Illustrated Books: Papers given at the fifteenth annual Conference on Editorial Problems, University of Toronto, 2-3 November 1979*. Ed. William Blissett. New York & London: Garland Publishing, 1980, 58-96.

Bentley 1988
——————. *Blake Records Supplement*. Oxford: Clarendon Press, 1988.

Bentley & Nurmi 1964
—————— & Martin K. Nurmi. *A Blake Bibliography*. Minneapolis: University of Minnesota Press, 1964.

Beyer 1947
BEYER, Werner W. *Keats and the Daemon King*. New York: Oxford University Press, 1947.

Bindman 1978
BINDMAN, David. *The Complete Graphic Works of William Blake*. London: Thames & Hudson, 1978.

Bircher & Straumann 1971
BIRCHER, Martin & Heinrich Straumann. *Shakespeare und die Deutsche Schweiz bis zum Beginn des 19. Jahrhunderts. Eine Bibliographie Raisonnée*. Bern & Munich: Francke Verlag, 1971.

Blake
BLAKE, William. *Complete Writings with variant readings*. Ed. Geoffrey Keynes. London, Oxford, New York: Oxford University Press, 1966.

Blake 1980

_____. *The Letters of William Blake with Related Documents*. 3rd ed. Ed. Geoffrey Keynes. Oxford: Clarendon Press, 1980.

Boase 1947

BOASE, T.S.R. 'Illustrations of Shakespeare's Plays in the Seventeenth and Eighteenth Centuries'. *Journal of the Warburg and Courtauld Institutes*, 10 (1947), 83-108.

Boase 1963

_____. 'Macklin and Bowyer'. *Journal of the Warburg and Courtauld Institutes*, 26 (1963), 148-177.

Boerlin-Brodbeck 1981

BOERLIN-BRODBECK, Yvonne. 'Eine Mutter mit Ihrer Familie auf dem Lande'. *Neue Zürcher Zeitung*, 29-30 August 1981, 65-66.

Boime 1987

BOIME, Albert. *Art in an Age of Revolution 1750-1850*. Chicago & London: University of Chicago Press, 1987.

Bourguignon 1936

BOURGUIGNON, Jean. *Napoléon Bonaparte d'après Arnault-Aulard-Chateaubriand*, [etc.]. 2 vols. Paris: Les Éditions nationales, 1936.

Boydell Catalogue 1803

BOYDELL, John & Josiah. *An Alphabetical Catalogue of Plates, Engraved by the most esteemed Artists, After the finest Pictures and Drawings of the Italian, Flemish, German, French, English, and Other Schools, which compose the stock of John and Josiah Boydell, Engravers and Printsellers, No. 90, Cheapside, and at the Shakspeare Gallery, Pall Mall; Preceded by an Account of Various Works, Sets of Prints, Galleries, &c. Forming part of the same stock*. London: [Boydell], 1803.

Bradley 1980

BRADLEY, Laurel. 'Eighteenth-Century Paintings and Illustrations of Spenser's *Faerie Queene*: A Study in Taste'. *Marsyas: Studies in the History of Art*, XX (1979-1980), 31-51.

Bray 1851

BRAY, Mrs. Eliza Anne. *The Life of Thomas Stothard, R.A.* London: John Murray, 1851.

Bronson 1938

BRONSON, Bertrand H. *Joseph Ritson: Scholar-at-Arms*. 2 vols. Berkeley, CA: University of California Press, 1938.

Brown 1979

BROWN, David B. 'Fuseli's Drawings for Jonson's *Masque of Queenes*'. *Burlington Magazine* (February 1979), 111-113.

Buchner 1873

BUCHNER, Karl. *Aus Den Papieren der Weidmannschen Buchhandlung*. Berlin: Weidmannsche Buchhandlung, 1873.

Calloway 1981

CALLOWAY, Stephen. *English Prints for the Collector*. Guildford & London: Lutterworth Press; Woodstock, NY: The Overlook Press, 1981.

Christie's 14 April 1992

CHRISTIE'S. *Drawings by Henry Fuseli, R.A. From a Private Collection*. 14 April 1992. London: Christie's, 1992.

Cohen 1964

COHEN, Ralph. *The Art of Discrimination: Thomson's* The Seasons *and the Language of Criticism*. London: Routledge & Kegan Paul, 1964.

Cohn 1924

COHN, Albert M. *George Cruikshank: A Catalogue Raisonné of the Work Executed during the Years 1806-1877. With collations, notes, approximate values, facsimiles, and illustrations*. London: Office of "The Bookman's Journal", 1924.

Collins Baker 1948

BAKER, C.H. Collins. 'Some Illustrators of Milton's *Paradise Lost*'. *Library*, 5th ser. 3 (1948), 1-21, 101-119.

364

Cunningham 1829-1833
CUNNINGHAM, Allan. 'Henry Fuseli', in *The Lives of the Most Eminent British Painters, Sculptors and Architects*. 6 vols. London: John Murray, 1829-1833, II, 260-320. (2nd enlarged ed. 1830-1833).

Dante 1972
DANTE ALIGHIERI. *La Divina Commedia*. Ed. & annotated C.H. Grandgent; revised Charles S. Singleton. Cambridge, MA.: Harvard University Press, 1972.

Dante 1980
_____. *The Divine Comedy*. Trans. C.H. Sisson. Manchester: Carcanet New Press, 1980.

Darwin 1981
DARWIN, Erasmus. *The Letters*. Ed. Desmond King-Hele. Cambridge: Cambridge University Press, 1981.

Delteil 1925-1930
DELTEIL, Loys. *Le Peintre-Graveur Illustré (XIXe et XXe siècles)*. Vols. XX-XXIX-bis: *Honoré Daumer*, I-XI. Paris: Chez l'Auteur, 1925-1930.

De Vesme/Calabi 1928
CALABI, A. *Francesco Bartolozzi; catalogue des estampes et notice biographique d'après les manuscrits de A. de Vesme, complétés d'une étude critique*. Milan: Guido Modiano, 1928.

Douglas 1903
DOUGLAS, R.J.H. *The Works of George Cruikshank, Classified and Arranged with references to Reid's Catalogue and their approximate values*. London: J. Davy & Sons, 1903.

Du Roveray I-IV
BENTLEY, G.E., Jr. & D.H. Weinglass. 'F.I. Du Roveray, Illustrated-Book Publisher 1798-1806. Parts I-IV'. Bibliographical Society of Australia and New Zealand *Bulletin*, XII, Nos. 1-4, 1988 (issued 1990).
I. D.H. Weinglass. 'The Life of a Huguenot Publisher and Connoisseur in London'. XII, No. 1 (1988), 1-19.

II. G.E. Bentley, Jr. 'The Amateur and the Trade'. XII, No. 2 (1988), 63-83.
III. G.E. Bentley, Jr. 'Du Roveray's Artists and the Engravers' Strike'. XII, No. 3 (1988), 97-146.
IV. G.E. Bentley, Jr. 'A Bibliography of His [*Du Roveray's*] Publications'. XII, No. 4 (1988), 167-186.

Easson & Essick 1972-1979
EASSON, Roger R. & Robert N. Essick. *William Blake, Book Illustrator: A Bibliography and Catalogue of the Commercial Engravings*. 2 vols. Normal, IL: The American Blake Foundation, Illinois State University, 1972, 1979.

Essick 1980
ESSICK, Robert N. *William Blake Printmaker*. Princeton, N.J.: Princeton University Press, 1980.

Essick 1983
_____. *The Separate Plates of William Blake. A Catalogue*. Princeton, N.J.: Princeton University Press, 1983.

Essick 1985
_____. *The Works of William Blake in the Huntington Collections. A Complete Catalogue*. San Marino, CA.: The Huntington Library, Art Collections, Botanical Gardens, 1985.

Essick 1991
_____. *William Blake's Commercial Book Illustrations. A Catalogue and Study of the Plates Engraved by Blake after Designs by Other Artists*. Oxford: Clarendon Press, 1991.

Euripides
EURIPIDES. *With an English Translation*. Ed. & translated Arthur S. Way. 'The Loeb Classical Library'. London: William Heinemann; Cambridge, MA: Harvard University Press, 1912.

***Farington Diary* 1978-1984**
FARINGTON, Joseph. *The Diary of Joseph Farington*. Eds. [Vols. I-VI] Kenneth Garlick &

Angus Macintyre; [Vols. VII-XVI] Kathryn Cave. 16 vols. London & New Haven: Yale University Press, 1978-1984.

Feaver 1981
FEAVER, William & Ann Gould. *Masters of Caricature from Hogarth and Gillray to Scarfe and Levine*. London: Weidenfeld & Nicolson, 1981.

Federmann 1927
FEDERMANN, Arnold. *Johann Heinrich Füssli Dichter und Maler 1741-1825*. Zurich & Leipzig: Orell Füssli Verlag, 1927.

Fielding 1905
FIELDING, Mantle. *Catalogue of the Engraved Works of David Edwin*. Philadelphia: Privately printed, 1905.

Frankau 1902
FRANKAU, Julia. *An Eighteenth Century Artist & Engraver John Raphael Smith, His Life and Works*. London: Macmillan, 1902.

Frankau 1904
_____. *William Ward A.R.A. James Ward, their Lives and Works*. London & New York: Macmillan & Co., 1904.

Fredericksen 1988
FREDERICKSEN, Burton B., assisted by Julia I. Armstrong & Doris A. Mendenhall. *The Index of Paintings Sold in the British Isles during the Nineteenth Century*. Santa Barbara, CA & Oxford: The Provenance Index of the Getty Art History Information Program/ABC-CLIO, 1988-. Vol. I. 1801-1805; Vol. II. 1806-1810.

Friedman 1974
FRIEDMAN, Winifred H. *Boydell's Shakespeare Gallery*. New York: Garland, 1976 (Ph.D. dissertation, Harvard, 1974).

George
GEORGE, Mary Dorothy. *Catalogue of Political and Personal Satires Preserved in the Department of Prints and Drawings in the British Museum*. Vols. V-XI [1771-1832]. London: British Museum, 1935-1954.

George 1959
_____. *English Political Caricature 1793-1832: A Study of Opinion and Propaganda*. Oxford: Clarendon Press, 1959.

Glaser 1922
GLASER, Curt. *Die Graphik der Neuzeit. Vom Anfang des XIX. Jahrhunderts bis zur Gegenwart*. Berlin: Bruno Cassirer, 1922.

Gradmann 1967
GRADMANN, Erwin. *Eidgenössische Technische Hochschule Zürich. Graphische Sammlung: Geschichte, Sammlungsbestand, Ausstellungen*. Zurich: ETH, 1967.

Grego 1880
GREGO, Joseph. *Rowlandson the Caricaturist: A Selection from Rowlandson's Works with Anecdotal Descriptions of his famous caricatures*. 2 vols. London: Chatto & Windus; New York: J.W. Bouton, 1880. (Reprinted: New York: Collectors' Editions, 1970).

Grunfeld 1969
GRUNFELD, Frederic V. *The Art and Times of the Guitar: An Illustrated History of Guitars and Guitarists*. New York: Macmillan, 1969.

Haenlein 1974
HAENLEIN, Charlotte. 'A Fuseli *Oedipus*, Lost and Now Found'. *Apollo* (October 1974), 321.

Hagstrum 1964
HAGSTRUM, Jean. *William Blake, Poet and Painter. An Introduction to the Illuminated Verse*. Chicago & London: University of Chicago Press, 1964.

Hahn 1982
HAHN, Karl-Friedrich. '"Füssli im Gesprach mit Bodmer": Ein Sokratischer Dialog'. In *Interaktionsanalysen: Aspekte dialogischer Kommunikation*. Ed. Gerhard C. Rump & Wilfried Heindrichs. Hildesheim: Gerstenberg Verlag, 1982, 177-206.

Hall 1985
HALL, Carol Louise. *Blake and Fuseli: A Study in the Transmission of Ideas*. New York & London: Garland Publishing, 1985.

Halsband 1980
HALSBAND, Robert. *The Rape of the Lock and its Illustrations 1714-1896*. Oxford: Clarendon Press, 1980.

Hamlyn 1978
HAMLYN, Robin. 'An Irish Shakespeare Gallery'. *Burlington Magazine*, 120 (August 1978), 515-529.

Hammelmann 1957
HAMMELMANN, Hanns 'Eighteenth-Century English Illustrators: Henry Fuseli RA'. *The Book Collector*, VI, 4 (1957), 350-360.

Hammelmann 1975
_____. *Book Illustrators in Eighteenth Century England*. Ed. T.S. R. Boase. New Haven: Yale University Press, 1975.

Hartmann 1969
HARTMANN, Wolfgang. *Die Wiederentdeckung Dantes in der deutschen Kunst. J.H. Füssli - A.J. Carstens - J.A. Koch*. Bonn: Rheinische Friedrich-Wilhelms-Universität, 1969. (Ph.D. dissertation).

Haydon 1960-1977
HAYDON, Benjamin Robert. *Diary*. Ed. Willard Bissell Pope. 5 vols. Cambridge: Harvard University Press, 1960-1977.

Hazard & Delteil 1904
HAZARD, N.A. & Loys Delteil. *Catalogue raisonné de l'oeuvre lithographié de Honoré Daumier*. Orrouy/Oise: N.A. Hazard, 1904.

Heath 1992
HEATH, John. *The Heath Family Engravers, 1779-1878*. Scolar: Aldershot, 1992.

Helvetisches Journal
HORNER, Jakob. 'Die Kunst Ausstellung in Zürich im Jahr 1802'. *Helvetisches Journal für Literatur und Kunst*. 1802, I, 162-171.

Hesiod
HESIOD. *Theogony*. Ed. M.L. West. Oxford: Clarendon Press, 1966.

Hill 1966
GILLRAY, James. *Fashionable Contrasts: Caricatures by James Gillray*. Introduced and annotated by Draper Hill. London: Phaidon, 1966.

Hodnett 1982
HODNETT, Edward. *Image and Text. Studies in the Illustration of English Literature*. London: Scolar Press, 1982.

Hoe 1911
HOE, Robert. *Sale of the Library...To be sold by Auction Beginning on April 24, 1911*. 4 Parts. New York: The Anderson Auction Co., 1911-1912.

Homer
HOMER. *The Iliad. With an English Translation*. 2 vols. Trans. A.T. Murray. 'The Loeb Classical Library'. Cambridge, MA: Harvard University Press; London: William Heinemann, 1965-1967.

_____. *The Odyssey. With an English Translation*. 2 vols. Trans. A.T. Murray. 'The Loeb Classical Library'. Cambridge, MA: Harvard University Press; London: William Heinemann, 1938-1942.

Horace
Horace. *Satires. With an English Translation*. Trans. H.R. Fairclough. 'The Loeb Classical Library'. Cambridge, MA: Harvard University Press; London: William Heinemann, 1926.

Horner 1917
HORNER, Friedrich. 'Briefe des Alumnats-inspektors Prof. Joh. Jacob Horner (1779-1831). Auswahl aus den Jahren 1794-1830; Ein Beitrag zu den Beziehungen Zürichs zu Goethe und Weimars klassischer Zeit'. In *Zürcher Taschenbuch*, 1917. (Reprinted: Zurich: Buchdruckerei Berichthaus, 1916).

Hufford 1982
HUFFORD, David J. *The Terror that Comes in the Night*. Philadelphia: University of Pennsylvania Press, 1982.

Hunt 1872
HUNT, Leigh. *The Autobiography, with Reminiscences of Friends and Contemporaries.* 2 vols. New York: Harper & Brothers, 1872.

Hunt 1973
HUNT, John Dixon. 'Milton's Illustrators'. In *John Milton: Introductions*. Ed. John Broadbent. Cambridge: Cambridge University Press, 1973.

Hutchison 1962
HUTCHISON, Sidney C. 'The Royal Academy Schools, 1768-1830'. *The Walpole Society*, 38 (1960-1962), 123-191.

Irwin 1966
IRWIN, David. *English Neoclassical Art: Studies in Inspiration and Taste.* London: Faber & Faber; Greenwich, CT: New York Graphic Society, 1966

Jackson 1915
JACKSON, F. Nevill. 'Balloon Caricatures'. *Connoisseur* (May-August 1915), 84.

Jaton 1988
JATON, Anne-Marie. *Johann Caspar Lavater: Philosoph, Gottesmann, Schöpfer der Physiognomik.* Zurich: SV International & Schweizer Verlaghaus, 1988.

Jonson
JONSON, Ben. *Works.* Ed. C.H. Herford & Evelyn Simpson. 11 vols. Oxford: Clarendon Press, 1925-1952.

_____. *Ben Jonson's Plays and Masques.* Ed. Robert M. Adams. 'Norton Critical Edition'. New York & London: W.W. Norton & C., 1979.

Juvenal
JUVENAL. *The Sixteen Satires.* Trans. Peter Green. Harmondsworth, Middx.: Penguin, 1967.

Kaplan 1988
KAPLAN, Paul H.D. 'The Earliest Images of Othello'. *Shakespeare Quarterly*, 39 (Summer 1988), 171-186.

Keay, 1974
KEAY, Carolyn. *Henry Fuseli.* London: Academy editions; New York: St. Martin's Press, 1974.

Klingender 1947
KLINGENDER, Francis D. *Art and the Industrial Revolution.* London: Adams & Mackay, 1947. (Reprinted: Ed. & rev. Arthur Elton. New York: Augustus M. Kelley, 1968. [Does not contain Fuseli illustration]).

Knowles 1831
KNOWLES, John. *The Life and Writings of Henry Fuseli.* 3 vols. London: Henry Colburn & Richard Bentley, 1831. (Reprinted: With a new introduction by D.H. Weinglass. Millwood, N.Y., London & Nendeln: Kraus Thomson, 1982).

Lambert 1987
LAMBERT, Susan. *The Image Multiplied: Five Centuries of Printed Reproductions of Painting and Drawings.* London: Trefoil Publications, 1987.

Lande 1983
McGILL UNIVERSITY LIBRARIES. *Catalogue of the Lawrence Lande William Blake Collection in the Department of Rare Books and Special Collections of the McGill University Libraries.* Montreal: McLennan Library, McGill University, 1983.

Lange 1991
LANGE, Thomas. 'Intramuralia', *Huntington Library Quarterly* 54 (1991), 88.

Letters
FUSELI, Henry. *The Collected English Letters.* Ed. David H. Weinglass. Millwood, N.Y., London & Nendeln, Liechtenstein: Kraus International Publications, 1982.

Litteratur und Kunst
Journal für Litteratur und Kunst. Ed. Johann Jacob Horner. Vols. I-IV. 1806.

Lonchamp 1920
LONCHAMP, F.C. *L'Estampe et le Livre à Gravures. (Un Siècle d'Art Suisse 1730-1830).* Lausanne: Librairie des Bibliophiles, 1920.

Macandrew 1959
MACANDREW, Hugh. 'Henry Fuseli and William Roscoe'. *Liverpool Libraries, Museums & Arts Committee Bulletin*, 8 (1959-1960), 5-52.

Man 1962
MAN, Felix. 'Lithography in England (1801-1810)'. In *Prints: Thirteen Illustrated Essays on the Art of the Print*. Ed. Carl Zigrosser. New York: Holt, Rinehart & Winston for the Print Council of America, 1962, 98-130.

Man 1970
_____. *Artists' Lithographs. A World History from Senefelder to the present day*. New York: G.P. Putnam's Sons, 1970.

Maré 1981
MARÉ, Eric de. *The Victorian Woodblock Illustrators*. London: Gordon Fraser Gallery, 1980; New York: The Sandstone Press, 1981.

Martin 1987
MARTIN, Philip W. *Mad Women in Romantic Writing*. Sussex: Harvester Press; New York: St. Martin's Press, 1987.

Mason 1951
MASON, Eudo C. *The Mind of Henry Fuseli. Selections from his Writings with an Introductory Study*. London: Routledge & Kegan Paul, 1951.

Mason 1961
_____. 'Heinrich Füssli und Winckelmann'. In *Unterscheidung und Bewahrung. Festschrift für Hermann Kunisch zum 60. Geburtstag 27. Oktober 1961*. Berlin: Walter de Gruyter & Co., 1971, 232-258.

Mason 1962
_____. *Remarks on the Writings and Conduct of J.J. Rousseau.—Bemerkungen über J.J. Rousseau's Schriften und Verhalten*. Zurich: Fretz & Wasmuth Verlag, 1962.

McCarthy 1965
McCARTHY, F.I. '*The Bard* of Thomas Gray: Its Composition and its Use by Painters'. *National Library of Wales Journal*, XIV, 1 (Summer 1965), 105-113.

Merchant 1959
MERCHANT, W. Moelwyn. *Shakespeare and the Artist*. London: Oxford University Press, 1959.

Miller 1990
MILLER, Dwight C. 'Another Drawing by Giacomo del Po for Milton's *Paradise Lost*'. *Master Drawings*, 2 (1990), 181-185.

Milton
MILTON, John. *Complete Poems and Major Prose*. Ed. Merritt Y. Hughes. Indianapolis: Odyssey Press, 1980.

Monthly Epitome
Monthly Epitome and Catalogue of New Publications. Vols. I-VIII. London: 1797-1804.

Monthly Mirror
The Monthly Mirror: Reflecting Men and Manners. With strictures on their epitome The Stage. Vols. I-XXII. London: 1795-1806.

Northup 1970
NORTHUP, Clark Sutherland. *A Bibliography of Thomas Gray*. New York: Russell & Russell, 1970.

Ovid
OVID. *Metamorphoses. With an English Translation*. Trans. Frank J. Miller. 2 vols. 'The Loeb Classical Library'. London: W. Heinemann; Cambridge, MA: Harvard University Press, 1977.

Paulson 1971
PAULSON, Ronald. *Hogarth: His Life, Art and Times*. New Haven & London: Yale University Press, 1971.

Plato
PLATO. *With an English Translation*. Trans. Harold N. Fowler. 'The Loeb Classical Library'. London: William Heinemann; Cambridge, MA: Harvard University Press, 1914.

Plutarch
PLUTARCH. *Lives. With an English Translation.* Trans. Bernadotte Perrin. 'The Loeb Classical Library'. London: W. Heinemann; Cambridge, MA: Harvard University Press, 1914.

Pointon 1970
POINTON, Marcia R. *Milton and English Art.* Toronto: University of Toronto Press, 1970.

Powell 1973
POWELL, Nicolas. *The Nightmare.* London: Allen Lane, The Penguin Press; New York: Viking Press, 1973.

Ravenhall 1980
RAVENHALL, Mary Dennis. *Illustrations of Paradise Lost in England, 1688-1802.* Ann Arbor, MI: University Microfilms International, 1980. (Ph.D. dissertation, University of Illinois at Urbana-Champaign, 1980).

Reid 1871
REID, George William. *A Descriptive Catalogue of the Works of George Cruikshank, Etchings, Woodcuts, Lithographs, and Glyphographs, with a List of Books illustrated by him.* 3 vols. London: Bell & Daldy, 1871.

Roberts 1990
ROBERTS, Marie. *Gothic Immortals: The Fiction of the Brotherhood of the Rosy Cross.* London & New York: Routledge, 1990.

Roe 1969
ROE, A.S. 'The Thunder of Egypt'. In *William Blake: Essays for S. Foster Damon.* Ed. Alvin H. Rosenfeld. Providence: Brown University Press, 1969.

Russell 1912
RUSSELL, Archibald G.B. *The Engravings of William Blake.* London: Grant Richards; Boston & New York: Houghton Mifflin Co., 1912. (Reprinted: New York: Benjamin Blom, 1968).

Russell 1963
RUSSELL, Norma. *A Bibliography of William Cowper to 1837.* Oxford: Clarendon Press, 1963.

Saunders 1989
SAUNDERS, Gill. *The Nude: A New Perspective.* New York: Harper Collins: 1989.

Schiff 1-1826
SCHIFF, Gert. *Johann Heinrich Füssli 1741-1825.* 2 vols. Zurich: Verlag Berichthaus; Munich: Prestel-Verlag, [1973].

Schiff 1961
_____. *Johann Heinrich Füssli, Ein Sommernachstraum. Einführung von Gert Schiff.* Stuttgart: Philipp Reclam Jun., 1961.

Schiff 1963
_____. *Johann Heinrich Füsslis Milton-Galerie.* Zurich & Stuttgart: Fretz & Wasmuth Verlag, 1963.

Schiff 1964
_____. 'Johann Heinrich Füssli in Zürich'. *Librarium: Zeitschrift der Schweizerischen Bibliophilen-Gesellschaft.* 7th Year, III (December 1964), 130-154.

Schiff-Viotto 1977
_____. & Paola Viotto. *L'opera completa di Füssli.* Coordinated Gert Schiff. Critical apparatus P. Viotto. Milano: Rizzoli Editore, 1977. (French ed.: *Tout l'oeuvre peint de Füssli.* Trans. Claude Lauriol. Paris: Flammarion, 1980).

Schroyer 1977
SCHROYER, Richard J. 'The 1788 Publication Date of Lavater's Aphorisms on Man'. *Blake/An Illustrated Quarterly,* XI, 1 (1977), 23-26.

Schroyer 1980
LAVATER, J.C. *Aphorisms on Man (1788) by Johann Caspar Lavater. A Facsimile Reproduction of William Blake's Copy of the First English Edition.* Ed. Richard J. Schroyer. Delmar, NY: Scholar's Facsimiles, 1980.

Schulte-Strathaus 1913
SCHULTE-STRATHAUS, Ernst. *Bibliographie der Originalausgaben deutscher Dichtungen im Zeitalter Goethes.* Munich & Leipzig: Georg Müller, 1913.

Shakespeare
SHAKESPEARE, William. *The Complete Plays and Poems. A New Text.* Ed. William Allan Neilson & Charles Jarvis Hill. Cambridge, MA: Houghton Mifflin Co., 1942.

Smith 1883
SMITH, John Chaloner. *British Mezzotinto Portraits, being a Descriptive Catalogue of these Engravings from the Introduction of the Art to the Early part of the Present Century.* 5 vols. London: Henry Sotheran & Co., 1883-1884.

Sophocles
SOPHOCLES. *With an English Translation.* Trans. F. Storr. Cambridge: Harvard University Press; London: William Heinemann, 1951.

Spectator
THE SPECTATOR. Ed. Donald F. Bond. 5 vols. Oxford: Clarendon Press, 1965.

Spenser
SPENSER, Edmund. *Works. A Variorum Edition.* Ed. Edwin Greenlaw, C.G. Osgood & F.M. Padelford. 9 vols. London: Oxford University Press; Baltimore: John Hopkins Press, 1932.

Stock 1982
STOCK, R.D. *The Holy and the Daemonic from Sir Thomas Browne to William Blake.* Princeton, N.J.: Princeton University Press, 1982.

Stock 1989
_____. *The Flutes of Dionysus: Daemonic Enthrallment in Literature.* Lincoln & London: University of Nebraska Press, 1989.

Stolk
STOLK, Atlas van, G. van Rijn & C. van Ommeren. *Katalogus der Historie-, Spot- en Zinneprenten betrekkelijk de Geschiedenis van Nederland..* Amsterdam: Frederik Muller & Co., 1908.

Strauss 1981
DÜRER, Albrecht. *The Intaglio Prints of Albrecht Dürer: Engravings, Etchings & Drypoints.* Ed.

Walter L. Strauss. New York: Kennedy Galleries & Abaris Books, 1981.

Tinker 1922
TINKER, Chauncey Brewster. *Young Boswell; Chapters on James Boswell, the Biographer.* Boston: The Atlantic Monthly Press, 1922.

Todd 1947
TODD, Ruthven. 'The Reputation and Prejudices of Henry Fuseli'. In *Tracks in the Snow, Studies in English Science and Art.* London: Grey Walls Press, 1946; New York: Charles Scribner's Sons, 1947, 61-93.

Todd 1971-1972
_____. 'Two Blake Prints and Two Fuseli Drawings with some possibly pertinent speculations'. *Blake Newsletter*, V, 3 (Winter 1971-1972), 173-181.

Todd 1972
TODD, William B. comp. *A Directory of Printers and Others in Allied Trades, London and Vicinity 1800-1840.* London: Printing Historical Society, 1972.

Tomory 1972
TOMORY, Peter. *The Life and Art of Henry Fuseli.* London: Thames & Hudson; New York & Washington, D.C.: Praeger, 1972.

Turner 1985
TURNER, Jean. 'Fuseli and Lavater: The Personification of Character'. *Athanor*, IV (1985), 33-41.

Twyman 1972
TWYMAN, Michael. *A Directory of London Lithographic Printers 1800-1850.* London: Printing Historical Society, 1976.

Updike 1981
UPDIKE, John. 'Impressions by John Updike: A Case of Overestimation'. *Realités* (January-February 1981), 39-41. (Reprinted: In *Just Looking: Essays on Art.* New York: Alfred A. Knopf, 1989, 30-32).

Virgil
VIRGIL. *Aeneid. With an English Translation.*

Trans. Henry R. Fairclough. 2 vols. 'The Loeb Classical Library'. London: William Heinemann; New York: G.P. Putnam's Sons, 1930.

Vovelle 1986
VOVELLE, M. *La Révolution française. Images et Récits 1789-1799*. Paris: Livre Club Diderot/Messidor, 1986.

Wakefield 1796
HOMER. *The Iliad* [&] *The Odyssey. Translated by Alexander Pope*. A New Edition, with additional notes by Gilbert Wakefield. 12 vols. London: T. Longman, et al., 1796.

Ward 1970
WARD, A.G., et al. *The Quest for Theseus*. London: Pall Mall; New York: Praeger, 1970.

Warner 1984
WARNER, Janet A. *Blake and the Language of Art*. Kingston & Montreal: McGill-Queen's University Press; Gloucester: Alan Sutton, 1984.

Weber 1966
WEBER, Wilhelm. *A History of Lithography*. New York, Toronto & London: McGraw-Hill, 1966.

Weinglass 1978
WEINGLASS, D.H. 'The Painter's Muse: Henry Fuseli and Maria Riddell'. *Gazette des Beaux-Arts* (September 1978), 75-83.

Weinglass 1980
_____. '*Johann Heinrich Füssli 1741-1825*'. *The Art Bulletin*, LXII, 4 (December 1980), 665-669.

Weinglass 1988
_____. '*Theseus Receiving the Thread from Ariadne; An Incubus Leaving Two Girls; Odysseus Between Scylla and Charybdis*'. In *From Liotard to Le Corbusier. 200 years of Swiss painting, 1730-1930*. Swiss Institute for Art Research, Ed. Zurich: Coordinating Commission for the Presence of Switzerland Abroad & the Swiss Institute for Art Research for the High Museum of Art, Atlanta, 1988. 66-71. Catalogue entries nos. 10-12.

Weinglass 1991
_____. '"Kann Uns zum Vaterland die Fremde Werden?" In der Emigration: Johann Heinrich Füssli'. *Neue Zürcher Zeitung*, 23/24 November 1991, 67-68.

West 1988
WEST, Richard Samuel. *Satire On Stone; The Political Cartoons of Joseph Keppler*. Urbana & Chicago: University of Illinois Press, 1988.

Whitman 1907
WHITMAN, Alfred. *Nineteenth century mezzo-tinters; Charles Turner*. n.p.: George Bell & Sons, 1907.

Worman 1987
WORMAN, Eugene C. 'George Virtue's New York Connection, 1836-1879'. *AB Bookman's Weekly*, 30 March 1987, 1350-1363.

Worman 1987a
_____. 'George Virtue and the British "Numbers" Game'. *AB Bookman's Weekly*, 15 June 1987, 2646-2657.

Wüthrich 1956
WÜTHRICH, Lukas Heinrich. *Christian von Mechel, Leben und Werk eines Basler Kupferstechers und Kunsthändlers (1737-1817)*. Basel & Stuttgart: Helbing & Lichtenhahn, 1956.

Wüthrich 1959
_____. *Das Oeuvre des Kupferstechers Christian von Mechel. Vollständiges Verzeichnis der von ihm geschabten und Verlegten Graphischen Arbeiten*. Basel & Stuttgart: Helbing & Lichtenhahn, 1959.

Zelle 1990
ZELLE, Carsten. 'Physiognomie des Schreckens im achtzehnten Jahrhundert. Zu Johann Caspar Lavater und Charles Lebrun'. *Lessing Yearbook*, 1989, XXI, 89-102.

III. EXHIBITIONS

Berlin 1986
Brosch, Renate, Joachim Müller, Gretel Wagner. *Shakespeare Buch und Bühne*. West Berlin:

Kunstbibliothek Berlin, Staatliche Museen Preussicher Kulturbesitz, 1986.

Bern 1991
Gamboni, Dario & Georg Germann. *Emblèmes de la Liberté: L'image de la république dans l'art du XVIe au XXe siècle*. 21ème Exposition du Conseil de l'Europe. Musée d'histoire de Berne et Musée des beaux-arts de Berne. Berne: Editions Staempfli & cie, 1991.

Cambridge 1965
Blanton, C.W. & M.H. Caviness, et al. *Sublimity and Sensibility: The Genesis of Romanticism*. 30 April-31 May 1965. Cambridge, MA: Fogg Art Museum, 1965.

Chicago 1978
Hutton, Richard W. & Laura Nelke. *Alderman Boydell's Shakespeare Gallery: An Exhibition of a Selection of the Engravings made After the Paintings Commissioned by Alderman John Boydell*. 4 October-26 November 1978. Chicago: The University of Chicago, David and Alfred Smart Gallery, 1978.

Cleveland 1948
PRASSE, Leona E. et al. *Catalogue of an Exhibition of the Art of Lithography Commemorating the Sesquicentennial of its Invention, 1798-1948*. 11 November 1948 - 2 January 1949. Cleveland, Ohio: The Cleveland Museum of Art, 1948.

Coburg 1989
Kruse, Joachim. *Johann Heinrich Lips, 1758-1817. Ein Zürcher Kupferstecher zwischen Lavater und Goethe*. Coburg: Kunstsammlungen der Veste Coburg, 1989.

Frankfurt 1988
Perels, Christoph. *Sturm und Drang*. Frankfurt Goethe-Museum, 2 December 1988-5 February 1989. (Düsseldorf 26 February-9 April 1989). Frankfurt: Freies Deutsches Hochstift Frankfurter Goethe-Museum, 1988.

Florence 1979
Tomory, Peter. *The Poetical Circle. Fuseli and the British*. Florence: Centro Di, 1979.

Glasgow 1990
Hunterian Art Gallery. *Prints & Printmaking*. Glasgow: Hunterian Art Gallery, University of Glasgow, 1990.

Hamburg 1974-1975
Schiff, Gert. *Johann Heinrich Füssli, 1741-1825*. Ed. Werner Hofmannn. Munich & Hamburg: Prestel & Hamburger Kunsthalle, 1974.

Hamburg 1989
Hofmann, Werner. *Europa 1789. Aufklärung, Verklärung, Verfall. Zum 200. Jahrestag der Französischen Revolution*. 17 September - 19 November 1989. Köln: DuMont, 1989.

Kansas City 1982
Weinglass, D.H. *Henry Fuseli and the Engraver's Art*. 3 October - 29 October 1982. Kansas City, Missouri: University of Missouri-Kansas City Library, 1982. (Friends of the Library Publication Series, no. 4). Distributed by Worldwide Books, Boston.

Kansas City 1989
_____. *Paradise Illumined: Fuseli, Stothard, Westall, and Burney, Milton's late 18th-century Illustrators*. An Exhibition on the occasion of the Central Renaissance Conference (5 to 8 April 1989). Kansas City, Missouri: University of Missouri-Kansas City Libraries, 1989.

Lawrence, Kansas 1971
Kingsbury, Pamela D., Vernon, H. Minor, et al. *Imagination and Vision. Prints and Drawings of William Blake*. 17 October-18 December 1971. Lawrence, KS: University of Kansas Museum of Art, 1971.

London, Boydell, 1789
BOYDELL, John & Josiah. *A Catalogue of the Pictures in the Shakspeare Gallery, Pall-Mall*. [Listing Pictures I-XXXIV]. London: Sold at the Place of Exhibition, 1789.

London, Boydell, 1790
_____. *A Catalogue of the Pictures, &c. in the Shakspeare Gallery, Pall-Mall*. [Listing Pictures I-LVI]. London: Printed by H.

Baldwin; And Sold at the Place of Exhibition, 1790.

London, Boydell, [1794?]

_____. *A Catalogue of the Pictures, &c. in the Shakspeare Gallery, Pall-Mall.* [Listing Pictures I-LXXXIII + 'Small Pictures' I-XLIX]. London: Printed for the Proprietors, And Sold at the Place of Exhibition, [1794?]. (Date cropped from copy in University of Missouri-Columbia Library).

London, Boydell, 1802

_____. *A Catalogue of the Pictures, &c. in the Shakspeare Gallery, Pall-Mall.* [Listing Pictures I-CLXII]. London: Printed by W. Bulmer and Co., for the Proprietors; And Sold at the Place of Exhibition, 1802.

London 1957

British Museum. *1757-1957 William Blake and his Circle. British Museum Bicentenary Exhibition.* London: British Museum, 1957.

London 1975

Schiff, Gert. *Henry Fuseli, 1741-1825.* Trans. Sarah Twohig. London: Tate Gallery, 1975.

London 1986

Scrase, David, Patricia Jaffé, Jane Munro, & Craig Hartley. *William Blake and his Contemporaries. A Loan Exhibition in Aid of the Friends of the Fitzwilliam Museum, Cambridge.* 11 June-11 July 1986. London: Wildenstein, 1986.

London, Heim, 1991

Cannon-Brookes, Peter, ed. *The Painted Word. British History Painting: 1750-1830.* London: The Heim Gallery; Woodbridge: The Boydell Press, 1991.

London 1992

Hamlyn, Robin. *William Blake: The Apprentice Years.* 13 May-16 August 1992. London: Tate Gallery, 1992.

Munich 1958

Halm, Peter. *Deutsche Zeichenkunst der Goethezeit, Handzeichnungen und Aquarelle aus der Sammlung Winterstein.* April-November 1958. Munich: Hirmer Verlag, 1958.

New Haven 1980

Alexander, David & Richard T. Godfrey. *Painters and Engraving: The Reproductive Print from Hogarth to Wilkie.* 26 March - 22 June 1980. New Haven: Yale Center for British Art, 1980.

New Haven 1981

Ashton, Geoffrey. *Shakespeare and British Art.* New Haven, CT: Yale Center for British Art, 1981.

New Haven 1982

Bindman, David. *William Blake: His Art and Times.* London: Thames & Hudson for the Yale Center for British Art, 1982.

New York 1974

Pierpoint Morgan Library. *Gifts in Honor of the Fiftieth Anniversary: An Exhibition.* 3 September-2 November 1974. New York: The Pierpoint Morgan Library, 1974.

New York 1981

Harding, Anneliese. *Eden Revisited: Graphic Works by German Romantic Artists.* New York: Goethe House, 1981.

Paris 1975

Schiff, Gert. *Johann Heinrich Füssli, 1741-1825.* Trans. Martine Perrot, Christine Casler & Jacques Chavy. 21 April-20 July 1975. Paris: Musée du Petit Palais, 1975.

Paris 1989

La Révolution française et l'Europe 1789-1799. 20th Exhibition of the Council of Europe. 16 March-26 June 1989. Paris: Éditions de la Réunion des musées nationaux, 1989.

Pescara 1985

Gizzi, Corrado. *Füssli E Dante.* Torre de' Passeri (Pescara); Castello Gizzi. September-October 1985. Milano: Mazotta, 1985.

Princeton 1969

Ryskamp, Charles. *William Blake Engraver. A*

Descriptive Catalogue of an Exhibition.
December 1969-February 1970. Princeton,
N.J.: Princeton University Library, 1969.

San Marino 1987
Essick, Robert N. *William Blake and His
Contemporaries and Followers. Selected Works
from the Collection of Robert N. Essick.*
November 1987 through February 1988. San
Marino, CA: Henry E. Huntington Library and
Art Gallery, 1987.

Stockholm 1990
Cavalli-Björkman, Görel & Ragnar von Holten.
Füssli. 4 October 1990-6 January 1991.
Stockholm: Nationalmuseum, 1990.

Washington 1988
GOULD, Lynn M. *Drawings on Stone: Early
European Lithography.* 12 June-4 September
1988. Washington, D.C.: National Gallery of
Art, 1988.

Zurich 1941
Wartmann, Wilhelm. *Johann Heinrich Füssli,
1741-1825. Zur Zweihundertjahrfeier und
Gedächtnisausstellung 1941.* [Bicentennenial
Exhibition]. Zurich: Kunsthaus, 1941.

IV. OTHER WORKS CONSULTED

ANDERSON, Ross, Lucy Oakley, & Cary
Mazer. *A Brush with Shakespeare. The Bard in
Painting: 1780-1910.* Montgomery, AL:
Montgomery Museum of Fine Arts, 1985.

BENNETT, Shelley M. *Thomas Stothard: The
Mechanisms of Art Patronage in England circa
1800.* Columbia: University of Missouri Press,
1988.

BRIGANTI, Giuliano. *I Pittori dell' Immaginario:
arte e rivoluzione psicologica.* Milano: Electa
Editrice, 1977. (Abridged English version:
Fantastic and Visionary Painting. London:
Bloomsbury Books, 1989).

CHANDLER, George. *William Roscoe of
Liverpool 1753-1831.* London: G.T. Batsford,
1953.

CHARD, Leslie F., II. 'Joseph Johnson: Father
of the Book Trade'. *Bulletin of the New York
Public Library,* 79 (Autumn 1975), 51-82.

CURWEN, Henry. *A History of Booksellers, The
Old and the New.* London: Chatto & Windus,
1873.

DÖRRBECKER, Detlef W. 'Blake and His
Circle: An Annotated Checklist of Recent
Publications'. [Annual Bibliography]. *Blake/An
Illustrated Quarterly,* 1977-

DYSON, Anthony. *Pictures to Print: The
Nineteenth-century Engraving Trade.* London:
Farrand Press, 1984.

EICHENBERG, Fritz. *The Art of the Print:
Masterpieces, History, Technique.* New York:
Harry N. Abrams, 1976.

ENGEN, Rodney K. *Dictionary of Victorian
Wood Engravers.* Cambridge: Chadwyck-
Healey, 1985.

ESSICK, Robert N. 'Blake in the Marketplace'.
[Annual review of auction and other sales of
Blakeana]. *Blake/An Illustrated Quarterly*
(formerly *The Blake Newsletter*), 1971-.

_____. 'Handlist of the Huntington Blake
Collection'. *Blake/An Illustrated Quarterly,* XI,
4 (Spring 1978), 236-259.

FITZWILLIAM MUSEUM. *The Print in England
1790-1930. A Private Collection.* Ed. Craig
Hartley & Susan Ridley. Cambridge:
Fitzwilliam Museum, 1985.

FOLGER SHAKESPEARE LIBRARY. *Catalog
of Prints, Engravings, Photographs, and
Original Art Materials.* 4 vols. Boston: G.K.
Hall, 1984.

FUSELI, Henry. *The Lectures* [I-XII]. In *Lectures
on Painting, By the Royal Academicians. Barry,
Opie, and Fuseli.* Ed. Ralph N. Wornum.
London: Henry G. Bohn, 1848, 337-560.

_____. *Sämtliche Gedichte.* Ed. Martin
Bircher & Karl S. Guthke. Zurich: Orell Füssli
Verlag, 1973.

_____. *Unveröffentlichte Gedichte von
Johann Heinrich Füssli.* Ed. Eudo C. Mason.
Zurich: Kunstgesellschaft, 1951.

GERMANN, Martin. *Johann Jakob Thurneysen
der Jüngere 1754-1803 Verleger, Buchdrucker
und Buchhändler in Basel.* 'Basler Beiträge zur
Geschichtswissenschaft. Band 128'. Basel &
Stuttgart: Verlag von Helbing & Lichtenhahn,
1973.

GODFREY, Richard T. *Printmaking in Britain: A
General History from its Beginnings to the
Present Day.* Oxford: Phaidon, 1978.

GRAHAM, John. 'Lavater's *Physiognomy*: A

Checklist'. *Papers of the Bibliographical Society of America*, LV (1961), 297-308.

GRAVES, Algernon. *The Royal Academy of Arts. A Complete Dictionary of Contributors and their work from its foundation in 1769 to 1904.* 6 vols. [Wakefield]: S.R. Publishers Ltd.; [Bath]: Kingsmead Reprints, 1970.

GRIFFITHS, Antony. 'A Checklist of Catalogues of British Print Publishers c. 1650-1830'. *Print Quarterly*, I, 1 (March 1984), 4-22.

_____. *Prints and Printmaking: An Introduction to the history and techniques.* London: British Museum Publications, 1980.

HOMER. *The Iliad.* Trans. Robert Fagles. Harmondsworth, Middx. & New York: Penguin Books, 1990.

_____. *The Iliad & Odyssey.* Trans. Alexander Pope. Ed. Maynard Mack. 'The Twickenham Edition of the Poems of Alexander Pope', vols. VII-X. London: Methuen; New Haven: Yale, 1967.

HUNNISETT, Basil. *A Dictionary of British Steel Engravers.* Leigh-on-Sea: F. Lewis, 1980.

_____. *An Illustrated Dictionary of British Steel Engravers.* Aldershot: Scolar Press; Brookfield, VT: Gower Publishing Co., 1989.

_____. *Steel-engraved book illustration in England.* London: Scolar Press, 1980.

KIESSLING, Nicolas. *The Incubus in English Literature: Provenance and Progeny.* Pullman, WA: Washington State University Press, 1977.

KÖNIG, Alfred. *Johann Heinrich Füssli 1745-1832.* ['Obmann Füssli'] *Weltanschauung eines Zürcher Politikers im 18. Jahrhundert.* Zurich: Orell Füssli Verlag, n.d.

LYLE, Janice. 'Handlist of the Essick Blake Collection'. *Blake/An Illustrated Quarterly*, XI, 4 (Spring 1978), 216-235.

LYLES, Anne & Diana Perkins. *Colour into Line: Turner and the Art of Engraving.* London: The Tate Gallery, 1989.

MASON, Lauris, Joan Ludman & Harriet P. Krauss, comps. *Old Master Print References: A Selected Bibliography.* White Plains, NY: Kraus International Publications, 1986.

MAYER, Joseph. *Early Exhibitions of Art in Liverpool.* Liverpool: Privately printed, 1876.

MEISEL, Martin. *Realizations. Narrative, Pictorial, and Theatrical Arts in Nineteenth-Century England.* Princeton, N.J.: Princeton University Press, 1983.

PALEY, Morton D. 'Handlist of Four Blake Collections'. *Blake/An Illustrated Quarterly*, XI, 4 (Spring 1978), 260-275.

PRESSLY, Nancy L. *The Fuseli Circle in Rome: Early Romantic Art of the 1770s.* New Haven: Yale Center for British Art, 1977.

RIGGS, Timothy A. comp. *The Print Council Index to Oeuvre-Catalogues of Prints by European and American Artists.* Millwood, N.Y.: Kraus International Publications, 1983.

RÜMANN, Arthur. *Die Illustrierten Deutschen Bücher des 18. Jahrhunderts.* Stuttgart: Julius Hoffmann Verlag, 1926.

RYCHNER, Max. *Rückblick auf Vier Jahrhunderte; Entwicklung des Art. Institut Orell Füssli in Zürich.* Zurich: Zum Froschauer, 1925.

SCHIFF, Gert. *Images of Horror and Fantasy.* New York: Harry N. Abrams, 1978.

SHAKESPEARE, William. *Selected Plays. With the Illustrations of Henry Fuseli.* Franklin Center, PA: The Franklin Library, 1981.

SMITH, John Thomas. *Nollekens and His Times and Memoirs of Contemporary Artists from the Time of Roubiliac Hogarth and Reynolds to that of Fuseli Flaxman and Blake.* Ed. Wilfred Whitten. 2 vols. London & New York: John Lane, 1920.

THIEME, Ulrich & Felix Becker. *Allgemeine Lexikon der bildenden Künstler von der Antike bis zur Gegenwart.* 37 vols. Leipzig: 1907-1950.

TYSON, Gerald P. *Joseph Johnson: A Liberal Publisher.* Iowa City: University of Iowa Press, 1979.

WITTREICH, Joseph A. 'Illustrators of Milton'. In *A Milton Encyclopedia.* Ed. William B. Hunter, Jr. 8 vols. Lewisburg: Bucknell University Press, 1978-1980, IV, 55-58.

INDEX OF ENGRAVERS

Many of the titles listed below have been abbreviated. For complete titles see entry headings. A letter appended to the number (e.g. **69V**) usually indicates a re-engraved or reissued plate.

Tiresias Appearing to Odysseus in the
    Underworld, 1804 185
Uriel Observing Satan's Flight, 1802 . . . **167A**
Uriel Observing Satan's Flight, 1808 . . . **167B**
Virtue Reclaiming Youth from the Arms of Vice,
    1807 268
Macbeth, Banquo, and the Witches, 1817 . 134

Burke, Thomas (1749-1815)
The Nightmare, 1783 67
The Nightmare, 1802   . . . . **67C**

Burnet, John (1784-1868)
Silence, 1820 . . . . **161A**

Caldwall, James (1739-1819)
Macbeth, Banquo, and the Witches, 1798 . 120

Callot, ---
Female Seated on a Demon, 1830
    (Litho) **69T**

Carbonneau, Jean-Baptiste-Charles (1815-*post* 1869)
Prospero, Ariel, Miranda and Caliban,
    1863 . . . . **117J**

Chapman, J[?ohn] (fl. 1790-1820)
The Night Mare, 1799 . . . . **69J**

Collyer, John (1708-1786)
Cain and Abel, 1772 26
Cain and Abel, 1803 . . . . **26A**

Copia, Jacques-Louis.--See Provost, Benoit-Louis

Corner, John (1768?-1825?)
Head of Christ, 1791 102

Couché fils, Louis-François (1782-1849)
Brutus à la Vue d'un Spectre, 1806 . . . . **40A**
Cain, 1806 . . . . **45A**
Un Chevalier [et] sa Maitresse qu'il vient
    d'assassiner, 1806 (Ezzelin and Meduna) **56A**
Deux Mains de grande Valeur physiognomique,
    1806 . . . . **63A**
Un Groupe Représentant Jésus-Christ Mourant, et
    à qui on Donne des Secours, 1807 . . . **57A**
Homme Assis, 1807 . . . . **61A**
Jeune Homme, 1807 . . . . **49A**

Le Magicien Balaam, 1807 . . . . **46A**
Une Main très-expressive, 1806 . . . . **62A**
Marie, Soeur de Marthe, 1807 . . . . **41A**
Martha Hess, 1806 . . . . **58A**
La Mort d'Abel, 1806 . . . . **44A**
Un Penseur, 1807 . . . . **59A**
La Pythonisse d'Endor, 1807 . . . . **48A**
Quatre Visages d'Après le Dante, 1807   **50A, 51A**
St. Jean, 1807 . . . . **42A**
Salomé, 1807 . . . . **52A**
Satan, 1807 . . . . **43A**
Un Satellite, 1807 . . . . **53A**
Sibylle, 1809 . . . . **60A**
Tête de Patriarche, 1807 . . . . **54A**
Une Tête très-expressive
    (The Escapee), 1807 . . . . **47A**
Un Trasteverain, 1806 . . . . **39A**

Cox, Thomas Jr.--See Richardson, James H. (fl. 1848-1880) & Cox, Thomas Jr.

Cromek, Robert Hartley (1770-1812)
Beatrice Eavesdropping on Hero and
    Ursula, 1803 194
Coriolanus Before Aufidius, 1804 216
Death of Cleopatra, 1804 218
Huon and Amanda Find Alphonso Dead, 1806 252
Huon Disguised as a Gardener Seen by the
    Sultana Almansaris, 1806 254
Iachimo Emerging from the Chest, 1804 . . 219
King Henry at the Deathbed of Beaufort,
    1803 210
Lear Carrying the Body of Cordelia, 1804 . 222
Penelope Holding the Bow of Odysseus,
    1806 241
Richard II in the Dungeon of Pomfret Castle,
    1803 205
Timon Cursing Athens, 1803 215

Cruikshank, George (1792-1878)
Napoleon Dreaming in his Cell at the Military
    College, 1814 (unsigned) **69M**
The Night Mayor, 1816 (unsigned) **69N**

Cruikshank, Robert (1789-1856)
Louis the Fat Troubled with the
    Night Mare, 1823 . . . . **69O**

Dadley, John (1767-*post* 1807)
The Creation of Eve, 1807 . . . . **174B**
Eros and Dione, 1807 . . . . **175B**

384

BOOKS CONTAINING ENGRAVED ILLUSTRATIONS AFTER FUSELI

For complete titles see catalogue entry headings. A letter appended to the entry no. (e.g. **263B**) usually indicates a re-engraved or reissued plate. An asterisk (*) indicates a pastiche.

INDEX OF PUBLISHERS

INDEX OF TITLES

For complete titles see catalogue entry headings

404

CONSPECTUS OF SUBJECTS

408

ACKNOWLEDGMENTS AND PHOTOGRAPH CREDITS

The illustrations were reproduced by kind permission of the libraries, museums, collections and private individuals listed below. Numbers are entry numbers. Photograph credits are indicated in parentheses. In the case of institutions, the photography may be assumed to have been done in house, unless otherwise noted.

1-8: Vanderbilt University Library
9-11: Author's collection (Hollis Officer Studio, Kansas City, Missouri)
Fig. 1: Reproduced in C.B. Tinker, *Young Boswell*, 1922, facing p. 60 (Hollis Officer Studio, Kansas City, Missouri)
12: Huntington Library
13: The British Museum (Paul Mellon Centre for British Art)
14-20: Author's collection (Hollis Officer Studio, Kansas City, Missouri)
21: The British Museum
22: The British Museum (Paul Mellon Centre for British Art)
23: Dr. Alfred Winterstein
24: The British Museum (Paul Mellon Centre for British Art)
Fig. 2, 25-30, 32-34: Dr. Williams's Library (Max Browne)
25A: The British Museum
31: The British Library
35: The University of Chicago Library
36: The Newberry Library
38: Zentralbibliothek, Zurich
39-63: The Newberry Library, Wing Collection
64: Kunsthaus Zürich, Graphische Sammlung
65-67, 67D: The British Museum (Paul Mellon Centre for British Art)

68: Author's collection (Hollis Officer Studio, Kansas City, Missouri)
69A, 69C: The British Museum
69E: Miriam and Ira D. Wallach Division of Art, Prints and Photographs, The New York Public Library
69G, 69H: British Museum
69I: Reproduced in Nicolas Powell, *Fuseli: The Nightmare*, pl. 42. London: Penguin, 1972
69J: The Huntington Library
69K, 69L: The British Museum
69M: Author's collection (Hollis Officer Studio, Kansas City, Missouri)
69N, 69P, 69Q, 69W, 69Y: The British Museum
69X: University of Pennsylvania
69Z: Glenn Book Shop, Kansas City, Missouri (Hollis Officer Studio, Kansas City, Missouri)
69AA: The Metropolitan Museum of Art, The Elisha Whittelsey Collection, The Elisha Whittelsey Fund, 1966
69CC: The British Museum
70: The British Museum (Paul Mellon Centre for British Art)
71: Kunsthaus Zürich, Graphische Sammlung
72: The British Museum
72B: Kunstsammlungen der Veste Coburg
73: The British Museum (Paul Mellon Centre for British Art)
73B: University of Illinois - Champaign Urbana Library
73D: Max Browne (Max Browne)
74: Kunsthaus Zürich, Graphische Sammlung
75: The British Museum (Paul Mellon Centre for British Art)
76: The British Library
77-78: The British Museum (Paul Mellon Centre for British Art)
79: Kunsthaus Zürich, Graphische Sammlung
80: The British Library

81: The Metropolitan Museum of Art, The Elisha Whittelsey Collection, The Elisha Whittelsey Fund, 1955
82: The British Museum (Paul Mellon Centre for British Art)
83: Hunterian Art Gallery, University of Glasgow
Fig. 3: Author's collection (Hollis Officer Studio, Kansas City, Missouri)
Fig. 4: The Yale Center for British Art, Paul Mellon Collection
84-110: Author's collection (Hollis Officer Studio, Kansas City, Missouri)
111-112: The British Museum
113: Kunsthaus Zürich, Graphische Sammlung
114: Author's Collection (University of Missouri - Kansas City Photographic Services)
115-116: Collection of R.N. Essick
Fig. 5: University of Missouri-Kansas City General Library
117-124: The British Museum (Paul Mellon Centre for British Art)
Fig. 6: The Ashmolean Museum, Oxford
125: The British Museum (Paul Mellon Centre for British Art)
125A: The Lewis Walpole Library, Farmington, Ct.
125B: Author's collection (Hollis Officer Studio, Kansas City, Missouri)
125E.: The British Library
126-128: The Huntington Library
129: The British Museum (Paul Mellon Centre for British Art)
130: The Huntington Library
131: The British Museum
Fig. 7, 131A, 132-134: Author's Collection (Hollis Officer Studio, Kansas City, Missouri)
133A: Witt Library, Courtauld Institute of Art
135: Öffentliche Kunstsammlung, Basel

136-139: Author's collection (Hollis Officer Studio, Kansas City, Missouri)
140: British Museum
140A: Kunsthaus Zürich, Graphische Sammlung
141-145: Author's collection (Hollis Officer Studio, Kansas City, Missouri)
146: Princeton University Library
147: Author's collection (Hollis Officer Studio, Kansas City, Missouri)
148: Collection of R.N. Essick
149: Author's collection (Hollis Officer Studio, Kansas City, Missouri)
150: Hornby Library, Liverpool City Libraries
151-152: The British Museum (Paul Mellon Centre for British Art)
153: Author's collection (Hollis Officer Studio, Kansas City, Missouri)
154: The British Museum (Paul Mellon Centre for British Art)
155-157: Author's collection (Hollis Officer Studio, Kansas City, Missouri)
158-160: The British Library
161-164: Author's collection (Hollis Officer Studio, Kansas City, Missouri)
165-170: The Huntington Library
Fig. 8: Philadelphia Museum of Art: Gift of Charles Zigrosser
171-172: The British Museum (Paul Mellon Centre for British Art)
173-177: Author's collection (Hollis Officer Studio, Kansas City, Missouri)

178: The British Museum (Paul Mellon Centre for British Art)
178A: The British Library
179: The British Museum (Paul Mellon Centre for British Art)
180-182, 182A., 183: Author's collection (Hollis Officer Studio, Kansas City, Missouri)
184-186: The British Library
187: Author's collection (Hollis Officer Studio, Kansas City, Missouri)
188: The Metropolitan Museum of Art, Harris Brisbane Dick Fund, by exchange, 1970
189-225: Max Browne (Max Browne)
226: The British Museum
Fig. 10: Collection of Detlef Dörrbecker
227-232, Fig. 11, 233-235, Fig. 12, 236-239, Fig. 13, 240-243: The Huntington Library
244-255, 244A., 248A: Author's collection (Hollis Officer Studio, Kansas City, Missouri)
256-260: The British Museum
261: Author's collection (Hollis Officer Studio, Kansas City, Missouri)
261B: The British Museum
262: Cambridge University Library. By permission of the Syndics
263-265: The British Museum (Paul Mellon Centre for British Art)
266: The British Museum
267A: The British Museum (Paul Mellon Centre for British Art)
267-274, Fig. 14, 275-283, 276A: Author's collection (Hollis Officer Studio, Kansas City, Missouri)

284: The Metropolitan Museum of Art, The Elisha Whittelsey Collection, The Elisha Whittelsey Fund, 1955
285-286: The British Museum (Paul Mellon Centre for British Art)
287: The British Museum
288: The British Museum (Paul Mellon Centre for British Art)
289: Kunsthaus Zürich
290: The Metropolitan Museum of Art, The Elisha Whittelsey Collection, The Elisha Whittelsey Fund, 1963
291: The Metropolitan Museum of Art, The Elisha Whittelsey Fund, 1953
292: Hunterian Art Gallery, University of Glasgow
293: The British Museum (Paul Mellon Centre for British Art)
294: Author's collection (Hollis Officer Studio, Kansas City, Missouri)
295: The British Museum (Paul Mellon Centre for British Art)
296: University of Michigan
297, 298: Author's collection (Hollis Officer Studio, Kansas City, Missouri)
299-301: The British Library
303: The British Museum
304-305: The British Museum (Paul Mellon Centre for British Art)
306: The British Museum

Addenda

93B, 303A.: Author's collection (Hollis Officer Studio, Kansas City, Missouri)

American Antiquarian Society, Worcester, Massachusetts: 181A

The Art Institute of Chicago, Chicago, Illinois: 288

Ashmolean Museum, Oxford:
73F, 125, 264, 265A, 298

Öffentliche Kunstsammlung, Basel: 29, 39-63, 67G, 77, 78, 79, 81, 82, 117-118, 121-124, 117A, 120A-121A, 123A, 135, 140A, 171, 188

Universitätsbibliothek, Basel: 1-8, 178B

Stadtbibliothek, Bern: 1-8, 117D-119D, 123D, 178B, 180-181, 226A, 263B, 276A, 285A, 288A, 293A, 298A, 299A

Bibliothèque Nationale, Paris: 69D, 69E, 69F, 69BB

Birmingham Shakespeare Library: 72A, 72B, 117-124, 120B-122B, 125B, 125C, 117F, 117G-118G, 122G-124G, 125I, 132-134, 165-170, 165B-170B, 189-225, 284A

Bodleian Library, Oxford University: 12, 17-20, 17A-20A, 17B-20B, 36-37, 68, 75, 75B, 76, 80, 84-110, 84A-110A, 114-115, 114-115A, 115D, 117-125, 117A, 120A-121A, 123A, 136-139, 141, 153, 155-157, 155A, 158-164, 165B-170B, 187, 189-225, 227-243 (Cowper), 244-255, 244A, 248A, 261C, 262, 299A-301A

British Library, London: 1-12, 17-20, 17A-20A, 17B-20B, 17C-20C, 17D-20D, 25-35, 25B, 26A, 30B, 27C, 30C, 36-37, 39-63, 39A-63A, 66, 67E, 67F, 67G, 68, 69J, 69M, 69X-69W, 69CC, 72B, 73, 73G, 75, 75A, 75B, 75C, 76, 77, 80, 80A, 84-110, 84A-110A, 114-116, 114-115A, 114B-115B, 125, 117A, 120A-121A, 123A, 120B-122B, 125B, 117D-119D, 123D, 117E-125E, 117F, 117K-118K, 124K, 126-130, 126A-127A, 126B-127B, 129B, 131A, 131C, 132-134, 136-139, 140A, 141-145, 153, 155-162, 161A-162A, 163-170, 165A-166A, 168A-170A, 165B-170B, 173-176, 173B-176B, 177, 178A, 180-225, 226A, 227-243, 227A, 244-255, 261, 263B, 265A, 267-274, 294, 298, 299-301, 285A, 288A, 293A, 298A, 299B

British Museum, London: 13-16, 21, 22, 24, 25A, 31, 32, 35, 65-67, 67C, 67D, 69A, 69B, 69C, 69G, 69H, 69K, 69L, 69M, 69N, 69O, 69P, 69Q, 70-72, 72A, 73A, 73C, 75-79, 81-84, 86, 88-96, 99-101, 104-108, 111-125, 125A, 131, 136-141, 151-152, 153A, 154, 155A, 159, 163-176, 174B-176B, 177-243, 240A, 240B, 244-260, 261B, 261C, 262-265, 265A, 266, 267A, 267-274, 285-288, 291, 293-295, 297-301, 299A-301A, 302-306

Collection of Max Browne, London:
73D, 77, 78, 121, 177A, 189-225, 244-255

Cambridge University Library: 9-10, 17B-20B, 75, 80, 80A, 114-116, 125B, 136-139, 153, 161-162, 161A-162A, 165B-170B, 173-176, 189-225, 244-255, 244A, 248A, 261C, 262, 284A, 299-301

The University of Chicago: 17B-20B, 25-29, 293A

Kunstsammlungen der Veste Coburg, Coburg, Germany: 72B

Collection of Detlef W. Dörrbecker, Trier, Germany: 75, 114-115, 114A-115A, 125-130, 153, 155-157, 162-164, 189-225, 227-243 (1810), 267-274, 284A

Dr. Williams's Library, London: 12, 25-35, 68, 84-110, 114-116, 114A-115A, 173-176, 173B-176, 306

Eidgenössische Technische Hochschule, Zurich: 36-37, 39-63, 40A-63A, 72, 70A-71A, 72A, 74A, 72C, 73E, 77, 78, 82, 131, 161-162, 171, 275-283, 289, 295

Collection of Robert N. Essick, Altadena, California: 11, 17-20, 66, 67D, 68, 70, 73A, 75C, 77, 78, 80, 81, 84-110, 114-116, 114A-115A, 117-124, 117D-119D, 123D, 132, 139, 141-149, 155-157, 161-162, 161A-162A, 163-164, 165B-170B, 171, 173-176, 173B-176B, 177, 177A, 178, 188-225, 226A, 244-255, 244A, 248A, 263, 263B, 264, 267-274, 284A, 285-286, 285A, 287, 288A, 293A

The Fitzwilliam Museum, Cambridge:
69C, 80, 83, 115-116, 125, 142-149, 226, 263-264

The Folger Shakespeare Library, Washington, D.C.: 9-10, 17A-20A, 72B, 85, 114-115, 117-125, 117A, 120A-121A, 123A, 125B, 125C, 117E-125E, 117F, 117G-118G, 122G-124G, 117H, 125I, 132-134, 136-138, 161A-162A, 165B-170B, 182-183, 189-225, 244-255, 244A, 248A, 288A, 305

121A, 123A, 125B, 125C, 117D-119D, 123D, 117D-125D, 131A, 139, 142-149, 155-157, 165-170, 189-225, 227-243, 227-243 (Cowper), 267-274

Rice University, Houston, Texas: 181A

Royal Academy of Arts, London: 114-115

Schweizerische Landesbibliothek, Bern: 1-8, 11, 13A, 36-63, 39A-63, 80, 84A-110A, 109B, 117A, 120A-121A, 123A, 161A-162A, 275-283, 289

St. Louis Mercantile Library: 125C

University of Southern California, Los Angeles, California: 125C, 284A

University of Tampa, Tampa, Florida: 173A-176A

Collection of Peter Tomory, Melbourne, Australia: 129B

University College, London: 161-162

Vanderbilt University, Nashville, Tennessee: 1-8, 131A

University of Virginia, Charlottesville, Virginia: 125C, 117D-125D, 131A, 131B

Victoria & Albert Museum, London: 67D, 68, 69G, 69J, 69Q, 69Y, 73, 73F, 78, 102-104, 108, 113, 139, 141, 153A, 155, 161A, 163, 165-170, 170C, 171-172, 178-183, 186, 188, 226-227?, 256-259, 263, 263A, 267-274-284, 286, 288, 293, 295, 299-300, 304, 305

Collection of Leland E. Warren, Manhattan, Kansas: 17D-20D

Collection of D.H. Weinglass & M. Carbonell, Kansas City, Missouri: 9-12, 13A, 14-20, 17A-20A, 17B-20B, 67C, 67F, 68, 69M, 69DD, 73A, 73F, 74, 70A-71A, 74A, 72C, 73E, 75, 78, 80, 84-110, 93B(Addenda), 114, 117-125, 125C, 117D-119D, 123D,117E-125E, 117J-118J, 131A, 132-134, 136-139,141-145, 147-149, 153, 155-157, 161-162, 161A-162A, 163-170, 165B-170B, 171, 173-176, 173B-176B, 177, 177A, 178, 180-183, 182A, 187, 189-193, 196-202, 205-212, 215-217, 219-222, 226A, 227-255, 244A, 248A, 261, 261A, 263B, 265A, 267-283, 275A-276A, 284A, 294, 297, 298, 299-301, 285A, 288A, 303A (**Addenda**), 305

Widener University, Wilmington, Delaware: 84A-110A

Collection of Dr. Alfred Winterstein, Munich, Germany: 23

Stadtbibliothek, Winterthur, Switzerland: 1-8, 36-37

Witt Library, Courtauld Institute, London: 88, 133A, 285A, 288A, 293A, 298, 298A

University of Wisconsin, Milwaukee, Wisconsin: 69V, 131B

Yale Center for British Art, New Haven, Connecticut: 9-10, 71A, &2C, 73E, 74A, 76, 77, 84-110, 113, 117-124, 125A, 117D-119D, 123D, 131, 171-172, 182-183 226A, 227-236, 239-240, 242, 263B, 265A, 275-280, 285A, 288A, 293A, 298-301, 299B

Yale University Libraries, New Haven, Connecticut 11, 17B-20B, 68, 80, 80C, 114-115, 114A-115A, 114B-115B, 125C, 117E-125E, 117H, 119H, 173B-176B, 227-243

Zentralbibliothek, Zurich, Switzerland: 1-10, 13A, 38-63, 39A-63A, 69AA, 72B, 75C, 80, 84-110, 84A-110A, 123D, 153, 155-160, 161A-162A, 165B-170B, 189-225, 275-283, 275A-276A, 295A, 296

Unknown locations: 69I, 69R-69T, 69U